Financing and Acquiring Park and Recreation Resources

John L. Crompton, PhD

Texas A&M University

Human Kinetics

Library of Congress Cataloging-in-Publication Data

Crompton, John L.
    Financing and acquiring park and recreation resources / John L.
Crompton.
      p.   cm.
    Includes bibliographical references (p.   ) and index.
    ISBN 0-88011-806-7
    1. Parks--United States--Finance.   2. Recreation--United States-
-Finance.   3. Parks--United States--Management.   4. Recreation-
-United States--Management.   I. Title.
    SB486.F54C76   1999
    333.78'16--DC21   98-8643
                                           CIP

ISBN: 0-88011-806-7

Acquisitions Editor: Scott Wikgren; **Developmental Editor**: Laura Casey Mast; **Assistant Editors**: Cynthia McEntire, Jennifer Goldberg; **Copyeditor**: Elisabeth Harbison; **Proofreader**: Sarah Wiseman; **Indexer**: Marie Rizzo; **Graphic Designer**: Nancy Rasmus; **Graphic Artist**: Sandra Meier; **Photo Editor**: Boyd LaFoon; **Cover Designer**: Jack Davis; **Photographer (interior)**: Pages 2, 16, 54, 176, 262, 290, 362, and 490 © Terry Wild Studios; pages 82, 314, and 410 © Mary Langenfeld; pages 110, 226, 340, 390, and 474 © CLEO Photography; page 148 © Martha McBride; pages 198 and 440 © Ron Way; **Illustrator**: Terry N. Hayden; **Printer**: Edwards

Human Kinetics books are available at special discounts for bulk purchase. Special editions or book excerpts can also be created to specification. For details, contact the Special Sales Manager at Human Kinetics.

Printed in the United States of America

10 9 8 7 6 5 4 3 2 1

Human Kinetics
Web site: http://www.humankinetics.com/

United States: Human Kinetics
P.O. Box 5076, Champaign, IL 61825-5076
1-800-747-4457
e-mail: humank@hkusa.com

Canada: Human Kinetics
475 Devonshire Road Unit 100, Windsor, ON N8Y 2L5
1-800-465-7301 (in Canada only)
e-mail: humank@hkcanada.com

Europe: Human Kinetics
P.O. Box IW14, Leeds LS16 6TR, United Kingdom
(44) 1132 781708
e-mail: humank@hkeurope.com

Australia: Human Kinetics
57A Price Avenue, Lower Mitcham, South Australia 5062
(088) 277 1555
e-mail: humank@hkaustralia.com

New Zealand: Human Kinetics
P.O. Box 105-231, Auckland 1
(09) 523 3462
e-mail: humank@hknewz.com

This book is dedicated to Marguerite Van Dyke
who has been the spirit of Aggieland
and the guardian angel of Aggies
in the Department of Recreation,
Park, and Tourism Sciences
for more than 25 years.

CONTENTS

Part III Support From External Sources

PREFACE

Twenty years ago, I coauthored a book with Dennis Howard titled *Financing, Managing and Marketing Recreation and Park Resources*. At the time, it was considered a ground-breaking text because it was the first book to develop the idea of public-private partnerships and to introduce concepts of marketing to the park and recreation field. It remained in print for almost 20 years—an extraordinary length of time for a textbook—and was used in the curricula of more than 100 colleges. Publishers consistently report that professionals do not buy textbooks, but professionals purchased more than 3,000 copies of that book.

When I committed to revising the book, it quickly became apparent that the project needed to be conceptualized again. The array of financing, managing, and marketing tools and techniques that park and recreation agencies use had increased dramatically in the 20 years since the original book was written. It was obvious that writing a state-of-the-art book of manageable size, which would incorporate all three of these elements of administration, was not feasible. The quantity of material would require separate volumes for each element.

My own interests are confined to financing and marketing and do not extend to management techniques. Hence, I decided to write independent books that focus on each of these two areas. My intent is to produce a similar state-of-the-art text in the marketing area in the next three to five years to complement this book about financing and acquisition. Hence, the contents of this book do not include discussion of pricing or of retailing and merchandising opportunities, even though both of these elements provide revenue that contributes to the financing of services in many agencies. It was decided that these topics would be discussed more appropriately in the subsequent volume on marketing.

Park and recreation managers are confronted with the certain reality of being required to do more with less. This has been their *modus operandi* for the past two decades, and there is no evidence to suggest it will change. The declining availability of traditional tax-supported revenue sources, coupled with escalating costs, has placed park and recreation managers under intense pressure to obtain the financial resources necessary to sustain the level of service expected by clientele groups, the general public, and elected officials. More than ever, managers must assume a proactive, rather than a reactive, role in confronting the fiscal challenges facing them. Agencies that will flourish will have managers who adopt an entrepreneurial approach, relentlessly seeking out new resources, as well as aggressively exploiting existing sources, to ensure that constituents receive the most effective service or experience possible. This book is intended to provide comprehensive coverage of the many traditional and innovative financing and acquisition tools and techniques that are available to park and recreation managers.

The book aspires to be a benchmark that documents the state-of-the-art financing and acquisition techniques in this field at the end of the 20th century. In this respect, it seeks to continue a tradition that was started more than 70 years ago by J.H. Weir in his classic treatise *Parks: A Manual of Municipal and County Parks*, which was published in New York in 1928 by A.S. Barnes and Co.

I have made an effort to inventory comprehensively the array of "hands-on" practical techniques and tools that are being used to finance and acquire the resources necessary to facilitate delivery of park and recreation services. Comparisons with Weir's volume and with the original Howard and Crompton text noted earlier offer insights into the remarkable ingenuity, creativity, and innovation that professionals in this field have exhibited in recent years for developing and acquiring the resources to deliver public park and recreation services.

research appointment that gives me one-third release time from teaching responsibilities; regular sabbatical leaves; graduate student assistance; substantial library, computing, and photocopying resources; travel support; and secretarial assistance. This creates a fertile environment for the nurturing of writing endeavors such as this. For me, writing is a joyful, enjoyable endeavor that I find deeply satisfying. It is more avocation than vocation. However, a project of this magnitude would not be feasible without the remarkable support that Texas A&M provides.

My mechanical writing tools consist of pen, yellow pad, scissors, and staple gun, which means that others have to undertake the onerous task of transcribing my difficult handwriting into typed form and safely securing the manuscript in the memory of a computer. Thus, special thanks are extended to Ms. Susan Buzzingham and Ms. Jelinda Pepper who exhibited both inordinate patience in interpreting my handwriting and consummate skill in organizing the material into its final typed form. Mr. Seong-Seop Kim has been my research assistant for six years while he completed two graduate degrees at A&M. He generously volunteered his wondrous computing skills and was responsible for preparing all the text's graphics for publication.

I have been privileged to have Ms. Marguerite Van Dyke as a secretary for more than 20 years. This book is dedicated to her because she contributes in innumerable ways to all my endeavors. She never has a bad day, the sun always shines on her world, she volunteers effusive assistance and affection, and she radiates positive vibes to all who enter her orb. Marguerite Van Dyke is a beloved legend among the students, staff, and faculty who have passed through the Department of Recreation, Park, and Tourism Sciences at Texas A&M University.

Dr. Peter Witt, the head of my department, has been marvelously supportive of this project as he has been of all my other endeavors. His intellectual and resource support, high energy and contagious enthusiasm, and friendship and encouragement were key factors in the great satisfaction that I derived from writing this book.

My thanks go to Human Kinetics for their willingness to publish this text. I was fortunate enough to work with Scott Wikgren as acquisitions editor and with Laura Casey Mast as developmental editor. The enthusiastic encouragement and professional expertise offered by both Scott and Laura were much appreciated.

Finally, my thanks go to my wife, Liz. Her support for my work has been unwavering over the past 30 years. I hope that this project will remind her of our wonderful five months in New Zealand, which I think gave some credibility to my oft-repeated claim that I really do lead a life that is well balanced between work and play!

PART I

FOUNDATIONS OF FINANCING AND ACQUISITION

INTRODUCTION: THE OPERATING ENVIRONMENT

In the past 20 years, every survey of public park and recreation practitioners that has sought to identify the field's major issues and challenges has reported that lack of finance is at the top of their list. It underlies many other sources of concern, such as deteriorating infrastructure, facility renovations, and the need to acquire and develop new areas, facilities, and services. In many jurisdictions, the tax funds that have been made available to deliver services have not been commensurate either with the demands of citizens for expansion of park and recreation services and for improvements in their quality or with the expectations that elected officials place on agencies.

The demand for park and recreation services has grown at a much faster rate than anticipated. For example, projections of outdoor recreation for the year 2000 that the Outdoor Recreation Resources Review Commission made in 1962 were reached by 1980. The range of services delivered is now more extensive than it has ever been, embracing the spectrum from heavily subsidized social welfare services to highly profitable revenue-generating and economic development activities. In the late 1970s, a group of Canadian park and recreation professionals anticipated the expansion in mission, range of services, and range of clientele served and the implications of those changes for organizational structures and service delivery modes. With remarkable foresight, they compared the typical characteristics of agencies and service delivery that prevailed in 1975 with how they anticipated these characteristics would evolve by 1995. Their vision is summarized in table 1.1, and it constitutes a useful overview of shifts that indeed did occur during that time period.

There is abundant evidence attesting to the need for additional services and facilities. During the past 20 years, voters in most jurisdictions have consistently approved bond issues resulting in the acquisition of substantially more park acreage and recreational facilities. For example, in the fall of 1996, voters cast ballots on 150 measures relating to parks, recreation, and conservation, and

---

Table 1.1   Changes in Organizational Structure and Service Delivery Modes From 1975 to 1995 (Projected in 1978)

1975	1995
Recreation Department	Department of Human Services
Narrow definitions of recreation and fitness	Broad definitions of leisure and human potentiality
Recreation in discretionary time	Leisure in any/all life spaces (meaningful, self-chosen activity)
Emphasis on child and youth	Market segmentation to focus on groups with greatest need
Public services universal	Equal services provided at all stages in life cycle
Attempts to provide leisure	Focus on preconditions to leisure (time, opportunity, capacity to choose)
Beginnings of joint use	Joint-planning, development, and management of public and many private facilities
Direct public sector provision	Indirect provision—public agency coordinates and refers
Perception of public agency as prime suppliers	Perception of public agencies as residual suppliers
Centralization	Decentralization
Professionals serving individuals	Community using all available human resources
Disciplinary perspectives	Interdisciplinary perspectives

Source: *The Elora Prescription: A future for recreation*. 1978. Envisaged by a group of concerned recreationists. Interpreted by Ken Balmer. Ontario, Canada: Ministry of Culture and Recreation, p. 22.

70% of these measures passed, authorizing a stream of more than $4 billion of new state and local money for these purposes.[1] By 1997, the aggregate value of new long-term bonds that municipalities issued annually for park and recreation projects had reached $1.37 billion, up from $270 million in 1987.[2] Nevertheless, a widespread perception that facilities are inadequate to meet citizens' demands still remains.

An enhanced understanding of ecology has accentuated the focus on protecting more land because it has led to the realization that ecosystems involving larger areas of land, rather than only isolated park areas, need to be protected. However, their sheer scale combined with the added complexities of their being in multiple ownership and different political jurisdictions makes the outright acquisition of ecosystems by a public agency difficult and expensive. The funding difficulties are further exacerbated by the greater variety of land types that agencies now seek to conserve. The land extends beyond scenic areas and athletic fields, which were often the sole interests two decades ago, to embrace landscapes such as endangered species' habitats, wetlands, greenways, river corridors, aquifer recharge zones, working farmland, long-distance trails, and urban shorelines.[3]

While acquisition of recreational facilities and park land has been expanding substantially, the costs of maintaining them has become disproportionately more onerous because of lower standards of visitor behavior and because of increased vandalism and littering that stems from proliferation of such technological "improvements" as disposable bottles and cans, spray paints, fast-food packaging, felt-tip pens, and filter-tip cigarettes. Resolving these problems requires intensive human labor, so the increased maintenance cost cannot be offset fully by improvements in equipment and mechanization.

Thus, park and recreation agencies at all levels of government typically provide many more services, maintain substantially larger acreages of land, and experience more vandalism and crime problems than they did two decades ago. Despite these major increases in responsibilities, which in some jurisdictions have more than doubled in the past 20 years, the number of full-time staff members that the park and recreation agencies employ increased by less than 10% during this time period.[4] This ability to "do more with less" is attributable partially to the major changes that have evolved in the ways in which park and recreation agencies finance their operations. These approaches are the subject of this text.

The changes were provoked by a dramatic shift in public attitudes toward government that emerged in the 1970s and early 1980s. This shift in attitude evolved into a national and international movement that advocated limitation of government spending and that generically has been termed "the tax revolt." This movement proved to be enduring, and fiscal conservatism is the defining external influence on park and recreation expenditures in many jurisdictions today. For this reason, a brief review of the tax revolt movement is provided here.

Evolution of the Tax Revolt[4]

The tax revolt movement developed as a reaction to more than 50 years of government growth during which public spending increased from one-tenth to one-third of the gross national product. During the early 1970s, state and local governments were the fastest growing employers in the economy. For example, even under two fiscally conservative governors, California's state budget grew at the rate of 12% annually in the decade preceding the passing of Proposition 13 in 1978. In addition to this increase in taxation, citizens were subjected to persistent and unprecedented double-digit inflation in the late 1970s that further slowed their growth in real incomes.

Taxpayers were angry and resentful of both substantial increases in property taxes that local governments levied and similar increases in federal and state taxes. They perceived that these tax increases were eroding their standard of living. Frustrated taxpayers felt powerless to attack directly federal or state taxes for which their remote, elected representatives were responsible. In contrast, taxpayers could access property taxes more directly through their actions because these taxes were established by more familiar, local, elected officials and, in some cases, could be influenced through voter referendum initiatives. In addition, the property tax was targeted because it was highly visible; it was not taken out at the source like many other taxes but was presented as a bill to property owners.

A series of opinion polls tracing the public mood over time documented a substantial decline in the public's confidence in government from the early 1960s to the late 1970s. The results showed a growing perception that governments wasted money, taxes were too high, government employees were highly paid and lazy, welfare services were fraudulently consumed, and many services were nonessential or inefficiently produced. A sizable proportion of the electorate believed that taxes could be cut without endangering "basic" or "essential" services; only waste and inefficiency would be eliminated by budget cuts.

The tax revolt commenced during 1975 and 1976 when the fraction of the gross national product accounted for by government fell for the first time in 50 years. Since that time, a substantial proportion of voters have been disinclined to approve any budget increases and have been inclined to favor the more frugal candidates in elections.

Early tax limitation laws were passed in New Jersey and in Rhode Island in 1976 and 1977, respectively, but the tax revolt did not gain a prominent place in the nation's psyche until June 1978 when voters in California passed the much more radical Proposition 13. (Proposition 13 sometimes is called the Jarvis-Gann Amendment after the names of its two major organizers.) Proposition 13 was a voter initiative that amended the state constitution. Almost two-thirds of the voters supported it. Total property taxes in California fell from $10.3 billion in fiscal year 1977-78 to $5.6 billion in fiscal year 1978-79, a decline of more than 45%.

Proposition 13 represented a dramatic watershed in government spending. It was noted at the time: "This is the new environment within which many recreation and park agencies now have to operate" (p. 37).[5] Immediately after it was passed, the *Wall Street Journal* in a lead editorial opined: "After the Jarvis-Gann earthquake in California, nothing can be quite the same in American politics. The voters are fed up with soaring taxation, spending and inflation, and are beginning to make their anger felt" (p. 20).[6]

Although the tax revolt was manifested most dramatically in California, the tax and expenditure limitation movement reverberated across the nation. It symbolized a dramatic retrenchment in the public attitude toward government spending and influenced not only local and state governments but also spending policies of the federal government. By the end of 1979, 22 states had reduced property taxes, 18 states had reduced income taxes, and 15 states had cut sales taxes. Overall, 36 different states had instituted some kind of reduction in property, income, and sales taxes or had

some type of spending limitations in place. Since that time, this type of legislation has multiplied. By 1990, only six states were not constrained by some form of tax limitation.[2] These statutory provisions have been reinforced by the political actions of elected representatives who recognized that survival in office depended on them demonstrating frugality to the electorate. At the federal level, the tax revolt led to reductions in intergovernmental transfers from the federal government to state and local entities, which exacerbated the problems of the latter.

The adverse impact of the tax revolt was reinforced in the early 1980s by the worst economic downturn since the 1930s, which further reduced government tax revenues. As the economy rebounded in the late '80s, budgets of many park and recreation agencies improved dramatically. Indeed, the period from 1985 to 1990 was the "Golden Era" of funding in the history of the field for local park and recreation agencies.[4] However, part of this increase was provoked by a compensatory need to pay for a backlog of infrastructure maintenance and for equipment replacement that had been deferred in the immediate aftermath of the tax revolt but ultimately had to be encumbered.

Effects of the tax revolt have been exacerbated by two other factors that have adversely impacted governments' ability to provide public resources for park and recreation services. First, in some jurisdictions, especially in large cities, the tax base has eroded. The middle class and industry, which were the main sources of property taxes, have moved to the suburbs. At the same time, poorer, socially dependent people have moved into the inner-cities. They require substantial subsidized public services but pay relatively little in taxes. Hence, total taxes collected by cities have declined, while demands for social services have increased.

The second factor is the impact of servicing the federal debt. Table 1.2 reports the exponential growth of this constraining factor in the last decades of the 20th century. The national debt is debt that the federal government owes. It now amounts to more than $5.4 trillion, which translates to more than $20,000 per person in the United States. Interest payments on the debt are nondiscretionary funds. Each dollar spent for debt service is a dollar that cannot be spent for traditional government services. As the debt increases, even larger cuts must be made in the discretionary part of the budget, of which park and recreation

Table 1.2   Impacts of the Exponential Growth in the Federal Debt

Year	Debt per capita	Annual interest on the debt (billions)	% of federal outlays
1970	$ 1,814	$ 19.3	9.9
1980	3,985	74.9	12.7
1990	13,000	264.8	21.1
1995	18,930	332.4	22.0

services are a part, merely to maintain the status quo.

A note about the information in table 1.2. The national debt of more than $5.4 trillion is funded in two main ways. Approximately two-thirds of it is financed by external marketable instruments. These may be in the form of Treasury Bills, which are issued for 12 or fewer months; Treasury Notes, issued for periods of 2-10 years; or Treasury Bonds, issued for more than 10 years (typically 30 years). Most of the remaining one-third of the debt is funded by the U.S. Treasury issuing non-marketable debt, derived by "borrowing" money from surpluses in the Social Security Trust Funds. Since these latter funds are not repaid by the Treasury, some officials who seek political advantage from belittling the magnitude of the debt disregard the one-third nonmarketable component of it. This enables them to state that the cost of servicing the debt is much less; typically, the figure quoted in the mid-1990s was 14% or 15% rather than the 22% shown in table 1.2. However, this action adversely impacts the viability of the Social Security Trust Funds. At some date early in the 21st century when the surpluses will be needed to meet the Funds' obligations, they will not be there.

In 1970, interest payments on the debt accounted for 9.9% of federal government outlays; however, 25 years later, these payments had increased to 22.0%. Interest payments on the national debt now exceed $1 billion each day. This amount is higher than the largest annual amount ever budgeted by the federal government from the Land and Water Conservation Fund program, which has been the major source of federal funds for acquisition and development in the park and recreation field and is discussed in chapter 11. In addition to reducing and terminating grant programs to state and local agencies, this squeeze has also caused the federal government to give state and local governments the responsibility of providing services that it can no longer afford to finance. These entities have to find new resources to fund the services, which, in turn, squeezes their financial capacity to support park and recreation services.

Recent efforts to reduce the annual deficit between federal government expenditures and income may stop the cumulative debt from growing larger if they are successful; however, a balanced annual budget will not shrink the existing debt. Without further annual deficits, the debt as a percentage of federal outlays may decline over time if other federal expenditures increase. However, the principal value of the debt is not likely to decline much at all.

Political and legal barriers to raising property taxes, combined with fewer federal and state dollars flowing to local governments, have put considerable pressure on the general funds of all types of local governments. Local park and recreation agencies continue to secure property tax resources from the general fund, but in order to retain existing service levels, they increasingly have to develop alternative financing sources to supplement property taxes.

The financial challenges with which many park and recreation managers were faced in the past two decades constituted perhaps the most severe challenge in the field's history. The situation confronting the National Park Service is fairly typical (figure 1.1). In constant dollars, the National Park Service budget declined by $635 million from 1978 to 1996, which represented a budget decrease of almost 50%. At the same time, annual visits increased by almost 40 million, and Congress created 79 new park units. Furthermore, the Park Service was required to accept numerous new

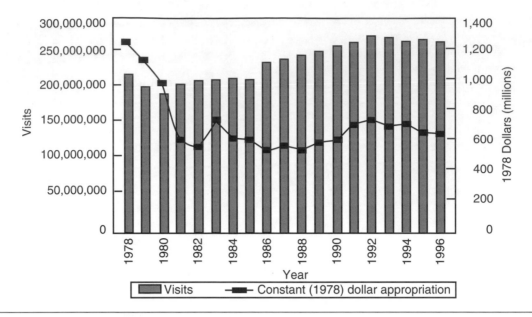

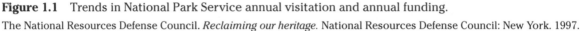

Figure 1.1 Trends in National Park Service annual visitation and annual funding.

The National Resources Defense Council. *Reclaiming our heritage.* National Resources Defense Council: New York. 1997.

responsibilities during those two decades. Some related to necessary environmental protection, such as the identification and removal of hazardous waste, while others related to issues of employee and visitor health and safety.[7] The following are illustrative examples of the new responsibilities.

Yosemite National Park received no additional funds in fiscal year 1994 to cover the $122,000 it had to pay to correct violations of Occupational Safety and Health Administration regulations and to clean up hazardous waste. In addition, the cost of more detailed background checks now required for law enforcement officers rose from less than $100 in 1991 to more than $3,000 in some cases for each check. As a result, Yosemite spent approximately $200,000 on background checks in fiscal year 1994 alone, accounting for about 6% of the

previous year's operating budget available after salaries and benefits.

Beginning in fiscal year 1992, Glacier National Park has had to spend an additional $20,000 each year to comply with Safe Drinking Water Act requirements.[7]

At the local level, the draconian plight of some agencies was illustrated by the parks department in New York. After experiencing waves of cuts throughout the 1980s, the department absorbed a 45% staff reduction between 1990 and 1994.[8] This caused the executive director of the Parks Council, a support group, to charge, "The city has in effect announced that it is not going to take care of its parks," and the city park commissioner to observe that further budget cuts would amount to "giving liposuction to a skeleton."[8]

Crisis in Philadelphia's Park System

Tax dollars in Philadelphia were inadequate to maintain the park system. The city faced mounting social problems, causing it to skimp on parks and allocate more resources to welfare and police, which it perceived as higher priorities. Much of the system's 8,700 acres was careworn. Picnic areas that once were mowed were reclassified euphemistically as "meadows." Trails, bridges, and retaining walls that were built as public works during the Great Depression were deteriorating.

The needs were spelled out clearly in a master plan that called for significant increases in operating and capital budgets. The plan reported that the city was spending less per capita on parks and recreation than many other major cities. The needs cited were basic: aggressive reforestation; more and better parking facilities; improved trails and roads; better lighting; better maintenance of culverts and drainage systems; and more picnic tables, shelters, and toilets. Nevertheless, the annual operating budget virtually had been unchanged for a 10-year period. Despite large increases in the overall city budget, capital funding had fallen by one-third, and staffing had fallen by 30%.

"The money has just not been forthcoming," the park commission president said. At the time of the interview he was worried about the removal of several hundred tires dumped beside a boarded-up, weather-beaten building that had not been used since a budget cut 20 years earlier disbanded the park's mounted police force.

The effects of cutbacks were evident around Memorial Hall, which was built for the 1878 Centennial Exposition and is now the park commission's headquarters. In front, the grass was neatly cut, the trees were pruned, and the trash receptacles were emptied frequently. However, 50 yards behind it, a fence was falling to the ground, a toppled tree lay unattended, and a rusted muffler rested by a rutted sidewalk.

The park system had come to rely heavily on the private sector. Officially, nearly 70 "friends-of-the-parks" groups had adopted sections of parks. Increasingly, they mowed ball fields and cleaned up after storms. Some groups, such as Friends of Pennypack Park with their "heavy-metal division," removed abandoned cars, refrigerators, shopping carts, and other debris. Some of the most significant landscaping projects were funded privately. For several years, the local William Penn Foundation paid for approximately 70 rangers to provide first aid and an aura of security; the six-year ranger training and employment program carried a $19 million price tag. However, private sources have their limits. One is that much of the park system borders distressed working-class neighborhoods that did not have much to give. "What's needed is more than the private sector can or should be expected to do," said a park commission member.

Many of the more than 60 historic buildings in the park system, which include mansions that were once summer houses of the well-to-do, had deteriorated, and no money was available for maintenance. To address this problem, park officials requested proposals for refurbishing some of these properties. Nearly 30 developers responded with proposals for bed and breakfasts, restaurants, conference and equestrian centers, and a residential work complex for artists. The idea was for developers to finance repairs of $250,000 to $1 million on each building and to pay rent to support other park buildings.

Clearly, the entrepreneurial thinking that advocated turning historic park properties into commercial enterprises was likely to be controversial, but no obvious alternative was available for maintaining and restoring them. Park officials were sensitive to possible accusations of turning public property into places accessible only to the well-to-do, so priority was given to developers who provided public access. Even potential critics came to recognize and accept the necessity of this entrepreneurial approach. Thus, the leader of the Preservation Coalition in Philadelphia was able to state: "If there's a mix with some things more accessible to people of a low-income level, it would appear to be a reasonable plan. But if every one of these historic houses became a very expensive bed and breakfast or a restaurant, there would be a hue and cry."

Adapted from Leslie Scism. Turning to developers to rescue parks: Philadelphia, strapped, sees no alternative. The New York Times. February 2, 1992, volume 141, page 29 (N). Copyright ©1992 by the New York Times Company. Reprinted by permission.

In these contexts, it was no longer sufficient for managers to be good stewards of resources that were entrusted to the agency and for them to spend wisely the tax money that they were given. The reduced availability of tax funds made it increasingly obvious that the public treasury would never have enough money to provide exclusively for the continued growing demands of citizens for more services.

Emergence of the Park and Recreation Manager as Entrepreneur

The conflicting demands of being asked to do more with fewer resources created a crisis. "Crisis in Philadelphia's Park System" is typical of the nature of the crisis that confronted many agencies and the conundrum with which they were confronted. Traditionalists yearned for more tax funds and protested that some of the proposed approaches to acquiring resources for development or maintenance of amenities were inappropriate. However, given the prevailing political climate, it was unrealistic to expect that the large increases in tax funds that would be required to operate in the traditional way would ever be forthcoming.

Thus, the field was forced to change its traditional ways of operating. Crises frequently force reappraisal of existing operating methods and persuade managers that yesterday's formulas for success often are neither effective nor efficient in meeting the needs and wants of today's clientele. Kevin White, a former mayor of Boston, once observed: "I hate these constant crises, but without them would we ever get anything done?" The Chinese explain the potential that a crisis offers for improvement through their written symbol for the word. This symbol comprises two characters: one indicating danger and the other indicating opportunity (figure 1.2).

Danger is an effective stimulus for action and change. Sometimes inertia and tradition blind people to new opportunities because either change is seen as requiring too much effort or they suffer from "trained incapacity"—that is, they were trained to do something one way and are incapable of perceiving that it could be done in other ways. The danger to survival inherent in this crisis forced park and recreation managers to broaden their

horizons and to think and act in a different way. Out of the crisis came creative pragmatism. The crisis was sufficiently severe and enduring for the field to acquire a new entrepreneurial mind-set and to develop an array of innovative funding and operating methods. It led to new standards of performance being established against which the efficiency and effectiveness of park and recreation agencies is now gauged. The result has been a quantum step forward in the field's maturity.

The new role that is characteristic of effective park and recreation managers is that of an entrepreneur who operates in a public sector environment. An entrepreneur is defined as someone who shifts economic resources out of an area of lower and into an area of higher productivity and greater yield.[9] Traditionally, the term was applied only to business people who operated in this way, but it now accurately describes the *modus operandi* of effective park and recreation managers. They seek creative, resourceful ways of using their scarce funds to leverage substantial additional resources through partnering with a wide range of business, nonprofit, and other government entities (figure 1.3). Managers then employ their management and marketing skills to ensure that these resources are used to yield the maximum possible social and economic benefits.

When any new service or facility is proposed, the starting point of managers with an entrepreneurial mind-set is to determine how it can be produced with minimal use of public funds and

Danger

Opportunity

Figure 1.2 The Chinese symbol for crisis.

Figure 1.3 To avoid closing facilities, partnerships with nonprofit and commercial entities will be needed.

resources. The service or facility is supported by a "can-do" positive attitude that managers adopt while pursuing the array of possibilities described in this text. The prevailing philosophy is "We have no problems, only exceptional opportunities." These managers are doers who are active and visible leaders in the community. They make things happen and do not look for excuses for not making the effort. They recognize that some failure is inevitable in entrepreneurial efforts but that it does not reflect badly on the initiator. The only real failure is failure to adopt this approach and to try vigorously to bring projects to fruition. This entrepreneurial mind-set and "can-do" attitude is illustrated in the Statement of Commitment developed by the Indianapolis Parks and Recreation Department, shown in figure 1.4. A challenge for any field is its ability to adapt to change and to manage it rather than to resist it. The range of funding and acquisition techniques described in this text is testimony to this field's ability to meet that challenge.

The entrepreneurial role does create additional difficulties for park and recreation managers because entrepreneurial actions may be incompatible with the democratic values and institutional roles to which they are required to adhere. Four types of tensions have been identified.[10] First, entrepre-

---

Statement of Commitment

The task before us now,

if we would not fade away

in the downward spiral

of diminishing funding, service, and

utilization,

is to shake off the mind set of

entitlement;

to stop waiting for others to lead;

and to rebuild Indy Parks

through advocacy and partnerships

with the community.

Figure 1.4 Statement of commitment developed by the Indianapolis Parks and Recreation Department.

neurial managers seek autonomy in the budget processes; they want freedom from rules, procedures, and control. This autonomy enables them to be more efficient, effective, and responsive to citizens' needs and unanticipated opportunities, but such autonomy is counter to the democratic value of accountability. Second, these managers are likely to have a vision of the future and a level of confidence for enacting it that is beyond the understanding of many of their citizens and other stakeholders. Hence, it may not survive public participation processes, and the managers may be tempted to avoid such processes to reduce contention and frustration. Third, partnership negotiations sometimes require secrecy if they are to be successful, but secrecy compromises open policy-making processes and the public's right to know.

Fourth, a relatively high level of risk may be involved; a project may fail and result in damage to the long-term public good. For example, when voters in Arlington, Texas, passed a $7 million bond issue to build Seven Seas theme park, they were informed that there would be no consequent tax increase. It was explained that a lease to operate the new park had been signed with the Six Flags Over Texas organization, which operated a nearby theme park, at an annual fee that was sufficient to pay all costs associated with the bond. However, three months before the park opened, when construction was almost complete, the parent company of Six Flags declared bankruptcy, which legally nullified the lease agreement. The city was left to operate the park with no expertise in doing so and no lease fee. Seven Seas ran at an operating loss for a few years before closing. Arlington taxpayers had to meet all of the $7 million bond payments as well as the operating losses, and they received no benefits.

Reconciling these four types of tensions requires unusual skill and sensitivity to the prevailing political environment. Certainly, they make the task of an entrepreneurial park and recreation manager substantially more difficult than that of peers in the private sector.

Orientation to the Text

The title of this text incorporates the words "financing and acquiring." These words highlight that the book's content is not limited to identifying alternate sources of money; it extends to methods of acquiring other resources, especially land. There is good reason for this. When dollars are available, they are used to purchase one of three types of resources: property; labor; or physical materials, facilities, and equipment. Economists call these three types of resources "the factors of production." Every park and recreation facility or service depends on inputs of some combination of these three factors of production. Hence, while money is obviously a fundamental resource, on many occasions substitute resources, such as property, personnel, or facilities and equipment acquired from others, may be equally as useful. Agencies use money to buy these factors of production. However, this text suggests a wide variety of other ways in which entrepreneurial managers can obtain these factors.

Figure 1.5 suggests that these factors of production may be substituted at least partially for each other. For example, if the availability of land (property) is restricted, it may be possible to compensate by using additional labor (personnel) or physical materials and equipment to construct indoor facilities, artificial playing surfaces, or floodlighting. This substitution may result in the same degree and quality of use as would have been forthcoming if the optimal amount of land had been available initially.

Methods of acquiring all three factors of production are discussed in the text, but emphasis is placed upon acquisition of land because that is usually the most scarce of the three factors. Hence,

it was perceived to be the most critical resource for park and recreation agencies to acquire. The array of new methods that have emerged for financing and protecting land have made possible the plethora of new partnerships that agencies have forged with individual landowners, nonprofit organizations, and businesses in the past two decades. These partnerships have increased recreational access and conservation of lands. They have moved the nation closer to the vision articulated by Stephen Mather, the first director of the National Park Service, of "a national system of parks."

The text is divided into three parts. Material in the remainder of this first part is intended to be a foundation upon which the content in the subsequent two parts builds. It consists of four foundation elements. Chapter 2 discusses public tax funds obtained from property and sales taxes. Traditionally, these taxes have been the primary sources of both operational and capital funds for local and state park and recreation agencies. They remain the most important asset that most agencies possess, and they constitute the basic resources used to leverage partnerships with other entities. The allocation of these funds is determined by an agency's budget (chapter 3), which is a financial plan that directs how the agency is authorized to spend its funds in a given year.

The third foundation element (chapter 4) describes less-than-fee simple techniques. Twenty

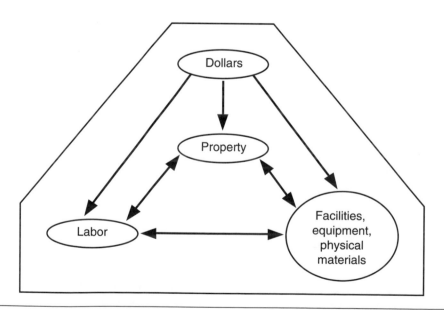

Figure 1.5 Dollars are used to purchase one of three factors of production, which may be substituted at least partially for each other.

years ago, these techniques were regarded as esoteric. Their potential applications were discussed occasionally in academic journals, but rarely were they used in the field. Today, they are used extensively instead of fee-simple purchases, as agencies recognize that there are many situations in which committing land needed for park and recreational purposes to full public ownership is neither possible nor desirable. Most public lands are in unpopulated areas of the country. Conversely, desirable private lands often are located near population centers. This makes private lands especially important in certain regions of the country, notably the East and South. America cannot be bought back. Public agencies can never hope to purchase large tracts of these lands, but partnerships with their individual and corporate owners using seed funds and less-than-fee simple techniques will lead to more land becoming accessible to the general public for recreational use. The increasing use of less-than-fee simple techniques has enhanced substantially the potential for partnerships with individual landowners, nonprofit organizations, and businesses.

Chapter 5, which concludes the foundation part of the text, addresses how to nurture a broad constituency beyond that of direct service beneficiaries, which are needed to secure resources. To do this, the field has to be repositioned so that it is perceived to contribute to alleviating the prevailing economic and social concerns in a jurisdiction.

The topic of part II in the text is direct partnerships. Agencies seek these partnerships to encourage other entities to share responsibility for

delivering services by investing some of their factors of production into the process. They are the primary means through which agencies leverage their production. Chapter 6 discusses the principles of privatization and partnerships and the challenges associated with reconciling the different value systems of potential partner organizations. Chapter 7 identifies the complementary assets that businesses and public agencies can contribute to partnership agreements. The remaining chapters in part II describe different types of partnerships with the commercial sector (chapters 8-10), with other public entities including grant aid from higher levels of government (chapter 11), and with nonprofit organizations (chapter 12). A summary of the types of direct partnerships that may be formulated is given in figure 1.6.

A complementary alternative to involving others in sharing responsibility for the actual delivery of services is to persuade them to provide resources that enable the agency to take sole responsibility for service delivery but to use fewer of its own resources in doing so. Part III discusses these external sources of support. This support may be in the form of assistance from volunteers (chapter 13), assistance from individuals or corporations (chapters 14-17), sponsorship from businesses (chapters 16 and 17), support from foundations which may be facilitative and technical (chapter 18), or support from foundations in the form of monetary grants (chapter 19). The multifaceted potential ways in which businesses, foundations, and individuals can provide external support are summarized in figure 1.7.

With business	**With other governmental agencies**	**With nonprofit organizations**
—Agency pump priming (with land, low-cost capital tax incentives, permit, and zoning controls)	—Schools	—Facilitation
—Land exchanges	—Other public agencies	—Coproduction (including vouchers and grants)
—Use of commercial facilities	—Federal and state grants	—Brokering
—Joint development		—Technical assistance
—Contracting out		—Opportunity referral
—Exactions (land dedication, fees in lieu, impact fees, negotiated planning gains)		

Figure 1.6   Types of direct partnerships.

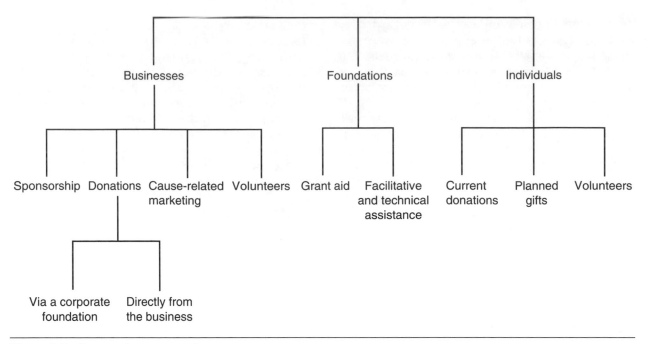

Figure 1.7 Support from external sources.

Summary

Managers of park and recreation agencies consistently have identified financing and acquiring resources as their major challenge. More than at any time in the history of the field, they are being required to provide a broader range of services targeted at a wider spectrum of users, to improve the quality of services, to maintain larger acreages of land, and to ameliorate the effects of more vandalism and crime. However, the tax resources that they are given are not commensurate with the cost of performing these additional tasks.

Fiscal conservatism is ensconced as the prevailing mantra of elected officials and is the defining external influence on park and recreation expenditures in many jurisdictions today. It emerged from the tax revolt movement that achieved momentum with the passing of Proposition 13 in California in 1978. From there, it reverberated across the nation. Tax limitation legislation is now prevalent at all levels of government. Its influence in reducing available tax dollars has been reinforced by erosion of the tax base in some major cities and by the magnitude of interest payments on the national debt, inhibiting the federal government's ability to fund discretionary programs.

The crisis created by the expectation that agencies should do more with fewer tax resources resulted in managers acquiring a new entrepreneurial mind-set and developing an array of innovative funding and operating methods. Effective park and recreation managers are entrepreneurs who operate in a public sector environment. However, that environment does contain constraints that make their task substantially more challenging than it would be if they were operating as an entrepreneur in the private sector.

Money is used to acquire some combination of the three factors of production: property; labor; and physical materials, facilities, and equipment. If money is not available to buy these factors, then an agency may use some of those factors that it possesses to forge partnerships with other organizations that are also prepared to invest some of their factors of production into providing park and recreation facilities and services.

References

1. Myers, Phyllis. 1997. Voters go for the green. *Greensense* 3(1): 3.

2. Myers, Phyllis. 1998. Park bonds continue upward trend. *Greensense* 4(1): 1.

3. Bendick, Robert L. 1993. State partnerships to preserve open space: Lessons from Rhode Island and New York. In *Land conservation through public-private partnerships*, edited by Eve Endicott. Washington, DC: Island Press: 149-171.

4. Crompton, John L. and Brian P. McGregor. 1994. Trends in the financing and staffing of local government park and recreation services 1964/65-

1990/91. *Journal of Park and Recreation Administration* 12(3): 19-37.

5. Howard, Dennis R. and John L. Crompton. 1980. *Financing, managing and marketing recreation and park resources.* Dubuque, IA: Brown.

6. *Wall Street Journal.* 1978. Editorial, June 8.

7. Natural Resources Defense Council. 1997. *Reclaiming our heritage.* New York: National Resources Defense Council.

8. Martin, Douglas. 1994. Trying new ways to save decaying parks. *New York Times*, November 15, A16.

9. Osborne, David and Ted Gaebler. 1991. *Reinventing government.* Reading, MA: Addison-Wesley.

10. Bellone, Carl J. and George F. Goerl. 1992. Reconciling public entrepreneurship and democracy. *Public Administration Review* 52(2): 130-134.

CHAPTER 2

PROPERTY TAXES, SALES TAXES, AND BONDS

Traditionally, property and sales taxes have been the primary sources for funding both the operational needs and the acquisition and developmental needs of local and state park and recreation agencies. In the first part of this chapter, the author describes these taxes and alternative ways in which they are applied. When agencies purchase park land or build facilities, they must usually borrow money. The latter part of the chapter reviews the most common mechanisms that park and recreation agencies use to acquire and develop such capital facilities.

General Property Taxes

For generations, the general property tax has been the backbone of local government finance. More than 96% of property tax revenues go to local governments. The property tax is to local government what personal and corporate income taxes are to the federal government. There has been some decline in its dominance, but it remains the pre-eminent source of finance at the local level. In 1932, property taxes provided local governments with 97% of their total revenues. Today, the aggregate figure has declined to approximately 80%, and the specific percentage now varies greatly between types of entities.[1] Municipalities have shifted to more reliance on sales taxes and various fees and charges, but counties and school districts remain reliant almost exclusively on the property tax.

The dependence of local governments and their park and recreation agencies on the property tax stems from lack of alternative revenue-generating options for most cities and counties. The potential of other taxes is limited. Local taxation of income, sales, or business could deter new business expansion and ultimately bring about shrinkage in the tax base. However, real property is immobile. Only a very substantial tax on land and buildings would induce people to move from their homes and places of work. Retail businesses must locate close to customers, and, once committed, manufacturing establishments tend to stay because even severe property taxes represent only a small part of their overall operating costs. In short, real property offers a dependable base upon which local governments can safely levy taxes.

Theoretically, the property tax is consistent with both the ability-to-pay principle and the benefit principle of taxation.[2] To the extent that the value of property owned increases with income, those with greater ability to pay will pay higher taxes. Property tax serves as a benefit tax because its revenues are used to finance local government expenditures on services that benefit property owners and increase the value of their properties.

Typically, a minimum of three government units—the school district, the city, and the county—impose taxes on the same property. Homeowners can expect to pay separate property taxes to at least three entities, and perhaps to as many as five or six entities, if the homeowner resides in several special districts.

All property owners bear the property tax, but churches, charitable organizations, educational institutions, and other governmental entities, such as state and federal institutions, are excluded from paying the tax in almost every state. Classes of exempt property also may include cemeteries (42 states), hospitals (40 states), and historic properties (13 states).[2] These exemptions can inflict substantial financial problems on some jurisdictions. Thus, for example, a major state university located in a small city requires extensive service support from the city but provides no taxes to pay for them. Extensive federal land holdings in an area can create similar difficulties. For example, in Montrose County, Colorado, 970,000 of the county's 1.4 million acres are federal lands, which in private ownership would yield substantial taxes. In recognition of the problem that federal lands create, Congress provides payment-in-lieu-of-taxes funds through annual appropriations to counties with such holdings. However, these mitigation amounts are substantially lower than amounts that would be obtained if the land were in private ownership. The U.S. Forest Service has a similar mitigation program whereby 25% of the revenue it receives from timber sales, campground charges, recreational activities, and grazing fees is distributed to affected counties.

Figure 2.1 shows a taxonomy of the types of property that may be subjected to taxation. The fundamental distinction is the difference between real property and personal property. Most variation across jurisdictions in which the property elements shown in figure 2.1 are taxed occurs in the personal property category, which includes everything that can be owned but that is not real property. It is difficult for appraisers to locate, inventory, validate, and value both tangible and intangible personal property. Because of these difficulties, it has been noted that personal property frequently "is exempt by law; sometimes, by local practice. Seldom is taxation complete"

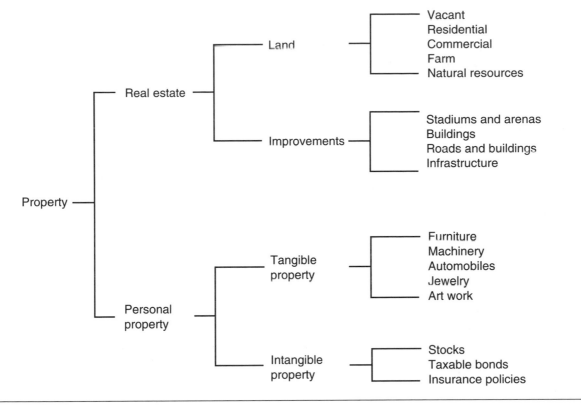

Figure 2.1 Types of property that may be subjected to taxation.

(p. 292).[3] Indeed, the personal property share of locally assessed taxable property declined nationwide from almost 16% in the early 1960s to less than 10% by the late 1980s.[4]

The value of real property is determined by estimating its taxable worth. These estimates are called assessments. The task of determining these property values is assigned to an assessor, who is either appointed or elected. It is the assessor's responsibility to list on the tax rolls each parcel of taxable property within the jurisdiction and, on a specified date each year (often January 1), to place a value on each parcel in conformity with assessment rules.

Current market value is defined as "the most probable price at which the property would be transferred in a competitive and open market under all conditions requisite to a fair sale, between a willing buyer and a willing seller, neither of whom is under any compulsion to buy or sell and both having knowledge of relevant facts at the time of sale"(p.16).[5] A state's tax law may or may not assess property at the current market rate. Indeed, in only 19 states is assessed value supposed to reflect 100% of market value. In the other states, the practice is to assess property at below prevailing market levels:

Some of the states define assessed value as a fixed percentage of market value. Examples range from 70% in Connecticut to 10% in Louisiana. In some states (New York, New Jersey, Delaware, and Maine), the ratio is determined and allowed to vary by local taxing unit. In 14 other states the assessment ratio varies by property class. Such tax systems are usually referred to as classified. In Colorado, residential properties are supposed to be assessed at 15% of market value, and all other properties at 29%. Similarly, in Arizona, residential properties are assessed at a lower rate (10%) than are agricultural properties (16%) or commercial and industrial properties (25%). Tennessee assesses commercial and industrial properties at 40% of market value, all other real property at 25%, and personal property at 30% of market value (p. 22).[2]

In Kay County, Oklahoma, the assessment ratio is 0.11. Thus, if a home is valued at $80,000, its assessed value for tax purposes in that county is $8,800. A tax rate of $5 per $100 assessed value would mean the homeowner would pay annual taxes of $440 to the county.

The intent of this practice is to create an illusion. Because the assessed value of the property is below market value, property owners may believe that they are getting a concession and, therefore, are less inclined to challenge the assessor's judgment. In fact, tax payment made by the homeowner is likely to be the same regardless of whether all properties in a jurisdiction are assessed at 100% or some lesser percentage of their market value.

> Under normal circumstances the overall assessment ratio has little impact on absolute property tax burdens because assessment levels can be counteracted by differences in the statutory tax rate. For instance, suppose a municipality seeks $5 million from its property tax and the market value of taxable property is $80 million. If the assessment ratio is 100%, a property tax rate of $6.25 per $100 assessed value will yield the desired money. If the assessment ratio is 50%, a property tax rate of $12.50 per $100 assessed value will produce the desired revenue. Low assessment ratios will produce compensating statutory rate adjustments (p. 227).[3]

The aggregate value of all the assessed property within a particular jurisdiction is referred to as the tax base. Once the tax base has been determined by assessment, the local government sets a tax rate to meet its revenue needs. Tax rates are usually expressed in terms of dollars and cents per $100 assessed value. The function of the property tax is to fill in the gap between the revenues that the agency's budget requires and the amount that the agency expects to derive from other local, state, and federal sources. Thus, tax rates are established by dividing the local government's budget (projected expenditures for one year) less anticipated income from nonproperty sources (e.g., sales taxes, fees, fines, federal and state funds, etc.) by the total assessed value of property. For example, assume that the total assessed value of property in a community is $400,000,000 and the tax revenue needed by a government unit amounts to $5,000,000:

(a) tax rate = $5,000,000 ÷ $400,000,000 = 0.0125

This may be expressed as a tax rate of $1.25 per $100 assessed value. The relationship between the budget and total assessed value always determines the tax rate. If a city increases its budget expenditures and the assessed value total remains stable, the tax rate goes up:

(b) tax rate = $6,000,000 ÷ $400,000,000 = 0.0150

Conversely, if the assessed value or tax base goes up and the city budget remains the same, the tax rate will go down:

(c) tax rate = $5,000,000 ÷ $500,000,000 = 0.0100

When the tax rate has been established, it is a simple matter to determine the amount of taxes that will be collected from individual homeowners. The calculation involves multiplying the approved tax rate by the assessed value of taxable property:

tax rate × assessed value = tax revenue due
from property

Thus, if a property has an assessed value of $100,000 and a tax rate of $1.25 per $100 of assessed value, then the annual tax to be paid by the property owner would be $1,250. Although the tax rate most frequently is expressed in terms of dollars and cents per $100 assessed value, it is expressed in some states as a millage rate in terms of mills per dollar of assessed value. A mill is $0.001. Thus, a millage tax of 1 mill per $1 assessed value is equivalent to a tax of 10¢ per $100 assessed value or $1 per $1,000 assessed value. Tax calculations using both of these approaches are shown in figure 2.2.

Property owners are obligated to pay their annual tax bill. If they fail to do so, then a tax lien can be attached to the property. This gives a jurisdiction the power to have the property sold and the proceeds from the sale applied to delinquent taxes, penalties, and accrued interest. However, if they believe it is too high, property owners have the right to protest and appeal the value at which their property is appraised for tax purposes. Each state establishes appeal procedures that jurisdictions must follow, and these are publicly announced. The procedures that property owners in Brazos County, Texas, must follow, for example, are specified in the announcement reproduced in figure 2.3, which appeared in the local newspaper.

The newspaper headline in figure 2.4 announces that the city council of College Station, Texas, decided not to raise the property tax in the coming year. Most residents in the community are likely to interpret this as meaning that the council is exercising tight cost controls and that residents' annual property tax payments will be the same next year as they were for this year. Claims of this nature are made frequently or implied by local elected officials and supportive media. However, such claims are likely to be grossly misleading

I. Assume that an independent park district establishes an annual tax rate of 1 mill per dollar on a homeowner's property that is assessed at $80,000. The amount the homeowner must pay is figured by multiplying the assessed value by the dollar amount of the tax rate:

$80,000 × $0.001 = $80.

II. The same tax rate may be expressed as 10¢ per $100 assessed valuation:

A. Divide the assessed value by $100:

$80,000 ÷ $100 = $800.

B. Multiply the result by 10¢:

$800 × 10¢ = $80.

Figure 2.2 Tax calculation examples.

Table 2.1   Announcement of an "Effective" Tax Rate

	Last year	This year
Average taxable home value	$72,265	$79,893
Tax rate	$1.61/$100	$1.61/$100
Tax	$1,163.47	$1,286.28

Note: The above table compares taxes on an average home in this taxing jurisdiction last year to taxes proposed on the average home this year. Your individual taxes may be higher or lower, depending on the taxable value of your property. Under this year's proposal, taxes on the average home would increase by $122.81 or 10.56% compared with last year's taxes.

---

because they ignore increases in the tax base. Later, in the body of the text in figure 2.4, the reporter notes that the city budget is actually $5.2 million higher (9.6%) for the next year. Further, a city official acknowledges that if the unchanged proposed tax rate is approved, it would mean higher property taxes for residents whose homes have increased in value.

Figure 2.4 and tax rate example (c) illustrate how it is possible in communities where land values are escalating for a government body to announce, rather magnanimously, to its taxpayers its plan to reduce the tax rate. Actually, its claim often is based on the assessed value of property having grown so much that the council can afford to reduce the tax rate substantially without losing any property tax revenue. Hence, it is probable that the actual tax that the property owner is required to pay will increase.

To counter the possibility that taxpayers may be misled in this way, some states require all taxing jurisdictions to announce publicly their proposed effective tax for the coming year and to hold public hearings to discuss it before approving it. The effective tax involves reporting the total tax change that will take place. A typical announcement is shown in table 2.1. It reports to taxpayers that, although the tax rate in the coming year remains the same, the taxes on an average home will increase by 10.56% compared with the taxes last year because of the increases in the appraised value of homes.

Revenues collected from the taxes that cities and counties levy usually are placed into the general fund of the respective government units. The general fund consists of revenue from multiple sources including property tax, sales tax, user fees, fines, and intergovernmental transfers. The general fund finances almost all government services including parks and recreation. To secure what it hopes will constitute its fair share of general fund monies, the local park and recreation agency must submit a formal request for funds, which usually is in the form of a budget proposal. In most cases, the local legislative authority determines budget approval of the specific amount of money that the agency receives. In the case of city government, this body would most likely be the mayor and city council. This process will be discussed in greater detail in chapter 3.

In contrast to city and county park and recreation departments that compete with other local agencies for funds from the general fund, there are some park and recreation agencies in the United States that have been granted the legal right to levy their own taxes. Generally, this authority is derived from one of two sources:

1. The enabling law that created them as special districts, such as in the case of park districts in Illinois, Colorado, Oregon, California, and other states. State legislative authority allows the park districts in Illinois, for example, to levy a tax not to exceed a total of 10¢ per $100 assessed value of property for park and administrative services and to impose an additional 7.5¢ per $100 assessed value limit for recreation services.

2. The passage of a special tax levy for parks and recreation by the voters in their jurisdiction. For example, the voters in Jefferson County, Colorado, supported a proposal to establish an open

Property Tax Protest and Appeals Procedures

The law gives property owners the right to protest actions concerning their property tax appraisals. You may follow these appeal procedures if you have a concern about:
- the value placed on your property
- any exemptions that may apply to you
- the cancellation of an agricultural appraisal
- the taxable status of your property
- the local governments which should be taxing your property
- any action taken by the appraisal district that adversely affected you.

Informal Review

Call or meet with staff appraisers at 1421 Waterfield #A101 (409-555-8731) Monday–Friday 8:00 am–5pm. Appraisal Review Board policy requires that you meet with a staff appraiser before the date of your hearing.

Review by the Appraisal Review Board

If you can't resolve your problem informally with the appraisal district staff, you may have your case heard by the appraisal review board (ARB). You must file a timely Notice of Protest by June 12. The ARB is an independent board of citizens that reviews problems with appraisal or other concerns listed above. It has the power to order the appraisal district to make the necessary changes to solve problems. If you file a written request for an ARB hearing (called a Notice of Protest) before the deadline, the ARB will set your case for a hearing. You'll receive written notice of the time, date and place of the hearing. The hearing will be informal. You and the appraisal district representative will be asked to present evidence about your case. The ARB will make its decision based on the evidence presented. You can get a copy of a protest form from the appraisal district office at 1421 Waterfield #A101, Bryan, Tx., or call 409-555-8731.

Note: You shouldn't try to contact ARB members outside of the hearing. The law requires ARB members to sign an affidavit saying that they haven't talked about your case before the ARB hears it.

Review by the District Court

After it decides your case, the ARB must send you a copy of its order by certified mail. If you're not satisfied with the decision, you have the right to appeal to district court. If you choose to go to court, you must start the process by filing a petition within 45 days of the date you receive the ARB's order. If the appraisal district has appraised your property at $1,000,000 or more, you must file a notice of appeal with the chief appraiser within 15 days of the date you receive the ARB's order.

More Information

You can get more information by contacting your appraisal district at 1421 Waterfield #A101, Bryan, Tx. (409-555-8731). You can also get a pamphlet describing how to prepare a protest from the appraisal district or from the State Comptroller's Property Tax Division at P.O. Box 13528, Austin, TX 78711-3528.

Deadline for Filing Protests with the ARB

Usual Deadline

On or before May 31 (or 30 days after a notice of appraised value was mailed to you, whichever is later). THE DEADLINE FOR FILING A PROTEST IS JUNE 12 FOR BRAZOS COUNTY APPRAISAL DISTRICT. Late protests are allowed if you miss the usual deadline for good cause. Good cause is some reason beyond your control, like a medical emergency. The ARB decides whether you have good cause.

Late protests are due the day before the appraisal review board approves records for the year. Contact your appraisal district for more information. THE BRAZOS COUNTY APPRAISAL REVIEW BOARD EXPECTS TO APPROVE THE RECORDS BY JULY 18.

Special Deadlines

For change of use (the appraisal district informed you that you are losing agricultural appraisal because you changed the use of your land), the deadline is before the 30th day after the notice of the determination was mailed to you.

For ARB changes (the ARB has informed you of a change that increases your tax liability and the change didn't result from a protest you filed), the deadline is before the 30th day after notice of the determination was mailed to you.

If you believe the appraisal district or ARB should have sent you a notice and did not, you may file a protest until the day before taxes become delinquent (usually February 1). The ARB decides whether it will hear your case based on evidence about whether a required notice was mailed to you.

Figure 2.3 Property tax protest and appeals procedures.

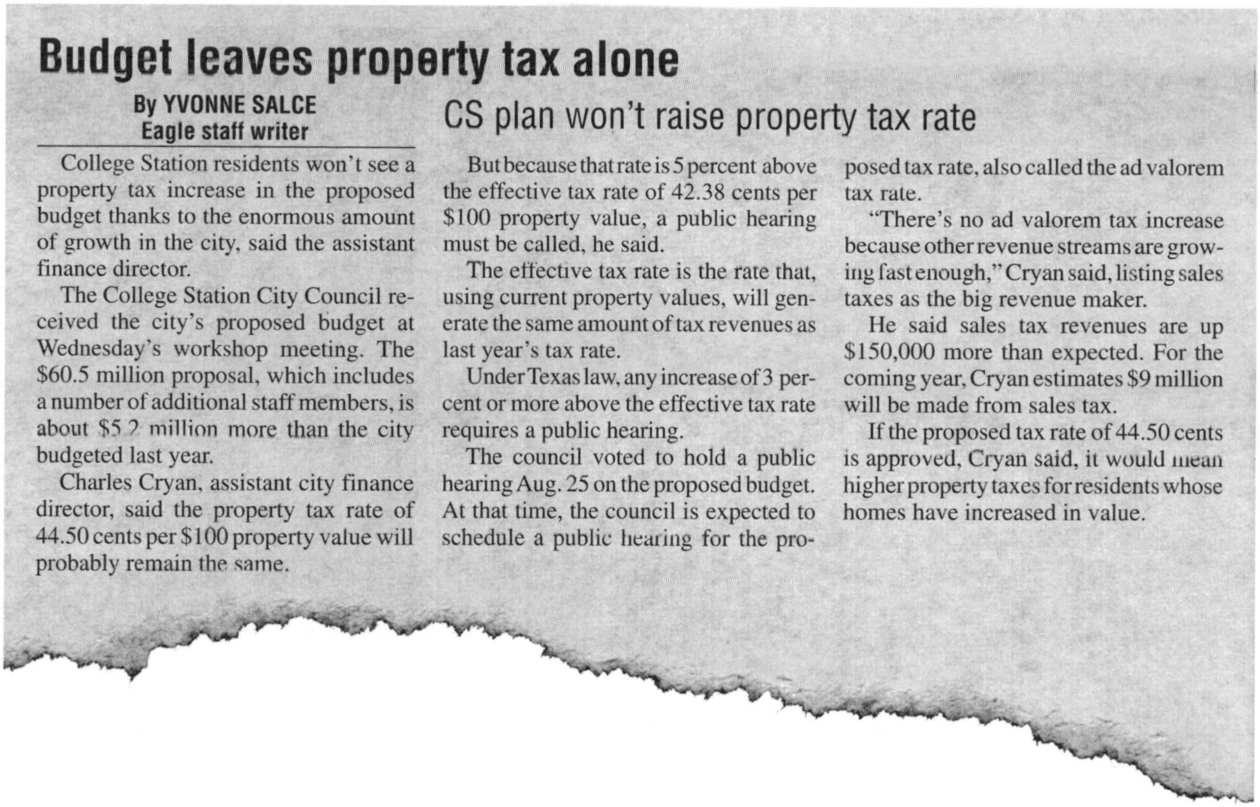

Budget leaves property tax alone

By YVONNE SALCE
Eagle staff writer

CS plan won't raise property tax rate

College Station residents won't see a property tax increase in the proposed budget thanks to the enormous amount of growth in the city, said the assistant finance director.

The College Station City Council received the city's proposed budget at Wednesday's workshop meeting. The $60.5 million proposal, which includes a number of additional staff members, is about $5.2 million more than the city budgeted last year.

Charles Cryan, assistant city finance director, said the property tax rate of 44.50 cents per $100 property value will probably remain the same.

But because that rate is 5 percent above the effective tax rate of 42.38 cents per $100 property value, a public hearing must be called, he said.

The effective tax rate is the rate that, using current property values, will generate the same amount of tax revenues as last year's tax rate.

Under Texas law, any increase of 3 percent or more above the effective tax rate requires a public hearing.

The council voted to hold a public hearing Aug. 25 on the proposed budget. At that time, the council is expected to schedule a public hearing for the proposed tax rate, also called the ad valorem tax rate.

"There's no ad valorem tax increase because other revenue streams are growing fast enough," Cryan said, listing sales taxes as the big revenue maker.

He said sales tax revenues are up $150,000 more than expected. For the coming year, Cryan estimates $9 million will be made from sales tax.

If the proposed tax rate of 44.50 cents is approved, Cryan said, it would mean higher property taxes for residents whose homes have increased in value.

Figure 2.4 Property taxes may increase without raising the tax rate.

Reprinted with permission of The Bryan-College Station Eagle, Bryan, TX.

space district and to authorize it to levy a 0.5% sales tax, the proceeds of which were to be spent "for planning, acquiring, maintaining, administering, and preserving open space, real property, or interests in open space real property for the use and benefit of the public." The tax generated approximately $25 million annually. Subsequently, voters extended the scope of the sales tax to permit the funding of recreational facilities. In this regard, the open space district aids the 11 cities and 10 park and recreation districts, which serve the 500,000 people in Jefferson County, with capital funds to build recreational facilities, but the other jurisdictions accept full responsibility for operating and maintaining these facilities.

In Boulder County, Colorado, multiple jurisdictions levy a designated sales tax for open space and park acquisition and operation. The Boulder County Open Space Department receives $7.5 million from a 0.25% designated sales tax, and their budget is supplemented further by $4 million from the county's general fund and $1 million from the Colorado lottery. The City of Boulder Open Space Department receives approximately $15 million from a 0.73% sales tax. Much of this money is used to purchase greenbelts around the city. As a result of these actions, Boulder now contains more than 40,000 acres of public open space—impressive for a city with a population of less than 100,000. Voters in the nearby cities of Louisville, Lafayette, and Broomfield also approved a 0.25% sales tax for open space acquisition in and around their jurisdictions.

Authority to levy taxes designated for the exclusive use of park and recreation agencies gives them fiscal independence. It means that they do not have to compete directly with other community tax-supported services to obtain resources from the general fund.

The Mechanics of Proposition 13

It was noted in chapter 1 that the tax revolt movement was launched essentially by the passing of Proposition 13 in California in June 1978. The success of Proposition 13 in lowering local taxation levels in California was attributed to it restricting increases in both the tax rate and the tax base and making substitution of an alternative source of taxation to compensate for lost property tax revenues very difficult. Its authors fixed the maximal property tax at 1% of the 1975-76 assessed value of the property and then mandated that assessed values could not be increased more than 2% per year based on the 1975-76 property value except on property that changed hands.

In sections 3 and 4 of the Proposition, the authors made it very difficult to replace these lost revenues by passing alternative taxes. First, at the state level, a two-thirds majority vote by legislators was required either to introduce new taxes or to increase taxes other than property taxes. New taxes based on the value or sale of real property were banned. Second, no new substitute taxes could be levied at the local level unless they were approved by a two-thirds majority in a referendum.

Text of Proposition 13

That Article XIII A is added to the Constitution to read:

Section 1.

(a) The maximum amount of any ad valorem tax on real property shall not exceed one percent (1%) of the full cash value of such property. The one percent (1%) tax is to be collected by the counties and apportioned according to law to the districts within the counties.

(b) The limitation provided for in subdivision (a) shall not apply to ad valorem taxes or special assessments to pay the interest and redemption charges on any indebtedness approved by the voters prior to the time this section becomes effective.

Section 2.

(a) The full cash value means the County Assessor's valuation of real property as shown on the 1975-76 tax bill under "full cash value" or thereafter, the appraised value of real property when purchased, newly constructed, or a change in ownership has occurred after the 1975 assessment. All real property not already assessed up to the 1975-76 tax levels may be reassessed to reflect that valuation.

(b) The fair market value base may reflect from year to year the inflationary rate not to exceed two percent (2%) for any given year or reduction as shown in the consumer price index or comparable data for the area under taxing jurisdiction.

Section 3.

From and after the effective date of this article, any changes in state taxes enacted for the purpose of increasing revenues collected pursuant thereto whether by increased rates or changes in methods of computations must be imposed by an Act passed by not less than two-thirds of all members elected to each of the two houses of the Legislature, except that no new ad valorem taxes on real property, or sales or transaction taxes on the sale of real property may be imposed.

Section 4.

Cities, counties and special districts by a two-thirds vote of the qualified electors of such district, may impose special taxes on such district except ad valorem taxes on real property or a transaction tax or sales tax on the sale of real property within such city, county or special district.

Section 5.

This article shall take effect for the tax year beginning on July 1 following the passage of this Amendment, except Section 3 which shall become effective upon the passage of this article.

Section 6.

If any section, part, clause, or phrase hereof is for any reason held to be invalid or unconstitutional, the remaining sections shall not be affected but will remain in full force and effect.

Before Proposition 13, the average effective property tax rate in California was approximately 2.5% of the market value. The 1% limitation meant that a formula had to be developed to distribute the cuts among all taxing entities. For example, if the values for the city, school district, and mosquito district were 1.5%, 0.8%, and 0.3%, respectively, the taxpayer would face a total 2.6% property tax rate. However, the 1% limitation meant that rates could no longer be set independently by each district and then simply aggregated. A complex system had to be devised to allocate these revenues.[2]

The Proposition created major inequities stemming primarily from the requirements of section 2(b). While new property owners were assessed at full market value, the assessments of existing property owners could be increased by only a maximum of 2% per year, so they paid much lower property taxes. This provision has sarcastically been called the "Welcome Stranger" clause.[3] The Los Angeles County assessor confirmed that by the 1990s rapid inflation of housing prices in many parts of California led to frequent instances of owners paying property taxes that were five times higher than the taxes paid for similar properties whose owners had possessed them before Proposition 13 was passed. Thus, a homeowner who was a long-time resident may be paying $500 per year, while a neighbor who recently moved into an identical property may pay $2,500 per year in property taxes. These disparities led to a challenge in the courts, but in 1992 the U.S. Supreme Court found that the assessment feature of Proposition 13 did not violate the equal protection clause of the Constitution.

Real-Estate Transfer Taxes

The general property tax is levied annually. It is used to finance the cost of ongoing operations and maintenance, and almost all local park and recreation agencies rely on it. In contrast, a real-estate transfer tax is levied only periodically: when property is sold and conveyed from one person to another. Although it is frequently discussed as a potential source of funding, relatively few local park and recreation agencies acquire resources from this type of tax, but it is emerging with increasing frequency at the state level for acquiring and developing parks and open spaces.

The philosophical justification for levying a real-estate transfer tax for parks and open spaces was well expressed by the commission that initially recommended its implementation for this purpose in Maryland:

> The idea behind the transfer tax is that the person who buys a home or other property for private use has hastened the decline in available open space land. By paying a tax at the rate of one-half of one percent of the property purchase price, that same person would help to support the buying of land which could be used and enjoyed by the general public.[6]

The real-estate transfer tax is used at the state level for park acquisition purposes in Maryland, Georgia, Florida, Arkansas, Illinois, North Carolina, South Carolina, Tennessee, and Washington. On every real-estate transaction in Maryland, for example, a tax of 0.5% is imposed. This generates approximately $25 million in a typical year for the state's Program Open Space because the rapid economic growth in the state has led to substantial activity in the real-estate market. The state has used the funds from this tax to acquire more than 150,000 acres for state and local purchase of parks, forests, natural-environment areas, natural-resource management areas, and wildlife-management areas.

Similarly, in Florida, the Land Acquisition Trust Fund provides for expansion of state park and recreational areas. The fund is financed annually from a relatively small proportion of the tax on real-estate transactions currently levied at the rate of $4.50 per $1,000 of assessed value and yields from $20 to $40 million per year for land acquisition. In Arkansas, the real-estate transfer tax rate of $1.10 per $1,000 sales value is used for acquisition and development of park, recreational, and cultural resources and yields approximately $4 million per year. A similar levy of $1 per $1,000 assessed value is imposed in North Carolina where it yields approximately $13 million annually for parks and natural areas. The tax has also been adopted to finance park acquisition by a small number of local governments like that of Spring Island, South Carolina.

Spring Island is a small, 3,000-acre island off the South Carolina coast, which is accessible from a neighboring island via a private bridge or by boat. The company that developed the island in the 1990s limited its development to 500 homes, a golf course, and tennis courts. It capitalized on the growing market for environmentally sensitive development and preserved much of the island's animal habitat and natural beauty. Part of this effort involved establishing a 1,000-acre native preserve that was owned and managed by the nonprofit Spring Island Trust, an entity created by the developer. The trust was supported financially by a 1.5% fee from the sale of each lot and a 1% transfer fee on subsequent sales. An extensive trail system linked each lot with a network of trails in the preserve. A full-time naturalist—half of whose salary was paid by the trust and half by the developer—managed the preserve.[7]

The real-estate transfer tax is a relatively reliable source of revenue, particularly in those areas where the population is growing and an active real-estate market exists. It is an appropriate source of revenue for park acquisition and construction because land development often decreases recreational opportunities at the same time that it creates a need for more recreational areas. For this reason, some have suggested that it should be called a growth-enhancement tax. In this respect, its conceptual justification appears to be strong and similar to that which underpins exactions,

which are discussed in chapter 10. However, there are two important distinctions. First, exactions are imposed only on initial property development, whereas a real-estate transfer tax is imposed on each occasion that the property changes ownership. Second, exactions usually apply only to residential dwellings, while a real-estate transfer tax generally is imposed on all types of property transactions. The rationale for imposing the periodic real-estate transfer tax rather than the one-time exaction is that park and recreation properties deteriorate with use and need periodic renovation even when they are well maintained. Exactions do not provide the ongoing source of funds necessary for such renovations.

There is conceptual justification for making the tax the responsibility of either the buyer or the seller of the property. As a current resident, the seller has enjoyed access to the facilities and contributed to their depreciation. Thus, the selling household should contribute to restoring them before its members leave. On the other hand, the

Preserving Open Space in Nantucket

Nantucket Island, which is off the coast of Massachusetts, protects about one-third of its 31,000 acres through various government agencies and the Nantucket Conservation Foundation. However, several years ago residents feared that the island's increasing popularity would threaten its rustic atmosphere. The number of building permits had accelerated, and property values had risen at 15% each year.

Land on the island is expensive. Even small building sites routinely sell for $250,000 or more. Authorities suggested that the island should "hitch the conservation wagon to the wild, runaway real-estate market." They proposed that a flat 2% of the purchase price on all real-estate transactions be used to pay for land conservation. In effect, those who bought or developed real estate also pay to protect land from development. At a special town meeting in 1984, island residents approved the concept by 446 to one. The island's chief planner commented: "Developers and brokers, summer people and year-rounders all saw it. If we didn't move fast and aggressively, everything that made Nantucket special and valuable would be gone." In the program's first six years it acquired $22 million that was used to purchase more than 1,000 acres, and the concept spread to other communities across New England.

The level of activity in the real-estate market dictates the amount of funds that will be available for acquisition of park and open space land. However, Nantucket authorities do not have to wait to purchase land until they have cash in-hand. When the program was launched, they issued $10 million of revenue bonds and subsequently issued another $18 million of bonds that were redeemed by the income stream provided by the real-estate transfer tax.

People who buy homes on Nantucket and who are required to pay the 2% tax usually do not complain about it. The program's administrator states: "We tell them, 'This is your insurance policy. This is going to protect your home. Why are you buying here? What do you want it to look like in 10 years?' People don't object. They understand it is for their children."

Adapted from James Stolz. Preserving open land Nantucket style. Country Journal. November/December, 1990; and Robert Guenther. Nantucket races developers to preserve its open spaces. The Wall Street Journal. March 27, 1985, page 33.

buyer enjoys immediate access to established park and recreational facilities but has made no capital contribution to them. This freeloading is eliminated if the buyer has to contribute through a real-estate transfer tax. There is also an important political consideration here. If the tax is made the buyer's responsibility, then most of the burden does not fall on current residents but rather on newcomers.

Using real-estate transfer taxes incorporates an inherently attractive financial balancing mechanism. Prevailing economic conditions substantially influence the private real-estate market. Because the real-estate transfer tax is tied to that market, the amount of revenue it generates also depends on economic conditions in the area. However, downturns in the economy do not necessarily reduce its purchasing power, even though the amount of available funds decline as real-estate market activity slows. In periods of slow real-estate activity, the cost of acquiring park land is likely to be less, particularly because a public agency is likely to purchase in cash. Therefore, less revenue is needed to purchase the desired land. Conversely, when the real-estate market is active, the tax generates more revenue, which is a necessity because land prices are also likely to be higher.

Sales Taxes

Sales taxes are the largest single source of state tax revenues and the second largest source of tax revenues for municipalities after the property tax. However, in some cities with large retail centers, sales tax receipts exceed those receipts received from the property tax. Local sales taxes tend to ride piggyback on taxes that the states levy, but the local rates are typically much lower than state sales tax rates. The combined local-state general sales tax rates usually range from 3% to 10% among the states, but the most commonly used local rates range from 1% to 2%. The dominance of sales taxes at the state level means that many state park and recreation agencies use the sales tax as a funding source. For example, the state of Missouri has two dedicated funds supported by a state sales tax that voters approved as constitutional amendments. The first is a 0.25¢ sales tax targeted to acquire and manage fish and game lands. The second is a 0.1¢ sales tax that produces about $26 million annually that is divided equally between the park system and the soil and water conservation program which are both adminis-

tered through the Missouri Department of Natural Resources. In 1996, citizens voted overwhelmingly to extend this state parks fund through the year 2008.

Most sales taxes are not applied to the sale of services but are imposed on nearly all transactions involving tangible products at the retail level. Typically, food for at-home consumption and prescription drugs are exempted to reduce the regressiveness of the sales tax. (A regressive tax is one that bears more heavily on lower-income groups than on higher-income groups.) In some states this exemption has been expanded to include clothing. Purchase of these essential items constitutes a higher percentage of the income of low-income families than of high-income families. Thus, if these items remain in the tax base, the sales tax would be strongly regressive. In some situations, sales taxes have particular appeal to local residents because a large proportion of them may be paid by visitors from outside the jurisdiction who, thus, effectively subsidize the park and recreation amenities designed mainly for residents' use.

Residents in the city of North Richmond Hills, Texas, voted to approve a park system master plan that contained $40 million of improvements to be financed by a 0.5¢ sales tax. Passage of the referendum was aided by a study showing that 60% to 70% of the sales tax revenue was generated by nonresidents who shop in the city, so they effectively paid most of the costs of these facilities. The city's park and recreation director observed: "It means $3.5 million a year for parks and recreation development, which is pretty fabulous for a city of 50,000." The first facility constructed was a $7.8 million family aquatic park that averaged more than 2,500 users each day in its first summer of operation, and revenues matched operation and maintenance costs.[8]

In Lake Havasu City, Arizona, the city council approved a 1¢ sales tax increase to finance construction of a 55,000 sq ft facility with a combination competitive-leisure pool, gymnasium, and other amenities. Since the city receives a large influx of visitors in the summer and winter, outsiders pay about 36% of the sales tax revenue. Likewise, nonresidents are charged more than residents to use the facility.[9]

In addition to general sales taxes that are levied on a broad spectrum of sales transactions, selected excise taxes may be enacted. These are imposed only on a limited set of products that are specified in the legislation authorizing them. The two types of selected excise taxes that are important sources of funds for the park and recreation field are hotel-motel taxes (sometimes called bed taxes) and manufacturers' excise taxes on specified recreational equipment.

The Hotel-Motel Tax

Like the general sales tax, the hotel-motel, or bed, tax is a state tax on which local jurisdictions ride piggyback. The combined rate usually ranges from 10% to 15% that is added to the price paid for a hotel or motel room. The tax is assessed only on the room price and not on the cost of food that the hotel serves or the cost of other personal services. Unlike a local sales tax, the local bed tax in most states does not require voter approval. In most cases, these funds are designated exclusively to promote and develop a jurisdiction's tourism industry. Conceptually, this tax enables visitors to a state or city to pay the costs incurred in the promotion that provides them with information and to pay some of the facility costs associated with meeting their tourism needs. However, note that many visitors to a community may be there for business rather than recreational reasons. These people, nevertheless, are required to pay this tax even though they make no use of these tourism services.

Hotel-motel tax revenues are sometimes used to finance park and recreational facilities and operations that may serve the needs of local residents as well as visitors. It may be argued that this revenue source can legitimately fund lifeguarding, fishing piers, and beach patrols in a resort area; costs associated with soccer or softball tournaments that attract people from other towns; or zoological parks that often are positioned as tourism attractions. The bed tax has been used widely to fund stadia that the public sector construct. For example, the Louisiana Superdome received proceeds from a 4% hotel-motel occupancy tax imposed in Jefferson and Orleans parishes, which compose the principle population service area of the stadium. The city of Atlanta increased its hotel-motel tax to finance the $200 million Georgia Dome. The Dome's debt and related fees were $18.3 million in the first year of operation, and the city raised nearly $11 million through the hotel-motel tax.[10] A variation of the hotel-motel tax for funding park and recreational facilities is described in "A Variation of the Hotel-Motel Tax in Flagstaff."

Pledging part of the hotel-motel tax to redeem revenue bonds for major recreational facilities is politically attractive for two main reasons. First, it does not require voter approval in most states, whereas approval is often required at the local level for general sales tax increases. Second, it transfers the costs of building (and sometimes also operating) a major recreational facility to out-of-town visitors. They do not vote on tax increases and are unlikely even to realize that the tax is underwriting those facilities.

A Variation of the Hotel-Motel Tax in Flagstaff

Flagstaff welcomes 2 million tourists each year who are attracted by easy access to the Grand Canyon, which is a 1-hour drive; skiing opportunities; the national forests; and the mountainous setting. Its population is growing rapidly at a rate of 8% each year. Newcomers have a way of calling for more services. Visitor spending provides a source of funds to meet those local needs.

In 1988, a citizen initiative was passed to raise $2 million per year. It is known as the "bed, board, and booze tax." While a hotel tax is common in Arizona, taxing restaurants and bars is not. These revenues are divided by the statute: 48% goes to tourism marketing; 16.5%, to economic development; and 32%, to beautification projects (the remainder is for administration). The winning argument for the initiative was that "the tax would provide amenities that citizens could not otherwise afford and would be paid for by people who do not live there."

Flagstaff's urban trail system, which connects neighborhoods, commercial areas, schools, and national forest land, is one of the tax's most popular benefits. The bed, board, and booze tax revenues contribute $110,000 each year to building the system, which is leveraged with Arizona's lottery-supported Heritage Fund and the federal Intermodal Surface Transporation Efficiency Act monies.

From Phyllis Myers. Financing parks and conservation. Greensense. Spring, 1995. 1(2), page 6.

Manufacturers' Excise Tax on Recreational Equipment

A manufacturers' excise tax on recreational equipment is an attempt to allocate the costs of providing recreation amenities to the users of those facilities. Two long-established taxes of this nature at the federal level are noncontroversial and widely accepted. The first of these taxes originally was called the Dingell-Johnson Fund but was subsequently revised and renamed the Wallop-Breaux Fund. It imposes an excise tax on fishing tackle and equipment, on trolling motors and fish finders, and on motor boat fuels, and it earmarks the funds for distribution to states for sport-fishing area restoration, coastal wetlands, and boating enhancement programs. This approach says: "Let's take tax money paid for certain products purchased by boaters and fishermen and use that money to develop more boating and fishing resources."[11] Revenues from the Wallop-Breaux Fund are distributed through federal grants to states. These revenues typically amount to between $300 million and $350 million per year, and they have been used in a variety of ways illustrated by the following examples:

- New artificial reefs and a restored kelp forest in southern California.

- Improved sport fishing off California's coast.

- Improved access to numerous lakes by building new boat launch ramps.

- Habitat improvements along rivers resulting in large increases in the fish population.

- Thousands of Pennsylvania youngsters each year learning about life in and around the water and about water safety and outdoor ethics through Keystone Aquatic Resource Education. The program was especially active in downtown Pittsburgh, reaching youth who might not otherwise have been exposed to fishing.

- Native brook and cutthroat trout reintroduced into streams and lakes in many states.[12]

This principle of taxing recreational equipment to provide facilities was incorporated into the Pittman-Robertson Act passed in 1937. To ensure that wildlife resources are restored and maintained, this act provides financial support derived from an excise tax on sporting arms and ammunition, archery equipment, pistols and revolvers, and related items. Each year this program typically generates approximately $200 million, distributed to the states for wildlife restoration and enhancement purposes.

The notable success of these programs has led others to suggest that if an excise tax on related equipment is appropriate for financing fishing, boating, and hunting opportunities, then the same logic should apply to other recreational opportunities, such as golf courses, tennis courts, running tracks, swimming pools, softball diamonds, soccer fields, and campgrounds.[11] Indeed, it may be argued that it is inequitable to require hunters, boaters, and fishermen to pay for their recreational opportunities through an excise tax while those who pursue other recreational opportunities are not required to do so.

The primary conceptual argument against wider applications of this type of excise tax is that it is too broad to operate as a closed-loop tax; that is, the tax revenues may not be reinvested in a facility that benefits its payer directly. Unlike the Pittman-Robertson and Wallop-Breaux Funds, which are limited to one type of recreation, a recreation trust fund would include many types of recreation. For example, the revenues accruing from taxes on baseballs and golf balls would go into the same account so that purchasers of baseballs would contribute to the development of golf courses and vice versa. The complexity of administering separate funds for taxes from equipment associated with each recreational activity and reallocating them exclusively for facilities related to that activity makes such a plan not feasible.

A further complication arises from recreational facilities and services being provided by both the public and the private sectors. The mixed delivery system leads to two concerns: the closed-loop issue and unfair competition. The closed-loop issue in this context is concerned with the fairness of using excise tax revenues to develop public facilities when the tax has been levied on equipment that may be used exclusively at private facilities.

An excise tax would not distinguish between products used at public facilities and those not. Golf clubs and tennis racquets are examples. Should a racquet used by someone who plays exclusively on the courts of a private tennis club be taxed when he or she would derive no benefits? The equity issue becomes even more dramatic with a $50,000 motorhome. Many never enter a public recreation area, utilizing only private campgrounds and RV resorts.[13]

This equitability concern also extends to public agencies, such as schools and colleges, that would pay taxes when they purchase recreational equipment even though they may not be eligible for grants from a trust fund. This concern might be resolved by providing exemptions for such entities, but it would add to the complexity of implementation.

The second public-private issue is that the trust fund would exacerbate unfair competition. The question likely to be raised by private sector suppliers is, "Why should we support this when the revenues will be used primarily to build public facilities, which will directly compete with our facilities, frequently undercut us on price, and steal our customers?" The traditional response would be that the two sectors serve different markets; after trying an activity in the inexpensive, basic public facility and finding that they have a commitment to the activity, some people decide to use a private facility. However, the legitimacy of this response may not be widely accepted. The Pittman-Robertson Fund and Wallop-Breaux Fund allocations generally have not raised such questions of unfair competition because they primarily sustain the mobile biomass of animals, fish, and birds, which benefits facility and service suppliers in both sectors.

A high level of visible support from all impacted constituencies is needed before a manufacturers' excise tax can be extended to finance other recreational facilities. The Dingell-Johnson Act was backed by a wide consensus of fishermen, conservationists, manufacturers, and others who noted the success of the Pittman-Robertson Fund and believed that a similar program for fisheries could be equally successful. Its extension to other recreational equipment has periodically received support from senior administration officials, such as the secretary of the Department of the Interior, and from coalitions of environmental groups and businesses that sell outdoor equipment.[14] However, such an extension is opposed by other politically influential equipment manufacturers who consider the potential benefits too indirect and too speculative to outweigh higher product costs and the costs of administering the tax. They point out that the price of recreational equipment would increase because manufacturers would add the tax amount to the price of their products.

For optimal implementation, a manufacturers' excise tax should be implemented at the federal level of government because this would strengthen the closed-loop nexus. The potential for this implementation is discussed in chapter 11. For example, it would be inequitable if the state were to levy the tax on a manufacturer in Texas when people in other states buy most of the products. The benefits would accrue to Texans but would be paid for by others. This situation is unlikely to discourage Texas legislators! However, the manufacturer would be disadvantaged relative to competitors in other states who did not have to pay the equipment excise tax. This may encourage the manufacturer to move the facility to another state to avoid the tax, and this potential to move is likely to discourage state legislators.

Despite the advantages of implementing the manufacturers' excise tax at the federal level, it has not occurred. At the state level, there are examples of sales taxes levied on recreational equipment and designated for park and recreational facility acquisition and development. However, these taxes are levied on retail sales and not on the manufacturers. The most comprehensive of these programs was enacted in Texas when the state legislature approved a state excise tax on sporting goods that were defined as items of tangible personal property designed and sold for use in a sport or sporting activity, excluding apparel and footwear except that which is suitable only for use in a sport or sporting activity and excluding board games, electronic games and similar devices, aircraft and powered vehicles, and replacement parts and accessories for any excluded item.

The dedicated revenues for parks and recreation under this law were capped at $32 million with amounts in excess of this directed to the state's general fund. Of the $32 million, 40% was allocated to state parks; 40% to local parks; and 20% to a capital contingency account.

This was not a new tax. Rather, revenues from the existing general sales tax on sporting goods were reallocated from the general fund to a dedicated fund for parks and recreation. Revenues from a cigarette tax previously had financed this dedicated fund, and these revenues were redirected into the state's general fund. Because no new taxation and no immediate loss to the state's general fund were involved, the new law gained widespread political support. Parks and recreation have benefited in two ways from these changes. First, a much stronger conceptual nexus exists between the parks and recreational facilities and sporting goods than exists between the facilities and cigarettes, which makes its defense easier if budget cuts or reallocations are suggested. Second, revenues from the cigarette tax are likely to decline as smoking decreases, whereas revenues from sporting goods are likely to increase in the future.

Benefit Assessment Districts

Until this point in the chapter, the discussion has assumed that property or sales taxes used to support park and recreation services are levied on the whole community. The following section describes a mechanism through which these taxes may be imposed only on a selected geographical area that benefits from a service.

In some enabling legislation, benefit assessment districts are also termed enhancement districts, special assessment districts, improvement park districts, special services districts, or business improvement districts. They are similar to special districts because they have defined geographical boundaries. However, they differ because they are funding mechanisms instead of governmental units, and they do not have management responsibilities. Local governments form them because most property owners within the district's boundaries want a higher level of service than the standard that the city provides. Hence, the property owners agree to assess themselves an additional property or sales tax to pay for this higher level of service. The tax is apportioned according to a formula designed to reflect the proportion of benefits that the property owners are accruing. For example, people whose property is located on the fringe of the district may be assessed less than people whose property abuts the park or facility. The benefit assessment district tax is identified separately on tax bills.

The higher level of service that taxpayers desire may refer to acquisition and development of new facilities, as well as to higher standards of operation and maintenance. In these cases, special assessment bonds may be issued to finance the capital improvements. Because the benefit is confined to a carefully defined area of the community, only those people who will benefit from the improvement bear the cost. The director of parks and recreation in New York City observed: "It's like upgrading an airline ticket to first-class."[15]

The requirements for establishing benefit assessment districts vary between states, but typically they are created by a petition from taxpayers representing 50% or two-thirds of the affected property. For example, the River Oaks community in Houston, which is relatively affluent, wanted a higher standard of esplanade maintenance than the city's standard 19-day maintenance cycle provided. They formed a special assessment district where the assessments pay for maintenance on a five-day cycle.

Some see park enhancement districts that are organized at a neighborhood level and are authorized to levy a small surcharge on real estate in the area as the key to achieving adequate maintenance and to revitalizing parks in major cities. The neighborhood can terminate the arrangement at any time it elects to do so. The city would collect the money but would turn it over to the park district. This arrangement can empower neighborhood residents by giving them more direct control over investments made in their parks.

Critics of benefit assessment districts express concern that they may create a two-tier system of parks. Some cite the experience of Minneapolis, which in the 1960s tried financing its parks with special assessments on residents living around particular parks. The superintendent of the Minneapolis Park and Recreation Board commented: "It totally disenfranchised the folks who couldn't afford parks.... The system became so imbalanced between rich and poor that there were uprisings by communities demanding their rights."[15,16] Minneapolis scrapped this system and reverted to a citywide charge on each property that was dedicated to park use.

Government agencies usually provide the additional level of service in benefit assessment districts, but in many large cities it has been initiated by business leaders and the areas termed business improvement districts. There are more than 1000 business improvement districts in the United States and Canada.[17] Business improvement districts frequently elect their own boards that take responsibility for the annual budget, hire staff, let contracts, and generally oversee operations. Much of their effort goes into cleaning up, landscaping, maintaining trees and flowers, and enhancing security. One mayor experienced in the work of business improvement districts explained the concept in the following terms: "The concept behind a BID is to treat the downtown like a mall with a mall manager. The mall manager is responsible for security, cleanup, beautification, joint marketing of the downtown special events and promotion."[18] A businessman involved with a business improvement district said: "Money can be raised on a voluntary basis, but you spend half your time doing it. With a BID you know what you have and you get to work."[15]

Bryant Park was a neglected, vandalized facility that had become a haven for drug dealers in the city of New York. A business improvement district was formed to maintain the park and focus on ongoing park improvements. The park has been restored with tall shade trees, lush green grass, and flower beds and is now considered a model park. At its summer peak, there are 55 employees working in Bryant Park in security, sanitation, gardening, and special events. All of them work for the business improvement district. The city paid one-third of the $18 million restoration costs, and foundations, philanthropists, and surrounding businesses financed the rest through the business improvement district. The businesses assessed themselves $1.2 million of Bryant Park's $2 million annual maintenance bill, while much of the remainder of the bill was raised in rental and concession fees from restaurants and special events held in the park. Businesses recognized that property values, and, hence, lease rentals, were closely tied to conditions in the park. Rents in nearby buildings increased dramatically after the park was redesigned and secured.[19]

The business improvement district approach has become widespread in the downtown areas of major cities. The 24 business improvement districts in the city of New York have a combined annual budget of more than $30 million. Hotel operators, theater owners, storekeepers, restaurateurs, service providers, office employees, developers, property owners, and property managers plan and manage urban services in their neighborhoods. These stakeholders pay for them as a cost of business because they are perceived as being essential to the area's economic vitality.[17]

Capital Funding Mechanisms

The development and expansion of park and recreation systems through the acquisition of park land and new facility construction at both state and local levels primarily has depended on the ability of agencies to borrow money. Most of these capital outlays have been paid for through the sale of long-term debt instruments, the most common of which are bonds. Bonds are defined formally as a promise by the borrower (the agency bond issuer) to pay back to the lender (the financial institution bond holder) a specified amount of money with interest within a specified period of time. The interest is expressed as a percentage of the principal (face amount of the bond) available for use during a specified period of time. Typically,

the contract specifies that interest payments will be made semi-annually.

The alternative to borrowing money is to adopt a pay-as-you-go approach, which offers the major advantage of substantial savings in interest charges. For example, the city of San Antonio adopted a pay-as-you-go approach for financing its Alamodome, which cost $174 million to build. Most of the money was raised by a five-year surcharge of an additional 0.5¢ on the local sales tax, which was approved by the city's voters in a referendum.[20] The project director estimated that if long-term general obligation bonds had been used, taxpayers would have paid a total of $435 million in principal and interest payments over the years of the bond issue. This would have required annual debt service payments of $17 million, which would have been equivalent to a 15% increase in the property tax.

However, there are two major disadvantages of using the pay-as-you-go approach to finance capital projects, which account for its relatively infrequent use. First, from a political perspective, the actions of many elected officials are guided by their desire to be re-elected. Thus, they perceive it to be advantageous to build major facilities today, to reap the political rewards from their construction, and to shift the costs of the facilities as far forward as possible so that political penalties associated with paying for them become the problem of their successors. Second, from an equity perspective, pay-as-you-go is likely to be inefficient and inequitable. With population mobility, some residents will pay the full cost of a facility from which they will receive no benefits if they later leave the community. Conversely, others moving into the community will receive benefits from an asset to which they made no financial contribution.

To issue long-term debt instruments, a municipality obtains legal authorization from either the voters or its legislative body to borrow money from a qualified lender. The lender can be any individual, organization, or group with money to lend at interest. Usually, the lender is an established financial institution, such as a bank; an investment service that may purchase bonds as part of its mutual fund portfolio; or, sometimes, an insurance company. When the financial institution lends the money to the public agency, the agency provides the lender with an appropriate number of engraved certificates (usually issued in multiples of $5,000 denominations). These redeemable certificates, or bonds, represent the legal obligation of the public agency (borrower) to pay back the certificate or bond holder (the lending institution) the amount borrowed together with a fixed rate of interest.

A fundamental rule associated with issuing long-term debt instruments is do not issue them for a maturity longer than the project's useful life. People should not be paying for a major park or recreational facility after it is no longer in use: "If the debt life exceeds useful life, the project's true annual cost has been understated and people will continue to pay for the project after it has gone. If the useful life exceeds the debt period, the annual cost has been overstated and people will receive benefits without payment" (p. 408).[3] The longer the maturity term, the higher the interest rate required to borrow for that period of time because borrowers have to compensate investors for locking up their resources for a longer time.

State statutes limit the amount of borrowing to which local government can commit. These limitations vary widely from one state to another. This restriction is generally referred to as the statutory debt ceiling. In almost all cases, the debt ceiling is expressed as a percentage of the total assessed value of property within a jurisdiction. For example, if a park and recreation special district has a total assessed value of $500 million and its statutory debt ceiling is limited to 3% of the assessed value, then it has the legal potential to borrow up to $15 million.

A taxonomy of the types of capital funding mechanisms that municipalities may use to finance the acquisition or development of a park or recreational facility is shown in figure 2.5. The most fundamental distinction in the type of debt that governments incur to fund capital projects is whether that debt is a full-faith and credit obligation or is a nonguaranteed obligation. The discussion in this section is arranged under these two headings.

Full-Faith and Credit Obligations

Full-faith and credit obligations have an unlimited claim on the taxes and other revenues of the government entity borrowing the funds. The burden of paying these debts is spread over all taxable property within the issuing government's geographical boundaries. When they are issued by a local government entity, the general obligation usually is secured by the property tax. State governments, which have a different tax structure, usually pledge revenue streams, such as sales or income taxes. In effect, the government unit makes an unconditional promise to the bondholder to secure or to pay back the interest and principal owed through its authority to levy taxes.

Figure 2.5 identifies the three most common forms of full-faith and credit obligations: general obligation bonds, certificates of obligation, and contractual obligations. Because general obligation bonds are issued with this full-faith and credit provision, they are regarded by many as the safest and most secure form of investment next to U.S. Treasury bonds. They offer greater security that bond principal and interest payments will be made

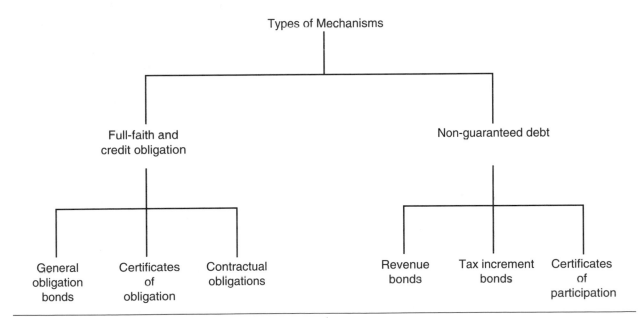

Figure 2.5 Types of capital funding mechanisms.

on time than do other types of bonds that are nonguaranteed. Hence, they bear a lower interest rate than equivalent nonguaranteed debts do.

The security that a government body's unconditional pledge of full tax support provides usually results in making the bonds easier to sell. The reduced risk, which is associated with the almost certain probability of reimbursement, increases the attractiveness of general obligation bonds to a greater range of potential investors. Ease of sale and reduced cost of tax-guaranteed general obligation bonds are significant advantages. However, because the sale of general obligation bonds represents an obligation that all taxpayers must meet, the government body desiring to issue them must first obtain voter approval. This requirement to obtain broad-based support from the electorate for new park and recreational facilities is a major challenge to agencies seeking the use of general obligation bonds.

In contrast to general obligation bonds, certificates of obligation and contractual obligations (see figure 2.5) do not require approval of the voters at a referendum, but both are still backed by the full faith and credit of a jurisdiction's tax base. The city council is required to publish a legal notice announcing a public hearing of their proposed use. The electorate can then petition the council requesting a public referendum on their use, but this rarely occurs. Certificates of obligation must be used for real property acquisition or improvements, whereas contractual obligations can be used for broader purposes, such as renovating a facility or purchasing major pieces of equipment.

These certificates usually are sold to local, rather than to regional or national, investors, and, as with general obligation bonds, the debt is retired over a given period of years with property tax revenues. These instruments typically are used in one of the following circumstances:

- A relatively small capital item is involved: for example, the purchase of a small building for additional office or maintenance space. The investment is considered to be too small to justify the cost of organizing a referendum to vote on it.
- If the capital purchase is not made quickly, then the opportunity to acquire it will be lost. There is insufficient time to go through the lengthy process of obtaining voter approval for the purchase.

- The council has doubts that voters would approve the purchase, but its members are convinced strongly that the project is in the community's best long-term interest.

The latter two conditions were present in the following example. In the early 1980s, the city of College Station used certificates of obligation to acquire 1,200 acres for $1.2 million. The intent was to reserve part of it for future development of a business park and to use the rest of it as a large natural park area. The land was located 3 mi south of the existing city boundary. The council doubted that voters could be persuaded to fund this purchase because its development seemed likely to be in the distant future and it was so far from the existing city boundaries. Further, developers were interested in acquiring the tract, and it likely would have been sold before a referendum could be organized. These factors persuaded the council to use this funding mechanism. The city grew rapidly and, by the late 1990s, extended out to this area. The 540-acre natural park consisted of attractive post-oak forest and savanna land. A business park and a large subdivision, featuring an 18-hole golf course, bordered it. Future generations will have cause to praise the vision of the council in acquiring such an outstanding natural park in this way.

Non-Guaranteed Debt

Park and recreation agencies are issuing non-guaranteed debt instruments with growing frequency. These are not backed by the full faith and credit of the government entity. Rather, they are sold on the basis of repayment from other designated revenue sources. If revenue from the designated sources falls short of what is required to make debt payments, the government entity does not have to make up the difference.

Non-guaranteed debt instruments have three major advantages. First, in most states, direct voter approval is not required because the general taxpayers are not being asked to pay these debts. Second, they are not considered statutory debts, so they do not count against the government entity's debt ceiling capacity. Third, if the revenue accrues directly from the project, then the people who most benefit from the facility pay for it.

Investors who buy these non-guaranteed instruments incur more risk, which means that the government borrowers have to pay higher interest rates to lenders than they would pay on full-faith and credit obligations. The difference in rates between full-faith and credit debt and non-guaranteed debt may be as much as 2%. In other words, it may cost 7% to finance a project using non-guaranteed debt as opposed to 5% if full-faith and credit mechanisms are used. The additional interest cost over the full period of the loan may be substantial. The difference between paying 5% and 7% on a 20-year, $1 million issue is almost $300,000.

Non-guaranteed debt is secured by a revenue stream from a designated source; however, a city often will accept either a real or a moral obligation to secure it. Accepting this obligation requires the city either to pledge legally or orally to appropriate from its annual revenues money that may be required to meet full debt service on the bonds if the designated revenue source does not provide it. The city does this for two reasons. First, it reduces risk and, hence, rate of interest that investors charge for the bonds. Second, even though a jurisdiction has no legal obligation to support non-guaranteed debt, a default would damage its reputation in the investment markets and make securing capital funds in the future more difficult and expensive for the jurisdiction.

A wide array of non-guaranteed funding mechanisms have been created, but the three that are likely to be most pertinent for development of park and recreational facilities are revenue bonds, tax-increment bonds, and certificates of participation (see figure 2.5).

Revenue Bonds

Revenue bonds are usually backed exclusively by revenue accruing from the project, which means that a facility has to generate sufficient funds to cover both operating and maintenance expenses and annual principal and interest payments. The bonds may be used to finance the construction of revenue-generating facilities, such as golf courses, campgrounds, marinas, athletic fields, and indoor tennis arenas. The income raised from the operation of these facilities through user prices, rental charges, and concessions is used to retire the revenue bonds. An illustration of a softball complex funded by revenue bonds is given in "Developing a Softball Complex With Revenue Bonds."

Investors usually require that a debt-service reserve fund be created to provide additional security in case projected revenues fall below the level needed to meet annual debt-service requirements. In such cases, this reserve can be used to make the required payment, and the reserve subsequently is replenished from any annual surplus revenues that exceed the amount needed for debt service. The reserve amount is usually equal to the maximal annual debt payment. In table 2.2, this reserve consisted of $36,000 derived from a one year collection of a $5 surcharge fee on the softball players before the revenue bonds were issued. Alternatively, the reserve fund may be created out of proceeds of the bond issue.

As a rule, revenue bonds for park and recreational facilities are much more difficult to sell in the open, or public, market than general obligation bonds are because investors prefer less risky opportunities about which they are better informed. As a result, park and recreation officials often are restricted to obtaining revenue bond financing by negotiating with a local financial institution.

Revenue bonds have been suggested as a mechanism for aiding the National Park Service to raise capital funds. Congress would establish a national park authority for the specific purpose of issuing national park bonds. The principal and interest payments would be redeemed by dedicating all revenues generated by the park system to this purpose rather than diverting them to the general treasury as is now done. These revenues approximate $150 million per year, which would be sufficient to service approximately $1.5 billion of new capital for park projects.[21]

Congress has not yet considered this comprehensive proposal, but revenue bonds have been proposed to solve problems at specific parks. For example, a bill proposing bonds to finance a new public transportation system at Grand Canyon National Park was introduced. The system would be paid for by a special surcharge of $2 on each visitor to the park. This surcharge would be sufficient to service specific funds for the building of a public transit system on the south rim of the canyon.[21]

Tax-Increment Bonds

More than half of the states now have enabling legislation authorizing tax-increment financing. Although the rules and limitations associated with it differ among the states, the basic concept is the same. The first stage is to designate an area that is in need of urban redevelopment as a tax-increment financing district. The local development authority or city then issues tax-increment bonds and uses the proceeds to purchase or acquire by eminent domain several parcels of property containing substandard buildings or structures; to clear the land; and to prepare the land for development by installing park, infrastructure, or other public

Developing a Softball Complex With Revenue Bonds

Johnson County, Kansas, used revenue bonds to develop an 80-acre, seven-field softball complex with three additional multipurpose fields (all irrigated) for soccer and for flag and touch football and with a 2.5-acre lake for fishing and ice skating, a jogging trail, a playground area, a concession stand, a restroom area, picnic shelters, and a parking lot. A federal Land and Water Conservation Fund grant of $246,000 was matched with $260,000 of revenue bonds to develop the complex. The county already owned the land, but they had no capital money with which to develop it. They would not back the bonds with a cross-pledge of tax revenues, so the revenue bonds had to be sold at full risk on the commercial market.

The Johnson County Softball Players Association was approached. They contacted their 4,500 members who agreed to pay a surcharge of $5 per player to provide the funds needed to repay the revenue bonds. This surcharge was in addition to the normal fee paid to Johnson County that covered all operating, maintenance, utility, minor improvement, and overhead costs. The athletic associations were pleased to cooperate because it meant that they would have additional facilities available for their use. The district had turned away more than 240 softball teams, and the park and recreation agencies in the Kansas metropolitan area had turned away 1,000 teams due to a lack of facilities. This was evidence of a substantial demand for new ball fields.

The bonds were redeemable from the revenues received from players and teams playing in the softball and soccer leagues and tournaments scheduled through Johnson County. Table 2.2 illustrates that revenues from this source were projected on a yearly average of 1.95 times the necessary income to cover the average yearly principal and interest payments required along with operation and maintenance costs. This income was derived from the approximately 6,000 players (3,000 in each of two seasons) who the county projected were likely to use the facility. A second source of security was unencumbered recreation fees derived from other recreational programs scheduled through the Johnson County Park and Recreation District. Because these had historically exceeded $100,000, this latter provision enabled the bonds to be rated AA instead of A.

The surcharge was imposed for one year before the county sold the bonds in order to demonstrate to the banks that the scheme was feasible. In that year, officials collected $33,000 from the $5 surcharge. This convinced a consortium of local banks to buy the bonds, which had a 15-year payback period at 8.5% interest. The park and recreation district agreed to place the $36,000 in a special reserve account as an additional source of security to the lending banks. This amount exceeded the highest yearly payment for interest and principal (see table 2.2) and was meant to be used only to prevent default of payment of principal and interest on the bond.

The complex proved to be a financial and recreational success. It generated substantial surplus revenues that the county reinvested in further capital improvements on the project.

improvements. The bond's principal and interest are paid by the tax increments, which are captured and dedicated to that purpose.

Tax-increment bonds are secured only by projected increases in revenues from existing and new development in the tax-increment financing district. Repayment is contingent upon increases in the taxable value of the property in the district. From the time that the tax-increment financing district is created, two sets of property tax records are maintained for it. The first reflects the value of property up to the time that the district is formed, and the second reflects any growth in assessed property value after the enhancements have been made. The second incremental portion of tax reve-

nues is used to pay for the cost of the enhancements.

The distinctive feature of tax-increment financing districts is that they rely on property taxes that revitalization projects in the district directly create. The projects pay for redevelopment costs that the public incurs. The tax base of the property in the designated area is frozen at its current level before redevelopment. All entities that have taxing authority, such as cities, counties, and school districts, agree to this freeze. (Remember that only the tax base, and not the tax rate, is frozen.)

Because rejuvenation of the district is likely to increase the value of their assets, landowners and residents have every reason to support the

Table 2.2 Financial Feasibility of Revenue Bonds

Year	#Annual seasonal softball teams	#Annual seasonal soccer/ football teams	Total teams	Team annual special assessment maintenance fee	Total gross revenue	Annual (1) facility maintenance expenses	Available for debt service	Bond issuance debt service	Annual (2) debt coverage
1	470	77	547	$84	$45,948	$5,000	$40,948	—	—
2	800	77	877	85	74,545	15,000	59,545	31,212.50	1.90
3	800	77	877	86	75,422	16,500	58,922	30,387.50	1.93
4	800	77	877	87	76,299	18,150	58,149	29,562.50	1.96
5	800	77	877	88	77,176	19,965	57,211	28,737.50	1.99
6	800	77	877	102	89,454	21,961	67,493	27,912.50	2.41
7	800	77	877	103	90,331	24,157	66,174	32,112.50	2.06
8	800	77	877	103	90,331	26,572	63,759	30,912.50	2.06
9	800	77	877	103	90,331	29,229	61,102	29,712.50	2.05
10	800	77	877	103	90,331	32,151	58,180	33,512.50	1.73
11	800	77	877	111	97,347	35,366	61,981	31,912.50	1.94
12	800	77	877	111	97,347	38,902	58,445	30,312.50	1.92
13	800	77	877	111	97,347	42,792	54,555	33,662.50	1.62
14	800	77	877	111	97,347	47,071	50,276	31,600.00	1.59
15	800	77	877	111	97,347	51,778	45,569	29,537.50	1.54
16	800	77	877	111	97,347	56,955	40,392	32,475.00	2.27*
							$902,701	$463,562.50	

Note: Average annual debt coverage is 1.95.
(1) Total gross revenues and annual facility maintenance expenses increase in annual team assessment to cover anticipated increases in annual costs.
(2) Actual debt service.
*Coverage for Year 16 includes $33,000 in Bond Reserve.

district's establishment. Other jurisdictions, such as school districts, cities, and counties, do not lose revenue by agreeing to freeze assessed property values because without rejuvenation this assessed value would decrease over time.

While state laws vary, all include a provision that enables each of the taxing jurisdictions to continue receiving the share of the taxes that they had collected in the past from the frozen tax base (see figure 2.6a). Each taxing jurisdiction first applies its tax rate to the frozen value then to a new property value. The revenues accruing from the difference between the two is the tax-revenue increment available that year for repaying capital debts that the project accumulated (see figure 2.6b). These incremental dollars go to the special district that issued the bonds. As assessed value in the district increases above the frozen tax base level, greater increments become available for retiring the redevelopment district's debts.

Tax-increment financing has not been used widely for funding park and recreational facilities, but the example from Portland on page 39 shows that this type of financing can be used successfully. Another illustration can be found in Edina, Minnesota, a suburb of Minneapolis and St. Paul. The city constructed an indoor park that enabled residents to engage in recreational activities in the

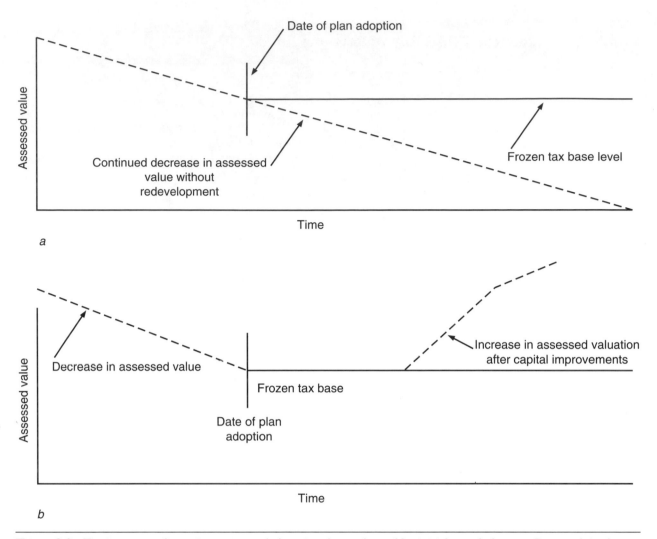

Figure 2.6 Tax increment financing: *a*, stage A: freezing the tax base (the initial stage); *b*, stage B: growth in the tax base after redevelopment.

winter even if they did not enjoy outdoor winter sports. Edinborough Park is a two-acre recreational area (approximately one acre is enclosed). It is a joint project involving private developers and the city of Edina, which also incorporates condominiums, office buildings, and a high-rise retirement complex.

The park, which is open to all Edina residents, includes a running track, swimming pool, multipurpose gymnasium, ice rink, and amphitheater. Its indoor landscaping consists of 9,200 trees, plants, shrubs, and flowers. The $6.5 million project was funded through tax-increment financing. Operating funds for the park are provided by user fees, as well as by interest generated from an escrow account, established with park dedication fees paid by each of the private developers involved in the overall project.[22]

Certificates of Participation

Certificates of participation involve a lending institution providing funds to an intermediary for major equipment, development, or open space acquisition. The intermediary serves as a trustee and holds title to the leased asset for the benefit of the investors who are the certificate holders. The financial institution is reimbursed over time from the lease fees that the government pays the intermediary. The intermediary is usually a nonprofit organization acting as a public-benefit corporation, but, in some circumstances, it may be a different government entity. If a public-benefit corporation is used, its directors are likely to be publicly spirited citizens deemed acceptable to the government entity. When the debt is paid, the facility becomes the agency's property. Certifi-

Using Tax-Increment Financing to Develop Waterfront Park in Portland, Oregon

The Portland Downtown Development Commission is the city's designated urban renewal and development agency. It is responsible for implementing the downtown waterfront urban-renewal plans that involve 300 acres on the west bank of the Willamette River, including a 35-acre, 1.5 mi linear park.

Before the city council adopted the downtown plan in 1972, Portland had already begun revitalization of an area near the waterfront through the traditional urban-renewal approach. Included was a civic auditorium, a pedestrian mall, and a new office and housing development along with a noted fountain designed by Lawrence Halprin. The success of these projects and the subsequent tax revenue created a positive atmosphere for more extensive redevelopment and encouraged the city to develop plans for the waterfront of the nearby Willamette River.

In 1974, the city council adopted two plans: the downtown waterfront urban-renewal plan and the Waterfront Park plan. The waterfront urban-renewal district sold $10 million in tax-increment bonds in 1976 and another $15 million in 1978. Funds generated from the sale of these two bond issues financed the first two phases of Waterfront Park, which involved preservation and improvement efforts in two abutting historic districts.

When the districts were established in 1974, their assessed value was $100 million, but by 1984 the assessed value had increased to $400 million. Waterfront Park has a 1 mi esplanade on the riverfront with plazas; extensive open grassy areas; pension and condominium projects; a recently completed public marina; and a large center for restaurants, retailers, entertainment, special events, and dance performances.

In addition to its waterfront project, Portland also used $1 million of tax-increment financing money as seed money to construct the $8 million Pioneer Square. This is a central public square with fountains, seats, and a pleasant environment that the parks department maintains.

cates of participation tend to be used as alternatives to bonds and, thus, possess relatively long maturities (more than 20 years). Income that investors receive from the leasing payments to the intermediary is tax exempt because the project serves a government purpose.

A referendum is usually not required because the lease agreement is not backed by the full faith and credit of the city, and certificates of participation do not count against a jurisdiction's debt ceiling. There is a moral, rather than a legal, obligation for the jurisdiction to pay the lease fee to the investors annually either from annual appropriations from the general fund or from a designated income stream. Hence, such certificates tend to be viewed as higher risk than traditional bonds and so tend to have higher interest rates. Typically, certificates of participation are rated approximately one letter grade lower than general obligation bonds. The meaning of these ratings is discussed in the next section of this chapter.

Washington State Parks raised $600,000 for major park development by using certificates of partici-

pation. The state treasurer served as intermediary by selling the certificates to private investors. The state park agency received the cash to do the improvements and paid its lease fee to the treasury with revenues that the new facilities earned. The state treasurer in turn paid the investors. The improvements technically are leased to the park system from the state treasury until the debt is repaid.[23]

The city of Corpus Christi, Texas, sold $5.3 million in certificates of participation to fund a new display for three replicas of Christopher Columbus' ships and an expansion at the Corpus Christi Museum of Science and History for an exhibit documenting the discovery of the Americas. The certificates were repaid out of annual appropriations and from the revenues that projects generated. The certificates of participation were guaranteed by the Corpus Christi Greater Business Alliance, which served as the intermediary.[24]

In the city of North Augusta, South Carolina, the Riverview Park Activity Center was funded by $2.4 million from the city's capital projects fund and $3.12 million in certificates of participation. A corporation named Riverview Park Facilities Incorporated was established, and its directors comprised the five members of the North Augusta Parks and Recreation Advisory Board. The North Augusta City Ordinance No. 92-02 stated:

> Whereas, in order to finance the cost of the Project, the City has determined to enter into a Base Lease Agreement whereby the City will lease the existing site whereon the Project will be constructed (the "Land") to RIVERVIEW PARK FACILITIES, INC. (the "Corporation"), and contemporaneously with the execution of such Base Lease, the City will enter into a Project Lease Agreement whereby the Corporation will lease back the Project together with the Land, as improved in the manner discussed above (the "Facilities") to the City; and WHEREAS the Corporation will assign its interest in the Project Lease Agreement to FIRST UNION NATIONAL BANK OF SOUTH CAROLINA, as Trustee for holders of Certificates of Participation in the Project Lease Agreement, which will provide the financing source for the Project (p. 1).[25]

The use of certificates of participation is growing rapidly, and the increase appears likely to continue. They are a means of surmounting legal and political impediments to the use of traditional bonds. Thus, their growth has been particularly prominent in states severely constrained in their ability to borrow funds by tax limits or expenditure limitation statutes.

> For instance, California local governments could borrow only after receiving approval from two-thirds of special referendum voters. In that environment, a one-third minority could prevent projects from having the support, including the willingness to pay a tax to finance the project, of the remaining voters. The COP provided easier access to capital markets without the referendum test; given the size of the state, the pressures on state and local governments there to provide services, and the rigidity of the debt constraint, it is no surprise that California has the largest share of the COP market.[26]

The ability to enter into these arrangements without voter approval is a controversial feature of certificates of participation.[27] In some jurisdictions, voters have opposed their use because they are not subject to citizen review and they dilute

the government's general resources. Because lease payments most often come out of a jurisdiction's general operating fund, however, this places a practical limitation on the amount of certificate of participation financing that a government can undertake. If the certificates became extensive, property taxes would increase substantially, and the public would make an outcry.

Certificates of participation do not legally bind a future government to continue the lease payments. They are conditional agreements subject to annual appropriations. If in any year the government entity fails to appropriate its lease payment, it can terminate the lease and vacate the facility that was financed through sale of the certificates. The intermediary lessor must then assume ownership of the equipment or facility and attempt to protect the investors' interests by finding another purchaser or lessee. The effect of certificates of participation is similar to that of a bond, but the arrangement is structured so that it does not violate constitutional limitations on borrowing or affect the debt ceiling. The steps in the issuance of certificates of participation are summarized in "Steps in the Issuance of Certificates of Participation."

Conducting a Bond Campaign

Persuading a majority of voters to support a bond issue is a major challenge confronting park and recreation personnel. The task is complicated because their actions are limited by both ethical and legal constraints. As public employees, park and recreation personnel are responsible to all taxpayers in the community who provide the resources that pay their salaries. Many taxpayers may be opposed to a proposed bond issue. Thus, because taxpayers pay the salaries of the park and recreation personnel, it is unethical for personnel to advocate directly a bond issue or to campaign for its approval. Their role must be limited to providing information about the proposal.

Similarly, it is illegal for a public agency to expend public funds to promote a partisan position in a bond election campaign. Again, an agency's role must be limited to disseminating information to the public, which is a fair presentation of relevant facts related to the bond proposals. Thus, the agency is not permitted to use public funds to purchase items advocating approval of the proposals, such as bumper stickers, posters, print advertisements, or television and radio advertisements. Public funds cannot be used to disseminate campaign literature prepared by private pro-

Steps in the Issuance of Certificates of Participation

Step 1. A corporation should be created by the government entity to buy the public facility or property.

Step 2. The corporation serves as a trustee and sells or issues certificates of participation to raise the money needed to purchase the facility or property.

Step 3. The government entity leases back the facility or property.

Step 4. The government unit "agrees" to appropriate money annually to meet the lease payments.

Step 5. The trustee holds the title of the facility or property for the benefit of the investors.

Step 6. At the end of the lease period when all payments have been made, the ownership of the facility or property passes to the governmental entity.

From Nancy J. Gladwell, James R. Sellers and J. Robert Brooks. Certificates of Participation as an alternative funding source for capital projects: A case study. Journal of Park and Recreation Administration. Copyright ©1997 JRPA/AAPRA. 15(4), page 33. Reprinted by permission.

ponents of the proposals. However, a park and recreation agency is authorized to make reasonable expenditures for the purpose of giving voters relevant facts to aid them in reaching an informed judgment when voting on the proposal. The illegality of using public funds to promote a favorable position on a bond issue was confirmed by the California Supreme Court when it ruled against William Penn Mott, who at that time was the director of the California Department of Parks and Recreation, for actions he authorized.

According to the complaint, the department's promotion of the bond issue took a number of forms. First, upon the plaintiff's request for information concerning the bond issue election, the department allegedly sent him materials written and printed by the public agency that "were not merely informative but presented promotional material in favor of the . . . Bond Act." Second, the department also allegedly sent the plaintiff "promotional materials written by Californians for Parks, Beaches and Wildlife," a private organization formed to promote the passage of the bond act. Third, the department allegedly expended state funds for speaking engagements and travel expenses to promote the passage of the act. Fourth, a three-person staff, established under the defendant's authorization to work specifically on the bond act, allegedly expended time and state resources to promote the passage of the act.[28]

The park and recreation director's role is to serve as a catalyst in the formation of a steering committee and to service the informational needs of the committee. Frequently, the committee will be charged with developing a list of priority projects that should be presented to the voters in a referendum. When this has been completed, the committee's role shifts to encouraging residents to vote in favor of the proposal. The committee's members and responsibilities will be appointed or confirmed by the jurisdiction's elected governing body.

Typically, the steering committee comprises residents who represent a broad spectrum of groups and interests and who command wide respect in the community. Their task is to mobilize the broad-based community support that is likely to be critical to the passage of a bond referendum. They should seek input from as many in the community as they can reach by undertaking a survey of registered voters, listening to their natural constituencies, holding open public forums, and receiving formal briefings from park and recreation department staff. A description of the work of a steering committee is given in "Role of a Steering Committee in Passing a Bond Referendum: The Crystal Springs Experience."

This steering committee makes recommendations to the elected governing body in the jurisdiction that makes a final decision on what should be included in the bond proposal. Because the elected body authorized the committee, it is rare that it rejects or extensively amends the committee's recommendations. If it did so, the committee may decide not to support the bond issue. Given their influence in the community, this lack of support could lead to its defeat. Members of the committee typically are invited to endorse publicly the bond

Role of a Steering Committee in Passing a Bond Referendum: The Crystal Springs Experience

The Crystal Springs Family Aquatic Center, operated by the township of East Brunswick, New Jersey, needed major renovation and expansion. Financial feasibility studies had been undertaken, but township officials needed to be sure that they were developing a facility that the community would support through a bond referendum.

Hence, they appointed an oversight committee that was charged with the responsibility of educating the public on all aspects of the project, receiving feedback, and reporting their findings to the mayor and council. A six-month time limit was established to facilitate a timely review of the question. The appointed committee members represented a broad cross-section of the community. Working with the Department of Recreation, Parks, and Community Services; the public library; and cable channel 8 (a local-access channel), the committee undertook an aggressive campaign.

The committee produced a 30 min informational video called "A Family Aquatic Center—the Public Question." It explained the family aquatic center concept and showed similarly sized projects around the country. The video explained the project's finances including projected operating expenses, bonding, and capital. The concept of a self-sustaining facility also was documented. The video was produced to standardize the information for public comment. During the campaign, the video aired eight times on channel 8. Additionally, free copies of the video were available at the video rental department at the library. All former study documents, concept plans, and financial studies were made available to the public for review at the library reference desk.

A series of six public hearings was scheduled. Each hearing included the video presentation, a question-and-answer period, and a public comment segment. Committee members volunteered to speak to all civic and fraternal organizations interested in the project. In all, more than 12 forums were held. All comments from citizens were included in the minutes of each public hearing, and they were recorded on citizen input sheets and placed in a binder known as the Red Book, which was available at the library reference desk for public review.

The oversight committee then met to review all comments and produced a document for formal presentation to the mayor and township council. The oversight committee's position paper included the consensus of the study committee and individual committee members' evaluation of the process and recommendations.

Based on all the feedback received, the position of the oversight committee was: "the Community is in favor of a Family Aquatic Center for Community Beach. . . . It must be functional, attractive, and affordable to serve the community." The oversight committee also urged that the Red Book of citizen input be used as a planning tool for the engineers of the project to ensure that residents' concerns be reflected in the design. The staff was to use the Red Book for operations and pricing concerns.

Taking on such an ambitious campaign was worthwhile on many levels for the community and made it easier for staff to solve problems and address issues. Rumors and misunderstandings about the project's size and scope were addressed and clarified. This resulted in a fair evaluation on the project. Many residents who favored the project had operational concerns relating to crowds, pricing, and behavior. Without an opportunity to express their concerns, residents would have reacted negatively to a referendum. By having their comments heard and documented, they were able to support such a project. Ultimately, when the decision was made to proceed, the community in general had bought in to the concept and could be a part of the design team. This resulted in a membership that felt responsible for their facility.

The referendum was passed and the project's attendance and financial viability exceeded projections when the facility opened.

Adapted from Judith L. Leblein. Judging community consensus without a referendum: The Crystal Springs experience. Parks and Recreation. *February 1995, pages 34-40. Copyright ©1995 the National Recreation and Park Association. Used by permission.*

proposal, and their endorsement usually accompanies the informational literature distributed. A typical endorsement is shown in figure 2.7.

Presenting voters with a bond proposal costing many millions of dollars for acquisition and development of park and recreational facilities is likely to be intimidating and may result in many voters expressing a negative reaction. Such large aggregate figures are misleading because they represent the amount that all taxpayers are being asked to contribute. Thus, it is important to present bond costs in terms of their impact on an individual taxpayer. Table 2.3 illustrates how this may be done. The owners of property assessed by this particular jurisdiction at $75,000 will be required to pay an additional $5.25 per year, or approximately 50¢ per month, to pay the debt charges on a $4 million park bond.

In addition to the cost of servicing the bond repayments, residents also need to be informed of how operating and maintaining the new facilities will affect their taxes. Thus, (in the bond issue illustrated in table 2.3) if it is estimated that operating expenses are $200,000, then residents should be informed that the ongoing tax implication for a home assessed at $100,000 is likely to be (for example) 35¢ per year. Presenting costs in terms of their implications for individual taxpayers gives voters a perspective that for "less than the equivalent of a cup of coffee a week," they can enjoy the benefits of many park and recreation improvements. In this regard, there has been widespread acceptance in the parks and recreation field of the pizza principle. This principle states that voters will not approve bond issues for park and recreation projects if their annual cost exceeds the price of a pizza! Headlines in promotional literature may include statements such as: "For less than 2¢ a day, you can substantially improve the community's quality of life." This type of perspective makes a bond proposal seem much more reasonable to the taxpayer than the aggregate price tag of millions of dollars.

Marketing theory offers three key concepts that are central for an effective campaign to pass a bond referendum. The first is market segmentation, which recognizes that residents are likely to have heterogeneous perceptions, attitudes, and interests toward park and recreational facilities. Thus, there will be some residents who will not support any proposals that they are asked to consider because, as a matter of principle, they are opposed to increases in taxation. Investment of resources directed at changing their mind is likely to be wasted. Rather, efforts should be targeted at those segments of the population likely to be most supportive, that is, those who are likely to benefit most from the proposal.

In Dubuque, Iowa, authors of a bond referendum for a softball and baseball complex compared voter registration lists with softball rosters and determined that a large number of softball players were not registered to vote. A small group of enlisted softball players established voter registration booths at all softball fields. Finally, they mailed postcards to softball players prior to the election indicating the impact on softball should the referendum fail.

In San Mateo, California, the park and recreation agency identified five distinct groups as likely "yes" voters; the campaign committee concentrated its efforts on getting these groups out to vote.

In Waterloo, Iowa, volunteers staffed a bank of 14 telephones from 10:00 A.M. until 9:00 P.M. for four weeks before the bond referendum. They called individuals who had participated in the recreation department's programs and activities. Using a prepared script and asking if people knew about the bond election and if they would vote "yes," they spent less than 1 min on average for each call. The volunteers also answered questions that were later compiled and distributed as most frequently asked questions and answers. A second call made on election day reminded individuals to vote and arranged rides to voting sites. The bond election passed with an 85% "yes" vote.[29]

The second central marketing idea is that of benefitizing. This involves addressing the question, "What's in it for them?" This question is

Table 2.3	The Effect of a $4 Million Bond Issue on Individual Homeowners' Taxes in a Hypothetical Jurisdiction

Property value	Annual tax increase	Monthly approximate tax increase
$ 50,000	$ 3.50	$0.25
$ 75,000	$ 5.25	$0.50
$100,000	$ 7.00	$0.75
$125,000	$ 8.75	$1.00
$150,000	$10.50	$1.25

College Station

Capital Improvements Program

A Message To Fellow Citizens From the Capital Improvements Committee

Dear Citizens of College Station:

On August 25, 1994, we were appointed by the College Station City Council to a Capital Improvements Advisory Committee. The charge to the committee was to study and make recommendations to the City Council and residents of the community for a general obligation capital improvements bond election. We met weekly for two months and studied an extensive list of capital projects that totaled over $56 million. We carefully examined the infrastructure and facility needs for College Station for the next several years. There were many needs that this committee felt were important, however; those included in this proposed bond package of $22.5 million were the most pressing over the next three to five years. We believe these are needed to maintain College Station's quality of life.

Based on current projections and assumptions, the proposed $22.5 million in capital projects can be funded without an increase in the property tax rate. There will be additional operational expenses associated with these propositions that may increase your taxes in the future. This is explained on page 14 of this brochure.

We hope you will carefully review this information and the following propositions. Each member of the committee is willing to answer any questions you may have. We encourage you to vote on March 25th and become a vital part of making College Station's quality of life a continuing success.

David Hickson, Chairman

Committee Members:

Sherry Ellison	Steve Aldrich	Peter Keating
Charles Thomas	Ron Silvia	Edsel Jones
Stacy Gunnels	Bill Swafford	A.C. Vinzant
Winnie Garner	Anne Hazen	Marci Rodgers
Joe Bergstad	Dick Birdwell	Tony Jones
Richard Talbert	Jim Hull	Greg Stiles

Please vote on March 25

Figure 2.7 Steering committee endorsement of a bond proposal.
City of College Station Voter Information, 1995.

relatively easy to answer for the groups who will use the proposed facilities, but there is also a need to identify benefits that may accrue to non-users. Some of these non-users may not recognize that they will benefit, and highlighting their roles as beneficiaries may persuade them to support the proposal. These non-user benefits are discussed in detail in chapter 5 and may include

- economic impact on the community created by nonresidents using the new facilities and spending money in the area while doing so;
- improvement of the community's general quality of life, which is a key factor in recruitment and retention of businesses and retirees, both of which may be central components of the community's economic tax base;
- increases in homeowners' real-estate values resulting from creation of new park land or open spaces; and
- alleviation of juvenile crime and delinquency by providing new opportunities for at-risk children and youth.

"The 'Safe Neighborhood Parks Act' in Dade County, Florida" example describes how the benefitizing theme was used to good advantage.

Like the residents, developers may find advantages to becoming active supporters of a park bond. For example, when Californians voted on Proposition 180, which authorized $2 billion for more than 400 park-land purchases, improvements, and cultural projects statewide, supporters raised more than $2 million to promote it. Contributions to the promotion fund included the following:

- The Irvine Company, a large landholder in Orange County, donated $60,000. The company had three parcels of land that would be purchased under the bond act for a total of $36 million.
- Avator Properties gave $10,000. The firm owned land at the base of the Santa Monica Mountains. At least $13 million of land in the area would be acquired if the bond referendum passed; however, not all of that money would go to Avator.
- Canyon Oaks Estates L.P. contributed $25,000. The bond would provide $5.8 million to complete the purchase of 662 acres of Canyon Oaks property in the Santa Monica Mountains.

- The Los Angeles Philharmonic Orchestra gave $60,000 to the campaign in the hope of ultimately winning $15 million for improvements to the Hollywood Bowl.[30]

The third central marketing idea is development of a strategic plan. Passing a referendum requires much more than developing some promotional pieces and then hoping that enough sympathetic residents will turn out to vote on election day. It calls for a carefully organized campaign, such as those described in "Role of a Steering Committee in Passing a Bond Referendum: The Crystal Springs Experience" and "The 'Safe Neighborhood Parks Act' in Dade County, Florida." Formulation of the plan should be based on research that identifies which segments of the community are likely to be responsive and unresponsive, what facets of the bond proposal are controversial, and what benefit appeals are likely to be most effective. The plan should address issues, such as how to disseminate information, how to contact prospective voters, how to involve the media, how to raise funds to support the campaign, and how to organize the bond's supporters to maximize their effectiveness.

The campaign should build momentum steadily toward reaching a peak in the week of the actual referendum. It should begin six to eight weeks before the referendum day. This allows sufficient time to generate the necessary support and still maintain the enthusiastic commitment of campaign volunteers. A good way to start the campaign is to hold a press conference to which representatives from all media are invited. Press packets containing prepared articles about the bond issue, illustrations, statistical data, and fact sheets would be made available to the media at this meeting. Media support is likely to be critical in the bond referendum and close liaison should be maintained with the media throughout the campaign.

The better informed a community is, the more likely it is that a bond issue will pass. Brochures, posters, telephone calls, newsletters, lightweight display boards, door-to-door solicitations, television and radio shows, video tapes, slide shows, electronic messages, media advertisements, bumper stickers, buttons, and pins may all play a role. Many agencies give details of the bond proposal by directly mailing literature to every resident or taxpayer, by paying for an insert in local newspapers, or by placing the material in retail stores and public buildings. However, the agency-sponsored material must be careful to be impartial

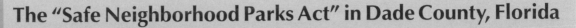

The "Safe Neighborhood Parks Act" in Dade County, Florida

A series of public meetings and three professionally taken public-opinion polls revealed that the major concern of Dade County residents was improving safety in their neighborhoods. These research efforts also revealed that most voters would approve a general obligation bond for park and recreation improvements if the cost to their household was no more than $7 to $10 per year. Based on this information, park advocates in the county built support for a $200 million general-obligation bond measure by calling it the Safe Neighborhood Parks Act, stressing its contribution to improving safety and pointing out that the average cost per household would be $8.34.

Under the general theme of neighborhood safety, several different types of parks and recreation problems were addressed. The following examples were included in the advocates' campaign literature:

- Safety and security upgrades. Of concern to many residents is the safety of the parks. Many things will be done to improve safety, such as adding security lighting, financing, pedestrian paths, and facilities for increased staff.

- Hazard remediation. A number of very old parks have problems that pose a threat to public health and safety. Hazards, such as asbestos, lead paint, underground storage tanks, and unsafe structures, need remediation.

- Recreational programs and facilities for children. Increasingly, the public is voicing its strong concerns over the lack of adequate leisure-time activities for children. As an alternative to delinquent behavior, recreational programs and activities keep young people involved in positive, character-building programs. Whether it is a sports team, a computer lab, or an art class, programs need facilities in which to operate.

- Completing parks that have not been finished. Parks that are underdeveloped and underused are invitations for criminal activity. Many projects have been started without sufficient funds to complete them. Although many neighborhoods reluctantly have adopted the attitude that "half of a park is better than no park," they deserve better.

- Building new parks in neighborhoods without them. Since 1970, Dade County's population has grown by more than 1 million. This means that entire communities have developed without adequate parks and open spaces. The problems have become so acute that children are denied a place to play and, instead, are more vulnerable to juvenile delinquency.

- Preservation of very old parks. Many of the parks are more than 40 years old and in need of extensive renovation. Whether it is painting, a new roof, a sewer-line hookup, or safety and fire code upgrades (just to mention a few), these parks must be saved from the ravages of time and generations of heavy use.

An example of the promotional material used in this campaign is shown in figure 2.8. The bond referendum was passed with 67% of voters approving it. This was the highest approval vote ever recorded on a tax measure in Dade County history.

and nonpartisan. Park and recreation bond proposals usually are incorporated as part of a larger package of proposals covering a range of service areas on which residents are asked to vote. A typical package is shown in figure 2.9, and a typical format for presenting information on the park and recreation elements within the overall package is shown in figure 2.10.

In addition to the written materials, every civic and community organization should be contacted,

and an offer should be made to present information about the bond issue at their meetings. Some of the individuals in these groups are likely to be important opinion leaders in the community. For this purpose, presentations of 5, 10, and 20 min should be prepared so that different time slots can be accommodated. Endorsements from these groups and from prominent community residents should be solicited and then publicized. When these endorsements are made public through

Vote YES for the Safe Neighborhood Parks Act

And You Will Get...

- **Youth Recreation** Facilities That Will Help **Reduce Juvenile Crime**
- More than **170 Safer Neighborhood** and **Regional Parks**
- To **Protect and Restore Biscayne Bay** and other important **Natural Resources**
- To **Restore And Repair Aging Park** and **Recreational Facilities**
- To Free-up money to **Create After-School Programs** to keep **Children Out Of Trouble**
- A **Citizens Oversight Committee** and **Annual Independent Audit** to ensure dollars go toward the projects approved by **YOU** the **Voters**
- An Ordinance that guarantees policymakers won't reduce parks budgets receiving these dollars.

For only 2 cents a day, the average homeowner provides $200 million to improve and make our parks safer.

"Idle kids with little or nothing to do are just a problem waiting to happen. Using the resources available through an effective park and recreation system can keep kids too busy to get involved with crime."

— Katherine Fernandez Rundle
DADE STATE ATTORNEY

If We Choose Right, So Will They...
VOTE YES on November 5th

For more information, call The Trust for Safe Neighborhood Parks, 860-7290

Paid for by The Trust for Safe Neighborhood Parks, Inc.

Figure 2.8 Sample flyer.

The Trust for Safe Neighborhood Parks, Inc.

Capital Improvements Program

College Station

How these propositions could affect your tax rate

Propositions	Projects	Capital Expenditures	Annual Operations/ Maintenance
1	Street Projects	$10,065,000	$ 11,400
2	Sidewalks/Bikeways and Northgate	$1,600,000	$99,000
3	Traffic Projects	$1,900,000	$10,000
4	Drainage Projects	$1,805,000	-0-
5	Library Services	$2,635,000	$178,000
6	Fire Station Relocation/ Land Purchase	$1,365,000	$10,000
7	Parks & Recreation Projects	$1,630,000	$146,000
8	Community Parkland Acquisition/Development	$1,500,000	-0-
	Total	$22,500,000	$ 454,400

The $22.5 million in proposed capital expenditures for this bond election WILL NOT increase your taxes. However, the operations and maintenance costs of the projects COULD increase your property tax rate by approximately 3.5 cents in the future. For example, the construction costs for a new street project, if approved, would be paid for with available funds, but additional funds to maintain it MAY require additional taxes at a later time.

Currently, 1 cent in the tax rate would generate approximately $135,000 in revenue. A 1 cent increase in city taxes will affect the total taxes on an $85,000 home by $8.50 annually.

Please vote on March 25

Figure 2.9 A typical bond package.
City of College Station Voter Information, 1995.

College Station

Capital Improvements Program

PROPOSITION #7

Parks & Recreation Projects

$1,630,000

GOAL: Citizens benefit from parks and recreational activities that are geographically and demographically accessible and serve a diversity of interests.

After extensive review by the Parks & Recreation Advisory Board, the CIP Committee, and the City Council, this proposition includes the following projects:

Lincoln Center/Wayne Smith Park Corridor $1,230,000
This item is a part of the Parks Master Plan and includes the construction of three youth baseball fields, a concession building, a parking facility, and lighting in the Lincoln Center area.

Park Facilities Upgrade/Renovation $200,000
This proposal is for upgrades and renovations at Bee Creek and Central Parks. The Bee Creek Park improvements include replacement of fences, backstops, dugouts and shelters, as well as the clean-out of the arboretum ponds. Central Park improvements include the renovation of the concession facility.

Neighborhood/School Park $200,000
This project would be constructed in conjunction with the elementary school scheduled to open in 1996 in south College Station near the Pebble Creek area. It would be similar to the neighborhood/school park at Rock Prairie Elementary. This type of dual-use public park facility has proved to be a wise use of taxpayer dollars.

Total $1,630,000

Please vote on March 25

Figure 2.10 A typical parks and recreation bond proposal within the overall bond package. City of College Station Voter Information, 1995.

advertising materials, many voters are likely to be reassured that the bond proposal has merit.

Convincing more people to vote "yes" than "no" in a bond referendum is likely to be a substantial undertaking. When the referendum outcome is known, it is important that all of the people who were involved in supporting it be recognized and publicly thanked for their efforts.

Mechanics of Selling Bonds

After a park and recreation bond proposal has been approved, other city officials and bond consultant specialists usually take responsibility for developing the financial, legal, and technical details that are required before the bonds can be offered for sale. Three tasks must be accomplished when preparing the bonds for sale: obtaining a bond rating, ensuring the financial transactions are completed efficiently, and ensuring the legal contractual language in the bond sale agreement is accurate. Jurisdictions usually hire bond-specialist lawyers and financial consultants to complete the latter two tasks.

Bond Ratings

The level of risk that investors incur strongly influences the interest rate that government entities will pay on their bonds. These bonds remain among the safest investments available; however, although very rare, defaults do occur. The largest default was on $2.25 billion of bonds issued by the Washington Public Power Supply System in 1983. Although it was many years ago, the memory of this large default reminds investors that investments in government bonds are not entirely risk free.

To provide potential investors with information regarding the degree of risk involved in a bond issue, two major rating agencies—Moody's Investors Service Inc. and Standard & Poor's—analyze an issue's risk of default and assign a credit rating to the bonds. The bond issuer pays for the rating. The rating agencies prepare an opinion of the borrower's credit quality (for full-faith and credit issues) or of the particular bond issue (for revenue bonds). Credit quality depends on the ability of the tax base or revenue source to generate the required debt-service payments while financing regular current expenditures. The agencies' ratings are distributed widely to the investment community and have a major influence on borrowing cost. An issue without a rating seldom will sell on national markets, but issues may not be rated if local markets will buy them.

The alphabetical rating systems used by the two agencies generally are considered to be equivalent, and the characteristics of a government entity that they consider when determining bond ratings are similar. An issue is assigned one of the ratings shown in table 2.4. To illustrate the impact of these ratings in one community, the difference between AA and AA+ ratings for a bond of $11.8 million over 20 years reduced the community's borrowing costs by 0.5%, which amounted to $850,000 over the life of the bond.[31]

In recent years, the influence of ratings on borrowing cost has been altered with the evolution of insurance for new municipal bond issues. In the early 1980s, less than 4% of new municipal bond issues were insured, but this percentage now has increased to more than 50%. Typically, an insurer agrees to guarantee the timely payment of principal and interest to investors in return for a one-time premium paid on the issue date of the bonds. The insurance enables a lower-rated issue to be sold at the level of a AAA rating. Fees for insurance fall somewhere between the interest payment that would be due on a bond issued with the jurisdiction's credit rating and the interest payments on a bond with the insurance company guaranteeing it as a AAA rating. The insurance allows the jurisdiction to harvest some of the interest-rate savings that the higher credit rating may confer. Typically, borrowers seek competitive bids on the insurance premium and have their bond offerings bid on both an insured and uninsured basis. This allows the market to determine the cheaper way to borrow.

Financial Advisors

If employed, financial advisors serve as a jurisdiction's impartial consultants on structuring and selling the bonds. Their primary responsibilities are to advise on the most feasible timetable for retiring the debt (this includes a maturity schedule and interest payment dates); the fee structure and methods necessary for supplying enough money to pay the principal and interest; and the relative acceptability of bids when sealed bids are opened. All states have laws that require general obligation bonds to be sold to the bidder offering the lowest net-interest cost at an advertised public sale. The bond consultants also assist in distributing the official notice of sale to potential lenders. Financial periodicals generally are used to ensure broad exposure. Prospective lenders (e.g., banks, investment houses, insurance companies) are invited to submit bids to the government entity detailing the terms under which they will lend the money.

Table 2.4 Credit Ratings by Moody's and Standard & Poor's

Moody's ratings	Symbol	Symbol	Standard & Poor's ratings
Investment grade			
Best quality, smallest degree of investment risk; referred to as "gilt edge."	Aaa	AAA	The highest rating. Capacity to meet debt payments is extremely strong.
High quality; smaller margin of protection or larger fluctuation of protective elements than Aaa.	Aa	AA	Strong capacity to meet debt payments; differ from the highest rated issues only in small degree.
Upper medium grade, many favorable investment attributes, but elements may be present that suggest some susceptibility to future risk.	A	A	Strong but more susceptible to adverse effects in circumstances and economic conditions than debt in higher rated categories.
Medium grade; neither highly protected nor poorly secured; adequate present security that debt payments will be met but may be unreliable over any great length of time.	Baa	BBB	Adequate capacity to meet debt payments, but adverse economic conditions or changing circumstances are more likely to weaken this capacity than in higher rated categories.
Speculative grade			
Judged to have speculative elements; not well safeguarded; very moderate protection of principal and interest, payments over both good and bad times. Element of uncertainty.	Ba	BB	Less near-term vulnerability to default than other speculative issues but faces major ongoing uncertainties or exposure to adverse economic conditions that could lead to inadequate capacity to meet debt payments.
Lacks characteristics of desirable investment. Assurance of debt payments over the long term may be small.	B	B	Greater vulnerability to default but currently has the capacity to meet debt payments.
Poor standing; may be in default or may have elements of danger in meeting debt payments.	Caa	CCC	Has current identifiable vulnerability to default. Is dependent on favorable economic conditions to meet debt payments. If these conditions deteriorate, it is not likely to have the capacity to meet debt payments.
Speculative in high degree; in default or other marked shortcomings.	Ca	CC	Economic conditions are deteriorating making bankruptcy a likely option.
Lowest rated class; extremely poor prospects of ever attaining any real investment standing.	C	C	Bankruptcy petition has been filed, but debt service payments are continued.
		D	Default. Debt payments are not made on the date due.

Sources: Standard & Poor's *Municipal Finance Criteria*. New York: Standard and Poor's, 1994, p. 4.
Moody's Investors Service, *An Issuers Guide to the Rating Process*. New York: Moody's Investors Service, 1994.

Bond Counsel

Bond counsel plays a critical role in an agency's attempt to attract the interest of potential investors in its bond issue. Bond buyers place great confidence in nationally recognized bond counsel, lawyers with proven records in working with bonds. Investors expect the bond counsel to help screen out unacceptable risks. Legal restrictions are prone to new interpretations and tests. It is the job of bond counsel to monitor and incorporate these changes into the advice and documents prepared for their clients' jurisdictions. Bond counsel will be called on to make numerous interpretations of federal laws and regulations, state constitutions and statutes, and local charters and ordinances. Even the smallest technical or legal error may result in invalidating an entire issue. There have been many unfortunate examples of jurisdictions having to resubmit their bond proposal to the voters because of inappropriate legal advice.

Summary

The property tax is the primary source of funding for local park and recreation agencies. Property values are determined by an assessor, and the aggregate value of all the assessed value within a particular jurisdiction is referred to as the tax base. After the tax base has been determined by assessment, the government entity sets a tax rate to meet its revenue needs. Property taxes may be increased either by raising the value of the tax base or by raising the tax rate. Proposition 13 in California was successful in preventing large property tax increases because it imposed limits on both these variables. A real-estate transfer tax is levied when property is conveyed from one person to another. It is not used widely at the local level by park and recreation agencies but is being used increasingly at the state level. It is a relatively reliable source of revenue, particularly in growth areas where the real-estate market is active.

Sales taxes are the largest single source of state tax revenues and the second largest source of tax revenues for municipalities after the property tax. Because nonresidents use some types of park and recreational facilities, designated hotel-motel sales tax revenues may be used to assist in financing those facilities. A second type of designated sales tax that has been advocated widely for developing recreation amenities is a manufacturers' excise tax on recreational equipment. This approach is analogous to a user fee. Those who purchase recreational equipment pay a tax that is used to develop facilities at which they use the equipment.

Areas within a community that desire a higher level of service than the standard that a jurisdiction regularly provides can achieve this service by forming a benefit assessment district and by paying higher property taxes to pay for the extra level of service. Most capital development and expansion of park and recreation systems has been financed through the use of bonds. Bonds formally are defined as a promise by the local government that is borrowing money to pay back a specified

amount of money, with interest, to the lender within a specified period of time. The interest payments on bonds makes them a more expensive method of financing than a pay-as-you-go approach, but, nevertheless, they are the preferred method of capital funding.

General obligation bonds are full-faith and credit obligations that are supported by the local government's authority to levy taxes. Hence, they are a very secure form of investment with minimal risk, enabling them to be sold at a relatively low interest rate. Certificates of obligation and contractual obligations also are backed by the full faith and credit of the tax base, but, unlike general obligation bonds, they do not require voter approval at a referendum.

In contrast, non-guaranteed debt is redeemed from designated revenue sources other than property taxes. For those bonds, if projected revenues fall short of what is required to make debt payments, the government entity is not obligated to make up the difference. The three types of non-guaranteed debt most frequently used to develop park and recreational facilities are revenue bonds, tax-increment bonds, and certificates of participation. Revenue bonds usually rely on revenue produced from the project to redeem them. Tax-increment bonds are redeemed by the increment of increase in property taxes occurring as a result of the amenity improvements paid for by the bonds. Certificates of participation require an intermediary, usually a public benefit corporation, that borrows the money from a financial institution and repays it with lease fees paid from the sponsoring government entity.

Park and recreation agencies are not permitted to use public funds to promote an advocacy position in a bond referendum. From both ethical and legal perspectives, their public position is required to be one of neutrality and limited to disseminating impartial information. Hence, the tasks of demonstrating needs, formulating priorities, and convincing voters to support a bond proposal are usually the responsibility of a citizen committee. The committee will attempt to stimulate grassroots involvement. The marketing concepts of segmentation, benefitizing, and strategic planning are likely to be central to a successful campaign to pass a bond referendum.

After a bond has been approved, specialized consultants and other city officials guide the process that leads to acquisition of the borrowed funds. This process involves obtaining a bond rating; structuring and selling the bonds; and ensuring that all aspects of the bond process, including the contractual language in the sales agreement, are legal and accurate.

References

1. Standard & Poor's. 1994. *Municipal finance criteria*. New York: Standard and Poor's Ratings Group.

2. O'Sullivan, Arthur, Terri A. Sexton and Steven M. Sheffrin. 1995. *Property taxes and tax revolts: The legacy of Proposition 13*. Cambridge, England: Cambridge University Press.

3. Mikesell, J.L. 1991. *Fiscal administration: Analysis and applications for the public sector*. Third edition. Pacific Grove, CA: Brooks/Cole.

4. Bell, Michael E. and John H. Bowman. 1991. Property taxes. In *Local government finance*, edited by John E. Peterson and Dennis R. Strachotta. Chicago: Government Finance Officers Association, 85-112.

5. Kozlowski, James C. 1995. Private property bill more demanding than Constitution. *Parks and Recreation* 30(5): 16-24.

6. Maryland Department of Natural Resources. "Program open space: Ten-year report 1969-1979." Unpublished manuscript.

7. Salvesen, David. 1994. Preservation through limited development. *Urban Land* 53(8): 66-68.

8. Schmid, Sue. 1995. Water world: It's water, water everywhere at a Texas water park. *Athletic Business* 19(10): 24.

9. Schmid, Sue. 1992. No stone unturned. *Athletic Business* 16(10): 23-27.

10. Howard, Dennis R. and John L. Crompton. 1995. *Financing sport*. Morgantown, WV: Fitness Information Technology.

11. Crompton, John L. and Jill M. Decker. 1989. Establishing a federal recreation trust fund: An analysis of the options with special emphasis on a manufacturers' excise tax. *Journal of Park and Recreation Administration* 7(1): 1-14.

12. Crandall, Derrick A. 1991. Buying fishhooks snags more federal fishing funds. *Trilogy* 1(4): 52-54.

13. Derrick A. Crandall to the chairman of the President's Commission on American's Outdoors, September 1986.

14. Crandall, Derrick A. 1997. Interior Secretary favors federal tax on outdoor gear. *Wall Street Journal*, September 17, section 1.

15. Martin, Douglas. 1994. Trying new ways to save decaying parks. *The New York Times*, November 15, A16.

16. Martin, Douglas. 1995. Who should pay for parks? Voices from those in the field. *The New York Times*, January 25, A18.

17. Houstoun, Lawrence O. 1994. Betting on BIDs. *Urban Land* 53(6): 13-18.

18. Jochum, Glenn. 1995. Jumping in the BID wagon. *Long Island Business News*, March 13, section 1.

19. Mouat, Lucia. 1992. Some green in New York's concrete. *The Christian Science Monitor*, July 31, 7.

20. Kormon, Richard. 1989. A matter of pride. *Sports Inc.*, February 20, 34.

21. National Resources Defense Council. 1997. *Reclaiming our heritage*. New York: National Resources Defense Council.

22. Minnesota's indoor park. 1987. *Athletic Business* 11(5): 15.

23. Myers, Phyllis. 1996. Washington state parks issues certificates of participation. *Greensense* 2(2): 6.

24. Barnes, Rosemary. 1994. City sells bonds to improve bayfront attractions. *Corpus-Christi Caller-Times*, December 21, B2.

25. Gladwell, Nancy J., James R. Sellers and J. Robert Brooks. 1997. Certificates of participation as an alternative funding source for capital projects: A case study. *Journal of Park and Recreation Administration* 15(4): 23-37.

26. Johnson, Craig and John Mikesell. 1994. Certificates of participation and capital markets: Lessons from Brevard County and Richmond Unified School District. *Public Budgeting and Finance* 14(3): 41-54.

27. Joseph, James C. 1994. *Debt issuance and management. A guide for smaller governments*. Chicago: Government Finance Officer's Association.

28. *Stanton vs. Mott*, 17 CA 3d. 206, 130 California Reporter, 697, 1976.

29. McLean, Daniel D. and W. Donald Martin. 1991. Blueprints for successful bond referendums. *Journal of Physical Education, Recreation and Dance* 62(10): 40-44.

30. Craft, Cynthia H. 1994. Land firms give green to parks initiative. *Los Angeles Times*, May 30, A1.

31. Lee, Robert D. and Ronald W. Johnson. 1989. *Public budgeting systems*. Rockville, MD: Aspen Publications.

BUDGETING PROCESSES

This chapter was written in association with Mark E. Havitz, Department of Recreation and Leisure Studies, University of Waterloo, Canada.

Most park and recreation personnel work in the field because they derive satisfaction from positively impacting a community. The extent to which they can achieve this noble end depends heavily on how many resources they can acquire. An increasing amount of these resources comes from partnerships or external sources, but most of them still are generated internally from a jurisdiction's tax base. Access to these internal resources is gained through the budget process, so success in this arena is of central importance. Hence, park and recreation managers spend much time and effort developing, defending, implementing, and monitoring budgets.

A budget is a financial policy and political plan that forecasts an agency's estimated revenues and expenditures for a given time period. It provides a detailed description of the agency's proposed expenditures (e.g., salaries, equipment) and purposes (e.g., provision of programs, preservation of open spaces) and assigns dollar amounts to each item or purpose. A properly drawn budget is more than just an accounting instrument. Elected officials use this basic direction-setting tool to direct the nature, type, and extent of services that an agency delivers to a community. It should allocate resources to programs and activities in a manner that most effectively reflects the desires of the community to be served. It should be an accurate reflection of the policy values and service priorities of an agency. In this respect, the budget is a management plan for meeting the organization's goals and objectives. An effectively prepared budget should accomplish the following:

- Provide a general statement of the financial needs, resources, and plans of the agency including an outline of all program elements and their costs and allocations for facilities and personnel.

- Inform taxpayers and budget officials of the amounts of money to be spent, the sources of revenue, and the costs of achieving agency goals.

- Help in promoting standardized and simplified operational procedures by classifying all expenditures and requiring systematic procedures for approving them.

- Serve as a means of evaluating the success of programs.

Budgeting is not a neutral exercise. It is a way to rationalize the allocation of scarce resources, and, thus, it involves priorities, choices, and trade-offs about what an agency will and will not do. Each budget decision requires a consideration of potential benefits that may or may not accrue to an agency and its constituents, but each decision also involves opportunity cost. That is, if the available money is allocated to one program, then another program cannot be funded, or it has to be funded at a lower level. Budgeting is highly emotional, complex, and detailed, and it involves much work. When policy makers decide whether to fund programs, they profoundly affect the lives of community members.

The chapter opens by differentiating between capital and operating budgets. This explanation is followed by a discussion of the characteristic roles and behaviors of major participants in the budgeting process and of the dominant influence of incrementalism in determining budgets. Five formats commonly used by park and recreation agencies are described: line-item, program, performance, zero-base, and entrepreneurial budgeting. The chapter concludes with a review of enterprise funds and of the time table and logistics of the budgeting process.

Capital Budgeting

Capital budgeting is concerned with the financing of long-lived physical improvements. This differentiates it from the operating budget, which addresses annual or routine activities financed from current resources. Capital budgeting refers to those one-time expenditures on major purchases that generally have a life expectancy of at least 10 years. These may involve repair and replacement of existing facilities and development of new amenities. Capital budgets almost always are developed independent of annual operating budgets. The use of separate budgets prevents the volatility that would occur, for example, to an agency's athletic division annual operating budget if costs for constructing a new gymnasium or ballpark were incorporated into it. Separation of operating and capital budgets also allows the park and recreation agency to make long-range decisions without having to be responsive to short-term exigencies.

Examples of items that may be included in a park and recreation agency's capital budget are construction of new tennis courts, renovation of an aquatics facility, and acquisition of a park site. To some extent, the size of the agency influences the decision as to whether an item should be a capital or an operating expense. For example, in small park and recreation agencies, vehicles may be classified as capital expenditures because of their high cost in relation to the department's regular supplies. However, in a large agency they are likely to be classified as routine operating expenses. If the agency operates 100 vehicles, it is likely to include the replacement of 10 vehicles each year as a routine operating expense because it is a recurring, rather than a one-time, expense. Almost every agency establishes some kind of arbitrary cut-off point that distinguishes operating from capital expenditures. A major exception to this procedure, however, are the federal agencies because the federal government does not have a separate process for deciding whether an expenditure should be classified as capital or current.

The annual capital budget is the plan for capital expenditures to be incurred in any given year. It is part of a plan that usually covers a five- or six-year time period and is called the capital improvement program. The capital improvement program prioritizes capital projects to be undertaken in the multiyear planning period and develops a fiscal plan to provide for the funding of those projects.

> The CIP should be a logical extension of a jurisdiction's comprehensive land-use plan. Typically, the CIP describes each capital project proposed for development over the planning period by listing the year it is to be started, the cost to be incurred by year, and the proposed method of financing. Based on these details about each project, annual cost schedules for capital expenditures, as well as summaries of financial requirements and resources (i.e., current revenues, general obligation bonds, intergovernmental assistance), are developed (p. 67).[1]

After a capital improvement program has been adopted, the development of capital budgets is relatively straightforward. As the first year's capital projects are completed, those projects scheduled in the capital improvement program for the second year become the starting point for discussion of projects to go in the new year's capital budget.

The capital budget makes the capital improvement program operational. The capital improvement program is a long-term plan in which the priorities of future projects can be changed; however, once it has been approved by the council, the annual capital budget is a legal document that authorizes specific projects in the fiscal year. When they review the priorities each year, elected officials can shift projects forward or backward in time in the capital improvement program to reflect changes in demands and available resources. The multiyear time frame of the program enables the planning, feasibility, surveying, land acquisition, and other extensive preliminary work associated with capital projects to be systematically programmed and undertaken in a timely manner.

Each year agencies submit project requests for inclusion in the capital improvement program. Projects that were previously included in the program but have not yet advanced to the capital budget are likely to require only revisions of cost estimates and descriptions of other new developments. For projects not in the program, extensive detailed justification, together with detailed costs and projected impact on future operating budgets, is likely to be required.

Because of their long time frames, capital budgets often result in facilities being provided on the basis of needs that were identified some years earlier. The citizens' needs and the agency's personnel change over time. Elected officials and agency administrators who take office at a subsequent time may feel frustrated because many service delivery decisions are dictated by facilities that their predecessors proposed and developed. Capital development decisions are not easily reversed. The market for used equipment is often limited and conversion of facilities to other uses may not be feasible. Further, structuring capital and operating budgets in widely different time frames may create problems. A facility that is initiated during a period of economic growth and population expansion may open just as the agency's operating budget is being cut and programming personnel are being terminated. Likewise, an agency may delay capital projects during difficult times only to find that it is unprepared to meet increased demand when the economic and social climate improves. When projects are in the capital improvement program, elected officials have several capital development options on how to proceed. Table 3.1 outlines these options.

Capital budgets should be reviewed after the construction or purchase of a project has been completed for two reasons. First, lessons may be learned that could lead to improvements in the capital budgeting process. Second, corrective actions may be identified that may improve current projects. A post-completion review should involve

- reviewing all assumptions that were formulated during the assessment period;

Table 3.1	Options in Capital Budgeting
Category	**Description**
Option to defer	An agency owns a piece of undeveloped property. The agency can wait X number of years to see if demand materializes for a comprehensive recreation center or for facility development on a smaller scale. Alternatively, it may sell the site or trade it for a site that is more conducive to meeting residents' needs.
Time-to-build option (staged investment)	Staging development as an incremental series of outlays creates the option to abandon additional development in midstream if new information is unfavorable. Each stage can be viewed as an independent option.
Option to alter operating scale (e.g., to expand; to contract; to shut down and restart)	If market conditions are more favorable than expected, the agency might expand the scale of the facility or accelerate resource utilization. Conversely, if conditions are less favorable than expected, it can reduce the scale of operations. In extreme cases, some programs may be halted and restarted.
Option to abandon	If market conditions markedly decline, then the agency can abandon current operations permanently and realize the resale value of the facility and other equipment-related assets. This option is seldom available since recreation facilities are generally use specific. For example, a swimming pool or skateboard facility cannot be converted readily to other uses, though a piece of large equipment (e.g., an ice resurfacing machine or water slides) may be sold to another agency.
Option to switch	If demand changes, the agency can change the output mix of some facilities (program flexibility). For example, Eugene, Oregon converted an equestrian arena into an indoor ice arena.

Adapted from: Trigeorgis, L. (1996). *Real Options: Managerial Flexibility and Strategy in Resource Allocation*. Cambridge, MA: MIT Press.

- comparing the actual resources consumed by the project with forecasts made during the initial assessment;

- comparing the actual outcome or performance of the project with forecasts made during the initial assessment in terms of effectiveness, equity, and efficiency; and

- reviewing conformance with agency policy and objectives.[2]

The Operating Budget

The remainder of this chapter focuses on the annual operating budget because this dimension of budgeting is more likely to impact managers at all levels in the agency each year. The operating budget is a financial plan that provides a detailed statement of all of the expenditures (e.g., personnel, supplies, etc.) necessary for the day-to-day operation of an agency for a one-year period. Multiyear (e.g., three- to five-year) operating budgets have been proposed as a means of enhancing

rational choice because agencies "have no idea what will happen to spending or revenues beyond the first or second year. In today's world, this is the equivalent of flying a 747 through the fog with no instruments" (p. 237).[3] One-year budgeting may result in short-sighted decision making because only the next year's expenditures are reviewed; overspending because disbursements in future years are hidden; conservatism because incremental changes do not open up larger future vistas; and parochialism because programs tend to be viewed in isolation. Nevertheless, the inertia of tradition, the desire of policy makers to retain relatively tight control of expenditures, the difficulty of projecting future needs over longer periods of time, and the amount of time that multiyear budget planning would consume mean that annual operating budgets remain the norm.

As part of its operating procedures, an agency will have a cash-flow, or running, budget. Cash-flow budgets provide administrators with a picture of their agencies' short-term financial needs and usually are updated on a quarterly or monthly basis. Cash-flow budget dilemmas are analogous to those dilemmas that individuals attempting to balance their personal accounts face. Although overall income may be sufficient to meet long-term financial obligations, it may be insufficient to meet expenses during certain short-term periods. Effective cash-flow budgeting involves estimating when revenues and expenditures occur to ensure that no times arise when a shortage of income means that an agency is unable to pay its bills. Cash-flow budgeting is most relevant for enterprise-fund operation (discussed later in this chapter) and for seasonal operations, such as winter sports (e.g., skiing) and summer activities (e.g., aquatics), in which income revenue may be uneven while fixed expenses remain constant. Cash-flow budgets are less critical for agencies and programs that primarily rely on tax revenues than for those that depend more on revenue from user fees because the former revenue source is likely to be more predictable and stable than the latter.

Roles of the Actors

Budgets reflect the relative power of different actors in the process to influence the outcomes. However, research indicates that certain universal behaviors characterize the process of developing an annual operating budget regardless of the type of budget used. Severe fiscal constraint is a key feature that conditions budgeting behavior in most jurisdictions. Law requires municipalities, counties, and special districts to balance their budgets. Expenditures are not allowed to exceed revenues; the budget must either provide for a surplus or be balanced. This requirement, more than any other condition, governs the behavior of participants in the budgetary process. For most of the past two decades the public has demanded tax cuts and, hence, budget reductions, but has not reduced demands for services. Thus, public officials have found it difficult to develop budgets that adequately meet service demands. In this environment, budget decisions are often predicated on the amount of money available rather than on what needs to be done.[4] It has been observed:

> Rather than using the budget for purposes of steering, that is, to determine new directions for city operations, budgeting becomes largely a maintenance activity. Its essential purpose is to keep expenditures within legal limits by assuring that administrators carry out past policies within acceptable boundaries (p. 201).[4]

Frequently, this results in the emergence of a "we/they" dichotomy between the principle actors in the budgeting process. The two camps are divided into budget spenders and budget cutters. The chief government executives (e.g., mayor, city manager, premier, governor) and many elected officials generally perceive the budget more as a device for curbing expenses and holding the line on tax increases rather than as a means for allocating resources. In contrast, most budget spenders (department heads and staff) hold a service-performance perspective. Meeting professional responsibilities and constituents' demands have a higher priority for them.

Traditional budget procedures have created circumstances whereby spenders typically request larger dollar amounts than the amounts that budget reviewers will allow. For example, a longitudinal study of the budgeting process in 19 state governments revealed that administrative agencies in each of the states requested substantial increases over their current annual appropriations (from 15% to 35%), while the governors concurrently pared their requests by a sizable amount (from 4% to 31%).[4] A significant finding of the study was that the governors and legislatures made the largest cuts in the budgets of those agencies that requested the largest percentage increases. However, it was also discovered that only those agencies that asked for a large increase were awarded substantial increases over their previous budgets. Those agencies requesting no additional funds received none.

This research illustrates a simple but important principle of budgeting: agencies must take the initiative in the budgeting process if they hope to secure adequate or additional financial resources. Under most systems, the universal tendency of agencies to request more than they expect to receive is based not only on the hope that they will gain additional funds, but also on an expression of their professional responsibility. Even if an agency head is unsuccessful in obtaining increased support, many administrators believe that they have at least carried out their professional obligation to communicate fully the resources needed by their agency to meet citizens' demands.

> The city engineer states that a path needs a railing or someone might be hurt; the fire chief feels the level of protection is in jeopardy because the city should have a new pumper; and the recreation superintendent believes the golf course should be seeded again as the city is competing with other

courses. Department heads feel they have done their jobs and relieve their anxiety merely by expressing their needs. Not only do they satisfy their own professional norms, but, by putting the monkey on the backs of the manager and council, they abate pressure from their employee and community constituents (p. 190).[4]

If a park and recreation director wants to change the priorities of an agency, he or she can do it much more easily, quickly, and painlessly if the agency's budget is expanding.

To fire incompetents, change inherited attitudes, turn around a misguided unit, or galvanize a tired one into action is a lot harder than getting more money, creating a new unit, staffing it with fresh people, and setting it off with enthusiasm in a promising new direction. In short, even the most selfless public servant can honestly say that he is better able to serve the public interest if he has a bigger budget (p. 24).[5]

Elected officials are sometimes suspicious that agencies may have selfish motives for maximizing their budget requests. Larger budgets may create more opportunities and stronger justification for larger salaries, higher status, and more perquisites. Managing a larger organization with many resources often results in a larger salary for the manager.[5] Similarly, a larger budget may result in bigger and nicer offices, more assistants, use of an agency vehicle, more invitations to join prestigious community organizations, and other status symbols. If some elected officials hold these suspicions of selfish motives, then they are likely to be particularly zealous budget cutters.

Balanced budget requirements and the often severe fiscal constraints facing government agencies have combined to make budgeting a conservative process. As a hedge against unanticipated events, balancing the budget generally means having at least a slight surplus on hand. A basic decision rule that budget makers have adopted, therefore, is to estimate revenues lower than they are actually expected to be. The park and recreation administrator, for example, will most likely incline to a pessimistic or conservative point of view when estimating the anticipated revenues from a golf course operation because of the many uncertainties that could disrupt normal income production. Because prolonged poor weather and damaged course conditions are im-

probable more often than not, the administrator will be faced with the pleasant task of disposing of a surplus.

Incremental Budgeting

Another nearly universal characteristic of budgeting in almost all government agencies is incrementalism, which is the tendency of budget participants to assume the previous year's budget level as a given and to concentrate only on that increment, or amount of change, (whether an increase or decrease) requested in an agency's budget. A prevailing assumption or norm that guides the actions of park and recreation administrators in preparing their budgets is that they will continue to receive what they already have and will get a fair share of any budget increase. Thus, managers usually use last year's budget as the starting point when formulating their requests.

A budget is a record of the past. Victories, defeats, bargains, and compromises over past allocations are reflected in the items included and, by inference, those left out. Once enacted, a budget becomes a precedent; the fact that something has been done before vastly increases the chances that it will be done again (p. 9).[4]

Rather than having to justify the entire or overall budget, park and recreation administrators focus their attention on any adjustments or deviations that they plan to make from last year's appropriation level. Beyond that base level, the size of the increase (or decrease) requested depends on the administrator's perception of what will be acceptable. In making this judgment, many factors are weighed, including the tone of the chief executive's budget instructions, which give guidance to the agency head as to the parameters within which he or she should work; whether the agency's budget increased, decreased, or remained stable in the previous year; and the amount of pressure that constituents can bring to bear on decision makers.

If the economy is relatively stable or growing, administrators generally select one of the three following budgeting strategies:

- Expand the base, adding new programs.
- Increase the base, inching ahead with existing programs.
- Defend the base, guarding against cuts in existing programs.

The selected strategy will depend on the budgeting climate in any given year. Unstable economies, high unemployment rates, and large budget deficits present park and recreation administrators with less desirable options. In recent years, the prevailing climate of fiscal conservatism has meant that many administrators have had only two choices:

- Decrease the base, inching back with small incremental cuts in existing programs.
- Erode the base, deleting existing programs.

Incremental budgeting has become firmly entrenched because of its attractiveness to those responsible for giving final approval to budget requests. Council members, commissioners, elected officials, and park and recreation professionals often find the simplicity of the incremental budgeting routine appealing. The limited incremental focus allows the predominantly part-time elected and appointed officials, who constitute the ultimate decision makers, to narrow down the potentially overwhelming and time-consuming budgeting process to a few simple decision rules. Two of the most time-honored spending rules on which they rely are the following: 1) Analyze last year's appropriations to see if there have been any increases requested and, if not, approve the items; and 2) If an increase is to be granted to an agency, it should be no larger than a given percentage of the previous year's appropriation. To aid decision makers in evaluating the merit of proposed incremental changes in the budget, it is usual to require that the cost implications of each new proposed program be described on a standard form, such as that shown in figure 3.1.

Although pressure from constituent groups can influence these decision rules, the incremental budgeting routine reduces to a minimum the occurrence of radical funding changes or deviations. Budgets may change over time, but they tend to change in a slow, orderly, uniform fashion. An important consequence of this condition is the realization that previous budget decisions determine present allocations. Due to the highly conservative bias of incrementalism, the spending priorities of most government units were established, in effect, many years ago. Many, if not most, of the spending decisions that budget reviewers make today are in reality an unconscious reaffirmation of decisions made in the past. By accepting past actions as a given and by usually permitting only small increments of change, budget

makers have made budgeting a stable and predictable process.

This reality has both positive and negative consequences. From a positive perspective, it makes little sense to ignore years of previous experience that have gone into the development and implementation of core offerings, such as learn-to-swim programs, older-adult fitness classes, and park maintenance practices, that are common to most park and recreation agencies. Tremendous amounts of financial and human resources would be expended if agencies were to reinvent themselves from the ground up on an annual basis. From a negative perspective, however, budgetary incrementalism hinders agencies' abilities to pro-actively address changes within their communities. For example, many departments serve expanded aging constituencies, people affected by changes in family structure, and populations whose racial and ethnic composition is changing. Programs that were relevant 20, 10, or even 5 years ago may now have only marginal relevance, but incremental budget practices may keep them in place. In 1924, a commentator observed:

> It must be a temptation to one drawing up an estimate to save himself the trouble by taking last year's estimate for granted, adding something to any item for which an increased expenditure is foreseen. Nothing could be easier, or more wasteful and extravagant. It is in that way obsolete expenditure is enabled to make its appearance year after year, long after reason for it has ceased to be (p. 172).[6]

Incremental budget cuts, which are a current reality for many agencies, also may have the insidious effect of decreasing levels of service quality, although this is often initially imperceptible. When applied across the board, incremental cutting weakens programs with little regard for community or agency priorities. Services do not contribute equally to satisfying citizen wants, and reduced resource allocations should reflect the different priorities that citizens assign to services. Making across-the-board cuts instead of achieving this goal tends to penalize past and current efficiencies. When cuts are made in this way, efficient divisions and agencies are likely to be penalized more than their poorly performing peers because they have already implemented the easy and obvious cuts. In inefficient divisions with plenty of "fat," the cut is much easier and much less painful to implement.

New Program Request Justification

Department _____   Fund _____

Program Description _____

Program Activities	Amount
Personal Services	
Payroll Fringes	
Contracted Services	
Materials and Supplies	
Other Charges	
Capital Outlay	
Total	

Revenue Projection	
Type	**Amount**
Estimated Cost/Benefit to City	

Personnel – Program Title	Salary	FTE	New or Existing

Figure 3.1   New program request justification.

Types of Operating Budgets

There are numerous approaches to formulating operating budgets. Five of the most frequently used formats are described in this section: line-item, program, performance, zero-base, and entrepreneurial budgeting systems. They have evolved sequentially, with line-item budgeting being the oldest and entrepreneurial budgeting being the newest.

Since the 1950s, a relatively major reform has been proposed about once each decade in an effort to overcome some of the perceived deficiencies of incremental line-item budgeting—performance budgeting in the 1950s, program budgeting in the 1960s, and zero-base budgeting in the 1970s. In the 1980s, there was a growth of what might be called automatic control budgeting in which voters and policy makers tried to impose statutorily prescribed formulas on revenues and expenditures, the most notable examples being Proposition 13-type laws. In the 1990s, another type of budgetary reform was proposed—entrepreneurial budgeting (p. 445).[7]

Each of these approaches has strengths and weaknesses. In each case, the highly publicized success of a few applications led to promises and expectations of universal applicability that were not attained.[8] However, each of these five approaches has had an influence on current budgeting practices. Thus, a survey of municipal government budgets reported that in addition to the pervasive presence of the line-item approach, elements of performance monitoring appeared in 75% of them; program budgeting, in 70%; and zero-base budgeting, in 30%.[9]

This section describes the respective properties, preparation requirements, limitations, and benefits of each of these most frequently used budget types. Most park and recreation agencies use hybrids of these budget types that incorporate features from several of them; few departments use any of them in their pure form. Indeed, it is rare to find any two jurisdictions that have adopted an identical budget format. Almost all of them have developed their own idiosyncratic versions: "Each local government's budgeting process is unique. . . . It is the product of geographical, historical, economic, political and social factors peculiar to that jurisdiction" (p. 45).[10] Thus, budgeting in public agencies follows no uniform practice.

Line-Item Budgeting

Line-item, or object class, is the oldest and most common form of budgeting used by government bodies. Its initial practice dates back to the reform movement of the early 1900s when the dominant concern was for fiscal control and accountability in the operation of government. Nevertheless, one survey reported that approximately one-third of local governments still use the line-item method exclusively and another 43% use line-item in combination with other methods.[11] Line-item budgeting has persisted because it is simpler, easier, more controllable, and more flexible than are many of the subsequent alternatives that have emerged.

The line-item budget appropriates a specific dollar amount to each object or item of expenditure listed in the budget. The agency is limited to spending no more than the dollar amount assigned to each of the items. It lists these items, line by line, just the way that they are paid out—an employee's salary is shown on one line; soccer balls, on another; fertilizer, on another; and so on. Rather than listing the objects of expenditure at random, the line-item budget systematically organizes all of the items into specific categories or accounts. The primary purpose of such a classification system is to define the main classes of expenditure by clear lines of demarcation and to develop subclasses that refine the nature of the principle category. The object of expenditure, or line-item, classification scheme that governments use most extensively is shown in figure 3.2.

The focus of line-item budgeting is on the allocation of funds, not on the service benefit outputs. As a consequence, a line-item budget makes it difficult to see a direct relationship between expenditures and output benefits or program results. When looking through a line-item budget, such as the one depicted in figure 3.2, it is impossible, for example, to determine exactly what amount is being spent on educational programs for preschool-aged children, educational programs for school-aged children, a new polar bear exhibit, improvements to the zoo's rainforest habitat, or other program areas. The costs associated with providing these activities are spread among the many separate expenditure categories of the budget.

Paradoxically, analysts of public finance suggest that this nonprogrammatic, fragmented emphasis is precisely what makes line-item budgets the preferred option of many budget participants. It is a control-oriented system. By virtue of the

Line-Item Budget Report

1000	**Personnel services**				$1,400,000
	1100	Salaries (full-time)		$789,800	
	1200	Wages (part-time)		$529,800	
	1300	Benefits		$ 80,400	
2000	**Contractual services**				$ 154,900
	2100	Communication and transportation		$ 8,000	
		2110 Postage	$ 4,800		
		2120 Telephone and fax	$ 3,200		
	2200	Substance, care, and support		$ 52,900	
		2210 Support of persons	$ 8,100		
		2220 Support of livestock	$ 35,400		
		2230 Care of vehicles	$ 9,400		
	2300	Printing, binding, and public relations		$ 23,500	
		2310 Printing	$ 6,300		
		2320 Computing and word processing	$ 3,500		
		2330 Binding	$ 3,200		
		2340 Advertising	$ 8,000		
		2350 Incentives	$ 2,500		
	2400	Utilities		$ 39,700	
		2410 Heat	$ 22,000		
		2420 Light and power	$ 8,900		
		2430 Water	$ 8,800		
	2500	Repairs		$ 27,500	
		2510 Equipment	$ 17,000		
		2520 Buildings	$ 10,500		
	2600	Custodial services		$ 3,300	
3000	**Commodities**				$ 545,600
	3100	Food for livestock		$317,100	
		3110 Grain	$ 66,900		
		3120 Meat	$152,800		
		3130 Fruits and vegetables	$ 97,400		
	3200	Veterinary needs		$ 88,800	
		3210 Supplies	$ 8,400		
		3220 Medicine	$ 73,000		
		3230 Equipment	$ 7,400		
	3300	Materials		$ 31,300	
		3310 Building	$ 9,900		
		3320 Road	$ 21,400		
	3400	Livestock		$108,400	
		3410 Purchase	$100,000		
		3420 Lease	$ 8,400		
4000	**Current charges**				$ 29,800
	4100	Rents		$ 6,300	
		4110 Buildings	$ 4,300		
		4120 Equipment	$ 2,000		
	4200	Insurance		$ 18,400	
	4300	Registrations and subscriptions		$ 1,200	
	4400	Taxes		$ 3,900	
5000	**Properties**				$ 21,500
	5100	Equipment		$ 3,000	
	5200	Buildings and improvements		$ 6,700	
	5300	Land		$ 11,800	
6000	**Debt payments**				$ 22,500
Total					**$2,174,300**

Figure 3.2 Hypothetical line-item budget for a municipal zoo. Additional subheadings would be developed in an actual budget. For example, line 1100 could be broken down further to show salary lines for the chief administrative officer, vice presidents, supervisors, managers, secretaries, etc.

piecemeal way in which budget items are presented in a line-item format, budget reviewers concentrate on changes in specific items, e.g., personnel, travel expenses, and supplies, that compose the programs rather than focusing on the various functions or programs that an agency provides. It has been noted:

> It is much easier [for budget reviewers] to agree on an addition or reduction of a few thousand or a million than to agree whether a program is good or not. It is much easier to agree on a small addition or decrease [in a specific item] than to compare the worth of one program to that of all others (p. 136).[4]

In this regard, line-item budgeting facilitates budget cutting processes, which is one reason why it has remained popular with decision makers. Because the link between expenditures and benefit outputs is so unclear, budget cutters are able to delete bits and pieces of an overall budget without being directly confronted with the consequences of their actions. They do not have to worry about the effects of their actions on a particular service when they are cutting or eliminating relatively small items that are not tied directly to service outcomes.

When decision makers make cuts, they usually enact the cuts first in those places that appear unlikely to affect a desirable program adversely. Departmental administrative expenses are often primary targets. However, such cutbacks may result in less monitoring of activities, less strategic planning, or less effort in soliciting external resources, which may be more costly than the money saved in the long run. Thus, line-item budgeting sometimes produces outcomes that run counter to agency goals regarding effectiveness, equity, and quality service delivery.

In summary, line-item budgets have three major weaknesses. First, they offer little information about the nature and level of services provided or about the resources needed to provide a specific level of service. Second, no formal process exists to force trade-offs and choices between programs and services. Third, no mechanism exists to predict the impact on performance or service level if changes in funding are made.

Program Budgeting

The intent of program budgeting is to present expenditures in the form of departmental functions or program packages. Rather than developing budgets in the traditional line-item form (e.g., salaries,

maintenance, supplies, etc.), the agency's expenditures are clustered into major program (activity) areas (e.g., aquatics, golf courses, greenhouse operations, recreational centers) or even into specific programs within these major areas (e.g., a learn-to-swim program, a golf tournament, a summer drop-in program for teens). A program budget emphasizes end outcomes rather than cost inputs. Using only major heading areas, figure 3.3 illustrates the basic difference between line-item and program budgets. Note that the budget total is identical using both the line-item and program formats.

The initial step in the program budgeting process is for key agency staff to identify each program that they provide. Once this program structure has been established, the next step is to determine all costs associated with the provision of each program. Many program budgets do not eliminate line items from budget statements; however, line items are placed under program-related headings. This involves recasting line items previously assigned to account classes (e.g., personnel services, commodities) and allocating them directly to the particular program. The staff, supplies, contractual services, and often overhead (e.g., rent, electricity) are taken out of the pure line-item budget format and are allocated to each program area. The resulting budget format combines the features of both line-item and program budgets.

Figure 3.4 on page 67 illustrates this combined format by taking the marketing and maintenance elements of this program area from the program format in figure 3.3 and allocating dollar amounts to them from the line-item categories. Table 3.2 on page 68 gives a more extensive illustration of a combined format featuring both line-item and program elements. Combining the output emphasis of the program budget with the accounting control detail of the line-item budget provides both park and recreation managers and taxpayers with a clearer picture of the range of services that will be undertaken and of their cost. Like the line-item budget, program budgets typically use an incremental approach whereby budget amounts for existing services are carried forward from one year to the next and increases or decreases to them are based on the amount of money available in a given year. Although it provides more information than a line-item budget, a program budget in its simplest form does not give administrators answers to important questions, such as, Why is the agency spending money on this program? What purpose will be served? What benefits will accrue to program participants and to the community?

Line-Item Format

1000	**Personnel services**		$1,400,000
	1100	$789,800	
	1200	$529,800	
	1300	$ 80,400	
2000	**Contractual services**		$ 154,900
	2100	$ 8,000	
	2200	$ 52,900	
	2300	$ 23,500	
	2400	$ 39,700	
	2500	$ 27,500	
	2600	$ 3,300	
3000	**Commodities**		$ 545,600
	3100	$317,100	
	3200	$ 88,800	
	3300	$ 31,300	
	3400	$108,400	
4000	**Current charges**		$ 29,800
	4100	$ 6,300	
	4200	$ 18,400	
	4300	$ 1,200	
	4400	$ 3,900	
5000	**Properties**		$ 21,500
	5100	$ 3,000	
	5200	$ 6,700	
	5300	$ 11,800	
6000	**Debt payments**		$ 22,500
Total			**$2,174,300**

Program Format

Support services		$ 758,900
Marketing	$108,400	
Maintenance	$455,300	
Projects	$195,200	
Administrative services		$ 569,200
Computer	$ 75,200	
Finance	$184,000	
Safety	$216,800	
Human resources	$ 93,200	
Biology and conservation		$ 846,200
Animal care	$390,300	
Veterinary needs	$281,900	
Nutritionist	$ 70,700	
Ground keeping	$103,300	
Total		**$2,174,300**

Figure 3.3 Comparison of hypothetical line-item and program budgets for a municipal zoo (abridged).

Performance Budgeting

Performance budgets place emphasis on the relationship between resource inputs and program outputs. Emphasis is not merely on the dollar amounts but rather on what is achieved with the money that is spent. The goal of the agency is to allocate money to the accomplishment of specific measurable units of performance. They develop the program budgeting process further by incorporating mission statements, objectives, and performance indicators for each program. Mission statements and objectives describe the medium- or long-range purposes of a program. Such statements indicate what the park and recreation agency hopes to accomplish with its programs over a specified period of time. These accomplishments are stated in terms of end benefits and address community needs or problems.

Thus, in addition to identifying program goals, managers in agencies using a performance budget format are requested to formulate performance measures for each activity or function. These indicators are intended to demonstrate progress toward achieving mission statements by quantifying output for each program. Types of performance indicators or criteria may include the following:

- Workload or output measures. (These may also be referred to as program size or vol-

Line-Item/Program Budget Format

Marketing		$108,400
Personnel	$ 77,300	
Salaries (full-time) $ 61,000		
Benefits $ 6,100		
Wages (part-time) $ 10,200		
Office supplies	$ 6,000	
Photocopies $ 3,800		
Telephone $ 1,000		
Fax $ 1,200		
Utilities	$ 2,100	
Research	$ 14,200	
Advertising	$ 8,800	
Maintenance		$455,300
Personnel	$417,100	
Salaries (full-time) $300,000		
Benefits $ 30,000		
Wages (part-time) $ 87,100		
Office supplies	$ 1,500	
Photocopies $ 1,000		
Telephone $ 400		
Fax $ 100		
Utilities	$ 18,900	
Supplies	$ 16,100	
Tools	$ 1,700	
Total		**$563,700**

Figure 3.4   A combined line-item/program budget.

ume indicators.) These measures assess basically how much is being done (e.g., numbers of acres of parks being maintained, number of hours of instruction, number of recreational center users served).

- Efficiency measures. They measure how well an agency is utilizing its budget resources. Usually, this type of indicator is expressed as a ratio of the amount of input (e.g., manpower or dollar cost) expended per unit of output. These measures provide some idea of the success with which input is converted to output (e.g., dollar cost per program, number of acres mowed per operator-hour, number of class hours pro-

vided per instructor year, cost per resident served).

- Effectiveness measures. Effectiveness is a measure of how well a program meets a need or achieves an objective. Effectiveness measures are often confused with efficiency measures. For example, trash cans may be purchased and installed more efficiently but still may not be effective in reducing the amount of litter in parks.

Illustrations of these types of performance measures used by the athletics and forestry divisions of the College Station Parks and Recreation Department are shown in table 3.3 on page 69.

The development of performance indicators is not easy to achieve and is likely to involve substantial effort:

In order to implement performance budgeting, one should use a cost-accounting system. A reporting system must also be developed to record cost items (personnel, supplies, equipment, and overhead) needed to perform work (input). From the data collected, the cost of performing units of work can be determined—that is, cost per acre of mowing park land, cost per mile of operating a vehicle, or cost per camper day for campers in a resident camp program (p. 42).[12]

The emphasis of performance budgeting is on outputs (e.g., programs, services, and benefits) rather than on expenditure inputs that characterize the line-item budget. It reflects more accurately and clearly how funds are being used. It should be quite evident to a person reading a program budget how much it costs to run a swimming pool or a golf course at a given performance standard level. By incorporating performance standards into the budgeting process and focusing on outputs, the emphasis shifts from control to management. This more meaningful and more informative budget document provides better information upon which to base decisions. The data supplied by the process of performance budgeting are particularly important to park and recreation administrators and elected officials who are removed from the operating processes of the agency. Those involved in operations can see the results and may regard this type of documentation or verification as redundant, but to decision makers who are removed from such direct contact, a performance budget is their only means of identifying and relating costs specifically to the work being performed.

Table 3.2   Combined Program and Line-Item Format

Object classification of expenditures	Administration	Athletics	Building and indoor centers	Swimming pools	Playgrounds	Special activities	Total
Regular salaries and wages	**$36,516**	**$11,400**	**$ 43,600**		**$ 14,800**	**$ 9,600**	**$115,916**
Professional	25,300	11,400	32,400		11,200	6,000	86,300
Other	11,216		11,200		3,600	3,600	29,616
Temporary salaries and wages	**960**	**6,800**	**18,800**	**25,028**	**87,200**	**11,180**	**149,968**
Professional		3,200	14,520	6,520	57,920	9,520	91,680
Other	960	3,600	4,280	18,508	29,280	1,660	58,288
Contractual services	**7,092**	**510**	**14,902**	**6,774**	**5,082**	**1,812**	**36,172**
Communication and transportation	4,680	330	450	170	930	450	7,010
Heat, light, power, and water	1,200		7,964	5,520	1,560	640	16,884
Printing, etc.	900	180	1,508	224	508	392	3,712
Repairs			4,200	860	1,524		6,584
Other services	312		780		560	330	1,982
Commodities	**6,450**	**2,920**	**10,278**	**6,956**	**12,296**	**3,120**	**42,020**
Offices	1,308	560	350	68	184	104	2,574
Fuel	920		4,360	364	128	172	5,944
Supplies	2,152	1,440	2,528	4,720	7,520	2,590	20,950
Materials	1,480	600	760	1,640	2,964	254	7,698
Repairs	590	320	2,280	164	1,500		4,854
Current charges	**700**	**268**	**640**	**950**	**390**	**150**	**3,098**
Insurance	220	148	572	920	360		2,220
Memberships	480	120	68	30	30	150	878
Properties	**760**	**3,270**	**12,400**		**6,112**	**1,520**	**24,062**
Equipment	760	2,350	5,280		5,520	1,520	15,430
Building improvements		920	7,120		592		8,632
Total	**$52,478**	**$25,168**	**$100,620**	**$39,708**	**$125,880**	**$27,382**	**$371,236**

Table 3.3   Performance Measures Used by the Athletics and Forestry Division

	Last fiscal year	This fiscal year	Next fiscal year
Athletics			
Input			
No. of permanent, full-time staff	2	2	3
No. of full-time equivalents	9.96	6	5
Athletic general fund budget/expenditure	$268,727	$274,201	$289,985
Athletic hotel/motel budget/expenditure	$41,126	$73,336	$70,766
Output			
Total revenue	$201,757	$192,925	$196,400
Total number of participants	17,038	17,804	18,204
No. of regional, state, and national tournaments	12	11	12
Efficiency			
Percentage of expenditures covered by revenue	65%	56%	54%
Estimated cost per participant	$18	$20	$20
Effectiveness			
Percent satisfied on customer survey	87%	90%	91%
Forestry			
Input			
Total forestry budget/expenditure	$319,275	$351,810	$361,871
No. of employees	9	9	9
No. of vehicles	4	4	4
No. of shops	1	1	1
No. sq ft beds	116,000	116,000	116,000
No. of irrigation systems	62	64	64
Output			
No. of worker-hours on municipal tree care	2,166	2,100	2,100
No. of worker-hours on horticultural maintenance	2,327	2,300	2,300
No. of worker-hours on irrigation system checks, repairs, and improvements	1,613	1,600	1,600
No. of worker-hours on special events	5,539	5,500	5,500
Efficiency			
No. of sq ft beds maintained per worker-hour	N/A	49.8	49.8
No. of worker-hours per irrigation system	N/A	25	25
Effectiveness			
Percent satisfied on customer survey	N/A	84%	90%
Percentage of work orders cleared within 10 working days	90%	90%	90%
No. of checks per year on irrigation systems	400 of 744	400 of 768	400 of 768
(percentage checked annually)	54%	52%	52%

Zero-Base Budgeting

Zero-base budgeting, which is another variation of program budgeting, received substantial attention when it emerged in the early 1970s. In its original form, zero-base budgeting was intended to provide an alternative to conventional incremental approaches. Rather than using current budget appropriation levels as the starting point when budgeting for the next year, zero-base budgeting required agencies to start from ground zero. Conceptually, this meant that even if an item was included in the current year's budget, it did not mean that it would appear in the following year's budget. Each year, an agency was required to look at its entire budget afresh and produce, if warranted, a better allocation of resources among its programs. Using this approach, basic questions confronting an agency were whether a current program was of sufficient value to be retained, whether it should be curtailed, or whether it should be replaced by a new program of higher priority. The zero-base budgeting approach required an agency to evaluate systematically all of its programs (existing as well as proposed) on the basis of output or performance criteria.

Two fundamental steps are involved in effectively implementing zero-base budgeting: formulation of decision packages and prioritization of decision packages. Decision packages are formulated so that management can evaluate them, rank them against other decision units competing for funding, and decide whether to approve them for funding.

The second major step in zero-base budgeting is prioritizing the identified decision packages in rank order. The initial ranking of decision packages usually is made at the level at which the packages are developed. Thus, the manager of each division or subdivision in the park and recreation agency evaluates the relative importance of the programs or operations that are his or her responsibility. The decision package rankings are then, in turn, reviewed by successively higher supervisory and administrative echelons in the agency. Each manager is responsible for preparing a consolidated ranking of decision packages from all units, divisions, or departments reporting to him or her. It has been found that a participative committee approach involving key personnel from each division is a useful method for establishing consolidated rankings.

When all decision packages are listed in order of priority, decision makers start at the top of the list, determine how much money is available, and incorporate into the budget those for which there is funding. They draw the budget line at that point, and those below the cut-off line are not funded. Thus, if 75 packages were proposed by a park and recreation agency, decision makers may fund packages one through 55 but not packages 56 through 75. In principle, this ensures that in an environment of scarce resources, the highest-priority decision packages are funded. Any subsequent change that emerges in the level of available funding requires only a shift in the position of the cut-off line.

There have been several criticisms of zero-base budgeting. The most prominent relates to the time and effort required to convert from a previous approach (e.g., line-item budget) to zero-base budgeting. Even after it has been established, the zero-base budgeting process is time consuming and bureaucratic relative to incremental budgeting approaches. A second criticism is that the priority ranking of an agency's decision packages may vary according to expected funding levels. That is, a $25,000 program may be ranked tenth among 20 options in a $2 million budget but ranked fifth in an $800,000 budget because several options initially ranked ahead of it may be too expensive to fit within the latter framework. Other potential problems include uncertainty and low staff morale arising from concerns about program continuity and employment status because of zero-base budgeting's emphasis on starting each budget cycle from ground zero.

The improvement in quality of management information derived from the use of the zero-base format when compared with the line-item approach is an important advantage. Its adoption is likely to provide all participants in the budget process with much greater insight into the relative usefulness of programs. However, the disadvantages of zero-base budgeting are so great that no agencies now use a pure version of it. Nevertheless, many agencies have developed modified versions of it in which they continue to use elements of the process. For example, some agencies use zero-base budgeting in the discretionary portions of their budgets. A small number of others use zero-base budgeting on an occasional basis (e.g., every five years) in order to review and revise the established past priorities inherent in their regularly used incremental procedures.

Agencies that use modified zero-base budgeting for discretionary portions of the budget have not shifted away from the incremental mode of operating, which was one of the early rationales for using zero-base budgeting. Rather their adaptation of it recognizes the reality that budgeting mainly is concerned with decisions made at the margin rather than with an agency's established core services. Typically, 85% or 90% of an agency's services, which constitute its uncontested core offerings, are not subjected to the zero-base budgeting approach. The relevant question that arises is: "Among the 10% to 15% of programs at the margin, is an increment in Program A more important than an increment in Program B or a previously funded item in Programs A, B, and C?"[13]

It is in creating trade-offs between existing marginal programs and new opportunities that zero-base budgeting is most useful. Its contribution is to make the preparation of alternative funding levels and different program alternatives a formal requirement in budget preparation so that elected officials can see all of the trade-offs involved when making budget decisions. From the point of view of elected officials and the jurisdiction's chief executive, it provides a system that permits meaningful comparison of programs between agencies as well as within agencies.

Table 3.4 shows a set of decision packages forwarded by the College Station Parks and Recreation Department to the city council as part of its annual budget. The city calls its decision packages service-level adjustments and requires them for all new funding requests. The department's various divisions are shown in the first column and each division's rankings are shown in the fourth column. The department's consolidated rankings are shown in the fifth column. The city manager receives similar decision packages from all other agencies. He or she leads the department heads in a participative exercise to integrate and rank decision packages from all of the departments' lists into a single master list. This is presented to the council as the staff's recommendation. The council accepts or reorders it as they wish and determines how far down the priority list to draw the funding line.

Entrepreneurial Budgeting Systems

Entrepreneurial budgeting systems, which are sometimes referred to as expenditure-control budgeting, target-based budgeting, or envelope budgeting, emerged in the early 1980s. The appeal of entrepreneurial budgeting systems is based in part on its control over the bottom line, which makes it popular with elected officials in times of fiscal constraint, and in part on its consistency with the trend toward decentralization and

Table 3.4   Prioritized Parks and Recreation Department Service Level Adjustments

| | | | Rank | |
Division	SLA	Amount	Div	Dept
Park operations	Central Park softball park lights and cross arms	70,000	1	1
Forestry	Landscape maintenance at Business Center, Northgate, Fire Station #1, library, utility billing	150,610	1	2
Park administration	Infrastructure replacement fund	50,000	1	3
Park operations	Wayne Smith baseball complex	80,897	2	4
Recreation	Bid out concessions/youth services coordinator	−55,669	1	5
Special facilities	Adamson Lagoon engineering fees	5,091	2	6
Park operations	Out-front mowers	16,000	3	7
Special facilities	Increase in O&M for CDBG van	5,091	2	8
Special facilities	Upgrade from 8- to 12-passenger van	6,781	3	9
Park administration	Directional signs for neighborhood parks	5,000	2	10
Total		333,801		

incentives. The basic concept underlying entrepreneurial budgeting systems is that elected officials set a budget ceiling for an agency without imposing any of the details that accompany traditional budgeting formats. The idea is that elected officials should focus on the big picture, not the details. The agency director then delegates authority for developing and implementing programs and services to staff members, who operate within the established budget limits. Thus, the budgeting system is centralized because policy goals are established and monitored by elected officials but is decentralized because individual agencies or units within agencies are given considerable discretion in how resources are allocated to achieve those goals. In return for this increased budgetary discretion, elected officials are likely to require strong evidence that an agency achieves its program goals efficiently.

Often an almost contractual agreement is negotiated between the council or central budget office and the operating departments in which each department lists and ranks its objectives, specifies indicators for measuring the achievement of those objectives, and quantifies the indicators as far as possible (p. 450).[7]

This type of strong performance accountability is essential with entrepreneurial budgeting systems because it ensures that elected officials retain responsibility for public policy and do not abdicate it to agency personnel. It ensures that in delegating more authority to administrators to decide how to pursue goals, elected officials do not inadvertently delegate decisions about what goals to pursue. An illustration of how entrepreneurial budgeting systems were implemented in the Texas Parks and Wildlife Department is given in "The Entrepreneurial Budget System Adopted by the Public Lands Division of the Texas Parks and Wildlife Department." In contrast to zero-base budgeting, entrepreneurial budgeting systems is

a top-down rationing process that is concerned with establishing priorities and limits at the top as a means to force choice among alternatives at the bottom. Agency staff can propose revenue enhancements, action designed to achieve productivity increases, and alternative means to avoid service and personnel cuts when targets cut into the base. Generally, departments have more autonomy under EBS than under other forms of budgeting (p. 52).[14]

The Entrepreneurial Budget System Adopted by the Public Lands Division of the Texas Parks and Wildlife Department

The Public Lands Division was responsible for the operation of all parks in the Texas state park system. With more than 500,000 acres and more than 24 million visitors each year, the Texas state park system is the fourth largest in the United States after the national park system and the state park systems of Alaska and California. The system encompasses 41 state parks, 44 recreational areas, 40 historic sites, and seven natural areas.

In 1991, the state legislature decreed that it would no longer provide tax support from the general fund for operation of the state parks. At that time, general tax funds composed 60% of the state parks' operating budget. The fiscal crisis confronting the agency was illustrated dramatically by its proposal to close 15 state park areas soon after these financial changes took effect. This action was averted, but it emphasized the need to adopt a dramatically different long-term approach to operating the parks.

Senior management encouraged park managers in the field to become more entrepreneurial. They challenged these managers to invest in programs that would either make money or save money and to provide services that would increase visitation and revenues. However, there was no system for rewarding those who responded positively to these exhortations. All budgeting was centralized; therefore, additional revenues and any cost savings went into the agency's central fund, and the park providing these additional resources received no direct benefits from them. The entrepreneurial budgeting system was initiated to address this problem. Its goal was to empower and reward individual park managers by giving them access to some of the extra resources that they generated.

The core of the entrepreneurial budgeting system was a contract between the park manager and the agency's senior management to meet certain performance standards. An expenditure ceiling was negotiated for the year. All savings achieved in a park in a given fiscal year were retained for the following year in that park. They were an enhancement to the park's budget in that following year and were not used to offset its budget. The savings and revenues could be invested at the park manager's discretion in enhanced programming, facility expansion, or park operational needs.

The park manager also committed to generate revenue that was equal to the previous year's revenue plus 0.5% to 3.0%. If the revenue target was exceeded, then the park retained 35% of each dollar over the target as an enhancement to its budget the following year. Of the remainder, 40% was retained by the agency for general funding of historic and ecological park units that were unlikely to attract enough visitors to be self-supporting, and 25% was reserved in a special account to finance the operation of new parks coming into the system. Park managers were given discretion in setting the park admission price and the prices for auxiliary services and programs.

As in any business venture, managers were also held responsible for shortfalls in revenue or overexpenditures. If target revenue figures were not met, then the following fiscal year's budget was reduced by that amount. The entrepreneurial budgeting system shifted responsibility for a park's operational and financial decisions from centralized control to field staffs in the parks, and it held park managers accountable for their decisions.

The system spawned attractive services that earn revenue. For example, visitors at Brazos Bend State Park enjoyed a 2 h nocturnal owl prowl for $3 per prowler. They watched alligators from a pontoon boat for $8 per person. At South Llano River State Park, a refurbished 1951 Chevy bus (donated by the local fire department) took visitors on wildlife safaris through the park for $3 per passenger. Huntsville State Park held an annual canoe rendezvous, Rocky Raccoon trail runs, and 50 mi and 100 mi fun runs that generated between $5,500 and $7,000 annually in additional funds. Activities such as these raised revenues without detracting from natural amenities. As an added safeguard to protect the parks' environment, regional managers had to approve all customer services proposed by field personnel so that protection of natural resources remained the first priority.

Overall, the entrepreneurial budgeting systems registered financial success. During the planning stage, department officials anticipated that the program would yield $1 million in additional revenue. By fiscal year 1995, additional revenue had reached $1.1 million and cost savings totaled nearly $685,000. The year before the entrepreneurial budgeting system began, nine parks raised more revenue than they spent. After three years of operating under the program, 22 parks took in more money than they spent.

From internal documents and interviews with managers of the Texas Parks and Wildlife Department and the Natural Resource Defense Council. Reclaiming our heritage. New York: National Resources Defense Council. 1997.

An agency's budget proposal is divided into two parts: the part that fits into the target, which will be funded, and the part comprising elements that do not fit into the target but that managers want or need. The agency must prioritize all items on the unfunded list, and it may or may not receive any of them. This approach requires agencies to prioritize at several levels: what items they will put in their target base budget and what items they will leave unprotected to compete with requests from other departments; how they will rank the items on the unprotected list; and how they will trade-off new programs with existing programs.[15]

In contrast to lengthy traditional line-item documents, the city council usually approves a short one- or two-page policy document that focuses on major goals it wants to achieve. The council may decide, for example, that citizens are particularly concerned about the condition of the parks, and, hence, they may increase the parks' budget by 10% but increase all other departments' budgets only by 5%. The council then monitors the agency's performance to ensure that their policy goals are met.

An entrepreneurial budgeting system is likely to have accounts for major program areas; however, if something breaks down or an opportunity arises, then money can be shifted from one account to another. An agency's budget typically is determined by a formula. For example, last year's amount increased by some percentage to account for inflation and population growth. The agency is required to maintain at least the same number and quality of services. New initiatives would receive additional funds. In this way, elected officials, and the city manager to some extent, move away from micro-management and toward greater attention to broad policy issues: "Department heads are, in effect, given block grants that demonstrate considerable trust in their judgment about the use of money and that allow a high level of autonomy in managing their departments" (p. 446).[7] Agency managers use a line-item or program format to track expenditures, but the format becomes an accounting device to help managers instead of a control device imposed by elected officials to constrain them.[3]

A result of this type of budget is that managers tend to adopt a different mind-set. Instead of focusing on how best to spend a line-item amount assigned to a particular program, the agency considers whether all of that amount is needed there or whether some of it could be saved and used elsewhere.[3]

This approach empowers agencies to pursue their missions unencumbered by previous budget expenditure priorities, which is a primary fault in incremental budgeting. Savings can be made in existing programs and used to initiate new services. This type of budget frees managers to move resources around as needs shift. It allows them also to keep all or some high proportion of what they did not spend from one year to the next. The freedom to reallocate funds fosters creativity and innovation. An added benefit of the system is that agencies have more time and resources to monitor their performance; they do not have to spend that effort on the laborious, time-consuming process of justifying long lists of detailed line items (which occurs in the traditional budgeting process). The relationship of entrepreneurial budgeting systems with other budgeting approaches has been summarized in the following terms:

> Clearly, the latest trends in budgeting contain elements of the earlier reforms. They contain performance measures from performance budgeting, functional categories from program budgeting, negotiation of objectives from management by objectives, and ranking of objectives from zero-base budgeting. But there are some differences between the old reforms and the latest ones. The latter are generally simpler, more streamlined, and require less paperwork and analysis. They involve more discretion by line managers than did the earlier reforms, and there is a much greater emphasis on accountability than under the older formats. Finally, the recent reforms are motivated by a desire to change fundamentally the culture of public management by turning bureaucrats into entrepreneurs. Previous budgetary reforms pursued legality, efficiency, and effectiveness. The present wave of budgetary reform aims to stimulate motivation. The new approaches incorporate most of the goals of the previous reforms, but they seek to achieve them through decentralized incentives that give program managers greater authority to combine resources as they think best but that hold the managers accountable for the results. These two qualities are virtually a definition of entrepreneurship (p. 450).[7]

Enterprise Funds

Almost all public sector revenues received from taxes, user fees, or other sources typically go into a centralized general fund from which elected officials allocate resources to pay for services. However, exceptions to this policy may occur in situations where an agency's intent is that the costs of providing services will be recovered from user fees, leases, or other sources of nontax revenue. In these cases, a separate accounting mechanism called an enterprise fund may be established. Historically, jurisdictions frequently have used enterprise funds to pay the cost of delivering utilities, such as water, sewer, or electricity; public car parking; or public transit systems. The movement toward greater reliance on user fees to pay for park and recreation services, which occurred after the tax revolt, resulted in many park and recreation agencies using enterprise funds for services such as golf courses, marinas, or recreational programs (see tables 3.5 and 3.6). These funds are particularly useful when there is a high demand for services from some groups but a strong opposition to paying for them by taxes from the general fund.

True enterprise funds are fully self-supporting so that revenues received from service users cover all costs associated with producing those services. These costs could include facility maintenance, debt charges, equipment depreciation, and administrative overhead. For example, in Bellevue, Washington, services in the park and recreation

Financing Recreational Programs From an Enterprise Fund

The Board of Johnson County Park and Recreation District in Kansas decided that all of its tax funds would be used for agency administration, park operation and maintenance, and park development. A parallel goal was that self-generating revenues would support fully all direct recreational programming. To facilitate this plan of financing, the district combined its fee-supported programs into the recreation enterprise fund and combined its tax-supported programs into the general fund.

The enterprise fund was the manifestation of a fee-support philosophy in which direct program costs were absorbed by user fees paid by participants who benefited from the programs rather than by the general taxpayer. Participant fees were also used to expand outdoor recreational facilities, especially athletic fields, by providing the funding source needed to retire revenue bonds. The enterprise fund's financial projections for the late 1990s are shown in table 3.5.

Table 3.5   Enterprise Fund Financial Projections

	1996	1997	1998	1999	2000
Revenue	$10,088,925	$10,673,789	$11,058,401	$11,361,388	$11,584,469
Operating expenses	$8,837,411	$9,192,734	$9,551,592	$9,742,959	$9,937,818
Net revenue	$1,251,514	$1,481,055	$1,506,809	$1,618,429	$1,646,651
Outstanding revenue bonds debt service	$936,121	$1,080,661	$1,117,125	$1,197,181	$1,176,708
Coverage	1.34x	1.37x	1.35x	1.35x	1.39x

agency's enterprise fund were required to generate revenues sufficient to recover the following costs:

- Direct program cost (100%), i.e., personnel, materials, supplies, contracts, capital outlays
- Indirect program costs (100%), i.e., maintenance expenses
- Department overhead (10.95%)
- City overhead (23.3%)
- Capital costs, i.e., all debt charges and rate of return based on fair market value of land and building[16]

Services in an enterprise fund are expected to be operated like a private business enterprise, and, in the private context, all of these costs would have to be met. However, in many jurisdictions enterprise funds with less rigorous conditions have been established and do not require some of these costs to be covered. The extent to which the general fund subsidizes an enterprise fund should match the benefits that the general public receives from the services as opposed to the benefits that users of the service receive.

Some agencies establish a separate enterprise fund for each service, e.g., one for golf, one for marinas, one for recreational programs, etc. Others, such as the illustrations shown in "Financing Recreational Programs From an Enterprise Fund" and table 3.5, use one enterprise fund for multiple services and programs. The latter approach offers much greater flexibility because services that generate a substantial surplus can be used to help support others that do not cover their entire costs. This increases the range of services that may be offered, but participants in high-surplus-generating activities may resent their resources being used to subsidize other activities.

Enterprise funds provide opportunities for managers to be creative. If a single fund is used for all services, then surpluses can be used as seed money to launch other programs that seem likely to be self-sufficient. Thus, new initiatives and program terminations can be implemented quickly in response to emerging and declining demands without managers having to go through the laborious and time-consuming process of developing justification for them and seeking funding approval through the general-fund budget process. They offer a source of resources for expanding existing programs and services, hiring new personnel, and purchasing additional equipment and supplies without having to compete with other agencies for funds to do this. If there is an income surplus in the fund at the end of the fiscal year, then it can be carried forward into the following year; however, elected officials are sometimes tempted to transfer any surplus into the general fund to offset expenditures on other services. Another way of achieving the same end of moving surplus revenues to the general fund is for an increased amount of indirect overhead expenses to be assigned to the enterprise fund. Finally, enterprise funds are popular with people who believe that some park and recreation services should be paid for by their users rather than by all taxpayers.

An innovative use of an enterprise fund was developed in Minnesota by the suburban Hennepin Regional Park District. The district established a park rehabilitation trust fund. Its purpose was to provide a stable source of funds to assure a program of park rehabilitation that would maintain the quality of the district's infrastructure. Daily- and annual-pass parking fees designated to the trust funded it. Because the rehabilitation costs were financed through these parking-fee funds, they became the responsibility of park users.[17]

Budget Preparation

A survey of municipal recreation managers highlighted both the perceived importance of budgeting and the potential concerns regarding budgetary processes.[18] Survey respondents ranked their involvement with planning and preparing budgets higher in importance than all other planning-related functions in the workplace. However, compared with their importance levels, scores reporting perceived proficiency in planning and preparing budgets were significantly lower. Budget planning was the only planning-related function of nine listed in which managers' perceived-proficiency scores were lower than their perceived-importance scores. This gap represents cause for concern and suggests the need for increased professional development opportunities on budget processes, especially because decentralized strategies, such

as entrepreneurial budgeting systems, are gaining popularity.

In most government agencies, the budget process officially is inaugurated with the development of a budget manual and calendar. The budget manual provides a standardized set of instructions and forms to be used in preparing the budget document. Its primary purpose is to facilitate a consistent understanding of what is expected from all participants in the budget process. The budget calendar establishes a time schedule for completing each phase in the budget preparation cycle from issuance of budget instructions to its adoption by the agency's governing body. In most jurisdictions, the budget manual and calendar are prepared annually by the chief financial officer under the direction of the jurisdiction's chief executive (e.g., city manager, county manager, governor) and distributed to all department heads. Agency heads and their staffs must adhere to the set deadlines.

A typical budget calendar is shown in figure 3.5. At the beginning of a budget cycle, the elected body develops the key fiscal, operational, and policy guidelines that will govern preparation of the budget.[10] These may define things, such as the upper tax rate that is acceptable, the level of salary increases for employees, the statement on level of fee increases, and an indication of what service and operational areas should be emphasized or de-emphasized to meet evolving priorities.

These guidelines will be incorporated into the budget instructions that the chief executive sends to department heads. In this case, it is assumed that the executive is a city manager rather than a county judge, mayor, or governor, for example. The budget instructions detail what the city manager expects to be accomplished in the next budget period: "Invariably, the message stresses frugality and the analysis of alternatives. The message also highlights the executive's priority programs. The inference is: If it is not on the list, it is not in line for major new resources" (p. 55).[10]

At the agency level, the director will request divisions and their sub-units to develop budget requests. The agency director's instructions will be consistent with those of the city manger, but will also reflect his or her own priorities for the agency. The mechanical part of the budget process is relatively straightforward because the city manager provides standardized worksheets and formats for the agency to complete. The more challenging part of the process is the visionary task of managers clearly articulating and selling

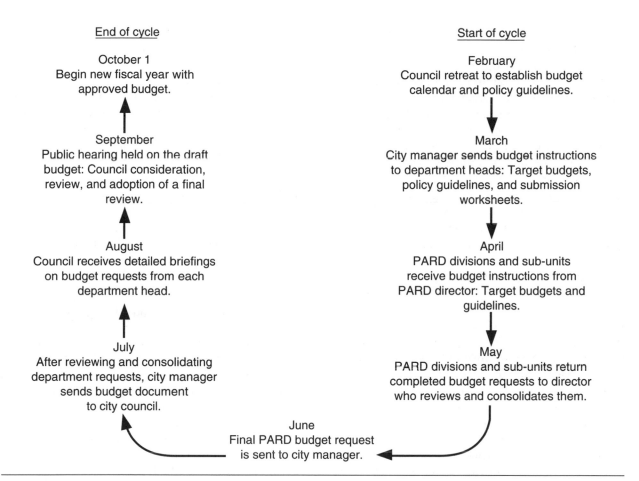

Figure 3.5   A typical local government budget calendar. *PARD*, parks and recreation department.

their programs' priority in the justification statements that typically accompany budget requests.

The park and recreation agency's budget requests are likely to be driven by the particular service demands of its constituents. In contrast, the city manager is likely to have a much broader vision of community needs and priorities and is required to achieve coordination and prioritization of the competing demands for resources. Hence, in consolidating the budget requests from all departments, the city manager will make adjustments to the proposed budget that the park and recreation agency submits.

When the budgets are returned to the city manager's office, there has been no discussion among agencies. Each has developed its own best case for resources that is independent of consideration for other service areas in the community. Agency heads are required to brief the city manager on their budgets and respond to critical analyses of them. These briefings provide the city manager with additional insight and aid in the decisions and trade-offs that have to be made in producing a consolidated budget for the jurisdiction.

The city council's role is responsive.[10] The initiative in budgeting lies with the city manager and agency directors, so council members have a tendency to feel inadequate, somewhat unprepared, and perhaps overwhelmed. Thus, after submitting the draft consolidated budget to the council, the head of the agency gives a similar set of briefings to the council. Public hearings are set to receive input from residents on the proposed budget. Typically, they are poorly attended and little input is forthcoming. After they are informed on the budget's content, the council often schedules workshop sessions to discuss, review, and insert amendments to the draft document before finally voting to approve it as an ordinance that sets the spending ceiling and authorizes all departmental budgets.

The agency head's performance at briefings before the city manager, before the city council, or at public hearings to interpret and justify the budget request is of critical importance. The manager must be prepared thoroughly because he or she will be asked to defend the value and purpose of the agency's programs in the presence of the media, constituent groups, and the general public. Park and recreation managers must be thoroughly familiar with their proposed budget and the justification for individual items. It is embarrassing if they fail to locate quickly needed budget materials or support documentation for items to which they are required to respond. A manager who provides unclear answers or poor documentation in response to questioning rapidly loses credibility.

The director generally begins budget presentations with a prepared opening statement highlighting previous agency achievements and accenting the scope, direction, and intent of the proposed budget. He or she is likely to use comparisons, ratios, trends, and other budget analysis methods to enhance the impact of the presentation. Ratios could be used, for example, to illustrate a positive relationship between program costs and user participation. Trends, such as rising costs or increasing attendance, could be plotted on graphs to emphasize important information or accomplishments. Changes or cuts to the budget may be made even after the most polished and informative of presentations. Revenue constraints, competing demands, and the fiscally conservative posture of many budget reviewers combine to make substantial increases an exception.

Budgeting is a year-round process. While the director and agency staff may be involved formally in the mechanics of preparing and presenting the budget for only a six-month period each year, effective budget development is the result of continuous long-range planning, review, and evaluation. To facilitate budgeting as an ongoing process, many park and recreation departments have established budget folders into which timely ideas, memos, and recommendations can be placed on a year-round basis. Rather than relying on imperfect recall, the administrator then has available a comprehensive, up-to-date information source when the official budget process is initiated. A formal reporting system should be created to encourage staff input into the budget folder.

Citizens' input should be a cornerstone of an agency's attempts to assemble budget information continuously. The analysis of residents' park and recreation preferences and their level of satisfaction with existing services provides an informative foundation upon which to make decisions regarding program priorities. If there are data to support budget figures, the chances of securing additional financial support for park and recreation services are likely to be greatly enhanced. For example, if an agency is able to demonstrate

that 75% of the community wants the new service, its request for funds is likely to have more credence in the eyes of elected officials.

The ability of an agency to sell successfully a proposed program or level-of-service change to its board is directly related to how well the agency lays the groundwork. The probability of receiving a favorable response is enhanced by preparing adequate justification data in the form of a clearly established and identified need for the service, a realistic appraisal of projected costs and operational requirements (e.g., manpower, equipment, etc.), and anticipated outcomes of the program (e.g., enhanced levels of satisfaction, increased numbers of people served, new skills learned, additional revenues realized).

Budget Monitoring

Managers working in a public agency are required to be good stewards of the public's funds. One dimension is careful monitoring of the funds with which they are entrusted to ensure that their actual expenditures do not exceed the amount allocated in the budget. Typically, they are assisted in monitoring the relationship between the amount expended and the amount budgeted by reports that emanate from the jurisdiction's finance department. In some jurisdictions, these are on-line and are available instantly to managers whenever they want to check their budgetary status. In other situations, managers receive a monthly statement documenting the current status of this relationship. Table 3.6 gives an illustration of this type of statement.

Table 3.6 compares budgeted and actual line-item expenditures and income in a performance fund (which is another name for an enterprise fund) for the month ending June 30 in a city whose fiscal year ends on September 30. Column 1 shows the total amount budgeted for the 12 months in that fiscal year. Current budget (column 2) refers to the amounts projected in the budget for the month of June, while current actual (column 3) reports actual income and expenditures in the month of June. Columns 4 and 5 compare the budgeted and actual June amounts in dollars and percentages. The remaining four columns show the year-to-date situation after nine months of the fiscal year have passed. Again, the budgeted and actual amounts are compared in terms of dollars and percentages and are reported in columns 8 and 9.

Ideally, columns 4, 5, 8, and 9 would show zero, indicating that actual expenditures exactly

Table 3.6 A Budget Monitoring Report

City of Waco, Texas, Recreation Services Performance Fund Statement of Income and Expenses

	Annual budget	Current budget	Current actual	Over/(under) Budget	Over/(under) Percent	Y-T-D budget	Y-T-D actual	Over/(under) Budget	Over/(under) Percent
Operating revenue									
Recreation fees	212,252	67,071	69,712	2,641	3.9%	166,614	169,364	2,750	1.7%
Contributions	100,000	42,800	(14,379)	(57,179)	-133.6%	72,800	43,296	(29,504)	-40.5%
Rent from real estate	—	—	(29,045)	(29,045)	—	—	4,290	4,290	—
Other	30,000	6,630	6,085	(545)	-8.2%	15,930	14,747	(1,183)	-7.4%
Commission on concession	—	—	4,003	4,003	—	—	5,832	5,832	—
Intergovernmental—state	—	—	6,886	6,886	—	—	42,939	42,939	—
Miscellaneous	10,000	3,410	3,937	527	15.5%	6,810	11,403	4,593	67.4%
Total revenue	352,252	119,911	47,199	(72,712)	-60.6%	262,154	291,871	29,717	11.3%
Operating expense									
Salaries and wages	118,527	9,525	24,678	15,153	159.1%	85,215	78,507	(6,708)	-7.9%
Employee benefits	29,960	2,269	3,995	1,726	76.0%	21,672	18,020	(3,652)	-16.9%
Purchased prof./technical	110,588	32,438	43,433	10,995	33.9%	67,174	110,774	43,600	64.9%
Maintenance	2,300	399	101	(298)	-74.6%	744	2,112	1,368	183.9%
Other purchased services	34,053	5,025	4,848	(177)	-3.5%	15,487	26,610	11,123	71.8%
Supplies	32,824	5,574	4,992	(582)	-10.4%	18,718	35,776	17,058	91.1%
Other	24,000	12,816	3,967	(8,849)	-69.0%	20,688	15,506	(5,182)	-25.0%
Total operating expenses	352,252	68,046	86,014	17,968	26.4%	229,698	287,305	57,607	25.1%
Capital outlay	—	—	0	0	—	—	10,356	10,356	—
Total expenses	352,252	68,046	86,014	17,967	26.4%	229,698	297,661	67,963	29.6%
Net income (loss)	—	51,865	(38,815)	(90,679)	-174.8%	32,456	(5,790)	(38,246)	-117.8%

Operating revenues of $291,871 are $29,737 more than budgeted with recreation fees over budget $2,750 and contributions under budget $29,504.
Expenses of $297,660 are over budget $67,962, resulting in a net loss of $5,789, which was $38,245 more than budgeted.
Total expenses are over budget by 29.6%; operating expenses are over budget by 25.1%.

matched those allocated in the budget. However, in reality, such precision is improbable and is not expected. Nevertheless, managers are required to adjust their operations to ensure that their budget is not exceeded by the end of the fiscal year.

The particular example shown in table 3.6 made managers aware that nine months into the fiscal year, actual performance substantially lagged behind budget projections. The apparent cause for this was excessive operational expenditures. The report suggests a need to severely curtail expenditures in the remaining three months of the fiscal year or to generate revenues beyond those projected. The latter strategy may have been feasible given that the summer months were the time when major income from athletic activities and special events was received and that many managers adopted the conservative position of deliberately underestimating their revenue projections to ensure their budget goals are met at the end of the fiscal year. Such worst-case revenue estimates assume extraordinarily adverse weather conditions, economic downturns, or unexpected competition from other suppliers, which, by definition, do not occur most of the time. Hence, in most years, more revenue accrues than is projected in the budget. In the case shown in table 3.6, managers were not alarmed unduly because they knowingly had brought forward some operational expenses that were budgeted originally for the months of July and August. Hence, they anticipated that actual expenditures in those forthcoming months would be substantially lower than those shown in the budget.

Summary

A budget is a financial policy and political plan that forecasts an agency's estimated revenues and expenditures for a given time period. It should allocate resources to programs and activities in a manner that reflects the community's desires. Because it involves choices and trade-offs, compiling a budget is often difficult and controversial.

Capital budgeting is concerned with financing major one-time, long-term improvements. The annual capital budget is the plan for capital expenditures to be incurred in a given year. It is part of a capital improvements program that prioritizes capital projects to be undertaken over a five- or six-year period and develops a fiscal plan for funding these projects.

The operating budget is a financial plan that provides a detailed statement of all expenditures necessary for the day-to-day operation of an agency usually for a one-year period. When developing a budget, most agency personnel focus on acquiring all resources needed to meet their clienteles' demands, so they are sometimes characterized as budget spenders. In contrast, city managers or other chief government executives and elected officials tend to be more concerned with tax increases and often are viewed as budget cutters.

Almost all budgets are incremental; that is, the previous year's budget level is the starting point for developing the current budget, and most effort is concentrated on the increment of increase or decrease requested compared with the previous budget. This means that many spending decisions, and, hence, service delivery decisions, are in reality an unconscious reaffirmation of decisions made in the past. Incremental budgeting makes radical shifts in funding priorities unlikely.

Five general types of operating budgets are recognized, but few agencies use any of them in their pure form. Most agency budget formats are hybrids of these five types, incorporating selected facets and attributes from each type; therefore, each agency's budget form is likely to be idiosyncratic and unique. Line-item budgeting is the oldest and most common form that government agencies use. Its focus is on the allocation of funds, not on service benefit outputs, so it is impossible to identify the relationship between expenditures and program results. This enables elected officials to make cuts without being blamed for their adverse impact on particular services. Program budgeting presents the costs associated with each program that the agency offers. It is common for agencies to adopt a budget format that combines the output emphasis of a program budget with the accounting detail that the line-item approach provides. Performance budgets place emphasis on the relationship between resource inputs and program outputs. Performance criteria expressed as workload measures, efficiency measures, or effectiveness measures are used to demonstrate the extent to which service goals that are funded in the budget are met.

In its original form, zero-base budgeting intended to be an alternative to incremental budgeting approaches by requiring agencies to start each annual budget cycle from ground zero. This proved to be too onerous in time and effort to be practical in its pure form, but some agencies have developed modified versions of it. These generally involve using zero-base budgeting to assist in the relatively discretionary decisions that involve trade-offs between new and existing services at the budget margins. The two key stages in zero-base budgeting are formulating decision packages and prioritizing them. The main strength of these types of budgets is that selecting from different program alternatives is a formal requirement, so trade-offs are clearly visible when making budget decisions.

Entrepreneurial budgeting is characterized by elected officials setting a budget ceiling and policy goals for an agency without imposing any of the details that accompany traditional budgeting formats. The agency has considerable discretion in how resources are allocated to achieve the goals. This approach is decentralized. It gives managers greater authority to use resources as they think best but holds them accountable for the results.

Enterprise funds may be established when the agency intends to recover the cost of producing a particular service or set of services from the revenues that users generate. True enterprise funds are self-supporting, so revenues pay the full cost of service production. Managers can be more creative and responsive if enterprise funds, rather than general funds, are used. They can implement new initiatives more quickly without having to justify them or compete for funding in the annual general-fund budget process.

Budget preparation is typically a six-month-long exercise. It is governed by a budget calendar establishing deadlines for each of the landmarks in the process and by a budget manual that gives instructions and standard forms for preparing the budget document. The chief executive officer sends out these documents after he or she has received policy direction from elected officials. Budget monitoring is facilitated by regular reports that compare budgeted amounts with actual expenditures and income. These enable managers to be informed continuously of their budget status, so they are able to make any adjustments necessary during the course of the year to ensure their budget targets are met at the end of the fiscal year.

References

1. Robinson, Susan G. 1991. Capital planning and budgeting. In *Local government finance: Concepts and practices*, edited by John E. Peterson and Dennis R. Strachota. Chicago: Government Finance Officers Association, 65-84.

2. *Post Completion Review*. 1994. New York: International Federation of Accountants.

3. Osborne, David and Ted Gaebler. 1991. *Reinventing government*. Reading, MA: Addison-Wesley.

4. Wildavsky, A.B. 1986. *Budgeting: A comparative theory of budgetary processes*. New Brunswick, NJ: Transaction.

5. Savas, Eric S. 1987. *Privatization: The key to better government*. Chatham, NJ: Chatham House Publishers.

6. Buck, A.E. 1934. *The budget in governments of today*. New York: Macmillan.

7. Cothran, Dan A. 1993. Entrepreneurial budgeting: An emerging reform? *Public Administration Review* 53(5): 445-454.

8. Barkdoll, G.L. 1992. Scoping versus coping: Developing a comprehensive agency vision. *Public Administration Review* 52: 330-338.

9. Poister, Theodore and Gregory Steib. 1989. Management tools in municipal government: Trends over the past decade. *Public Administrative Review* 49: 240-248.

10. Sprecher, Lon. 1991. Operating budgets. In *Local government finance: Concepts and practices*, edited by John E. Peterson and Dennis R. Strachota. Chicago: Government Finance Officers Association, 45-64.

11. Cope, G.H. 1986. Municipal budgetary practices. *Baseline Data Report* 18(3): 1-13.

12. Deppe, Theodore R. 1983. *Management strategies in financing parks and recreation*. New York: Wiley.

13. Draper, Frank D. and Bernard T. Pitsvada. 1981. ZBB—looking back after ten years. *Public Administrative Review* 41: 76-83.

14. Lynch, T.D. 1995. *Public budgeting in America*. (Fourth Edition). Englewood Cliffs, NJ: Prentice Hall.

15. Garner, W.C. 1991. *Accounting and budgeting in public and nonprofit organizations: A manager's guide*. San Francisco: Jossey-Bass.

16. Odden, Howie, Lee Springgate and Roger Hoesterey. 1994. Entrepreneuring and enterprise: Bellevue's burgeoning benefits. *Parks and Recreation* 29(11): 44-48.

17. Christian, John W. 1987. Financing infrastructure maintenance through public trusts. *Parks and Recreation* 22(4): 42-44.

18. Smale, B.J.A. and W. Frisby. 1992. Managerial work activities and perceived competencies of municipal recreation mangers. *Journal of Park and Recreation Administration* 19(4): 81-108.

CHAPTER 4

LESS-THAN-FEE SIMPLE APPROACHES

Ownership of a parcel of land can be conceptualized as a bundle of rights. These include elements, such as the right to sell or bequeath the land; the right to keep others off of it; the right to use it for farming, ranching, recreation, or timber production; the right to extract minerals from it; and the right to erect buildings and other structures on it. Taken together, all rights constitute the full fee. A less-than-fee interest consists of one or more rights or of specifically defined parts of rights. The most commonly acquired less-than-fee interests include access rights (right-of-way easements), development rights (conservation or scenic easements), and mineral rights.

Less-than-fee approaches are discussed relatively early in this text because many of the partnerships discussed in subsequent chapters involve less-than-fee, rather than fee-simple, arrangements. In the past, park and recreation agencies almost exclusively acquired full fee-simple ownership of the lands that they administered. However, in recent years, less-than-fee simple mechanisms have gained in popularity because it has become apparent that committing to full, public ownership of all the land needed for park and recreational purposes is neither possible nor desirable.

It is not possible to own all of the land needed because the amount of money required is not available to pay for the initial costs of buying land or for the ongoing costs of maintaining it once it has been acquired. The use of park and recreational lands continues to grow exponentially; the price of land has risen rapidly in recent years, but the availability of funds to purchase and maintain park land has increased only marginally. These conditions make the greater use of less-than-fee approaches inevitable.

When it is possible to purchase full ownership, it may not be desirable. One authority has observed:

> The primary consideration in choosing a technique for protecting a given area is to ensure that it is adequate for achieving the public purpose. The appropriate method will generally call for the minimum necessary level of control by government and the maximum permissible level of choice for private land owners. Often the method chosen will entail lower public costs than full fee acquisition. But appropriateness rather than cost should be the primary criterion (p. 482).[1]

There are at least four reasons why it may not be considered desirable always to purchase land in fee simple. First, at times, transferring the land from private to public ownership for recreational use may destroy some of the vital qualities that make it aesthetically attractive. This view was articulated to a generally unresponsive park and recreation field as long ago as 1963 when William Whyte stated:

> The public do want parks, but intuitively it is the living, natural countryside they seek, and they will respond to a program that articulates this. To present open space action almost purely in terms of conventional park acquisition does not touch this nerve, and the vision of institutionalized open space that it conjures up is a somewhat sterile paradise (p. 19).[2]

Second, if land is purchased in fee simple, it must be maintained at the taxpayers' expense, which is frequently a costly burden. Third, the less-than-fee simple approach does not take land off the tax rolls. It may result in the land being assessed at a lower rate, but the entire potential tax base is not lost.

Fourth, less-than-fee simple methods are likely to be less disruptive, for they do not deprive anyone of their right to remain on the land. Indeed, as later discussion in this chapter illustrates, they may permit a landowner to derive substantial monetary gains from the property and, at the same time, to continue using it as it has been used in the past. This philosophy was articulated by one experienced conservationist in the following terms:

> Protection of natural areas is no longer a matter of buying land and building fences. Here on the Virginia coast, the islands, marshes, and seaside farms are tied to the local economy. People have made a living fishing and farming here for centuries. So any program protecting natural resources also has a human component. Resource conservation and economic vitality are parts of the same puzzle; you can't address one without the other.
>
> This realization has caused a sea change in the way conservation organizations do business in the 1990s. The us-against-them attitude of the 1970s and early 1980s gradually has given way to partnerships between business and conservation and to the development of sustainable industries that provide jobs and economic vitality without damaging natural resources (p. 40).[3]

Less-than-fee simple approaches offer ways of working with people who own desirable open spaces so that private interests are protected and public park and open space goals are met. These approaches facilitate partnerships between public and private interests.

At one end of the continuum in figure 4.1 is the status quo, i.e., no formal mechanism is used to protect desirable open space. The land is in the landowner's fee-simple ownership, and maintenance of the open space is dependent entirely upon the owner's goodwill. "Reliance on Landowner Goodwill" shows an example of this type of arrangement. At the opposite pole of the continuum is full-fee purchase by a public or nonprofit entity of all rights in the land. Between the poles of the continuum, the four types of less-than-fee approaches, which are the focus of discussion in this chapter, are arrayed in an order reflecting the level of permanence they convey on the park and open spaces that they are used to protect. Exactions and donations could also be inserted on the continuum as approaches that yield a similar level of

permanence as the fee-simple (full-fee) purchase. They are omitted because they are discussed separately in subsequent chapters of this text.

In some cases, the isolated use of a particular less-than-fee approach is inadequate to resolve a particular resource protection problem; rather it is their combined potential that makes them effective. Thus, after separate discussion of each of the four approaches, the chapter concludes with illustrations of greenline parks that characteristically incorporate and integrate several less-than-fee approaches.

Differential Taxation Assessment

After Maryland introduced differential taxation assessment in 1956, it was adopted by every other state. It enables owners of designated types of land to petition for their land to be assessed at current-use value rather than at market value. All of the state statutes designate agriculture as a qualifying use for this program. A lesser number of states include forest use in their designation, and

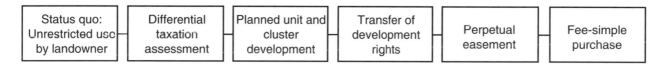

Figure 4.1 A permanence continuum of approaches for acquiring park land.

![tree icon]
Reliance on Landowner Goodwill

The chairwoman of the Lewisboro Horsemen's Association Trails in Westchester County, New York, relied on the beneficence of homeowners to establish and sustain a complex horse-trail network through private property in Lewisboro. She said: "We're approaching homeowners to get permission to clear trails through their property. So far the response has been enthusiastic. We hope eventually to hook up with the trail systems in our neighboring towns of North Salem and Bedford."

The model for such a trailway system is the Bedford Lanes Riding Association, which was founded in the early 1920s and which now has 175 mi of trails for walking, cross-country skiing, and horseback riding. A member of the association said: "We've never held an easement or right-of-way agreement. Just an informal arrangement with the landowner, and when the land changes hands, we approach the new owner and explain that we've always been here and if they don't want it, we can reroute the trail." They almost always agree.

Adapted from Mary McAleer Vizard. Trading development rights for goodwill. New York Times. September 19, 1993, section 10, page 9.

a growing number of states, such as Arizona, Hawaii, Maine, Minnesota, and Texas, authorize inclusion of natural, scenic, recreational, and historic resources and of wildlife habitat.

Current-use value means that farmland, for example, is assessed at agricultural production value, i.e., what a farmer can pay for the land and still make a viable living from it. Similarly, land designated for recreational, park, or scenic use is assessed at its value for those uses. If the land were taxed at its market value rather than its use value, the tax assessment would be based on the highest and best use of the land. Frequently, this would be much higher because of the land's development potential, especially if it were located close to an urban area. In some cases, these taxes might be high enough to force landowners to sell the land for development purposes, even though they may not really want to do so.

Differential assessment does not necessarily contribute to an increase in the amount of park land that is directly accessible to the public. However, it is intended to preserve open spaces close to urban areas and to enhance the aesthetic quality of the environment.

Three types of differential assessment programs are in use:

- Pure preferential taxation by which property is assessed on the basis of its current use value, as opposed to its market value, with no associated penalty for conversion to development. Landowners prefer this method because it requires no commitment from them to keep their land in its existing state in the future.

- Deferred taxation is similar to pure preferential assessment, except that the taxes are only deferred. Thus, if land is converted to a non-eligible use, a sanction is imposed on the landowners consisting of the taxes that they were excused from paying (typically for a period between the previous two to five years) together with an interest penalty. This payment, or rollback, of taxes is intended to act as a deterrent to withdrawing from the program. This type of program operates, for example, in New Jersey, Massachusetts, and Texas.

- Restrictive agreements require the participant to sign a contract with a public agency that restricts the owner to keeping the land in an eligible use, such as recreational, park,

and scenic land, for the duration of the contract (typically 10 years). In return for this, the participant receives a current-use value assessment. This type of program operates, for example, in California.

Differential taxation has been used in some urban areas. For example, in metropolitan Dade County, Florida, an ordinance was passed to encourage owners of large, private tracts used for scenic outdoor recreational or park purposes, such as golf courses, bay fringes, wetlands, or other ecologically sensitive areas, to commit their land to nondevelopment. Owners of such lands could petition the county for their land to be assessed at its current-use value by guaranteeing that the parcel will not be developed or used for anything other than outdoor recreational or park purposes for a minimum of 10 years. The ordinance provides for penalties if development should take place during the agreed upon moratorium period.

It has been argued that differential assessment often encourages land speculation instead of effectively protecting land for its recreational use or scenic value. For example, speculators may purchase land on the fringe of urban areas in anticipation of development in five or 10 years. In the interim period, they may lease the land to a neighborhood farmer so that it qualifies for the reduced, current-use tax assessment. This is frequently 5% to 10% of the market value. The lease will often be set at a level that is sufficient to pay the taxes on the property in the interim years before it is developed.

The inclusion of a rollback clause requiring payment of back taxes with interest is not likely to deter abuse of this mechanism because property taxes generally are only between 1% and 3% of market value. If no interest is charged, the payment of back taxes is the equivalent of an interest-free loan to the owner because the taxes have been deferred and no penalty incurred. An interest charge is a true penalty only to the extent that it exceeds the rate that the landowner would have had to pay if the money were borrowed from a commercial lending institution. The prospect of paying several thousand dollars in back taxes and interest is not likely to be a significant deterrent to a developer because the owner can raise the money from the capital gain accruing from sale of the land. The deferred tax provision makes it easier to retain the property for many years until the selling price reaches the desired high level.

In many states the requirement to pay back taxes is waived if the land is sold to a public entity. The rationale is that the sale price to the jurisdiction is likely to be discounted by the amount of the rollback taxes that would be paid if the rollback provision was enforced. Hence, the public indirectly receives these rollback funds through the discount incorporated in the purchase price of the land. This mechanism means that it is possible for a landowner to receive a higher net price by selling the property at a substantially discounted price to a public entity than by selling it at fair market value to a commercial buyer.

The city of College Station sought to purchase 150 acres on the city boundary for use as a regional athletics complex. The city offered $1.5 million for the property. The land was appraised on the tax rolls at only $26,000 by the tax assessor who calculated that to be its agricultural value. Texas had a five-year rollback provision. The five years of back taxes and interest on them at 8% owed to the city, county, and school district amounted to approximately $275,000. This meant that if the landowner elected to sell the property to a commercial entity, he or she would have to receive $1.775 million in order to match the net return obtained if he or she sold the property to the city for $1.5 million.

Empirical evaluations of differential taxation assessment programs suggest that they do not stop the conversion of open spaces over time.[4] In figure 4.1 this approach is shown as being relatively nonpermanent because it encourages a holding action rather than a permanent solution. Occasionally, this holding action may furnish time for efforts to be made to secure more permanent protection of a resource, but most differential assessments appear to have become a source of subsidy for land speculators. William Whyte, who first brought many of the less-than-fee approaches to national prominence in his book *The Last Landscape* published in 1968, commented on the limitations of differential taxation assessment at that time when only seven states had passed enabling legislation:

> I think [the public] are being had . . . The public is not getting what it is paying for. What it is getting is the appearance of open-space preservation. These laws were passed in good faith, but in effect if not in intention, they are creating new speculative pressures on the countryside (p. 102).[5]

Planned Unit and Cluster Developments

Zoning authority is derived from a unit of government's police powers. Traditionally, it has been used to define what activities may take place in certain areas. However, zoning authority can be used to do more than regulate activities and their locations within an area. It can also be used to create and protect a wide range of public amenities. In 1954, the U.S. Supreme Court in *Berman v. Parker* held: "It is within the power of the legislature to determine that the community should be beautiful as well as healthy." This case underscored zoning legitimacy for protecting aesthetic values. In 1975, further legal endorsement for this function came from a federal appeals court that upheld the city of Petaluma, California's "desire to preserve its small town character, its open spaces and low density of population."[6]

In recent years, an increasing number of public agency officials and planners have recognized that their control of zoning ordinances provides a strong negotiating tool that can be used to increase park and recreational opportunities. However, it is a political axiom that laws and regulations can change when politicians and judges change, so zoning ordinances can be amended or abandoned relatively easily. Indeed, more recent court cases have suggested that a regulatory program based on zoning to preserve open spaces appears assailable as an uncompensated taking of private property for public purposes, which is unconstitutional.[7] Thus, in figure 4.1, zoning is shown as offering a more permanent solution to resource protection than differential taxation assessment offers, but it is shown as offering less permanent protection than other less-than-fee approaches offer.

The terms planned unit development and cluster development frequently are used interchangeably, but cluster development usually refers to smaller tracts than the tracts to which planned unit development refers. Standard zoning and subdivision ordinances have encouraged development of subdivisions comprising uniform building lots usually laid out in a grid pattern, which incorporate relatively little park land or open space. Cluster zoning is designed to create public open space close to residences without either the developer or the public jurisdiction incurring the cost of purchasing additional land. Its adoption permits a developer to reduce lot sizes and consolidate lot layouts on the portions of a tract that are most suited for building. Houses can be built closer together than local zoning would normally allow, provided that the total density is not raised. The portion of land left open must remain undeveloped permanently. The developer is able to avoid areas on which it would be difficult to build and to retain areas of attractive natural vegetation.

The consolidation of lots means reduced capital costs to the developer because there will be less land to clear, fewer streets, storm sewers, waterlines, and sanitary sewers. The developer can use these savings to build larger homes or additional amenities into them, to reduce closing costs, or to reduce the sales price. Each of these actions is likely to give a developer a competitive edge over developers who build houses using the conventional approach. Savings also accrue to the public jurisdiction that will inherit the development when it is completed because the consolidated infrastructure will reduce long-term costs of maintaining things, such as utilities, water supplies, and roads. The difference in layout between

A. The conventional approach

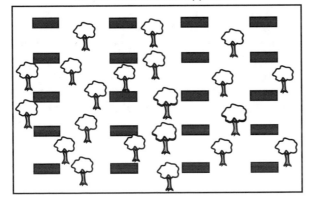

B. The clustering approach

Figure 4.2 Comparison of conventional with clustered layout of a 20-lot subdivision.

a conventional and a clustered subdivision comprising 20 homes is illustrated in figure 4.2.

Cluster development is not restricted to townhouses, apartments, or condominiums. It may offer single-family homes, each on a down-sized lot. Indeed, it has been pointed out that the classic New England village settlement pattern is an example of clustered single-family homes, with the central green constituting the permanently preserved open space.[8] An example of an up-scale development that embraced cluster zoning is the town of Bedford on Long Island, New York. The town used large-lot zoning to maintain open space, an important issue for the residents. In recent years, the strategy of large-lot zoning has been replaced by cluster zoning. Cluster zoning allows developers to put a greater density of housing units on less land than large-lot zoning allows as long as a large portion of the land remains open and available for public use.

One successful open-cluster development in Bedford is Bedford Ponds, a former sand and gravel excavation site. It was agreed that the homeowners association would own and maintain the 59 luxury housing units being built on 28 acres of the site, and would have the exclusive use of the surrounding 85 acres. Housing units range from one bedroom with a study to three bedrooms, typically costing around $600,000. The terrain is sloped deeply and rugged. Most of the land is lush and heavily treed, but wetlands and sand pits remain as reminders of its previous life as a sand and gravel quarry. The property's environmental sensitivity made it a challenge to develop.

Bedford was offered the former sand and gravel quarry for hiking, cycling, and fishing, but the town declined because of the maintainance and insurance costs. However, officials, recognizing the importance of keeping the land open, sought to preserve the property. The Bedford Ponds development increased the marketablility of the property while preserving the beauty of the open land.[9]

Compared with conventional subdivision of equivalent property, one model clustering plan yielded five times more open space. It also reduced the length of necessary streets by 10% and reduced the total length of required sewer lines by 25% (see table 4.1).[10]

In exchange for the concession of being allowed to cluster, a developer designates a portion of the tract as open space, so even though lot sizes are reduced, the net result is a feeling of openness. Cluster zoning ordinances typically require that open space be adequately maintained, and they

Table 4.1	Comparison of Conventional Subdivision With Cluster Subdivision

	Conventional subdivision	Cluster subdivision
Number of lots	108	108
Open space	10%	50%
Linear feet of streets	5,400	4,900
Linear feet of sewer lines	5,400	3,900

restrict the uses permitted on the open spaces. They permit provision of a level of park and recreational facilities superior to that which is possible in a traditional subdivision. Ordinances are likely to require that between 50% and 80% of a tract be set aside as a continuous belt of open space. Many people place a high value on views of and access to permanently protected open space, so the open space often increases the dollar value of the adjoining residential properties.

Allowable densities in these developments are based on two factors: 1) the savings that will accrue to both developer and government jurisdiction and 2) local market forces. For example, in Howard County, Maryland, it was found that the local housing market valued a one-acre house lot with adjacent open space created by the cluster development as equal to a typical three- to five-acre house lot without adjacent open space.[11]

Authors of a study that compared cluster-zoned developments to traditionally zoned developments in two Massachusetts communities reported that the percentage change in the selling price of houses over a 10-year period was slightly higher in the cluster developments.[12] In these two communities, the traditional lots were two and five times larger than the cluster lots, but purchase of an average home in the cluster developments yielded a higher rate of return on investment than one purchased in the conventional developments.

Open space deriving from cluster zoning may be held publicly or privately, and it carries a deed restriction prohibiting further development. Often this restriction is in the form of a conservation easement. A developer is unlikely to want to retain ownership and management of the open space that this mechanism creates because it offers no future profit opportunities, requires the payment of property taxes, and requires ongoing maintenance costs. Thus, the developer usually will seek to pass title for the open space either to a homeowners association that is established by the developer or to a public agency.

If a homeowners association takes responsibility for these amenities, then each resident is assessed his or her share of the cost of management of the amenity area. In such situations, it is usual for the public agency to reserve the right to assume responsibility of the open space resources if they are not adequately maintained and to assess each owner for the cost of municipal maintenance.

In some jurisdictions, government takes responsibility for determining the appropriate ownership and use of the amenities based on public need. This model is followed in Fairfax County, Virginia. The Fairfax County ordinance gives the county the right of first refusal on any cluster-created open space that has not otherwise been reserved for schools or other public uses. The right allows the county either to request dedication of the open space to the county or to recommend dedication to a homeowners association. More than 35% of the 17,000 acres of public park land that the county owns has been acquired by dedicated open space created as a result of cluster zoning. In addition, Fairfax County has an unusually large amount—more than 13,000 acres—of privately owned open space. Most of that space was dedicated by developers to homeowners associations at the recommendation of the Fairfax County Park Authority.

Some communities regard open space and park land as sufficiently valuable to justify offering extra density as a bonus to induce a developer to choose a cluster approach, such as in the Jackson Hole, Wyoming, area where there is great concern for protecting the spectacular Grand Tetons region:

> The Teton County ordinance has a generous cluster provision, allowing developers who place conservation easements on at least 50 percent of their parcel to receive a density bonus up to 100 percent. For instance, the owner of a 300 acre parcel zoned for one unit per three acres who gives an easement on 150 acres to the county, can build 200 units on the remaining 150 acres instead of the 100 normally permitted. A few large-scale

Transferable Development Rights Program in the New Jersey Pine Barrens

Locally known as the Pine Barrens, the New Jersey Pinelands encompasses 1 million acres between Philadelphia and Atlantic City in parts of seven counties and all or part of 52 municipalities. It embraces almost one-quarter of New Jersey's total land area. Ecologically significant areas include its oak forests, pine stands, bogs, cedar swamps, marshes, and agricultural lands for cranberry and blueberry cultivation. Suburban and second-home development and the Atlantic City boom threatened the ecosystem of the Pinelands in the 1970s and prompted support for a regional approach to growth control and environmental protection. This support led to federal legislation establishing the Pinelands National Reserve in 1978, authorizing creation of a regional planning body charged with developing a comprehensive management plan for the reserve. In 1983, the United Nations designated the Pinelands as an international biosphere reserve.

The Pinelands Development Credit program is a key element of the comprehensive management plan. The development credits are transference of development rights intended to redirect development from sensitive areas to areas that can better accommodate growth and to allow landowners in the most restricted areas to share in the benefits of increased land values in the receiving areas. The plan is the largest in scale and perhaps the most complicated transference of development rights scheme ever implemented.

Credits were allocated to landowners in the designated preservation area district according to a formula that recognized the land's current use and its suitability for future development. Credits were calculated on the basis of 39-acre increments. Uplands or woodlands generally received one credit for each 39 acres, although some woodlands that were needed to protect the watershed received two credits per 39 acres. Wetlands were judged to have the least development potential and received 0.2 credits per 39 acres. A developer who buys a credit has the right to build an additional four residential units in areas designated for development. Property owners who sell their development rights are required to record a deed restriction limiting future use of the land.

In Burlington County, which is one of the Pineland's jurisdictions, a Pinelands development credit bank was established. The county issued $1.5 million in bonds to create the bank—the Burlington County Conservation Easement and Pinelands Development Credit Exchange—to stimulate the private market and to serve as buyer of last resort in cases of hardship. The bank exchanged, purchased, and resold the rights for $10,000 plus costs. The $10,000 price was established by calculating the value to a developer of one additional unit of housing.

With the exception of the Burlington County bank, an organized system of development credit exchange does not yet exist in the Pinelands. Buyers and sellers have been brought together by word of mouth, and developers have purchased rights from restricted sites owned by them and have applied these rights to developable sites also owned by them. At first, realtors resisted listing development credits, but an interest in them gradually emerged.

Adapted from Richard J. Roddewig and Cheryl A. Inghram. Transferable Development Rights Programs: TDRs and the Real Estate Marketplace. *American Planning Association: Chicago, Illinois, pages 5-6. Copyright ©American Planning Association. Used by permission.*

Pine Barrens." Transference of development rights is shown as being a relatively permanent less-than-fee simple approach for creating park space, but it is also a complicated, lengthy procedure with high administrative costs, which is difficult to explain to residents. In addition, it requires enabling legislation at the state level as well as enacting an ordinance at the local level. The concept has generated considerable discussion in the planning literature, and its implementation is gaining momentum. For example, by the mid-1990s, 27 transference of development rights programs had been identified in California.[16]

Easements

At the beginning of this chapter, it was noted that ownership of land consists of a bundle of rights that a landowner is permitted to exercise. An easement enables a landowner to exercise one or more of those rights. In 1900, easement provisions were incorporated into a Massachusetts planning act, and, during the same period at the urgings of Frederick Law Olmsted, a number of scenic easements were acquired in California.[5] However, the first major statutory support for easements did not emerge until Congress passed the Capper-Cramton Act in 1930 that authorized easement acquisition along the streams and parkways of the national capitol area. In the 1930s, the National Park Service acquired scenic easements along many stretches of the Blue Ridge and Nachez Trace Parkways, but these early examples were rare and spasmodic. The use of easements gained momentum with a 1964 IRS ruling that the gift of an easement was tax deductible. This momentum accelerated with the widespread publicity given to William H. Whyte's influential book *The Last Landscape* published in 1968 in which Whyte advocated greater use of easements.

The oil crisis in the 1970s alerted people to the high speculative value of oil and gas mineral rights. Hence, many were reluctant to sell or donate property in fee simple because they did not want to forego revenue that would accrue to them if minerals were found on their property. This gave further impetus to conservation easements because they enabled landowners to retain speculative rights, while selling or donating other rights to the property.

The use of easements is now increasing exponentially as they become more familiar to a larger number of lawyers, land-use planners, and landowners. The National Park Service has acquired easements on more than 80,000 acres in almost 100 different park units.[18] The federal Farmers Home Administration agency administered a program passed by Congress whereby the agency forgave delinquent farm debts on wetlands and highly erodible lands in exchange for the farmer placing conservation easements on the property. The easements prohibited plowing, draining, or splitting the land for non-agricultural purposes. With more than 100,000 delinquent borrowers, it seems likely this could lead to substantial expansions of easements.[19] Similarly, the 1996 federal farm bill incorporated the wetlands reserve program that authorized the Natural Resources Conservation Service to protect 1 million acres of agricultural wetlands on farms and ranches across the country. It provided funds for the agency to do this by purchasing permanent easements, by purchasing 30-year easements, or by engaging in cost-share restoration agreements. In addition, the current federal tax laws, which are discussed later in this section, provide more incentives to landowners to consider easements.

These federal actions provide evidence that "The conservation easement is no longer an interesting notion or an innovative idea. It is a proven, pragmatic, voluntary land-saving technique that is powerfully resonant with our dual traditions of individual responsibility and community action" (p. 831).[19] In the last decade, several million acres of land have been placed in easements by public agencies and by land trusts. The Maryland Environmental Trust alone has negotiated more than 300 easements in that period.

A distinguishing feature of easements is that the landowner retains title to the land and may sell it, lease it, bequeath it to heirs, or whatever else he or she chooses, for the landowner relinquishes only those rights that are stated in the easement agreement. The greatest strength of easements is their flexibility. They are negotiated individually and tailored to meet a landowner's emotional, personal, and financial objectives. However, all easements run with the land, which effectively binds not only the original landowner who executes the easement but also all subsequent purchasers or heirs to the land.

The following subsections on easements start by differentiating between affirmative and negative easements and between term and perpetual easements. This is followed by a discussion of the factors that landowners and agencies are likely to consider before entering into an easement agreement. Finally, the section concludes with suggested strategies for expediting easement acquisition.

Affirmative and Negative Easements

If an easement authorizes something to be done on a landowner's property, then the easement is affirmative. The most common types of affirmative easements are those that permit limited pedestrian access by the general public, which is often along a specific trail or corridor, for fishing, hunting, canoeing, nature study, or scenic hiking. Frequently, these easements provide access to beaches, rivers, or forest lands. For example, most of the Bureau of Land Management's acquisition program is devoted to purchasing easements that will allow the public to cross private lands in order to access the bureau's public lands. This is necessitated by the fragmented land ownership pattern in most of the western states where many roads and trails providing access to public lands cross state and private land.

If an easement prohibits a landowner from doing something on his or her property, the easement is negative. A negative easement may be called a conservation, scenic, open space, facade, or historic preservation easement. The name relates to differences in the way it works. For example, a conservation easement is likely to be a negative easement under which a landowner agrees to conserve the resource by giving up development rights on it and the right to remove vegetation or add building extensions. The most extensive conservation easement on record is 130,000 acres on Ted Turner's ranch in Montana.

Generally, the covenants in a negative easement limit the number and location of structures and the types of commercial and industrial activity, and they specify what can be done to the surface of the land and its natural growth. Every easement is tailored to the needs of the individual landowner so that no two easement agreements are likely to be identical. Thus, negative easements may be drafted to conform to almost any situation, such as restriction against development; restriction against cutting down trees; restriction against altering land use or form within a certain distance of a stream, coast, or road; restriction against mining; restriction against putting up a structure that would block a view; or, in the case of historic structures, restriction against alteration of exterior features.

The following examples illustrate the use of negative easements.

At Piscataway Park, Maryland, the National Park Service acquired scenic easements to 2,450 acres of largely upper-class residential land to protect the views from Mount Vernon, just across the Potomac River in Virginia.[20]

At San Antonio Missions National Historic Park, the agricultural scene around Mission Espada is compatible with the objectives of the park, and it is desirable that such use continue. There, farming and cattle grazing is a continuation of the historic scene. Therefore, all that is needed is assurance that it will not be replaced by some incompatible use. The acquisition of development rights through easements was perceived by the National Park Service to be the best way to protect that land.

The ponds of the North American prairies are the breeding grounds of the continent's most sought-after ducks. These ducks are migratory, breeding mainly in Canada and wintering in Central America. Most of the hunting takes place in the United States. The breeding habitat was threatened because the ponds are mostly on farmland, and the farmers were tempted to fill them to increase grain production. Elimination of these ponds would severely reduce the duck population and perhaps lead to the extinction of some species.

Congress authorized the U.S. Fish and Wildlife Service through the waterfowl protection area program to acquire small wetlands. It was obvious that there would be neither sufficient funds nor political support for the purchase in fee title of sufficient area to meet the wetland preservation objectives. Therefore, an easement was designed to purchase the landowner's right to drain, fill, or burn wetland areas. The program has been accepted by more than 20,000 willing sellers involving more than 1.2 million wetland acres with total payments of more than $33 million.[21]

Negative easements are used frequently in connection with river corridors. If the primary attraction is the scenic beauty of a river, there is no need for the land abutting the river to be owned; it needs only to be protected. Perhaps the most ambitious plan relying on easements and similar agreements is the Great River Road that was launched in Wisconsin in the 1950s. It envisages a scenic and recreational corridor on both banks along the full length of the Mississippi River. Today several hundred miles of the river's banks are covered by the terms of easements.

It is possible for an easement simultaneously to be both affirmative and negative. For example, an affirmative easement permitting right of access and a negative easement restricting development may both be negotiated on the same piece of property.

Term and Perpetual Easements

Easements may be granted for a term of a fixed number of years or in perpetuity. A term easement may provide a park and recreation agency with time to acquire resources to buy the land or to persuade a future owner to make the easement perpetual. For example, the Lake Champlain Islands Trust and the Vermont Land Trust, which are both nonprofit conservation organizations, negotiated a five-year conservation easement with the owner of a 14-acre island in Lake Champlain. The owner wanted to experience living under the restrictions and to become better acquainted with the land trusts before considering a permanent commitment.[13] State-enabling statutes generally authorize any length of term desired by the parties, but a few require a minimal length, such as 5 (Virginia), 10 (Michigan and California), or 15 years (Montana).[22] A term easement is likely to be subjected to a rollback provision, similar to that included in many states' legislation for differential taxation assessments, which were discussed at the beginning of this chapter.

To obtain a federal tax deduction for the contribution of a conservation easement, the easement must be granted in perpetuity. In perpetuity easement agreements are permanent because they legally bind all present and future owners of the land. Thus, they are shown in figure 4.1 as being close to a fee-simple purchase in terms of permanency. The easement always goes with the title to the land thereafter. Almost all negative easement agreements are in perpetuity in order to guarantee preservation of the resource. However, affirmative easements often are negotiated for term periods. This permits a landowner to refuse access beyond a specified future time period; therefore, if users abuse the resource or if the arrangement does not function to his or her satisfaction, it can be terminated.

Ostensibly, it appears that a perpetual easement is always likely to be the more desirable alternative for a park and recreation agency. However, it has been suggested that enacting such a permanent land use control raises a moral and ethical question:

> To what extent is any owner of an interest in land justified in imposing his or her will upon the future use of land by the community, even though needs may change and the desires expressed in the legal instrument directed toward preserving the land become obsolete? (p. 84)[23]

If the property loses its environmental value in, for example, 200 years' time because the species it was designed to protect have disappeared as a result of surrounding development, then it may be a responsible decision for the agency to sell the land for development and use the money elsewhere to further its conservation goals more effectively. This predicament has been recognized, and an easement may be extinguished by judicial proceedings, in the event of an "unexpected change in the conditions surrounding the property" that make "impossible or impractical the continued use of the property for conservation purposes."[24] It also is possible to amend the terms of a perpetual easement if the changes do not result in net degradation of the conservation values that the easement is designed to protect. For example, the Maryland Environmental Trust approved an amendment to an easement that it held for a 300-acre property where the easement reserved for the landowner the right to build private educational and recreational camp facilities on 23 designated acres. The amendment replaced this right with the right to build one single-family residence with accessory structures confined to a two-acre site, which substantially reduced the potential development impact on the property.[22]

Landowner Considerations in Negotiating an Easement

In most cases, a landowner's primary consideration is likely to be the financial benefits that may be obtained from negotiating an easement agreement. The extent of these will depend on an easement's value. Financial value of an easement is determined by its effect on the market value of a property. An easement will reduce market value to the extent that it limits its development and use potential. Its financial value is equal to the difference between the fair market value of the property it encumbers before the granting of the restriction and the fair market value of the encumbered property after the easement is granted. An appraiser will define fair market value as the highest and best use, that is, the most profitable likely use of the land. Traditionally, this has been calculated in the context of the potential for future development, the limitations of existing zoning, and economic feasibility.[25] Land planners play a key role in easement donations. Their task is to develop a plan showing maximal profitable development of the property before and after the easement encumbrance. The following examples illustrate the before-and-after approach to valuing easements.[26]

Riverview is a 200-acre property that could be sold to a developer for $3.5 million. The developer would then subdivide the property, build homes on it, and sell homes and house lots. If Riverview were subject to a conservation easement so that it could not be subdivided, then the development potential would be non-existent and the value of the estate would be reduced to $1 million. Thus, the value of the easement donation is $2.5 million, which represents the income tax deduction that would be allowed to the donors. (These deductions are discussed in chapter 14.)

Alternatively, the owners may decide to retain the right to do some limited development at Riverview in the future. They could donate a conservation easement that reserved the right for them to build four more houses there, which would be subject to certain restrictions and limitations. If their house and lot were assessed at $900,000 and each of the four reserved lots were assessed at $150,000, then the total value of the property after the easement would be $1.5 million. Thus, the value of the easement donation would be $2 million.

Most disputes about the financial benefits accruing to landowners from making easement contributions revolve around the appraisers' calculations of an easement's value. Thus, the appraiser's reputation, experience, and training are critical. The appraiser must be able to present and defend effectively an easement valuation in tax court and IRS audits. Ideally, fair market value should be determined from a "substantial record of sales of easements comparable to the donated easement."[27] However, given that easements are not bought and sold in any organized, market-like fashion and that the set of situations determining their value is so diverse, typically no such record will exist.[25]

Appraisers use three basic methodologies to calculate easement values,[25] and different appraisers are likely to reach different conclusions as to an easement's value. Detailed discussion of them is beyond the scope of this text. However, in general terms, a before-and-after value is likely to be used, so value will depend upon the extent of the property rights relinquished as well as the type and location of the land. Thus, if a negative easement that removes development rights on land close to a growing city or suburb is negotiated, then the easement may be worth almost as much as the land itself. However, if the same easement is enforced in a rural area where there are no development pressures, then its financial value may be low. Examples in Florida illustrate the potential for variations in price.

The Florida legislature authorized $30 million for the purchase of development rights. The state acquired these rights on 30,000 acres in Alachua and Volusia counties for $12.5 million, which represented 28% of the land's market value. The price was relatively low because the seller, Georgia-Pacific Corporation, wanted to keep the land undeveloped as long as the Atlanta-based company could continue to harvest timber. In contrast, the price offered to landowners for development rights in the Green Swamp, a 500,000-acre rural mosaic of environmentally sensitive wetlands, pasture, citrus groves, and watermelon fields that the state wanted to protect, was typically more than 75% and in one case was 91% of market value. These high percentages reflected the amounts needed to compensate owners for the money they would lose if they could not develop the land, which had strong development potential. These high percentages were criticized: "I just can't imagine paying 90% or even 75%, as being supportable—the state usually buys land outright for 85% to 95% of market value. To pay that much for development rights doesn't make sense." In rebuttal, others pointed out that analyzing the price of development rights as a percentage of market value was not entirely fair because the equation ignored the state's savings on land management and the effect on property-tax revenue.[28]

A limitation of the before-and-after approach to determining financial value is that it ignores the intrinsic value of the easement. Hence, negative easements prohibiting development rights on rural areas or affirmative easements providing access rights may have little value when this form of approval is used, so there is no incentive for a landowner to sell or donate them. However, such easements may have considerable conservation or recreational value. To counter this anomaly, Maryland has initiated an alternative system whereby easements may also be valued according to their significance to the organization purchasing them.[29] Thus, the greater the public benefit from access to trails or water, or the more attractive the land resource being protected, the greater the amount the landowner is paid for the easement.

Financial benefits from an easement agreement may accrue to the landowner from three sources. First, if a perpetual easement is donated to a park and recreation agency or tax-exempt organization exclusively for conservation purposes, then the donor can claim a charitable donation equal to the value of the easement, which can be used as a deduction against state and federal income taxes. Easement donations would be treated in a similar way to the donation of property in fee simple, which is discussed in chapter 14. However, if an easement has the effect of increasing the value of other property that the donor or a relative of the donor owns, then the amount of the donation value must be reduced by the amount of the enhancement in value of the other property. Conservation purposes must meet one of the following four tests defined by the IRS:[22]

1. Preservation of land areas for outdoor recreation by, or for the education of, the general public. This category inevitably

requires public access, which many landowners have no interest in permitting.

2. Protection of relatively natural habitats of fish, wildlife, or plants or similar ecosystems.

3. Preservation of open space including farmland and forest land for scenic enjoyment or pursuant to an adopted governmental conservation policy; in either case, such open space preservation must yield a significant public benefit.

4. Preservation of historically important land areas or buildings.

Most landowners do not offer public access and are not concerned with habitat protection or with historical preservation, so it is the open space standard (the third test listed) that is the most frequently used criterion. In urban contexts, scenic enjoyment may be difficult to establish, so the primary test is frequently to ask whether the easement donation is furthering clearly delineated government policy. If a government agency accepts an easement, then it is ipso facto likely to be considered a donation consistent with government policy.

The financial benefit of the income tax deduction is increasingly being used by conservation easement buyers. These individuals purchase a property as a second home because of its hunting, fishing, or other recreation amenities and immediately place a negative easement on it giving up development rights. The effect is to reduce substantially the purchase price. Consider the following example.

A wealthy individual from a major city pays $5 million to purchase a ranch that she intends to use for hunting, fishing, and other recreational purposes. She is in the highest federal income tax bracket (39.6%) and state income tax bracket (5.4%). If the easement is valued at $2 million, then she will receive a 45% deduction on her income tax for that year, i.e., $900,000. In essence, this has lowered the purchase price to $4.1 million. Because the major attraction in purchasing the property was its recreation attributes, the easement is unlikely to adversely affect its long-term future sale price.

A particularly entrepreneurial approach targeting these individuals was initiated by the Montana Land Alliance, which organized trips for potential conservation easement buyers. Staff and supporters of the alliance who were interested and were experts in trout fishing made contact with fishermen in major cities on the East and West coasts. They agreed to locate suitable properties on trout streams for those interested and then brought the city dwellers out to review the properties. These people bought properties and put easements on them because they were fishermen interested in pristine opportunities and were wealthy enough to benefit from the income tax deductions. The alliance executed 39 of these types of easements in a single year in the mid-1990s!

In some instances, a relatively large tract may be acquired by a nonprofit organization, which then puts together a conservation buyer group whose members purchase individually owned parcels and benefit from the lower per-acre cost that larger packages make possible.

A second financial benefit stems from an easement agreement reducing a property's value because it no longer has development potential. Land cannot be taxed for a use that the property owner cannot perform legally. Thus, the property's assessed value for tax purposes will be commensurably lower. This will result in a landowner paying less property taxes than he or she would have paid before the easement agreement.

A reduction in estate (inheritance) taxes is a third source of potential financial benefit to a landowner. Estate taxes are imposed on the value of the deceased's property based on its highest and best use at the time of the owner's death. Thus, for example, the estate taxes on a 600-acre property consisting of visually attractive mountain pasture may reflect the value of 60 10-acre ranchettes that could be constructed on it rather than its existing use value as a recreational retreat. Federal law grants an exemption for inheritance taxes to each taxpayer. Until 1997, this exemption amount was $600,000, but it was gradually increased with effect from 1998 so that by the year 2007 it will reach its new ceiling of $1 million. These gradual increases equate to adjustments for annual inflation of approximately 3%. However, for family farms and small businesses, the exemption ceiling was fixed at $1.3 million in 1997 and will remain at that amount. This is especially germane to park and recreation agencies because their land acquisitions are often negotiated with the owners of family farms. Above these exemption amounts, the tax rate rises rapidly from a minimal level of 37% to a high marginal rate of 55%, which is applied when estates reach a value of $3 million or more. These tax rates are shown in table 4.2.

nonprofit organization ownership, these revenues would be foregone.

Holding an easement is like owning land in a partnership. A U.S. Fish and Wildlife Department administrator noted: "From a practical point of view, there is no such thing as a perpetual easement if there is not a commitment to enforce the terms of the easement . . . acquiring the easement is the easy part" (p. 87).[22] Another administrator commented: "With every right acquired . . . a corresponding responsibility is assumed" (p. 93).[22] Thus, when an agency acquires an easement, it incurs the costs of enforcing it. Ongoing associated costs may include supervision; resource deprecation; lawsuits; and, in some instances, bad publicity, which an agency may get when seeking to enforce an easement. An experienced easements administrator observed:

> Some agencies ignore the reality that easement and land acquisitions have inbred constant and long-term costs and obligations associated with them. . . . The Wyoming Game and Fish Department philosophy is that the acquisition cost is considered to be a one-time "cost of doing business," while the maintenance and monitoring costs are a long-time commitment to the goals and objectives precipitating the acquisition. It is the long-term annual monitoring and maintenance costs that can erode an agency budget (p. 24).[22]

The keys to effective prevention of easement violations are the following:

- A good relationship and regular contact with the property owner. This is especially important after the property is transferred from the original easement donor to heirs or other owners. Most conflicts over easements occur with subsequent owners of a property and not with the original donors.

- A clear agreement that the landowner easily understands. Many violations are the result of misunderstanding and ambiguity rather than willful transgressions. Resentment may be nurtured by differing interpretations of the terms of an easement. For example, along the Blue Ridge Parkway, the terms of the scenic easements sold to the National Park Service in the 1930s stipulated that no new buildings would be constructed without agency permission and that no trees were to be cut without prior

agency approval. Immediately, there began to arise disputes, some of which reached the courts, over what distinguished a building from a mere shed and over where to draw the line between tree cutting and brush clearing.[20]

- An easement document with clear and enforceable restrictions.

- A program of regular, systematic, and well-documented monitoring.[22] Monitoring easements costs money, but being required to seek legal redress to enforce them because a good monitoring system is not in place is likely to be much more expensive. Furthermore, in some instances recourse to the legal system cannot protect the resource. After a scenic woodland has been cleared, the legal system cannot bring it back!

If easements are violated and the easement holder does not bring suit within the period of time required in the state's statutes, the right to bring an enforcement action expires. As a result, the easement will be extinguished through the holder's inaction. This is the primary legal and practical reason why adherence to the provisions of an easement must be monitored consistently on at least an annual basis.[22]

Views on the use of easements may vary within an organization according to individual responsibilities. Senior managers and policy makers concerned with formulating agency strategy and overall budget concerns may be attracted to the concept of easements. In contrast, field managers who have to resolve the operational difficulties that may arise may be less enthusiastic. An easement agreement signed with a sympathetic, supportive landowner may be opposed by subsequent owners of the land, who may seek ways to abuse it. They may regard careful monitoring as harassment. In such situations, field service personnel find themselves in the emotionally traumatic position of being in the middle of disputes between landowners and recreationists, often with only limited control over either.

An experienced administrator of easements in the National Park Service summarized the trade-offs involved in acquiring easements in the following terms:

> Observers of the [National] Park Service's land protection program often want to know at what point is it more "cost effective" to buy land in fee instead of an easement. This simple

question has only one simple answer: it depends. . . . For both fee and easement acquisitions, there are direct and indirect expenses: costs of purchase, administrative expenses, maintenance of improvements and access, monitoring and enforcement, and payments in lieu of taxes to local governments. . . . One clear conclusion is that there is no simple formula to decide if fee or easement is preferable. An easement costing 10% of the estimated fee value may not be a good deal if it fails to protect the resource, or provide for needed public use. An easement that costs 90% of the estimated fee value may be an excellent deal if it protects a historic structure without burdening the government with maintenance responsibilities, keeps the building in use and on the tax rolls, and avoids the need for condemnation (p. 23).[22]

Part of the reluctance to use easements at the local level is attributable to most local park and recreation managers having had no experience with them. Because easements are unfamiliar, managers lack confidence and are suspicious of them. The problem is compounded because the legal, appraisal, and property skills that they need are not likely to be under the direct control of park and recreation managers and have to be solicited and coordinated with other departments. In contrast, federal and state agencies frequently have this expertise available within their departments and have had experience in working with easements. Similarly, nonprofit organizations devoted to preserving land because of its scenic or conservation values often have expertise in this area and have made extensive use of easements.

Strategies for Expediting Easement Acquisition

This section describes two different strategies that have reduced the cost and expedited the acquisition of easements and that may be generalized to other contexts. The first strategy is to purchase in fee simple and re-sell with an easement or to pre-empt. The second strategy illustrates the potential of an escrow account approach.

Establishing an Easement via Fee Simple

There is some evidence that suggests that the cost of acquiring an easement can be reduced if a park and recreation agency or nonprofit organization acquires unrestricted land by fee purchase, attaches the desired easement to it, and then re-sells or leases the land subject to the easement.[33] Generally, it is not possible for government agencies to engage in the buying and selling of real estate in this way. Such transactions have to be undertaken by a nonprofit organization. The resale price will almost certainly be lower than the purchase price because the easement is likely to decrease the market value of the land. Thus, a nonprofit organization has to be prepared to absorb the difference between the buying and selling prices, as well as to finance the total initial purchase cost, of the real estate during the time period until it is re-sold.

Other countries, such as France and Norway, have adopted a concept called the right of pre-emption. In France, this mechanism enables a municipality or the state to intervene and pre-empt a sale in designated areas of public concern whenever designated land is sold to someone intending to change its use. In the United States, the concept is similar to the common practice in the private marketplace of the right of first refusal. In Norway, the conditions for pre-emption are different. There, it is applicable for use in areas that have been developed privately but that the government has decided should be returned to the public domain over a period of time and should be protected from development in the interim. It works in the following way. When a willing seller and buyer have negotiated an agreement, the municipality has the right to pre-empt the sale. However, it must offer the seller the same price he or she would have received from the agreement with the buyer. The municipality then offers to lease the property, with desired easements attached to it, to the buyer at a rate that is sufficient to redeem the annual payments on the publicly borrowed money that the municipality used to finance the scheme. This is likely to be considerably less than the buyer would pay if he or she were to commercially borrow money from a bank.

Thus, the usurped buyer is able to enjoy living on the property while paying lower monthly payments and without having to provide a down payment. The buyer's money that would have been used as a down payment can be invested elsewhere to build up equity. The lease payments redeem the money that the municipality borrowed. Over a 25- or 30-year period, the municipality would have protected the property through easements and ultimately acquired it at no direct cost to its taxpayers.[32]

Putting Easements in Escrow: The Blackfoot River Corridor[34]

The Blackfoot River in western Montana is one of the nation's best trout streams. It is used intensively not only by fishermen but also by swimmers, tubers, floaters, and campers. It was the landowners' desire to retain their agricultural way of life and to maintain the natural state of the river. This intention was being threatened by the emergence of recreational subdivisions in the area and the exponential growth in the river's popularity with recreational users. As a group, they did not want to be forced by escalating land values and accompanying property and estate taxes into selling their land for development purposes. The landowners were prepared to preserve the tradition of reasonable public use of their private land along the river, but "farmers got tired of getting off their tractors and running down to deal with trespassers" (p. 180)[13] Fire, vandalism, and livestock harassment were among the problems the owners faced from unwelcome visitors. The Blackfoot was considered for designation as a Wild and Scenic River, but because of local opposition and because local protection was being discussed, the U.S. Department of the Interior withdrew its proposals.

With a sense of enlightened self-interest, the landowners perceived that if the private sector voluntarily provided recreational access to the river, the potential of imposed public access through governmental action would be blunted. Thus, a task force that included representatives of all concerned landowners and public land managers was formed. A recreation management plan encompassing 30 mi of river frontage emerged. The plan identified frontage ownership, delineated a conservation corridor, and identified access points to the river.

The landowners agreed to donate those property rights along the river that could significantly impair the natural, scenic, or aesthetic quality of the resource, such as the right to subdivide, to clearcut timber, to dredge, or to establish feedlots. However, the landowners kept all other agricultural and forestry rights, such as the option to selectively harvest timber, to graze livestock, to cultivate crops, and to irrigate.

One important problem had to be addressed before the plan could be implemented. Landowners were reluctant to grant an easement because they had no guarantee that their fellow landowners would also cooperate in the plan. If a landowner granted an easement and the neighbors did not, then he or she merely had contributed to enhancing the value of abutting property because of the guarantee of adjacent open space that the easement provided. Hence, before any single landowner would grant an easement, there had to be an assurance that all others would do likewise.

This assurance was provided by establishing an escrow account, which was managed by the Nature Conservancy. Landowners agreed individually to the specific terms of the conservation easement as it pertained to their property, and the document was put into escrow. Any landowner could inspect the documents signed by the other landowners to ensure that suitable flank protection was afforded his or her property. If some easements had not been granted at the end of a specified time period, those landowners who had granted easements would be free to choose whether they wanted the easement to be implemented or whether they wanted to invalidate it.

Easements were first sought for a 10 mi pilot segment. When this was achieved, the Nature Conservancy expanded its goal from the 30 mi envisaged in the original plan to protecting 50 mi of the river. Affirmative term easements for 10-year periods were negotiated with landowners to provide access points to the river. At the end of the 10-year period, these were either renewed or canceled. The Montana Department of Fish, Wildlife, and Parks polices the area, empties trash barrels, and educates the public about the special nature of the recreational corridor.

This principle may be equally applicable in the context of establishing urban greenbelts in which the fragmented ownership and small lot size make it unlikely that landowners would agree to an easement unless they could be assured that adjacent properties could be similarly preserved. It requires coordinating multiple donations of negative easements linked together in a plan in which the instruments of conveyance are held in an escrow until all the participating landowners have committed to the plan.[35] Model escrow agreements needed to implement this type of approach have been developed.[36]

The Emergence of Greenways

Greenways are corridors of protected open space managed for conservation and recreational purposes. This generic term encompasses considerable diversity that is exemplified by the five major types of greenways:[37]

1. Urban riverside greenways that usually are created as part of (or instead of) a redevelopment program along neglected, and often run-down, city waterfronts

2. Recreational greenways that feature paths and trails of various kinds, often of relatively long distance, based on natural corridors as well as canals, abandoned railbeds, and other public rights-of-way

3. Ecologically significant natural corridors, usually along rivers, streams, and (less often) ridgelines, to provide for wildlife migration and species interchange, nature study, and hiking

4. Scenic and historic routes, usually along a road or highway (or, less often, a waterway), with the most representative of them making an effort to provide pedestrian access along the route or, at least, places to alight from a car

5. Comprehensive greenway systems or networks that usually are based on natural landforms, such as valleys and ridges, but sometimes are simply an opportunistic assemblage of greenways and open spaces of various kinds to create an alternative municipal or regional green infrastructure

They can be as elaborate as a lengthy, paved hiking-biking-riding route or as simple, natural, and ecologically important as a stretch of stream bank left wild. The intent has been described in the following terms:

> To use river-sides and stream courses that have been floodplain-zoned against development, to use abandoned railroad beds and canal towpaths, to use high-tension lines and even sewerline rights-of-way, to use old roads untrod and new roads unbuilt, to use mandatory recreational land dedications by subdividers, to use pieced-together ridgeline open spaces—in short, to use anything linear they can lay their hands on to provide the greenways for a skein of paths and trails crisscrossing within and leading out of metropolitan America (p. 93).[37]

Greenways are not new. The concept grew out of the work of Frederick Law Olmsted, who coined the word parkway in 1865 and was the designer of some of the nation's first linear parks. It evolved with the development of the Appalachian Trail in 1921, the urban parkways of the 1930s, and the British concept of greenbelt areas around neighborhoods and communities. The term greenway is derived from taking a syllable from the words greenbelt and parkway.[37] The term first appeared in the 1950s, but it was brought into common use and given national prominence in 1987 by the President's Commission on Americans Outdoors.

The commission reported that there was a clamor for outdoor recreational facilities closer to home.[38] Their response was a vision of a system of recreational corridors: "fingers of green that reach out from and around and through communities all across America" (p. 142). They called for a "prairie fire of local action" (p. 73) to implement the vision and recommended that "communities establish Greenways, corridors of private and public recreation lands and waters, to provide people with access to open spaces close to where they live, and to link together the rural and urban spaces in the American landscape" (p. 142). The fire was ignited, a ground swell of public support emerged, and greenways have since been developed in hundreds of communities across the country.

In many urban areas, developing greenways often involves negotiating with multiple public and private sector landowners. Success requires creativity and persistence. The exponential increase in the number of greenways emerging in the 1990s was greatly facilitated by the availability of major funding for trails, bicycle paths, and walkways provided by the Intermodal Surface Transportation Efficiency Act in 1991 (discussed in chapter 11) and by the increased confidence of park and recreation agencies in using easements. Easements are a primary mechanism for developing greenways, especially in urban areas where land is less available and is expensive to purchase. Hence, the shift in perception from easements being an innovative, but rather esoteric, idea to being accepted as a proven, fundamental tool (which has occurred in recent years) has been of critical importance in the emergence of greenways.

Greenways may provide three main types of benefits to a community: recreation, transportation artery, and biotic diversity. From a recreational perspective, greenways are better suited than traditional parks for the linear forms of outdoor recreation (e.g., hiking, jogging, bicycling, inline skating, horseback riding, cross country skiing, and ordinary walking) in which many North Americans engage today.

As a transportation artery, greenways may serve as an alternative means of connecting people to the work place, the market place, historic and cultural attractions, and other modes of transportation. They may link open spaces, tie increasingly urbanized populations to experiences in the outdoors, interrupt the monotony of strip development, and bind neighborhoods closer together. This integrating role may also result in enhanced community support for park and recreational projects. Thus, Joe and Beth Smith may not pay much attention to a proposal to develop a park 5 mi away; however, if that park is linked to a greenway system that winds its way through their community, the likelihood of them becoming enthusiastic supporters for the park project is enhanced.

Aldo Leopold noted: "Everything is connected to everything else." Greenways that link isolated parks like beads on a string form an overall network for life-sustaining movements. Greenways may provide habitat for a diversity of plant and animal species and may provide the migratory corridors necessary for their survival and the maintenance of biodiversity. Biologists and ecologists are placing growing emphasis on the problem of island populations of wildlife and plants in isolated reserves. They are stressing the need for natural corridors that enable species interchange from one isolated area to another so the island populations will not die out. This interchange is the essential component of biological diversity and, therefore, ecological stability.

> Decades of land development around our conservation areas and the isolation of remnant populations of wildlife by gigantic systems of roadways, powerlines, pipelines, and strip development are increasing the ecological problems with which we must deal (p. 113).[37]

This fragmentation, not simply the lack of wildlife refuges, is now taking a heavy toll on wildlife. A special plea is made for the function between land and water as the best location for wildlife corridors: "Numerous species of fish, amphibians, reptiles, mammals, and birds not only live there, but they also use these riparian or stream-side woods as landscape thoroughfares" (p.113).[37]

Greenline Parks

The protection of scenic landscapes often involves areas that are working and living environments for people. The concept of greenline park planning has emerged as a means of protecting these types of environments. Greenline parks, which are also known as national reserves, may incorporate all of the less-than-fee approaches that have been discussed in this chapter. These areas contain a mix of public and private land that comprehensively is planned, regulated, and managed by an authority set up specifically to preserve recreational, aesthetic, ecologic, historic, and cultural values. Greenline parks are living landscapes. They not only protect landscape values and facilitate recreational use but also permit within their boundaries certain economic activities that are commensurate with the concepts of a recreational experience and a living landscape. Within the greenline, public and private lands, towns, villages, farms, tourist attractions, and a host of other historic and cultural areas and activities coexist. These activities preserve the economic base of the region and are an integral part of its overall attraction.

Fee-simple acquisition in these parks is limited to relatively small, high-intensity use areas. Affirmative easements are used to link fee-simple acquired areas along watercourses and trails. Negative easements are purchased to preserve critical scenic views.

> If there are sufficient chunks of public-access recreation lands augmented by linear systems involving trails and watercourses, the outdoor recreation need can be satisfied. In existing parks—national, state, and local— only a fraction of the land is intensively used. In many cases five percent or ten percent. The rest is ambiance. It is hardly logical then for the public to deplete its treasury to buy land in fee when it is not intensively used (p. 17).[39]

The greenline park idea emphasizes intergovernmental planning cooperation, with federal, state, and local levels each having their own distinct functional and spatial responsibilities; however, each level cooperates with the others in overall planning. There can be no standard format because each park has to be sensitive to the unique requirements of each area and of the state and local government units that will administer those areas. However, land-use regulation is one of the keys to their success. Because it is the state level of government that possesses the power to control land use, greenline parks must be primarily a state-level initiative.

Any federal government involvement is limited to supplying initial capital as incentives to state, regional, and local entities. This money is used for research and planning, start-up costs, payments in lieu of taxes to local governments, easements, and fee-simple acquisition of critical, small, intensively used sites.

Models

The greenline park concept is not new. It has been applied extensively in England and Wales. In the United States, the outstanding example of this concept is the Adirondack Forest Preserve that contains 6 million acres of which only 42% are owned publicly. It was established in 1894 when the New York legislature drew a blue line around a substantial region within the Adirondack Mountains in order to protect the vast watershed of the Hudson River.

Early visitors to this area, which is a five-hour drive from the city of New York, were appalled by the rate at which trees were being logged. Their concern merged with worries of the state's industrialists that the Hudson would begin to silt up as whole mountains eroded and that the waterways (which were the state's economic lifelines) would deteriorate. These two factions combined in the state legislature to produce this landmark legislation. The legislation stated that the area "should be forever kept as wild forest lands. It shall not be leased, sold or exchanged, or be taken by any corporation, public or private, nor shall the timber thereon be sold, removed or destroyed."[40] The preserve is currently administered by the Adirondack Park Commission, which has major responsibility for the administration of public land and great regulatory power over the use of private land within its area of responsibility. It acquires some land by fee purchase, accepts gifts of land and easements, develops design controls, and regulates land use based on a comprehensive plan.

The Adirondack Park has been established for a long time. Perhaps the most ambitious greenline park in more recent times is the Pine Barrens area of New Jersey, which occupies one-fifth of New Jersey. The transferable development rights program in the Pine Barrens was described in "Transferable Development Rights Program in the New Jersey Pine Barrens" on page 92. The area is close to Philadelphia and, within its 1 million acres, there is a large amount of privately owned land. The park was established to protect the unique ecologic and cultural features of the area. It is under the control of the Pinelands Commission, which is modeled after New York's Adirondack Park Commission. Technical assistance and funds

for planning (not to exceed $3 million) and land acquisition (not to exceed $26 million) were authorized by federal legislation. If the traditional approach of full-fee acquisition of all private lands had been adopted, the cost probably would have exceeded $500 million.

Although primarily a conservation measure, the Pinelands plan was intended to manage growth and not to stop it. In its first five years, the commission approved permits for only 149 new houses in the sensitive 368,000-acre core, called the preservation area, but in the more diverse 568,000-acre protection area surrounding the core, permits for 17,297 houses and 697 new commercial buildings were approved.[41] The commission has no control over the balance of the national reserve, which remains under local jurisdiction.

The Pinelands approach has become the norm in recent additions to the national park system. In the case of the Alaskan additions, which include Aniakchak National Monument, Berring Land Bridge National Preserve, Cape Krusenstern National Monument, and Gates of the Arctic National Preserve, the private land allows indigenous cultures or already established towns to flourish without the inhibiting restrictions of public land ownership. Much private land also came into the national park system through the establishment of national wild and scenic rivers. For example, the New River Gorge unit in West Virginia included more than 54,000 acres of private land, of which only a small fraction is to be transferred to public ownership. Park planning calls for the rest to remain under essentially unchanged uses. Many of the new parks established near urban areas included large tracts of private land. Cuyahoga Valley, which includes 12,000 acres of federally owned land, includes more than 14,000 acres of private land. Public agencies will acquire some of this private land, but much will remain under current patterns of private use. Jean Lafitte National Historic Park and Preserve contains slightly less than 15,000 acres of federal land and more than 13,000 acres of private land.[20]

Advantages and Disadvantages

Experiences in the United States and England suggest at least seven advantages of a national reserve approach:[42]

1. A wider range of living landscapes, such as historic fishing villages and farming communities, may be protected through a greenline approach than through exclusive

public land acquisition. For example, the unique sheep farming and private recreational activities of the English Lake District have been maintained. The approach facilitates the protection of whole regions and ecosystems, so an area may be managed as a whole landscape.

2. The reserve approach guarantees that a comprehensive approach to planning will take place and mobilizes all levels of government to protect the areas involved.

3. The costs of establishing a reserve are much lower than if public land acquisition is the only protective measure used for an entire area. In addition, acquisition cost may be phased over a longer period of time.

4. The costs to government agencies of operation and maintenance will be reduced because the private landowner will undertake most of this.

5. Political support for establishment of an area with a mix of public and private lands may be greater than for exclusive public ownership, which requires landowners to vacate their lands and deprives local units of government of real-estate tax revenues for lands within park boundaries. It provides a means of keeping certain land on the tax rolls and in economic production while protecting identified values.

6. The private business sector may be relied upon to provide on private land many of the required visitor services, such as restaurants, motels, hotels, and intensive-use recreational facilities (e.g., ski tows). Reliance upon the private sector to provide needed accommodations, services, and intensive-use recreation may be cost effective and may increase landowner and local support for the park concept.

7. The maintenance of local private commercial and industrial activities can help maintain the economic viability of an area and its essential community character.

On the other hand, the experiences in both the Unites States and England suggest the following four limitations of a reserve concept:

1. Although initial acquisition costs are lower, the amount of land ultimately available for active public use is smaller. This is an important consideration in urban areas where recreation demand may quickly outstrip existing public recreational facilities. With limited land available for public recreation, intensive use exceeding natural carrying capacities can be expected for some areas with resulting crowding and destruction of natural vegetation.

2. Landowner opposition to a greenline area may be strong, particularly during its first years of operation. For example, several attempts have been made to abolish the Adirondack Park. The regulation of private land may be opposed with particular vigor where intensive use of public land spills over into adjacent private land resulting in trespassers, litter, and vandalism. Local opposition complicates enforcement of restrictions.

3. Tight regulation of undeveloped portions of reserved areas may channel development problems into adjacent settings, causing such problems there also unless careful plans and regulations are applied.

4. Development controls may not be tightly monitored and enforced, resulting in gradual deterioration of the area.

Summary

Fee-simple ownership of land involves owning all rights associated with a property. In many contexts, funds are not available for agencies to purchase in fee simple all of the land that their residents want for park and recreational purposes. Further, purchase in fee simple may destroy some of the qualities that make the land aesthetically attractive, may mean the land must be maintained at taxpayers' expense, may mean the land will be taken off the tax rolls, and may be more disruptive to the lifestyles of the landowners.

Differential taxation assessment enables landowners to have land assessed at current-use value rather than at market value. Three basic types of differential assessment are used. The least restrictive is pure preferential assessment, which is followed by deferred taxation and then restrictive agreements. Differential taxation is intended to preserve open spaces close to urban areas and, hence, to enhance the aesthetic quality of the environment. However, it tends to be a holding action rather than a permanent solution, and most differential assessments appear to have become a source of subsidy for land speculators.

Encouragement of planned unit and cluster development permits developers to reduce lot sizes and consolidate lot layouts on portions of a tract that are most suited to building. This reduces their infrastructure and construction costs. In exchange for this concession, the developer is typically required to designate from 50% to 80% of the tract as permanent open space.

A transferable development rights program creates a market for development rights. Development rights on an area that is desired to be protected can be sold by landowners in that area to owners of land in an area that has been designated as appropriate for development. This enables relatively large areas of a community to be protected at little or no cost to the community, and development can be concentrated where it is most appropriate.

Easements in their various forms have emerged as popular less-than-fee procedures. Affirmative easements authorize something to be done on a landowner's property. Most frequently, these permit public access. Negative easements prohibit a landowner from doing something on his or her property. Often a negative easement relates to development rights. Perpetual easements permanently bind all present and future owners of the land to the terms of the easement. Term easements apply only for a fixed number of years.

The financial value of an easement is measured by comparing the property's value before and after the easement is enforced. Financial benefits from an easement agreement may accrue to a landowner from a reduction in income taxes, if the easement is donated; in property taxes; and in estate taxes. Landowners also receive the satisfaction of having protected something of value for others to enjoy.

Compared with fee-simple purchases, easements offer an agency the advantages of retaining a property owner's goodwill and of lower purchase and maintenance costs. Despite the potential benefits of using easements, there are occasions when the cost of monitoring them is so great that it outweighs the financial savings accruing from their use. Two strategies that may expedite easement acquisition are to purchase in fee simple and re-sell with an easement and to use an escrow account to store easement agreements until all impacted landowners have agreed to a project.

The potential effectiveness of easements for facilitating increased park and recreational opportunities has been controversial in the past. Some said that easements do not work. Others con-cluded that they work effectively and that the widespread failure to adopt them reflected adversely on park and recreation managers. It is clear that they will be used with increasing frequency in the future and that they may emerge as the primary mechanism for preserving open spaces. They became increasingly prominent as the movement to create greenways gathered momentum in the 1990s. They are likely to be particularly effective when they are used with a variety of other mechanisms in the way exemplified by the greenline parks concept.

References

1. Coughlin, Robert E. 1981. An overview of less-than-fee simple and other innovative protection techniques. *Workshop on public land acquisition and alternatives*. Committee on Energy and Natural Resources, U.S. Senate. Washington, DC: Superintendent of Documents.

2. Whyte, William H. 1962. *Open space action, outdoor recreation resources review commission study report 15*. Washington, DC: Superintendent of Documents.

3. Badger, Curtis J. 1995. A revolution in the business of conservation. *Urban Land* 54(6): 40-45.

4. Bergstrom, John C. and John R. Stoll. 1985. Southern differential assessment programs: Issues, status and policy. *Journal of Farm Management and Rural Appraisal* 49(2): 34-39.

5. Whyte, William H. 1968. *The last landscape*. New York: Doubleday.

6. Siehl, George H. 1990. *Scenic landscape protection*. Washington, DC: Congressional Research Service, The Library of Congress, Report #90-525 ENR. November 13.

7. Johnson, Scott K. 1995. Urban land trusts: Using conservation easements to preserve urban open space. *The Back Forty* 6(1): 16-20.

8. Arendt, Randall. 1988. *"Open space" zoning: An effective way to retain rural character*. Amherst, MA: Center for Rural Massachusetts.

9. Vizard, Mary McAleer. 1993. Trading development rights for goodwill. *New York Times*. September 19, section 10: 9.

10. Rohan, Patrick J. 1994. *Zoning and land use controls*, Volume 2. New York: Matthew Bender, 12.

11. Brabec, Elizabeth. 1992. On the value of open spaces. *Scenic America Technical Bulletin* 1(2): 12-14.

12. Lacy, Jeff. 1990. *An examination of market appreciation for clustered housing with permanent open space.* Amherst, MA: University of Massachusetts, Center for Rural Massachusetts.

13. Stokes, Samuel N. and A. Elizabeth Watson. 1989. *Saving America's countryside: A guide to rural conservation.* Baltimore: Johns Hopkins University Press.

14. Goldberger, Paul. 1986. When air rights go underground. *New York Times*, December 21, H14.

15. Tindall, Ronald and Thomas Peterson. 1981. The open space workbook. *Parks and Recreation* 16(5): 44.

16. Pruetz, Rick. 1993. *Putting transfer of development rights to work in California.* Point Arena, CA: Solano Press.

17. Petrillo, Joseph E. 1981. Statement at *Workshop on public land acquisition and alternatives.* The U.S. Senate Committee on Energy and Natural Resources, Subcommittee on Public Lands and Reserved Water. Washington, DC: Superintendent of Documents, 422-423.

18. Brown, Warren. 1993. Public-private land conservation partnerships in and around national parks. In *Land conservation through public-private partnerships*, edited by Eve Endicott. Washington, DC: Island Press, 104-128.

19. Miller, Anita P. and John B. Wright. 1991. Report of the subcommittee on innovative growth management measures: Preservation of agricultural land and open space. *The Urban Lawyer* 23(4): 627-649.

20. Foresta, Ronald A. 1984. *America's National Parks and Their Keepers.* Washington, DC: Resources for the Future.

21. Hester, Eugene F. 1981. Statement at *Workshop on public land acquisition and alternatives.* The U.S. Senate Committee on Energy and Natural Resources, Subcommittee on Public Lands and Reserved Water. Washington, DC: Superintendent of Documents.

22. Diehl, Janet and Thomas S. Barrett. 1988. *The conservation easement handbook.* San Francisco: Trust for Public Land.

23. Brenneman, Russell L. 1967. *Private approaches to the preservation of open land.* Washington, DC: The Conservation and Research Foundation.

24. Treasury Regulation 1-170A-14 (g)(6)(i).

25. Goldman, Lonnie. 1995. Conservation easement appraisal methodologies and their acceptance by the courts. *The Back Forty* 6(1): 1-16.

26. Small, Stephen J. 1992. *Preserving family lands.* Boston, MA: Landowner Planning Center.

27. Treasury Regulation 1-170A-14 (h)(3)(i).

28. Binkley, Christina. 1996. Florida Journal: Development rights plan looks great—on paper. *Wall Street Journal*, February 28, F1.

29. Dennis, Pamela M. 1993. A state program to preserve land and provide housing: Vermont's housing and conservation trust fund. In *Land conservation through public-private partnerships*, edited by Eve Endicott. Washington, DC: Island Press, 172-194.

30. Hutton, William T. 1996. Basic principles of federal income and transfer taxation. Presentation at *Workshop on maintaining private lands with conservation easements.* Austin, TX, April.

31. Small, Stephen J. 1996. Preserving family lands. *Land and People* 8(1): 14-15.

32. Handler, Frank. 1981. Statement at *Workshop on public land acquisition and alternatives.* The U.S. Senate Committee on Energy and Natural Resources, Subcommittee on Public Lands and Reserved Water. Washington, DC: Superintendent of Documents.

33. Reilly, William. 1981. Statement at *Workshop on public land acquisition and alternatives.* The U.S. Senate Committee on Energy and Natural Resources, Subcommittee on Public Lands and Reserved Water. Washington, DC: Superintendent of Documents.

34. This case study is adapted from Goetz, Hank. 1984. A cooperative approach to river management: The Blackfoot experience. In *Land-saving action*, edited by Russell L. Brenneman and Sarah M. Bates. Covelo, CA: Island Press, 3-7.

35. Johnson, Scott K. 1995. Urban land trusts: Using conservation easements to preserve urban open space. *The Back Forty* 6(1): 16-20.

36. Knight, Robert M. and Andrew C. Dana. 1993. Model escrow agreement. *The Back Forty* 3(5): 10-17.

37. Little, Charles E. 1990. *Greenways for America.* Baltimore: Johns Hopkins University Press.

38. The President's Commission on Americans Outdoors. 1987. *Americans outdoors: The legacy, the challenge.* Washington, DC: Island Press.

39.　Little, Charles E. 1975. *Greenline parks: An approach to preserving recreational landscapes in urban areas*. Committee on Interior and Insular Affairs, U.S. Senate. Washington, DC: Superintendent of Documents.

40.　McKibben, Bill. 1995. *Hope, human and wild*. Boston: Little, Brown.

41.　DePalma, Anthoney. 1986. New Jersey is winning its battle in the Pinelands. *New York Times*, August 10, section 4, 6E.

42.　Kusler, John A. and William Duddleson. 1978. Alternative federal strategies for strengthening state and local urban outdoor recreation and open space programs including the establishment of Greenline parks. *National urban recreation study technical report series*, Volume 1. *Technical report*, Number 2, Washington, DC: Superintendent of Documents.

CHAPTER 5

REPOSITIONING THE FIELD TO CREATE A BROADER CONSTITUENCY

The single most important task in securing additional resources for park and recreation services is to develop and nurture a broader constituency. In many communities, it is clear that resources will only be forthcoming when support for the field goes beyond existing users, visitors, or participants who directly benefit from the services delivered. These groups have been the dominant focus of agencies' efforts in recent years. However, while servicing them is a central element of the mission, in many jurisdictions they have proven to be too narrow a constituency for sustaining or securing additional public resources.

User satisfaction, while necessary, is not an adequate indicator of the success of park and recreation agencies. Most taxpayers are not frequent users of these services, and, thus, many of them have difficulty understanding why these services should be supported. The prevailing sentiment is often: "If only some segments of our community use park and recreation services, then why should the rest of us have to pay for them?" This is one of the messages that the tax revolt highlighted. Additional support is dependent on building awareness not only of the on-site benefits that accrue to users but also of the off-site benefits that accrue to non-users in communities.

Hence, it is important to understand how to nurture the broad support necessary before innovative financing and acquisition techniques can be implemented. Lack of strong support from a broad constituency makes it much more difficult not only to secure tax funds but also to acquire external resources, such as donations, sponsorships, and foundation grants, and to negotiate partnerships with other entities.

The key to gaining this support is a concept termed *positioning*. Positioning refers to the place that parks and recreation occupies in the minds of elected officials, nonprofit and business decision makers, and the general public relative to their perception of other services that are the field's competitors for public tax dollars (and sometimes for foundation and other private source funding). The term *position* differs from the term *image*; position implies a frame of reference. Perceptions of the field are compared with those of other public services in which elected officials may invest. When seeking additional resources, the position of a park and recreation agency in stakeholders' minds is likely to be even more important than the reality of what the agency does in the community.

It has been noted that the provision of park and recreational opportunities for their own sake still lacks political clout.[1] They have to be shown to solve community problems before politicians see them as being worthy of funding, especially if funding is to be directed from another city function or new money is to be allocated. The present position of park and recreation services that has existed in the minds of stakeholders for several decades is that they are relatively discretionary, nonessential services. They are nice to have if they can be afforded after the important, essential services have been funded.

Elected officials in the United States and Canada tend to hold the erroneous belief that most to all of the benefits of leisure accrue to the individuals who use leisure services and that there are few to any spin-off benefits from this use to society in general. This contrasts with their views about the social merits of other social services (e.g., education, health services, police and fire protection, transportation) for which these elected officials acknowledge large benefits to society beyond those that accrue to the direct users of those services. Therefore, these officials have improperly adopted for leisure services the principle of public finance, which dictates that only limited public funds should be allocated to a social service that does not promote the general welfare.[2]

Another commentator noted that in recent decades the basis for operating public park and recreational programs shifted from the original rationale, which focused on meritorious social outcomes, to a more narrow notion that such services are provided because people want them.[3]

Performing a necessary service for the public at large is an essential thing for a profession. This performance goes far beyond responding to the demands of particular user groups. Thus, the key to new vitality and securing additional resources for park and recreation services is to reposition them so that they are perceived as contributing to alleviating problems that constitute the prevailing political concerns of policy makers who are responsible for allocating tax funds. Only when they are so repositioned will park and recreation services be perceived positively as part of the solution to a jurisdiction's problems rather than perceived as having no impact or even perceived negatively as a drain on its tax resources.

One adage holds that people support only those programs and services that touch them directly or from which they can see some benefits.[4] Repositioning is an attempt to respond to this sentiment. However, repositioning is a difficult task because it involves shifting a widely held, long-established attitude towards the field. Further, there are pragmatic difficulties in shifting to this mode. An agency cannot immediately abandon many of its current tasks and switch those resources to strengthen its repositioning efforts. If this were done, existing clienteles would probably make a loud outcry. Such shifts can only be implemented over time. Hence, repositioning is likely to take many years of effort, but as one commentator has observed: "The divide in government between 'essential' and 'non-essential' service is going to get greater and greater. We are standing in the middle of that divide and need to jump as it widens" (p. 17).[5]

The Set of Repositioning Strategies

There are three strategies that agencies can pursue to achieve this repositioning.[6] They are not mutually exclusive; rather, all three should be embraced simultaneously. The first strategy is real positioning, which means that an agency changes what it does. This may involve not only changing its program offerings but also changing the types of alliances and partnerships that the agency forms and changing the community forums in which it becomes involved. Real positioning is the foundation upon which all actions rest. An agency must not try to be something it is not. If it aligns with an issue, an agency must structure its services and engage in cooperative partnerships that are compatible with its alignment promises.

The second strategy is competitive repositioning. This means altering stakeholders' beliefs about what an agency's competitors do.

Psychological repositioning is the third strategy. This type of repositioning means altering stakeholders' beliefs about what an agency currently does. It has been suggested that park and recreation agencies have a labeling problem.[7] Agencies are labeled based on the means used, i.e., recreation, rather than the ends that they aspire to achieve, i.e., contributing to alleviation of economic and social problems. In the past two decades, emphasis was placed on providing the means, while the ends were forgotten. Psychological repositioning involves bringing outcomes to the forefront so that when the words "parks and recreation" are mentioned, people immediately think of them as wanted outcomes or benefits. This is illustrated effectively in the area of tourism

where public investments in promoting tourism or developing new tourism opportunities are associated in people's minds with economic development, which most consider to be a highly desirable outcome, as in the following example.

The city had plenty of money for economic development, but the council could not be persuaded to commit $1.5 million for a 150-acre youth athletic field complex for which there was a clearly demonstrated need. The proposed site was adjacent to two major highways and would be well suited for tournaments in sports, such as soccer, rugby, baseball, softball, tennis, and lacrosse. Hence, its supporters regrouped and repositioned the project as an outdoor special-events center. This terminology resonated with the council because the city had both an existing indoor special-events center and a conference center, and they were recognized widely to be good investments in economic development because of the nonresident visitors that they attracted. Representatives of the hotel-motel association, convention and visitors bureau, and chamber of commerce came to a council meeting to lobby for the athletic complex because its supporters pointed out that the city frequently could hold tournaments bringing in from 300 to 500 people each weekend from other towns. Once it was repositioned into this economic development context and viewed as an outdoor special-events center, the council approved resources to acquire the site. They also recommended that some hotel-motel tax funds be used for this purpose, reducing the amount needed from taxpayers.

It should be emphasized that providing a program and getting participation in it do not lead automatically to the outcomes desired. A prerequisite for psychological repositioning is that the services must be designed and structured carefully so that they do deliver the desired outcomes. If this prerequisite is being met, then implementing psychological repositioning will not require changes in existing service delivery. Rather, the task is to demonstrate and inform stakeholders of the benefits that a community derives from these services in terms that consistently align and associate the services with alleviating community problems. To do this, managers have to measure and communicate the success of their existing programs in alleviating the problems that are of concern in a jurisdiction. Elected officials are likely to require convincing indicators of a program's success before investing tax dollars in its continuation or expansion.

There is an aphorism in the parks and recreation field that states: "What gets measured gets done." This means that there must be a shift in the measures needed to assess an agency's effectiveness. No longer should agencies and stakeholders only use efficiency measures (i.e., number of programs, participants, acres mowed, or park acreage); rather, the measures should relate to benefits that the agency provides to the community.

In 1991, the notion of benefits-based management was introduced to the field.[2] It represented the managerial application of more than two decades of pioneering work in identifying and measuring the psychological outcomes resulting from individuals engaging in recreational activities. Benefits-based management directs that designing a service should start by focusing on outcomes. Real repositioning occurs by structuring services in a way that will deliver those outcomes, and psychological repositioning occurs through communicating in outcome terms instead of in terms of the types and numbers of park and recreation services and opportunities provided per se. Together these strategies constitute the essence of benefits-based management. An illustration of a program designed to prevent deviant behavior among youth that embraced these principles is given later in the chapter in "An Illustration of Benefits-Based Management: The Totally Cool, Totally Art Program" on page 131.

Aligning With Community Concerns

A foundation of strong and widespread support will only be built if park and recreation agencies contribute to the achievement of central political and community goals. The most prominent political problems that decision makers face will vary across jurisdictions. However, in almost every community, they are likely to include economic development and alleviation of social problems.

Economic development is viewed as a means of enlarging the tax base. The enlargement provides more tax revenues that governments can use either to improve the community's infrastructure, facilities, and services or to reduce the level of taxes that existing residents pay. It is seen also as a source of jobs and income that enables residents to improve their quality of life. Park and recreation agencies can reposition by demonstrating their central role in economic development in one or more of the following six ways: attracting tourists, attracting businesses, attracting retirees, enhancing real-estate values, expanding retail sales of equipment, and stimulating urban rejuvenation. In

the context of social problems, an agency's repositioning may involve focusing on issues, such as alleviating the problems associated with youth crime, unemployment, or nonchallenging employment; reducing environmental stress; or on lowering the cost of health care.

The selection of which of these issues an agency elects to focus upon depends on the community's priorities and the agency's personnel and facility resources. A cardinal rule is that an agency should reposition by aligning with only one or two of these community issues. Establishing a position in residents' minds requires prolonged focus. Without a concentration of resources to support the selected repositioning strategy, it will not succeed. Aligning with multiple issues may be tempting, but such efforts are unlikely to be successful. The probable outcome of diffusing resources in this way is that a fuzzy, confused position, similar to that which currently exists, will emerge.

Contributing to Economic Development

This section of the chapter offers a brief review of the potential for park and recreation agencies to reposition by aligning with one or more of the six economic development strategies.

Attracting Tourists

Figure 5.1 shows a simplified model of the tourism system. This model indicates that tourists use some mode of transportation to travel to attractions, which are supported by various kinds of services. The attractions and support services provide information about their offerings to target groups whom they have identified as potential tourists.

This tourism system is activated by attractions. Only in rare cases do people leave their home milieu and travel some distance by automobile, airplane, or ship because they want to stay in a particular hotel or dine at a particular restaurant in a different locale. Most of the time, the desire to go to a destination on a pleasure trip is stimulated by its attractions.

A taxonomy of attractions likely to activate pleasure travel is shown in table 5.1. Almost all of these attractions are developed, and in most cases are operated, by the public sector or by nonprofit organizations. A large proportion of them are likely to be the responsibility of park and recreation agencies. This leads to the conclusion that, in most communities, pleasure travel is a business

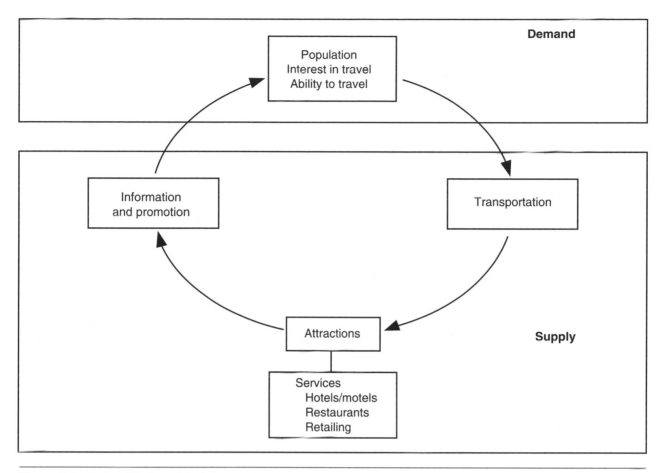

Figure 5.1 A simplified model of the tourism system.

Adapted by permission from Clare A. Gunn. *Tourism Planning.* 2nd edition. Taylor & Francis: New York. 1988.

Table 5.1 A Taxonomy of Tourist Attractions

Arts	Heritage places	Parks	Recreation	Arenas	Other
Theaters	Ethnic cultural places	National	Events and festivals	College sports	Gambling
Art galleries	Shrines, churches	State	Aquatic and coastal	Professional	places
Museums	Historical sites and	Regional	areas	franchises	Cruise ships
Performing	structures	Local	Outdoor recreations,	Concerts and	
groups	Educational institutions	Beaches	e.g., camping,	exhibitions	
Music	Industry factory tours	Theme parks	fishing, hunting		
concerts			Sports, e.g., golf,		
			tennis, skiing,		
			sailing, softball		
			Fitness and wellness		
			centers		

that the public sector drives, and park and recreation agencies are central to that business.

This is the antithesis of the general public's and the tourism field's conventional wisdom. Most people appear to be under the misapprehension that tourism is the almost exclusive preserve of the commercial sector. The commercial sector offers essential transportation; support services, such as accommodations, restaurants, and retailing; and information and promotion dissemination (see figure 5.1). However, the public sector primarily provides the attractions that activate pleasure travel. Disney World and Disneyland may attract more than 40 million visitors per year, but this number represents only 12% of the visitor days recorded in the national parks and less than 3% of visitor days to all federal recreational areas (including those operated by the U.S. Forest Service, U.S. Army Corps of Engineers, National Park Service, U.S. Fish and Wildlife Service, and Bureau of Land Management). The annual number of visits to state parks is approximately 740 million, and this number, in turn, is minuscule when compared with the number of visitors to regional, county, and local parks and beaches.

From the beginning, park managers have recognized widely the centrality of parks to tourism. Some of the first federal park managers encouraged railroads to construct lines to the parks and to develop large, luxurious hotels in them. In his report to the secretary of the Interior in 1918, the first National Park Service director, Stephen Mather, said: "It would seem that as soon as possible tourist travel not only should be sanctioned, but heartily encouraged" (p. 76).[8]

Tourism agencies, such as convention and visitor bureaus, undertake studies of tourists' economic impact to demonstrate tourism's contribution to a community's economic development. As part of their psychological and competitive repositioning strategies, park and recreation agencies should emulate them and identify the economic impact that is attributable to the facilities and services they provide. Typically, most agencies present only a financial balance sheet rather than an economic balance sheet. The differences between these two approaches explain why legislators and the general public are under the misapprehension that park agencies lose money while tourism agencies make money.

Figure 5.2 illustrates the conceptual reasoning for developing economic balance sheets to supplement the financial information. It shows that residents of a community give funds to their city council in the form of taxes. The city council uses a proportion of these funds to subsidize production of an event or development of a facility. The facility or event attracts nonresident visitors who spend money in the local community both inside and outside of the facility that they visit. This new money from outside of the community creates income and jobs in the community for residents.

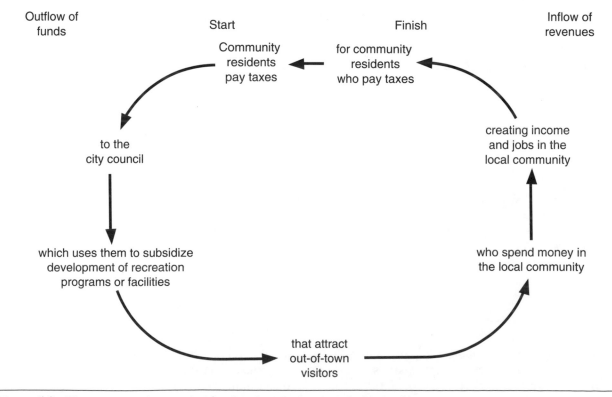

Figure 5.2 The conceptual reasoning for developing economic balance sheets.

This completes the cycle; community residents are responsible for creating the funds, and they receive a return on their investment in the form of new jobs and more household income.

The traditional financial balance sheet assumes that the cycle shown in figure 5.2 starts and ends with the city council rather than with a community's residents. This is narrow and misleading because it includes only the taxes and revenues that accrue to local government from the event or facility. Such a narrow definition suggests that the council should receive a satisfactory return on its investment from lease fees, admission revenues, increased sales tax revenues, and other revenues. However, this approach is flawed conceptually because the money invested does not belong to the council; rather, it belongs to the city's resi-

dents. Although it is efficient for the residents' investment to be funneled through the council, the return that residents receive, and not only the proportion of the total return that filters back to the council, is important. The purpose of economic impact studies is to measure the economic return to residents.

The difference between the two approaches is illustrated in "A Comparison of Economic Return and Financial Return From an Amateur Softball Association's Men's 40 and Over Fast-Pitch National Tournament." The park and recreation department's financial balance sheet shows a net loss of $9,375 from the tournament. However, if the agency used an economic balance sheet, as tourism agencies do, then it would show a net return of $273,000, $511,000, or $150,000 depending on

A Comparison of Economic Return and Financial Return From an Amateur Softball Association's Men's 40 and Over Fast-Pitch National Tournament

Context

All 37 teams that qualified for the tournament were from outside the local area. The average number of players per team was 15. Some players brought family and friends with them, so the average size of the contingent associated with each team, including the players, was 21. Because it was an elimination tournament, the length of time that the teams stayed in the community varied from two to six nights.

Economic Return

A survey of the players revealed the following:

Total expenditures in the local area by players and their family and friends = $287,000.

An input-output model that calculated multipliers concluded the following:

Total economic impact on sales = $525,000
Total economic impact on personal income = $164,000

Financial Return

Income to the city parks and recreation department from entry fees = $4,625
Costs incurred by the department, including manpower, to host the event = $14,000
Net financial loss to the city = $9,375

Pay-Back Period

The cost of constructing the softball complex was almost $2 million. Based on economic return to residents in terms of personal income, the capital cost of the complex will be repaid after 13 similar tournaments.

From John L. Crompton and Seong-Seop Kim. 1998. It's all in the presentation: Did the park and recreation agency lose $9,375 or gain $525,000. California Parks and Recreation. 54(2): 34-39.

whether economic impact was reported in terms of direct expenditures, sales impact, or personal income impact. (These figures were calculated by taking the gross amounts shown and subtracting from them the $14,000 that hosting the event cost.)

There is frequently confusion and misunderstanding on deciding which of the three economic impact measures shown in "A Comparison of Economic Return and Financial Return From an Amateur Softball Association's Men's 40 and Over Fast-Pitch National Tournament" should be used.[9] It has become commonplace for tourism agencies to report economic impact in terms of sales generated. In the author's view, this is of no value to elected officials or residents. It is used because it generates the highest economic impact number, but residents are not likely to have any interest in sales generated. As the model in figure 5.2 emphasized, residents are likely to be primarily interested in how the tournament impacted them in terms of personal income. Tourism agencies rarely use this measure because it is so small compared with the sales impact and with the direct expenditures amount. In this case, it is more than three times smaller than the sales impact. Nevertheless, it is the most meaningful indicator to residents because it shows them how much return they received from their investment (see figure 5.2). Residents in the jurisdiction paid the capital and operating costs of the softball complex, and their concern should be with how many new dollars coming into the community from visitors participating in the tournament end up as income to residents.

The capital cost of the softball complex was almost $2 million, which means that if the personal income measure is used, then the investment would pay for itself after 13 similar tournaments. How many other investments is a jurisdiction likely to have that pay for themselves in two years (assuming six or seven tournaments per year) and that continue to contribute $1 million to residents annually for the next 20 years? Agencies that undertake this type of economic impact study, using a representative sample of services or events that attract visitors to their jurisdiction, and that present these data in the form of an economic balance sheet to their stakeholders are likely to demonstrate that they make money for the community. This contribution to economic development is likely to reposition them favorably in the minds of legislators and the general public.

In addition to this psychological repositioning strategy, agencies also could engage in real re-positioning by adopting a more aggressive entrepreneurial approach to soliciting tourism business for the community. This could involve developing packaged services for visitors. Figure 5.1 highlights the dependency of park and recreation agencies on other components in the system for attracting pleasure tourists. The right side of figure 5.1 suggests that managing facilities and services involves facilitating transportation. It does not stop at the front gate! The challenge is not merely to provide services that people want; it is to package them so they can be accessed conveniently.

For example, in every area there are numerous organizations that have a program chair whose challenge is to develop a program of activities for the group. Park and recreation agencies have a smorgasbord of offerings available to meet those groups' needs. Packaging means that the agency links with a transportation source and necessary support services, such as a restaurant and hotel (if an overnight stay is involved), and offers a fixed price for the total experience to targeted groups. Thus, if an agency offers a fishing trip to senior citizen groups, the package may include a chartered bus, lunch, fishing poles, and a staff person who meets the chartered bus and provides interpretation and assistance with bait, fishing, cleaning fish, and so forth. Targeting groups from outside of the community with packages would further help to reposition an agency as a central contributor to tourism and economic development.

Strong linkages with a jurisdiction's tourism agency also may help reinforce the real repositioning strategy. If these organizations have a positive position in stakeholders' minds, then closer links with them by a park and recreation agency is likely to lead to some of their positive image being conveyed to the agency by association. Such linkages make pragmatic sense because the two organizations often have complementary assets. Tourism agencies typically have funds available for promotion that are scarce at most park and recreation agencies. For example, the Metro Dade County Parks and Recreation Department in Florida had an arrangement with the Dade County tourism agency whereby the tourism agency paid for a series of brochures providing information on the department's cultural, athletic, and recreational attractions. In contrast, tourism agencies rarely become involved in directly producing programs and services. Thus, some departments, for example, cooperate with tourism agencies to fund special-event coordinators who are responsible for organizing and soliciting sponsorship for special events in the community. The tourism agencies recognize that park and recreation departments have the expertise and a mandate to organize special events but frequently lack the funds to launch and promote them effectively. They help fund the position, provide initial seed funds for some events, and promote all events.

Changing their name is another action park and recreation agencies may consider in psychologically repositioning themselves more centrally to claim ownership of their contribution to tourism's economic impact. In the United Kingdom, the most common agency title is department of leisure services, and it is common practice for a division of tourism to be part of such a department. Another common title is the department of leisure amenities and attractions. In the United States, the states of Arkansas and South Carolina have a department of parks, recreation, and tourism, recognizing the close links between them. If it is not possible for political reasons to incorporate the word tourism into the department's title, then the taxonomy in table 5.1 suggests a change to the Department of Attractions or to the Department of Recreation Amenities and Attractions would enhance perceptions of an agency's central role in tourism.

Attracting Businesses

Substantial shifts in American industry have occurred in the past decade with the movement from traditional manufacturing industries to smokeless industries. Many of these industries may be characterized as footloose because they are perceived to be less constrained and more flexible in their choice of location than traditional manufacturing companies are. The principle resource of footloose companies is their employees. The financial performance of these companies is relatively independent of location decisions. They are not tied to raw materials, natural resources, or energy supplies. The absence of these resource constraints means that these companies are perceived to be excellent prospects for relocation by cities seeking to expand their tax base. For this reason, a large number of communities and states attempt to attract footloose companies, creating a highly competitive environment. The importance of these sources of tax base growth is emphasized by the aggressiveness with which communities or municipalities actively recruit and compete for new industry. Indeed, more than 10,000 economic development groups operate in cities and counties in addition to state government agencies operating in this capacity.

The importance of quality of life in business location decisions has been repeatedly documented.[10] The success of many businesses depends on their employees, particularly those businesses in the intensely recruited high-technology, research and development, and company headquarters categories. These types of businesses are information factories whose viability relies on their ability to attract and retain highly educated professional employees. The deciding factor of where these individuals choose to work is often quality of life in the geographic vicinity of the business. No matter how quality of life is defined, park and recreational opportunities are likely to be a major component of it. There are no great cities in North America or elsewhere in the world that do not have great park, recreation, and cultural systems. Great is defined not in terms of size but in terms of people's desire to live there. Great park, recreation, and cultural systems and great cities are synonymous.

The profound influence that park and recreation amenities have on people's preferred living locations can be illustrated by a simple exercise that the author has undertaken with literally hundreds of different groups. First, all members of the group are asked to write the place that they would like to live given their druthers (that is, their preferred place, ignoring pragmatic concerns, such as job, family, language, and heritage). After this task has been completed, each of them is asked to write in one sentence why they picked that place. When responses to this second task are analyzed, results are invariably similar. More than 80% of participants will cite some dimension of park, recreational, or environmental ambiance in their responses.

For many people, once they attain a threshold level of income, improvements in quality of lifestyle become more important than increases in salary. For example, a $15,000 raise in salary may not be sufficient to persuade a professional who has strong social networks in Place A, where he or she earns $70,000 with a company, to move to a similar company in Place B if the location offers similar lifestyle opportunities. However, the same individual may be enticed to move from the company in Place A to a similar job in Place C for a $5,000 salary increase if Place C offers superior lifestyle opportunities. Because park and recreation amenities are important lifestyle elements to many, it is not surprising that many company representatives recognize them as being important in attracting and retaining professional and executive employees.

The importance of park, recreation, and open space amenities was reported in a study of key decision makers from 174 businesses that had relocated, expanded, or been launched in Colorado in the previous five years.[10] Small-business decision makers were influenced particularly strongly because they reported that quality of life was their main reason for locating there. Among six elements that were used to measure quality of life, these small-business decision makers ranked the element of park, recreation, and open space amenities as being most important. They located their businesses where they could enjoy a preferred lifestyle. This finding is especially salient because analysts constantly reiterate that future growth in the United States' economy is likely to come primarily from small businesses.

It has been noted that many small companies set profit goals for themselves that are not optimum but are merely good enough.[10] They could earn higher profits, but this would involve adverse trade-offs for employees and owners in their quality of life. Hence, they satisfice, i.e., they accept a somewhat lower level of remuneration. One observer has commented: "The new breed of entrepreneur is less like the swashbuckler out for the quick hit and more like the pilgrim looking for a better life" (p. B2)[11]

There is substantial evidence that park and recreational opportunities play a role in the location decisions of many businesses that communities vigorously recruit. Real repositioning requires an agency to become part of a community's strategic marketing effort to attract businesses. Few park and recreation departments show an interest in their community's efforts to recruit and retain businesses. If they become involved in these forums, it draws attention to the role of their amenities in the relocation decisions of some companies. Their involvement should extend to identifying the facilities and services that businesses seek and to advocating that they be provided as part of the community's economic development effort. The importance of community ambiance in business location decisions provides park and recreation managers with leverage to advocate community commitment to features, such as greenways, urban tree planting, underground rather than surface wiring, tree protection ordinances, and demanding exaction requirements.

Strategic place marketing involves "designing a community to satisfy the needs of its stakeholders. . . . If small business constitutes the engine of the job generation process, then places should promote those things that facilitate small business growth" (p. 12).[6] Historically, most jurisdictions have been product driven rather than market driven in their efforts to persuade companies to locate in their communities.[12] That is, they have focused on selling their community as it is rather than on adapting the community to meet the changing needs of relocating companies. This approach markedly contrasts with how most viable organizations now operate. In communities seeking to attract footloose companies, especially small businesses, part of a market-driven approach involves real repositioning by investing in park and recreation amenities.

Responsibility for business recruitment in most communities has been assigned to an economic development agency. Competitive repositioning could involve subtly challenging the myth that these organizations have created about their high level of influence on company location decisions. Frequently, they claim credit for bringing XYZ company to town. The reality is that they rarely influence the company's decisions that result in it narrowing its list of prospective communities to a small set of between two and five communities. Narrowing the list usually occurs before community economic development organizations are contacted or have any awareness that a particular company may be planning to relocate. Typically, they become involved only in this final stage in a company's decision process. At that stage, their role is to serve as a conduit through which companies conveniently can request specific information from those communities that they are considering; to host and coordinate visits to the community by company officials; to coordinate company requests for easements and planning permissions; and to coordinate the negotiation of incentive packages that their community is prepared to offer.[12] If this more limited role becomes recognized as the real function of economic development organizations, then the scope of their operations may be scaled back and more funds released for providing amenities that companies seek.

Psychological repositioning could involve soliciting testimonials from senior executives that attest to the role of park and recreation amenities in relocation decisions. In many decision-making public forums, emotion prevails over logical analysis, and visible testimonials can be important elements in repositioning a department.

Attracting Retirees

It has been observed: "There is a new clean, growth industry in America today—the industry is retirement migration" (p. 7).[13] In 1990, approximately one in eight Americans were 65 years of age or more, and this ratio is projected by the Bureau of the Census to increase to one in five by 2050. Two related concomitant trends are accompanying this rapid increase in the number and proportion of seniors. First, individuals are retiring earlier. For example, in 1948, almost 50% of all men aged 65 or more were in the labor force, but by the 1990s, this figure had fallen below 15%.[14] Second, a growing proportion of retirees are relatively wealthy. Indeed, in terms of per-capita disposable income in the United States, the 55 to 59, 60 to 64, and 65 to 69 age cohorts are wealthier than any other five-year age-range cohorts.

These trends have caused many jurisdictions to view retention and recruitment of retirees as a strategy for stimulating their economies. Although most retirees remain in the same area in which they spent much of their lives, a substantial number change location when they retire. For example, between 1985 and 1990, more than 1.9 million Americans aged 60 years or more changed their state of residence.[11] Members of this mobile retiree cohort have been termed GRAMPIES.[15] The acronym is derived from the following trends: *growing* numbers of people are living longer, more people are *retiring* earlier, they are more *active* in lifestyle and consumption, and they are *monied* people who are *physically* and emotionally *in excellent shape*.

There are more than 100 local governments or chambers of commerce with active marketing programs designed to attract retirees, and the number is increasing rapidly. The appeal of retirees to communities stems from a realization that if 100 households come to a community in a year, each with a retirement income of $40,000, they have an impact similar to that of a new business that annually spends $4 million in the community. Some communities believe that retiree relocations are more desirable than business relocations for a number of reasons, some of which are identified in the following paragraphs.

Social Security and pension benefits of retirees are stable and not subject to the vicissitudes of economic business cycles. This income comes from outside the community, but retirees spend it locally, so it stimulates the economy and generates jobs. Not only do they increase the tax base, but retirees tend to be positive taxpayers. That is, they characteristically use fewer services than they pay for through taxes. Immigrating retirees are not likely to strain social services, health-care services, the local criminal justice system, or the natural environment.

Retirees transfer significant assets into local investment and banking institutions. For example, in Texas the total annual net income (i.e., gains from immigration assets minus losses from emigration assets) from migrants aged 60 years and more between 1985 and 1990 averaged more than $150 million.[13] These assets expand the local deposit base that can be used for commercial and industrial financing. Retirees provide the community with a pool of volunteers. They tend to be substantial contributors to churches and to local philanthropic and service organizations.

From the perspective of economic development investments, targeting resources at recruiting retirees, rather than exclusively at corporations, has at least two major advantages. First, retirees do not require economic incentive packages comprising such elements as tax abatements, low-interest loans, subsidized-worker training programs, and infrastructure improvements, which are often standard prerequisites to a corporate relocation.

Second, capital improvements made as part of a retiree recruitment effort are likely to focus on quality of life issues, such as recreational opportunities, beautification, ambiance, or support services, which will also benefit existing residents. Capital investments targeted at recruiting corporations involve large outlays for things, such as developing industrial and business parks, access roads, and utilities. In contrast to the retiree investments, local residents are likely to receive relatively few direct benefits from these facilities. Hence, the risk associated with recruiting corporations is higher because if the corporate strategy fails, then the community receives a much poorer return on its investment than the return it receives if the strategy of attracting retirees fails.

Extensive empirical evidence has been reported, recording the propensity of younger, affluent retirees to migrate to areas rich in amenities, particularly those with a warm climate and recreational opportunities. The central role of recreational opportunities in attracting them is consistently reiterated.[16] Among many who have recently retired, there is a desire to initiate a lifestyle change to a more recreation-oriented way of life. These retirees have an image of how they want to live in retirement and seek environments that facilitate that lifestyle. These sentiments are exemplified by the growing number of specialist retirement settlements, such as the Sun City and Leisure World communities, that have emerged in various parts of the country. These communities invariably emphasize in their promotion the array of opportunities they provide for engaging in recreational activities.

The central importance of recreation amenities to these mobile retirees has implications for all jurisdictions including those that are not actively seeking to attract new retirees. From an economic perspective, it is as important to retain existing retirees as to recruit new retirees. If they fail to provide a comprehensive set of recreational opportunities comparable with those available in other locations, communities may lose their GRAMPIES. From this perspective, an agency can reposition its provision of services for retirees as being an investment in the community's economic health as well as in the personal well-being of the beneficiary users of these services.

Enhancing Real-Estate Values

Government officials frequently seek to strengthen the tax base of their communities by encouraging development. Development is seen by many as a panacea for the problem of rising costs of community services at a time when federal and state aid to local communities is being reduced. The conventional wisdom is that development, not preservation of open space, brings prosperity and that parks are expensive for public entities to provide.

The challenge for park and recreation agencies is to pursue a psychological repositioning strategy that raises stakeholders' awareness of the fallacies in this conventional wisdom. Three types of costs for providing parks are usually identified: acquisition and development costs, operating and maintenance costs, and the opportunity cost of the loss of property tax income that jurisdictions would have received if the land had been developed for other purposes. The third cost is cited by people who point out that because the park land is publicly owned, it is exempt from property taxes. In contrast, if it were commercially developed, then it would generate property taxes and, thus, reduce the amount assessed on all other property owners in the jurisdiction to pay for local public services. This type of rationale and analysis is flawed.

People frequently are willing to pay a larger amount of money for a house located close to a natural, low-intensity-use park than they are for a comparable house farther away. The enhanced value of this property results in its owner paying higher property taxes to governments. If the incremental amount of taxes paid by each property that

is attributable to the presence of the park is aggregated, it is often sufficient to pay the annual debt charges required to retire the bonds used to acquire and develop the park. In these circumstances, the park is obtained at no long-term cost to the jurisdiction. An illustration of how this may work is given in "An Illustration of How Incremental Increases in Property Taxes May Pay for the Acquisition and Development of Parks." This conceptual example shows that the annual debt charges associated with creating a park may be covered by the increment of property taxes from the premium value attached to homes close to the park.

Three points relating to "An Illustration of How Incremental Increases in Property Taxes May Pay for the Acquisition and Development of Parks" should be noted. First, the illustration assumes no state or federal grants are available to aid in the park's acquisition and development. If they were available to reduce the community's capital outlay, then the incremental property tax income stream would greatly exceed that required to service the debt payments. Second, the incremental property tax income will continue to accrue to the community after the 20-year period during which the debt charges will be repaid. Third, a park of this size is likely to improve the quality of life and, thus, the value of property beyond Zone C; however, because this value is likely to be relatively small, no attempt was made to capture this additional tax income in the example.

This concept of park land adding value is the same principle as that used by private developers who incorporate golf courses into their projects. They forfeit the revenue that would be forthcoming from the sale of lots on the 150 acres of land needed for the course. If one-acre lots were sold at $40,000 each, then the loss to the developer of 150 acres would be $6 million. In addition, the developer may pay another $4 million to construct the course on this land. The developer makes this $10 million investment because the presence of the golf course causes the sale price of the other lots in the development to increase sufficiently to ensure that the investment is more than recouped.

A consistent stream of studies reporting this value-enhancing effect of parks has appeared as far back as Frederick Law Olmsted's documentation of the impact of Central Park on surrounding real-estate values in New York. This is reported in "The Impact of Central Park on Adjacent Real-Estate Values." Olmsted's analysis was fairly simplistic and primitive, but it initiated this line of thinking. More contemporary analyses that have

An Illustration of How Incremental Increases in Property Taxes May Pay for the Acquisition and Development of Parks

Costs

- Acquisition and development of a 50-acre natural park area with some appealing topographical and vegetation features (see figure 5.3).
- Assume cost of acquisition and development (e.g., fencing, trails, supplementary planting, some landscaping) is $20,000 an acre, so total park capital cost is $1 million.
- Annual debt charges for a 20-year general obligation (G.O.) bond on $1 million at 5% are approximately $90,000.

Income

- If properties around the park are 2,000 sq ft homes on half-acre lots (40 yd × 60 yd) with 40 yd frontages on the park, then there would be 70 lots in Zone A (30 lots along each of the 1,210 yd perimeters and 5 lots along each of the 200 yd perimeters).
- Assume total property taxes payable to city, county, and school district are 2% of the market value of the property.
- Assume market value of similar properties elsewhere in the jurisdiction beyond the immediate influence of this park is $200,000.
- Assume the desire to live close to a large natural park creates a willingness to pay a premium of 20% for properties in Zone A; 10%, in Zone B; and 5%, in Zone C.

Thus, the incremental income from property taxes attributable to the presence of the park (approximately $98,000) is sufficient to pay the annual debt charges (approximately $90,000) for acquisition and development of the park (see table 5.2).

Table 5.2   Property Taxes Pay Annual Debt for Acquisitions and Development of the Park

Zone	Market value of each home	Incremental value attributed to the park	Total property taxes at 2%	Incremental property taxes attributed to the park	Aggregate amount of property tax increments given 70 home sites
Outside the park's influence	$200,000	0	$4,000	0	0
A (20% premium)	$240,000	$40,000	$4,800	$800	$56,000
B (10% premium)	$220,000	$20,000	$4,400	$400	$28,000
C (5% premium)	$210,000	$10,000	$4,200	$200	$14,000
					$98,000

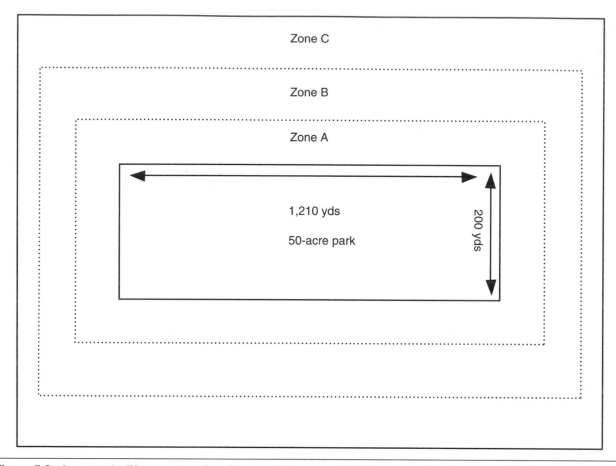

Figure 5.3 Layout of a 50-acre natural park area with topographical or vegetation features or both.

The Impact of Central Park on Adjacent Real-Estate Values

Frederick Law Olmsted was aware that the city of New York would be concerned about the costs of both land acquisition and the construction of Central Park. To justify the expenses, Olmsted tracked the value of real estate in three wards surrounding the park from 1856 (when the project commenced) to 1873.

By the end of 1873, Central Park had cost the city $13.9 million comprising $5 million for land acquisition and $8.9 million for capital improvements. Olmsted assumed that without Central Park, the property values in the three wards surrounding the park would have appreciated at the same rate, i.e., 100%, as property in other city wards during this 18-year time period. The 1856 appraised value of the three wards was $26.5 million, so a 100% increase would have valued them at $53 million in 1873. However, their actual appraised value in 1873 was $236 million. Olmsted proposed that the tremendous increase in property value was attributable to the existence of Central Park.

The property taxes accruing to the city from these increased values in 1873 amounted to $5.2 million. The annual debt charges on the bonds issued to finance Central Park were $800,000, so the annual net profit received by the city from the development of Central Park in 1873 was $4.4 million.

Adapted from Tim Fox. Urban open spaces: An investment that pays. *Neighborhood Open Space Coalition: New York. 1990.*

incorporated sophisticated statistical techniques and econometric models have reached similar conclusions. Typical of such studies was one that examined the net cost of greenbelt purchases around the city of Boulder. The authors concluded:

> The annual aggregate property value for the neighborhood was approximately $5.4 million greater than it would have been in the absence of greenbelt. This increment resulted in an annual addition of approximately $500,000 to the potential neighborhood property tax revenue. The purchase price of this greenbelt parcel for the city was approximately $1.5 million, and thus, the potential property tax revenue alone would allow a recovery of initial costs in only three years (p. 215).[17]

There is an adage stating that much of the value of properties on the tax roll is acquired from properties that are off the tax roll. The creation of natural park areas is, in fact, one of the most cost-effective uses of land. In contrast to natural parks that may lead to a net gain in government tax receipts, land developed for housing frequently results in a net loss to jurisdictions. That is, the cost of providing public services to occupants of the new houses exceeds the amount received from them in taxes. The services that they require include education (construction and operation of schools), sewers, drainage, street maintenance, police and fire protection, courts and jails, health and welfare, and parks and recreation. Thus, development of land for housing is often more expensive to government than development of that same land as a natural park. This is illustrated in further detail in "An Illustrative Comparison of the Net Cost of Servicing a Residential Development and a Natural Park Area."

Expanding Retail Sales of Equipment

It is estimated that leisure expenditures account for about $1 of every $8 spent by the American consumer and that 5 million jobs in manufacturing, retailing, and service industries depend on recreation. An agency can psychologically reposition by pointing out its contributions to the economic well-being of these industries.

The single most influential factor in determining demand for park and recreation services is probably the availability of opportunities to access them. Even though ice skating is a recreational activity that millions enjoy, very few of these skaters reside in Texas. Texans have a good reason for their lack of participation; Texas has no natural ice areas and few ice rinks. If ice rinks were constructed in every community in Texas, as they are in some northern states, then there would probably be a quantum increase in the number of Texas ice skaters. Once ice rinks were built, a demand would be created for equipment used in ice skating, ice hockey, and other ice activities. The facilities would stimulate production and retailing of these products.

This illustration is used to point out that the economic viability of equipment retailers in a community and of manufacturers of all types of recreational equipment relies heavily on the availability of park and recreational facilities at which the equipment can be used. The nexus between

---

An Illustrative Comparison of the Net Cost of Servicing a Residential Development and a Natural Park Area

On the 50-acre site, assume a density of three homes per acre and a property tax rate of 2% of market value on these $200,000 homes. Thus, annual property tax revenue equals $600,000 (50 × 3 × $4,000).

Assume that the cost of servicing these residences is 14% higher than the property taxes received.[a] Thus, the annual net loss to the community for servicing this residential development is $84,000 ([(114 ÷ 100) × $600,000] − $600,000).

Because the operation and maintenance cost of a 50-acre natural park is likely to be lower than $84,000, it is a less expensive option to service than a housing development on the site.

[a]This figure is derived from Commonwealth Research Group Inc., *1995 Cost of Community Services in Southern New England*: Chepachet, Rhode Island: Southern New England Forestry Consortium Inc.

equipment sales and facility provision is recognized when a manufacturers' excise tax is imposed on recreational equipment in an attempt to allocate the cost of providing recreation amenities to the users of these facilities. (This was discussed in chapter 2.)

The impact of limitations in the supply base to sales of recreational equipment has long been a concern of those in the pleasure boat industry. By some estimates, 200 marinas are closing each year and only 75 are opening.[18] Many operators of small family-owned marinas are located on the coast, and their businesses provide a basic living but no more. They now find themselves owning prime waterfront property worth millions of dollars if they sell it to developers for residential projects.

Without the public sector providing boat slips, the private sector finds it difficult to sell boats. In some parts of the country, there are not enough slips available to satisfy the number of people who want to moor a boat where it has access to salt water. For example, many harbors in the Northeast have waiting lists of several years.[19] The problem has been exacerbated by increased sensitivity to the environment. Historically, many marinas were built in wetland areas, which is no longer permissible. One result of this supply constraint is that small-boat owners do not trade-up. An industry official commented: "People are not buying larger boats because they can't find a place to keep them. So they're using smaller boats they can launch from a boat ramp. That's all well and good, but it does have a retarding effect on the industry" (p. 27).[19]

Stimulating Urban Rejuvenation

In many cities, parks and major recreation developments, such as aquariums, marinas, entertainment centers, cultural centers, convention centers, gaming venues, sports complexes, and urban weekend retreats, have been centerpieces of urban revitalization efforts.

Newark, once the nation's manufacturing capital, became the emblem of everything wrong with urban America. In 1996 it was at the top of *Money* magazine's "Ten Most Dangerous Cities" list. The cornerstone of city leaders' strategy for reversing the city's fortunes was to invest $180 million in building the New Jersey Performing Arts Center that opened in 1997 on a 12-acre site in downtown Newark. Two commentators observed: "Local social activists criticized the project, saying the money would be better spent on housing or schools. In the end, the only thing Newark has

going for it is the bizarre fact that performing arts centers really do seem to jump-start downtown recoveries" (p. 74).[20]

The role of the Performing Arts Center in repositioning Newark was clearly articulated by the center's president who stated: "This is the big idea: to change the way people think about Newark. It's not the place where you get your car stolen; it's where you go to concerts" (p. 74).[20]

One of the early types of catalysts in the 1980s were aquaria. Baltimore's National Aquarium opened in 1981 and was a central anchor in rejuvenating the Inner Harbor area. It became Maryland's leading tourist attraction and a model from which other cities drew inspiration. Subsequently, more than 20 large American cities developed large aquariums: "Everybody is interested in aquariums because of the urban renewal that goes on around them. Civic leaders have begun to realize that all 'living museums'—aquariums, zoos, botanical gardens—can help cure an ailing economy" (p. 29).[21]

Examples of types of recreational facilities that have been used to transform rundown central downtown areas into exciting, vibrant, livable places are given in "Types of Recreation Amenities That Have Been Used To Revitalize Downtown Areas." It has been noted:

These kinds of places have a ripple effect. For example, Coors Field, the open-air baseball stadium in Denver, improved land uses in a several-block radius. New Orleans' Rivergate casino had similar effects in its downtown neighborhood. Downtown entertainment districts tend to experience rapid growth after achieving a critical mass (p. 48).[22]

The characteristics of "an exciting new development project—the urban entertainment destination" (p. 6)[23]—that emerged in the mid-1990s are described in "Emergence of the Urban Entertainment Destination" on page 128. These entertainment centers frequently feature new technologies developed by the telecommunications, electronics, and computing industries.

The pioneer of this trend to use recreation amenities to rejuvenate downtown areas was San Antonio with the development of its Paseo del Rio, or River Walk. This linear park project was conceptualized and initiated in the late 1930s and early 1940s by the Works Progress Administration. However, it remained a lushly landscaped, but crime ridden, environmental corridor with most of the abutting buildings turning their backs to the river until the late 1960s. Its development accelerated in

Types of Recreation Amenities That Have Been Used To Revitalize Downtown Areas

- Cultural facilities, such as aquariums, science and industry museums, children's museums, performing arts centers, and libraries. Cities that have developed such facilities include Cincinnati, Cleveland, Columbus, Dallas, Denver, Jacksonville, Newark, New Orleans, and Tampa.
- New or expanded convention centers. Cities that have taken this route to attracting visitor business to downtown include Atlanta, Columbus, Dallas, Minneapolis, New Orleans, Philadelphia, and Tampa.
- Entertainment districts. Examples include Inner Harbor in Baltimore, the Flats in Cleveland, the Brewery District in Columbus, the West End in Dallas, Lower Downtown (Lodo) in Denver, Jacksonville Landing in Jacksonville, the Riverfront in New Orleans, Church Street in Orlando, Arizona Center in Phoenix, and Fifth Avenue in San Diego. In fact, almost every first- and second-tier city in the country is attempting to develop a downtown entertainment district.
- Casinos. This is an emerging land use for downtowns. After construction in New Orleans, others were planned for Chicago, Dallas, Houston, Philadelphia, and Pittsburgh.
- Waterfront destinations. Among the cities that have planned downtown waterfront locations for entertainment and retail activities are Cincinnati, Cleveland, Jacksonville, Miami, New Orleans, Philadelphia, and Tampa.

From J. Robert Brown and Michele Laumer. Comeback cities. Urban Land. August 1995, pages 46-51, 83. Copyright ©Urban Land Institute. Used by permission.

earnest with the World's Fair held in the area in 1968. Since that time, it has been extended periodically to embrace more of the city's downtown area. The project successfully persuaded businesses that had turned their backs on the river and regarded it as an eyesore and a nuisance to turn around to face it and recognize it as a special asset.

The river has been transformed into a park area with a remarkable, special ambiance. The city capitalized on this by building its convention center in the area, and the River Walk's ambiance has been a major factor in San Antonio's emergence as a leading convention destination. The River Walk became the leading tourist attraction in the state of Texas. The extensive array of hotels, restaurants, and leisure activities along the River Walk provide an urban focus for the city.

"Using Public Investment in Recreational Facilities To Rejuvenate Downtown Cleveland" on page 129 and the following examples are intended to illustrate both the key role of park and recreational facilities in stimulating economic development in deteriorated urban areas and the public-private partnerships needed to undertake these successful transformations.

Centennial Olympic Park in Atlanta was the focal point of a plan to capitalize on momentum from the 1996 Olympics and to revitalize the downtown area. The 21-acre park site served as the social center at the Olympics and was one of the Games' key legacies to Atlanta. It was the largest park built in the urban area in 25 years. The post-Olympics plan was to enhance 80 acres surrounding the park on the downtown's western edge. The goal was to transform downtown Atlanta from a 9:00 A.M.-to-5:00 P.M., five-day week city to a 24 h, all-week city by encouraging recreation, entertainment, and residential development in this area.

In Philadelphia, revitalization of the 2.5 mi central waterfront along the Delaware River was initiated by the investment of $50 million of public funds to develop the Great Plaza. This was a multitiered, tree-lined amphitheater with a view of the river. Subsequently, the Amazon Club opened its doors on a pier and targeted young people looking to dance, socialize, and have fun after work. It was a great success and stimulated a development spree of 15 new bars and restaurants in the area. The public sector helped this momentum by renovating and reopening the Independence Seaport

Emergence of the Urban Entertainment Destination

Within little more than one year, there has been an unprecedented upswell in development plans and announcements for entertainment destination projects from Miami to Seattle. During this period, nearly every major entertainment company has established development teams to evaluate, plan, or develop urban entertainment districts—the entertainment industry's term for leisure and entertainment destinations as distinguished from its core film, television, recording, and theme park products.

During the same period, at least 12 of the largest, most successful developers in the United States have announced projects that will use entertainment as an anchor or as a magnet to enhance retail, hospitality, residential, or mixed-use development. Melvin Simon & Associates, the Mills Corporation, Gerald Hines, the Rouse Company, Maguire Thomas Partners, and Himmel & Company are just some of the major developers who are introducing projects that will ultimately define the scope, scale, and content of entertainment destinations into the next century. Gaming companies, film exhibitors, hospitality groups, sports franchises, technology creators, retailers, restauranteurs, and a diverse range of entrepreneurs are emerging with a startling array of concepts, components, and projects. From the $250 million Broadway on the Beach in Myrtle Beach, South Carolina, to the Third Street Promenade in Santa Monica, California, a vast sweep of activity is underway, involving partnerships of developers, investors, entrepreneurs, large-scale entertainment companies, and municipalities.

One of the most interesting aspects of this entrepreneurial industry is the public sector's leadership in fostering the creation of entertainment destinations as a catalyst of urban revitalization efforts. Some of the most notable examples include Yerba Buena Gardens in San Francisco; 42nd Street in New York; and, the granddaddy of them all, the Inner Harbor in Baltimore. The recent opening of the $38 million Blockbuster-SonyMusic Entertainment Centre at the Waterfront on the Camden, New Jersey, waterfront is an example of the public-private collaboration that often serves as the foundation for many of these innovative urban destinations.

The abrupt emergence of this new industry has taken many people by surprise. Indeed, apart from the active players themselves, many seasoned development experts and practitioners are only vaguely aware of the swirl of excitement and activity that, in many cases, is just below the surface. The speed with which deals are being put together and the diversity of the plans and projects that are being contemplated are breathtaking. Although the effects of these projects are likely to be wide-ranging, they are little understood. Do urban entertainment destinations represent a fin de siecle development fad or do they reflect the nascent reemergence of America's downtowns and commercial districts as major entertainment centers? We believe it may be the latter.

From Michael D. Beyard and Michael S. Rubin. A new industry emerges. Urban Land, *supplement. August 1995, pages 6-7. Copyright ©Urban Land Institute. Used by permission.*

Museum, a 100,000 sq ft cultural center. Extensive condominium and retail development occurred after the leisure elements were created to attract people to the area.

In Pittsburgh, transformation of the blighted area at the point where the Allegheny and Monongahela Rivers merge to form the Ohio River began in the early 1980s, and a riverfront was a central feature. Private developers were attracted to the site by the proposed master plan but made their investments contingent upon the city developing a park known as Allegheny Landing. This park slopes to the river and forms a natural bowl where people gather for concerts and events or enjoy the view across the river. The riverfront was restructured into a landing stage for a marina and included an attractive fishing pier. When this was done, the private sector invested more than $50 million in the area to develop office buildings.

In Baltimore, the city's Inner Harbor redevelopment featured park areas, a convention center, an aquarium, and a highly praised new baseball stadium for the city's professional franchise. Waterfront Park in Portland was the rallying point for that city's rejuvenation, and the 1,700-boat marina at Long Beach, California, was a central feature of

Using Public Investment in Recreational Facilities To Rejuvenate Downtown Cleveland

In the mid-1970s, Cleveland was nicknamed by some the Mistake on the Lake (Lake Erie). It was a symbol of urban blight and an example of all that could go wrong in an aging blue-collar town. In a 1975 ranking of the 58 largest American cities, Cleveland was second-worst in terms of economic and social problems. The image of Cleveland was framed poignantly by the fires on the Cuyahoga River, which were fed by locally generated pollutants.

The subsequent renaissance of downtown Cleveland was driven by the investment of public funds in recreation developments. These included the $362 million Gateway sports complex; Jacobs Field, a 42,000-seat, open-air, baseball stadium; Gund Arena, a 21,000-seat basketball arena; Playhouse Square Center, Cleveland's theater district in which three former vaudeville houses and theaters were restored and two more such restorations were planned; the Steamship Museum; the Rock-and-Roll Hall of Fame; the Great Lakes Science Center; and the Great Lakes Aquarium. This is now an area of vitality, which is a stark juxtaposition to the earlier foreboding and desolate ghost-town ambiance.

These primarily public sector investments stimulated extensive private sector development in nightclubs, bars, and restaurants; in conversion of old warehouses into condominiums; and in apartments. As a result, Cleveland's nickname changed to Miracle on the Lake.

From J. Robert Brown and Michel Laumer. Comeback cities. Urban Land. August 1995: pages 46-51, 83. Copyright ©Urban Land Institute. Used by permission.

that city's redeveloped waterfront. The extensive downtown renovation of Denver was anchored by the new Elitch Gardens amusement park, which moved the park from the city's suburbs, and Coors Field baseball stadium.

The real repositioning opportunity in urban rejuvenation for park and recreation agencies mirrors that associated with business relocation decisions. An agency should seek to become actively involved in economic development forums, with redevelopment councils, and with economic development organizations. Agency personnel should be a community's best repository of knowledge and information of trends elsewhere in the recreation field in both the public and the private sectors. At the same time, through their understanding of the community's needs, they should also be best equipped to identify the types of developments in private recreation and entertainment that are most likely to be viable in that context.

Psychological repositioning may be achieved by the agency's personnel taking leadership in articulating the potential role of recreational facilities in a rejuvenation strategy. Key stakeholders in the community may not be cognizant of its centrality. By creating the vision and arousing awareness, interest, and excitement for the concept, agencies may be successful in psychologically positioning

themselves as leaders in the community's urban rejuvenation effort.

Alleviating Social Problems

Park and recreation services emerged as a social movement at the end of the 19th century. They were spurred by the public's interest in protecting its unique natural resources and the plight of immigrant children.[4] These services were viewed as a means through which social ends could be achieved. It was recognized that the field could make a substantial contribution to society by alleviating or resolving the consequences of contemporary social problems, even though it had limited capacity to address their root causes (which would require changing the structural arrangements of society). Hence, the field traditionally has had a social mandate stemming from negative conditions that affect society.

In recent decades many practitioners and the general public lost sight of this social mandate. Adverse financial conditions forced agencies to become more efficient and effective in their operations, but operational concerns supplanted concerns about mission and values.

By becoming good managers, park and recreation professionals may have done themselves and their systems a disservice. They were more concerned about how they were to perform than why the performance was necessary. This is not an indictment of the need to be effective managers, rather an expression of the times when technique and procedures seemingly were more important than reasons for service (p. 8).[4]

Agencies may achieve repositioning by designing services and highlighting their potential for attaining social ends (especially those of paramount community concern) in ways that save public funds. They can achieve these savings by decreasing costs of law enforcement, social welfare, and health care. Five social ends to which park and recreation agencies can contribute are discussed in this section. They are the alleviation of youth crime, the effects of unemployment, the effects of nonchallenging employment, environmental stress, and the cost of health care.

Youth Crime

There is a long tradition of using park and recreational programs to alleviate youth crime. Indeed, a desire to alleviate delinquent behavior stimulated much early public recreation provision at the beginning of the 20th century. For example, in 1910, the chief planner for the city of Chicago observed: "Police records show an extraordinary decrease of youthful crimes in the neighborhood of playground parks" (p. 147).[24] In the mid-1990s, approximately 1.7 million Americans were incarcerated, which was three times more than in 1980. This was the highest per-capita rate in the world by far and was ten times the rate of incarceration in Western Europe and Japan. The weekly net increase in those going to prison was 1,250. A substantial proportion of this population consisted of young people. The cost to taxpayers of this increased reliance on incarceration was enormous. Spending on prisons exceeded $25 billion each year and was rising faster than all other state expenditures.

Park and recreation agencies are uniquely positioned to be a primary community resource for addressing this issue for at least three reasons:

- First, recreational centers and park areas (where many gangs and deviant youth congregate) are distributed widely across communities and, thus, can be used as service centers for addressing gang- and youth-related problems.

- Second, an agency's personnel are experienced in establishing empathetic relationships with their clients.

- Third, recreational activities are inherently appealing to large segments of youth in general, including at-risk youth, and, thus, offer a vehicle for assessing and positively influencing positive social behavior. An experienced, roving leader who works with at-risk youth said: "I'm interested in the whole kid, in helping him do better in life. Recreation is just the hook to get into a relationship with them. It is what I use to collar them. If I organize a basketball game, they are there. You have to have some way to get them in. If I told them to meet me in church or school, I wouldn't get any of them, but ask them to play basketball and they will be there. However, slowly but surely I can then get them into different community organizations as our relationship strengthens" (p. 90).[25]

If youth crime is a significant issue in a community, then a park and recreation agency may engage in real repositioning by redirecting some of its resources to develop a high-profile, substantive initiative of new or revamped services for at-risk youth. Services would be designed and structured carefully to provide positive alternatives for youth who might otherwise engage in criminal activity. Critical elements in the structuring are likely to be social support from adult leaders, leadership opportunities for youth, opportunities to give intensive and individualized attention to participants, facilitation of a sense of belonging to a group, youth input and decision making in programs, the provision of challenging and interesting activities, and opportunities for community service. An example of a program structured to prevent youth engaging in criminal behavior is described in "An Illustration of Benefits-Based Management: The Totally Cool, Totally Art Program."

Another approach to real positioning is to identify agencies and organizations in the community that are currently perceived as being effective contributors to ameliorating youth crime and to align the park and recreation agency more closely with them. For example, the effective prevention work of the Boys and Girls Clubs is widely acknowledged by elected officials at both local and national levels. Thus, by cooperating and aligning closely with this organization, park and recreation

An Illustration of Benefits-Based Management: The Totally Cool, Totally Art Program

The Totally Cool, Totally Art program was initiated by the Austin Parks and Recreation Department. Through the program, visual arts classes were offered to teens twice each week (on Monday and Wednesday or on Tuesday and Thursday) at nine park department recreational centers. Each session lasted four weeks, each site offered six sessions, and each session featured a different art medium. The objectives it was designed to achieve (expressed in benefit terms), the means for achieving the objectives, and the effectiveness measures used to evaluate the program are summarized in table 5.3.

Objectives of the program included providing teens with a safe place to participate in constructive activities, thereby developing a sense of belonging (column 1). The program was designed to increase teens' art knowledge and skills and their interest in art as a possible career field. Other objectives were to increase teens' trust and respect for other teens and authority figures, to increase teens' ability to work cooperatively and to communicate effectively in a group setting, and to use art as a medium to stimulate meaningful relationships with adult mentors (both artists and teen leaders).

At each site, the Totally Cool, Totally Art program began at approximately 4:30 P.M. with a 1 h tutoring program or other activity organized by the teen leader at the host center. From 5:30 P.M. to 7:30 P.M., a practicing artist, with the assistance of the teen leaders, offered a class in a particular art medium. Participants signed up for as many sessions as they wanted. The target group size at each site ranged from 8 to 20 participants. For some of the sessions (claymation and computer animation) where specialized equipment or facilities were required, teens were transported to a specialized arts center for that portion of the program. At the end of the program, an open house was held at which the teens' art work was displayed, and family, friends, and the public were invited to attend.

Evaluation measures of the program included program workload (participation), efficiency (cost per participant-hour), quality (participants' ratings of the quality of selected elements of the program, e.g., program leaders, facilities, etc.), and effectiveness (the degree to which program goals were achieved). The protective factors scale, which was developed to measure effectiveness by assessing the extent to which intended benefits were delivered, was a key element in the evaluation procedures.[a] The chart, which is shown as table 5.3, identifies the subscales of the protective factors scale that were relevant to measuring program outcomes.

Development of this chart helped program supervisors, teen leaders, and artists to communicate better what benefits they were trying to deliver through the program, to relate better the program activities to the program goals, and ultimately to see the relevance of particular evaluation strategies. The process kept the program leaders clearly focused on program outcomes and helped funders (in this case the city council) evaluate the effectiveness of their investment in these programs.

[a]The protective factors scale is described in Peter A. Witt and John L. Crompton. 1997. The protective factors framework: A key to programming for benefits and evaluating for results. *Journal of Park and Recreation Administration*, 15(3). pp.1-18.

agencies may acquire some of these positive perceptions by association and consequent osmosis and may use them to enhance their own position in decision makers' minds.

Psychological repositioning could involve pointing out the cost efficiency of prevention strategies compared with the costs of incarceration. Figure 5.4 on page 134 offers an effective way of psycho-

logically positioning the cost efficiency of prevention programs.

In the context of at-risk youth, an agency's primary competitor for public funds is most frequently the police department. Thus, a competitive repositioning strategy could involve subtly and sensitively pointing out the fallacies inherent in the public and conventional political perception

Table 5.3 The Totally Cool, Totally Art Program

Objectives	Means for achieving objectives	Means for measuring objectives

Safe places/sense of belonging: to increase teens' sense of belonging and teens' feeling that they have safe, positive, and creative environments in which to participate during available free time.	a) create positive, supportive art class and mentoring environment.
	b) provide environment that respects the creativity and ability of each participant.
	c) provide opportunities for teens to be responsible and make positive choices through their participation in art activities.
		Protective factor subscales:
		  Neighborhood resources
		  Interested and caring adults
		  Sense of acceptance and belonging
		Other effectiveness measures:
		  Repeat attendance, and willingness to recruit other teens to join the program

New experiences: to provide opportunities for new experiences in order to increase participants' knowledge, skills, and possible interest in art as a career field.	a) provide opportunities for youth to be exposed to and to participate in a variety of art mediums.
	b) provide professional artists and quality arts supplies and equipment for teens to enable them to gain an appreciation of and skills in the visual arts.
	c) provide opportunities for teens to expand their imagination, creativity, and self-confidence through their involvement in art activities.
	d) provide teens with information about other community arts opportunities and possible career choices for people who are interested in the arts (e.g., resource lists, field trips, guest speakers, planning other arts activities).
		Protective factor subscales:
		  Neighborhood resources
		  Value on achievement
		  Positive attitude toward the future
		  Perceived competence in art
		Other effectiveness measures:
		  Rating of "Overall, my experience in the program was . . ."

Respect/trust: to increase teens' trust and respect for other teens, adult mentors, artists, and other authority figures.	a) provide opportunities for youth to interact with adult role models (e.g., center staff, artists, and other adults) who keep their word and create a supportive learning atmosphere.
	b) utilize both recreation center teen leaders and artists as collaborative program leaders so teens can benefit from contact with different artists while maintaining consistent contact over time with center teen leaders.
	c) provide opportunities for youth to interact with other teens in an environment that encourages respect and trust.
	d) provide opportunities for teens to create and strengthen friendships with other teens.
	e) provide opportunities for teens to learn responsible behavior through care and use of art supplies and equipment and through following curriculum directions and rules.
	f) provide opportunities for teens to act responsibly in the storage and protection of their own and others' art work.
		Protective factor subscales:
		  Ability to work with others
		  Ability to work out conflicts
		  Models for conventional behavior
		  Interested and caring adults
		Other effectiveness measures:
		  Ratings of
		  Knowledge, teaching ability, and preparation of teen leaders and artists
		  Impact of program on ability to care for art supplies and equipment, care for their own art work and art work of others, and respect the artistic and creative choices of others

Objectives	Means for achieving objectives	Means for measuring objectives

Team work/communication: increase teens' ability to work cooperatively with other teens and communicate effectively in a group.	a) encourage opportunities for teens to share ideas, supplies, and other resources and to resolve problems and conflicts through collaborative efforts.
	b) provide opportunities for teens to improve their ability to communicate and gain feedback about their ideas, thoughts, emotions, and experiences through their art work.
	c) provide opportunities for teens to learn about the activities and involvements of other program participants through program newsletters.
	d) provide opportunities to gain knowledge about and better understand cultural diversity through discussion of art from various cultures and historical periods.
		Protective factor subscales:
		    Ability to work out conflicts
		    Ability to work with others
		    High controls against deviant
		      behavior

Art education: to increase teens' ability to make creative and positive choices through self-expression.	a) provide an opportunity for teens to learn new or strengthen existing visual arts education concepts and skills.
	b) provide opportunities for teens to make creative choices about the content and product of their own artistic endeavors.
	c) provide opportunities to discuss and analyze the criteria and decision making processes used to select art work for exhibition at the open house.
	d) provide opportunities for teens to gain recognition and increase their pride in their accomplishments through exhibiting some of their art work at the culminating open house event.
	e) provide experiences through the arts that relate to math, history, language, etc. and thereby increase interest in school.
		Protective factor subscales:
		    Positive attitude toward the
		      future
		    Perceived art competence
		Other effectiveness measures:
		    Ratings of:
		    Impact of program on ability
		      to use imagination, share
		      ideas with others, finish
		      projects

that more vigorous law enforcement, more police, and more prisons are the best solution to the juvenile crime problem.

The potential return to jurisdictions investing in prevention programs can be calculated by tracking reductions in crime and ascribing a financial value to them. During the past decade, the clearance rates reported annually by law enforcement agencies nationwide for major offenses by juveniles who were less than 18 years of age have been remarkably stable at 20% to 21%. An offense is declared cleared or solved when at least one person is arrested and charged with its commission. The major crimes to which these statistics relate are murder and non-negligent manslaughter, forcible rape, robbery, aggravated assault, burglary, larceny theft, motor vehicle theft, and arson. However, the 20% to 21% clearance rate overestimates the proportion of crimes cleared because data from the Federal Bureau of Investigation indicate that many major crimes are not reported to the police. The level of underreporting includes 50% of all violent crimes, 30% of personal thefts, 41% of household crimes, and 75% of motor vehicle thefts.[26] Hence, for the purposes of this discussion, it has been assumed that 14%, rather

It costs approximately $30,000 to incarcerate a juvenile offender for one year.

If that money were available to the Parks Department, we could:

Take him swimming twice a week for 24 weeks, *and*

Give him four tours of the Zoo, plus lunch, *and*

Enroll him in 50 Community Center programs, *and*

Visit Oxley Nature Center twice, *and*

Let him play league softball for a season, *and*

Tour the garden at Woodward Park twice, *and*

Give him two weeks of tennis lessons, *and*

Enroll him in two weeks of day camp, *and*

Let him play three rounds of golf, *and*

Act in one play, *and*

Participate in one fishing clinic, *and*

Take a four-week pottery class, *and*

Play basketball eight hours a week for 40 weeks after which we could return to you:

$29,125 and one much happier kid.

Figure 5.4 An example of psychologically repositioning the cost efficiency of park and recreation programs for at-risk youth.

Bob Jennings. Naturalist. Oxley Nature Center. Quoted in the City of Tulsa's Marketing Plan.

than 20% to 21%, of youth crimes are solved. Of these, approximately one-third are acquitted or dismissed. Of the 9% to 10% of juveniles who are convicted, approximately one-half receive sentences that do not involve incarceration.

Obviously, incarceration is an essential component in alleviating juvenile crime. However, if only 5% of the juveniles committing crimes are incarcerated and 95% of them remain available to engage in more crime, then a strategy focused predominantly on incarceration cannot solve the problem! If this is pointed out and repeatedly reiterated to stakeholders, especially elected officials, then there is likely to be a realization that for major progress to be made, resources have to be allocated to prevention programs that target the overwhelming majority who are not arrested and incarcerated. Further, the evidence clearly indicates that early and consistent prevention efforts have the best chance of diminishing the need for more costly measures later.

Competitive repositioning may be reinforced by citing findings that show citizens' support for prevention programs. For example, the data in

figure 5.5 indicate far more support for investing funds on youth prevention programs than for using these resources to put an additional 100,000 police officers on the streets, which was the action taken by Congress and the Clinton administration at that time.

Psychological repositioning requires agencies to measure and then to communicate the success of their programs in positively changing the behavior of at-risk youth. The city of Fort Worth provided an illustration of how this may be done effectively. The city used a holistic approach involving coordinated action from a number of city departments to address the problem of serious gang-related crime. The Fort Worth Parks and Community Services Department (which includes recreation) played a central role in the effort. Table 5.4 shows data that compare the number of serious offenses in 1994 (before the program was launched) with the number in 1996 (two years after the initiative was implemented).

The 26% improvement, reflecting 180 fewer offenses, was dramatic. In addition to the human savings in personal and social suffering that accrued, the monetary savings to the community were likely to be substantial. The Criminal Justice Policy Council of Texas reported that the cost of keeping Texas Youth Commission clients in institutional facilities at that time was $119.49 per day, or $43,494.00 per year.[27] These costs underestimated the expense of incarcerating youth because they did not include court costs (e.g., judges, prosecuting and defense counsel, and all associated staff), police costs associated with making an arrest, or the cost of the juvenile crimes to victims and their families. Compare these costs with an annual cost of $170 per child (which was reported at that time in a survey of approximately 200 park and recreation agencies) for servicing at-risk youth with year-round recreational programs.[28] If a park and recreation agency could successfully keep even one of 256 youth served from being incarcerated in an institutional facility, then it saved the community money. Those are pretty good odds!

In Fort Worth, if the 180 fewer offenses had been committed by 100 young people, for example, and if all of these individuals had been arrested and incarcerated, then using the Texas Youth Commission's data, the cost of incarcerating them for one year would have been more than $4.3 million. Given the gravity of the offenses, it appears reasonable to hypothesize that each of the individuals could have been incarcerated for an average of 10 years. With this assumption, the costs

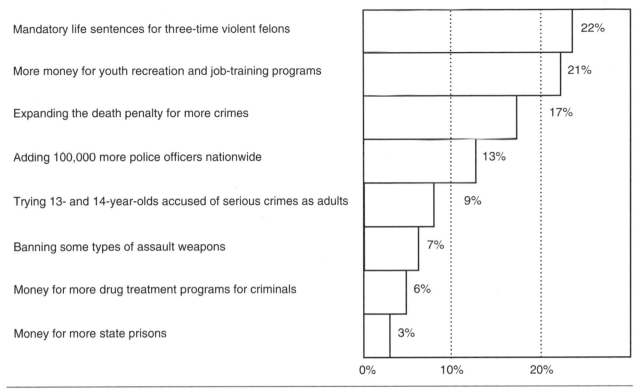

Figure 5.5 Which proposal would be most effective in reducing crime in this country?

Data from a nationwide telephone survey of 1,682 adults age 18 and older conducted by the *Los Angeles Times*, 1994.

Table 5.4 Change in the Number of Serious Gang-Related Offenses Committed in Fort Worth Between 1994 and 1996

Category	1994	1996	Percent of change
Capital murder/murder	37	7	–81%
Aggravated sexual assault	3	5	67%
Robbery/aggravated robbery	116	91	–22%
Criminal attempted murder/aggravated assault	421	294	–30%
Burglary	43	42	–2%
Theft	35	37	5%
Auto theft	25	24	–.5%
Totals	680	500	(26.48)%

then escalate to $43 million (ignoring the time value of money). The total investment of city funds in this at-risk youth initiative was $430,000 and $678,000 in fiscal years 1994-95 and 1995-96, respectively. This was supplemented with $156,000 and $278,000 in the respective years from private sources. Thus, the return on each dollar invested by the city was $39 ($43 million ÷ $1.108 million). These calculations do not take into account cost savings that are also likely to have accrued from at-risk youth not engaging in other less serious crimes not considered in table 5.5. This level of return made the investment unbeatable! Certainly the level of return makes it easy for elected officials to justify to their constituents the use of tax money to retain and expand their investment in this program.

The exactness of the numbers is not important. It does not matter if in some jurisdictions juvenile incarceration costs are lower, if city investment is greater, or if the magnitude of crime reduction is lower. The magnitude of the return on investment is so large that even quite major changes in the variables are unlikely to affect the principle.

Unemployment

Contemporary unemployment is largely structural in origin, and threatens to persist. Its main causes are the decline and closure of major sections of traditional industry . . . coupled with the introduction of labor-saving technology (p. 47).[1]

In 1969, only 7% of the labor force in the United States was unemployed or underemployed, but 20 years later, this figure was almost 17%.[14] The underemployed population is growing more rapidly than the unemployed population. Underemployed refers to those people who work part time but desire to work full time. This has resulted from businesses preferring to hire part-time employees to avoid the cost of fringe benefits and to have their existing staff work overtime to avoid the cost of hiring and terminating new employees in response to changes in economic conditions. These changes in the nature of the economy mean that there are jurisdictions and specific target groups where unemployment is a major social problem.

The unemployed work force who are measured in official statistics are adults at least 16 years of age who are not employed, are available for employment (not injured or ill), and actively are seeking employment. This definition reveals the relatively conservative nature of official unemployment statistics because it excludes people who are not actively seeking employment. Although fluctuations in the state of the national economy influence unemployment statistics, they remained remarkably consistent among young males in the 15-year period shown in table 5.5. Given the conservativeness of the official definition of unemployment, the data in table 5.5 suggest that there is a major opportunity for agencies in some locales to target unemployed youth, who in many instances are likely to be the same individuals described in the previous section as being at risk.

Unemployment is usually an unpleasant, unwelcome experience that is personally devastating to individuals, often leads to a deterioration in their physical and mental health, and increases the likelihood that these disaffected people—especially the young unemployed—will engage in behavior that is disruptive to society. Park and recreation agencies have a long tradition, dating back to the depression years of the 1930s, of responding to the needs of the unemployed by providing programs, activities, and job opportunities for them. However, a survey of 254 park and recreation departments in American cities in the 1990s, concerned with identifying their efforts to reach the unemployed, concluded that departments "do a poor job of addressing the needs of unemployed people" (p. 32).[29] The authors reported that only 1% of all responding agencies provided programs specifically for unemployed constituents. Less than 40% of agencies even offered price discounts for the unemployed, and this percentage was generally higher in communities

Table 5.5 Percentage of Range of Young Males Unemployed, 1980 to 1995

| | 16-19 years old | | | 20-24 years old | |
	High	Low		High	Low
All	21.5	16.3		12.5	9.1
Hispanic	27.5	19.5		13.2	9.1
Black	40.2	30.9		23.8	17.1

Source: U.S. Bureau of Labor Statistics. *Employment and Earnings.* January issues annually 1980 to 1995.

with low unemployment than in those with high unemployment! These findings reinforced findings of another study that concluded: "The results suggest that the leisure service delivery system does not have a good understanding of the barriers to increased participation by the unemployed" (p. 125).[30]

Participation in recreational programs cannot be a satisfactory substitute for a job.

What work removes, leisure cannot replace. This is most obvious in the case of income, and indeed the poverty of the unemployed is a prime constraint on their leisure. Far from taking on new and varied leisure interests to absorb the time freed from work, financial restrictions mean that for most unemployed people, previous leisure patterns are curtailed (p. 158).[1]

Further, many of those who are most likely and frequently to be unemployed are not leisurely literate; that is, they do not have a repertoire of recreational skills or interests. Nevertheless, there may be an opportunity for repositioning because park and recreation services targeted at the unemployed can fulfill some of the functions traditionally supplied by employment for some individuals and, thus, contribute to alleviating this social problem.[1]

- At the simplest level, they can fill time. This may reduce the potential for societal disruption: "That 'the devil makes work for idle hands' has long been feared to be more than merely proverbial, and so 'idle hands' must be provided with things to do and reasons to get involved" (p. 131).[1]
- Everyone needs to feel needed. Many people derive this feeling from their jobs. It has been observed that employment provides both a social setting and an identity to people in their broader social relationships. Thus, when people are introduced for the first time, one of the opening questions is likely to be, What do you do? Inability to offer a work response to the question often leads to problems of self-worth and identity. Park and recreational programs may partially alleviate this by fostering an interest and involvement in something the individual perceives to be worthwhile. This may incorporate the development of skills, achievement of results, and a sense of purpose.

- Most people are accustomed to organizing their daily and weekly routines around externally imposed time constraints. Structure is regarded by many as a basic human need, and the loss of structure has been found by some to be the most psychologically destructive consequence of unemployment. Participation in regularly scheduled programs may provide some semblance of this structure.
- They can foster and sustain friendships and a sense of belonging.

These benefits are exemplified in comments made by unemployed people who have participated in such programs:

— "It's enjoyable company, you make friends. At the beginning I did it to pass the time, now I do it because I really enjoy it."

— "I think the program is an excellent idea and gives people who are unemployed something to look forward to, as well as getting them out of the house."

— "Before I went I hated myself because I wasn't putting anything into society, but now I feel fit and more sure of myself."

— "I have become more confident with people since starting these activities" (p. 139).[1]

Real positioning would involve linking with unemployment and social welfare agencies to develop holistic strategies for alleviating the problem. Empirical studies have confirmed that park and recreational activities have the potential to change the lives of some unemployed people by providing the basis for an alternative lifestyle, resulting in relatively contented unemployment. For example, one researcher concluded: "This study does suggest that leisure activity has a role to play in helping unemployed people gain satisfactions that were previously obtained through work" (p. 125).[30] Their numbers may be relatively small, but the influence may be major. For some others, such programs may offer temporary relief from the boredom and frustration of unemployment. The success of these services, as with the at-risk youth programs, depends on the leadership of those responsible for delivering them. Their job is not only to deliver recreational programs to this target group but also to engage in outreach work, to get to know and understand unemployed people, and to offer services that meet their needs.

If financial barriers to participation can be removed, it seems likely that park and recreational programs can have some mitigating effect on the experience of unemployment because:

> The losses incurred in unemployment are closely matched in typical motivations for taking part in leisure activities. Quests for identity, purpose, activity, social contacts, self-confidence, self-esteem, relaxation, and physical and mental well-being—and even, at the most basic level, the search for something to do—are the established stock-in-trade of the psychology of leisure. If unemployment leaves these needs unmet, leisure ought partly at least to be able to fulfil them (p. 92).[1]

Some agencies are reluctant to target this group for philosophical reasons. For example, one respondent to a survey noted: "The answer to unemployment and low income is to help people help themselves, not to make them thrilled with their present circumstances" (p. 32).[29] Encouraging involvement of the unemployed in recreational programs is helping them to help themselves. Further, those people officially recognized as being unemployed by definition include only able-bodied adults who are actively searching for work. This tendency to view the unemployed as blameworthy for their plight and as being lazy spongers on welfare who live at the expense of decent working people is becoming less widespread as more people have acquaintances in their social circles who have been subjected to unemployment. It touches the professional and managerial classes much more lightly than the poor, but even here it is a growing reality.

The real and psychological repositioning obtained by developing recreational programs for the unemployed has been accentuated by some agencies that have moved directly into job training.

The Tampa parks department hired two crews in summer employment programs. Each crew consisted of 15 youth between 14 and 18 years of age who were unemployed, from low-income backgrounds, and at risk or in legal trouble. The first crew worked constructing boardwalks and fishing piers for 4 h per day and 20 h per week under the guidance of a professional carpenter. They were also required to go for 2 h each day to a local vocational school to improve their reading and writing skills. The second crew were integrated into existing park crews and assigned a mentor.

They also worked for 20 h per week and were involved in a customized training program learning to read and to do math by using grounds-maintenance-type problems and activities. They were also taught how to open a bank account, to use a computer, to design a landscape plan, and to identify plants.[31]

Nonchallenging Employment

For a growing number of Americans who are employed, the potential for deriving satisfaction from their work is small. Many people have had to reduce their aspirations and to take jobs for which they technically are overqualified, with a result that they find the work boring, frustrating, and generally not satisfying. Further, there is evidence that the risk of unemployment causes people to stay in jobs they dislike and even to forego the opportunity of a better job elsewhere because they fear loss of seniority would leave them more vulnerable to being made redundant in the new organization at the first economic downturn.

Table 5.6 shows projections made by the U.S. Bureau of Labor Statistics of the occupations that are likely to experience the largest job growth between 1994 and 2005. This list is illustrative of the shift away from a manufacturing economy toward a service economy. The only categories that are not relatively low level in status and pay are registered nurses, general managers and top executives, and systems analysts. Basic psychological needs that many people derive from their work will be difficult to acquire in positions such as cashier, janitor, and cleaner. Such needs may include self-esteem, prestige accruing from peer-group recognition, ego satisfaction of achievement, a desire to be successful, excitement, and self-worth. These needs are derived from the feeling of being important and having responsibility.

For the growing number of people in those types of jobs, these basic psychological needs will be obtained in their familial or leisure milieus, or they will not be obtained at all. Like the youth at risk and the unemployed who were discussed in the previous subsections, the low-paid, low-status employed constitute a potentially disaffected, alienated group with a need to find meaning for their lives in a leisure milieu. This is the meaning of the leisure revolution. It has nothing to do with the availability of time; rather, it has to do with where people find their reason for being. For many, it is found increasingly in a leisure rather than a work context.

Table 5.6   Occupations Preferred to Have the Largest Job Growth 1994 to 2005

Occupation	Employment (1,000)		Percent change 1994-2005
	1994	2005	
Cashiers	3005	3567	18.7%
Janitors and cleaners	3043	3602	18.4%
Retail salespersons	3842	4374	13.8%
Waiters and waitresses	1847	2326	25.9%
Registered nurses	1906	2379	24.8%
General managers and top executives	3046	3522	15.3%
Systems analysts	483	928	92.1%
Home health aids	420	848	102.0%
Guards	867	1282	47.9%
Nursing aids, orderlies, and attendants	1265	1652	30.6%

Source: U.S. Bureau of Labor Statistics.1995 *Monthly Labor Review*, November.

The list showing major new job categories also explains in part why poverty rates among the employed are soaring.[5] In 1980, 20% of all people aged 18 to 24 years who worked full time did not earn sufficient income to exceed the federal government's official poverty-level criterion. By the mid-1990s, this figure had increased to almost 50%. Approximately one-half of the people aged 18 to 24 years who work full time are officially classified as poor. The implications for park and recreation agencies are clear.

As sociologists say, their life chances are going to be considerably diminished. They will be primary clientele for local recreation and park agencies but only if they are paid attention to. Many of them have not been socialized into using local recreation and park services. They need to be, not only because there is ample evidence that they lack leisure skills, but also because their options in terms of using the commercial sector are going to be very limited. They also need to be listened to (p. 18).[5]

The real and psychological repositioning opportunities associated with aligning to alleviate youth crime and the effects of unemployment can be extended to include those in nonchallenging employment.

Environmental Stress

Uncomfortable environmental stress is a condition experienced daily by many who live or commute in urban or blighted areas. The stress may involve both psychological emotions, such as frustration, anger, fear, and coping responses, and associated physiological responses that use energy and contribute to fatigue. Its detrimental impact to health and well-being may be manifested in characteristics such as headaches, tension, short temper, aggressive temper, low morale, and increase in number of sick days away from work.

Surroundings influence individuals' outlook on life, their sense of well-being, and ultimately their attitude and behavior toward others. Different outdoor environments can have quite different influences on inflicting or ameliorating stress, and parks and natural vegetation have long been known to have a restorative effect by fostering psychological well-being. In 1865 Frederick Law Olmsted wrote insightfully about stresses associated with cities and job demands and argued that viewing nature was effective in inducing recovery from such stresses: "Olmsted's instinctively-based ideas about the restorative effect of nature formed an important part of his influential justification for providing pastoral parks and other nature in America's cities, and for preserving wilderness such as the Yosemite Valley for public use" (p. 204).[32]

Parks have been aptly described as still eyes in the hurricane of the city, as safety valves for the release of the tensions of modern life, and as the city's lungs which enable people to breathe in relaxation and escape pressure. When overcrowded; surrounded by a harsh, callous, and perhaps deteriorating physical environment; or harassed, human beings frequently show traits of aggression. This has led to the following suggestion:

It is time to consider the environmental conditions that may promote hostility and antisocial behavior. This is not meant to minimize the negative impacts of chronic unemployment, drug addiction, broken homes and the general feeling of hopelessness that pervade many inner-city communities. Nevertheless, many urban problems may come down to a simple question: Are our attitudes and behaviors resulting from them influenced by the physical environment in which we live and work? . . . It is surprising that programs that permit residents to introduce nature into inner-city neighborhoods are rarely listed among priority approaches for addressing urban problems (p. 52).[33]

The authors of more than 100 studies of recreational experiences and urban nature areas have reported that stress mitigation is one of the most important verbally expressed perceived benefits. Urban settings that prominently include vegetation are less stressful than settings that lack a natural component. Such settings for urbanites may include, for example, viewing trees or flowers through a window in a workplace or residence, lunching in a park, or driving on a tree-lined boulevard or on roads with landscaped vegetation medians.

Stress managers will tell you that one of their most successful techniques for reducing stress is visualization. If you ask them what people visualize when they wish to relax, they never say parking lots or freeways or baseball stadiums. What do they mention? . . . forests and mountains and sea-coasts.

So, if this is what reduces stress and gives people a sense of emotional stability, why not take it seriously? Maybe what we need in every city are more parks and gardens and more places where people can physically connect with what is natural and peaceful rather than with purely imaginary landscapes or some form of virtual reality (p. 24).[34]

Conclusions demonstrating the therapeutic value of natural settings have been derived not only from psychological studies but also from physiological measurements of cardiovascular activity, including heart rate and blood pressure; skin conductance, which the autonomic nervous system controls; and muscle tension, which the central nervous system controls. The physiological studies tend to be given greater scientific credibility, especially by the court system.

In an early classic study of this genre of using physiological measures completed in 1984, the authors found that hospital patients recovering from surgery had more favorable recovery courses, including shorter hospital stays, lower intake of potent narcotic pain drugs, and more favorable evaluations by nurses, if their windows overlooked trees rather than a brick building.[31] Authors of studies researching patient anxiety in a dental clinic and using self-analysis and heart-rate data suggested that patients felt less stressed on days when a large mural depicting a natural scene was hung on a wall of the waiting room than on days when the wall was blank.[32] These findings from studies of health-care facilities are paralleled by results from prisons suggesting that cell-window views of nature are associated with lower frequencies of prisoner stress symptoms, such as digestive illness and headaches, and with fewer sick calls.[32] These physiological studies strongly suggest that recuperation from stress occurs much faster and more completely when individuals are exposed to natural rather than urban environments. The leading researcher in this field suggested "that even short duration leisure contact with nature might be important to many urbanites in fostering restoration from mild stressors such as daily hassles or annoyances" (p. 83).[35]

The cost of environmental stress in terms of work days lost and medical care is likely to be substantially greater than the cost of providing and maintaining parks, urban forestry programs, and oases of flowers and shrubs. The harshness of the physical environment in many urban areas may contribute to the sense of social deprivation, anger, and aggressive temper that lead to antisocial behavior. Agencies providing these restorative amenities can psychologically reposition by pointing out the recuperative benefits that accrue, and other agencies could engage in real positioning by becoming advocates for such amenities.

Cost of Health Care

The United States spends more than $400 billion annually (which is approximately 14% of its gross national product) on the medical enterprise, and containment of medical costs has become a high-profile political problem.[3] It will be a continuing priority of government entities and other institutions that are responsible for meeting these costs. This may provide park and recreation agencies with a repositioning opportunity.

There has been growing recognition that the key to curtailing health costs lies in prevention of illness so it does not have to be treated by the expensive medical system. One manifestation of that awareness is the more than 350 hospital-operated fitness centers that now exist.[36] These wellness centers are attractive to hospitals because managed care is giving them strong incentive to keep patients healthy and limit costly medical procedures. Members pay fees that tend to be substantially higher than fees paid to ordinary private fitness clubs, so most of these hospital-operated centers are profitable.

The most significant advances in public health have been in the prevention, not the treatment, of disease.

> Our state of health is largely determined by how we live our everyday lives, our behaviors, emotions and, sometimes, our luck. Doctors are not a very important part of health care, although they can sometimes help. What is most important is our own personal habits and our collective social actions (p. 59).[3]

Health is not merely the presence or absence of disease but a continuum representing all levels of vitality from the utmost to the lowest endpoint (euphoria to death!).[37] Healthy refers not only to physical well-being but also to the status of a number of related processes. It involves a holistic integration of the physical, emotional, spiritual, intellectual, and social dimensions of people's lives. If any of them are unbalanced, then it can lead to individuals seeking help from the health-care system. Frequently, the popular view of the contribution of park and recreation agencies to health is limited to their potential for improving physical fitness through exercise. This is a myopic perspective because their role in facilitating positive emotional, intellectual, and social experiences is well documented.

It has been observed that people with high levels of wellness are likely to act during their free time rather than merely to be acted on.[7] Such action must be thought of holistically rather than just in terms of physical behavior. Psychological repositioning would involve pointing out that park

and recreation agencies offer opportunities for people to act. These contrast with vicariously experienced, passive entertainment that involves being acted upon by television, narcotics, or displays in a shopping mall. These things do not provide the challenge, arousal, creation, complexity, or stimulation that may emerge from active engagement in recreational activities.[7]

If people's main motivation for engaging in activities is a belief that it will be good for them, they are likely to quit after a short time period irrespective of whether the activity is dieting to lose weight, joining exercise classes to become fit, or eating only foods that are good for them. The only enduring lifestyle changes are likely to be those in which activities are undertaken for the intrinsic enjoyment and satisfaction that they yield. Such intrinsic values are a central goal of park and recreation services. Thus, psychological repositioning could suggest that park and recreation services are, in essence, health services.

> These services provide sustained opportunities by which citizens can increase their physical fitness, reduce stress, reduce substance abuse, meditate, learn new skills which lead to higher self-esteem, lessen social isolation and depression and do many other things which improve health. They also provide parks and open spaces which improve air quality, moderate temperature and provide opportunities for tranquility (p. 74).[3]

The prevailing fiscal concern relating to the cost of health care, and the potential of park and recreation services for alleviating it, may provide agencies with an opportunity to reposition by making their services the means through which people achieve wellness. For many agencies, no real repositioning in terms of service offerings would be necessary because they already are delivering these services. However, additional real repositioning may be achieved by linking with health organizations in the community that have an existing high profile in this area. There are many precedents of health organizations partnering with park and recreation agencies to fund and operate facilities and services that have measurable health outcomes. Examples are given in chapter 8.

Competitive repositioning may be facilitated by a financial comparison of the relative efficiency of park and recreation services and medical procedures in addressing health issues.

> The cost-to-benefit ratios are compelling. For an annual tax fee of $50 to $60 per person, a

typical local park and recreation agency provides a wide array of health-enhancing services. The amount paid for a typical heart bypass operation ($60,000, for example) would fund local government park and recreation services for approximately 1,200 people for one year at $50 per person per year. Of those 1,200 people, 948 people would use such services, based on national data relating to the use of public park and recreational facilities; the non-users would also derive considerable benefits. If you were in charge of improving health and wellness services for the American public and had a shrinking pool of money to do so, who ya gonna call? (p. 105)[38]

There are two pragmatic difficulties to surmount in moving from the strong conceptual arguments to effectively repositioning through aligning with the movement to contain health-care costs. The first challenge is structural. Institutional concern for the cost of health care is the domain of federal and, to a lesser extent, state governments; employers; insurance companies; and medical industries. The cost is not on the list of many local governments' concerns because most of them do not have direct responsibility for delivering or funding health-care services. Thus, any cost savings would not improve their budgets.

The second challenge is empirical. A substantial body of evidence documents the benefits that arise from participation in regular physical activity, particularly with reference to the incidence of cardiovascular disease. This evidence has been derived from two types of studies. Authors of epidemiologic studies have observed populations on a longitudinal basis over many years and have compared levels of cardiovascular disease of people in those populations who do and who do not exercise. These studies have been complemented by experimental studies in which groups were given exercise regimens of varying frequency, duration, and intensity; the results were compared with control groups who did not engage in the regimens.

Nevertheless, assessing the extent to which these results, or results relating to dimensions of wellness other than physical fitness, could be attributed to services and facilities that park and recreation agencies provide would be extremely difficult to measure. This is the same measurement problem that has confronted major companies that have made, or have considered making, substantial investments in wellness programs and facilities. Available evidence is inconclusive.

One company president typified the ambivalence of the empirical data related to corporate fitness centers when he observed: "We're having trouble quantifying how beneficial it could be to productivity and to our employees' health. We think that the benefits outweigh the downsides, but we don't know" (p. 30).[39] Despite the lack of hard evidence that they save money, many large companies have adopted the wellness concept. Driven by runaway insurance costs and absenteeism, executives tend to justify the programs with the type of commonsense arguments noted earlier in this subsection. For many companies, the 10% of employees with expensive problems, such as

General Motors' FitnessWorks Wellness Center

General Motors and the Henry Ford Health System opened an $11 million corporate wellness center, FitnessWorks, in downtown Detroit. The 75,000 sq ft center accommodated General Motors' employees with all of the amenities associated with state-of-the-art health clubs: cardiovascular and strength-training areas; a gymnasium; a jogging track; racquet courts; swimming pools; an aerobic studio; and extras, such as a batting cage, a juice bar, saunas, and steam rooms. However, it also includes the Henry Ford LeVine Cardiac Wellness Center, the Henry Ford Occupational Health Center, and the Henry Ford Center for Athletic Medicine—three facilities operated by Henry Ford Health System, a $2 billion health-care organization that serves 20,000 employees in southern Michigan and northern Ohio.

Both groups had high hopes for the center: Henry Ford Health System, because it had a major financial stake in the health of its 500,000 health maintenance organization members; and General Motors, because it had made lopping 20% off its $5 billion annual health-care bill a priority.

Adapted from Andrew Cohen. Putting wellness to work. Athletic Business. March 1997, page 29.

heart disease, account for 70% to 80% of their total medical bill. Averting even a few of these cases could create huge savings. It seems likely that park and recreation agencies seeking to reposition by aligning with containment of health costs would have to rely on similar arguments to make their case.

Summary

Nurturing a broader constituency base through repositioning the field is perhaps the single most important task in retaining or securing more resources for park and recreation services. The task involves moving the field away from its present position of being perceived as relatively discretionary and nonessential to a position where even off-site stakeholders regard it as being a central contributor to alleviating the prevailing economic and social problems in a jurisdiction. Three strategies may be pursued to achieve this shift. Real repositioning means that an agency changes what it does. This may involve changing its program offerings and changing the types of alliances and partnerships it forms and the community forums in which it becomes involved. Competitive repositioning involves altering stakeholders' beliefs about what an agency's competitors do. Finally, psychological repositioning means altering stakeholders' beliefs about what an agency currently does.

The starting point for repositioning an agency is to ask the question: "What are the most important political concerns in this community?" When these have been identified and prioritized the next question is: "With which of these concerns can this department align itself and contribute to addressing?" An agency should focus on one or two of these concerns that it is best equipped to address. If its efforts are dissipated by trying to align with a greater number of issues, then the result is likely to be a fuzzy, confused position rather than a clear position in stakeholders' minds.

In some cases, real repositioning is not necessary because the agency already is addressing a major political concern. However, it may not be receiving public and political credit for its efforts because either they are not sufficiently visible or they are overshadowed by the involvement of other agencies who are perceived as being more effective. In these situations, the challenge is to align more closely with those effective agencies (real repositioning), to measure and communicate the effectiveness of the agency's efforts (psycho-logical repositioning), and to subtly lower the public's perceptions of the contributions of other agencies who are competitors for funds and who have created myths and exaggerated their effectiveness (competitive repositioning).

The most prominent issues confronting elected officials will vary across jurisdictions, but they can be classified generally into the two categories: economic development and alleviation of social problems. Park and recreational facilities and services can contribute to economic development in at least six ways. The most obvious way is their central role in tourism. Attractions activate the tourism system; they are what cause tourists to visit a selected destination. A large proportion of the attractions that stimulate pleasure travel are likely to be the responsibility of park and recreation agencies. As part of their psychological repositioning strategy, agencies should produce economic, as well as financial, balance sheets showing their role in bringing new dollars into the community. They may also consider changing the agency's name so that it better represents its central role in tourism. They could engage in real repositioning by packaging their services and promoting them to potential visitor groups.

Quality of life in an area is a primary concern for both footloose businesses and retirees when they seek a new location. Park and recreation amenities are central components of quality of life. Indeed, there are no great cities that do not have a great parks, recreation, and cultural system. Among retirees, these amenities and a year-round warm climate dominate all other criteria. Among businesses, small business owners are influenced particularly by the quality of park and recreation amenities because their owners are likely to select a location where they can enjoy a preferred lifestyle.

Natural parks in urban areas are a cost-effective use of land. Unlike other uses, such as residential subdivisions, they are frequently profitable investments for governments because they generate more tax revenue than they cost to acquire, develop, and operate. This net surplus is derived from the increment of tax revenue that is attributable to the higher value of property surrounding such parks when compared with the value of similar property elsewhere in the area.

The facilities that public agencies provide are crucial to the economic viability of recreational equipment vendors and manufacturers. An absence or shortage of such facilities will lead to reduced equipment sales. A final contribution of park and recreation amenities to economic development is their role in urban rejuvenation. In many American cities, they have been the centerpiece of such efforts.

The park and recreation field has had a long-established social mandate to alleviate negative conditions that affect society. This was somewhat neglected in the years following the tax revolt. Repositioning the field involves designing services, highlighting their potential for achieving social ends that are of paramount concern to citizens and elected officials, and liaising with organizations in the community that have a high profile in this area. Services aimed at reducing youth crime by targeting at-risk youth have become a major focus of many agencies. Effective psychological repositioning is dependent on evidence that these programs are successful, and multiple sources of such evidence are now available. Critical variables in the success of these programs are likely to be social support from adult leaders, leadership opportunities for youth, opportunities to give intensive and individualized attention to participants, facilitation of a sense of belonging to a group, youth input and decision making in programs, the provision of challenging and interesting activities, and opportunities for community service.

Park and recreation services can contribute to alleviating problems caused by unemployment and underemployment through filling time, providing an interest and a sense of involvement in something worthwhile, and fostering friendships and a sense of belonging. Large numbers of those in full-time employment are in low-paying, low-status positions that do not offer opportunities for fulfilling basic psychological needs. Like the unemployed, such people will acquire those needs in their familial or leisure milieus, or they will not obtain them at all.

The harshness of the physical environment in many urban areas may contribute to the sense of social deprivation, anger, and aggressive temper that lead to antisocial behavior. Parks and recreation can have a restorative effect on uncomfortable stress that such adverse environmental conditions cause. Urban settings that prominently include vegetation are less stressful than settings that lack a natural component. The cost of environmental stress in terms of work days lost and medical care is likely to be substantially greater than the cost of providing and maintaining parks, urban forestry programs, and oases of flowers and shrubs.

Finally, park and recreation services can contribute to the high-profile issue of containing health costs by their potential for facilitating holistic health involving people's physical, emotional, intellectual, and social well-being. These are traditional agency goals. As prevention increasingly is recognized as the key to reducing health-care costs, opportunities may be available to reposition services as being an effective mechanism for containing health costs.

References

1. Glyptis, Sue. 1989. *Leisure and unemployment*. Milton Keynes, England: Open University.

2. Driver, Beverly L. and Donald H. Bruns. 1998. Concepts and uses of the benefits approach to leisure. In *Leisure studies at the millennium*, edited by Tim Burton and Edgar Jackson. State College, PA: Venture Publishing.

3. Godbey, Geoffrey. 1991. Redefining public parks and recreation. *Parks and Recreation* 26(10): 58-61, 74.

4. Sessoms, H. Douglas. 1993. Justification for our services: Have we lost our way? *Trends* 30(4): 6-8.

5. Godbey, Geoffrey. 1994. Extraordinary change: A few implications for recreation and parks. *TRAPS Magazine* Spring: 16-18.

6. Kotler, Philip, Donald H. Haider and Irving Rein. 1993. *Marketing places: Attracting investment, industry, and tourism to cities, states and nations*. New York: Free Press.

7. Godbey, Geoffrey. 1993. The contribution of recreation and parks to reducing health care costs: From theory to practice. *Trends* 30(4): 37-41.

8. Zeigler, Jeffrey B., Lowel M. Caneday and Priscilla R. Baker. 1992. Symbiosis between tourism and our national parks. *Parks and Recreation* 27(9): 74-79.

9. Crompton, John L. 1995. Economic impact analysis of sports facilities and events: Eleven sources of misapplication. *Journal of Sports Management* 9(1): 14-35.

10. Crompton, John L., Lisa L. Love and Thomas A. More. 1997. Characteristics of companies that considered recreation/parks/open space to be important in (re)location decisions. *Journal of Park and Recreation Administration* 15(1): 37-58.

11. Seltz, Martin. 1994. More businesses set up shop in Western U.S. *Wall Street Journal*, May 23: B1-2.

12. Decker, Jill M. and John L. Crompton. 1993. Attracting footloose companies: An investigation

of the business location decision process. *Journal of Professional Services Marketing* 9(1): 69-94.

13. Longino, Charles F. 1995. *Retirement migration in America*. Houston: Vacation Publications.

14. Schor, Juliet B. 1992. *The overworked American: The unexpected decline of leisure*. New York: Wiley.

15. Van der Merwe, S. 1987. GRAMPIES: A new breed of consumers comes of age. *Business Horizon* 30(6): 14-19.

16. Haigood, Traci L. and John L. Crompton 1998. The role of recreation amenities in retiree relocation decisions. *Journal of Park and Recreation Administration* 16(1): 25-45.

17. Connell, Mark R., Jane H. Lillydahl and Larry D. Singell. 1978. The effects of greenbelts on residential property values: Some findings on the political economy of open space. *Land Economics* 54(2): 207-217.

18. Lyons, Richard D. 1986. Boatslip owners buoyed by soaring resale prices. *New York Times*, November 16, Section 8, 2.

19. Barthold, Charles. 1987. Looking for a dock for the day sailor. *New York Times*, January 10, Section 3, 4.

20. Malone, Maggie and Malcolm Jones. 1997. A true urban legend: Newark seeks salvation in an arts center. *Newsweek*, October 27, 74.

21. Lublin, Joann S. 1985. Forget big convention halls: Now cities see aquariums as urban renovation tools. *The Wall Street Journal*, November 22, section 2, 33.

22. Brown, J. Robert and Michele Laumer. 1995. Comeback cities. *Urban Land* 54(8): 46-51, 83.

23. Beyard, Michael D. and Michael S. Rubin. 1995. A new industry emerges. *Urban Land* Supplement: 6-7.

24. Lewis, N.P. 1923. *The planning of the modern city*. Second edition. New York: Wiley.

25. Crompton, John L. and Peter A. Witt. 1997. The roving leader program in San Antonio. *Journal of Park and Recreation Administration* 15(2): 84-92.

26. Federal Bureau of Investigation and the Office of Justice Programs, U.S. Department of Justice. 1994. Crime Statistics. *Congressional Digest* June-July: 167-168, 192.

27. Arrigona, N. and T. Reed. 1995. *Texas correctional cost per day, 1993-94*. Austin: Criminal Justice Policy Council.

28. Espericueta-Schultz, Lorina, John L. Crompton and Peter A. Witt. 1995. A national profile of the status of public recreation services for at-risk children and youth. *Journal of Park and Recreation Administration* 13(3): 1-26.

29. Havitz, Mark E. and Clarence Spigner. 1993. Unemployment, health and leisure: The role of park and recreation services. *Trends* 30(4): 31-36.

30. Reid, Donald G. 1988. The needs of the unemployed and the ability of leisure providers to respond. *Society and Leisure* 11(1): 117-148.

31. Witt, Peter A. and John L. Crompton. 1996. *Recreation programs that work for at-risk youth*. State College, PA: Venture Publishing.

32. Ulrich, Roger S., Robert F. Simons, Barbara D. Losito, Evelyn Fiorito, Mark A. Miles and Michael Zelson. 1991. Stress recovery during exposure to natural and urban environments. *Journal of Environmental Psychology* 11: 201-230.

33. Hull, Richard J. 1994. Psychological and physiological benefits of greenspace. *Golf Course Management* 62(8): 50-53.

34. Roszak, Theodore. 1995. The greening of psychology: A conversation with Theodore Roszak. *Land and People* 7(1): 23-26.

35. Ulrich, Roger S. 1984. View through a window may influence recovery from surgery. *Science* 224: 420-421.

36. Stone, Brad. 1997. Rx: Thirty minutes on the StairMaster twice weekly. *Newsweek*, March 17, 46.

37. Paffenbarger, Ralph S., Robert T. Hyde and Ann Dow. 1991. Health benefits of physical activity. In *Benefits of leisure*, edited by B.L. Driver, Perry J. Brown and George L. Peterson. State College, PA: Venture Publishing, 49-57.

38. Godbey, Geoffrey. 1997. Recreation and parks in a changing world: Becoming a health service. *Parks and Recreation* 32(3): 91-105.

39. Cohen, Andrew. 1997. Putting wellness to work. *Athletic Business* 21(3): 29-38.

PART II

DIRECT PARTNERSHIPS

CHAPTER 6

THE EMERGENT PARADIGM: PRIVATIZATION AND PARTNERSHIPS

Partnerships have become more important because people expect government, citizens, and industry to work together to solve common problems. Problems are too complicated and too expensive to handle on your own. So partnerships have simply become a way of life. You simply don't have any choice if you want to get things done.[1]

The seven chapters that compose part II of the text (chapters 6-12) discuss direct partnerships between park and recreation agencies and business enterprises, nonprofit organizations, or other government agencies. This first chapter in part II initiates the discussion by reviewing the characteristics of privatization and partnerships, which are recurrent themes in the following chapters. These two concepts are interrelated, but they are not synonymous. It is possible to engage in privatization actions that do not involve partnering, for example, when public park and recreational facilities are sold to a business. Similarly, it is possible to have partnerships without privatization, for example, when the arrangement is with another public agency.

Widespread acceptance of both concepts has emerged as agencies have sought to change from their role of direct service deliverers. The early sections of the chapter review the frustrations associated with direct delivery, which is the traditional model of agency service delivery, and of the different political agendas that converged to advocate privatization as a superior alternative. This review is followed by a discussion of the inefficiencies associated with monopolistic service delivery and the distinction between provision and production of a service, which advocates perceive to be central tenets of the privatization philosophy.

The challenge for park and recreation agencies seeking to develop partnerships with business enterprises is to create a climate in the agency and in the community that is conducive to nurturing them. Hence, in the latter part of this chapter, two major actions that agencies can take to foster this favorable environment are discussed.

The spheres of business and government traditionally have been viewed as distinctively different in terms of philosophies, objectives, reward structures, and codes of conduct. Relations between them have not always been cordial. If any antipathy that prevails is not removed, then partnerships are unlikely. Hence, the first task confronting an agency desiring to expand its partnering activities with businesses is to encourage a positive attitude among agency employees and elected officials toward the potential contribution of commercial enterprises. To do this, the involved parties must reconcile and accept as legitimate the different value systems that prevail in the two sectors. The discussion of this issue extends to reviewing strategic and organizational adjustments that will be required to make partnerships work effectively.

It is useless to laud the benefits of partnerships if agencies engage in activities that engender distrust and alienation. Thus, a second task is to remove any suspicion that the public agency is competing unfairly with commercial businesses in the services it delivers. In the past, this issue was especially contentious in the provision of campsite areas and of recreational and fitness centers, but now these allegations are emerging also in a number of other service areas. A perception of unfair competition is likely to result in animosity from the business community and to negate the possibility of partnerships with it.

Frustration With Direct Service Delivery

The traditional role of park and recreation agencies was to provide services directly rather than to deliver them in partnership with others. The agency solicited input and advice from users, the general public, and other stakeholders, but it took exclusive responsibility for planning and producing all of the services that it offered. In effect, the agency preassembled from within the organization all of the ingredients needed to deliver a service (e.g., facility, equipment, materials, maintenance, leadership, etc.) and created packages of participation opportunities. The citizens' task was then to pick and choose cafeteria style from the array of opportunities made available to them.

The emergence of the tax revolt in the late 1970s and early 1980s resulted in many jurisdictions considering alternative models of service delivery to supplement or replace the traditional direct delivery approach. The initial momentum for this rethink was stimulated by frustration with the high cost and inflexibility associated with the traditional model. The traditional model requires an agency not only to finance fully all land acquisition and capital improvements but also to hire relatively large numbers of full-time personnel to perform specialized delivery tasks. Typically, two-thirds of an agency's budget is committed to personnel salaries and benefits, and personnel have long-term (maybe lifetime) tenure under the civil service guidelines that prevail in most government organizations. In addition, terminating ineffective employees is difficult for many agencies because of lengthy, convoluted grievance and disciplinary procedures requiring extensive, detailed documentation that civil service regulations mandate.

These limitations inhibit an agency's flexibility and agility so it is less able to respond to shifts in citizens' demand priorities, and they compromise the agency's ability to deliver quality services. In the traditional model, opportunities to hire staff with different skills that may be needed to respond to shifts in demand only arise when resignations occur. Personnel who have specific skills and who were hired to directly deliver a particular service may be reluctant and ill equipped to work in a different service area. Consider the following scenario.

Throughout the 1980s, many park and recreation agencies were told to do more with less. They often achieved this by focusing on target markets with the ability and willingness to pay prices high enough to cover most service costs and by reducing resources invested in high-subsidy social benefit programs. Employees were hired with entrepreneurial skills that could contribute to this objective. In some of these communities, the political mandate in the early 1990s was to do something about juvenile crime and delinquency. However, agencies that had focused for a decade or more on revenue production from middle-class target markets often did not have staff with the skills to implement effectively this resurrected social mandate. Thus, they lacked the flexibility and agility to respond effectively in the short term.

This inflexibility has led to growing support for the maxim: "The fewer government employees, the fewer personnel problems." It is easier to change contractors than to change employees.

In addition to the inherent inflexibility associated with hiring full-time personnel whose skills are tied to the direct delivery of a specific service, public agencies' agility is inhibited by both the enabling legislation that proscribes the scope of their authority and powers and by the bureaucratic regulations and procedures that govern their actions. These legislative and procedural constraints have been imposed because they are in the public interest. They are necessary to ensure adherence to the public agency's responsiveness to its mandate, to reassure elected officials, who represent the citizens responsible for providing public funds, that their policy directives are being implemented; and to demonstrate accountability for those funds.

Despite the frustration that many park and recreation managers feel about the system of checks and balances that characterize a bureaucracy and create cumbersome administrative procedures and extensive paperwork, such a system is needed because an agency is required to account for each penny of public funds. It has been noted that

> a little dishonesty in government is a corrosive disease. It rapidly spreads to infect the whole body politic. Yet the temptation to dishonesty is always great. People of modest means and dependence on a salary handle very large sums of public money. People of modest position dispose of power and award contracts and privileges of tremendous importance, e.g., construction jobs, zoning laws, and building codes, to other people. To fear corruption in government is not irrational. This means, however, that government bureaucracy, and its consequent high costs, cannot be eliminated. Any government that is not a "government of forms" degenerates rapidly into a mutual looting society (p. 214).[2]

Thus, regulations designed to prevent politicalization, patronage, or corruption often become red-tape that inhibits efficiency. Adherence to them means that there are facilities and programs that make it impossible for public agencies to finance and manage efficiently with the direct-delivery model. These services can be operated optimally only through collaborations with nonprofit and commercial organizations that are not subject to these constraints.

The inhibiting impact of bureaucratic procedures was illustrated by the renovation of the Wollman Memorial Skating Rink in Central Park, New York. After its concrete floor buckled, the Wollman Rink closed for two years for renovations at a cost of $4.9 million. Over the next six years, the city spent $12.9 million on various repair efforts, and the renovation was still incomplete. At that point, city officials proposed to spend an additional $3 million to complete the project over the next two years. Donald Trump, a major New York developer, volunteered to undertake the remaining work for no more than $2.97 million and to complete it in one year. He completed it for $2.1 million in 5.5 months. The surplus was used to renovate the skate house and to landscape the area. The major reasons for the city's cost overruns and delays were the delays in signing contracts and sequencing the work of four different contractors. Under a New York state law, which did not apply to private contractors, state and local agencies were required to hire separate contractors for plumbing, construction, electrical, and heating and ventilation work and to use the lowest bidder. As a private contractor, Trump was not subject to this law.[3]

The Emergence of Privatization

The emergence of privatization was a natural response to these perceived limitations of direct provision. At the same time, it embraced two pervasive tenets of American lore: "Government is inherently wasteful because it lacks the incentive of the profit motive" and "Private enterprise is inherently efficient because inefficiency is not tolerated in the marketplace." Privatization incorporates all activities that reduce the role of the public sector in the financing, production, or management of services or assets. It involves the replacement of public resources with private investments. This definition has been made operational in a variety of ways.

The purest form of privatization is divestiture of assets, which means selling existing public park and recreation properties to nonprofit or commercial entities. For example, the British Columbia provincial government in western Canada sold Manning Park Lodge and the Gibson Pass ski facilities near Vancouver. The Minister of Lands, Parks, and Housing stated: "selling these facilities gets government out of a business that can best be run by the private sector" (p 244).[4] Advocates of privatization from outside of the field look at recreational facilities and frequently argue that extensive divestiture of them should take place.

> "Load shedding" could be carried out for a whole range of recreational activities, such as golf and swimming. Facilities that are publicly owned could be sold to private bidders and operated as ordinary private businesses, selling their services to the public at large or functioning as nonprofit membership organizations that are prohibited from engaging in discriminatory practices. The rationale for doing so is that the benefits accrue directly to the users with little spillover to society at large. There is little reason for government to provide these goods at collective expense,

> and every reason for the aficionados to band together for mutual enjoyment under their own rules and at their own expense (p. 235).[5]

To this point, such advocates generally have been ignored and divestiture of this type is rare. Contrary to the view expressed above, many citizens do perceive spillover benefits to accrue to society at large. They perceive public provision of recreational facilities to be an important element in a community's quality of life, in its economic development, and in the alleviation of community social problems. Thus, the sale of such facilities is likely to arouse substantial opposition and inflict an unacceptable level of political cost on elected officials who propose such actions.

More common forms of load shedding by agencies involve encouraging business entrepreneurs to invest resources into four areas: financing, developing, and perhaps operating facilities and services often in some type of partnership with the agency; contracting out the operation, maintenance, and management of facilities and services to businesses or nonprofit groups; enforcing exactions that require developers to provide public park and recreational facilities at their expense; and encouraging community groups and nonprofit organizations to assist in production of the services they desire. Each of these facets of privatization is discussed in subsequent chapters of this part of the text. Some people use the privatization term more expansively, so it also embraces the acquisition of external resources that supplement agency funds in the form of donations, sponsorships, foundations' support, or volunteers. These types of external resources are discussed in part III.

Privatization is as old as government, but the first call for its use as a deliberate public policy can be traced to Peter Drucker's book, *The Age of Discontinuity*, published in 1969.[2] Drucker noted the disenchantment with government performance, observing: "the record of the last thirty or forty years has been dismal" (p. 203).[2]

> There is mounting evidence that government is big rather than strong; that it is fat and flabby rather than powerful; that it costs a great deal but does not achieve much. There is mounting evidence also that the citizen less and less believes in government and is increasingly disenchanted with it (p. 198).[2]

It was these sentiments that led to the tax revolt emerging a few years after he wrote this. Drucker advocated the handing over of operating tasks to nongovernment organizations, a process for which he coined the term reprivatization because:

> The tasks which flowed to government in the last century because the original private institution of society, the family, could not discharge them, would be turned over to the new, non-governmental institutions that have sprung up and grown during the last sixty to seventy years (p. 218).[2]

Reprivatization was viewed as a means of reversing the widespread disenchantment and growing cynicism with government and of restoring strength and performance capacity to it.

The Convergence of Political Agendas

Drucker's insights were acclaimed and quoted but were not much acted upon for another decade. Privatization was only widely embraced and adopted in the 1980s when an extraordinary confluence of political agendas came together. By this time, the prevailing direct-delivery model was being subjected to extensive criticism from people at both ends of the political spectrum. Conservatives considered it to be costly and inefficient, and liberals regarded it as being bureaucratic and inflexible. Hence, there was a coalescence of support for it, albeit for very different reasons from diverse political forces.[5] These forces are summarized in table 6.1. They represent a convergence of agendas that tend to be associated with the conservative right wing of the political spectrum (i.e., ideological, commercial, and pragmatic forces) and with populists, many of whom are likely to view themselves as standing toward the liberal left wing of the political spectrum. Pragmatists and populists view privatization as a means to an end, whereas commercial and ideological advocates regard it as an end in itself.

Pragmatists sought a more cost-effective government and saw privatization as a means to that end. The exigencies that the tax revolt forced upon many park and recreation agency managers galvanized them into becoming pragmatists and shifting from their traditional mode of thinking. They embraced strategies such as contracting out services because its reason for existence was to improve efficiency (see chapter 9). This entails either reducing costs while holding quality at the same level or improving the quality while holding costs at the same level.

Populists saw privatization as a means of achieving a better society through giving people greater power to satisfy their common needs while diminishing the power of large public and private bureaucracies. They were concerned that there was too much institutional encroachment on voluntary efforts. Populists recognized that winning support for park and recreation services was more

---

Table 6.1 The Forces Behind the Emergence of the Privatization Movement

Force	Goal	Reasoning
Pragmatic	Better government	Prudent privatization leads to more cost-effective public services.
Ideological	Less government	Government is too big, too powerful, too intrusive in people's lives and therefore is a danger to democracy. Government's decisions are political, thus are inherently less trustworthy than free-market decisions.
Commercial	More business	Government spending is a large part of the economy; more of it can and should be directed toward private firms. State-owned enterprises and assets can be put to better use by the private sector.
Populist	Better society	People should have more choice in public services. They should be empowered to define and address common needs, and to establish a sense of community by relying more on family, neighborhood, church, and ethnic and voluntary associations and less on distant bureaucratic structures.

Source: Eric S. Savas. 1987. *Privatization: The key to better government.* Chatham, New Jersey: Chatham House Publishers.

about emotions than motions. They regarded relationship building as the essence, not a by-product, of strategy. What people do not understand, they will not value. What they do not value, they will not support. The argument is encapsulated in the following observation:

> If the Victorians had eaten roast dodo for Sunday brunch, then the poor hapless creatures would undoubtably still be with us. The point being, that if you want to conserve something, the best way to do so is by making it worth people's while. No one had any kind of vested interest in the survival of the dodo, so it didn't (p. 3).[6]

It follows that the best way to secure the future of park and recreation services is to broaden the base of people who invest effort, energy, and resources into their well-being.

Direct service delivery meant that agencies undertook actions that ensured programs were available, but they forewent the opportunity to get individuals emotionally and passionately involved in fulfilling a park and recreation agency's mandate. Without emotional and passionate support, an agency is unlikely to thrive in the political decision-making arena. The more commitment, energy, and sweat individuals invest in assisting an agency to produce services, the stronger their commitment to the agency's cause is likely to be. Only those who are strongly committed tend to become active advocates in the political arena. Hence, populists saw privatization as a means of encouraging coproduction of services (see chapter 12) and broadening public support for the agency.

In contrast to the pragmatists and populists, those who advocated privatization on ideological or commercial grounds viewed it as an end in itself rather than as a means to an end. The goal of commercial interests was to obtain more business by taking over some of the agency's financing, production, or operating roles. They viewed privatization as a mandate for them to exploit profitable business opportunities that they perceived existed in a park and recreation system (see chapters 8 and 9) and as a platform from which they could launch attacks on services in which they perceived an agency to be competing unfairly with them. (This is discussed later in this chapter.) Both of these were legitimate goals to explore. These goals could lead to a wider range of park and recreation services being made available

in a jurisdiction and to efficiencies in an agency's delivery of service.

Finally, for those who approached the issue ideologically, privatization was a political agenda aimed at ensuring that government played a smaller role than private institutions played. They believed that government's role in service production had become too dominant. They were concerned that managers in public agencies were seeking out more areas to colonize and on which to impose their expertise in order to build up their empires. Trends in the park and recreation field appeared to offer some support for these concerns because the number of full-time personnel in local agencies increased from 117,000 in 1970 to 145,000 in 1978, which was when the tax revolt gathered momentum.[7] Ideologists saw privatization as a way of halting or reversing this trend.

Recognition of the Inefficiencies Associated With Monopolistic Direct Delivery

A central tenet of privatization is that it should be used to inject competition into the service delivery system. In many communities, a park and recreation agency is the only producer of facilities, such as parks and swimming pools, and of recreational activities, such as softball and soccer. In these situations, an agency is a monopolistic supplier of the services that it produces. Irrespective of whether they are in the public or private sectors, monopolies are notoriously inefficient because they lack the incentive that competition provides to be responsive to clienteles' demands. Such organizations are unlikely to undertake innovations or changes that may increase quality or decrease costs because this requires additional effort and risk taking, and there are no incentives in terms of rewards or punishments for monopolistic organizations to do this. If employees do improve performance, they receive few material gains, and if they do not, there are few adverse consequences.

Over time, insularity from competitive pressures encourages managers and employees in these organizations to become unresponsive, complacent, and, in some instances, callous and arrogant. As the sole producer of a service, a monopolistic organization is in control and may succumb to the temptation to act in ways that further the interests of its managers and employees rather than those of its clienteles. For example, in a monopoly, prestige, salaries, and promotion tend to be correlated with the size of a manager's staff and budget. The consequences of this in the context of public sector monopolies have been expressed in the following terms.

> If a public agency manager underspends the budget or utilizes workers more productively, the manager is likely to be penalized with a smaller budget and staff (in relative terms) in following years, and the manager's salary and career progression will be hampered. Alternatively, if the manager's budget increases substantially, a higher salary and career progression are likely. The economic losses that result from less efficient spending are passed on to others—the taxpayers. In the public sector, then, managers tend to be rewarded for inefficiency and penalized for efficiency (p. 77).[8]

Similarly, the effect of collective bargaining agreements is likely to be different on monopolistic organizations than on those that operate in a competitive environment.

> Collective bargaining rarely drives employee compensation above the market rate in competitive industries because both management and the union are constrained by competitive economic pressures. On the other hand, collective bargaining may drive employee compensation above the market rate in government because there is no competition for labor rates and because above-market costs are passed on to taxpayers. Management has little incentive to maintain strict control of costs because taxpayers are required to pay the bill. This accounts for the tendency of public employee compensation to rise at a greater rate than that of employees in the private sector (p. 78).[8]

The inefficiency and unresponsiveness of monopolies has resulted in their being aggressively resisted and forbidden by law in the private sector. However, traditionally this policy of opposing monopolies has not been extended to the public sector.

> How strange. We vigorously oppose monopolies in the private sector and enforce laws to break up monopolies and conspiracies that would restrain competition; we know that the public interest suffers without the goal of competition and in the absence of

alternative choices. However, in the public sector, perversely, we often have chosen monopoly and prohibited competition in the mistaken belief that competition constitutes wasteful duplication (p. 250).[5]

The privatization movement is a manifestation of change in this paradoxical attitude toward private and public sector monopolies. It recognizes that a primary obstacle inhibiting an agency's performance is the structural problem of monopoly. From this perspective, the central issue in the privatization debate is not whether a park and recreation agency can produce a service more efficiently than a nonprofit or commercial supplier. Rather, it is how to induce competition into the delivery system that would optimize efficiency irrespective of the source of the supply. Certainly, simply transforming a service from an agency to a private sector supplier that is also a monopolist is unlikely to yield improvement in either quality or cost savings.

When a park and recreation agency is a monopolistic supplier of a service, improvements in performance can come only through exhortation and an appeal to employees' pride and professionalism. They may agree to improve their performance, but they cannot be forced to do so. A review of an agency's performance by senior managers, consultants, or external evaluators may identify potential efficiencies. However, an agency is unlikely to perform optimally without the discipline imposed by benchmark measures of quality and cost derived from bids of alternative suppliers. If competition is introduced through privatization, then efficiencies derive from the positive and negative incentives associated with competition rather than from the commands and directives of senior managers or elected officials.

Privatization means that a park and recreation agency is no longer viewed as a sole source supplier. If it fails to match the lower cost and higher standards that alternative producers offer, then there is a clear implication that responsibility for the service may be given to others, which is likely to have consequences relating to security and status. This threat is likely to stimulate advocacy for structural change within an agency. Barriers that inhibit efficiency, such as bureaucratic procedures, traditional practices, centralized regulations, and traditional hierarchical organizational frameworks, may be reviewed and revised in the quest to enable an agency to remain viable when measured against other producers.

Awareness of the Distinction Between Provision and Production

Drucker was the first to articulate the distinction between provision of a service and its production. That is, he differentiated between the decision making and the doing roles of government. He argued that the purpose of government was to focus the political energies of society, dramatize issues, present fundamental choices, and make decisions from among them. He perceived these functions to be quite different from doing: "Any attempt to combine governing with 'doing' on a large scale, paralyses the decision-making capacity. Any attempt to make decision-making organs actually 'do' also means very poor 'doing'" (p. 217).[2] He advocated what he recognized was a "heretical doctrine" (p. 233)—that nongovernmental organizations are responsible for the actual doing, that is, for performance, operation, and execution of service delivery. The role of the agency was seen as being analogous to that of an orchestra conductor.

> The conductor himself does not play an instrument. He need not even know how to play an instrument. His job is to know the capacity of each instrument and to evoke optimal performance from each. Instead of being the performer, he has become the conductor. Instead of doing, he leads (p. 219).[2]

There is growing awareness of Drucker's original insight of the distinction between an agency's recognizing a need for a service to be provided and the agency's producing it. This has led to a recognition that service delivery involves two independent decisions. The first decision is about whether a park and recreation agency has a responsibility to ensure that a particular service is provided. If the answer to that question is affirmative, then the second decision to be made relates to who should produce it. Traditionally, the direct-provider model prevailed, whereby agencies produced services that they believed should be provided; however, now more agencies are evaluating alternative production options, recognizing that often there is a superior alternative.

This shift changes a park and recreation agency from being a seller of services to being a facilitator or buyer of services. From this perspective, its allocations of public funds are seen not as expenditures but rather as investments requiring active consideration of the trade-offs between alternative production options.

The word *government* is derived from a Greek word meaning helmsman.[5] This suggests that the job of a park and recreation agency is to steer the boat and not to man the oars! Steering means selecting the course or direction to be taken, and the rowing metaphor refers to the direct delivery of services. The boat, equipment, or crew of oarsmen from within the park and recreation agency may not be the strongest or best available in a particular context.

Senior park and recreation managers spend much of their time fighting fires that operational problems create rather than in long-term strategic-policy planning. Their attention is focused on the production rather than on the more important provisional policy decisions. It has been observed:

> Large staffs require supervision, and civil service rules and limits make it difficult to manage and divert attention to people problems. Supervision time subsumes long-term planning time, illustrating Gresham's Law of Planning—that trivia drive out planning. Likewise, decision makers can have their attention diverted from policy matters to administrative issues. Their attention span is limited, and routine matters quickly fill up an agenda (p. 56).[3]

The essential function of a park and recreation agency is to determine whether a service should be made available to the public. Subsequently, the agency may decide to produce what it has determined should be provided, but it equally well may decide it should arrange for others to produce it. The provision decision addresses social goods, contending values, who should benefit and who should pay, equity, income redistribution, and other issues that are inherently political. In contrast, the production decision is mainly an economic issue that addresses how the political service objective can be delivered most effectively and efficiently.

An agency does not have to control the resources needed to deliver a service; rather, its efforts should be focused on controlling and monitoring the nature and quality of what is delivered. One of the characteristic features of this field is the plethora of organizations in each of the public, nonprofit, and commercial sectors that produce park and recreation services. Each community likely will have organizations that, in defined areas, offer a more efficient service production alternative to direct delivery by the park and recreation

Collaboration on Programs for At-Risk Youth in Portland

The city of Portland decided to provide more resources for recreation services targeted at at-risk youth. After this initial steering decision was made, the Portland Parks and Recreation Department convened a series of summit meetings of all organizations in the public, nonprofit, and commercial sectors involved in producing youth services to shape a coordinated delivery strategy. The summits identified resources needed and those available from each of the organizations including facilities, equipment, funding sources, transportation, participants, volunteers, mentors, and training.

The goal was to ensure that each at-risk child in the city was served by someone. With approximately 50 youth-serving organizations collaborating in this way, this goal was realistic. The department sought to use its resources to strengthen the work that these organizations were doing. If the department had used its resources exclusively for direct delivery, it could have reached only a small proportion of the total and may well have duplicated the delivery efforts of other organizations. The specific benefits derived from this collaboration included

- expanding available services by cooperative programming and joint fundraising and grant programs;
- providing better services to clients through interagency communication about client needs, referral programs, and client case management;
- developing a greater understanding of client and community needs by seeing the whole picture;
- sharing similar concerns while being enriched by diverse perspectives that different members from varied backgrounds bring to the collaboration;
- reducing interagency conflicts and tensions by squarely addressing issues of competition and turf;
- improving communication with organizations within the community and, through those organizations, with larger segments of the community;
- mobilizing action to effect needed changes through collective advocacy;
- achieving greater visibility with decision makers, the media, and the community;
- enhancing staff skill levels by sharing information and organizing joint training programs;
- conserving resources by avoiding unnecessary duplication of services; and
- decreasing costs through collective buying programs and other collective cost-containment opportunities.

---

agency. It is efficient and effective to work with others in service areas in which they excel.

An example of how this approach may be made operational is given in "Collaboration on Programs for At-Risk Youth in Portland." It illustrates that after the responsibility to provide has been accepted, an agency's influence and resources may best be used to encourage collaboration and establishment of a shared vision among alternative producers rather than to provide direct service. This may lead to rationalization of services that were duplicated and better integration of complementary efforts. If it is deemed that additional services are needed, then the agency's role may be to induce other producers to supply them by

providing incentives in the form of seed resources, by partnering directly with other producers to deliver them, or by assisting individuals and organizations to produce services for themselves.

In this way, an agency seeks to meet policy objectives through leveraging its resources by supplementing them with resources that other service providers supply. This means that a central element of the modus operandi in today's effective park and recreation agencies is the development of partnerships with other public entities at local, state, and federal levels; with commercial entities; with organizations in the non-profit sector; and with individual volunteers and supporters.

A city manager in California indicated that before his city would sanction direct delivery of a service, there had to be negative answers to each of the following five questions:

1. Can this service be purchased less expensively from another jurisdiction?

2. Can the city enter into a joint management arrangement with one or more other jurisdictions to provide the service less expensively?

3. Can the city participate with an existing special-purpose government agency or special district to provide the service less expensively?

4. Can the city buy the service less expensively from a private firm, nonprofit agency, or individual?

5. Can a new service provider be created less expensively?[3]

The increased involvement of other service providers with park and recreation agencies has resulted in a progressive and pervasive integration of public, nonprofit, and commercial service suppliers. Organizations within each sector are increasingly dependent on effective interaction with organizations in the other sectors. There is recognition that the financing or management of facilities or programs proposed by an organization in one sector may often be produced more effectively and efficiently, and in some instances may only be viable by partnering with entities in another sector.

Reconciling Value Systems of Agencies and Businesses

Agencies are mandated to serve the whole community, especially its most disadvantaged members. Hence, their traditional value systems are concerned with social outcomes and benefits that are relatively intangible and difficult to measure. In contrast, the value systems of business organizations, whose assistance may be sought when privatizing services, focus on the tangible, easily measured outcomes of financial return on investment, and their mandate is to maximize return to their stockholders. This means that their services tend to be targeted narrowly at those segments from which the business perceives the highest return on investment is likely to be realized. Clearly, there is inherent potential for frustration, friction, and conflict between those working in these two different value systems.

Tensions are heightened by the different environmental milieus in which the two sectors operate. It was noted earlier that public agencies are constrained by bureaucratic procedures that are necessary to ensure accountability for their expenditure of public funds. Thus, while a business may want to proceed with a project immediately, a park and recreation agency may be required to engage in an extensive planning process involving wide public participation, lengthy legislative approval procedures, extended budgetary hearings, and frequent consultation with elected officials. These checks and balances, which accountability necessitates, cause delays and may cause potential business partners who do not understand how government works to perceive a park and recreation agency as lacking commitment to the project, being slow moving, or being indecisive. In contrast, the survival of commercial organizations is predicated on their ability to be flexible and to respond quickly to opportunities that arise in the marketplace.

The lack of flexibility in park and recreation agencies is reflected in their budgetary procedures. Typically, operating budgets are fixed before the start of the fiscal year, and there is little latitude for them to take advantage of unforeseen opportunities that may arise.

Suppose that in October a ski resort offers free instruction and lift passes for disadvantaged youth in city programs. The program will begin in December, but the city must produce the funds to cover transportation and equipment rental. With a traditional budget system, it is unlikely that the agency could respond until the next fiscal year when it may or may not be successful in persuading elected officials to include it in the annual budget. By then, almost a year will have passed, and the ski resort may have retracted the offer.[9]

This sort of delay makes it difficult to be responsive to new opportunities. A similar situation is likely to prevail for capital projects. A business probably can borrow funds quickly for a promising investment, but an agency interested in partnering with it may have to wait a long time for resources to be authorized by legislative authority or bond referendum. If more than one public agency is involved in a partnership, the problem is compounded because city, county, state, and federal agencies may all have different fiscal years and budget-planning cycles.

These distinctive differences between the two sections often lead to the formation of negative stereotypical attitudes that impede the development of partnerships. In the author's experience, both popular perceptions of government inefficiency and private sector efficiency are exaggerated grossly. Media opportunities and media actions have helped build the view that public and private organizations represent opposite poles of the efficiency continuum.

There is a segment of the population, including some managers in the commercial sector, who perceive park and recreation agencies as being wasteful, unresponsive, tradition-bound, incompetent, and inefficient bureaucracies that are staffed by people who have never had to meet a payroll and who sometimes seek to frustrate the legitimate goals of business. Much of this perception is derived from public agencies being required to operate openly and to give the media full access to all of their actions. Freedom of information acts and government-in-the-sunshine laws are deliberately written to guarantee public and media access to whatever is done by the officials who act in the public's name. They are designed to ensure that the public agencies are fully accountable to their taxpayer bosses for their actions.

In contrast, private organizations, for the most part, are entitled to keep their decision processes and actions confidential. Hence, media focus all of their investigative reporting efforts on public organizations because the rights of privacy that prevail in the private sector preclude public access. It has been suggested: "If the affairs of private corporations were equally accessible to public view, the media would expose private inefficiency with the same vigor they now devote to public waste" (p. 304).[10] However, even if equal accessibility were available, two reasons make it unlikely that the media would shift their investigative focus to the private sector. First, the financial consequences of inefficiencies in private organizations adversely impact only the shareholders of those entities and not all residents in the community. Thus, the moral imperative is not as strong. Second:

The media are themselves part of the fraternity of private enterprises, so while prominent media spokesmen have repeatedly and explicitly declared it their responsibility to take an adversary posture toward agencies and officials of government, none has expressed a comparable sense of obligation to expose the shortcomings of private enterprises (p. 306).[10]

In some segments of the population and among some park and recreation managers, commercial enterprises are viewed with distrust and suspicion. They are regarded as exploitive, overly concerned with private gain, and devoid of sensitivity to social issues and community well-being. Much of the stereotypically negative attitude toward commercial enterprises arises from misunderstanding the concept of profit. To some, it has the unfortunate connotation of unfair exploitation. However, it probably is viewed more appropriately as a combination of four types of costs.[11]

First, profit is the genuine cost of a major resource, namely capital. Relatively few businesses in the park and recreation field actually generate sufficient revenue to cover their basic cost and to give them a return on investment that exceeds the return that they could derive from investing their money in the stock market! Most small businesses in this field are operated by individuals who value the opportunity that the business provides to live a preferred lifestyle operating recreational areas, such as a campground, marina, or fitness center. Their businesses typically generate an annual operating surplus sufficient to give the owners an adequate standard of living but too low to provide a market return on the value of the equity that they have invested in land, structures, and major equipment.

Second, profit is a necessary cost of insurance. The insurance risks associated with events such as fire or theft are widely recognized as costs that a business must cover. The risks of investing in a business and sustaining it in times when there are economic downturns are no less real. A function of profit is to provide sufficient resources to enable a business to withstand unforeseen adverse market conditions.

Third, profit is the cost of investment in tomorrow's jobs, for profits are a primary source of resources for expanding the size or range of the enterprise or for investing in new ventures. Fourth, profit is the cost of employee pensions because businesses fund pension schemes from these resources. Further, many of the funds in which public employees' pensions are invested in turn invest some proportion of those resources in development projects and in the stock market, so park and recreation employees have a vested interest in the profitability of businesses! Indeed, employees are the major capitalists in the United States if capitalist is defined as the owner of the means of production: "Through their pension funds, the employees of American businesses own . . . between one-third and two-fifths of the equity capital of American industry" (p.183).[12]

When profit is viewed as a series of costs, there is no inherent conflict between profit and social responsibility. Indeed, it is not the business earning a profit appropriate to its genuine costs of capital, to the risks of tomorrow, and to the needs of tomorrow's worker and pensioner that rips off society; rather, it is the business that fails to do so.[11]

Creation of a favorable partnership climate requires park and recreation personnel to abandon any remaining vestiges of self-image that portray them as the good-guy protector of the public good working against the bad-guy forces of the commercial sector. Indeed, in many communities the bad guy is widely perceived to be government, and involving businesses in direct partnerships may build public support for the park and recreation agencies.

Even if negative stereotypes of the commercial sector do not exist in an agency, managers may still be reluctant to enter into partnerships with it.

> Agency officials often feel that they are on the front lines, encumbered by bureaucracy, politics, the press, and insufficient resources. It is difficult to take risks in such an environment, whether real or perceived. Working cooperatively with private sector organizations is a risk outside of normal government operations (p. 164).[13]

Much of the perceived risk is associated with giving up control. If a park and recreation agency commits to seeking partnerships, then an inherent corollary of that commitment is a willingness to compromise the degree of control it can exercise over the service delivered. Businesses have to be able to demonstrate to investors and bankers that they have sufficient control to operate the venture successfully before they can acquire the capital necessary to develop it.

A key factor in control is the length of a contract or lease. When the length is short, for example, less than five years, control largely is retained because the arrangement is periodically evaluated to ensure that it remains in the public interest. Long leases mean surrendering control of a public resource for 10 years or, more frequently, for 25 to 30 years. Such long leases are needed when the commercial sector invests substantially in capital assets in order for developers to have time to amortize successfully all of their capital improvements and secure an acceptable return on their investment. At the same time, a long-term lease provides the agency with evidence of the operator's long-term commitment to the project. The adverse consequences of short leases are illustrated by the following case.

Private enterprise develops major ski areas on land leased from the U.S. Forest Service. Private capital formation for construction of ski recreational facilities was handicapped by the 80-acre, 30-year lease limits set by Congress. The Forest Service responded to these limits by restricting the 80 acres to areas that contained lifts, buildings, and related structures and by issuing additional annual permits, for which it had authority, for the skiable terrain that ranged from 200 to 10,000 acres. Leasing by annual permits without renewable options was a major problem. Bankers, venture capitalists, and other financial organizations looked with suspicion at an arrangement whereby an investment could be lost if the annual permit was not renewed.[14]

To succeed, partnerships with the commercial sector require mutual respect that may not come easily. A park and recreation agency's reputation for fairness, thoroughness, competence, and professionalism is likely to be of central importance to gaining the confidence of the business community. Building trust so that both sides appreciate the value systems and objectives guiding the other's actions is likely to take time and require considerable skill and vision. Understanding and reconciling the different philosophies can occur only through communication and liaison. The best way to foster this is through the development of institutional forums whereby both sides come together to engage in active listening, to describe the constraints and opportunities associated with their services, and to discuss how they might join together to extend them.

Partnerships depend on park and recreation managers who will go out on a limb, bend the rules, or push the envelope to expand their vision beyond tradition. They will only commit to partnerships if they believe the chemistry and level of trust with their prospective partners is strong.

Key phrases from park and recreation managers engaged in successful partnerships include the following: "The group dynamics are right," "We complemented each other," and "There was a willingness to give up turf and a give and take." One manager noted: "You can't get too bound up in our regulations. That's one way to turn off the private sector fast."[1] Trust and confidence between the partners is likely to grow as interaction progresses because the organizations become more familiar with one another and, therefore, they are able to demonstrate reliability and commitment to each other. As trust levels increase, problems with delays that bureaucratic procedures cause tend to dissipate because agency officials perceive that there is less risk in bending the rules.

Making Partnerships Work

Initially, financial necessity nurtured recognition of the distinction between provision and production among many agency managers. As noted in chapter 1, at times of a perceived crisis, procedures and ways of doing things that seem entrenched tend to be reviewed and revised, creating more flexibility and opportunity. A perceived crisis helps senior managers to win support for privatization and partnering and to move their personnel beyond turf concerns about control, conflicting interests, and contrasting cultures. It makes moot any arguments from reluctant personnel that the agency could have done it as well, or better, alone. However, as one manager who was widely experienced in developing partnerships observed, financial necessity alone does not ensure that successful partnerships will ensue.

> Partnerships can fail because the parties become too eager to close a deal before they have squared their visions (Why are we building a new facility?) and missions (Once we build it, what are we going to stand for?). Some people partner just because of financial reasons, but that is not the only reason to do it. The real reason is that you want to solve a community problem and create a better quality of life, and you want to find a partner who can complement your strengths and improve on your weaknesses—and everybody has both (p. 35).[15]

There must be complementarity and reciprocity in a partnership arrangement so all partners

benefit from the collaboration and cooperation. Three types of benefits may accrue from a partnership in addition to financial considerations. First, there may be efficiencies involving removal of service duplication or use of complementary assets and strengths to jointly deliver services. Second, a partnership may enhance stability because future continuation of a service may be more probable when multiple parties make a commitment to it. Third, a partnership may confer enhanced organizational legitimacy on one or more of the partners. For example, in communities where there is widespread resentment of government, linking with nonprofit or commercial organizations may improve a park and recreation agency's reputation and image. Conversely, in other contexts where some of the actions of businesses have aroused adverse citizen reaction, their linkage with a park and recreation agency may serve to alleviate it.

Where the direct-delivery model is used, park and recreation agencies tend to be evaluated by what they do. Separation of the provision and production decisions, however, means that the evaluation criterion shifts to how well they prioritize services to be delivered, how well they work with other producers to accomplish public purposes, and how well they select among the available service alternatives. In those instances where multiple suppliers can produce a particular service, the park and recreation agency's task is to ascertain the combination that will offer the most comprehensive service to the targeted market at the desired quality and price and to ascertain how that combination can best use its resources and influence to implement this optimal delivery strategy. For example, if a policy decision has been made that all children in a community should be taught to swim, the task is to optimize the production potential of the options that are available. These may include

- direct delivery by the agency that hires instructors to teach classes in its own pools;

- the agency contracting with private instructors, Young Men's Christian Association (YMCA), American Red Cross, fitness club, or other entity to teach classes in the agency's pools;

- other organizations leasing space at the park and recreation agency's pools and taking responsibility for arranging and teaching the classes;

- the agency organizing and teaching classes, using either its own employees or contracted instructors, in pool space leased from a nonprofit organization (e.g., YMCA), a commercial health and fitness club, a motel, a school, or some other entity; and

- nonprofit and commercial organizations offering classes for the general public and the agency subsidizing those children unable to afford the classes.

There are costs associated with using partnering rather than direct delivery. Not only do the parties lose some control and autonomy of decision making, but they also have to invest effort and resources into coordination and liaison with the other parties. This may be substantial if multiple organizations are involved. The increase in organizational complexity and diffusion of responsibility complicates both financing and managing the service.

The success of partnerships depends on how the parties work together, but each partner also has to ensure that its own organization's objectives are met in the arrangement. Each entity's negotiators are responsible for meeting the expectations that their stakeholders hold about the outcome. Because the cooperating parties may have different outcome objectives, this frequently causes friction in partnership negotiations. A consequence is that partnerships often take longer than anticipated to come to fruition. The likelihood of acceptable compromise positions being agreed is likely to depend on the extent to which there is mutual trust and understanding and the effectiveness of communication. There are no generalizable formulas for forging partnerships because personalities, local conditions, state and local enabling laws, community values, and other factors vary widely. However, the two elements of mutual trust and effective communication appear to be common guiding principles that underlie successful partnerships.

Ultimately, the personalities of individuals involved in a partnership and the personal relationships they forge determine its effectiveness. If attempts are made to consummate partnership arrangements without a genuine commitment from those who will be responsible for executing them, then the arrangements will be undermined and fail. Mutual trust and understanding usually grow over time. They stem from familiarity and successful experiences of working together. This suggests

that partnerships are most likely to flourish in jurisdictions where leadership in key organizations in the public, nonprofit, and commercial sectors is relatively stable, enabling networks of trusting interpersonal relationships to evolve. Indeed, for this reason, development of partnerships in a community is best viewed not as a series of independent projects but as a continuous process.

With multiple parties involved, confusion and misunderstanding easily can emerge over goals, funding, timing, division of responsibilities, and a host of other issues. Effective communication alleviates these problems. Communication should start with clear articulation of the outcomes each partner seeks from an arrangement and the common vision and purpose the partners share for it. Sometimes this initial step is overlooked because it is assumed that each partner is aware of the others' goals and aspirations. Overlooking the first step may lead, for example, to a park and recreation agency interpreting a partner's expectations in a manner that is consistent with the outcomes that the agency seeks although this interpretation may be incorrect. Throughout the negotiation process, written documentation should be continued because points that were initially clear and agreed may not be recalled accurately 12 months later.

There may be some people who do not accept partnerships as their preferred strategy and who regard them as an action of last resort only to be explored when funds for direct delivery are not available. The following response to them was offered by the long-time director of the New Hampshire state parks system:

> The list of reasons for not entering into park partnerships is impressive: absence of authority; lack of support from the agency; risk of failure; loss of control; fear of complexity; conflict avoidance; uncertain ability to follow through; risk of liability; fear of budgetary retaliation; and philosophical resistance. "It won't work here!" "We tried it once!" "It's impractical!" "It's unprofessional!" Against this formidable barrage of thumbs down, partnerships offer this convincing rebuttal: THEY WORK! (p. 24).[16]

The Unfair Competition Issue

Two decades ago, it was possible to identify park and recreation services that were widely recognized to be the prerogative of the private sector and those services that were considered to be the responsibility of the public sector. In many areas, those lines of demarcation have now become fuzzy, overlap is common, and the number of contexts in which the sectors offer competitive programs is growing. The problem today is not defining boundaries between the sectors to determine who should be providing what services because the sectors are now too irrevocably intermeshed for that. Rather, the need is to rethink how they might interact and work together more effectively and constructively so their efforts are complementary rather than duplicative.

Three factors have contributed to blurring these sector boundaries. First, a host of new activities have emerged, such as aerobics, mountain biking, power walking, in-line skating, skate boarding, street hockey, jet skiing, beach volleyball, and cardiovascular machines. These were not offered two decades ago by either sector. Because there was no established supplier tradition for these activities, in some areas response to the new demand came from the public sector, and in others it came from the private sector.

A second factor was the reduced availability of public funds, which caused agencies to broaden their range of offerings by expanding into revenue-generating activities that previously were considered the exclusive preserve of private operators. The need to generate revenue was so sufficiently central to the survival of some agencies that it superseded any philosophical position that they may have held with regard to avoiding competition with the private sector.

The third factor encouraging sector overlap is a corollary of the higher prices most agencies now charge for services. It is not possible to give away cake and expect people to rush into the bakery business at the same time. Thus, if user prices are heavily subsidized, then an agency, in effect, is preventing the private sector from offering a similar service. If quality and convenience are equal, a participant is likely to use the lowest-priced service. When the price of a public recreation service is raised, the private sector is more likely to offer a competitive program because this action creates greater opportunity for generating a satisfactory return on the investment.

The blurring of traditional service boundaries has resulted in an increase in the number of charges made against public agencies alleging that they are engaging in unfair competition by offering services similar to those provided by commercial businesses. The charge of unfairness stems from the advantages that enable park and recreation agencies to offer programs of a given quality at a lower price. These include paying no property, sales, or income taxes; being self-insured; financing improvements with tax-exempt funds rather than borrowing money at commercial rates; not being required to cover debt charges with operating revenues; and receiving free advertising from the agency. If the public sector also were required to recover full costs, then businesses would be much less concerned. The potentially devastating impact of this competition is illustrated by the following examples.

Lafayette, Colorado, has a population of 15,000. The city built a $4 million fitness facility with three pools, steam rooms, a whirlpool, dry saunas, racquetball courts, a gymnasium, an indoor track, a fitness center with free weights and cardiovascular equipment, and babysitting services. When it opened, three private fitness clubs operated in Lafayette. After one year, one had gone out of business; a second saw its membership decline from 500 to 250; and the third, which was an aerobics studio, was unable to maintain the numbers it needed to justify proceeding with an expansion to which it had previously committed.[17]

Gore Mountain Ski Center, a public facility operated by the state of New York, received an annual tax subsidy of $50,000 each year and was constructed with tax-free bonds. It applied for $246,000 in federal grants to help fund a $2.87 million capital extension that involved installing snow-making machinery and other equipment. The balance of the capital was raised by issuing tax-free bonds. With these advantages Gore Mountain charged $400 for a family season pass. The four commercial resorts in the area charged an average of $1,125 for the same pass because they had to pay commercial prices for investment capital and received no assistance from federal grants. They also had to show a reasonable return on their investment. Thus, the publicly operated state project gradually forced the commercial operations out of business. An editorial in the *Wall Street Journal* commented: "By a sort of Gresham's law of competition, we have noticed that state enterprises in the mixed economy tend to drive out private enterprise."[18]

A federally funded campground was constructed at Pueblo Reservoir in Colorado at a cost of more than $5 million. In the immediate area of Pueblo, there were three privately owned campgrounds with marginal occupancy rates that were struggling to remain solvent. They were forced to close after the federal facility opened.[19]

These kinds of competitive actions by the public sector not only adversely impact existing businesses in a specific area but also may dissuade other entrepreneurs from establishing new recreation services elsewhere due to fear that a public agency may open near them and drive them out of business.

While competition with commercial operators may present significant philosophical, ethical, and political problems, agencies are not required legally to refrain from such competition. Under the general power authorizing them to provide park and recreational opportunities for citizens, agencies (if they choose to do so) legally can provide facilities and programs similar to those that private businesses offer. Thus, the courts generally have rejected suits brought by businesses alleging unfair competition, confirming that agencies have no obligations to businesses who suffer from such actions.[20]

The state of Colorado responded to concerns that recreation special districts were developing facilities that were traditionally the domain of the private sector by passing a statute that stated:

> No district shall construct, own, or operate any bowling alley, roller skating rink, batting cage, golf course on which the game is played on an artificial surface, or an amusement park which has water recreation as its central theme, unless the board of such district receives approval for such project from the board of county commissioners of each county which has territory included in the district. The board of county commissioners shall disapprove the facility or service unless evidence satisfactory to the board of each of the following is presented:
>
> (I) The facility or service is not adequately provided in the district by private providers;
>
> (II) There is sufficient existing and projected need for the facility or service within the district;
>
> (III) The existing facilities or services in the district are inadequate for present and projected needs;
>
> (IV) The district has or will have the financial ability to discharge any proposed indebtedness on a reasonable basis; and

> (V) The facility or service will be in the best interests of the district and of the residents of the district.

This was designed to safeguard the interests of private recreation suppliers in the state.

Regardless of the legal and ethical issues raised by unfair competition, there are two pragmatic reasons why agencies should avoid it. First, the presence of fair competition by private suppliers may stimulate the agency to improve performance in terms of both responsiveness to user demands and of minimizing costs. It was noted earlier in the chapter that competition that erodes an agency's monopoly status as service supplier may improve its efficiency. Second, most park and recreation agencies are unable to satisfy fully all of the demands expected of them. If some of these demands can be met by the private sector, then agency resources can be redirected to meet other needs.

Most of the allegations of unfair competition in this field have been made in the context of campgrounds or recreation and fitness centers, and these issues are discussed in the next two subsections. The third subsection gives illustrations of the wide array of contexts in which the issue has emerged, and the final part of this section reviews the unfair competition disputes that have arisen between fitness clubs and nonprofit organizations such as YMCAs.

Campgrounds

The most contentious debate on the unfair competition issue in the parks and recreation field has raged in the area of camping. Both the public and private sectors have a long history of providing camping services, but more than two-thirds of all campers go to public campgrounds. The private sector argues that a substantial proportion of campers go to public, rather than private, campgrounds merely because they are cheaper as a result of being subsidized heavily by public funds. Public agencies often justify subsidized campgrounds on the basis that they are necessary to provide access to the parks for moderate- and low-income families. However, data consistently show that most users of these facilities are from higher-income households.

Private campground operators argue that there is no rationale for the government to be in the lodging business. They point out that if there were a rationale, then its involvement logically should

Unfair Competition in Campground Provision

The intricacies and difficulties of a public agency's relationships with commercial recreation operators have long been recognized. They were illustrated by a conflict that occurred between the Tennessee Valley Authority and commercial campground operators in the area. The authority's official policy toward commercial operators was summarized in the following statement:

> It is not our intention to compete with private operations. . . . In fact we would like to feel we are doing everything we can do to encourage and assist developers of the commercial areas so that a wide range of outdoor recreation opportunities will be available on TVA lakes.

At the same time, the Tennessee Valley Authority believed it had commitments toward the general tax-paying public:

> It is TVA's belief that it has an obligation to assure that the public has adequate opportunities for free access to TVA lakes which were created with public funds.

This statement was further elaborated:

> TVA's general policy concerning recreation development on TVA lakes is to provide the land without charge to states and local governments for the development of parks, access areas, and other recreation facilities. The improvement and maintenance of these facilities are conducted by the states and local agencies. Because TVA lakes were created with public funds, we feel an obligation to make their waters available to everyone.

Hence, the Tennessee Valley Authority sought to encourage commercial development in order to expand the total range of recreational opportunities available, but, at the same time, it wanted to provide free service to the general public who had provided the facilities with their tax funds.

The commercial campground operators conceded that the authority had an obligation to ensure that public waters were accessible, but they believed this mandate should be defined narrowly and should not include the provision of a range of amenities. The Tennessee Valley Authority conceded that it incorporated amenities but stated: "The facilities are not designed to compete with private operations." The commercial operators were emphatic that in fact it did compete. Their views were represented by the following statement from a campground operator:

> TVA encouraged us to open a campground on our lakefront land. Soon after we were licensed and open for business, TVA began developing free public use areas and has continually added more facilities to attract people into them. These areas are developed on beautiful waterfront land. They have paved roads, concrete pads and picnic tables, fireplace grills, flush toilet facilities, drinking fountains, garbage cans, water pipes which are capped but not difficult to connect a hose to, and outdoor pavilions. White sand is hauled in and spread on some banks to make sandy beaches. Paved launching ramps with paved parking areas, fishing piers, etc., are provided.

The operator further assessed the impact of this development on commercial campground operators in the area:

> These free public use areas hurt the private campground operators in many ways. Many have been forced out of business entirely, others have phased out camping and increased marina or other phases of their business to compensate.
>
> Many, many times, when our advertising has brought in vacationing tourists, they stay a day or two with us, then they tell us that our campground is lovely, that we have been very nice to them, etc., but why should they pay to stay here when there are free places just down the road?

Compiled from an exchange of letters published in National Campground Owners Association News. *May 1977.*

be extended from campgrounds to public motels, public hotels, public gas stations, public restaurants, public ski lifts, or public anything. The primary purpose of public park agencies is to provide and preserve park lands, and they believe agencies should confine their efforts to those tasks.

However, public sector agencies do have a mandate to make their lands accessible for public enjoyment, which may include providing camping opportunities on them. In addition, they have a long tradition of operating campgrounds, so there is an expectation among the camping public that they will do this. The tension between the two sectors has a long history, as the case in "Unfair Competition in Campground Provision" illustrates. The dilemma in this case is fairly typical except that, in today's environment, the public camp area would not be free but would likely be priced lower than the commercial facility. In the case the Tennessee Valley Authority did not have the resources to provide all the desired recreational facilities at its lakes. Hence, it sought to encourage commercial enterprise to provide some of these facilities. However, because the Tennessee Valley Authority lakes were constructed with public dollars, the agency felt an obligation to provide the public free access to them. Permitting free access effectively discouraged commercial enterprise from assisting in providing facilities at the lakes.

The case for removing the public sector's unfair competition may be convincing, but the political reality of the strength of special-interest groups makes it difficult to achieve. Existing camping groups are large, well organized, and effective in lobbying elected officials and senior managers. Thus, organizations such as the Good Sam Club and the National Campers and Hikers Association are likely to turn out large numbers of members to lobby and testify in support of more public camping facilities and against any increase in their price. Many park managers would like to raise camping fees because the additional revenues would contribute to improving their agencies' financial resources, but the strength of special-interest lobby groups has often thwarted their efforts.

In recent years, many campers have sought higher levels of human comfort in their camping experiences. They now travel in recreational vehicles and mobile homes and prefer the comforts of readily available hot and cold water, electric, sewer, and cable television hookups to the in-

conveniences of roughing it. This has resulted in both public and private campground operators substantially increasing their level of investment in campgrounds. As the required level of investment has risen, the difficulty of securing a return on that investment has increased, and private operators have become more vociferous and strident in expressing their opposition to public provision. The public sector originally met its mandate to make park lands accessible by providing basic amenities limited to washrooms, drinking water, and sanitary stations. The private sector believes that there should be no elaboration of that basic role into investing in more luxurious facilities, especially if there are private campgrounds located nearby.

Many public campgrounds have an inherent advantage in that they are located on scenic public lands in close proximity to magnificent natural resources. This inherent advantage over private campgrounds is enhanced by a number of other factors that private operators regard as being unfair favorable treatment of public campgrounds.

• Prices at public campgrounds do not reflect the agency's cost of providing or operating them and are frequently below the fee charged in the private sector. These low rates effectively establish limits on what private campgrounds can charge even when there is no direct competition from a nearby public facility. This limit occurs because campers have an expected or referenced price in their mind based on their experiences elsewhere, and they are likely to reject a price that is not reasonably consistent with their previous experience. The losses that public campgrounds sustain are subsidized by general taxpayers, including the private tax-paying campground owners, who receive no benefits from them.

• Public campground operators are not required to pay property, sales, or income taxes as private operators are required to do.

• Double standards sometimes exist for publicly and privately operated campgrounds, with the public facilities often having to contend with less-burdensome regulations and policies associated with issues such as zoning, construction, sewage, and sanitation. Thus, for example, many public campgrounds are not held to the same sanitary standards that are enforced on private owners. This sometimes occurs because the regulations do not always apply to public campgrounds. In other cases in which the regulations do apply, they may not be enforced as strictly because of the fraternal relationship between public agencies.

- Public facilities often do not meet the restroom standards that private campgrounds must meet in either quality or number.

- Public campgrounds receive free advertising and promotion from public agencies including brochures, magazine advertisements and stories, literature, mentions in agency-produced television programs, and promotion from agency booths at outdoor shows.

- Public campgrounds rarely have problems persuading highway authorities to provide signs informing travelers of their existence and location, but such signage is much more difficult for private campgrounds to obtain.

Private campground operators would like these treatment inconsistencies to be removed and for public campgrounds to be established as enterprise funds. The enterprise fund would require that the public campgrounds generate sufficient revenues to cover all of their operating costs, regular depreciation on their capital improvements, interest and debt charges against the value of the land, and an amount in lieu of paying taxes. This would remove the unfair elements of competition and result in a substantial increase in the prices and revenues of public campgrounds. Private campground owners believe these changes would help the whole industry (both public and private sectors).

Recreational and Fitness Centers

New recreational and fitness centers that public agencies construct are emerging as another primary focus of the unfair competition debate as they evolve beyond basic gymnasia and pools to incorporate a higher-quality level of provision in response to citizens' expectations of an increased level of sophistication. Private health and fitness club owners allege that many proposed new recreational centers are indistinguishable from their facilities and serve only to drive them out of the market place. Some of their more extreme spokespeople ask: "Why should government build public recreational centers, when they don't build public foodstores or pharmacies?" Others more reasonably ask: "Is the city going to build and operate its own movie theaters and bowling centers as well as recreation centers, since they are also recreation facilities?"

Public agencies argue that because community recreational centers usually are financed with general obligation bonds that have to be approved by a referendum, the public's willingness to finance these centers indicates that citizens do not perceive that the private sector is meeting their demands. Competing public recreational centers generally are defended on the grounds that they aim at target markets, such as families, seniors, and children, in the community that do not have access to commercial facilities, whereas commercial operators primarily target young adults ranging from 16 to 30 years of age. For example, a spokesman defending the decision of the city of North Richmond Hills, Texas, to build a $7.8 million fun water park stated: "The park is not meant to compete with the large commercial water parks that target teens with their high-adventure rides, but is for families, particularly those with young children. We wanted elements that mom and dad would get out with the kids and interact together."[21]

In Boise, Idaho, the West Family YMCA/Boise City Aquatic Center was the result of a three-way partnership between the city, which paid $5 million of the $9.4 million construction costs; the YMCA, which paid the rest of the construction cost and operates both the city's aquatic center portion and its own fitness center portion of the facility; and a research park, which donated the land. The facility's manager stated: "Part of the Y's mission is to help provide for those who would otherwise not be able to afford it." That closely conforms to what the city wants to do by making recreational facilities very affordable. However, it was perceived differently by community health and fitness club owners in the area. One of them described it as "one of the most lavish health clubs in the area which has been responsible for putting four clubs out of business since it opened." Another club owner stated: "It was presented as a place for our youth to learn solid values and strengthen body, mind and spirit, as a way to counteract the influence of gangs. Who can complain about that? . . . But in actual fact, they're catering to middle- and upper-class adults. From our point of view, what they are doing is using their special treatment through their tax exemptions, and the fact that they don't have a mortgage to pay. They were given this facility by the community, and are using these advantages to unfairly compete with the tax-paying businesses in the fitness industry here in Boise."[22]

Often, the different targeted segments identified by the public sector are perceived to be unable to afford the private sector facilities, which usually offer a higher level of personal service. Indeed, some see community recreational centers as places at which some people are introduced to activities; when they feel more confident and committed to them, they may move to commercial facilities seeking a higher-quality experience.

"Defeat of a $25 Million Bond Proposal for a Family Recreational Center" reports the response of fitness club owners who led a successful campaign to defeat a $25 million bond proposal for a family recreational center in Southfield, Michigan. A similar campaign in Fairfax County, Virginia, was not successful, but it emphasized the convincing arguments that can be made by the fitness industry against new public recreational centers. In the Fairfax County case, the private sector recreation suppliers authored a 16-page report documenting how the county park authority was directly and unfairly competing with them when it proposed to build four new recreational centers. The report was entitled, *Unfair, Unfair, Unfair Competition: How The Fairfax County Government and Fairfax County Park Authority Directly Compete Against Private Recreation*. The first two paragraphs of the report stated:

We are optimistic this document will make governmental agencies aware of the unfair situation that occurs when non-taxpaying public facilities compete directly against private taxpaying facilities, and will encourage responsible public officials to pass legislation that would prohibit any government recreation facility to locate within a specific distance of an existing private facility. This type of legislation would give the Fairfax County Park Authority a clear guideline and prohibit the park system from competing unfairly or duplicating recreation which is already provided by a tax paying business.

In Fairfax County there are numerous privately owned recreational facilities. . . . Competition in the leisure/recreation field has become increasingly fierce due to many factors; however, when you consider normal business expenses and the additional burden created by trying to compete with the very government you pay taxes to, it is difficult to understand why any new recreational businesses would enter the market. It should be noted that hundreds of privately-owned recreation/leisure facilities are competing for the same recreation/leisure dollar. A large general public is needed to support and patronize these businesses for them to succeed. As the County continues to expand into

Defeat of a $25 Million Bond Proposal for a Family Recreational Center

Proposal A on the ballot in Southfield, Michigan, sought a 20-year bond issue of up to $25 million to expand the existing civic center sports arena, which contained a 30-year-old ice rink, into a family recreational center and to renovate the existing space. This would have added a 1.09 mill tax to taxpayers' bills, so the owner of a $92,000 home (average for Southfield) would pay $50.14 each year. The proposed facilities included

— a three-court gymnasium;

— an elevated jogging track;

— an indoor-outdoor aquatic center with a leisure pool and a second pool for lap swimming;

— a second full-sized ice arena with 1500 spectator seats and a studio ice facility for figure skating;

— a senior citizen center;

— a teen center; and

— meeting rooms, kitchen facilities, food services, and locker rooms.

(continued)

Fitness businesses in the community quickly organized to oppose it. "We pay a lot of taxes and pay a lot of people and we will be hurt by this," said the general manager of Franklin Fitness & Racquet Club. "We've been a solid business operation in this community for 25 years," he said. "You don't want to start competing with the city which is using donated land and doesn't pay taxes to itself. If the measure passes, we and other clubs through the increased taxes we'd be paying, in effect would be subsidizing a competitor. Is there a need to tax 100% of the people for what 5, 10 or even 15% are going to use?"

The city authorities argued that they had an obligation to provide recreational facilities for their citizens, to which the fitness club general managers responded: "Maybe, but to what degree? When does it stop? Sure cities provide recreational facilities, but at what level? Would they want to provide bowling? Should they build a movie house?"

"There's a misunderstanding that may be there," said the assistant city parks and recreation director. "They feel we're being competitive, but we're not. We have a family atmosphere, not a club atmosphere. We feel we can bring in fun for young people, toddlers and adults. There would be no full-blown fitness program or body-building facility. . . . We don't think we compete for the same clientele. We offer an introduction to people to the things they do at the private clubs. In that regard, we may actually be helping them because people try something out and if they find out they like it they might want to sign up with a club."

Franklin Racquet Club celebrated its 25th anniversary that year by dedicating a new $1 million basketball-volleyball floor. "Basketball leagues are flourishing here on weekends and in the evenings," the club's manager said, "but volleyball hasn't yet gotten so popular here. And if the city winds up with a new basketball/volleyball gym what will that mean to places like Franklin? It definitely will affect our business. We can't grow like we want to. If someone could afford a league over here and get it at half-price over there—even if they could afford the higher price— why wouldn't they go there? We may not have made that $1 million investment if we knew we'd have been competing with the city."

At approximately the same time that this proposal was announced, the city, in conjunction with Providence Hospital, opened a new wellness center at its Beach Woods Recreation Center. They filled an existing 12,000 sq ft room with equipment. They charged $250 per year for membership and hoped to attract from 300 to 350 members. Four physiologists, who were not employed by the hospital, were available to members, each working 20 h per week in the center.

The fitness clubs developed a brochure that emphasized reasons the bond proposal should be rejected (see figure 6.1). This brochure gave no indication that the fitness clubs planned and funded the campaign. The group registered itself as Friends Opposed to Proposal A. This strategy was designed to ensure that the residents objectively reviewed the points raised. If this had not been done, some recipients may have dismissed the campaign as merely the disgruntled efforts of a narrowly vested commercial interest.

The fitness group invested approximately $20,000 in their opposition campaign that included the following:

- A brochure mailed to each household in Southfield (see figure 6.1)—printing, postage, and mailing cost $6,500
- Brochure inserts in the *Detroit Free Press* and *News for Southfield*—$3,000
- A full-page advertisement in the *Free Press and News*—$4,200
- A full-page advertisement in the *Southfield Observer*—$2,500
- Individuals handing out a brochure outside voting areas on the day of balloting—$2,000

As a result of their efforts, Proposal A was defeated overwhelmingly by 5,582 votes to 2,055 votes.

Here's what you **Need** to *know.*

✔ Currently *you are paying an average of $80 a year* in taxes to support Parks and Recreation. Should Proposal A pass - *your taxes will increase to $130.*

✔ Why should all the taxpayers pay for something that *only a small number* of the residents will use. Nationally only 5-10% of the population use recreational facilities. Shouldn't millages regarding police, fire, streets and schools be the focus since they *affect the majority?*

✔ *No independent feasibility study* or resident survey was done to determine whether a new facility is indeed needed.

✔ *There will be increases* in liability and property insurance costs as well as an increase in personnel and maintenance costs. Each year since 1989 the Parks and Recreation Budget Expense statement has shown increases for a total of 24.5%.

✔ *Additional millages will be necessary* for the increases in operational costs.

✔ Southfield *already has* 800 acres devoted to Parks and Recreation. The Beech Woods Recreation Center already has a wellness/center in operation. Aerobics and dance classes *are being taught* in various facilities throughout Southfield. There are outdoor and indoor pools available for use. Plus basketball courts are located throughout the city.

✔ Our study found that the city has had *money transferred* from other categories such as the General, Library and Major street funds to *balance the Parks and Recreation budget.* They also have depended on grants from the government to increase the revenue category.

✔ Each year *millions of dollars* of the Parks and Recreation budget go to maintain and improve existing facilities. It only seems reasonable that additional millage will be required to fund maintenance of new facilities. If not, will areas such as street repair, equipment purchases for police and fire departments *suffer to pay these costs?*

✔ Each year there are *millions of dollars* in capital improvements that have to be made to maintain and improve existing recreational facilities. Will additional millages become necessary to support future capital improvements as the Parks and Recreation facilities expand; or will other areas such as street repair and equipment purchases be delayed in order to not increase taxes?

Remember on April 25, the City Council is asking you to approve spending an extra $25 Million

VOTE NO!
On Southfield Proposal A

Sponsored by Friends Opposed to Proposal A

Figure 6.1 "Friends Opposed to Proposal A" brochure.

Friends Opposed to Proposal A, Southfield.

the revenue-producing recreation field, the recreational dollar is further diluted, which eventually will bankrupt some businesses and certainly discourage others that hope to build additional facilities.[23]

Other Public Sector Contexts

The unfair competition issue is endemic to the park and recreation field because of the broad range of services offered by many agencies. As the blurring of traditional sector responsibilities increases, the range of contexts in which the issue emerges is likely to be extended. The case in "Unfair Competition by the National Park Service?" and the following examples give an indication of the extent of the issue.

The University of Colorado at Boulder operated an outdoor program for its students. The owner of a Boulder adventure travel company filed a complaint that it was undercutting his business by offering low-cost outdoor trips. The owner said that he could not compete because the university's program was subsidized by both student fees and by equipment and vehicles owned by the State of Colorado: "The University should be dealing in education, not adventure travel."[24]

Should an agency develop its own nurseries to supply public parks with plant materials when there are commercial companies which offer this service? The U.S. Forest Service raises about 150 million trees each year at 12 nurseries around the country. It has been growing seedlings for nearly 80 years for reforestation purposes. Some of the nursery jobs—fumigating, weeding, harvesting—are done by private contractors as is some of the planting. When the agency started raising its own seedlings around the first part of the 20th century, there were no private sector resources. However, the American Association of Nurserymen contends that operating tree nurseries is a commercial activity that should be left to the private sector.[25]

The Marine Command at Camp Pendleton, California, saw nothing wrong with a base recreational program that included sail-boat rentals, a diving school, whale-watching cruises, and sport-fishing trips. However, all of these competed with local businesses that could provide these activities for the 37,000 marines and their 10,000 dependents on the base. The base refurbished a surplus harbor tugboat for diving, fishing, and whale-watching trips. As a result, boat operations in nearby Oceanside lost nearly 100 trips each year that the marines and their dependents used to charter from them.

Camp Pendleton charged $11 per person, including tackle, for a one-day fishing trip, whereas local operators typically charged $29 per person. However, the U.S. Marine Corps got its boat for free, did not have to pay $10,000 to $15,000 each year to insure it, and was not required to make a profit. The operators argued that this constituted unfair competition.[26]

Nonprofit Organizations

Allegations of unfair competition have extended beyond the public sector to embrace nonprofit organizations, such as YMCAs. Like public park and recreation agencies, nonprofit organizations have been impacted by an adverse financial environment, heightened competition for private giving, changing clientele groups, and expectations for higher-quality services. Many have responded by changing from their traditional role of charitable, donation organizations to operating in a commercial style to generate a source of dependable operating revenue.

Traditionally, YMCAs offered basic no-frills facilities in urban areas and targeted their programs at low-income youth. Hundreds of YMCAs continue to serve the poor, aged, underprivileged, handicapped, and youth and are clearly public charities. However, in some areas, the YMCA has moved away from this model and has constructed modern fitness centers that cater to downtown businessmen or middle-class suburbanites. These are physically and operationally indistinguishable from commercially operated fitness and health clubs. These new facilities use commercial advertising that focuses on selling memberships and not on appeals for volunteer and financial help for the needy. In form and format, their advertisements are often no different from those of commercial facility operators.

The unfair competitive advantage that the YMCAs enjoy stems from a myriad of special privileges granted under federal, state, and local laws and regulations governing them. These include:

Exemption from federal income taxation under Section 501 of the Internal Revenue Code. Nonprofits also enjoy exemption from state and local income and property taxes, and many are exempt from state unemployment compensation regulations. They benefit from significantly lower nonprofit postal rates. In addition, a nonprofit organization enjoys a special status in the marketplace; tax-exempt status makes an organization especially attractive to prospective customers.[27]

The conceptual rationale for these exemptions is that the YMCAs are providing social services that would otherwise have to be provided by government, so it is appropriate that they be subsidized in this way. However, fitness club owners argue that these new YMCAs render few, if any, charitable services; allocate only small proportions of their revenue toward financial assistance or subsidized programs targeted at low-income groups; and target their services at those who can pay substantive fees. The YMCA points out that it needs to have some profitable programs, even if such programs compete with private businesses, because they are a major revenue source for providing services to the needy.

The Association of Quality Clubs, which is a trade group representing more than 1,500 commercial fitness and health businesses, estimates that the tax and regulatory advantages mean that a $3 million nonprofit fitness facility would enjoy an annual operating cost advantage of more than

$500,000 compared with the annual operating cost of an identical private club.[28] Accordingly, the Association of Quality Clubs has challenged the tax-exempt status of some of the new-model YMCAs. Their executive director articulated their case in the following terms:

> We argue that YMCA recreation and fitness centers are not tax-exempt by reason of what they do (providing such facilities), but rather by reason of whom they are serving. YMCA facilities whose services are focused primarily on taking care of youth, the elderly, the poor, the handicapped, etc., deserve every tax break they receive. On the other hand, YMCA facilities whose services are primarily focused on providing recreational and fitness services to affluent suburban communities or an upscale business and professional clientele are not public charities and ought not be tax-exempt.[29]

This fundamental principle has been accepted as the key factor by courts that have ruled in these cases.

The focus of the court cases to this point has been the legitimacy of the YMCA's exemption from local property taxes. The most prominent case

Unfair Competition by the National Park Service?

In New Orleans commercial tour operators and nonprofit groups, such as the Friends of the Cabildo (which is the primary support organization for the Louisiana State Museum), complained that they could not compete with tours that rangers from Jean Lafitte National Historic Park and Preserve offered. The commercial and nonprofit organizations charged $7 to $10 for their walking tour of the French Quarter, and the National Park Service did not charge for the tour. Part of the park's mandate is to "portray the development of cultural diversity" in southern Louisiana, and to do this, it has established a small cultural center at several locations in the area, including the French Quarter of New Orleans. At this site it offered tours, lectures, arts performances, and interpretive programs.

A spokesman said tours "duplicate almost exactly the same tours that for-profit groups offer. . . . In effect, the National Park Service designates the French Quarter, the Garden District and the cemeteries a national historic park, but it takes no responsibility for them and contributes nothing to their upkeep. There's no way the rest of us can compete with their budget." The superintendent of Jean Lafitte Park said: "We don't feel we are competing. We feel we are enhancing tourism in the French Quarter by making visitors aware there is more to the Quarter than Bourbon Street. . . . When tourists see a uniformed park service ranger in the French Quarter, it helps them realize this is a unique historical area."

From Bruce Eggler. Tourgroups: Park Service stealing turf. The Times Picayune. September 24, 1989, page 4. Copyright ©The Times Picayune. Used by permission.

concerned the Columbia-Willamette YMCA's Metro Fitness Center located in Portland. The Oregon Supreme Court ruled that this center should be placed on the tax roles because too few of its services could be defined as charitable. Indeed, only 5% of its revenue went toward financial assistance. This ruling required the YMCA to pay $150,000 in annual property taxes from which it had previously been exempt. However, two years later its property-tax exemption status was restored when it changed its name to Metro Family YMCA, expanded beyond its adult fitness focus by adding 20 new programs for youth including drug and alcohol rehabilitation and alternative education, and increased the level of financial assistance to extend to 33% of its members.

In some states, the YMCA has engaged in substantial lobbying to protect its tax-exempt status. In Illinois and Kansas, for example, this has resulted in laws being passed confirming the YMCA's tax-exempt status, provided they are committed to serving people "without regard to ability to pay."

Summary

There has been a movement away from a park and recreation agency being the exclusive direct provider of facilities and services toward an agency forming partnerships with other entities to produce these amenities. Two primary reasons for this shift were a desire to reduce the high cost and inherent inflexibility associated with hiring full-time personnel whose skills are tied to direct delivery of a specific service and a desire to avoid the constraining influence of bureaucratic procedures and regulations.

Most partnerships involve privatization, which is defined as all activities that reduce the role of a park and recreation agency, or increase the role of the private sector, in the financing, production, or management of services or assets. Support for privatization comes from four forces: pragmatists, populists, businesses, and ideologists who favor smaller government.

Irrespective of whether they occur in the public or private sectors, monopolies are prone to be inefficient, unresponsive, and self-serving. In many communities, park and recreation agencies are monopolistic suppliers of services. A central function of privatization is to induce competition into the delivery system so agencies and other suppliers will be efficient, responsive, and guided by the wants and needs of clientele groups.

There is growing awareness of the distinction between an agency's recognizing a need for a service to be provided and the agency's producing it. The role of a park and recreation agency increasingly is seen as being analogous to a helmsman who steers the boat but who may requisition equipment or oarsmen from elsewhere to row if they can do so more efficiently and effectively. It seems likely that in every community there will be organizations that, in defined areas, offer a more efficient service production alternative to direct delivery by the park and recreation agency.

Before entities from the public and commercial sectors will enter into direct partnership and pool their resources to deliver a service, a favorable supportive environment for such partnerships has to be present. The first challenge is for the potential partners to recognize and accept as legitimate their different value systems. Public agencies are mandated to serve the whole community, especially its disadvantaged members; are concerned with social outcomes and benefits that are relatively intangible and difficult to measure; and are constrained by bureaucratic procedures that are necessary to ensure accountability for their expenditure of public funds. Commercial organizations are mandated to serve their stockholders by maximizing their return on investment, which is frequently obtained by focusing on narrowly defined, responsive target markets, and they are relatively flexible with the ability to respond quickly to new opportunities. The different value systems may result in negative stereotypes and attitudes between those working in the different sectors. Removing these stereotypes and attitudes and building the mutual respect needed for partnerships to succeed requires the establishment of forums to facilitate communication and liaison.

There must be reciprocal benefits accruing to all parties in a partnership arrangement if it is to be successful. In addition to financial considerations, benefits may include efficiencies from removal of service duplication or use of complementary assets, enhanced stability for the service, and enhanced organizational legitimacy for the parties involved. Ultimately, the personalities of individuals involved in a partnership and the personal relationships that they forge determine its effectiveness.

A second factor that may inhibit the formation of partnerships is allegations of the public sector engaging in unfair competition with businesses. Public agencies have advantages that enable them to deliver services at a lower price than commercial enterprises can. The advantages include paying no property, sales, or income taxes; being self-insured; financing improvements with tax-exempt bonds; not being required to cover debt charges with operating revenues; and receiving free advertisements and promotion. The most contentious allegations of unfair competition from the public sector have been made in the context of campgrounds and of recreational and fitness centers, but the issue is being extended to a growing number of other areas. Similar disputes have arisen between commercial health and fitness clubs and YMCAs.

References

1. Sellin, Steven and Debbie Chavez. 1994. Characteristics of successful tourism partnerships: A multiple case study design. *Journal of Park and Recreation Administration* 12(2): 51-62.

2. Drucker, Peter F. 1969. *The age of discontinuity*. New York: Harper & Row.

3. Rehfuss, John A. 1989. *Contracting out in government*. San Francisco: Jossey-Bass.

4. Whitsum, Dave. 1988. Leisure, the state and collective consumption. *The Sociological Review* 33: 229-253.

5. Savas, Eric S. 1987. *Privatization: The key to better government*. Chatham, NJ: Chatham House Publishers.

6. Terry, Liz. 1997. Roast Dodo. *Leisure Management* 17(11): 3.

7. Crompton, John L. and Brian P. McGregor. 1994. Trends in the financing and staffing of local government park and recreation services. *Journal of Park and Recreation Administration* 12(3): 19-37.

8. Cox, Wendell and Samuel A. Brunelli. 1992. *Environmental partners: public private partnerships for the environment*. Washington, DC: American Legislative Exchange Council.

9. Crossley, John C. 1986. *Public-commercial cooperation in parks and recreation*. Columbus, OH: Publishing Horizons.

10. Sundquist, James L. 1984. Privatization: No panacea for what ails government. In *Public-private partnerships*, edited by Harvey Brooks, Lance Liebman and Corrine S. Schelling. Cambridge, MA: Bullringer, 303-317.

11. Drucker, Peter F. 1975. The delusion of profits. *Wall Street Journal*, February 5, 10.

12. Drucker, Peter F. 1981. *Managing in turbulent times*. London: Pan Books.

13. Bendick, Robert L. 1993. State partnerships to preserve open space: Lessons from Rhode Island and New York. In *Land conservation through public-private partnerships*, edited by Eve Endicott. Washington, DC: Island Press. 149-171.

14. Bedami, Nick. 1986. Testimony to the President's Commission on American's Outdoors. Unpublished paper.

15. Cohen, Andrew. 1996. Togetherness. *Athletic Business* 20(10): 31-37.

16. LaPage, Wilbur F. 1994. *Partnerships for parks*. Tallahassee, FL: National Association of State Parks.

17. Martinsons, Jane. 1994. The new kids on the block: Parks and rec departments. *Club Industry* May: 20-26.

18. *Wall Street Journal*. 1975. Editorial, September 12.

19. Oertle, V. Lee. 1981. Let free enterprise do it Mr. Reagan. *Woodall's Campground Management* 12(1): 3.

20. Kozlowski, James C. 1993. Authorized public recreation may legally compete with private facilities. *Parks and Recreation* 28(9): 36-44.

21. Schmid, Sue. 1995. Water world: It's water, water everywhere at a Texas water park. *Athletic Business* 19(10): 24.

22. Cohen, Andrew. 1996. Togetherness. *Athletic Business* 20(10): 31-37.

23. Weisiger, Harry. 1983. *Unfair, unfair, unfair competition: How the Fairfax County government and Fairfax County Park Authority directly compete against private recreation*. Distributed to members of the Fairfax County Park Authority, VA. October.

24. Light, Samuel. 1989. Outdoor program faces legal challenge. *Colorado Daily*, January 25: 1.

25. Jacobs, Sanford L. 1984. Tree nurseries reflect battle against federal competition. *Wall Street Journal*, April 30, section 2, 33.

26. Jacobs, Sanford L. 1985. Local firms say a marine base has stolen their customers. *Wall Street Journal*, October 14, section 2, 17.

27. De Marcus, Rachel. 1985. Nonprofit commercialism: A growing problem. *IRSA Club Business* November: 57-58.

28. Mehegan, Sean. 1994. Back on the hot seat: Congress eyes nonprofits' competition with business. *Non-Profit Times* August: 4-8.

29. McCarthy, John. 1990. Competition for the sports dollar—A response to Mr. Cousins. *Non-Profit Times* February: 20-21.

CHAPTER 7

THE COMPLEMENTARY ASSETS OF PARK AND RECREATION AGENCIES AND BUSINESS ENTERPRISES

The Disney Ice Arena

The Disney Ice arena, which opened in 1995, was a joint venture between the city of Anaheim and Disney Corporation. The project's four objectives were to provide

1. a vital resource for underserved youth in the area through the Disney GOALS program (Growth Opportunities through Athletics, Learning, and Service);
2. community programs that offered free skating and other activities for seniors and free hockey and figure-skating instruction to local high school students;
3. a fully equipped training center for the Mighty Ducks of Anaheim, a National Hockey League franchise; and
4. a focal point for local and regional hockey leagues and exhibition games.

In addition, Disney Ice offered paid public skating, spectator seating, a food court, and conference and recreational rooms for events ranging from business meetings to birthday parties.

The genesis for the ice rink occurred when the Walt Disney Company purchased a National Hockey League franchise in December 1992. Its popularity led Disney to consider creation of a community-based ice rink that would also serve the Mighty Ducks (the hockey franchise). For Disney to build and operate a community-based, dual-rink facility and to provide high-quality skating programs at reasonable fees, it required a partnership with the city of Anaheim. City officials were enthusiastic about the idea and offered land adjacent to the Anaheim Civic Center for the facility. The city envisaged this would create a focal point in the downtown development district, and it was only minutes away from Disneyland and the Anaheim Convention Center. The financial plan required Disney to give the city a specified number of ice hours and services in return for the city contributing the land. The actual figures were predicated upon the projected value of the land over time and the real cost of the free skating time and the services that Disney would provide to the city. The programs and services, which include youth hockey and figure skating lessons and senior citizen activities, were to be renegotiated with the Anaheim Department of Parks and Services on an annual basis.

Disney GOALS was established as a 501(c)(iii) organization to offer a free, nonprofit program providing organized ice, field, and in-line hockey activities; interactive learning; and community service.[a] It was targeted at youths ranging in age from 6 to 18 years. It was viewed as a healthy alternative for underserved youths in low-income neighborhoods who were subject to gangs and violence. Anaheim deeded the 3.2-acre site to Disney GOALS, which then leased the land to Disney Development Company, for $50,000 each year plus 500 h of free ice time. Thus, GOALS had income from the property that could be used for ongoing programs.

Disney Ice has 90,000 sq ft of space. The glass-enclosed entrance fronts a large plaza designed for community functions and activities and painted in the Mighty Ducks' colors. A 3,000 sq ft pro shop and Mighty Ducks superstore (where visitors can purchase top-of-the-line figure skating, ice hockey, and in-line hockey equipment and National Hockey League merchandise) are located to the right of the entrance. Rental skates are located on the left with plenty of seating room throughout the area. As visitors walk through the entrance hall, they see an 85 ft × 200 ft, National Hockey League-sized rink to the left and a 100 ft × 200 ft, Olympic-sized rink to the right.

From the Disney Development Company, Burbank, California.

[a]The characteristics of a 501(c)(iii) organization are described in chapter 18. The number refers to a paragraph in the Internal Revenue Service Code that defines a particular type of nonprofit organization.

commercial development in the 5,900-acre park. They argued that it would defile and damage the integrity of the battlefield site. One critic complained that the plan amounted to "a rape of the battlefield." Many considered the 307 ft National Tower built inside the park in the 1970s as a tourist observation structure to be a shocking eyesore.[3]

Park lovers tend to be protective of the natural qualities of parks and to regard the construction of recreational facilities within them to be incompatible and destructive. These views were expressed as early as 1916:

> Playgrounds are a foreign element in parks, disturbing and incompatible. Attempted amalgamation between parks and playgrounds results always in the annihilation of one, which in the past has never proven to be that of the playground. . . . Play and display will not fraternize.[4]

A more contemporary observer expressed his concern in the following terms:

> Historically, the key value of parks was considered to be the opportunities they provided for aesthetic appreciation of open space

and closely related passive or contemplative activities. As competition for limited urban space has continued to increase over the years, these parks were judged to be the most logical and least expensive locations for the siting of a variety of new structures and developments. Thus, such facilities as swimming pools, stadia, sports fields, tennis courts, and playgrounds, were located in parks. . . .

Parks are created as places of beauty, outdoor spaces of refreshment intended to serve as a foil for man-made urban environments. The earnest wish that visitors will find renewed belief and hope in the marvelous harmony of natural systems is never far from the consciousness of any park manager. Parks are repositories for natural beauty, and should serve as living demonstrations of how beauty, order and harmony can be made an integral part of every facet of the urban environment. . . .

We have tended to lose sight of the necessary role of parks in urban areas. The reason for their existence is not recreation. Parks do exist, in part, as open spaces where a variety

A Backlash to the Commercialization of Parks

The Metropolitan Dade County Parks and Recreation Department is widely recognized as one of the nation's outstanding agencies. Like many others, it has been required to accept substantial additional responsibilities but has not been provided with additional tax funds commensurate with fulfilling those responsibilities. In the past decade, the land that the department managed increased more than 50%, from 8,700 to 13,500 acres, while its tax revenues actually shrunk when adjusted for inflation from $27 million to $24 million. Hence, the agency's managers had no alternative except to raise additional funds by encouraging private businesses to operate in some of the agency's parks.

This created a passionate backlash from park lovers and stimulated a campaign for a charter amendment that would have required county voters' specific approval before any commercial structure larger than a snack stand was placed in a park (see figure 7.2). The leader of this movement called what was happening to Dade parks an "ecological Chernobyl. This is a nightmare. I don't think the public has realized how much of this is going on." One of his associates observed:

> The county sees park property as a way to steal from the parks budget and invest in the tourism budget. They're leasing out our birthright. The tennis stadium may be the biggest example, and you know they've even rented space so used cars could be sold in a park, but my personal favorite is Santa's Enchanted Forest at Christmastime. This is in Tropical Park. They charge you $8 so you can see a drunken spider weaving up and down stringing the lights. This gaudy display is the tackiest thing I've ever seen in my life. The county has been shameless in this. Every time there's been the slightest bit of land available, they've had this urge to make money on it.

The agency's director responded that his department desperately needs the $165,000 that the Christmas attraction poured into the county coffers just as it needs the other concessions to help keep the parks going as the budgets continued to be squeezed. "I need money to pay for cutting the grass," he said.

The director pointed out that throughout the county, neighborhoods were crying out for more services in their parks from tot lots to ballfields. With no tax money available, new ways of securing financing had to be found. These included inviting bids from private companies to build ball fields on west Dade County park land. The selected company would get its money back by charging the teams that use the fields.

Working arrangements with private businesses that allowed them to operate in the parks resulted in substantial revenues accruing to the agency. For example, the Sundays on Key Biscayne, which was an expansion of what was once a little snack shop on park land, generated $350,000 each year to the agency. The restaurant at Haulover Beach in north Dade County netted the county $157,000. The beach grill managed by Christy's at Matheson Hammock earned the department $84,000.

From John Dorshner. Keep off the grass: Must Dade's parks be paved to be saved? The Miami Herald. *July 29, 1992, pages 8-12. Reprinted with permission of* The Miami Herald.

JIM MORIN'S VIEW

Figure 7.2 Jim Morin's View.

Copyright 1992 *The Miami Herald.* Reprinted with permission.

of recreational activities can occur. However, the dominant reason for a park's existence is not as a space on which recreation activities occur.[5]

Another illustration of the backlash that may occur when park land is used to encourage private investment is given in "A Backlash to the Commercialization of Parks."

Low-Cost Capital

A park and recreation agency can borrow money at a lower interest rate than a commercial organization can. If the public organization can make this relatively inexpensive money available to a business enterprise, it can constitute a substantial financial incentive. For example, a reduction of 3% in the annual rate of borrowing from a commercial lender, compared with the interest payable on municipal bonds, may mean a reduction of $100,000 or more in annual debt payments on a $3 million loan. In effect, the public agency replaces the bank as the lender. By using this capacity, a local agency may be able to transform a nonfeasible project into a viable venture.

The reason that local governments can borrow money at lower interest rates is that most municipal bonds, unlike corporate bonds, are tax exempt. The interest paid to bond holders is free from all federal income taxes and usually from those in the state in which they are issued (if the state has an income tax). This results in substan-

tial tax advantages for those in the highest income brackets. Thus, table 7.1 indicates that an investor whose marginal tax rate is 39.6% (that is the rate on the last dollar earned, and this was the highest level of taxation paid to the federal government at the time this book was written) should be as willing to purchase a municipal bond offering 5% interest as to purchase a corporate bond offering 8.28%. Taking away the 39.6% federal income tax that would have to be paid on the 8.28% return would leave a taxable yield to the bond investor of 5%.

Table 7.1 illustrates that the higher a bond holder's tax rate, the more attractive tax-exempt bonds become. The taxable equivalent yield of a tax-exempt bond is calculated by using the following formula:

$$\text{taxable equivalent yield} = \frac{\text{tax-free yield}}{100\% - \text{tax bracket }\%}$$

For example, an investor in the 31% tax bracket who is considering investing in a 6% tax-exempt bond would receive a taxable equivalent yield of 8.7%:

$$\text{tax equivalent yield} = \frac{6\%}{100\% - 31\%} = 8.7\%$$

The tax-exempt provision allows governments to offer their bonds more cheaply than private firms can and to provide investors equivalent after-tax returns on their investment. In effect, this

Table 7.1 The Yield Required on a Taxable Investment to Equal the Yield on a Tax-Exempt Investment for Four Different Tax Rates

Tax-exempt yields	Taxable yield equivalents			
	28%	31%	36%	39.6%
2.00%	2.78%	2.90%	3.13%	3.31%
2.50%	3.47%	3.62%	3.91%	4.14%
3.00%	4.17%	4.32%	4.69%	4.97%
3.50%	4.86%	5.07%	5.47%	5.77%
4.00%	5.56%	5.80%	6.25%	6.62%
5.00%	6.94%	7.25%	7.81%	8.28%
6.00%	8.33%	8.70%	9.37%	9.93%
7.00%	9.72%	10.14%	10.94%	11.59%

means that state and local public facilities funded by bonds receive a federal subsidy because their interest income is exempt from federal income taxes. Although the cost of borrowing differs widely depending on the fiscal strength of a public agency and its credit rating, that cost invariably will be lower than the cost of borrowing from a commercial organization.

In the past, the most common way to facilitate commercial access to public sector capital was for the two parties to sign an agreement under which the public agency built a facility with its capital to the commercial operator's specifications and leased it to the operator at a price that enabled bond repayments to be met.

The city of Arlington, Texas, adopted this principle when it passed a $7 million bond issue to construct Seven Seas marine theme park. The city agreed with Great Southwest Corporation, which owned and operated the nearby Six Flags Over Texas theme park, that Great Southwest would advise on the initial design and subsequently lease and operate the marine park. Great Southwest guaranteed the city a minimum of $700,000 per year, which was sufficient to cover all bond repayments. Unfortunately, for reasons essentially outside its control, Great Southwest was forced to withdraw from the project after construction had commenced, leaving the city of Arlington to manage the park. Nevertheless, the feasibility of the principle involved was demonstrated clearly.

Leaseback arrangements of this type offer the lessee at least four important advantages:

— The lessee is free from providing capital financing for the development.

— The rental is tax deductible as an operating cost.

— The rental amount is reduced because of the government owner's ability to finance the development with tax-exempt bonds.

— The lessee does not have to pay property taxes on the development because it is owned municipally.

The magnitude of savings to businesses from these types of arrangements on large scale projects, such as construction of a new baseball stadium for a professional franchise, could be very high: "A $225 million stadium built today and financed 100 percent with tax-exempt bonds might receive a lifetime federal tax subsidy as high as $75 million, 34 percent of construction costs."[6] The lifetime federal subsidy represents the amount the federal treasury foregoes by allowing the business to benefit from tax-exempt bonds rather than requiring it to finance the venture with non-exempt bonds.

However, the ability to enter into these kinds of arrangements using these private-purpose tax-exempt bonds was substantially curtailed by the 1986 Tax Reform Act. It stated that bonds generally are not to be recognized as being tax exempt by the IRS if more than 10% of the bond proceeds are used by a nongovernmental entity and more than 10% of like debt service is secured by property used directly or indirectly in a private business. This stipulation means that these types of lease-back arrangements now are relatively rare. More frequently, governments now use their low-cost capital to assist commercial entities by directly funding part of their project. This approach to pump priming a project may be in the form of money or in-kind resources. Often these resources are used to assist a project by developing infrastructure for it that reduces development expenses associated with elements, such as roads, sewers, water, and utilities.

Downtown Camden, New Jersey, developed the Blockbuster-Sony Music Entertainment Center as part of a strategy to attack urban blight in a city with the third lowest per-capita income in the United States. Sony and Blockbuster Corporations joined with Pace Entertainment Corporation to form a company called Pavilion Partners, which agreed to commit $31 million and the expertise to build and run the entertainment complex. However, it was contingent on the public sector also making major contributions. Thus, Camden County agreed to commit $15 million for road and transit improvements, site clearances, and land acquisition. In addition, through its Casino Reinvestment Development Authority, its economic development authority, and the Urban Development Corporation, the state agreed to contribute an additional $11.5 million. In return for its investment, the state insisted on a number of conditions. Most of the workers had to be hired from the city of Camden, and, although Pavilion Partners planned to recoup its investment by presenting big-name acts, the state and county insisted on provisions that would also allow local acts and arts groups to use the facility.[7]

Denver voters approved a $14 million bond referendum that funded floodplain improvement and road infrastructure to entice Elitch Gardens—

Infrastructure Aid for Disney's Proposed Discover America Theme Park in Northern Virginia

The Walt Disney Company announced that it planned to develop a 3,000-acre resort on farmland near the town of Haymarket (population 375) in Prince William County, which is 35 mi southwest of Washington, DC. The site was 6 mi from Manassas National Battlefield Park, and its central focus was a 100-acre park with the theme of American history. The park would contain such features as virtual reality battles and a Lewis and Clark raft ride. It was projected to attract an average of 30,000 visitors each day. In addition, the development was to have almost 2 million sq ft of offices and shops, more than 2,000 houses, a 200-acre golf course, and 1,340 hotel rooms. Disney believed it would generate 6.3 million visitors each year and could bring substantial economic benefits to the area. Its construction was projected to create 19,000 jobs, and its operation would result in 2,700 permanent jobs. It was projected that $36 million each year would accrue in tax revenues for the state. Thus, Disney approached the Virginia legislature and persuaded them to contribute $158 million of state funds to the project in infrastructure support, worker training, and other incentives. Without this support, Disney indicated that the project would not proceed.

The mutual benefits to both sides and the risks that the public authorities would incur were summarized by one local commentator in the following terms:

> Prince William County and the state of Virginia have been asked to join in a quasi-business partnership with Disney's America. The citizens of Virginia will invest in the new city by buying the infrastructure—schools, roads, water, sewage, utilities, police, jails, solid waste and fire protection—necessary to its realization, and in return Disney will pay back dividends on their investment in the form of taxes on its profits and assets, which will presumably exceed the investment in infrastructure. The citizens will own the infrastructure that they build for Disney, but won't be able to sell it—their only possible return will come from taxes. Disney says these taxes will average about $36 million a year, or about $1 billion for the state and county over the next 30 years—although it can't say when those profits will begin, or indeed whether there will ever be profits at all.
>
> The citizens will take a lot of risk in this deal. The infrastructure could be in place for years before it's known if the project is destined to succeed, and if it fails the citizens will have gambled big and lost.

Soon after the Virginia legislature approved the infrastructure support, Disney abandoned plans for the development for two reasons. First, the venture was subjected to substantial negative national publicity that was damaging Disney's image. Critics argued that the development would damage important Civil War sites and would trivialize and sanitize American history. Second, law suits were filed by environmentalists who were concerned with the project bringing overcrowding, road congestion, and pollution to the area. Resolution of these suits was likely to delay opening of the development until well beyond the scheduled date and to lead to more negative publicity.

Adapted from Richard Squires. Disney's Trojan Mouse: A corporate colony paid for by gullible locals. The Washington Post, January 23, 1994, page C1.

Denver's oldest and largest amusement park—to consider moving to a downtown location. Its original 28-acre site in the city was landlocked completely by surrounding residential communities, making it impossible for Elitch Gardens to grow. The new 67-acre site had been a vacant railyard surrounded by decaying buildings. The injection of city funds was the catalyst that stimulated a $95 million investment in the new facility, which was completed in the mid-1990s.[8]

A large-scale example of this type of arrangement is given in "Infrastructure Aid for Disney's Proposed Discover America Theme Park in Northern Virginia."

Tax Incentives

The ability of the public sector to substantially reduce the property tax payments of commercial enterprises can be a powerful inducement to encouraging their participation in a partnership. These incentives most commonly take the form of tax abatements. A tax abatement is an agreement between a public jurisdiction and a commercial operator that the jurisdiction will forego at least some of the property taxes on a proposed new development for a given period of time. This incentive is used either as a competitive strategy to encourage a business to locate in a community or, more commonly in the context of parks and recreation, to encourage development of a facility that would not be viable if it were to pay property taxes in full.

The terms of a tax abatement are negotiable and may range from a waiver of some proportion of taxes for a short period (while the business builds up its clientele) to absolution of all property taxes for an extended period of time. Abatement programs exist in almost all states. Typically, if a community has a policy to grant abatements, they are awarded whenever requested; they routinely constitute part of a community's incentive package in negotiations with commercial enterprises. The length of the time period varies according to the state enabling the legislation. For example, the usual period in New York is 10 years, and the period in Ohio is 20 years. The conceptual rationale for tax abatements is that the overall long-term economic benefits the park and recreation project creates justify the tax relief extended to the commercial developer.

The city of New York arranged a tax abatement for a vertical tennis club—10 courts stacked two to each floor—that was constructed at 333 East 60th Street. The tax abatement was granted because the city believed that the project would create jobs and strengthen its economy. Normal property taxes would have been $243,000 each year. Under the terms of the tax abatement arrangement, the developer paid only half that amount the first year and five percentage points more each year until the full tax level was reached in 10 years. The tennis courts, together with a health spa, a tennis boutique, a restaurant, and a cabaret that were housed on the ground and basement floors of the building, were expected to create 225 new jobs. The company that operated the facility had been approached eight times to manage a tennis club in New York but had found the proposals unacceptable until the tax-abatement arrangement was proposed. This narrowed the risks of the venture by bringing down the costs.[9]

Although the use of tax abatements is widespread, some jurisdictions have discontinued them for three reasons. First, most businesses taking advantage of them already were located within the jurisdiction and were receiving them when they moved to a new site or expanded at their existing site. Thus, the tax revenue was being forfeited, but any benefits that accrued from job creation probably would have occurred without the incentives. Second, they were perceived as discriminating unfairly against established businesses in the community. Consider the following example.

A new $3 million health and fitness club is granted a tax abatement for 10 years, meaning that it does not have to pay the property taxes of $50,000 each year for which it normally would be liable. Similar clubs that have been operating in the city for many years pay property taxes. The new facility is able to offer its services at a lower price than the long-established clubs, which threatens their survival, because it pays no property taxes, making its costs of operation substantially lower.

The third reason that some jurisdictions have discontinued tax abatements is because businesses receive full city services even though they pay no property taxes. Therefore, their share of the taxes is unfairly shifted to existing taxpayers who subsidize them.

Control Over Permit and Zoning Processes

Nowhere is the adage "Time is money" more relevant than with respect to development projects. Invariably, one of the most challenging, and often time-consuming, aspects of the development process is meeting the various preconstruction permit requirements.

The ability to expedite permit applications has become increasingly important. The impact of government legislation and regulations is felt by the private sector from the initial planning of a project through to its development and operation phases. The development of a park and recreational facility by a private company is subject to myriad regulations and requirements that a great number of government agencies administer. The complexity of the situation for a large project is illustrated in figure 7.3. It shows the steps that would have confronted the San Francisco professional baseball franchise if it had proceeded with a proposal to build a new baseball stadium in the China Basin, which it investigated in the 1990s. The site was owned by two public agencies, the state of California and the San Francisco Port Commission. The author who developed this chart concluded: "It is simply inconceivable that the Giants could have a new ballpark without the city managing the process" (p. 17).[10]

Imagine a private firm setting out to build a ballpark in China Basin on its own. Starting in the upper left corner, figure 7.3 describes the steps with which the firm would be confronted in simply acquiring a site. Initially, a tract of land (large by any measure) would have to be assembled. As figure 7.3 indicates, once a site has been selected, elected government officials would be required to act. The colossal height of a coliseum would require a zoning variance by the zoning board, by the San Francisco Board of Supervisors, or by an initiative. Because the building of stadia is controversial, local politicians prefer an initiative that provides approval by the voters through a referendum. Therefore, site assembly would probably involve a referendum.

If the ballot measure were approved, as figure 7.3 illustrates, a host of further approvals from the city would be required to meet environmental remediation and traffic mitigation requirements, culminating once again with a vote of the board of supervisors.

If that hurdle were passed, figure 7.3 imagines what would have to happen next if this very large site were acquired. Many agencies would have to sign off, and once again the board of supervisors would have to give its assent. Getting environmental, safety, and traffic approvals and the acquisition of the state land definitely would be easier if an organ of government, for example, the Port of San Francisco, were the agency applying. Government agencies have credibility before other public agencies, and probably before the press and public also, that private firms do not have. It is hard to imagine a private firm working through the 28 steps indicated in figure 7.3 without the prior agreement of the mayor and a majority of the board of supervisors.[10]

These kinds of challenges exist even for smaller projects that, at first glance, seem relatively simple to expedite. For example the Indianapolis Parks and Recreation Department wanted to build a 120-slip marina in Eagle Lake Park, which is a large park located on a reservoir. The marina was not economically viable; therefore, the marina was packaged with a restaurant whose potential profitability made the whole project feasible, and proposals were solicited. A 25-year lease was awarded to a local restaurant owner for an annual amount that was equal to 15% of the property's appraised value. In the first year, the city received $106,000. However, completion of the development was delayed by the permitting process, and the operator had to pay interest on his financing for an entire year with no revenue accruing as a result. Permits from the following agencies were required:

- Indianapolis Parks and Recreation Department, which finalized the contracted lease agreement.
- Indianapolis mayor's office, which reviewed the arrangement to ensure it was in the public's interest.
- Indianapolis Department of Public Works, with whom all infrastructure improvements to the site had to be negotiated.
- U.S. Army Corps of Engineers, which had to approve all marine structures and flows into its reservoir.
- Federal Aviation Authority, which operated a nearby airport and with which the cost of bringing water out to the site from their pipe system had to be negotiated.
- National Park Service because the park had been acquired with matching funds from the federal Land and Water Conservation Fund. Before parts of it could be leased to a private operator, a similarly sized site (10 acres) had to be acquired by the city in close proximity and dedicated as park land in mitigation. Neither the city nor the restaurant owner had the funds to do this, so the city had to acquire a donation to meet this requirement.

Obtaining all of the necessary permits and permissions to proceed frequently is a frustrating process that discourages many developers. A public jurisdiction is likely to be able to assist in expediting this process. The public agency working from within the government system can push

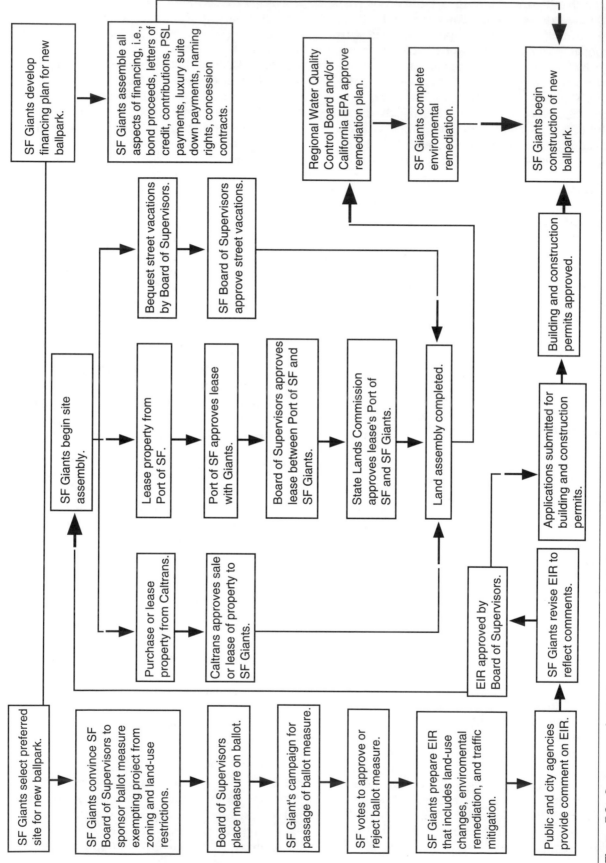

Figure 7.3 Steps toward private construction of a ballpark at China Basin in San Francisco. *SF,* San Francisco; *PSL,* personal seat license; *EIR,* engineering investigation report; *EPA,* Environmental Protection Agency.

much more effectively for rapid permit approval than can private firms operating outside the structure of government.

Control over land use through zoning is a basic asset that most local governments possess. Land-use zoning substantially impacts the value of land, and changes in it can greatly amend a project's viability. If a business purchases land that is zoned for agricultural purposes, then the land's cost and its value are likely to be much lower than if it were zoned for development because the income potential of agricultural land is significantly lower. If the zoning is changed after it has been purchased at a price reflecting agricultural use and if the land is then used to develop a park and recreation project (so the operator does not use land already zoned for development), then the cost to the business will be much lower, making it potentially more profitable. A business may seek to negotiate zoning changes by offering a desired public park and recreation amenity in exchange.

In 1997, the National Recreation and Park Association opened The Ahrens Institute, which was its new $3.5 million headquarters building located in a 120-acre model park in Loudoun County, Virginia. The county leased a five-acre site for the structure to the National Recreation and Park Association for a rent of $1 per year. It acquired the 120-acre site from Belmont Land Corporation, who agreed to donate the 120 acres to the county in return for receiving approval to rezone parts of a 4,000-home community that the company was planning to develop nearby.

Lee County, Florida, received a proposal from a developer who offered to donate 150 acres of land for a public golf course that the county wanted to construct provided that the county approve a rezoning of the surrounding property for a 400-unit residential development.[11]

Niwot, Colorado, lies 5 mi northeast of Boulder in an area of rapid growth. A developer owned a 158-acre tract, some of which Boulder County wanted to acquire as part of its plan for a greenbelt around Niwot. Existing zoning permitted one-acre home sites on 18 acres of it and two houses per 35 acres on the remaining 140 acres. An agreement was negotiated, resulting in the developer conveying 102 acres, which were valued at more than $400,000, as a donation to the county for use as a perpetual open space and conveying an additional 8 acres to the Niwot community as a park on which he agreed to construct two public ballfields. In return the county agreed to rezone the remaining land to permit more intensive development.[12]

Commercial Sector Assets

The commercial sector has five types of assets that it could contribute to a partnership with a park and recreation agency. There are many instances where these assets will not be needed because the agency is able to provide them itself. However, there are other contexts in which harnessing them may enable a nonfeasible service to become feasible or an existing service to be delivered more efficiently, effectively, or equitably. These assets are: the ability to raise capital, specialized management expertise, reduced labor costs, adaptability to scale of service, and reduced liability risks.

Ability to Raise Capital

Most park and recreation agencies have a list of desired capital improvement projects that far exceeds their available funding resources. The only way that some of these projects will ever come to fruition is if private funding is forthcoming. Further, an agency usually has to engage in an extended process of soliciting public input, acquiring support of legislators, and gaining approval of residents in a referendum before it can obtain capital resources. This lengthy procedure makes it difficult to respond in a timely fashion to unanticipated opportunities that may arise in the marketplace. In contrast to these agency limitations, a business can raise capital quickly, provided it can demonstrate to directors, investors, or bankers that the venture is likely to generate a satisfactory return on investment.

There are many opportunities for commercial investments in park and recreational facilities that would improve the existing amenities for visitors and reduce an agency's cost of operating them. Campgrounds in state and federal parks are an example. The users of these parks often travel in expensive recreational vehicles or mobile homes and prefer the comforts of readily available water, electricity, sewer, and cable television hookups to the inconveniences of roughing it. Many of these campers also are equipped with boats, mountain bikes, dune buggies, all-terrain vehicles, and other sophisticated equipment, and they desire to be in facilities where they can obtain fuel, repairs, supplies, and other services. Ancillary amenities such as gasoline stations, restaurants, convenience stores, and boat storage sometimes are not available close to a park because, in remote areas, they are only viable if developed in association with campgrounds that are large and attractive enough to support a threshold amount of visitation. Leasing selected camping areas in state and federal parks to commercial entities experienced in operating campgrounds could result in an injection of capital to upgrade the facilities and provide these additional amenities that state and federal agencies lack the resources to provide.

Angel Island State Park near San Francisco was the biggest money loser in the California state park system, bringing in only $350,000 to offset an operating cost of $900,000. The state park system awarded a 15-year lease contract to operate concessions there to Angel Island Company, a subsidiary of California Parks Company, which operated concessions in 15 state and federal parks in northern California. The company immediately invested $500,000 in upgrading facilities to encourage greater visitation. The range of concessions was expanded to include motorized tours in open-air trams; improvements in food service, which included an application for permission to serve beer and wine; and mountain bike rentals. In its first year of operation, the company doubled the former operator's gross revenues. Other services being considered were bed-and-breakfast lodging, overnight tents and cabins, a small conference center, and historical attractions at the island's Civil War vintage Camp Reynolds.[13]

Capital improvements of this nature could not be funded by the state park agency, but their availability resulted in increased revenues from the concession leading to a reduced operating subsidy for the park and an enhanced experience for many visitors.

Specialized Management Expertise

Commercial entities sometimes bring a different perspective to service provision. Traditionally, park and recreation agencies have provided services designed to offer opportunities for self-development, self-expression, self-improvement, character development, or social interaction. However, the recreation preferences of many individuals incline toward escapism, fantasy, or role playing. These preferences are reflected in the popularity of computer games, virtual reality simulation, television, spectator sports, theme parks, urban entertainment centers, resorts, and other recreational opportunities, which generally are supplied commercially. The commercial sector

has considerable expertise in developing and operating facilities that offer these kinds of benefits. Participation in partnerships with them to provide this type of entertainment may enable park and recreation agencies to provide an enhanced set of services that their residents desire and to generate revenue that will help offset an agency's operating costs.

California State Parks officials negotiated with private developers to have them construct a $23 million resort on the beach in Crystal Cove State Park in Orange County. The resort was to be built on public park land, and the developers were to receive a 55-year lease, giving the project an unusually high level of permanency. Park officials described the development as a boutique resort hotel, with average room rates of $225 each night, a restaurant, and three swimming pools. It was to be similar to the Inn at Ventana and Post Ranch Inn in the Big Sur area, two of the most exclusive lodgings on the California coast. However, both of these hotels operate on private lands. California State Parks proposed the project because the agency would receive 5% of the resort's annual gross receipts, which were projected at approximately $1 million per year.[14]

Clearly, developing and operating a recreational facility of this magnitude requires specialized management knowledge that is likely to be beyond that available in the state parks agency. The expertise of commercial enterprises in managing resorts of this type, arenas, stadia, convention centers, and similar major centers is widely acknowledged, especially when there is extensive involvement in food, beverages, souvenirs, or other retailing. Even if they have in-house expertise in these types of operations, public agencies often are constrained by a plethora of red tape, rules, and regulations that restrict their ability to operate such services efficiently and effectively.

Often, commercial companies that specialize in a particular service area can lower operating costs because of superior purchasing power with suppliers, especially if they operate a network of similar facilities. For example, a company managing several arenas is likely to be more successful at attracting top entertainment talent than an agency manager responsible for only one facility would be. A large company may also have an array of marketing skills, cost controls, and other systems that have proven effective at similar facilities, whereas an agency manager of a single facility may have to reinvent the wheel. An experienced park and recreation agency manager in charge of food and beverages highlighted the importance of such systems:

> I am not for one moment suggesting that people who work in food and beverage are one iota more dishonest than anyone else in this imperfect world. But these staff, and anyone who comes into contact with them in the course of their work, from delivery drivers to the customers, are dealing in cash, food and drinks. I can't think of three more temptingly tradable or consumable commodities handled together!
>
> It is for very good reasons that the best commercial vendors spend an enormous amount of time and money establishing effective and efficient control systems. When these are well monitored they ensure a tight grip on the business. I have looked at food and beverage operations where a 10% royalty from a good contractor would have far exceeded a presumed 30% profit from "our own people" for reasons of control alone.[15]

There is a long tradition of businesses providing concession services in public parks, especially in the areas of food, beverages, and accommodation. These are not core elements of a park and recreation agency's mandate, but they are important auxiliary support services for visitors. Agencies' bureaucratic processes and accounting procedures make it difficult for them to manage these types of commercial trading operations efficiently, and the specialized expertise needed for their management often is not available within agencies. In the past, many agencies were satisfied to see concessionaires providing services for visitors, and they regarded any revenues accruing to the agency as a secondary concern. That has changed, and the revenue potential of concession agreements has become a primary emphasis.

The magnitude of the change was illustrated by the new concession contract negotiated by the National Park Service for Yosemite National Park in the mid-1990s. For 30 years the old concessionaire paid 75¢ of every $100 in gross sales to the government. The new concessionaire, Delaware North Co., agreed to pay $20 of every $100 of gross sales. Delaware North had to buy out the old concessionaire, the Yosemite Park & Curry Co., for $61 million in compensation for decades of construction and repairs. It also agreed to spend an estimated $16 million to clean up 28 leaking underground gasoline and oil tank sites in the park. From the new agreement, approximately $4 million each year funded major improvements in the park.

Even in the case of facilities that park and recreation agencies traditionally have managed, situations are likely to arise in which agencies do not have personnel with the necessary training, experience, and equipment to effectively operate specialized facilities, such as ice rinks, indoor tennis centers, arenas, golf courses, and ski areas. In small communities, the problem may be particularly acute. For example, if they operate only a single outdoor pool in the summer months, agencies may find hiring, training, and supervising lifeguards difficult. In these situations, partnering with an established private firm to draw upon its depth of technical expertise has obvious advantages.

A large business with specialized expertise in a given service area may be better able to attract good managers to be responsible for the service than some public agencies are. Such an organization can offer that manager a career path with promotion to larger facilities and more responsibility, whereas a park and recreation agency frequently can only offer promotion to a relatively restricted level unless other duties outside the area of expertise are included. Further, the organization will have other trained managers with new ideas to replace the current manager when he or she resigns or is promoted, whereas an agency will have to invest effort and resources in recruiting from outside or will have to promote an assistant who may not be as able.

The American Golf Corporation provides a good example of how one firm has parlayed its management expertise into becoming the world's leader in public golf course management. "The American Golf Edge" indicates that the company offers a public agency a range of unique services designed to enhance both operating efficiencies and the quality of the golf experience. Rarely does a park and recreation agency responsible for operating a golf course have the resources or expertise to furnish such a complete array of specialized services.

American Golf Corporation has become the largest golf course management company in the world. The privately held corporation operates more than 250 golf courses. The company specializes in revitalizing golf courses for which

The American Golf Edge

American Golf has been the world's leader in public golf course management for the past 20 years. We have provided excellence in every facet of our operations and continually strive to stay on the leading edge of all developments in the golf industry.

We are able to provide services like no other management company because of the expertise found in our corporate personnel and our management and operations techniques.

Some of our unique human resources are

- the construction department. This department supervises all designs and construction of new site facilities and renovation of existing buildings. Our staff has extensive experience in

    — landfill construction. One example is Mountain Gate Country Club, a 27-hole private country club located in Los Angeles.

    — drainage reconstruction. Inadequate draining is a problem on many courses. We have had experience with every type of drainage problem across the country. One example of our redesign and construction can be found at Fullerton Golf Course in Fullerton, California.

- agronomy expert. Our in-house agronomy expert supervises and advises all regional and course superintendents nationwide in the proper care of trees and turf.

- training. This department ensures that all new employees are thoroughly trained in American Golf procedures, policies, and philosophy.

- employment opportunities. Career opportunities and competitive wages are offered nationwide (based on nationally collected salary survey information).

- the marketing department. All corporate marketing, advertising, promotion and public relations direction, as well as pro-shop merchandise coordination, falls under this umbrella. Where possible, central buying results in tremendous price savings for all American Golf pro shops.

Adapted from The American Golf Edge. *Produced by American Golf Corporation, 1633 26th Street, Santa Monica, CA 90404.*

governments do not have capital funds. American Golf's approach involves initial investment (sometimes reaching $1 million) to improve the course and related infrastructure, dramatically increasing rounds of play through enhanced service quality and vigorous marketing, and reducing costs largely through more flexible and cost-effective use of personnel.

The company's takeover of four municipally owned golf courses in Detroit illustrates the benefits of private sector expertise. It entered into a 20-year lease agreement with the city of Detroit Recreation Department to operate four of the six city golf courses. The courses consistently had lost money for the city. Operating losses of close to $600,000 had to be covered by monies from Detroit's general fund. The contract required American Golf to spend close to $2 million for improvements,

including clubhouse renovations, new irrigation systems, landscaping, bunker restoration, and drainage work. In addition, the terms of the agreement stipulated that American Golf pay the city $50,000 in the first year of the lease, increasing to $200,000 by the fifth year. In return, the possessory lease provided American Golf with exclusive operating rights to the four courses. American Golf's regional director acknowledged the risks for his firm: "We'll lose money for six years." [16] However, American Golf's strategy was to recoup losses as the dramatic changes in the courses drew people back. The company's goal was to attract 10,000 more golfers per year to each of the courses. The use of its own employees, who were paid considerably less than unionized city workers; sales from concessions; and equipment rentals also helped create efficiencies.[16]

It is important to note that the city of Detroit excluded two of its six golf courses from the management agreement with the American Golf Corporation. As noted in chapter 6, jurisdictions that encourage some level of competition among service providers produce substantial savings from contractors. In this case, the city induced competition between the courses that American Golf Corporation operated and those that the city maintained in-house; this action gave both service providers incentive to produce high levels of service.

Reduced Labor Costs

The labor-intensive nature of park and recreation services makes the cost of personnel a major element in the cost of service delivery. The bargaining agreements that public employee unions negotiate, the longevity of many agency personnel, and the protection that civil service regulations afford the employees frequently mean that their wages are substantially higher than those that businesses pay. For example, when Indianapolis contracted out its 12 golf courses, the contractors hired staff at an average of $7 per hour, whereas the city's average cost for the same positions was $18 per hour plus an incremental amount per hour for overtime when employees worked more than 40 h each week.

When agency and business wage rates are similar, agencies typically pay from 30% to 35% in fringe benefits to employees for things such as health insurance, retirement, sick leave, and maternity leave. Many businesses, in contrast, are not required to maintain such a high level of overhead. Federal and state laws may require commercial operators to pay Social Security and payroll taxes but not employee medical or pension benefits. As a result, payroll overhead costs for private firms average 12% to 15%. The approximately 20% savings advantage in overhead costs that many businesses enjoy allows them to provide the same level of service much more economically than a public park and recreation agency can. In addition, their exemption from civil service requirements provides them with greater flexibility in determining level of pay, fringe-benefit payments, and a mix of full- and part-time personnel.

Even when businesses pay their employees as much as public agencies both in salary and fringe benefits, they are able to save in labor costs. One

empirical study reported that these savings emerged because businesses

- used less labor,
- had about 5% less absenteeism,
- made managers responsible for equipment as well as labor,
- used younger workers (who tend to cost less),
- used more part-time labor,
- terminated more employees (which is probably why there was less absenteeism), and
- used more capital equipment (which may be why less labor was needed).[17]

The following example illustrates how one park and recreation agency overcame a difficult staffing cost problem by taking advantage of the flexibility afforded a private business.

A publicly managed golf course in Alameda County, California, operated on a 13 h summer schedule, opening at 6:00 A.M. and closing at 7:00 P.M. All maintenance activities were performed by public employees of a regional park and recreation authority. The employees formed a bargaining unit, affiliating with the American Federation of State, County, and Municipal Employees, which is a public employee labor union. The labor contract established between the federation and the park authority stipulated a standard workday of 8 h for full-time employees. Compliance with the contract required the park authority to commit two separate 8 h shifts of maintenance and operations personnel to the golf course. The park and recreation authority estimated that under this agreement, staffing costs at the golf course would increase as much as 21%.

Faced with an intractable situation, the agency made the decision to contract out the operation of the golf course to a specialized management firm. An advertisement placed in the *Wall Street Journal* produced several legitimate bidders. A long-term lease (five years with four, five-year renewable options) was awarded to a private firm with a successful track record in operating and maintaining golf courses. The agreement called for the management company to provide more than $600,000 in capital improvements over the first five years of the lease. By applying a more flexible personnel schedule to accommodate actual work demands and, at the same time, not being obligated to pay as high an overhead (e.g., retirement, vacation, and hospitalization benefits), the park authority estimated that the private firm reduced labor expenses at the golf course by as much as 50%. The end result was that the golfing public benefited from an enhanced resource. At the same time, the park authority freed approximately $400,000 each year in public monies, which previously were committed to paying golf course personnel, to apply to other service areas of concern.[16]

Adaptability to Scale of Service

The commercial sector is often better equipped to deliver services that require large numbers of part-time employees for short time periods. The bureaucratic procedures required of agencies to hire and pay part-time employees is sometimes lengthy, cumbersome, and onerous, whereas it is generally easy for businesses to do this. Thus, it may be efficient for an agency to partner with businesses for producing special events or highly seasonal services.

Partnerships with a commercial entity are also likely to be beneficial when an agency cannot take advantage of economies of scale. A business serving multiple organizations is likely to be able to purchase state-of-the-art equipment and materials at a lower price and is likely to be able to use them more efficiently than a single park and recreation agency can because the business services a larger number of units. An agency may not be able to justify purchasing equipment that will sit idle for much of the year. Examples of gains accruing to public agencies as a result of partnering with businesses include equipment for conveying workers to the tops of tall trees for tree trimming or for maintaining tall structures and the economies of scale available to large companies like American Golf Corporation.

Each year American Golf Corporation may purchase more than 3,000 golf carts for the 250 golf courses it operates, and this volume enables the company to negotiate a substantially lower purchase price per cart than any park and recreation agency can. This scenario is repeated for its purchase of all other types of golf course maintenance equipment and of clothing and supplies sold in pro shops.

A related advantage that sometimes accrues to large commercial companies is that they may be able to take advantage of federal business tax laws, which may permit rapid depreciation of new equipment and offer investment tax credits for its purchase. These types of regulations make it advantageous for companies to acquire new equipment, and this translates into greater operating efficiency (although, conversely, it should be noted that unlike public agencies, they are required to pay sales tax on equipment).

Reduced Liability Risks

An increasingly attractive incentive for park and recreation agencies to enter working partnerships with private organizations is that such a collaboration can substantially reduce their liability risks. Most liability suits arise from careless or reckless acts (negligence) that result in unintentional harm to an injured party. The decline in the doctrine of sovereign immunity, which historically prohibited units of government from being sued, has resulted in cities, counties, and school districts being more vulnerable to negligence claims. Now examples of liability awards that park and recreation agencies have paid range up to several million dollars. The increased threat of such catastrophic claims has necessitated that agencies purchase expensive insurance premiums.

A key question, then, for agency managers is how can they minimize the possibility of a financially catastrophic claim being made against their agency. Because liability insurance premiums largely are based on the estimated degree of risk facing an agency, any actions that it can take to reduce level of exposure to risk should lead to reduced premium costs. Park and recreation agencies have found privatization to be an effective strategy for minimizing their liability risks and, therefore, the costs associated with insurance protection. Increasingly, agencies are structuring partnership agreements in order to transfer as much of the risk and responsibility for liability as possible to the commercial or private operator. Typically, the transfer of liability risk is conferred in the lease agreement establishing a partnership. The following sample is drawn from an actual lease agreement established between a municipality and a commercial operator for the maintenance and operation of a recreational complex:

> CLAIMS. The contractor shall hold harmless the city and all of its agents, employees and officers from any and all damages or claims of any kind or nature, that may be made or may arise directly or indirectly from the performance of duties by the contractor, its

agents and employees, including but not limited to any claims which may arise either directly or indirectly from the use of any equipment or tools which the city may lease or sell to the contractor. The contractor shall appear and defend any action or suit instituted against the city arising in any manner out of the acts or omissions defined herein above. The contractor's duty to indemnify hereunder shall include all costs or expenses arising out of all claims specified herein, including all court, and/or arbitration costs, filing fees, and attorney's fees and costs of settlement.[16]

The excerpt identifies two provisions key to effective transfer of liability risks. The first element establishes that the park and recreation agency will be held harmless in the event of a negligence claim. The intent is to release the agency from all liability risks. However, while crucial, the hold-harmless clause alone may not provide ironclad protection. A standard provision is to add an indemnification clause stipulating that if the hold-harmless agreement is not completely adequate—for example, if the park and recreation agency is found liable of contributory negligence—the commercial operator would pay any damages that the agency owed. Thus, the private contractor exclusively bears responsibility and costs related to liability concerns.

One of the reasons that many park and recreation agencies hire independent contractors to teach recreational classes is to transfer to them the tort liability, eligibility for worker's compensation, and the accompanying costs associated with insurance coverage. However, it is important to ensure that this relationship is executed properly. Just having a person sign a statement that he or she is an independent contractor is not enough. If a worker is classified as an independent contractor but is determined by the IRS to be an employee, then the agency not only fails to transfer its risk liability but also can be required to pay an average of more than $3,000 in back taxes, including a percentage of the employee's Social Security payment.[18] The key issue in determining status of an independent contractor is control. The Federal Tax Code makes the distinction in this way:

An employer is able to exercise control over both methods and results. In general, if an individual is subject to control over the

objectives of his or her services, but is free to choose the means and methods, he or she may be defined as an independent contractor.

Thus, the IRS may classify an independent aerobics instructor, for example, as an agency employee rather than as an independent contractor if

- the agency determines class times and location and provides a set routine for selected music to the instructor;
- the instructor is not in a position to realize a profit or suffer a loss as a result of his or her services (if the remuneration level is dependent on number of participants in the aerobics class, that constitutes profit or loss and would be indicative of independent status);
- the agency hires, supervises, and pays assistants that the instructor uses; or
- the agency includes the instructor in its employee health plan or provides any other types of employee benefits.

These four criteria are illustrative of 15 criteria that the IRS reviews when determining whether a person is an employee or is an independent contractor. There is no clear line of demarcation between employee and independent contractor status. No single criterion alone will be the deciding factor; rather, the decision is based on an overview of all of them taken together.

Summary

Park and recreation agencies have four major assets that can be used to prime the pump and leverage commercial investments. A willingness to use them judiciously is central to creating a favorable climate for direct partnerships with businesses. First, they own large tracts of land, much of which is attractive with respect to location, access, and commercial value. If this land is leased for a nominal fee of $1 per year, for example, then a project that was nonfeasible because of the high cost of land may become viable when that cost is removed.

A park and recreation agency can borrow money at a lower interest rate than a commercial organization can. If it elects to make this relatively inexpensive money available to a business, then what appeared to be a nonfeasible project may become a viable venture. In the past, this money could be channeled to businesses by an agency building a facility to specifications set by the business and then leased to the business at a price that enabled bond repayments to be met. Tax reform has now made such arrangements much more difficult. Governments are now more likely to use their taxing power and low-cost capital to provide direct funding for a project either in the form of money or in-kind resources used to assist the development of infrastructure.

A third pump-priming asset is the ability to grant tax abatements that free a business from its requirement to pay property taxes for a specified period of time. Finally, the public sector's control over permit and zoning processes can be used to encourage a park and recreation business to develop a project. This control enables these processes to be expedited and, in some cases, even changed or waived, which substantially reduces the commercial financing costs and risks associated with the proposed venture.

The commercial sector has five types of assets that it can contribute to a partnership arrangement with a public agency. First, it has the capacity to raise capital quickly and easily, provided it can be demonstrated that a project is likely to generate a satisfactory return on the investment. Second, it has management expertise in specialized areas that may not be efficient for an agency to acquire through hiring personnel with these skills. Third, labor costs often are lower in terms of both salaries and fringe benefits. Fourth, it often is much easier for a business than for an agency to hire and pay part-time workers who may be required to handle one-time services or short peak seasons. Further, businesses serving multiple organizations may be better able to take advantage of efficiencies associated with economies of scale. Fifth, the involvement of businesses may enable park and recreation agencies to reduce substantially their vulnerability to liability claims by passing such risks to their business partners.

References

1. Clements, L. Davis. 1989. Involving the technical expert in the collaborative process. Paper presented at Annual Meeting of Society for Applied Anthropology. April 5. Santa Fe, NM.

2. Osborne, David and Ted Gaebler 1992. *Reinventing government.* Reading, PA: Addison-Wesley.

3. Pound, Edward T. 1997. Gettysburg plan gets a second look: Foe's counterattack puts pressure on park service. *USA Today*, October 28, A4.

4. Burnap, G. 1916. *Parks: Their design, equipment and use.* Philadelphia, PA: J.B. Lippincott Company.

5. Reid, Leslie M. 1976. A call for national reexamination of municipal recreation and park organizations. Presented at the Sixth National Symposium on Parks, Recreation, and the Environment. Chicago, IL. March.

6. Zimmerman, Dennis. 1996. *Tax-exempt bonds and the economics of professional sports stadiums.* Washington, DC: Congressional Research Service. The Library of Congress.

7. Strauss, Robert S. 1995. Urban entertainment center opens in New Jersey. *Urban Land* 54(10): 15-16.

8. Stern, Julie D. 1995. An amusement park moves downtown. *Urban Land* 54(8): 13-14.

9. Stone, Michael. 1977. Tax abatement approved for vertical tennis club to be built in New York; first such facility in US. *New York Times*, May 12, B2.

10. Agostini, Stephen J., John M. Quigley and Eugene Smolensky. 1996. Stickball in San Francisco. Presented at the Brookings Conference on Investment in Sports Facilities. October.

11. Winton, Pete. 1994. Developers scramble for shot at public golf course. *Fort Meyers News-Press*, August 3, 1 and 16.

12. Trust for Public Land. 1985. Creative acquisition of parklands: Strategies for financing open space. *Proceedings of the western governor's association and trust for public land; joint sponsored workshop.* Denver, CO: October 16-18.

13. Carlsen, Clifford. 1994. Private company is putting pearly gates on Angel Island. *San Francisco Business Times*, 2 September, 6.

14. Schoch, Deborah. 1997. Pricey resort planned at state park. *Los Angeles Times*, August 5, section A, 3, 17.

15. Urquhart, John. 1986. Catering: To contract or not? *Leisure Management* 16(5): 21-22.

16. Howard, Dennis R. and John L. Crompton. 1995. *Financing sport.* Morgantown, WV: Fitness Information Technology.

17. Stevens, B. 1984. *Delivering municipal services efficiently: A comparison of municipal and private service delivery. Summary*. U.S. Department of Housing and Urban Development. New York: Ecodata

18. Wong, Glen M. 1996. Contract law: Improperly classifying employees as independent contractors can be costly. *Athletic Business* 20(10): 10-14.

CHAPTER 8

PARTNERSHIPS WITH THE COMMERCIAL SECTOR BEYOND PUMP PRIMING

Unfortunately, seldom is the owner of a desirable tract enthusiastic about (or even interested in) exchanging his or her land for surplus public holdings. Far more frequently, another landowner shows interest in acquiring the surplus holdings. To resolve this conundrum, a second type of exchange incorporating a third party or external agency may be used. Using such arrangements, the money accruing from the sale of park land in place A is used to buy park land in place B. Congress incorporated such an arrangement into the Santini-Burton Act to facilitate land exchanges between Las Vegas and the Lake Tahoe region.

Under this act, the U.S. Bureau of Land Management was authorized to sell to private developers isolated tracts of land in Las Vegas that it could not manage because the tracts were in the middle of the city. The money was used to buy private land around Lake Tahoe, high in the mountains on the California-Nevada border where development was causing pollution and severely damaging the area's fragile environment.

In this case, Congress was, in effect, the third party. It enacted specific federal legislation to authorize the exchange because, like many other agencies, the Bureau of Land Management was barred from selling public land. However, these agencies are often permitted to trade their lands, and a third party foundation or trust, such as the Trust for Public Land, may be used to expedite the exchange. These exchanges are likely to work as follows:

— The public agency identifies to the foundation the parcel of private land it wants to acquire, and the foundation options it.

— The agency identifies land it owns that it is prepared to designate as surplus to its requirements and is prepared to trade.

— The foundation finds a buyer for the agency-owned land.

— The foundation exercises the option and acquires the private parcel. It then exchanges it for the agency-owned parcel, which is sold to the identified buyer. This is illustrated in the following example.

A 540-acre tract of prime development land valued at more than $3 million and located in Little Cottonwood Canyon in the Wasatch Mountain range of Utah was offered for sale when the landowner died and the heirs could not afford to hold the property. It was an important part of the watershed that provided Salt Lake City's water supply, a popular rock-climbing area, and a home to a wide variety of animals and birds. For these reasons, the U.S. Forest Service wanted to acquire it and absorb it into the adjacent Wasatch National Forest, but it lacked the funds to do so. The Forest Service did have tracts of land in the area that it identified as surplus to its requirements. The Trust for Public Land was invited to purchase an option on the canyon property and to find buyers for the surplus tracts. Receipts from the sale of the tracts were used to meet the sale price that the canyon's heirs sought.

The third type of voluntary exchange is the trade-out, or quid pro quo, approach, whereby a park and recreation agency grants authorization for a commercial entity to do something and, in exchange, receives some type of in-kind resource.

Under its city charter, Cincinnati is allowed to sell or exchange land without seeking voter approval. Hence, the city was able to convey 6.85 acres of property valued at $596,000 to the Kroger Company. The land contained a small park with old facilities, including a small pool and ball fields, that needed major renovation. It was located in the Hartwell Business District that was a redevelopment area, and Kroger wanted to build a large general retail store on the site. In exchange for the land, Kroger agreed to construct recreational facilities equal in cost value for the city, in accordance with the city's specifications, on an adjacent site that the city also owned. The new facilities included a large indoor pool complex, three ball fields, and playground equipment. Users of the recreational facility were permitted free use of the Kroger store's parking lot.

In Nashville, the Metropolitan Board of Parks and Recreation engaged in a land exchange with Hospital Corporation of America. The corporation provided $12 million plus 10 acres of land enabling the board to build the 112,000 sq ft Centennial Sportsplex facility containing high-quality aquatic, ice arena, fitness, and tennis complexes. This facility replaced an existing tennis and ice-arena complex. In return, Hospital Corporation of America received 10 acres of urban Centennial Park, which it needed to connect two of its major health-care facilities. With its newly acquired land, the corporation planned to build a $100 million hospital and medical center complex, which would generate substantial additional property taxes for the city.[3]

Mitigation Land Exchanges

In recent years, mitigation, which is an involuntary form of land exchange, has been mandated in a growing number of federal, state, and local government statutes. For example, the federal Water Pollution Control Act, often referred to as the Clean Water Act, could require developers to compensate for any damage or loss inflicted on wetlands by replacing or providing substitute resources or environments. Mitigation is a payment imposed on developers and polluters, requiring them to compensate society for their negative impacts on the environment. The compensation may be in the form of land or money that is used to buy land or land-related natural resources to offset their negative actions.

On-site mitigation is mitigation that takes place in the same locale in the watershed or ecosystem as the impacted area. On-site mitigation is preferred; however, if on-site measures are impossible, then off-site mitigation may be required. This has spawned the concept of mitigation banking. In the context of wetlands, mitigation banking is defined as the intentional creation, restoration, or enhancement of a wetland to protect a habitat for the purpose of compensating for losses from development. Thus, many agencies or nonprofit organizations develop plans that provide for creating, restoring, or enhancing wetland areas, and developers contribute their mitigation funds to these projects.

In some cases, major nonprofit conservation organizations have purchased and assembled banks of land, which they sell to public agencies when the agencies receive mitigation funds from developers. These approaches enable a large area of wetlands or an ecosystem to be acquired in mitigation for the despoilation of perhaps dozens of relatively small tracts of land; this practice is often advantageous from both a conservation and an efficient management perspective. The following examples illustrate mitigation exchanges.

A court settlement created the Platte River Whooping Crane Maintenance Trust with $7.5 million in mitigation funds from a consortium of midwestern power companies. The trust was designed to offset the effects of the Glenrock, Wyoming dam and power plant by providing for

Negotiated Mitigation by Disney

For years, developers gazed longingly at the 8,500-acre Walker Ranch, 15 mi south of Walt Disney World Resort in central Florida. The property was located ideally for houses and shopping centers; however, its woods, prairie lands, and wetlands were the home of 15 endangered and threatened species including the greatest concentration of active bald eagle nests in the southeastern states. A creative effort by the Walt Disney Corporation, federal and state regulatory agencies, and the Nature Conservancy resulted in the ranch becoming a preserve and an environmental learning center.

The effort began when Disney decided to try a new approach to developing 10,000 acres of its property, which included wetlands areas, as it expanded the Disney World Resort. Instead of seeking government approval parcel by parcel and negotiating wetland mitigation compensation on each, Disney asked regulatory agencies for permission to build on the whole tract during the next 20 years. To compensate, Disney officials offered to help preserve an entire ecosystem—the Walker Ranch—and to place a conservation easement on an 8,300-acre area of its property at Disney World.

Government officials agreed to the plan, provided that a conservation group manage the ranch. The Nature Conservancy agreed to do this and its staff prepared a management plan that was accepted by all of the parties for the property. Disney then bought the ranch, renamed it the Disney Wilderness Preserve, and donated it to the Nature Conservancy, which restored damaged parts of the tract and preserved the entire ecosystem. Disney agreed to fund restoration and management of the preserve for 20 years and established a $1 million endowment for stewardship after that period ended. They also agreed to build and fund an environmental learning center to educate the public about restoring and safeguarding ecosystems. Conservancy officials estimated that the total value of Disney's financial commitment to the project was between $35 million and $45 million.

From Jeff Porro. Saving Disney's land. Nature Conservancy. March/April 1993, page 32. Copyright ©1993 The Nature Conservancy. All rights reserved. Used by permission.

downstream land acquisition to protect critical migratory bird habitat in Nebraska.[4]

Congress directed the federal Bonneville Power Authority to spend about $1 billion in mitigation funds in four states—Washington, Montana, Idaho, and Oregon—to mitigate for losses to fish and wildlife habitat incurred in the course of constructing dams along the Columbia River. Most of the funds were used for hatchery improvements, but some also were used to acquire wetlands.[4]

Wetlands were purchased on San Francisco Bay with $2.7 million in mitigation funds from a major oil company. These funds were part of a larger settlement between the oil company and the Sierra Club Legal Defense Fund to mitigate for the company's pollution of San Francisco Bay.[5]

In the city of Poway, California, a local golf course developer paid $300,000 in mitigation for removing wildlife habitat. This money was used as part of the financing to purchase a 400-acre natural canyon site with significant wildlife habitat.[5]

The Walt Disney Corporation engaged in a negotiated mitigation exchange in which the company agreed to acquire and protect an ecosystem in return for approval from government regulatory agencies to build on property that it owned. This case is described in "Negotiated Mitigation by Disney" on page 203.

A similar arrangement was negotiated with the Irvine Company, a large commercial developer, for a project in Orange County, California. The company agreed to set aside 21,000 acres of prime land for a nature reserve. In exchange, it received a no surprises guarantee from federal, state, and local officials that it could build residential and commercial developments on other parts of its tract without facing endless legal battles over the federal Endangered Species Act. The nature preserve was designed to shield nearly 40 troubled species from extinction. It was to be managed by a nonprofit corporation, whose board of directors included property owners; federal, state, and local regulatory agencies; and three public members. A $10.6 million endowment by the private and public participants would fund it, and an independent panel of scientific consultants would advise it.

Transportation projects account for a relatively large proportion of mitigation exchanges because of their frequent impacts on wetlands. Florida state transportation officials acquired two large tracts of land as mitigation for the 44 mi, $477.5 million Suncoast Parkway north of Tampa. One tract was a 3,636-acre ranch adjacent to a protected area already managed by the state, and the second

tract consisted of 6,700 acres. The acquisition costs were financed from tolls on the highway.[6]

Using Existing Commercial Facilities

The barriers and incentives to park and recreation agencies using commercial sector facilities vary according to whether the partnerships are concerned with recreational facilities or classes, urban neighborhood parks, or land beyond the urban environment. The issues involved in each of these contexts and a discussion of the potential for negotiating use of utility company lands are presented in this section. The section concludes with consideration of the strategy of public agencies taking control of existing commercial operations that are faltering.

Recreational Facilities or Classes

Fairmont Lanes was a $3 million bowling center in Midland, Texas. It was not used for this purpose to a great extent until after 5 P.M. During the day, it was used as a senior citizen center organized by the Midland Parks and Recreation Department. The long, wide, carpeted lobby was ideal for walking and permitted about 10 laps to 1 mi. Other areas were set up for various table games, and free coffee and a large-screen television were available. The bowling center benefited from the establishment of a Senior Citizen's Bowling Club that formed, sales from a snack bar, pool rooms, and positive word-of-mouth publicity about its operation.

A country hotel wanted to build a nine-hole golf course with clubhouse facilities and a golf driving range as an added attraction for its guests. To convince their bankers that these new facilities would generate a guaranteed income, the owners entered into a partnership with a local public agency. The hotel owners built the facilities on their own land. The agency rented 80% of the time periods at the course for an agreed fee for five years. The agency controlled the prices charged during their operating periods and retained all income. The hotel was responsible for maintenance and was able to offer its guests use of the facilities during the prime 20% time it retained.[7]

Illustrations of extended use of commercial facilities by park and recreation agencies such as those described are not common, but there appears to be little reason why more of these types of partnerships should not be forged. The more common type of partnership with commercial facilities is limited to recreational classes scheduled for tightly defined, relatively short time periods. Commercial facilities that could be used for this purpose include those providing activities, such as horseback riding, gymnastics, racquetball, aerobics, bowling, ceramics, golf, roller skating, photography, sailing, fishing, skiing, and dancing. Classes, such as swimming and tennis, may be offered at motel or apartment complex facilities.

Typically in these types of arrangements, the park and recreation agency promotes the class or activity and registers participants. In some cases, the agency may provide bus transportation and supervisory staff for the activity, but class instruction usually is provided by the commercial operators who often will have the best instructors in the area. The park and recreation agency contracts for a class with the operator. Class prices are set to cover the cost of the contract with the operator and the agency's overhead. The agency's staff are likely to be present for the first one or two sessions to ensure that there are no administrative loose ends, to ensure that the class is being delivered as promised, and to facilitate introductions.

An additional dimension is that the park and recreation agency may be able to schedule classes at off-peak times. This suggests that its clients will pay a reduced rate for using the commercial facility, while the operator will welcome the business. From the agency's perspective, these types of partnerships keep fixed costs low because there is no building overhead and the permanent instructional staff costs are minimal. These arrangements allow maximal flexibility in programming so that the agency can respond to market shifts. From the client's perspective, the agency serves as a broker who joins clients with recreation providers who can meet their needs. Commercial operators are likely to welcome park and recreation agency use of their facilities because, from their perspective, the agency is serving as an unpaid agent, efficiently reaching client groups who are attractive potential prospects to the operator. In addition, businesses receive considerable promotional exposure because the park and recreation agency advertises their locations when it advertises program offerings.

Because the agency is promoting a large number of class offerings in both its own and commercially owned facilities, there are economies of scale, and the promotional cost per class is low. If an individual operator tried to reach the same number of potential users with a promotional communication, the cost may be prohibitive. The primary challenge of the commercial sector is to persuade people who are interested in an activity to investigate their facility. They expend substantial promotional dollars and effort to do this because having prospects see the facility is the critical first step in persuading them to become regular users. With this recreational class arrangement, the park and recreation agency delivers people interested in the activity to the facility at no cost to the operator. At the same time, program participants are able to sample recreational opportunities at a relatively low cost without a long-term membership commitment.

Many of these people feel comfortable participating under the auspices of a park and recreation agency because they are familiar with it, but they may feel some intimidation about venturing into an unfamiliar commercial establishment. This participation with a park agency enables them to try the facility at no financial or embarrassment risk, and if they like it, they subsequently may enroll as a regular user. They are unlikely to make the substantial investment normally required to use a commercial facility without experiencing it first.

Urban Parks

In the context of urban neighborhood parks, short-term leases with landowners may be negotiated at a nominal rate to make use of vacant space that may not be scheduled for development for some years. For example, it is common practice for some major retail and hotel chains to buy land in growth areas a long time in advance of the date on which they plan to build on it. In the interim period, this land may be leased for a nominal amount by an agency and may be used on a temporary basis for athletic fields.

Plano, Texas, leased 30 acres of undeveloped prime industrial property from a major real-estate developer at no cost and developed soccer fields. The lease was indefinite, but the developer could terminate it with 30 days' notice. The only improvements made by the city were minimal grading and seeding, some irrigation, and the installation of goal posts that could be removed and reused when necessary.

On Third Street in downtown Los Angeles, a soccer field was constructed on a site that had been a long-time eyesore. The neighborhood was Latino with half the population less than 18 years of age. The primary sport was soccer, but no playing fields existed. This site was leased for a nominal amount from Cathay City Developments, which did not anticipate developing the land for another 10 years.

The park board of the city of Dallas on occasion has used vacant lots in areas without parks. Simple permission-to-use letter agreements are signed with cooperative owners. Either party can cancel the agreement within 30 days. This allows the board to install playground equipment that can be removed easily on short notice. The board promises to return the property to its original state at the request of the owner. Owners of such lots have the satisfaction and public relations benefits of seeing their land used for community good, and, at the same time, they have not lost ownership of the property. Use of a vacant lot in this way prevents it from degenerating into an overgrown, weedy, unsightly distraction, convincing many owners to participate in the program. The Dallas park board has been able to provide play equipment without capital outlay for land purchase. Various communities, in turn, have received a small neighborhood park when purchase of one was perhaps impossible.

Looking for park land in densely populated urban areas means taking advantage of opportunities wherever they can be created. In New York, for example, some residents have made use of roof tops for private gardens, landscaped terraces, and even swimming pools. New Yorkers speak of tar beaches by which they mean sunbathing areas on house roofs. Similarly, commercial buildings may construct private garden areas on roofs for aesthetic purposes. Thus, Rockefeller Center has four gardens located on the seventh story roof on which people can look down, but they are not open to the public. A 10,000 sq ft garden, which is open to the public, was constructed at the Metropolitan Museum of Art. It features large sculptures set against an attractive view of Central Park's tree tops and the city skyline.

The potential of this roof-top tradition of creating private, small-scale parks was expanded in the development of Riverside State Park in Harlem, described in "Riverside State Park." In Japan, several public parks have been constructed on the roofs of sewage plants, but this is the first large-

Riverside State Park

The 28-acre Riverside State Park located in West Harlem was built on the 0.5 mi-long roof of the North River Water Pollution Treatment Facility at a cost of $129 million. The park was promised to Harlem residents in exchange for them allowing the $1 billion treatment plant to be built in the late 1960s. Other New York neighborhoods had rejected the plant because of concerns about it emitting foul odors. Thus, in essence, the park was a mitigation payment to win residents' support for the treatment plant. Construction of the park began in 1987 and was completed in 1993. People enter the park by two bridges linking it to Riverside Drive at West 138th and 145th Streets. They can access the site by walking to it or by riding a public bus. There is little car parking provision because the community felt strongly that it did not want people to come by car.

The park's 28 acres were designed to meet the recreational needs of the Harlem community, which had few recreation amenities. At elevations ranging from 5 ft to 69 ft above the Hudson River, the state-of-the-art recreational, athletic, and cultural center offers unparalleled views of the Hudson River north to the George Washington Bridge and south to the city's sky scrapers; an indoor 50 m and two outdoor pools; a 400 m, eight-lane running track; an indoor rink for ice skating in winter and in-line roller skating in summer; facilities for soccer, softball, and football; 12 outdoor tennis courts; a 1,270-seat gymnasium with facilities for basketball, volleyball, gymnastics, and martial arts; locker rooms for more than 1,000 people; picnic tables, fountains, a greenhouse, and a community garden; an 834-seat auditorium for cultural events; and a waterfront restaurant.

Admission to the park is free, although there are nominal charges for the rink and pool facilities. The staff of 160 includes 40 state park patrol officers who secure safety in the complex. The limited access to the park makes monitoring and security relatively easy. It is open year-round for 18 h each day and averages 10,000 visitors each day, increasing to 15,000 to 20,000 during weekends.

From Kirsten A. Conover. Relax on a rooftop. The Christian Science Monitor. July 9, 1993, page 10; and Alexander Garvin and Gayle Berens. Urban Parks and Open Space. The Urban Land Institute: Washington, DC. 1997.

scale park in the United States built in this manner. It is a pioneering example of how public facilities might be developed on privately owned assets, which other jurisdictions may seek to emulate, albeit on a smaller scale.

Resources Beyond the Urban Environment

The demand for outdoor recreation in the United States is likely to continue to grow. Given the reduced federal commitment to land acquisition, more pressure is emerging for privately owned lands to supply recreational resources, particularly in the eastern third of the United States where publicly owned lands are relatively scarce.

Many large companies, for example Crown Zellerbach and other lumber companies in the Northwest, allow the public to use their lands. They issue maps to facilitate access by assisting prospective visitors to identify the private road systems. Their lands are open for public hunting and fishing, and they publish brochures to inform the public about picnic and recreational areas. However, landowners tend to be less willing to permit such casual access. Acreage held by industrial forest owners that is open for public recreation has dropped substantially. In 1960, 96% of industrial forest land was open to public access, but by 1990, the amount had fallen to less than 50%. This declining trend has continued.

Increasingly, public access to private lands is being facilitated by more formal arrangements. Most states have programs to encourage private landowners to allow access. These programs include some states that lease private land. Government leases of access rights usually are purchased with designated money received from special fees or access stamps. In Michigan, for example, the Department of Natural Resources facilitates snowmobile access to more than 90,000 acres of private lands using funds from snowmobile registrations to compensate landowners. They also have implemented a program that requires all hunters in the southern portion of Michigan to purchase a public-access stamp. The revenues for this program are used to lease land in that part of the state. As a result, 600 farms encompassing more than 55,000 hectares are open to Michigan residents for hunting.

Most leasing by landowners, however, is not with government agencies. Rather, it is with individuals or with clubs and organizations for the exclusive use of their members. This type of private leasing has a much stronger economic appeal to landowners, and it is estimated that one-third of all private rural land in the United States is leased to private individuals or groups for their exclusive recreational use.[8]

Despite such efforts, much land remains closed to public use. The reasons most frequently cited to explain why large, private landowners are not willing to allow public use of their lands relate to concerns about liability, property abuse, and protectionism.

The Liability Issue

Legally, users of land can be classified into one of three categories: trespassers, licensees, or invitees. The three categories imply increasing protection for the visitor, and the extent of a landowner's liability varies according to which of these three categories a visitor is assigned:

- A trespasser is defined as a person who enters or remains on property without the owner's consent. As a general rule, owners owe trespassers no duty of care except to refrain from willfully or maliciously injuring them.

- A licensee is any person who enters property with the permission of the owner. A licensee may be a social guest of the landowner who pays no fee for access. A property owner's duty of care to licensees is to provide adequate warnings of hidden or latent hazards on the premises.

- Highest on the protection scale is the invitee. Invitees are persons asked onto the owner's property for purposes connected with the owner's business or for the mutual economic interest of both parties. A recreation lessee who pays a fee to use private property is an invitee. Owners are responsible for protecting invitees from unreasonable risk or harm. As such, they must inspect their property periodically to discover hidden dangers and either remove them or warn visitors of their presence.

These common law rules have been modified by the enactment of recreational use liability statutes in all states except Alaska. The state statutes have their genesis in a model act drafted in 1964 by the Council of State Governments. The purpose of these statutes is to encourage landowners to make their property available for public recreation by limiting their liability for user injuries. Under common law, the casual recreational user (such as a hunter who is granted free access to private land) is classified as a licensee. Under recreational use liability statutes, this status is downgraded to that of a trespasser. The landowner is liable only for willful or malicious failure to guard or warn against a dangerous condition. However, if users are charged a fee, then this negates the recreational use statute protection, and landowners are then treated like any other commercial enterprise. An exception to this is the Florida liability law that provides continuing protection even when a fee is charged, providing the landowner meets certain criteria for wildlife habitat management. A similar expansion of protection to other states would increase the likelihood of more private lands being made accessible to public use.

These statutes minimizing landowner liability appear to have had limited impact on landowners' public-access policies. In Michigan and New York, two states where modified statutes have been in place for many years, landowner surveys continued to find increased access restrictions as well as concerns expressed over liability. It has been suggested that the reason these statutes are unsuccessful in encouraging landowners to allow public access is that most landowners and lawyers do not know that recreational use statutes exist.[9] Indeed, a survey of all state wildlife agency chief executives reported that only 22 of them were aware of their state's legislation minimizing landowner liability for injuries sustained by hunters.[10]

Those who do know about the statutes often are not concerned about whether they have a successful defense to a recreational injury lawsuit. Their concern is much more basic; they want to know if they can be sued. Unfortunately, the answer invariably is yes with or without limited immunity provided by a recreational use statute. As a result, the lower landowner standard of care (from ordinary negligence to willful or wanton misconduct) imposed by the recreational use statute will not encourage most private individuals to open their lands to public recreational use.[9]

Thus, any solution to the liability issue on private recreational lands must address the landowner's very real concerns about being sued. Whether the result is a win or a loss, it has been said that a lawsuit is the worst thing that can happen to an individual with the exception of death or serious illness. Therefore, the challenge to encourage more public recreational access to private lands is to somehow insulate the private landowner from the costs attendant to a lawsuit.[9]

Lease agreements to provide public recreational land can be negotiated more easily with private landowners if a public agency agrees to defend and indemnify the private landowner. This means that the private landowner may still be sued, but the public agency will hold the private landowner harmless, absorbing the cost of defending the lawsuit. This incentive was discussed in chapter 7. In this way, private landowners will feel less threatened by potential liability when they open their lands to public recreational use. Further, a public awareness campaign is needed to educate private landowners about the immunity available to them under existing recreational use statutes. If this strategy is to be widely adopted, the recreational use statutes should be amended where necessary to extend such a lower standard of care to public entities as well as to private individuals. If this is done, then government agencies will be more willing to enter into a lease agreement whereby the public entity agrees to hold the private landowner harmless when liability must be based upon proof of willful or wanton misconduct.[9]

When a landowner does not expect to use land in the foreseeable future, it may be possible to avoid liability problems by the use of determinable title. The use of determinable title requires the landowner to sign over the land to a public agency for a fixed period of time, after which it reverts back to the owner. This enables the landowner to open lands for park and recreational use by the public without risk of incurring liability, without paying property taxes, and without giving up the right to use the land for some other purpose in the future.

Property Abuse

Major concerns related to granting public access, reported in a national survey of private and corporate landowners, included littering, fire, vandalism, and crop damage attributed to public users. In New York, 97% of landowners who restricted access did so in part because of problems they experienced with irresponsible recreationists, particularly hunters and snowmobilers. Statistical analysis of Wisconsin data revealed that the most important predictor of access restrictions among southern Wisconsin forest owners was the number of problems with public users they reported.[11]

Three approaches have been used in efforts to resolve property abuse problems. First, the use of private lease agreements with clubs and with individuals giving these recreationists exclusive rights to use the private land provides them with a vested interest in maintaining the quality of the resource. Second, some states have made substantial efforts to develop educational programs that inform recreationists of access laws and proper behavior on private land.

The third approach was initiated in New Jersey by that state's Open Land Management Act. The principles incorporated in this approach have been used successfully for more than half a century in Great Britain. Under this act, landowners may enter into agreements, called access covenants, with the state agency guaranteeing public access to their land. If a property owner will open up his or her land to the public for one of several types of outdoor activities, the state will in turn provide funds to eliminate the problems and hazards to the property owner. The recommended length of these covenants varies according to the amount of the grant and the ownership status, but the minimal period is one year. In return, landowners are eligible for grants and in-kind assistance to improve access and are guaranteed reimbursement for damages to their properties.

The arrangements are supervised by district wardens who decide on what and where to use the funding and who oversee development and maintenance of all participating properties in the program. Emphasis for grants is on providing trail access and facilities for passive recreation. The problems and hazards that the Open Land Management program covers include repair or replacement of damaged facilities and vandalized property of the landowner or adjacent landowners caused by public use, removal of accumulated trash, and payment of the premiums on any extra insurance liability the owner wants to take out.[12]

Protectionism

A third limiting factor that inhibits public use of private lands is the growing protectionism movement. Owners' values affect their recreational access decisions. State programs offering legal or financial incentives for opening private land may be pointless if directed toward owners who have a strong desire to retain all recreational use of the land exclusively for themselves. Because values represent deep-seated beliefs, it may be difficult to influence the access decisions of owners whose policies are based on a value hierarchy emphasizing protectionism.

There is evidence of an increase in the private land ethic under which landowners believe that their property resources should provide benefits only to them and their invited guests.[11] Increasingly, rural property is being purchased primarily for personal recreational enjoyment rather than for ranching or agricultural purposes. These owners are reluctant to allow public access. Such hobby farming is likely to be most prevalent on the urban fringe and in areas with great aesthetic value. Unfortunately, these are the very locations where the demand for outdoor recreation is likely to become most critical in future years.

Using Utility Company Lands

Utility company lands are often overlooked as a source of potential park and recreational opportunities. However, many utilities have a large water base, miles of transmission line rights-of-way, and substantial amounts of undeveloped property. Further, these resources often lie close to urban populations. Some utility companies are receptive to requests for recreational use of these resources, particularly the rights-of-way.

A utility company usually secures a right-of-way under one of two legal arrangements. The first method is by easement, which was discussed in detail in chapter 4. In this situation, the company does not own the land but merely has the right to run its lines across the property. Therefore, the company cannot grant permission to use the right-of-way for recreation. Rather, permission has to be sought from each individual landowner along the right-of-way. This requires a tedious, and often unsuccessful, effort, especially when the land is being used for other purposes, such as farming.

Second, when the company owns the right-of-way, the company can grant permission for it to be used for recreation. However, often these rights-of-way are leased to adjacent landowners. In other cases, there is reluctance to grant affirmative easements because of concern about liability. Granting an easement means that users become invitees for whom the utility company is required to exhibit a higher standard of care to safeguard itself from liability. Nevertheless, opportunities for their recreational use exist throughout the country.

The Indianapolis Parks and Recreation Department leased a corridor of land from the Indianapolis Water Company, which is a public utility. The department developed a greenways corridor plan, and one of the prime corridors was the towpath lying adjacent to a canal that forms a part of the company's water resources. The initial lease was for a 2.5-year period, but it was extended by mutual agreement of the parties. It was leased to the department for $1 per year. This lease differed from a perpetual easement because the company did not give up any permanent rights. From the city's perspective, this meant that the water company was not eligible for any downward adjustment of property taxes. The water company required the department to pay for comprehensive liability insurance, which protected both the company and the agency against claims for personal injury and property damage. In addition to relieving the company of liability concerns, the lease required the department to maintain the towpath and to control public access to it, which relieved the company of these responsibilities. Any erosion of the canal banks attributable to this public access became the department's responsibility.

California's East Bay Regional Park District had collaborative arrangements to lease 25,000 acres from four water management districts in the region. It managed the lands to enhance the public's visual and recreational opportunities including boating and fishing. Restrictions were imposed that ensured protection of the water supply. The utilities continued to pay taxes on the lands, which comprised about one-third of the park district's extensive holdings.[4]

The Denver Urban Drainage and Flood Control District provided part of the funding to construct and maintain hiking and bicycle trails along Denver's Platte River greenway. Because the district's mission was served by the increased physical access that the trails provided to the river and creek system for maintenance workers and vehicles, it funded gravel trails and took responsibility for structural maintenance. Local governments paid the increased costs of upgrading or maintaining trails for recreational purposes.[4]

Before it can proceed with development of a hydroelectric power project, a utility company has to receive a license from the Federal Energy Regulatory Commission. As part of their submission, utility companies are required to incorporate a recreation plan showing how the considerable water and land resources associated with hydroelectric projects will be developed and operated for recreational use. To secure license approval, a utility needs the support of local and state officials and interest groups. Recreation opportunities are likely to be a major concern, and a utility's willingness to provide such opportunities may be key to winning the necessary support. The utility company may operate and manage the rec-

reational opportunities at the project itself, or it may lease them to other agencies to operate.

Public Sector Takeover of Commercial Facilities

The takeover of a faltering commercial leisure business should not be viewed as a public bailout. Rather, it should be viewed as an opportunity to retain an existing recreational asset that will otherwise disappear. Takeover is an appropriate strategy if a commercial entity closes and the type of recreational opportunity that it offers either is not offered by another supplier in the area or can be used to service a market segment that is presently not being reached with that opportunity. However, sometimes takeover opportunities have to be foregone because an agency cannot respond quickly to market forces and the business or lending institution is unable to wait for the time-consuming referendum process necessary to authorize bonds for capital investment.

The takeover of facilities such as golf courses, ski facilities, or ice rinks is unlikely to be very controversial because they are consistent with the public's image of the types of facilities that are appropriate for government to provide. For example, the town of Eastchester on Long Island purchased the financially ailing Lake Isle Country Club with its 18-hole golf course, five pools, eight tennis courts, and large banquet hall. The wording of the referendum that approved the town purchasing the facility required it to be a self-sufficient operation. It could not look to local tax revenues to support its $2.4 million budget. However, the complex did not have to yield a return on equity or meet debt charges associated with the purchase cost, so it was easier for the complex to be self-sufficient than for the previous private operator who had to recover capital debt and equity costs.[13]

A further financial advantage that accrues to a public agency when it takes over a facility is that the facility may be eligible for grants for capital improvements from federal or state programs, which are not available when the facility is operated privately. Thus, the Lake Isle complex received more than $750,000 in capital grants from the federal Land and Water Conservation Fund's matching grant program. The grant funds and the low interest rate of public debt mean that these improvements cost substantially less than half of what they would have cost a private operator.

Unfortunately, park and recreation agencies often fail to consider takeover of less-conventional ailing commercial recreational facilities. Sometimes such unconventional facilities can effectively complement existing public opportunities. For example, a number of commercial amusement parks have closed, and park and recreation agencies subsequently have taken them over. Many of these amusement parks reflected marginal profitability rather than operational losses but were not viable because of a poor cash flow position and lack of revenue for reinvestment. Instead of permitting the resources to be lost, it may be appropriate for park and recreation agencies to lease or purchase them in order to preserve the range of available opportunities. This type of park should be considered as worthy of public agency support and subsidy as the traditional city park, for it may be appreciated by as many of the population as the traditional park is. In addition, these commercial facilities may constitute a part of the cumulative attraction that encourages tourists to visit a jurisdiction.

Although it was motivated by a desire to prevent traffic congestion rather than to save a recreational opportunity, one of the most visible examples of a public agency taking over a commercial enterprise occurred in Santa Clara, California. Marriott Corporation operated the Great America Theme Park in Santa Clara. The park was profitable, but the value of its 200-acre site increased dramatically with the high-technology boom in Silicon Valley. The city was concerned that Marriott would sell the park for its land value. If that occurred, it was likely that the site would be occupied by more office and industrial buildings that substantially would worsen an already serious traffic congestion problem. The city calculated that alleviating the problem would cost much more than the $90 million Marriott was asking for the park. Hence, the city purchased the park to pre-empt the traffic problem. It then contracted with King's Entertainment, which operated several large theme parks, to manage Great America. Five years later, the city sold the park, but not the land, to King's Entertainment for approximately $50 million. In addition, King's Entertainment agreed to pay $5.3 million each year for at least 50 years to lease the land.

A commercial enterprise developed Lake Pleasant Lodge as an elaborate tourist center in Maricopa County, Arizona. It eventually fell on hard times. The Maricopa County Park and Recreation Department purchased the facility and renovated it. The center now is open as an outdoor education center targeted at school and youth groups.

The city of Dallas took over the Majestic Theater in order to safeguard the last remaining example of vaudeville theater in the city. The Majestic, which opened in 1917, had been converted to a movie theater. However, because it was located downtown away from hotels and because of the emergence of multiple screen theaters in the suburbs, its commercial viability waned, and it was closed. Because it had no obvious alternative commercial use, the owners offered it to the city, which accepted the donation. The city renovated the theater using $2 million of bond money and $1 million raised by the private sector, and it became home for the Dallas Ballet Company. The theater is now operated by a nonprofit organization that receives an annual subsidy from the city, and it is a prominent element of the city's arts area.

A park and recreation agency may be able to operate a facility that commercially fails because the purchase price that an agency pays for a takeover may be substantially less than the original cost or the asset value of the operation as a going concern.

Consider the situation confronting a bank that is forced to foreclose on a specialized recreational facility, such as a ski lift, because the operator is unable to make contributions toward the loan payments. The equipment has minimal resale value, and the bank is unlikely to have either the expertise or the inclination to operate the ski lift. Thus, the bank may be receptive to an offer from a park and recreation agency to purchase it for 50% of its cost, for example, because this would enable the bank to recoup at least some of the capital it loaned the operator to build the facility. In addition, by enabling the facility to continue to operate, the bank is contributing to maintenance of the area's economic health and quality of life, both of which are important to the bank's long-term profitability.

There are two major, but often overlooked, factors that are likely to impede the success of a takeover. First, a public agency's operating expenses may be substantially higher because their existing policies often require agencies to pay higher salaries and more fringe benefits to employees than the commercial sector pays. The second factor relates to management style and attitude required to operate a traditionally commercial facility. Consider the following case.

When Homassa Springs Nature Park, a 50-acre amusement and nature park, was listed for sale because of financial reverses, a private buyer could not be found. The residents of Citrus County,

Florida, voted to acquire it using revenue bonds. The $3.8 million bonds were to be repaid from operating revenue generated by the park and, if necessary, to be supplemented by general funds. Thus, the county purchased an existing commercial enterprise the residents believed to be a valuable county asset. Upon purchase, the county set up the park as an enterprise account separate from the general fund. It retained the same manager and staff employed by the private owner. At the time the park was purchased, a citizen committee was appointed to help prepare policy guidelines for the initial transition. This committee provided much sound business direction.

Despite this guidance, the negative aspects associated with public agency operation became evident in the first year. Personnel, purchasing, accounting, auditing, pricing, and advertising policies had to conform to county regulations. The park was a public entity, yet to function as a private enterprise, it needed to be emancipated from the bureaucratic constraints of a public agency. Initially, as would be expected, there was the mother hen syndrome of close scrutiny that almost jeopardized the enterprise's economic viability. In response to these problems, a separate board, similar to a board of directors, was established with authority to oversee all aspects of the park's operations. This alleviated many of the initial difficulties.[14]

Joint Development With the Commercial Sector

In this third category of partnerships with the commercial sector, five types of arrangements are discussed. The first category is multiparty partnerships in which an agency serves as primary broker and ultimate manager of a facility that is at least partially funded and used by other entities. The second type of partnership is more limited. It focuses on expansion of an existing park and recreational facility undertaken by a commercial entity, which is prepared to invest in improvements to expand use of that facility in exchange for the right to lease it or to operate it at off-peak times. The third type of partnership is commercial sector pump priming, in which a commercial entity offers some of its assets as an inducement for the public sector to make major investments in park and recreational facilities. The fourth type is leaseback arrangements by which a commercial developer agrees to finance and develop a facility or major equipment and to lease it to the park and recre-

ation agency at a previously agreed rent. The fifth type of partnership is multiple exploitation of a resource, which occurs when an agency cooperates with commercial operators to exploit a resource in such a way that it leads to the development of a park and recreation amenity.

Multiparty Partnerships

In multiparty partnerships, a park and recreation agency takes the lead in conceptualizing and subsequently implementing ventures that involve several financial partners from both the public and commercial sectors. These types of arrangements are exciting and have enormous potential. However, they are complex and difficult to implement because the agency is acting in an imaginative and entrepreneurial fashion with a variety of different organizations but is constrained by public sector rules and procedures. Substantial investment of effort is required in initially formulating a shared vision and a viable action plan, in convincing elected officials of its worth, in persuading other organizations to participate, and in continually negotiating amendments to the original action plan to accommodate the specific needs of participating organizations. Given the complexities of such schemes, it requires managers of unusual talent to bring them to fruition.

The following example describes a relatively simple arrangement involving a park and recreation agency, a school district, and a commercial developer. An indoor court complex was constructed and operated by a commercial group on land secured by a lease at $1 per year from a park and recreation agency for a 10-year period. At the end of this period, the facility reverted to the agency. The developer offered the school district use of the facility from 9 A.M. to 10:30 A.M. and from 2 P.M. to 3:30 P.M. for each day the school was in session for a 5-year period. An advanced payment was negotiated with the school district. This arrangement provided the school district with inexpensive discount playing time when spread over the full period of 5 years and provided the developer with initial equity capital to help finance the project. The times allocated for school use were times at which the operator did not expect to attract other users. Thus, although per-student charge was very low, it probably generated more revenue than would have been received if there were no school use. At the same time, students were introduced to the facility and taught to play the racquet games so that they became potential future users.

As hospitals move into the wellness business, a growing number of park and recreation agencies are forging relationships with them to jointly develop facilities. This joint development avoids the expense of duplicating efforts by institutions that are located in close proximity to each other. Elmhurst Park District in Illinois contacted Elmhurst Memorial Hospital to find out if it wanted space in a tennis facility that the district was expanding into a multipurpose health and fitness center. The hospital agreed to lease 5,000 sq ft of the 77,000 sq ft Courts Plus facility and to pay the $288,000 cost of equipping that area. Their area houses the hospital's Life Plan program, which consists of health education, physical therapy, and phase three cardiac rehabilitation. The Life Plan staff have access to the district's track and fitness facilities at certain times.

The hospital pays the district $64,000 each year for use of the facility. It has a substantial budget to promote its Life Plan program, and, because it is in the district's facility, some of those promotional benefits spin off to the district. The Life Plan program also provides the district with a feeder source for new members. After completing cardiac rehabilitation in the Life Plan program, approximately half of the people enrolled in it purchase memberships in the district's facility and continue to exercise on their own.[15]

"Establishing a Public Golf Academy Through Multiple Partnerships" describes a more complex joint development involving the city of Indianapolis, a commercial operator, the United States Golf Association, and philanthropic donations from civic-minded major businesses.

One of the most common approaches to developing tourism real estate has been timesharing. Timesharing enables individuals who desire to own property at a resort area to purchase a selected number of weeks per year at a condominium rather

Establishing a Public Golf Academy Through Multiple Partnerships

Indianapolis had no public facility for teaching golf and no course on which learners could practice. Thus, the Indianapolis Parks and Recreation Department envisaged creating a golf academy, which was to be a teaching facility incorporating six elements.

1. A clubhouse approximately 14,400 sq ft in size that included a pro shop, concession area, a covered 80 ft × 20 ft training area with 18 tee positions, a training video viewing area, a club fitting and repair area, a classroom, and two golf simulators.

2. An outdoor, lighted driving range with 40 outdoor tee positions.

3. A practice putting green.

4. A pitching practice area.

5. A sand-trap practice area.

6. A nine-hole, par-three training golf course with greens built to Professional Golf Association standards but with holes not exceeding 150 yd in length. Regular courses intimidate learners because of the level of difficulty and their tendency to slow play, frustrating experienced golfers behind them. The nine-hole facility would alleviate this problem.

The golf academy's mission was to expand the exposure of golf to Indianapolis' residents, particularly to young people. Total projected cost of the project was $1,750,000. To bring it to fruition, resources were pooled from four partners: the park department, a private golf course operator (R.N. Thompson & Associates), the United States Golf Association, and the Indianapolis corporate community.

The park department issued a request for proposals, inviting private operators to lease a 35-acre site for 15 years for the purpose of funding, constructing, and operating the golf academy. The site was located in Riverside Regional Park, which was a 680-acre park incorporating both a wide range of recreational facilities and extensive passive areas. The site was highly visible from major traffic arteries, and it was situated in a lower-income, racially diverse area with moderate gang activity. Within 1.5 mi of the site were three golf courses. There was no other driving range in the area, and this component of the academy was seen as the cash cow undergirding the financial viability of the venture.

The park department established a 501(c)(iii) organization, the Indianapolis Junior Golf Foundation, to own and govern the project for two reasons.[a] First, the academy was intended to be a self-sufficient, but nonprofit, venture with any surplus funds being reinvested to fund capital improvements, improve promotion, and offer additional training opportunities for youth. To operate in this manner, it needed to be free of political interference from the city council. Second, if the city directly operated the academy, the city would likely have more difficulty persuading corporations to contribute to its construction

In response to the request for proposals, R.N. Thompson & Associates were selected. The company was a major real-estate developer in the Indianapolis area, had developed four residential golf courses, and owned and operated four other daily-fee golf courses and a private golf academy in the area. Thompson agreed to pay a lease fee to the park department of 10% of the first $500,000 gross receipts; 7%, between $500,000 and $750,000; and 5%, in excess of $750,000. This lease fee went into the park's golf enterprise fund and was reinvested in golf. Thompson also agreed to contribute $450,000 toward design and construction of the academy and to operate it for a management fee set at an amount necessary to reimburse actual maintenance and management expense. R.N. Thompson & Associates were entitled to additional compensation if specified performance goals were exceeded.

R.N. Thompson & Associates were required to maintain a capital improvement fund of at least $40,000 each year to reinvest in the academy's operation and to appoint a full-time experienced general manager, who was acceptable to the park department and was a licensed, Class A, Professional Golf Association golf professional. The lessee could not sublet or assign the lease to anyone else under the contract terms because the city's long relationship and shared vision with Thompson were viewed as key to the venture's success.

The United States Golf Association contributed a grant of $300,000 to the golf academy. Additionally, it provided technical assistance with the design, construction, and operation of it. The association recognized that much of the current boom in golf was attributable to the baby boomer cohort reaching the prime age for golfers. They believed that 7% of adults played golf. Given the smaller numbers of people in age cohorts following the baby boomers, a larger proportion of them would have to be players if the demand for golf was not to fall. The association saw minority groups as a main target market because minorities were substantially under-represented among golfers and were the fastest growing demographic segments.

The golf academy site was easily accessible to minorities in Indianapolis. Prices and quality standards were controlled by the park department through the contract with Thompson, and a variety of measures were used to permit economically disadvantaged youth to earn green fee credit as an alternative to paying the academy's fees. The academy was available to all youth regardless of their access to funds. The United States Golf Association invested in similar programs targeted at minority youth in San Diego, Dallas, and New Orleans. If these pilot projects were successful in expanding the number of minority golfers, the association was likely to increase substantially its investment by extending the program to other cities.

The final partner was the corporate community in Indianapolis from whom the park department solicited $1 million to raise the balance of the funds. The department did this by working with the Indianapolis Corporate Community Council, comprising major businesses that annually selected quality-of-life projects to support. Appeals to the corporate community were based on the belief that if golf is made available to inner-city youth, then acquisition of the skill to play golf and participation in junior tournaments will assist in building self-esteem, confidence, and good social characteristics. This involvement would provide an alternative to joining local gangs. The golf academy's development was phased so that the clubhouse's indoor components were constructed while corporate donations were solicited to complete the project.

[a]The characteristics of a 501(c)(iii) organization are described in chapter 18. The number refers to a paragraph in the IRS Code that defines a particular type of nonprofit organization.

than having to purchase a whole condominium unit. This enables the purchase price to be shared by a number of buyers (52 of them if each buys one week), and maintenance of the unit is the responsibility of a management company. How a county park and recreation agency planned to use the timesharing principle to finance the building of an indoor recreational center is described in "Developing a Recreational Center Using the Timesharing Principle." This approach would have provided a new facility for the use of residents at no cost to the sponsoring county agency.

Jackson County Parks and Recreation Department near Kansas City used the multiparty partnership concept to construct two sports complexes, which cost approximately $4 million each, using a form of revenue bonds. The following example briefly describes the cooperative agreement at one of these, the Longview Sports Complex.

The department entered into a cooperation-and-use agreement with the Junior College District of Metropolitan Kansas City, under which the district sold 10 acres of its Longview Community College Campus to the county for $1. The depart-

ment agreed to develop a modern sports complex on the site and grant the college priority time in the building from 8 A.M. to 4 P.M. on weekdays during regular fall and spring semesters. The college paid $100,000 each year for this building-use time and equally shared the costs of utilities and maintenance with the department. In addition, the department preleased space in the building to a day-care center, which serviced children of the many older students who attended the college; several large corporations, which preleased time in the building for their own corporate recreational programs; a pro-shop operator; and concession operations. The income from these preleasing arrangements with other partners was supplemented by revenues accruing from the department's own classes, programs, and leagues to make the total project viable for funding with a form of revenue bonds.

A multiparty partnership may be forged by combining facilities with high and low revenue-generating capability into one package. Hence, the package as a whole is self-supporting, but within it there may be specific components that lose money.

Developing a Recreational Center Using the Timesharing Principle

Seven of a number of corporations who were invited to participate agreed to buy exclusive use of part or all of a proposed recreational center for their employees at selected times on weekdays from 11:00 A.M. to 1:00 P.M. and from 5:00 P.M. to 8:00 P.M. At other weekday times and on weekends, the facility would be available for use by all residents of the county. The facility would be operated and managed by the county at all times.

The capital cost of the facility was approximately $3 million. Each corporation agreed to pay $100 per day per hour for the exclusive use of the facility's space. This space and time was purchased in advance for a five-year period with an option under which it could be renewed for a further five-year period. The presold space and time allocations from the seven corporations provided all of the initial finance needed to construct the building.

The county had negotiated with a private developer to lease a park site to him for a 15-year period, and he agreed to build the facility. He would then lease it back to the county in order to take advantage of depreciation on the structure. The county agreed to pay him a lease fee based on the debt charges on the building that were covered by the presold time shares purchased by the seven corporations.

Although the county commissioners were informed fully of the progress of the intended development, they refused to support it in the end because they were reluctant to grant the developer an exclusive 15-year lease on county property. The developer required an exclusive lease because, if for some reason the scheme failed, he had to be able to use the building for some other purpose in order to generate revenue to pay the annual debt charges on the building for which he would be liable. After being rebuffed by the commissioners, the developer took the feasibility data that the county staff had assembled and proceeded to build the facility elsewhere and manage it himself as a private venture.

This type of packaging is illustrated in the following joint development.

A city owned a large outdoor swimming pool that was no longer functional. It was located on a valuable commercial site at a major highway intersection. Proposals were solicited from the commercial sector for development of the site, but the proposals had to focus on leisure provision and had to include a $5 million new indoor-outdoor aquatic complex. The aquatic facilities were to be built at no cost to the city. The commercial components included in the selected proposal were a 10-screen multiplex cinema; a night club; 40-lane, 10-pin bowling center; and restaurants. The city owned and operated the aquatic complex, while the developer's profits from the commercial elements built on the site were sufficient to pay debt charges on the capital cost of the new pool complex.[7]

This strategy is being pursued with increasing frequency by arts institutions that are turning to real-estate developers for solutions to their chronic money problems. The early lead in this movement was provided by the Museum of Modern Art in New York. Like many other cultural institutions, the museum experienced financial difficulties, with annual expenditures exceeding income by almost $1 million. To ease its financial difficulties, the museum permitted a developer to construct a luxury condominium project, known as Museum Towers, on top of a new gallery wing. The profits from the sale and rentals of condominiums made a major contribution to solving the museum's financial quandary.

This precedent encouraged other arts institutions, including the Jewish Museum of American Folk Art and the Whitney Museum, in the city of New York to pursue real-estate projects that involved exploiting their development rights.[16]

Expansion of Existing Facilities

Expansion of an existing facility may be achieved with the assistance of a business that is prepared to invest in improvements, renovations, or expansion of the facility in exchange for the authority to lease the facility or to operate it at off-peak times. An example of a partnership that resulted in major renovation of a moribund public asset is described in "Developing the Chelsea Piers Complex in New York." "Expanding a Velodrome to Include Go-Carts" on page 219 illustrates how an existing facility may be adapted by additional investment to accommodate new activities. In this case, a velodrome was adapted so that go-cart racing could also take place there.

More commonly, this type of joint venture has occurred in northern states and has involved the commercial developer in covering an existing facility for winter use. The city of Oak Park, Michigan, leased land to a commercial operator for a 10-year period with the lessee having an additional two successive five-year options to extend the lease. The lessee paid 5% of gross sales to the city for rent. The developer constructed and operated a five-court indoor tennis facility, including a permanent support building; five asphalt courts; and a five-court air-supported structure. The city provided all utilities to the site and prepared the site for contractors.

Developing the Chelsea Piers Complex in New York

Piers 59 to 62 between the city of New York's 17th Street and 23rd Street are historic. Built in 1910 to serve the major passenger liners, the piers extend 0.75 mi along the Hudson River. Views from these four piers include the Statue of Liberty and the Verrazano-Narrows Bridge to the south and include the George Washington Bridge and New Jersey Palisades to the north. They contain magnificent two-story structures that were designed to accommodate the needs of departing ocean liner passengers. These structures are large indoor spaces (120 ft wide and 840 ft long) with no columns. However, by the early 1990s, these four piers were no longer used and were in danger of falling into disrepair.

A city-state agency, the Hudson River Park Conservancy, leased 30 acres containing the piers to a developer for 49 years for $157,000 each month, which was adjusted annually for inflation. The lease payments were used to maintain bike paths, gardens, playgrounds, promenades, and playing fields. The lease payments were expected to generate approximately $70 million in revenue for the conservancy over the 20-year period.

The developers invested $90 million (of which $25 million in improvements was made by subtenants) in adapting the structures on the piers for leisure use. They estimated that constructing similar facilities from scratch would cost $250 million and noted that obtaining building permits would be impossible. The development was completed in four years from bidding to opening, which is remarkably fast for a project of this scale in New York. The absence of new construction was key because it reduced the number of community groups who had to be involved in the process. The elements of the complex included the following (see figure 8.2):

- Pier 59 included a 200 yd golf driving range with 52 weather-protected hitting stalls in four tiers, a pro shop and training-center locker rooms, meeting rooms, a putting green, lounges, and a restaurant grill and lounge. This was one of the most technically advanced driving ranges and teaching centers in the world and could be used regardless of the weather conditions.

- Pier 60, which was covered with large structures, contained the 150,000 sq ft Sports Center featuring a 0.5 mi indoor jogging track; a banked six-lane, 200 m competition track with arena seating for 1,500 spectators; three basketball courts; volleyball courts; a 15,000 sq ft rock-climbing wall that was the largest in the Northeast; a fully equipped locker room; six-lane, 25 yd swimming pool; boxing ring; steam and sauna rooms; a waterfront restaurant; and a sundeck. It was designated the Summer Games Sports Center.

- Pier 61 contained the Sky Rink that had two ice-skating rinks with seating for 1,600 spectators (including two heated sky boxes). Floor-to-ceiling windows in the two ice rinks offered spectacular views of the Hudson River.

- Pier 62 featured two outdoor, regulation-sized, in-line and roller skating rinks for roller hockey league play or, when the rinks were combined, for public skating. At the water's end of Pier 62 was a public park that the developer funded and managed.

- The headhouse associated with the piers stretched from 22nd Street to 18th Street and housed the Silver Screen Studios, which was a 300,000 sq ft center for film and television production, and a 90,000 sq ft field house containing an Olympic-quality gymnastics training facility, a 40-lane bowling facility, rock-climbing wall for children, two basketball courts, two artificial turf playing fields, and four batting cages.

Along the 1.2 mi perimeter of the Chelsea Piers, dinner boats, charter boats, luxury yachts, and a sailing school were to be accommodated. Private marina facilities were planned. The development also featured two destination waterfront restaurants: The Crab House and Chelsea Brewing Company with seating capacities of 600 and 300, respectively, and 500 parking spaces.

Even without using the sports facilities, pedestrians could walk throughout the project along Sunset Strip, which was a walkway that ran parallel to the river. From there they could enter any of the commercial spaces: the stores, the cafe, the seafood house, and the microbrewery. They could watch the sports at the outdoor facilities, including the roller rink and the golf club; they could sit in the park at the end of Pier 62; and they could sit on any of benches that dotted the esplanade. Chelsea Piers attracted from 8,000 to 10,000 visitors daily and became a stop on New York Apple Tours. The complex was kept immaculately clean, which was one of several management ideas that the developers freely admit they stole from Disney. Badges for all 600 employees (including owners, managers, and the 150 part-time employees) bore only a first name. Chelsea Piers had its own security force, but the limited entrances helped eliminate problems by providing natural checkpoints.

This imaginative, expanded use of a moribund public facility made productive use of the city's waterfront, stimulated economic development in the area, revitalized historically significant structures, and created a host of new recreational opportunities for New York residents at no cost to the taxpayer.

Adapted from Vilma Barr. The Chelsea Piers complex. Urban Land. August 1994, pages 38-41; and Alexander Garvin and Gayle Berins. Urban Parks and Open Space. The Urban Land Institute: Washington, DC. 1997. Copyright©The Urban Land Institute. Used by permission.

Leaseback Agreement for an Indoor Ice Rink

The city of Dublin, Ohio, and Columbus Hockey Inc., owners of the East Coast Hockey League franchise, the Columbus Chill, entered into an agreement to develop a $3.3 million indoor ice rink. The 60,000 sq ft facility included two ice surfaces (one National Hockey League-sized surface measuring 190 ft × 85 ft and one Olympic-sized surface measuring 200 ft × 100 ft), pro shop, skate rental area, video game room, public locker room, and concession area. In addition, the ice arena housed offices for the Chill's management staff and a team locker room and training facility.

Impetus for establishing a new ice rink came from the Chill, who were finding it increasingly difficult to reserve adequate ice time for team practices at the one ice rink in the metropolitan area of 1.4 million residents. So great was the demand for ice at the single arena owned and operated by the local state university that the Chill were limited to 1 h practices, often at 5:00 A.M. or 6:00 A.M. Analysis of the area's imbalance between supply and demand led management of the hockey team to develop a proposal for creation of a permanent facility that could be used beyond the team's practice needs to accommodate the apparent demand for youth and adult hockey, figure skating, and speed skating in central Ohio.

The Chill approached the city of Dublin with a joint-development proposal in which the hockey team would build and operate the ice arena but lease back initially up to 20% of the facility's ice time to the city. In return for utilization privileges, the city agreed to lease an eight-acre parcel of land (market value of $400,000) to the Chill for 25 years at $1 per year.

The reciprocal benefits from this partial leaseback arrangement were extensive. The city received the following:

— A state-of-the-art community resource that served the ice-skating needs of its residents year-round at minimal taxpayer expense

— A regional attraction with the potential to lure thousands of overnight and day-use visitors each year to the city to attend tournaments and annual events conducted at the ice arena (and with the potential for considerable benefits for the local economy)

— More than 30 h per week of exclusive ice time for programs conducted and supervised by the Dublin Parks and Recreation Department

— Complete possession of the facility when the lease expires after 25 years

On the other hand, benefits to the Chill included the following:

— Substantially reduced development costs, in which land acquisition expenses were borne entirely by the city and many infrastructure costs, such as utility hookups and access roads, were shared (total savings could amount to more than $500,000).

— A leaseback agreement giving the Chill almost complete management autonomy. All income from concessions, video games, pro-shop sales, rink rental (including the modest fee charged the city for its exclusive use), and public skating belonged entirely to the hockey team.

— A permanent facility that completely accommodated practice and office personnel needs.

organically dead. The city offered to sell fill to the contractor from the lake bed that it wanted to dig out as part of a plan to revive the lake. This excavation would have cost the city $650,000. The contractor removed 700,000 cu ft of fill from the lake bottom in accordance with a configuration the city mandated. He paid $1.5 million for the privilege, and the lake was resuscitated. He also put in 1 mi of city-standard access road to make it easier for him to haul out fill and give the city improved access to the lake.

A number of jurisdictions have followed the precedent set by DuPage County Forest Preserve District in allowing part of their land to be used as a landfill site to generate revenue and then using this money to develop recreational facilities on the site when the landfill is full. This is described in "Creation of a Winter Sports Hill From Trash."

Riverview, Michigan, constructed a Mount Trashmore, rising 200 ft above some of the flattest terrain in the state. It provided tobogganing, sledding, and beginning skiing opportunities for the local community. Artificial snow machines and a tow rope were installed. A similar venture was undertaken by the Maryland National Capitol Park and Planning Commission at their 220-acre Sandy Hill Creative Disposal Project.

The initial excitement associated with the joint development of these Mount Trashmores has been tempered by more than two decade's experience operating them. The DuPage Forest Preserve District's development of Mount Hoy was a pioneering effort, and during their years of operating it, a number of problems emerged that were not anticipated at the outset. First, the responsibilities associated with managing a landfill are much greater today than they were when the project was launched more than two decades ago. More awareness exists of the dangers of pollutants seeping into the water table. Plus, two decades ago, no requirement to separate household waste and hazardous waste existed. Consequently, the district had to establish a cleanup fund of several million dollars to remove hazardous waste. The Environmental Protection Agency now requires landfill sites to be monitored continually, and there are ongoing costs associated with providing these status reports.

Second, once the Forest Preserve District had established a precedent, it was under pressure to view sanitation disposal as one of its obligations.

Creation of a Winter Sports Hill From Trash

The Roy C. Blackwell Recreational Preserve is administered by the Forest Preserve District of DuPage County, Illinois. It was purchased as a disused gravel pit with 1,300 acres surrounding it. The area, known as the Badlands, was badly scarred and in need of scenic rehabilitation. Funding was raised for purchase of the land, but no finance was available for development of the site. Unprocessed gravel, which had not been economical to extract, remained in the pit. However, as the price of gravel rose, it again became profitable to extract this unprocessed gravel. It was sold to commercial operators, and the profits were used to help excavate the lake in accordance with a master plan that had been developed.

Subsequently, officials of DuPage County Department of Public Works approached the Forest Preserve District seeking assistance in locating a new landfill site. The Forest Preserve District's excavation caused the problem of how to dispose of large deposits of blue clay that were extracted with the gravel deposits. It was determined that the impervious clay could be used as a protective barrier for trapping natural decomposing material in a landfill. Thus, a 40-acre site located on top of a 55 ft waterproof bed was selected for development of the landfill. Designers created a system by which cells were filled with waste material and then encased in clay so residue from the refuse was unable to leak into the subsoil where it might pollute underground or adjacent-lake waters.

The floor of each cell forming the base was leveled and covered with 2 ft of impervious blue clay. This was keyed into walls or berms of clay forming two- to four-acre cells. The berms were made 20 ft thick at the base and narrowed to 15 ft at the top as they were built. The cell walls were 5 ft to 10 ft high, and as the solid waste was deposited, Mount Hoy (known locally as Mount Trashmore) emerged. At 150 ft, it is the highest point in DuPage County.

When first conceived, the hill was to become a ski and toboggan hill; however, subsequent changes in its design led to it being used only for sledding and tubing. As part of the Blackwell master plan, a swim beach was constructed on the site to provide a summer recreational activity. It was located at the bottom of the hill's southern slope.

Upon completion of Mount Hoy, two additional sites were located on other district holdings. By contract, solid waste disposal firms deposited solid waste at the two sites over a 19-year period. This work was done in accordance with the recreation plan for the original Blackwell development. The district was paid 10% of gross refuse royalties over the first 10 years. Over the 19-year period, the Forest Preserve District expected to realize more than $10 million in royalties.

Consequently, two more landfills followed Mount Trashmore in the Forest Preserve District at Greene Valley and Mallard Lake. As a result, the district has had to expend substantial effort in managing landfills and sanitation problems, which has dissipated efforts and resources directed at its major mission of park and recreation provision.

Third, the design of Mount Hoy was not effective. It was intended primarily for outdoor winter sports, but the final shape was like an airfoil, which caused snow to blow off quickly. Also, trees would not grow on the hill because of the extensive winds, low topsoil, and escaping methane gas created by the decomposing garbage.

In contrast to its experience with sanitation, the Forest Preserve District has continued to exploit successfully gravel excavations to generate revenue and develop lake areas. It has contracted with gravel companies to develop five 30-acre lakes that are up to 40 ft in depth.

Construction of golf courses on landfills has become increasingly common. More than 60 landfill golf courses exist nationwide.[22] The first such courses were created in the 1960s when there were few federal and state regulations regarding closure procedures. As a result, many of the early landfill courses were built with very little fill soil, and problems with settlement, leachate (liquids), and gases were prevalent. The negative impact of landfill gas on course landscaping was of particular concern (e.g., oxygen displacement in the root zone), but now effective systems have been designed to extract this gas from disposal sites. Continuing improvements in construction techniques in recent years have made these facilities viable.

The problems associated with developing landfill golf courses make them expensive. However, three factors suggest their number is likely to increase. First, landfills in some communities are the only areas of open space remaining that are sufficiently large to accommodate golf courses. As demand for the game grows in major population centers, landfills become an attractive option. Second, such sites are not considered prime property, meaning that the land is relatively inexpensive. Third, federal regulations require that closed landfills must be monitored closely for a minimum of 30 years. This requirement limits their potential uses and brings golf to the forefront with an increasing number of city planners and engineers seeking a solution to the final phase of managing a landfill, that is, how the land should be used after the landfill is closed.

Summary

Realignment of lands between a public agency and commercial entities may create recreational opportunities that previously were unavailable. Land exchanges are frequently complex to enact and take years to bring to fruition because of the difficulty in ascribing an agreed value to them, the need to solicit public input, the amount of staff time and effort required, and the possible requirement for a public referendum seeking approval. There are three types of voluntary exchanges: the direct barter of lands; use of third parties; and a trade-out, or quid pro quo. Mitigation is usually an involuntary form of land exchange that increasingly has been mandated for developers and polluters, requiring them to provide compensatory natural resources for those resources that they have negatively impacted.

In the urban context, existing commercial recreation businesses have strong incentives to negotiate with public agencies to permit the use of their facilities to teach various types of recreational classes. Some landowners in urban areas also are receptive to short-term leases at a nominal rate to enable a vacant space, which is not scheduled to be developed for some years, to be used by an agency for athletic fields or a neighborhood park. Beyond the urban area, the reduced federal commitment to land acquisition is leading to more pressure to open privately owned lands for public recreational use, particularly in the eastern third of the United States where publicly owned lands are relatively scarce. The major issues to be addressed before such lands are opened concern liability, property abuses, and protectionism.

Utility companies own large bodies of water, transmission line rights-of-way, and substantial undeveloped property. These resources often are close to urban populations, and some utility companies are receptive to requests from public agencies to manage these resources for recreational use. Takeover of a business by a park and recreation agency may be appropriate if the commercial operation will otherwise close and if the recreational opportunity offered is either not available from another supplier in the area or can service a market segment that is currently not being reached with that opportunity.

The third category is joint development. Five different types of joint development arrangements are recognized. The first type is the multiparty partnership in which a park and recreation agency takes the lead in conceptualizing and implementing developments that involve several financial partners. Second, existing facilities may be expanded by inviting a business to invest in improvements and expansion of a facility in exchange for the right to operate that facility at off-peak times. This most commonly occurs in northern states and involves the developer in covering an existing facility for winter use. Commercial pump priming, which is the third type, involves a business using some of its assets to entice a park and recreation agency to make a relatively large investment in a facility from which the business will also gain. In leaseback arrangements, the fourth type, a developer finances and develops a park or recreational facility in accordance with an agency's specifications and then leases it to the agency at a previously negotiated annual rent for an extended period of time. The fifth type of joint development partnership is multiple exploitation of a resource. Commercial interests are permitted to exploit a public resource following agency guidelines. Money accrued from the sale of this right is used to improve the facility for recreational use.

References

1. Porro, Jeff. 1993. Finding refuge in the wetlands. *Nature Conservancy* 43(2): 30.

2. Hertz, Ken. 1994. Landswapping: It could benefit everyone. *Parks and Recreation* 29(5): 53-57.

3. Schmid, Sue. 1991. This land is your land. *Athletic Business* 15(4): 36.

4. Myers, Phyllis. 1993. Financing open space and landscape protection: A sampler of state and local techniques. In *Land conservation through public-private partnerships*, edited by Eve Endicott. Washington, DC: Island Press, 223-257.

5. Poole, William. 1993. Preserving urban and suburban gardens and parks: The Trust for Public Land its Partners. In *Land conservation through public-private partnerships*, edited by Eve Endicott. Washington, DC: Island Press, 61-82.

6. *Greensense* 2(2). 1996. Mitigation sweeteners pay for open space. Editorial: 1.

7. Simmonds, Brigid. 1994. *Developing partnerships in sport and leisure: A practical guide*. London: Longman.

8. Cordell, H. Ken, James H. Gramann, Don E. Albrecht, Scott Withrow and Robert W. McLellan. 1985. Trends in recreational access to private rural lands. In *Proceedings 1985 national outdoor recreation trends symposium II*. Clemson, SC: Department of Parks, Recreation, and Tourism Management, Clemson University, February 24-27, 166-167.

9. Kozlowski, James C. 1986. The challenges: Legal views on liability. In *Recreation on private lands workshop proceedings*. Dirksen Senate Office Building, Washington, DC: Superintendant of Documents, 27.

10. Wright, Brett A. and Ronald A. Kaiser. 1986. Wildlife administrators' perceptions of hunter access problems: A national overview. *Wildlife Society Bulletin* 14(1): 33.

11. Gramann, James H., Don E. Albrecht, Thomas M. Bonnicksen and William B. Kurtz. 1985. Recreational access to private forests: The impact of hobby farming and exclusivity. *Journal of Leisure Research* 17(3): 234-240.

12. Barry, Susan J. 1984. Public access: Private property protection. *Parks and Recreation* 19(5): 43.

13. Steinborg, Jacques. 1993. Public park is too private to suit the government. *The New York Times*, August 13, B1.

14. Clarke, Marion L., Robert Grist and James D. Mertes. 1987. County nature conservancy joint venture. *Parks and Recreation* 22(8).

15. Schmid, Sue. 1995. The best medicine: Park districts find a cure for hospital competition. *Athletic Business* 19(4): 18.

16. Guenther, Roger. 1984. Novel links with developers give arts institutions a boost. *Wall Street Journal*, April 18, section 2, 33.

17. Winton, Pete. 1994. Developers scramble for shot at public golf course. *Fort Myers News-Press*, August 3, 1, 16.

18. Crossley, John C. 1986. *Public-commercial cooperation in parks and recreation*. Columbus, OH: Publishing Horizons.

19. Marchant, Ward. 1995. Open range: Municipalities and developers coordinate their respective interests to fuel a public golf boom in Colorado. *Golf Course Management* 63(7): 41-42.

20. Beaver, Roger L. 1985. Privatization nets multiple returns in West Lafayette. *Parks and Recreation* 20(12): 40-43.

21. Schmid, Sue. 1992. No stone unturned. *Athletic Business* 16(10): 23-29.

22. Saunders, Doug. 1996. Fulfillment: Case studies indicate that former trash dumps are viable solutions to golf's projected growing pains. *Golf Course Management* 64(3): 116-124.

CHAPTER 9

CONTRACTING OUT SERVICES

This chapter was written in association with Mark E. Havitz, Department of Recreation and Leisure Studies, University of Waterloo, Canada.

Very few organizations are completely self-sufficient to the extent that they generate everything they require in terms of goods and services. In this respect, park and recreation agencies are no different from other enterprises. Contracting out shifts responsibility for production of park and recreation services away from an agency's employees to an outside organization that is paid to provide them. The variety of organizations to which responsibility may be shifted includes not only commercial businesses but also nonprofit entities, such as community groups, YMCAs, Boys and Girls Clubs, and service clubs.

Park and recreation agencies have a long history of contracting out for the production of technical professional services such as architectural and landscape design, comprehensive planning, and construction. Similarly, the contracting out of concessions dates back at least to the act designating Yellowstone as a federal protected area. This act authorized the Secretary of the Interior to lease small parcels of park land where accommodations for visitors could be built and operated. By 1880, eight years after Yellowstone was created, it contained seven frontier-type log cabins, a small hotel, horse-riding and pack-train facilities, guides, and stage lines.[1] The principle of contracting with the private sector to produce these types of services rarely has been controversial.

After the tax revolt movement, the list of contracted-out professional services expanded to include recreational program activity classes and maintenance services requiring highly specialized and expensive equipment that agencies could not afford to purchase. These services included urban tree trimming, equipment maintenance and repair, specialized garden or turf maintenance, and garbage collection from facilities. Over time the list expanded further as some agencies adopted a policy of evaluating the cost effectiveness of contracting out all non-core support functions including services such as print shop, concessions, staff training, parking lot, security, accounting, bookkeeping and data processing, custodial, nursery, research, marketing, and dispatch call. Finally, as the Indianapolis situation described in "The Contracting-Out Revolution in Indianapolis" indicates, the evolution reached a point where contracting out in some agencies was considered for all services including core functions such as park maintenance and recreational facility management.

The major advantage agencies perceive from not contracting out and retaining direct delivery is control. They are able to control decisions, such

The Contracting-Out Revolution in Indianapolis

When a new park and recreation director was hired by the recently elected mayor in Indianapolis, his instructions were to reduce costs and improve service quality. Contracting out was a primary tool for achieving this. After two years, the number of full-time equivalent employees had fallen from 770 to 236, and the net operating cost of the department had been reduced from $22 million to $19 million. The fall in net operating costs was not commensurate with the reduction in employee numbers because the agency still had to pay for services that were contracted out. Further, operating savings were reinvested into renovating deteriorating facilities. At the same time, the quality of park and recreation services improved substantially on all objective measures including customer-satisfaction surveys, mystery-shopper surveys, and number of complaints.

One-third of the mowing work was contracted out to several different contractors. Their work was monitored by private inspectors who were hired to measure it against performance standards specified in the contracts. The agency's employees were efficient in mowing large open park areas that required large equipment and allowed them to stay on the machines for relatively long time periods. They were inefficient when they had to constantly travel, loading and unloading equipment, to maintain relatively small neighborhood parks. Hence, it was these smaller facilities that were contracted. The contractors were typically small, local, landscaping firms whose main source of business was mowing people's yards. The department previously mowed on an 11-day cycle in the summer, but the cost savings from contracting out enabled all mowing to be done on a six-day cycle. Other savings were invested in purchasing new equipment to replace the inefficient 10-year-old equipment typically being used. Much of the savings came from the contractors' not having to pay the department's unionized employees' relatively high overtime rates. As a result of contracting out, the department's parks equipment inventory was reduced from 400 pieces to 200 pieces.

Half of the urban forestry work was contracted out. The remainder was retained to create competition and to retain capacity to respond to emergencies, such as tornado damage or contractor failure.

A recreational center, which had a large kitchen area, was contracted out to a catering company. It held a liquor license and used the kitchens extensively for special functions, such as wedding receptions and parties. The contractor created events and programming based on this asset. The center's net operating loss was previously $60,000 per year; however, in the second year of the contract, this loss was transformed into a net operating surplus of $133,000 derived from the 18% of gross revenues paid to the department by the contractors. Space that the contractor did not use was offered back to the department for a fee and used for regular recreational programs at the center.

The city's 12 golf courses were contracted out to 12 different operators. The changes resulted in an aggregate increase of 175,000 rounds annually and a $4 million annual net gain to the city in the second year of the contracts.

Three of the city's 20 swimming pools were contracted out in the summer. Bids were received from retired individuals who had previously been pool managers; by the YMCA; and by university and high school pool staffs, whose pools were closed in the summer because no students were in school.

Other services that were contracted out (and which agency staff had performed previously) included printing, graphics, concessions, internal daily cleaning of buildings, research, and production of promotional literature.

as price, scheduling, service quality, and shifts in service priorities, without having to negotiate with a contractor about every decision. If the service is profitable, there also may be a belief that direct delivery maximizes revenues because all profits are retained by the agency rather than shared with a contractor.

On the other hand, advocates of contracting out point out that in areas such as recreational activity classes independent contract instructors will strive to build their clientele. Most of these instructor contracts guarantee instructors a percentage of enrollment fees (typically, 60% or 70% to the instructor and 40% or 30% to the agency). Thus, instructors make more money as classes increase in size. Further, lack of demand results in cancellation of a program and no remuneration to the instructor. These arrangements enable an agency to offer virtually any program for which there is a demand, even highly specialized activities, without tax support.

Contracting out frees agency staff resources and dollars for other purposes. It may not only save money, but also remove the headaches and hassles associated with day-to-day management. In the context of concession operations, for example:

scheduling of hourly part-time employees, purchasing perishable foodstuffs or imported souvenirs, determining what stands are open, determining whether the sanitation policies are enforced, and determining who might be stealing cash are all items that many agency managers do not want to oversee even with a qualified concessions manager on staff (p. 214).[2]

Further, agencies do not have the freedom to establish autonomous purchasing and personnel procedures, which a contractor can do. This freedom is especially important in revenue-producing services in which success is often dependent on an ability to respond rapidly and efficiently to changes in market volume and preference.

Four conditions have been identified that generally must be satisfied before an agency will seriously explore the feasibility of contracting out a service:

1. The agency is under serious fiscal stress.

2. It seems likely that substantial monetary savings could accrue from contracting without reducing quality or level of services.

3. It is politically feasible, given the power of the service's constituencies, i.e., both employees and client groups.

4. Some precipitating event makes it impossible to continue with the status quo.

The first three factors have been widely recognized, but in many instances, it is the fourth factor that is indispensable to successful implementation of contracting.

The mere availability of large and much-needed savings by privatizing is necessary but by no means sufficient to assure adoption of this approach. Generally, some other factor must be present that elected officials can seize as an opportunity to create the political consensus that makes privatization feasible (p. 256).[3]

In chapter 7, the potential advantages of commercial enterprises were identified to be availability of private capital, specialist management expertise, reduced labor costs, adaptability to scale of service, and reduced liability risks. Any or all of these advantages may contribute to an agency's decision to analyze the feasibility of contracting out a particular service.

There are some inherent characteristics of park services that make them particularly appealing targets for contracting out.[4] First, much park maintenance work requires only moderately skilled employees who do not require extensive training or high levels of education. Often contractors have lower wage and fringe benefits than public agencies have for these personnel partly because they are less unionized and because relatively rapid turnover tends to keep commercial rates at the low end of the scale. Second, there are usually several companies with the capacity to offer these services, and, thus, more competition for contracts occurs. Third, the services are tangible (a certain number of trees trimmed or acres mowed per service cycle), so agencies are confident of being able to measure contractor performance and ensure quality levels. Finally, some park services, such as tree trimming, require expensive capital items that an agency may underutilize but that contractors may be able to spread over multiple contracts with other entities.

As the number and variety of service contracts has grown, the controversy associated with contracting out has grown. It tends to be particularly acrimonious when services have had a long tradition of being delivered directly by the agency and when management of recreation services beyond activity classes is involved; these more directly impact client groups than operation and maintenance functions do, and developing specifications for them is more difficult. The conclusion drawn from two decades of controversial experience with contracting out in this field is that contracting out is likely to be successful in selected contexts when it is applied thoughtfully and is properly developed, implemented, and monitored. It is neither the panacea advocated by some politicians, consultants, and professionals nor the recipe for disaster pronounced by others. Indeed the uniqueness of situations in different communities makes it likely that the contracting out of a given service in one community may be a success while in another community it may be a failure.

Many illustrations in this chapter report successful contracting-out experiences, but sometimes this form of privatization is not successful. This is illustrated in "A Negative Contracting-Out Experience," which describes one facility's bad experience with contracting out and offers some insight into why this strategy may fail. In the context of horticulture, similar reservations were expressed by the director of an internationally renowned arboretum in Philadelphia:

> Private contractors cannot resist the temptation to put routine jobs such as mowing in the hands of the cheapest labor. But these people know nothing about gardening. With their mowers they can do permanent damage to trees or chop down bulb foliage before the bulbs have fully matured. You only see the damage when it is done, and some of it is irreparable (p. 11).[5]

One of the consequences of the increased tendency to contract out has been the stimulation of new specialized businesses. As the vignette in "Providing Lifeguards: A Company Success Story" on page 232 illustrates, it offers a new type of employment opportunity for people in parks and recreation who possess specialized knowledge and an entrepreneurial temperament.

This chapter develops a systematic process for making decisions related to contracting out. The process illustrated in figure 9.1 on page 233 consists of six main stages. The first issue is the potential for cost savings because this is the primary reason for contracting out. If the costs of contracting out are estimated to be at least 20% lower than those currently incurred by the agency in delivering a service, then the analysis should proceed. The second stage is to confirm that alternative producers of the service are available because, without them, the issue is moot. Third, much of the controversy in a contracting-out debate usually revolves around the issues of displacement of existing personnel, control of prices, and equity. If any of these three issues are not resolved, then the acrimony and level of political agitation may be strong enough to cause a contracting-out

A Negative Contracting-Out Experience

The new city recreational center was a comprehensive building with two gymnasia, basketball courts, fitness facilities, sauna, three swimming pools, aerobic rooms, and a children's nursery. Incorporated also were a large cafeteria and kitchen facilities to service the large number of center users. These catering facilities were designed to a high quality. It was regarded as essential that they provided a service commensurate with that offered in the remainder of the building, viz. of the highest possible standards. In addition, these facilities were required to produce a net operating profit.

It was decided before the center opening that the catering would be contracted out. A small firm was given a three-year contract based upon the following terms:

- The firm would have exclusive rights for all catering in the building.
- They would provide a service in accordance with an agreement drawn up.
- They would pay the council a 14% return on gross receipts.
- The council would pay for gas, electricity, water, replacement of fixed equipment, and general maintenance.

The assistant director of the city's park and recreation department recalls the sequence of events that followed:

Things didn't go in accordance with our wishes and in consequence we did not enjoy three totally successful years. It may be argued that the contract should have been terminated, but that ubiquitous word "reasonable" seemed to thwart us at every turn. Who does define what is a "reasonable" return, what is a "reasonable" service, and what are "reasonable" prices? The major benefits which did materialise included:

- No direct involvement with the service.
- A "reasonable" financial return which reached $20,000 in the final year.

The drawbacks which became evident were:

- Remoteness of decision makers. The on-site managers (and there were eight during the contract period) had little authority and, therefore, decisions were a long time forthcoming and changes to meet emerging needs were equally slow.
- The company operated the section with little regard to service, but with emphasis almost exclusively on profit (although I believe the two can and should go hand in hand).
- A virtual ignorance of the special catering requirements within a recreation center.

After three years and following a number of "head to heads" with the company, it was decided to readvertise the franchise. The idea of self-catering at that stage was vetoed by the Council. Since we had had unsatisfactory results with Contract Caterers, a "Management" caterer was appointed. It was impressive to hear of returns of $40,000, use of company resources and expertise, exercising control without direct involvement etc., but in reality things never went right from the start.

The company seemed to lack an understanding of the clientele who use a recreation center and the whole organisation appeared to be swamped by bureaucracy (and they call Local Government bureaucratic!) meaning very little was achieved at "the sharp end." Whilst it is fair to say that standards did improve, the financial results were disastrous. The first year's trading yielded a "profit" of $10,000, whilst the second year ended with the Council losing $4,000. Whilst the company to their credit offered to recompense the Council this figure against their management fee, clearly the writing was on the wall.

It was time for a change. Following reports to the council it was decided to go "in-house." It could be justifiably said that we had seen five years of operation and, therefore, knew what was required and what to expect. However, to counter that, surely this experience is what outside companies should bring to an operation from day one.

In more ways than one it can be said that the venture has been successful. "Profits" are now at their highest (almost $34,000 last year based upon the same criteria as the contract caterer) and the service not only has improved, but is more aligned with what the people want. Decisions are arrived at quickly, changes and amendments to service, prices, and menus can happen almost immediately and any criticism (or praise) can be dealt with promptly. What has also been discovered is the feeling that the catering is a part "of us" and, consequently, dual use of staff is possible and a more harmonious approach is evident.

I am sensible enough to appreciate that it wouldn't work for everyone. I firmly believe that it is necessary to have experienced staff. I have been amused to see and speak to people who, because they can spread a jelly sandwich, make coffee and pour a beer, think that they are expert caterers. These people should leave it to others and not delude themselves. However, I think it's a fallacy to use the argument of wastage, pilfering and dishonesty against direct control, because if it is happening to you, you should be able to take swift and decisive action. If it's happening to you through a third party you might not even know about it or at best, it will take some time to resolve. One final thought has to be that if there are so many companies chomping at the bit to step in and run your catering—there must be some money to be made. Why let others have it? With good management you could be enjoying all of it, not just a percentage.

Adapted from P.R. Collins. Catering: To contract or not, or one man's meal is another man's poison. Leisure Management. 1986. 16(8), page 11. Copyright ©The Leisure Media Company. Used by permission.

Providing Lifeguards: A Company Success Story

Jay Hennick was young, energetic and ambitious. At 16 years of age and in the ninth grade, he needed pocket money. Twenty years ago with $1,000 that he borrowed from his father, he started his own business: supplying lifeguards to swimming pools in apartment complexes. "I remember I was getting 45¢ an hour when I started" said Hennick. "The business initially was seasonal until buildings started installing indoor pools. At that time no one else was doing it." His first job, which was part time, came after he had answered an advertisement in *The Star*.

Soon, the landlord was asking him to find lifeguards for other buildings that he owned, and Hennick borrowed the $1,000 to fund the payroll until he got paid. He formed Superior Pool, Spa, and Leisure and started advertising for lifeguards. Then, he began making sales calls on other apartment buildings, condominium developments, and municipal offices. From there, he expanded to include property managers, offering to open pools in early summer, maintain them throughout the season, provide lifeguards, and close them in the fall. The average contract was $1,600 for a season. The company now has revenues of more than $2.5 million each year.

Adapted from John Picton. Company made its first splash with lifeguards. Toronto Star. February 1994, page 14.

proposal to be abandoned. Stage four is soliciting input from all impacted stakeholder groups, and only if there is evidence of widespread support is the proposal likely to proceed.

Fifth, key decisions to be made in formulating a contract include how to safeguard the agency against the contractor's failing to deliver the service; using the invitation-to-bid or request-for-proposals approach for selecting a contractor; choosing a fixed-price, commission, or fixed-price-with-incentives type of payment option; determining the size and scope of the contract; and ascertaining the content details that should be included in the contract.

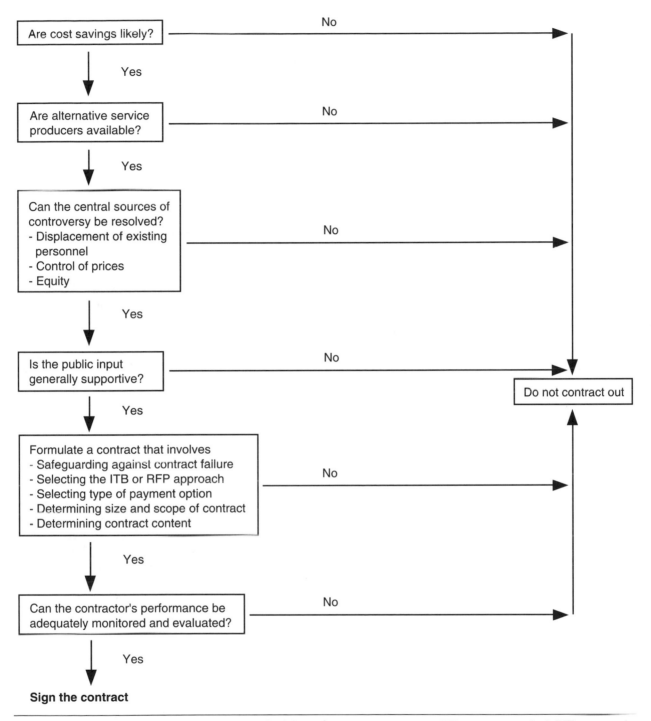

Figure 9.1 A systematic approach to making decisions about contracting out. *ITB*, invitation to bid; *RFP*, request for proposals.

The sixth stage is monitoring and evaluating the contractor's performance to ensure that the specified standard of service is delivered. The chapter concludes with a case study illustration of how one park and recreation agency integrated the principles espoused in the chapter when it planned and implemented a major contracting-out program for park maintenance work.

Individual agencies are likely to have developed adaptations of this strategic approach. "Specific Tasks Undertaken by One Agency To Implement Its Contracting-Out Program" gives an illustration of one such variation developed by the Los Angeles

Specific Tasks Undertaken by One Agency To Implement Its Contracting-Out Program

I. Prepare contracting plan.
  A. Inventory department activities.
  B. Determine if legal to contract.
  C. Determine if possible to contract.
  D. Prioritize and develop plan.
  E. Assign in-house task force to complete tasks.

II. Prepare performance standards and monitoring plan.
  A. Define required services.
  B. Gather data.
  C. Determine economic value of activities.
  D. Develop performance requirements.
  E. Write performance standards.
  F. Design monitoring requirements.
  G. Write monitoring plan.

III. Conduct contract solicitation.
  A. Determine method of solicitation (invitation to bid or request for proposals).
  B. Circulate draft solicitation documents.
  C. Prepare vendor and advertiser list.
  D. Conduct public advertisement.

IV. Conduct cost analysis.
  A. Prepare in-house cost estimate.
  B. Submit in-house cost estimate to finance staff.
  C. Submit in-house cost estimate to department head.

V. Evaluate and select contractor.
  A. Select evaluation team.
  B. Conduct solicitation evaluation.
  C. Determine if service will remain in-house.
  D. Conduct pre-award survey.
  E. Select contractor.

VI. Negotiate and award contract.
  A. Select negotiation team.
  B. Make preliminary selection.
  C. Negotiate contract.
  D. Send draft and checklist for department sign off.
  E. Send final contract to governing body for approval.

VII. Implement monitoring program.
  A. Prepare monitoring evaluation schedule.
  B. Conduct monitoring and record observations.
  C. Document unsatisfactory performance.
  D. Take appropriate action.

County Department of Parks and Recreation for implementing its contracting-out program. This agency was a pioneer in contracting out services in this field. The list identifies seven internal technical tasks that the agency undertook and the key elements that are needed to perform each task. This list does not incorporate the broader strategic issues that are considered in figure 9.1.

Analyzing the Potential for Cost Savings

The most frequent motivation for contracting out is a desire to improve efficiency. This entails either reducing costs while holding quality at the same level or improving level of quality while costs remain constant. As the Indianapolis case described in "The Contracting-Out Revolution in Indianapolis" indicated, the magnitude of efficient improvement may be substantial. Another example, given in chapter 18, reports that a nonprofit organization that was contracted to operate five public golf courses for the city of Baltimore was able to reduce the number of employees from 120 to 60 while simultaneously improving golfers' satisfaction levels, increasing the annual number of rounds played by more than 90%, and saving the city $5 million over a 10-year period. Similarly, the case described at the end of this chapter reports that over an eight-year period, the parks division in Kansas City reduced its mowing costs from $43.50 (which was the cost of direct service) to less than $17.30 per acre for each mowing cycle on 1,600 acres of contracted-out park land, saving the city more than $575,000 each year. Possible reasons for these types of cost savings are summarized in "Reasons Why Contracted Service Delivery May Be Less Expensive Than Agency Delivery."

The only way to determine if there are identifiable efficiencies that could be rectified by contracting out is to undertake a comparative cost analysis. In some jurisdictions, such cost comparisons are mandatory. For example, almost all federal agencies are required to do them and to contract out services if the expected savings exceed 10% of the personnel-related costs of performing the work in-house. At the same time, agencies that want to assume functions currently performed by a contractor have to demonstrate that they are able to save at least 10% on the cost of personnel and 25% on the cost of facilities and materials that the government would have to begin

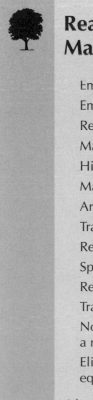

Reasons Why Contracted Service Delivery May Be Less Expensive Than Agency Delivery

Employ only persons needed and pay only market-rate wages.

Employ part-time and temporary workers to cover peak periods.

Reward employees based on performance.

May provide less-extensive fringe benefits packages.

Hire for skills as needed.

May have better management information.

Are willing to take risks.

Trade off the use of labor versus equipment.

Retain only equipment that is used.

Spread equipment costs over many jobs.

Rent specialized pieces of equipment as needed.

Trade off purchased and leased equipment.

Not required to spend budgeted funds by the end of the fiscal year; can carry them over to a new fiscal year without losing them.

Eligible for tax credits on equipment purchased and for depreciation allowances on equipment.

Adapted from International City Management Association. Service Delivery in the 90s: Alternative Approaches for Local Governments. *International City Management Association: Washington, DC. 1989.*

providing. Presumably, this 10% margin was selected because it was deemed adequate to cover the agency's personnel costs of administering and monitoring a contract. In the author's view this difference is too marginal to justify all of the political, human, and organizational upheaval that often accompanies a shift to contracting out. As a rule of thumb, experience suggests that overall cost savings should be at least 20%—without considering the cost to the agency of monitoring the contract—to make contracting out worthwhile.

The sources of costs that should be included in comparisons are identified in "Cost Sources Used in Comparison of Agency and Contracted-Out Delivery." When making comparisons, some agencies fail to include costs for contract preparation, administration, monitoring, and renegotiation. Similarly, the cost of contractors' using in-house facilities such as storage sheds, maintenance shops, or equipment may be inadvertently omitted. Such omissions make the contracting-out option appear more favorable. On the other hand, when

Cost Sources Used in Comparison of Agency and Contracted-Out Delivery

Agency Costs

1. Direct provision
   - Personnel (number and type). Costs should include salaries, wages, fringe benefits, overtime, and cost-of-living trends.
   - Services and supplies, such as gas, oil, phone, paper, and electricity (costs per unit).
   - Debt service and capital outlays and equipment.
2. Support (for direct provision)
   - Personnel (number and type). Costs should include salaries, wages, fringe benefits, overtime, and cost-of-living trends. Only those positions that would be eliminated or reduced by contracting should be included.
   - Facilities and equipment (additional requirements only and incremental costs).
   - Services and supplies (gas, phone, and electricity).
3. Indirect costs associated with items 1 and 2
   - Contract service.
   - Departmental administrator.
   - Operating division administrator.

Contracted-Out Costs

1. Contract
   - Cost of purchasing services from a contractor.
2. Support (preparation and monitoring of contract)
   - Personnel (number and type). Costs should include salaries, wages, fringe benefits, overtime, and cost-of-living trends.
   - Facilities and equipment (additional requirements only and incremental costs).
   - Services and supplies (gas, phone, and electricity).
3. Other adjustments
   - Sale value of government equipment if government chooses contracting.
   - Local government's employee severance costs.
   - Contractor's use of agency facilities or equipment.

Adapted from International City Management Association. Service Delivery in the 90s: Alternative Approaches for Local Governments. *International City Management Association: Washington, DC. 1989.*

costing direct delivery by the agency, fringe benefit items such as sick leave, vacation time, and retirement plans are sometimes omitted. On occasion, contractors' wage scales may be as high or higher than those of a park and recreation agency, but fringe benefits are likely to be 12% to 15% of salary compared with 30% to 35% for agency employees. Hence, accurate computation is critical for there to be a realistic cost comparison.

A common source of error in cost comparisons is a failure to include all of an agency's indirect and overhead costs in the calculations. Many comparisons do not extend costing beyond the direct costs and fringe benefits of personnel, immediate support staff, and materials associated with producing the service. Figure 9.2 illustrates why this will result in a substantial underestimate of the real costs involved. Determining the real costs of services has not been required in the past, and few park and recreation services have a cost-accounting system that enables indirect costs to be determined easily.

Figure 9.2 indicates that typically there are four layers of cost that should be included in determining the real cost of a park and recreation agency producing a service. Central service functions may include executive administration of the jurisdiction, purchasing, accounting, budgeting, personnel, and data processing. A park and recreation department may benefit from each of these centrally supplied functions, so a proportion of their operating costs should be attributed to the agency. A park and recreation department's indirect costs are those associated with the agency's administration, such as the director's office, planning, and administration. The costs of these functions and the costs of central services have to be equitably allocated to each of the agency's operating divisions. Finally, each operating division's costs (including the share of central and departmental costs that it has been assigned) have to be allocated to each of the services offered by the division. Thus, accurate costing goes beyond the direct costs associated with a service to identifying the three layers of indirect costs and allocating them to successively lower echelons of the agency to develop a true service cost. All of these indirect costs will be included in bids that contractors submit because only by covering all costs can commercial enterprises remain solvent.

Since most park and recreation agencies do not have access to a formal cost-accounting system that accurately identifies indirect costs, they frequently have to resort to cost finding, a less-rigorous alternative. Cost finding involves taking available financial data and recasting and adjusting it to derive an estimate of a service's costs. It extracts data from budgets, analyzes detailed transactions (e.g., payroll records, invoices, contracts), reviews cost-accounting data that may be available from other agencies and interpolates from it, and conducts staff interviews, both from within the department and from central services, to ascertain the best estimates of these costs. Data from multiple sources is collected, assembled on worksheets, and analyzed to estimate individual service delivery costs.

Ascertaining the real costs of producing a service and comparing them with the cost of contracting out is in itself a valuable exercise. It provides the park and recreation agency with a benchmark or yardstick against which it can measure the relative efficiency of its operations. Indeed, it is likely to be the first time in many agencies that elected officials, managers, and employees become aware of the true cost of a service. For this reason, managers and employees should be given the opportunity to show what they could do rather than what they are currently doing. This may be done by giving them a minimum of six months, and preferably up to one year, after these data become available to try to reduce the cost of their operation before making a decision to contract out a service.

Availability of Alternative Service Producers

After identifying potential cost savings, an agency's next logical step is to find out if a number of alternative, qualified service producers are available to bid if work is contracted out. The larger the

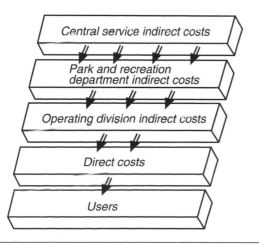

Figure 9.2 Different types of costs incurred in delivering a park and recreation service.

pool of potential bidders, the more competition that is likely to be generated, and the greater the efficiency increases that are likely to emerge. Typically, in the park and recreation field, there is a strong relationship between size of contract and number of bidders, with smaller contracts securing more interest from local contractors. Clearly, work put out to contract should be packaged to bring it within as wide a range of contractors as practical. Thus, it has been suggested:

> If a community is small or isolated, local officials may doubt whether there are any local providers large enough to deliver the service. But for parks and recreation services, many types of providers are potentially available, including neighborhood or condominium associations, school districts, nonprofit organizations, sports leagues, and arts organizations. Dividing a larger task into smaller pieces can encourage small providers to contract with the local government. Park maintenance can be broken down into tree trimming, mowing, and horticulture; or the area to be served can be split to encourage small providers to participate in contracting (p. 104).[6]

Alternative service producers may include other public agencies as well as business and nonprofit organizations. The kinds of pro-active efforts that may be required to create a pool of bidders are illustrated in the Kansas City case study at the end of this chapter. Although standard official advertising announcements may attract large contractors, it is likely that a more aggressive outreach effort will be needed to reach small contractors, who often submit lower bids. These outreach efforts may extend to training workshops that offer small businesses advice on how to submit effective bids; on city procedures; on reporting requirements; and on how to complete the bidding documents, which are often lengthy and formidable to those lacking experience with them. An agency's ability to solicit bids will also depend on reputation gained in the treatment of its past contracts and contractors, including fair and timely payment and smooth resolutions of differences in contract interpretation.

In the Kansas City case, the strenuous effort made to attract the interest of a large pool of qualified contractors invariably resulted in a relatively large contingent attending the pre-bid conference for qualified bidders. The superintendent of parks described one of the benefits of having a large attendance at the pre-bid conference:

> We'll have a room full of contractors and we'll lay out last year's bids and they're all looking around the room at each other and saying, "Wow, there's a lot of people here and the prices are low, so I probably shouldn't go up much" (p. 20).[7]

Central Sources of Controversy

This section discusses three issues that are likely to be controversial if a decision is made to contract out an existing service: displacement of the existing labor force, control of prices, and equity. If any of these issues remains unresolved, then it is possible that, irrespective of the potential cost savings, the level of political opposition will be sufficiently strong to cause abandonment of the proposal to contract out a service.

In considering each of these three issues, the central task is to arrive at a compromise in contracting out that is fair to all stakeholders involved: that is, fair to the taxpayer who pays for the service if it remains subsidized; fair to employees who have invested their careers with the agency; and fair to service recipients who have expectations about price and standard of quality.

Displacement of Existing Personnel

It has been estimated that approximately 40,000 people in full-time and permanent part-time positions are now in the private sector doing work that was done in-house by public park and recreation agency employees two decades ago.[8] Hence, displacement of personnel has emerged as a major issue associated with contracting out. Contracting out often is perceived by senior agency managers and elected officials as being advantageous because it permits them to sidestep bureaucratic barriers that cause direct delivery to be inefficient. These sentiments are likely to be particularly prominent in larger jurisdictions where the extensive system of checks and balances needed to ensure control and accountability of funds may substantially impede the efficiency and effectiveness of service delivery. Contractors do not have to follow civil service rules and regulations in hiring, promoting, terminating, or disciplining employees and, thus, can more easily reward employees for good performance and dismiss them for bad performance. Hence, a central reason for sidestepping the bureaucracy may be to make changes in organizational structures, personnel, and remuneration systems.

If a decision is made to contract out, then what happens to existing employees in the agency who currently perform the service function? Several questions arise.[9] Who gets jobs with the new management? Are the current workers protected? What do collective agreements require? Should staff be invited to bid on the work? Even if the efficiency case for contracting out is convincing, the agency must alleviate adverse political and human consequences of the decision and the potential negative impact on staff morale. Indeed, if the displacement issue is not resolved satisfactorily, the merits of contracting out likely are to be forgotten in the recrimination and bitter arguments over job losses. Displaced employees often garner considerable sympathy from both citizens and elected officials, and their displacement can become a volatile political issue. Analyses demonstrating the case's merits are not likely to impress individuals whose job security and status are at stake. Further, there may be an adverse impact on the morale of other employees. They may become cynical and less committed because they now feel exposed to the threat of termination or because they perceive that their future career ladder and prospects for advancement within the field have been curtailed.

Employees are likely to make intense efforts to save their jobs through internal opposition, civil service rights, appeals to conscience, and direct political activism. If they are supported by a union, then the opposition may be particularly fierce. Unions' interest extends not only to protecting the best interests of their members but also to protecting its corpus because union jobs in an agency may be replaced by non-union jobs with contractors. The potential politicization of the issue by unions is exemplified in the advertisement shown in figure 9.3, which appeared in the *Toronto Globe and Mail*.

Underlying this political problem, there is the human and moral dimension of how to treat displaced employees. In many cases, the decision to contract out is not a reflection of inadequate employee performance but rather a recognition of wage costs, technological advances, or the cost of new equipment.[4] Personnel may be good employees trapped in a bad system: people who are as dedicated and talented as their peers in the private sector but whose effectiveness and efficiency is inhibited by archaic bureaucratic procedures within which they are required to operate. It may be more efficient to contract out; however, if

these employees have served the agency well for many years, then they have earned the right through their dedication, commitment, and loyalty to be treated fairly.

Thus, for political, humane, and moral reasons, both agencies and contractors are likely to want to do the right thing for people who are to be displaced. Strategies they may elect to achieve this include the following:

- Offer a golden handshake or severance pay to employees if they volunteer to resign from the agency.

- Require contractors to hire employees at existing salary levels. This may cause their bids to be higher, but over the long term, voluntary attrition or termination for poor performance will enable rationalization to take place.

- Reassign employees to positions elsewhere in the park and recreation agency or in

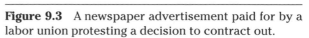

Your Provincial Parks . . . FOR RENT!

Silver Lake, Fitzroy, Rainbow Falls, Sturgeon Bay, Sauble Falls . . . 19 parks so far have been rented out and it's just the start.

When parks are leased, workers lose jobs, students lose work experience, communities suffer.

Will commercial operators keep up the park environment, provide security, keep camping fees at affordable levels?

We paid for a parks system accessible to all. It makes no sense to hand it over to private business.

Please write to

Mike Harris, MPP
Minister of Natural Resources
Queen's Park
Toronto
M7A 1W3

Help stop the rental of our parks.

Sponsored by Provincial Parks Workers. OPSEU

Figure 9.3 A newspaper advertisement paid for by a labor union protesting a decision to contract out.

Copyright ©1985 Ontario Public Service Employees Union. Used by permission.

other departments of a jurisdiction for which their skills are appropriate. This frees the contractor to pay market rates and hire new employees, and savings should emerge from this approach.

- Make displaced staff redundant, but require contractors to interview and appoint from all those affected. This makes it likely that good employees will be hired again.

Control of Prices

The second controversial issue is likely to be pricing. As an alternative or complementary strategy to cost reduction, a contractor's financial goals may be met by generating additional revenues from price increases. Whereas cost reduction focuses inwardly on the agency and its structures, revenue generation focuses outwardly on participants' ability and willingness to pay for services. An agency has to decide whether to retain control of prices, and if it does retain control, it must decide whether it should authorize a price increase. Its response may vary. For example, an agency deciding that at-risk adolescents are a top service priority may not permit a contractor to raise prices for those services. However, there may be a willingness to sanction such increases if they are associated with improved services for older adults or if the agency is under pressure to reduce a large operating deficit.

The pricing issue requires making a fundamental strategic decision regarding the question: Does the agency want to delegate control over revenue to the contractor? If the answer is affirmative, then the contractor will benefit from higher revenues created by increased patronage or higher fees. In this case, the agency would transfer all financial risk to the contractor whose profit would depend not only on cost control but also on optimizing patronage and fees. Alternatively, the agency could opt to retain control over price and not authorize a price increase. This choice may be preferred if there is evidence that social benefits would likely be diminished if fees were not controlled. These decisions will influence the amount of revenue that the contractors offer an agency in their contract bids. Generally, agencies that seek to keep prices low are likely to find it more difficult to embrace contracting out than agencies that are more tolerant of higher prices.[9]

Contracting out may offer a means of encouraging revenue generation because people are accustomed to businesses changing the market rate; however, there is often an expectation that a park and recreation agency will subsidize the service and charge a relatively low price. If an agency raised prices to market level, it likely would be strongly contested, but such actions taken by a contracting business may be less controversial. This is exemplified in "A Contracting Organization That 'Creamed' the Market," which is discussed in the next section.

Equity

The impact contracting out has on equity is the third controversial issue to be addressed. Efficiency gains are likely to be achieved easily if a contractor is allowed to confine service delivery to relatively responsive target markets. The modus operandi of business is to target responsive market segments and ignore nonresponsive segments. However, park and recreation agencies are mandated to service all segments of the community, especially the disadvantaged, often the most unresponsive. Indeed, it has been argued that in prioritizing indicators of an agency's performance, "primary concern should be given to equity, then to effectiveness, and finally to efficiency" (p. 168).[10] Service delivery to specific groups may be defined and mandated in the contract. However, if incentive remains for the contractor to avoid servicing higher-cost target segments, it places a substantial burden on contract monitoring.

This contractor preference has resulted in the emergence of the term "creaming" because agencies have noticed contractors are most interested in services that are easy to deliver to users who are easy to serve, and they tend to ignore services that are more difficult to deliver or customers who are difficult to serve.[9] Thus, for example, contractors prefer to maintain grounds in neighborhoods that do not have graffiti and vandalism problems. A contractor specializing in the management of recreational centers confided to the author that his company had three criteria to be met before the company would consider contracting:

1. The agency's elected governing body had to be philosophically supportive of contracting out.
2. The recreational facilities being contracted had to be relatively new and high quality.
3. The target market had to be relatively affluent.

Although creaming has a negative ring to it, the responses by park and recreation personnel to the example in "A Contracting Organization That 'Creamed' the Market" suggest that this connotation may be misleading. In this case, contracting out resulted in extensive sponsorship resources being made available, ensured that those who had the ability to pay market rates were not receiving subsidized service, and freed agency resources to focus on serving other target markets.

Equity is concerned with who gets what. If contracting out resulted in creaming without agency resources being available to service other segments that previously had received a service, then equity is likely to become a contentious issue. This may often occur inadvertently as the following example illustrates.

An agency in southern California operated a park that contained a lake with a beach for swimming, which was popular with local residents. Visitation was approximately 200,000 people per year, revenues totaled $400,000, and operating expenses were $500,000. The agency was approached by a commercial water park company that offered $500,000 each year to lease the area

for a 10-year period. Being under substantial political pressure to reduce its operating deficit, the agency accepted the offer. Visitation to the commercial water park was also about 200,000 per year. The agency transformed a $100,000 annual deficit into a $500,000 surplus (a net gain of $600,000), which is a substantial gain in efficiency. However, the equity issue was not addressed. Were the water park visitors who paid $15 admission to the water park the same people who paid $2 admission to the lake swimming and beach area? It seems unlikely. If not, what happened to the original visitors? Were there similar opportunities near by that they could use, or was this experience now no longer easily available to them?

Soliciting Public Input

Contracting out threatens the status quo and, hence, is likely to be controversial and fraught

A Contracting Organization That "Creamed" the Market

Sport and Social Clubs of the United States operated in 20 cities and had 250,000 participants each year in its mainly coed floor hockey, volleyball, touch football, softball, golf, tennis, soccer, and basketball leagues. The emphasis was social rather than competitive. It contracted space for indoor and outdoor facilities from park and recreation agencies and practiced "creaming" by focusing on a narrow, distinctive demographic group: urban, 21 to 35 years of age, 90% single, 85% white, median income of $40,000.

An advertisement in *Advertising Age* aimed at corporate sponsors bore the headline, "We can put Generation X in the palm of your hand!" A major advantage of the organization over park and recreation agencies was that it did not offer youth, single-sex adult, or senior programs, so its efforts were highly targeted. This was attractive to sponsors targeting Generation X, and with programs in 20 cities and high numbers of participants, the company's market reach was appealing to sponsors. Their most visible sponsor was Anheuser-Busch, which, as a beer producer, would not have been permitted by most park and recreation agencies. (This is discussed in Chapter 15). Other major sponsors included Gatorade, Chrysler, Spalding, and Reebok.

Park and recreation agencies with which Sport and Social Clubs appeared to compete did not view its creaming strategy as being a problem. Typical observations included the following:

- "I am not sure they would ever be a threat to our program because it seems there is always a demand for more programs than tax dollars can pay for" (Denver).

- "I wouldn't consider them a competitor, simply from the standpoint that there are enough people in this city who we don't touch that someone should be able to touch" (Detroit).

- "Their games are almost intramural. They don't wear uniforms, they don't have as many guidelines as we do, they have no officials. It's all social; it's basically unorganized recreation" (Atlanta).

- "If we pick up these games, we're going to have to add staff and sometimes it's easier to just make money by charging them for using our fields rather than add staff" (Minneapolis).

From Andrew Cohen. Social service: Are for-profit sports clubs your partners or competitors? Athletic Business. July 1995, pages 16-18. Copyright ©Athletic Business. Used by permission.

with infighting, interest group politics, and maneuvering. Users of services will be concerned about price and quality implications, while employees will be concerned about their jobs. In addition, some of these stakeholders, as well as some managers and elected officials, ideologically and philosophically may be opposed to the principle of privatization and its contracting-out manifestation.

Hence, a community needs plenty of time to consider the prospect of contracting out, the reasons for selecting this option, and opportunities to articulate reservations. Before they can proceed with contracting out, the agency and elected officials have to respond to the concerns and satisfy them to the extent that there is general community acceptance and support for contracting out. The set of impacted stakeholders from whom input should be solicited may include

- agency elected officials, managers, and employees;
- unions and professional associations;
- athletic and cultural associations;
- nonprofit organizations, such as the YMCA;
- operators of commercial park and recreation services;
- community groups and service clubs;
- taxpayer action groups; and
- the general public.

Only if the views, opinions, and concerns of these groups are heard and addressed will they have ownership in the contracting-out decision and support it. To proceed in the face of strong adverse reactions, especially if they come from employees and unions, is likely to be unwise. If these people are not committed, it is relatively easy for them to undermine a contracting-out decision in a host of overt and subtle ways. Further, if there is substantial opposition and political infighting, some potential contractors may not submit bids in order to avoid the negative repercussions of being the focus of a controversy.

At the end of this stage, managers have to decide on whether to proceed. Figure 9.4 shows a tool used in some agencies to summarize the pros and cons of contracting out a service. It provides a useful overview and a starting point for a discussion leading to a final recommendation. A manual with this summary chart gives guidelines on criteria to use when scoring each of these nine decision factors.

Formulating the Contract

After a decision to contract out has been made, an agency has to decide on the form of contract it wants to offer. This involves discussion of five issues that are presented in this section: safeguarding against contract failure, selection of an invitation-to-bid or request-for-proposals approach, types of payment option, size and scope of contract, and contract content.

Safeguarding Against Contract Failure

Before proceeding with development of the contract, a decision has to be made on how the service will be delivered in the event of contractor failure. Although most contractors perform effectively, there is a need to safeguard against disruption if a contractor should fail to deliver to acceptable standards and have to be terminated or if a contractor has to withdraw because of strikes or bankruptcy. If a park and recreation agency has dissolved its own labor force, the service may have to be discontinued. Sometimes this concern is sufficient to persuade against contracting out. Contractors are usually required to post a performance bond, which is sufficient for an agency either to hire replacement labor and equipment or to purchase them from another contractor. This usually ranges from 5% to 15% of the contract's value. However, money availability does not help if alternative labor, equipment, or service suppliers cannot be acquired.

There are two ways that park and recreation agencies can plan for this contingency. First, responsibility for service production may be contracted to several different suppliers. This is most common in large jurisdictions in which it is feasible and efficient to offer contracts in different geographical areas. For example, in Indianapolis, the city's 12 golf courses were contracted out to 12 different operators. If failure by any one operator occurred, then the service could be assumed by one of the other contractors by expanding its operations to the course not served. Similarly, Kansas City divided the 3,100 acres of parks that it contracted for mowing services into 50-acre segments, and it limited the number of segments that a contractor could mow to three. The parks superintendent noted: "It can be cumbersome when you're looking at 20 different contractors, but we're very comfortable with it. If we get a contractor who is not doing well, then I only have to worry about that 150 acres" (p. 20).[7]

		Pro-government provision			Pro-private provision		
〜	Market strength	−3	−2	−1	+1	+2	+3
✛	Political resistance	−3	−2	−1	+1	+2	+3
$	Cost efficiency	−3	−2	−1	+1	+2	+3
★	Quality of service	−3	−2	−1	+1	+2	+3
👥	Impact on employees	−3	−2	−1	+1	+2	+3
⚖	Legal barriers	−3	−2	−1	+1	+2	+3
✎	Risk	−3	−2	−1	+1	+2	+3
🕐	Resources	−3	−2	−1	+1	+2	+3
✍	Control	−3	−2	−1	+1	+2	+3

Department _____   Composite score_____

Program/activity _____   Evaluator _____

Notes _____

_____

_____

_____

_____

_____

_____

_____

Figure 9.4   A tool used to summarize the pros and cons of contracting out.

In the context of recreational classes, one manager articulated to the author another reason why some agencies prefer to contract with multiple instructors to teach in a given activity area:

> We have learned over the years never to give one type of class to only one instructor because he or she may put a fence around it and march off with it and all the students. For example, a ballet instructor may develop a good class over time, build up a cadre of loyal followers, and then go private with the class, by-passing the agency. The agency loses momentum and struggles to recreate a viable option for the few remaining students and for newcomers. Thus, we prefer to contract with several ballet instructors who teach one or two sections each, rather than with one instructor who teaches all of them.[8]

An alternative approach to safeguard against contract failure is for an agency to engage in partial contracting, whereby it shares delivery with contractors both to inject competition into the process and to protect against service failure. This can be used when it is not feasible or economically efficient to use more than one contractor. It also has the advantage of enabling the agency's personnel to retain a feel for the service that may be lost when there is no direct contact with it. There are various modifications of this option. Thus, an agency could retain a limited amount of equipment and cross-train employees so that they could partially fill the gap if service is interrupted.

A second modification is for the park and recreation agency to retain ownership of some or all of the capital equipment (e.g., vehicles, mowers) needed for a service and to lease this equipment to the contractor. A third modification is to structure the contract to permit an agency to take over equipment in the event of a default. If the agency had to take a service back from a contractor, it then would need only to provide employees for it to be functional.[9]

Contract failure may extend beyond failure in service delivery to embrace failure to garner long-term efficiencies. This occurs with low balling, which means that a business may make an unrealistically low bid to obtain a contract, knowing that it will lose money in the short term. If an agency removes all of its own service capacity after the contract has been won, the contractor may be the only entity with experience in producing the service. Having achieved this dominant status and gotten the agency dependent on its expertise, the contractor then substantially raises the bid when the contract comes up for renewal. This strategy can only work if there is no effective competition from the agency or other contractors.

Selecting the Invitation-to-Bid or Request-for-Proposals Approach

Two approaches are available for selecting contractors. The invitation to bid is usually preferred when a service can be defined precisely and several potential contractors are available. The focus of this approach is cost reduction, and the contract is awarded to the lowest bidder. The invitation to bid will include items such as statements about bidder qualifications, service specifications, place for the official bid and price, and information about deposits or performance bonds that may be required. It will specify when and where the sealed bids will be opened, and an agency generally is required to accept the lowest bid unless there are good reasons for not doing so.

The request for proposals is an alternative approach that tends to be used when the service cannot be defined easily and differences in service type, level, or quality are possible. Typically, the agency specifies the basic tasks it wants done, and the request for proposals allows bidders the option of suggesting improvements that will enhance service delivery by incorporating elements or methods that the agency did not consider. It provides flexibility for an agency and competing contractors to be creative in designing the operation and any improvements to the service under consideration. For example, when contracting recreation services, an agency may want potential contractors to propose the activity mix that they can provide or believe will best meet the community's needs. The agency is not locked into having to accept the lowest bidder. It is a negotiated approach whereby both parties engage in discussion about range of service, specifications, costs, and other elements. Usually evaluation of a request for proposals is more comprehensive than using only the cost criterion. For example, the illustration in "Evaluating Request for Proposals to Manage Indianapolis' Golf Courses" on page 246 indicates that the evaluation of request for proposals to operate Indianapolis' golf courses weighted net income to the city at 50% and seven nonrevenue criteria at 50% in the final decision.

Types of Payment Option

The three methods of paying for contracted services that park and recreation agencies use most frequently include firm fixed-price, commission, and fixed-price-with-incentives contracts.

In firm fixed-price contracts, contractors quote a single price for performing a service. They are responsible for any cost overruns but benefit from any cost savings generated. The contract includes detailed specifications of the work to be done. For a contractor to make a profit, the service has to be produced efficiently within the quoted price. This type of contract usually is preferred for contracting park maintenance services. The mowing contracts developed by the Kansas City Division of Parks, which are described in the case study at the end of this chapter, were fixed-price contracts.

A commission contract is used for services that are profitable. It provides for a contractor to pay an agency a percentage of the contractor's gross receipts. The contractor pays all operating costs and collects all revenues. This type of contract typically is used for food and beverage concessions and for profitable services, such as golf. The advantages are that it removes financial risk to the agency, is relatively simple to audit, and removes the agency from responsibility for daily operating decisions. Potential contractors include the gross percentages that they are prepared to pay in the bid document. The example shown in figure 9.5 is adapted from the request for proposals used by the city of Indianapolis when it was selecting contractors for its golf courses.

Sometimes when profitable services are contracted out, an agency may use the contractor as a source of capital. For example, the request for proposals may require the contractor to construct and equip a golf club house or a food and beverage area at the facility, or it may require him or her even to do noncontract-related improvements, such as restroom facilities or interpretive displays. This may be the only way that an agency can acquire resources for these improvements. However, the contractor must earn a return on the investment. Thus, if the contract is used as a source of capital, then the commission percentage offered in the bids will be commensurately lower.

The primary purpose of contracting out is to improve cost efficiency. To optimize this, there should be incentive for performance improvements. Fixed-price-with-incentive contracts start with an agreed price for the service but provide the contractor with incentives to improve performance. For example, if the contract is for equip-

Contractor shall remit the following to the department:

1. _____% of the gross revenue received from greens fees and pass surcharges at the golf course.

2. _____% of the gross golf course revenue received from the rental of golf carts and pull carts.

3. _____% of the gross revenue received from the food and vending concessions at the golf course.

4. _____% of the gross revenue received from the sale of all merchandise, merchandise gift certificates, and golf supplies sold in the golf course pro shop.

5. _____% of the gross revenue from the operation of the driving range.

Figure 9.5 Compensation to the agency from a commission contract.

ment maintenance, the contractor's bid price will be for meeting the contract's specifications related to elements, such as performance levels, downtime, and spare-part costs. If these specifications are exceeded and result in cost savings or improvements in service quality, then the contractor is eligible to receive additional payments. Sometimes the agency and contractor will share the savings at an agreed ratio, for example, 40% to the contractor and 60% to the agency.

An emerging form of the fixed-price-with-incentives contract used in services such as concession operations, provides for the contractor to receive a management fee, which typically is stated as a percentage of gross receipts (while the incentive is stated as a percentage of net profits). The concessionaire supplies all personnel, supplies, and equipment, and the agency reimburses the concessionaire for those costs. The agency retains all profits after these costs and the incentive payment have been deducted. This formula enables the agency to retain relatively strong control of the service and to have input into the contractor's operation. This arrangement

eliminates the typical adversarial relationships found in so many contracts. Many times under commission contracts the agency makes demands that cost the contractors additional payroll or product cost. The agency makes these decisions for the overall good of the facility, but the contractor sees it as a negative financial influence to its profits while

Evaluating Request for Proposals to Manage Indianapolis' Golf Courses

Two sets of criteria were used to evaluate the request for proposals to manage Indianapolis' golf courses. The first category was revenue projections, and these accounted for 50% of the weight in the final decision. The second set of criteria involved nonprice attributes. These also accounted for 50% of the weight in the final decision. The seven nonprice criteria are described in this section.

Management skills were defined as the availability of effective management systems and methods appropriate to the successful management of the golf course. Potential contractors needed to provide evidence that they had a sufficient number of competent personnel with appropriate management skills. Examples of general guidelines for the evaluation of proposals included the following:

- Is the management structure focused on meeting the contract requirements as outlined in the request for proposals?
- Is the organization's structure appropriate for this contract?
- How much daily contact will the professional have involving operations?
- What quality control measures for customer service are identified?

The second area, *existing track record*, referred to the potential contractor's previous record of completing work projects to the required standard, on time, and within budget. The general guideline for this evaluation was: Based on their existing track record, is the contractor likely to perform satisfactorily for the duration of the contract?

Technical skills encompassed the competence of the personnel and the proposed contractor with particular regard to their skills and experience in comparable technical areas. Technical skills included pro-shop operations, concession operations, course maintenance, operation experience, equipment maintenance experience, and driving range experience. Technical skills applied only to the proposed course personnel other than the professional; management skills were not included in this category. General guidelines included the following:

- What technical skills are deemed necessary for this contract?
- Is the level of technical skill sufficient to achieve the quality required?
- Is there confidence in the proposed personnel?
- If skills are barely sufficient, can they be improved by cross-training within the contractor's organization?

Resources included the equipment available, the facilities, and golf course property that the contractor proposed to use. Subcontractors identified as being used for the contractual work were considered resources available to the contractor. General guidelines included the following:

- Does the contract propose the correct and sufficient amount of supplies and equipment to undertake the work?
- Is the proposed facility adequate enough to provide the required services?
- Are the proposed labor resources sufficient to cover the golf course and the responsibilities described for it in the request for proposals? (Judgment and productivity levels should be avoided.)
- Are adequate financial resources proposed to operate the course?

Relevant experience referred to the potential contractor's previous experience in contract works of comparable scale and content. It specifically related to the person's or company's experience in managing golf courses. General guidelines included the following:

- Recent experience is much more valuable than historic experience.
- Has the contractor undertaken this type of work before?
- Can the contractor modify existing experience to this type of work?
- If applicable, is the contractor able to shift from existing management responsibilities to the required responsibilities as outlined in the request for proposals process?

Methodology referred to the procedures and methods the contractor proposed to use to achieve the specific end result. The contractor needed to demonstrate an understanding of the job and the best way to achieve the desired results. General guidelines included:

- Has the contractor proposed an appropriate methodology to accomplish this type of work?
- Does the submission focus on the needs of the contract?
- How are records and information to be assembled?
- How will regular reports to the city's golf administrator be undertaken?
- How will quality control be assured?

Quality of the proposal related to the question, Does the proposal meet the requirements of the request for proposals so that the evaluators can appropriately address the points needed to make a sound decision? General guidelines included the following:

- No specific pieces of information outlined in the request for proposals can be omitted from any proposal.
- Capital improvement priorities must be outlined.

Each proposal was graded relative to the seven nonprice attributes using a four-point scale: 0 equals entirely inadequate; 1, below average (barely adequate and would need improvement if selected); 2, average (minor deficiencies not likely to adversely affect operations); 3, good (all requirements fully covered); and 4, excellent (all requirements met to an outstanding degree). The evaluation team eliminated all proposals that rated 0 on any of the seven criteria.

From Leon Younger. *Private management of golf courses. In Mark E. Havitz (ed.). Models of Change. Venture: State College, PA. Pages 48-56. 1995. Copyright ©Venture Publishing, Inc. Used by permission.*

still having to pay the same commissions to the agency (p. 217).[2]

Size and Scope of Contract

The size and scope of contracts range widely, but they can be classified generally into four categories.[9] First, facility-based contracts cover all operational aspects of a facility and its immediate surrounds or of specific activities within the facility. Second, activity-based contracts relate to a specific activity that can be contracted out at one or more sites. For example, an agency could contract out catering operations at six of its recreational facilities. The third category is area-based contracts that cover park and recreation services delivered within a specified geographic area. Small contractors and nonprofit and community organizations are more likely to bid on area-based contracts than on contracts requiring services to be delivered throughout the whole jurisdiction. The Kansas City mowing contracts discussed earlier in this section were of this type. The final category is comprehensive contracts that cover a large number or all services offered by an agency. "Contracting Out the Operation of all Park and Recreation Services in Ingersoll, Ontario" describes a contract of this type.

Contract Content

Detailed discussion of a contract's content is beyond the scope of this text and will vary according to the particular service involved and state and local laws. However, the template shown in "Typical Content of a Contract for Park and Recreation Services" illustrates the type of items included in a typical contract.

Developing documentation, seeking contractors, and evaluating bids takes a considerable amount of time and effort. Although much depends on the systems and procedures in place within each agency, the checklist of tasks and associated times given in table 9.1 provides an indication of the timeframe needed and the complexity of the contracting-out process.

Monitoring the Contractor's Performance

In figure 9.1 monitoring is shown as the final stage in the contracting-out decision process. If the developed contract is too complex or vague for the contracted work to be monitored effectively with the resources that the agency has available,

Contracting Out the Operation of all Park and Recreation Services in Ingersoll, Ontario

Ingersoll has a population of 9,600 and is located 100 mi west of Toronto. The town had a 30-year-old arena with an ice pad and an auditorium. It maintained approximately 100 acres of passive and active park land, which included several soccer pitches, seven baseball diamonds (four of which were lighted), and two outdoor tennis courts. More recently, the council constructed a $3.7 million indoor leisure pool and fitness center called the Victoria Park Community Centre.

A vocal group who opposed the decision to build the Victoria Park Community Centre continued to attack the Ingersoll Park and Recreation Department's operation of it after the center opened because the agency's budget increased substantially with the need to staff the new facility. In response to this pressure, the town accepted a proposal from Recreation Services International Inc. to take responsibility for managing all of the department's services for a five-year period at an annual cost saving of $125,000 to the town. Highlights of the agreement included the following:

- The operator assumed total control of the management and operation of the arena, parks, and the Victoria Park Community Centre.
- The operator assumed all employees, the collective bargaining agreement, and all outstanding grievances. There were three grievances, including a partially completed arbitration hearing.
- The town maintained ownership of all facilities and equipment.
- The town was responsible for capital repairs to buildings and capital replacement of equipment.
- The operator was responsible for all normal equipment and building maintenance.
- The operator was required to obtain council approval to make improvements, renovations, or additions to facilities.
- The operator was required to obtain council approval to increase user fees or to reallocate ice time for youth hockey or figure skating.
- The operator was to maintain the level of maintenance and service that the town previously provided.
- The operator received all revenue and paid all accounts.
- The operator posted a performance bond for $100,000 for the term of the contract.

Although there were initial concerns by user groups about a lack of public consultation and potential for declines in service and maintenance, there were no major complaints after the contract was implemented. Items that were not considered in the initial negotiation or that required clarification were resolved amiably. The operator aided this transition by appointing the town's former parks and arena director as its manager and by retaining all other management personnel. This helped ensure a good relationship with the town, which was exemplified by the operator's manager attending meetings of the town's senior management team.

then a contract should probably not be consummated. Although responsibility for producing a service can be contracted, accountability for its quality always remains with the park and recreation agency. If a contractor performs poorly, the public rightly will blame the agency and expect it to restore service quality. Indeed, citizens and users of the service are unlikely to differentiate between the agency's employees and the contractor's employees. In essence, this means that if the contractor fails, the agency fails. Hence, when the contractor starts work, the agency's parallel monitoring role commences.

Good contract management embraces regularly inspecting the contractor's work to ensure performance standards are being met, negotiating modifications to the contract if both parties recognize these are necessary, and terminating the contract if performance quality is unsatisfactory. The two most frequently noted problems with contracting out are contractor unreliability and the difficulty of monitoring contracts: "These two problems may be but two sides of the same coin, since unreliable contractors may simply be contractors who anticipate weak monitoring" (p. 48).[4]

Typical Content of a Contract for Park and Recreation Services

The Content of the Preamble Should Include

- the date of the agreement;
- the names of the parties to the agreement;
- the definitions of significant terms;
- the place of signing;
- the legal authority for the contract; and
- the general purpose of the contract.

The Core Conditions Should Include

- the term of the contract and of extensions, if applicable;
- the services to be provided, with reference to the specification;
- any variations or changes to the agreement;
- reference to the specification and any other schedules;
- appointment of the auditor;
- control and management;
- staffing;
- insurance;
- performance surety;
- ownership and rights of entry to the premises;
- the financial basis of the agreement and profit sharing, if any;
- financial recording and reporting;
- invoicing and payments;
- successors and assigns;
- agreements and contracts in force;
- quality control, default, and termination; and
- arbitration.

Many of these items require schedules or appendixes that set out details. These schedules usually are attached to the end of the contract.

Table 9.1	Tasks and Times Required for the Steps in the Contracting-Out Process Once a Decision to Proceed Has Been Made

Task	Time required
Develop strategic plan and timetable	4 weeks
Draft the contract	4-10 weeks
Produce the specification	8-20 weeks
Prepare the Request for Proposals (RFP)	1-2 weeks
Produce tendering instructions	1-2 weeks
Produce an information package for bidders	2-4 weeks
Advertise the request for bids	1-2 weeks
Prepare for and conduct bidders' meeting and site meeting	2-4 weeks
Receive proposals	3-6 weeks
Evaluate proposals	3-5 weeks
Research proponents' financial status and seek technical reference	2-4 weeks
Short-list the best proponents	1-2 weeks
Interview the short-listed proponents	2-3 weeks
Select the best proponent	1-2 weeks
Negotiate final details	1-2 weeks
Sign the contract	1-2 weeks
Implement the contract and monitor compliance	N/A

Many of these tasks can be undertaken simultaneously. However, the process is complicated and is likely to take between 25 and 40 weeks to complete.

The contractor should be regarded as a partner and not as the enemy. An adversarial perspective is likely to be counterproductive to both parties. Feedback is as important to contractors as it is to the agency, for without it they do not know if the agency considers the service to be of high or low quality. Good communication is crucial, particularly during the first few months. The communica- tion process starts at the pre-bid conference to which all interested qualified bidders are invited for the purpose of clarifying the agency's intent in the contract and identifying potential problem areas. This meeting typically will be conducted by the personnel responsible for monitoring the contractor's performance.

Ironically, scarcity of resources, a prime stimulus for contracting out, also contributes to reducing its potential by inhibiting monitoring. Monitoring is not free. Even a relatively sketchy and incomplete effort involves expenditure of time and resources. The imperatives of day-to-day operations often push monitoring aside. Park and recreation agencies face continuing dilemmas of reducing services to clients or reducing administrative costs. The latter are the first to be reduced, restricting the resources available for monitoring.

Wide variation exists in estimates of monitoring costs, but a reviewer of these estimates concluded:

Assuming that the cost of contract administration is considered separately from monitoring, a crude estimate of monitoring costs is from 5 to 10 percent of the contract cost. Accurate monitoring of cost estimates would require at least rudimentary cost accounting, and most jurisdictions have no desire or intention to do such cost accounting (p. 96).[4]

The key to effective monitoring is to write specific performance standards into the contract so that both sides know the evaluation criteria to be used. The performance standards should be performance or output oriented when possible rather than task or input oriented. For example, in a tree-trimming or park-mowing contract, the specified standards should be outputs in terms of number of trees trimmed and acres mowed in a given time period rather than inputs, such as number of hours worked and extent of equipment used.

Four types of monitoring may be used. The challenge is to select the combination of approaches that will provide the most information given the resources available. The first approach involves reviewing contractors' reports and records that describe work undertaken during the previous time period. Agencies typically require contractors to provide regular reports—often monthly—that address the following issues:

- Attendance figures (by activity or by area)
- Number of programs or activities conducted
- Complaints and actions taken to resolve them

- Problems and solutions
- Revenue (by activity, by day, or by week)
- Expenditure (by activity or by cost center)
- Noteworthy events or activities
- Forthcoming events or activities
- Seasonal phenomena, such as Christmas, or spring preparation of sports fields[9]

In addition to these regular reports, the agency should review periodically the following:

- Plant maintenance records
- Cleaning schedules
- Staff attendance records (who worked and when)
- Preventive maintenance records
- Activity attendance sheets
- Reports of fire drills, fire inspections, and health inspections
- Complaint registers
- Program schedules
- Records of users' attendance[9]

The frequency with which an agency reviews records is likely to decline as the contract progresses and trust is established.

A second monitoring mechanism is to review complaints. Effort should be made to communicate to citizens where to send complaints. They may go either to the agency or to the contractor, but each party must promptly inform the other about them. The contractor must have a system in place to ensure that they are processed speedily and that citizens are notified of the actions taken, and the agency needs to monitor how quickly and how well they are addressed.

Some agencies do not engage in any other monitoring, assuming that user complaints will ensure performance. This is fallacious. The absence of complaints cannot be interpreted as demonstrating a high level of satisfaction because, as long as the service does not deteriorate below some minimal satisfaction level, many people will not make an effort to comment. Indeed, most dissatisfied people do not complain. Instead, they either quit using the service or use an alternative service if one is available. However, they do tell their friends of their dissatisfaction; therefore, negative word of mouth about the park and recreation agency disseminates through the community, and because no complaint was made, the agency remains un-

aware of it! Hence, aggressive, proactive monitoring is needed more than a reliance on processing complaints.

Inspection of work, which may be done with or without a contractor's knowledge, is a third monitoring approach. These inspections usually include a rating scale and form on which to note problems and comment on quality of service. A typical scale would be

A = work exceeds specification requirements;

B = work meets specification requirements;

C = work is only marginally satisfactory;

D = work does not meet specification requirements; and

E = work is unsatisfactory.

Some agencies use a mystery-shopper approach to inspections. For example, Indianapolis monitored its contracted golf courses by training a cadre of volunteer mystery shoppers who were experienced golfers and members of the Society of Retired Executives. There was no expense to the city. The volunteers inspected the courses while playing golf on them. When they handed in their completed inspection forms to the contract administrator, they were reimbursed their green and cart rental fees. Figure 9.6 and "Quality Standards Graded From Eagle (2) to Triple Bogey (7)" show the rating forms that were used. The latter specifies the quality standards that were expected. Alongside each item, the mystery shopper golfers wrote a score using the scoring system shown at the bottom of figure 9.6. The ratings and comments were reviewed each week with the contractor and a time period by which the problems would be resolved was agreed upon.

The final monitoring tool is surveys of users and citizens. Sampling procedures and how to develop survey instruments is beyond the scope of this text, but a note of caution is appropriate. Directly asking people what they think of the quality of a particular service often is not helpful. As long as their level of satisfaction is within some adequate range, most will answer positively. A high percentage of favorable evaluations or satisfied responses does not necessarily reflect a high level of satisfaction, only a lack of dissatisfaction. Indeed, clients almost always report high satisfaction and favorable evaluations even for ineffective programs. Only if the service becomes excessively bad are citizens likely to respond negatively to generalized questions.

Golf Course: <u>Whispering Hills</u>   Date: <u>6/5</u>   Time: <u>2:30</u>   Rater: <u>Kack</u>

Weather Conditions: <u>Warm   80°   Sunny—Last rain 6/2</u>

Item rated	Score	Comments
Entrance	3/5	Sign at Senouc Rd is not readily seen from west
Parking lot	4	Improved since last visit
Club house	3	Much landscaping work done — flowers planted, beds mulched
Pro shop	3	Reasonable selection at various prices
Locker room	4	Clean
Rest rooms	4	Clean
Restaurant	4	Clean, looks nice
1st tee	4	New plantings, mulch added by RR ties
Tees	5	Some tees have weedy grasses
Fairways	4	Decent stand of grass
Greens	3	Consistent, soft
Bunkers	4/5	Being edged today
Roughs	4	Good but some holes still have ruts, bare spots in rough
Ponds/creeks	4	Have been weed eated
Trees/shrubs	5	Trees still need weed eating — especially Pines
Cart paths	3	Finished in 94 — collars of paths have ruts in places
Driving range	4	New area sodded
Preserve areas	4	A few natural areas but not designated as preserve
Carts	4	
Cart barn	4	Under clubhouse
Maintenance building	4	OK for now — be careful not to let area look messy
Club racks	4	Available at clubhouse
Signage	3	

General comments: <u>Eight dead trees on 3rd hole — 3/4 dead trees #5</u>

<u>Drink water available & cold</u>

- **2 Eagle—Excellent**
- **3 Birdie—Very good**
- **4 Par—Good**
- **5 Bogey—Fair**
- **6 Double Bogey—Poor**
- **7 Triple Bogey—Unacceptable**

Figure 9.6   Mystery-shopper rating scale.

Case Example: Contracting Out Maintenance and Mowing Services[11]

Many of the guidelines and principles discussed in the chapter were exemplified by the Kansas City Parks and Recreation Department in its contract maintenance program. The agency's park maintenance managers faced problems similar to those confronted by many other agencies. Support from the general fund had decreased consistently for many years. Initially, it was possible to offset these decreases by increasing funds from other sources;

Quality Standards Graded From Eagle (2) to Triple Bogey (7)

A. Customer service
1. Tee times are scheduled easily.
2. Bag stand is near clubhouse to drop clubs.
3. Receipts are given for fees.
4. Rules and regulations, including dress codes, are displayed attractively.
5. Information on passes, leagues, lessons, etc., is available readily.
6. Score cards, pencils, etc., are available readily.
7. Hole signs with yardage, par, etc., are well placed.
8. Ball washers are operational.
9. Towels are available at ball washers.
10. Benches are adequate in number and well placed.
11. Trash containers are available on the course.
12. Wildlife management areas are designated with appropriate signage.
13. Cold water is available on the course.
14. Pace of play is monitored appropriately.
15. Dress code is enforced.
16. Shoe cleaners are available at clubhouse entrance.

B. Staff
1. Professional staff are clearly identifiable.
2. Staff consistently greet customers.
3. Staff members present neat and clean appearance.
4. Staff members are knowledgeable and communicate clearly.
5. Ranger is friendly and courteous.

C. Clubhouse
1. Clubhouse is clean and swept.
2. Lighting fixtures are operating.
3. Restroom floors are clean and swept.
4. Sink and toilet fixtures are clean and without odor.
5. Restroom supplies are available (e.g., soap, toilet tissue, towels).
6. Grounds are landscaped nicely.

D. Pro shop
1. Shop is adequately stocked and merchandise is displayed attractively.
2. Pricing is competitive with comparable municipal golf courses.

E. Snack bar and concession area
1. Concession area is clean.
2. Menu board is clearly visible.
3. Food and drink prices are stated clearly on menu board.

F. Grounds

1. Entrance is clearly visible.
2. Entrance is well landscaped.
3. Parking lot is clean and well maintained.
4. Parking lot has designated handicapped slots.
5. Area surrounding clubhouse is groomed and landscaped neatly.
6. Area surrounding maintenance building is groomed and landscaped neatly.
7. Maintenance building is neat and clean.
8. First tee is nicely landscaped and attractive in appearance.
9. Tee boxes are well maintained, with multiple markers where space allows.
10. Grounds and bunkers are maintained in a professional manner.
11. Greens are consistent in speed, appearance, and playability.
12. Fairways are distinguishable from rough.

G. Golf carts and cars

1. Adequate quantity and quality of rental golf cars and pull carts are available for the course.
2. Car is clean and refueled or recharged.
3. Car is undamaged (e.g., seats, body dents, etc.).
4. Car performs well at all speeds and in all directions.
5. Car is equipped with score cards and pencils.

H. Driving range, if applicable

1. Hitting surfaces are well maintained.
2. Balls are clean and uncut.
3. Lighting is functional, if applicable.
4. Adequate rental clubs are available.
5. Yardage signs are in place for 100, 150, 200, and 250 yd.
6. Hitting area safety features are in place.

I. Business operations

1. Where required, employee Professional Golf Association credentials are maintained in good standing.
2. All transactions are entered properly into the department-provided cash registers.
3. Cash registers are available for daily polling.
4. All business provisions of contract with the department (e.g., insurance; compliance with federal, state, and local laws and regulations; nondiscrimination, etc.) are performed consistently.

however, the potential of these sources ultimately was exhausted, and real budget decreases were inevitable. The budget problem was compounded by rising costs of labor, equipment, and materials. The minimum wage paid to seasonal part-time staff was not competitive, making it difficult to fill positions. The agency's part-time work force generally was poorly educated and often unmotivated.

Further, the agency had a financial responsibility to pay unemployment benefits to former employees, even though many worked for only six months per year. These problems were exacerbated by the age of many facilities and pieces of equipment. Facilities built in the 1930s by the Works Progress Administration and Civilian Conservation Corps had deteriorated, and old equipment, such as heating and cooling systems, was inefficient and unreliable.

At the same time, Kansas City residents were demanding more and better services. Almost 90% of respondents to a citizen survey requested additional park and recreation services, but only 23% favored increasing taxes to pay for them. These circumstances stimulated the agency to investigate alternative strategies for maintaining the parks. A reduction in the level of maintenance was considered but was rejected as being unacceptable to the public. Another option of shifting resources to maintenance from other department service areas was similarly rejected as nonfeasible. The only realistic option appeared to be contracting out.

Planning and Preparation

Management negotiated an agreement with union representatives on the maximal level of contracting out mowing and trimming. The intent was to free the agency's permanent employees from these responsibilities and to concentrate their efforts on more-skilled tasks. To do this, the department developed a career enhancement program, tailored to meet the additional training needs of each employee.

The agency formulated eight objectives to guide the contracting-out program:

1. To develop closer ties with neighborhood and community groups. Facilitative arrangements with several neighborhood associations were negotiated, whereby the associations subcontracted to undertake park maintenance tasks using agency funds. Neighborhood residents developed a sense of stewardship in their parks. By adding their own volunteer time and effort to resources that the department supplied, they further enhanced the overall appearance of the parks.

2. To curb the rising cost and size of government. Rather than assume that contracted services were cheaper than directly delivered services, the program required a comparison of costs incurred by both pubic and nonpublic sector maintenance crews.

3. To provide services such as electrical and plumbing needs and irrigation installation and repair that may be beyond the skills of the existing in-house labor force.

4. To increase the flexibility of the existing labor force. Skilled agency employees were to be freed for more complex tasks by not being tied down with nonskilled routine duties.

5. To support the commercial sector so maintenance contractors would become effective supporters of the Department of Parks and Recreation in bond and levy elections.

6. To develop a business constituency supportive to parks and recreation and, in particular, to the department. In addition to local contractors, local suppliers of maintenance equipment and chemicals were supported by the program.

7. To avoid the purchase or rental of costly equipment that would be used on a limited basis. Seldom-used equipment, such as tree spades and drill seeders, and complex equipment prone to breaking down, such as street sweepers, would be contracted from private landscape companies.

8. To shift some worker's compensation and general liability insurance costs to independent contractors. Although these costs were included in all private bids, the amount expended on the agency's full-time employees for these purposes far exceeded the amount included in the bids from external producers.

A cost comparison between in-house and contracted services was undertaken. Before undertaking this exercise, the agency had only a vague idea of the real costs of its services because of inadequate cost-accounting procedures. Their analysis of these costs included five elements:

1. All direct labor costs, including wages, overtime, and benefits

2. Clerical and other support costs

3. Training and licensing costs

4. Other operating costs that supported service delivery (e.g., liability insurance, uniforms, equipment maintenance and repair)

5. The portion of equipment depreciation attributable to each service or program

Following this internal audit, the agency determined the likely contract costs for services that potentially could be done by outside organizations. Again, five elements were considered:

1. Direct payments to the contractor for services rendered. These costs varied on situational factors. For example, mowing costs were not spread equally over warm-weather seasons but instead were dependent on other variables, such as rainfall levels. Accordingly, a range of estimates was developed for all potential contracts.

2. Costs involved in preparing contracts and writing specifications.

3. Costs involved in monitoring and administering contracts during the course of a year.

4. Cost for developing and administering alternative plans should the contractor fail to complete the project or service satisfactorily.

5. Costs for bid advertisement and promotion.

A sample cost comparison developed by the department is shown in figure 9.7. It shows that the average cost per acre for mowing and litter collection was $48.81 if the agency did the services and $22.99 if a contractor did them. Thus, annual savings accruing to the agency from contracting out the 1,600 acres negotiated with the unions amounted to $578,368.

During this costing exercise, it was found that private contractors had four distinct advantages over public agencies. First, their personnel costs were generally lower. For example, the agency was mandated from previous negotiations with unions to pay annual cost-of-living allowances; however, this was not an obligation of most potential contractors. Second, the agency was required to assign certain jobs to certain employees as a result of civil service regulations and union agreements, but private contractors had much more flexibility. Third, the private sector was not encumbered with bureaucratic procedures for purchasing equipment and supplies, so contractors could make purchases in a more efficient and timely manner. Fourth, specialization allowed for economies of scale. For example, a contractor may do extensive curb and gutter work and thus make frequent use of pouring molds; however, the purchase of such equipment by the agency would be costly and inefficient because of the relatively few occasions on which it would be used.

Another result of the costing exercise was an identification of the types of situations when contracting was most likely to be beneficial. Most obviously, contracting was beneficial when travel time and costs were high because the areas to be maintained were isolated or in outlying parts of the city. Such situations were relatively frequent in Kansas City because its 10,000 acres of park land were spread over a large (316 sq mi) geographical area. Contracting was preferred when the special-

In house

Labor	+	Equipment	+	Materials
$20.50 mowing		$3.07 hourly costs		$1.20 gasoline, oil,
23.00 litter control		0.48 repair costs		and trash bags
0.12 clerical support		0.12 depreciation		0.32 uniforms, other
$43.62		$3.67		$1.52

Total in-house cost: $48.81 per acre

Contract

Direct payment	+	Labor	+	Materials	+	Advertisement
$19.00		$1.38 inspection		$1.92 gasoline, oil		$0.11
		0.58 clerical support				
$19.00		$1.96		$1.92		$0.11

Total contracted cost: $22.99 per acre

Cost difference (contract vs. in-house): $25.82 per acre

Total savings per year:

1,600 (no. of contracted acres) × 14 (mowings per year) × $25.82 (cost difference) = $578,368

Figure 9.7 Cost comparison of mowing and litter collection.

ized skills or equipment required were likely to be underutilized in the long term; when additional seasonal assistance was needed; and when new technology was being tested or equipment obsolescence was probable. For example, the agency was able to evaluate the quality of new mowers by monitoring how they performed for the contractors.

Contracting was deemed most desirable in situations when the need for public contact was minimal. Departmental experience suggested that city employees handled public contact better than contracted employees did. However, some contact was inevitable, and most citizens were likely to assume that contractors' employees worked for the city. Hence, the park maintenance contracts specified that contracted employees must wear uniforms and respond to citizens' complaints and comments within certain time parameters.

Implementation

Meetings were scheduled with union officials and members before implementing contracting out. Assurances were made that the primary intent was not only to upgrade maintenance of the park system but also to increase promotability of the current work force through training and reassigning personnel to more skilled and complex jobs.

After the work activities suitable for contracting had been selected, a complete inventory of all units in the system was conducted. This inventory of acreage was verified with official legal documentation so future disagreements between the agency and contractors regarding the number of contracted acres were forestalled. The derived level of service was specified, and care was taken to ensure that the specifications were complete, concise, and enforceable. All potentially ambiguous terms were defined. For example, explicit definitions of terms such as *production rate*, *inclement weather*, *maintenance cycle*, and *grounds maintenance project area* were included. Particularly important common terms, such as *trash* and *litter*, were also defined in order to minimize potential confusion. The contracts addressed issues of who, what, and where and addressed when work was to be performed. Figure 9.8 on page 258 shows the template of the general contractor maintenance specifications developed.

The contracts were segmented by size, scope, and geographic location within the city. This practice allowed contractors of various sizes and resources to compete successfully for different jobs, and the practice encouraged bids from regionally-based contractors who could offer economies related to time and travel. Contracts clarified the special skills or expertise required, detailed the expected appearance of contractors' on-site employees, and specified cleanup standards expected of contractors. Finally, they listed potential damage against which contractors should guard; identified situations posing health or safety hazards to park users and gave instructions on avoiding the situations; and detailed the expected level of communication between agency and contractor.

Payment to the contractor was based either on a measure of output or on a fixed price and included penalties for nonperformance. For example, the city retained the right to fine contractors for damages they inflicted incidentally to park property or for work that was incomplete or below standard. Thus, contractors were fined $259 per day if a mowing cycle was completed but the quality of the job remained unsatisfactory. The agency's contracts normally ran for one year with options to renew for one additional year. The renewal option typically was accepted for 96% of contracts, indicating that contractors generally were satisfied with the arrangements.

It was recognized that strict and consistent enforcement was critical to maintaining the program's integrity and its long-term success. Initial relationships between contractors and inspectors were established at pre-bid meetings. Once contracts had been signed, regularly scheduled meetings between contractors and inspectors were the norm. Inspectors documented problems in writing as a matter of policy. In addition, photographic documentation was collected if deemed necessary, and enforcement by inspectors was backed by the threat of executing the cancellation clause that was in each contract. Poor enforcement would result in deterioration of facility and program quality, increase in future costs needed to bring facilities and programs back up to standard, and damage to the agency's reputation. It also could result in lower bids being submitted in subsequent years by less professional contractors believing that they did not have to fulfill contractual obligations.

Encouraging many qualified businesses to bid for the work was key to the program's success. The agency built its initial list of bidders from Yellow Page listings and aggressive newspaper ads. In addition, previous suppliers of related services were contacted, discussions were held with other public agencies who had contracted for similar

Scope of work

Work shall consist of specified grounds maintenance activities upon specified Parks, Recreation and Boulevards properties within each defined area as scheduled.

Definitions

a. Grounds Maintenance Project Area shall refer to specific geographic area(s) of the City designated to receive specified grounds maintenance services. See Section 2-E.

b. Maintenance Schedule shall mean the time periods established for the project year within which all prescribed maintenance activities for each area shall be completed.

c. Maintenance Cycle shall refer to each time period in the mowing schedule for the project year. Each time period is defined by a beginning and ending date, in which all prescribed maintenance activities for each area shall be completed.

d. Area Inspector shall mean the duly authorized representative of the Director of Parks, Recreation and Boulevards who shall monitor the contractors' progress within the Grounds Maintenance project area he/she is assigned to.

e. Inclement Weather shall mean rainy weather or when the condition of the soil is such that the rutting of property will not allow cutting of grass to be accomplished satisfactorily.

f. Production Rate shall refer to the amount of acres to be maintained per day based upon the total number of acres identified as remaining to be maintained in the mowing cycle.

   The production rate shall be calculated in the following manner:

$$\frac{\text{Total acres identified to be maintained}}{\text{No. of days remaining in the mowing cycle}}$$

   For purposes of this contract, the minimum production rate shall be 25 acres per day.

g. Trash and Litter shall mean *any debris* within the Grounds Maintenance Project area such as paper, cans, bottles, limbs three (3) inches or smaller in diameter, rocks, etc. which is not intended to be present as part of the landscape. Inclusive of entire project area including streets, sidewalks, curbs, hillsides, ditches, etc. . . . *Removal of debris will require sweeping of hard surface areas such as sidewalks and driveways.*

h. Litter Removal cycle shall mean the removal of trash and litter from the assigned Grounds Maintenance Project area as determined by the area inspector. The issuance of a work order for Litter Removal only does not require mowing, trimming, edging, etc.

i. Trimming shall refer to the cutting or removal of all plant material immediately adjacent to or under park structures, trees, poles, tables, signs, fences, shrub beds, etc. Also includes removal of all plant material from expansion joints and any other cracks in curbs, sidewalks (both sides), driveways and any other concrete surface within the right of way.

j. Edging shall refer to the vertical removal of any and all plant material which encroaches over or onto sidewalks (both sides), curbs, steps, driveways and pavements. Edges shall be vertical, minimum depth of one (1) inch, and minimum width of one-quarter (1/4) inch.

k. Chemical Trimming shall refer to the use of a herbicide (such as Round Up and/or an approved equal containing a preemergent such as Surflan or an approved equal) as an alternative to the physical removal or cutting of plant material from areas to be trimmed. Approval for the application of herbicides must be obtained from the Area Inspector prior to herbicide application. Application must be in compliance with the Missouri Pesticide Use Act.

l. Scalping shall refer to any action which results in the mowing of any turf area below a three and one half (3-1/2) inch height down to and including the soil.

m. Shrub Beds shall mean any purposefully planted domestic, ornamental plant growth.

n. Foreign Growth shall include all weeds; thickets and noxious plants as defined in Chapter 18, Article VIII, Section 18.170, Code of General Ordinances.

o. Mulch or Tree Rings shall refer to those areas adjacent to trees, shrub beds, and other purposefully planted landscape areas in which all plant growth is removed.

p. Sucker Growth shall mean the incidental, vegetative growth arising from the bases and lower trunk areas of trees which are not essential to the overall well-being of the plant.

Figure 9.8 Grounds maintenance service specifications.

services, and leads were secured from professional associations. Generally, as the bidding pool grew larger, the bids were likely to be lower. Typically, 20 to 25 bidders competed for mowing contracts, and 10 to 12 of these businesses were successful.

A notice was directly mailed to contractors that included date, time, and location of the agency's pre-bid conference and bid opening for maintenance services. The notice specified what must accompany bids and listed the agency's contact who would provide additional assistance and would answer questions. The pre-bid meeting usually lasted between 1 h and 2 h and took place in the off-season, allowing maximal preparation and participation by agency staff. This timing also ensured that contracts were awarded and secured before the start of the mowing season. The previous year's tabulation of bids received was laid out for visual inspection, and a slide presentation, detailing quality expectations, was shown. Departmental mowing inspectors from the city's four maintenance districts conducted the pre-bid conference, thus allowing them an opportunity to establish their expertise and authority. In addition, the arrangement allowed inspectors to develop a rapport with bidders and to take them on tours of potential mowing sites. Several criteria were used to select contractors including past performance, level of expertise, suitability of equipment and facilities, possession of appropriate licenses and permits, and insurability. Figure 9.9 outlines the time line for the bidding process.

The department was especially sensitive to issues related to departmental morale and employee training. With respect to morale, it was deemed critical to separate the park areas maintained on contracts from those maintained by in-house crews. Interaction between the two groups was minimized to reduce any possibility of conflict.

The contracting program allowed the park maintenance division to meet its stated commitment to park mowing schedules despite the budget reductions. Most park land was on at least a 7- to 14-day schedule. At the same time, the contracting program was a successful vehicle for starting and supporting small businesses. Several companies

January

- Formal process of receiving bids and awarding contracts based on lowest and best bid basis.

February

- Process contract documents.

March

- Meet with contractors individually

April

- Initiate preseason service (e.g., edging).
- Issue notice to proceed.
- Complete contract approval process.

May

- Begin full-service operations on a routine cycle.
- Perform comprehensive inspections.

June

- Continue inspections, evaluations, and counseling as necessary.
- Begin making a record of possible changes for next contract(s).
- Same as prior month.

July

- Same as prior month.
- Establish contract schedule for next season.

August

- Same as prior month.

September

- Prepare budget for next contract season.
- Same as prior month.

October

- Finalize draft of contract documents and specifications for next contract season.
- Begin closure of current contracts.
- Establish fall and winter schedules for services, if applicable.

November

- Have draft of contract documents approved.
- Advertise for next season's contractual service.
- Print contract documents and specifications.
- As current season contracts expire, process final payments and return performance bonds.

December

- Conduct pre-bid conference for next season's contracts.
- Meet with potential contractors for next season to inspect service areas.

Figure 9.9   Project time line.

From Mark E. Havitz. *Models of Change.* Copyright ©1996 Venture Publishing, Inc. Used by permission.

were formed specifically to bid for park mowing contracts. Some of them were able to purchase capital equipment on the basis of winning these contracts and subsequently moved on to win other contracts in both the public and private sectors.

Three questions were asked by personnel charged with conducting contract evaluations: "Was the contract cost effective or were there additional cost consequences?" "Did the contract and specifications need to be revised?" "Did the scope of contract services need to be increased or decreased?" Figure 9.10 clearly indicates that the agency successfully decreased mowing- and litter-related maintenance costs on a cost-per-acre basis over an eight-year period.

Summary

Contracting out is a shift in responsibility for production of a service from an agency to an outside organization that is paid to provide it. Although long used for selected professional services, the range and variety of service contracts has grown dramatically recently. The increased use has resulted in increased controversy, but contracting out is likely to be successful in selected contexts when applied thoughtfully.

A systematic decision-making process relating to the desirability of contracting out starts with an analysis of its potential for cost savings. The major challenge in undertaking an analysis of delivering a service directly or contracting it out is to ensure that all of the costs associated with each alternative are included in the analysis. If cost savings of at least 20% seem likely, then an agency's next logical step is to find out if a number of alternative, qualified, service producers are available to bid if work is contracted out. The larger the pool of bidders, the greater the efficiencies from contracting out are likely to be.

Three sources of controversy are likely to arise. If they are not resolved, the political agitation may be sufficiently strong to cause a contracting-out proposal to be abandoned. The first controversial issue is the decision on what happens to displaced employees who previously delivered the service.

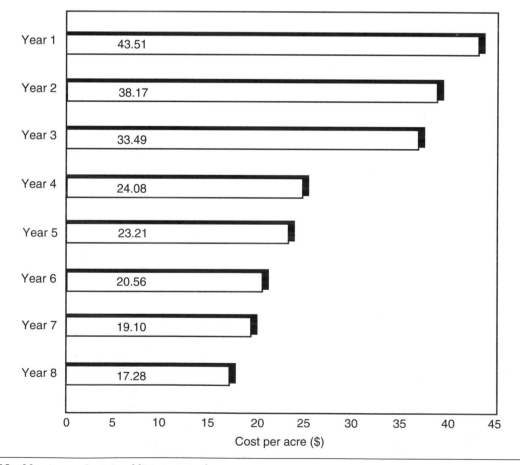

Figure 9.10 Mowing and minimal litter control.

The most viable options are to offer severance pay to those who voluntarily resign, require contractors to hire employees, redistribute them to positions elsewhere in the park and recreation agency or in the jurisdiction, or require contractors to interview and appoint from all those affected. A second controversial issue is likely to be pricing. If an agency relinquishes control of price decisions or authorizes substantial increases, then criticism from service users can be expected. A third source of criticism may arise if a contractor focuses resources exclusively on relatively responsive target markets in order to reduce costs and increase revenues and ignores the agency's mandate to equitably serve all segments of the jurisdiction. Input has to be solicited from all impacted stakeholders, and their concerns have to be addressed. If controversy remains and there is not general community support at this stage, then the contracting out proposal should not proceed.

If the agency decides to proceed with contracting out, five decisions have to be made relative to the form of contract an agency wants to offer. First, it has to identify how service delivery will be safeguarded in the event of contract failure. This can be done either by spreading responsibility for service production among several different suppliers or by engaging in partial contracting whereby the agency shares delivery responsibility with a contractor. Both alternatives ensure that a service could be assumed by another supplier if a contractor failed. A second decision relates to whether an invitation-to-bid or request-for-proposals approach should be used to select a contractor. A third decision is the type of contract to offer. The most common alternatives are a firm fixed-price contract in which a single price is quoted for delivering a service; a commission contract, whereby an agency is paid a percentage of the contractor's gross receipts; or a fixed-price-with-incentive contract, which starts with an agreed price for the service but provides the contractor with incentive to improve performance. A fourth decision relates to size and scope of the contract. Four types are usually identified: facility-based, activity-based, area-based, and comprehensive contracts. Fifth, the contract's detailed content has to be specified.

Although an agency may contract responsibility for producing a service, it always remains accountable for its quality. Hence, monitoring the contractor's performance is a critical element in successfully contracting out a service. The key to effective monitoring is writing specific performance standards into the contract so both sides are aware of the evaluation criteria to be used. Four types of monitoring may be used: reviewing contractor reports and records, reviewing complaints, field inspections of the work, and surveys of users and citizens. The combination of approaches selected will provide the best information given the resources available.

References

1. The Conservation Foundation. 1985. *National parks for a new generation.* Washington, DC: The Conservation Foundation.

2. Howard, Dennis R. and John L. Crompton. 1995. *Financing sport.* Morgantown, WV: Fitness Technology Systems.

3. Savas, Eric S. 1987. *Privatization: The key to better government.* Chatham, NJ: Chatham House Publishers.

4. Rehfuss, John A. 1989. *Contracting out in government.* San Francisco: Jossey-Bass.

5. Rose, Graham. 1991. Keeping a wary eye on royal parks. *The London Sunday Times,* July 28, C11.

6. International City Management Association. 1989. *Service delivery in the 90s: Alternative approaches for local governments.* Washington, DC: International City Management Association.

7. Schmid, Sue. 1992. Contracting for savings. *Athletic Business* 16(7): 20.

8. Crompton, John L. and Brian P. McGregor. 1994. Trends in the financing and staffing of local government park and recreation services 1964/65–1990/91. *Journal of Park and Recreation Administration* 12(3): 19-37.

9. Panther, Nigel J. 1996. *Contracting out municipal recreation services: A practical guide.* Stittsville, ON: Panther Associates.

10. Crompton, John L. and Charles W. Lamb. 1986. *Marketing government and social services.* New York: Wiley.

11. Lampone, Steve. 1995. Successful and effective contracting of maintenance services. In *Models of change,* edited by Mark E. Havitz. State College, PA: Venture Publishing: 36-56.

CHAPTER 10

ACQUIRING RESOURCES THROUGH EXACTIONS

Exactions qualify as a type of direct partnership between park and recreation agencies and developers; however, they differ from the types of partnerships discussed in previous chapters. In the case of exactions, developers are mandated to commit resources to parks, but in the case of the previously discussed partnerships, the arrangements were voluntary. Many developers are resentful of exaction ordinances because they are mandatory. Nevertheless, they have emerged as a primary funding source for park acquisition and development in many communities.

A park exaction is a local government requirement imposed on subdivision developers or builders, mandating that they dedicate park land or pay a fee to be used by the government entity to acquire and develop park and recreational facilities. In a few jurisdictions, the requirement has been extended to include such public services as child-care facilities. Exactions are a means of providing park and recreational facilities in newly developed areas of a jurisdiction without burdening existing city or county residents. They may be conceptualized as a type of user fee because the intent is that the cost of new parks should be paid for by the landowner, developer, or new homeowners who are responsible for creating the demand for the new facilities.

Under the terms of an exaction ordinance and as a condition of approval for a permit to subdivide or build, developers may be required to deed a portion of their land, pay a fee based on its equivalent value, or pay a development impact fee to the public jurisdiction for park and recreational purposes without receiving any compensation. The thinking behind this requirement is that because new development generates a need for additional park and recreation amenities, the people responsible for creating that need should bear the cost of providing the amenities. In essence, the public sector is transferring the cost of providing public amenities to the private sector. This approach has become an attractive alternative to conventional methods of financing park and recreation amenities to many government officials.

The first type of exaction that governments used was mandatory dedication. The earliest records of mandatory dedication are found in the historic charters issued by the king or queen, colonial legislatures, and state legislatures for the establishment of new towns and villages. These charters required that a common green or central plaza be set aside for the good and use of all. The earliest enabling bill was passed by the legislature of the state of Washington in 1907. (The governor vetoed it, so it did not become law.). This bill stated that no plot of land of 10 acres or more in area inside a city boundary or within 5 mi of a large city and 1 mi of a small city "shall be filed or recorded by any public official, unless a plot or plots of ground containing not less than one-tenth of the land in the plat, after deducting streets and alleys, shall be dedicated to the public for use as a park, common or playground, with the like effect that streets and alleys are dedicated to the public" (p. 490).[1] However, despite this early beginning, only since the 1970s have exactions emerged as a primary tool for acquiring park and recreational resources. The stimulus of the tax revolt inhibiting the use of property taxes for acquisition and development contributed to their widespread adoption.

The precedent for requiring dedication of streets, sewers, water drainage, utility easements, and school sites was well established before it was extended to include parks. The authority of municipalities to enact exactions for parks is derived from the developmental control authority granted to local government entities by state legislation. Under these so-called police powers, a municipality reviewing a residential subdivision plat (development application) may require the developer to construct and dedicate public facilities necessary to ensure the public's health, safety, and welfare. In approximately 20 states, this exaction authority has been made explicit by enabling acts specifically authorizing exactions as a precondition of subdivision or building approval.[2] In the remaining states, courts have inferred the authority to impose park exactions from a broad interpretation of legislation.

Alternative Forms of Exactions

Figure 10.1 indicates that the three principle forms of exactions are land dedication, payment of a fee in lieu of deeding land, and impact fees. They have evolved sequentially. The earliest exactions were confined to land. In response to limitations of this approach, fees in lieu were imposed. Most recently, impact fees have emerged. This evolution represents an incremental broadening of the concept of exactions and the types of costs they are intended to cover.

The current situation is the result of an evolutionary process whereby the policies that first gain legal and public acceptance provide the foundations for new policies creating an archaeological mound, in which earlier

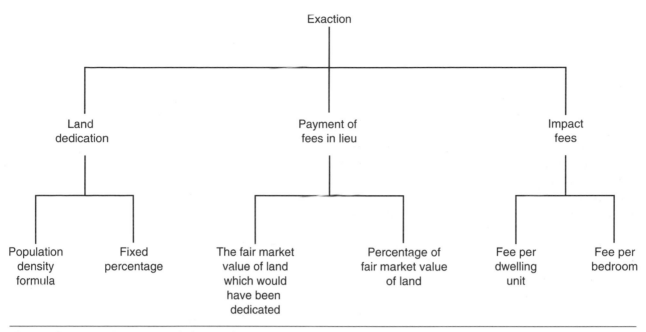

Figure 10.1 The three principle forms of exactions include land dedication, payment of a fee in lieu of deeding land, and impact fees.

layers are rarely abolished or amended; they continue to exist concurrently with the new forms (p. 25).[3]

The broadening of the exactions concept was documented in a survey of 573 municipalities designed to elicit information about park and recreation exactions.[4] Traditionally, park exactions were imposed only on residential development. However, the survey revealed that among municipalities that imposed exactions, approximately one-quarter extended them to commercial, office, and industrial developments as well as to residential developments. The tendency to extend exactions in this way varied dramatically between states. For example, extended exactions were imposed by approximately 90% of cities in Minnesota, while they were not evident in any cities in Texas. Further, park exactions historically were used to provide neighborhood parks, but the survey found that more than 75% of communities that have exaction ordinances are now using fees from this source also to acquire, develop, or renovate community and citywide parks.

Exponential increases in the extent and magnitude of exactions in recent years, especially impact fees, reflects a marked shift in views about the local benefits of growth. Before the mid-1970s, the prevailing conventional wisdom was that new, private, real-estate developments were important to the fiscal health of a community and that public investment in park and recreation and in other infrastructure improvements was desirable because it encouraged such development. In the decades since that time, this viewpoint increasingly has been superseded.

According to the new conventional wisdom, growth rarely produces sufficient revenue at constant tax rates to compensate host jurisdictions for its associated public costs. Localities generally face rising marginal costs for new infrastructures as they grow. Their existing infrastructure costs much less per unit of capacity on average. . . . Ordinary voters are likely to experience tax and fee increases for the benefit of newcomers, as well as negative changes in the quality of community life (p. 2).[5]

Exactions increasingly are viewed as a strategy for removing these inequities by requiring real-estate developers to underwrite public investments that their projects generate. As voters have become increasingly hostile to tax increases, some communities have been seeking to ensure that new development "pays its own way."[5]

Land Dedication

If an ordinance requires dedication of land, the amount to be dedicated may be determined in one of two ways. First, a fixed percentage of the total land area to be dedicated may be used. Its major advantages are simplicity and ease of computation. A typical ordinance might state, A minimum of 5% of the gross land area of subdivisions of more than 50 lots or 25 acres shall be dedicated for public parks or playgrounds.

The actual percentage required varies widely and may range from as low as 3% to as high as 10%. (Ten percent appears to be the upper range that the courts will accept.)[6] The major disadvantage of the fixed-percentage approach is that, although the park needs generated obviously will be different, the standard remains the same whether the subdivision is a single family development or a multiple family complex.

The courts increasingly have rejected ordinances based on a percentage dedication of land. Because subdivisions may be of very different densities, percentage dedication places burdens on developers that are not necessarily commensurate with the park needs that their homes will create. For this reason, an alternative approach called the population-density formula emerged. This approach requires the developer to deed a specified acreage per 1,000 people in the area or to deed land according to the number of residents who live there. Density is usually expressed as the number of dwelling units per acre (see table 10.1).

This approach has the important advantage of relating park needs directly to the number of people in a given geographical area.

The dedication of land has three major weaknesses. First, the size of the acquired land is limited by the size of the developer's project. Because most projects involve a relatively small acreage and because most ordinances require only a fraction of that acreage to be dedicated, only small fragmented spaces are provided. Such spaces offer

limited potential for recreation and are relatively expensive to maintain.

Second, the location of dedicated land is determined by the location of the development, which may not conform to the location designated in a city's park and recreation master plan. Third, the dedicated land may not be suitable for park development. The best residential land and the best park land frequently are characterized by well-drained soils, moderate slopes, and large tree vegetation cover. The developer often will seek to dedicate the land least suitable for building upon, which is also likely to be unsuitable for park use.

Fees in Lieu

For the reasons given in the previous two paragraphs, ordinances usually authorize a community to require developers to contribute cash instead of dedicating land. These cash payments are termed *fees in lieu*. There are two methods of assessing these fees in lieu (see figure 10.1). First, the fee may be a percentage of the total fair market value of the land being developed. For example, the ordinance might state: The fee in lieu shall be equal to 5% of the average fair market value of the land in the subdivision.

Second, the fee assessed may be substantially equal to the fair market value of the land that otherwise would have been dedicated using the population approach. For example, the ordinance might state: The subdivider shall pay to the municipality for the recreation fund a sum based on the fair market value of the land that otherwise would have been dedicated and in proportion to the density of population in the subdivision.

In some cities where the dedication requirement is based on a fixed percentage rather than on density, developers are charged an additional exaction fee whenever they receive an upgrade in zoning. A typical fee in California would be $2 per square foot. The fee typically goes into a trust fund for public improvements, and parks are a part of those improvements. This additional fee is imposed because a change to denser zoning or commercial zoning brings into the area more people who require extra services.

Impact Fees

Recreation impact fees (also known as capital recovery or development fees) are a direct outgrowth of mandatory land dedication requirements and fees in lieu. They differ from land dedication and fees in lieu because they are collected at the

---

Table 10.1 Density as Number of Dwelling Units Per Acre

Density (dwelling units per acre)	Park land (% of subdivision area)
1-5	8
6-10	13
11-15	15
16-20	17
Over 20	20

building permit stage rather than at the time of subdivision platting (i.e., when the land is approved for development). Hence, they are paid by the builder rather than by the developer. The courts' acceptance of fees in lieu opened the door to the emergence of impact fees. They are adopted most commonly in cities that are growing rapidly, have expanding tax bases, and have a strong local economy. In areas of rapid growth, impact fees can generate substantial funds. For example, in the mid-1990s, Metropolitan Dade County, Florida, was generating between $500,000 and $1 million each month from impact fees for park and open space acquisition and development. The impact fee may be imposed on a per-bedroom or a per-dwelling basis (see figure 10.1), and when the fee is imposed on commercial property, a per-square-foot basis may be used. Most agencies use the per-dwelling basis because it is easier than keeping track of the number of bedrooms, particularly in large agencies monitoring multiple developments simultaneously.

The impact fee has four major advantages over the fee-in-lieu approach. First, because it is collected when a building permit is issued rather than when the land is platted, the impact fee can be applied to developments that were platted before an impact fee ordinance was passed. (Grandfathering frequently occurs and exempts developments approved before the new ordinance was passed.) This is important in a state such as Florida where hundreds of thousands of vacant lots were platted before the passing of dedication ordinances by local governments.[7] Without impact fees, these developments would not pay their fair share for parks.

A second advantage of impact fees is that they "can be applied to condominium, apartment, and commercial developments which create the need for extra-developmental capital expenditures, but which generally escape dedication or in lieu fee requirements because of the small land area involved" (p. 34).[8]

Third, the intent of land dedication and fees in lieu was for developers to provide park land within or close to their developments, which met the close-to-home needs of their new homeowners. However, impact fees embrace a broader vision including paying for needs, such as regional parks, that are external to a particular subdivision but derive from multiple new subdivisions. In the past in the United States, these types of facilities were most likely to have been financed by general obligation bonds, but the public's resistance to tax increases has provided a powerful stimulus for the expanding use of impact fees.

Fourth, impact fees may be assessed for development as well as acquisition, which frequently is not authorized by land dedication or fees-in-lieu ordinances. This feature makes them an attractive alternative to bonds for financing new park development or major renovations. The movement to impose impact fees has been encouraged by a realization that the expense of developing a site for use as a park substantially exceeds the land cost. Hence, some local governments have moved away from requiring an undeveloped site or an equivalent amount of cash and have begun to formulate the exaction requirement as being a site fully developed with necessary facilities. For example, in Roseville, California, there is a mandatory land dedication requirement of nine acres per 1,000 people (which may also be met by a fee-in-lieu payment), but in addition there is a development impact fee of approximately $1,600 per residential dwelling to pay for developing the dedicated land into a park facility.

Agencies often negotiate with developers to have them construct the facilities for which the impact fees of the agencies would be used. This is likely to be cost efficient for both parties because, rather than the agency having to request bids for the work, developers can use their labor and equipment, which is already on site.

The tendency to move to a more comprehensive and inclusive recovery of costs is demonstrated in the following advice for establishing impact fees.

> To avoid shortfalls in their park development funds, communities, when calculating park impact fees should be sure to include the value of planned facility improvements to be located on acquired park lands. Also, the costs of providing road access and utilities to the perimeter of the site can be legitimately added to the site acquisition cost in establishing park fees. Because land values can vary significantly across the city, it is also advisable to set park fee schedules by regions. This will not penalize lower land value areas where most affordable housing is constructed, and it will capture the value from higher land value areas where most luxury housing is usually located. Austin's [Texas] park fees, for example, are half as high in the eastern part of the city as they are in the west, while fees in central Austin are 25 percent lower than they are in the west (p. 295).[9]

However, resistance from developers has meant that this goal of fully funding park and recreation amenities in new areas has been frustrated. For example, in Florida the cost per dwelling of providing water, sewerage, drainage, police, fire, library, school, park, recreational, and other community facilities to a new development has been estimated to average more than $20,000.[10] However, average impact fees for these services are between $3,700 and $4,700 according to the Home Builders Association of Mid-Florida.[11] In most cases, impact fees have not been set at a high enough level to cover the full capital costs of the park and recreational facilities demanded by new development. Their low level also may be explained by a desire to minimize the likelihood of litigation by developers and to be easily defensible in court if necessary: "Over time, as confidence about the legality of impact fees has grown, most early adopters have become far bolder, and new adopters have felt free to set higher rates from the outset" (p. 40).[5]

Although impact fees are relatively new, they are diffusing rapidly across the United States, and at least 19 states, representing approximately half of the country's population, have adopted legislation enabling a development impact fee.[12] An illustration of how one prominent park and recreation agency determines the impact fees is shown in "Calculating a Park Impact Fee." The range of amenities the fees are being used to fund has expanded. For example, in some communities, they are imposed for libraries, child care, or museums.[8] Their use has been most prevalent in Colorado, Florida, and California. In Colorado they have been used for several decades, whereas in Florida they emerged as a response to the fiscal problems associated with the very rapid growth of the past decade. Impact fees in California were identified as a new revenue source after Proposition 13, and now two of three builders report that they pay them.[13] In California, impact fees differ from those levied elsewhere in the United States because they are enacted as taxes rather than as part of a city's police power authority. The effect of this is that their use is less restrictive, and they are not required to meet the legal tests of reasonableness discussed in the following section of this chapter. Thus, for example, the city of Ventura, California, was able to implement a recreation impact fee on all new residential, commercial, and industrial development in the city for the purpose of acquiring and developing a 45-acre, area-wide park (which was estimated to cost $5 million) on

the east end of the city. This fee was imposed in addition to existing mandatory dedication requirements for local park acquisition.

Recoupment Impact Fees

Recoupment fees are emerging as an extension of the basic impact fee. *Recoupment* means: "the proportionate share of the capital improvement costs of excess capacity in existing park and recreation areas where such capacity has been provided in anticipation of the needs of new development" (p. 157).[14]

It is often cost efficient for a community to require, and in some cases develop, park land or hike-and-bike trails in advance of its residents' needs. Negotiation with landowners at times when activity in the real-estate market is slow, when a bargain sale opportunity becomes available, or when the land is beyond the community's existing developed areas may result in good park and recreational land being purchased at a relatively low price. It is also likely to be easier to acquire substantial tracts of 50 to 300 acres, for example, at this time than after development extends to these outlying areas. In effect, these acquisitions represent excess capacity to the community's current needs. Similarly, community amenities, such as libraries, auditoriums, or arenas, may be constructed with excess capacity in order to accommodate future needs created by new homeowners. Providing this excess capacity is likely to be supported by developers because it makes new developments more attractive to homeowners.

It is unreasonable to expect current residents to pay for this excess capacity through property and sales taxes when they are being acquired for future residents. One commentator observed:

> If new development is assessed its proportionate share of the cost of new parks that benefit new development, why not assess new development for its proportionate share of the cost of parks already built to accommodate new development but paid for by current taxpayers who do not benefit from excess capacity. In fact it is politically unwise in these times of fiscal restraint to have current taxpayers generate benefits that only new development reaps (p. 7).[8]

Regular impact fees are reserved for the payment of new facilities and generally are designated for neighborhood- and community-level facilities. A few communities (e.g., Loveland, Colorado) have initiated recoupment fees that may be levied in

Calculating a Park Impact Fee

To withstand a challenge in the courts, an impact fee must meet the criterion of rational nexus (discussed in the next section of the chapter) and must be consistent with the existing level of parks provision in the community. The recommended formula for calculating an impact fee for park land is

$$\text{average park land value} \times \text{acres per person service level}$$
$$\times \text{ number of units} \times \text{average persons per unit}$$

In the jurisdiction from which this example was derived, the community was divided into nine geographically defined park benefit districts in order to meet the rational nexus criterion. Thus, all impact fees collected within each benefit district must be spent within that district. In this jurisdiction, the impact fees were designed only to pay for neighborhood and community parks. They did not extend to regional facilities.

The land in each park benefit district was assessed using current values. The average cost of acquiring an acre of land in each benefit district is shown in table 10.2.

The agency undertook a study to identify the existing service level of publicly provided neighborhood and community parks in the jurisdiction. This indicated that they were provided at the rate of 2.75 acres per 1,000 people (i.e., 0.00275 acres per person). Hence, this was the level of service for new provision that the impact fees were designed to retain.

Census data were used to project the number of people currently living in different types of dwelling units in each benefit district. The numbers are shown in table 10.3 on page 270.

Thus, for example, the required impact fee for a single-family detached house in district 5 would be

$$\$139,533 \times 0.00275 \text{ acres} \times 3.285 = \$1,260.51$$

In addition to acquiring park land, impact fees are intended to pay for the cost of improving the new land for use as a park. The agency's data from recent construction of neighborhood and community parks showed this cost averaged $42,000 per acre. The impact fee required for a single-family detached house for park improvements in district 5 would be

$$\$42,000 \times 0.00275 \times 3.285 = \$379.42$$

Thus, the total impact fee required would be

$$\$1,260.51 + \$379.42 = \$1,639.93$$

Data for the formulas used to compute the impact fees are revised

— each year to reflect increases or decreases in land costs (see table 10.2),

— every five years to reflect changes in number of people residing in different types of dwelling structures (see table 10.3),

— every five years to reflect changes in the jursidiction's minimal service level (currently 2.75 acres per 1,000 people), and

— every three years to reflect increases or decreases in the cost of park construction (currently $42,000 per acre).

With the approval of the agency's director, a fee payer may provide land and improvements in lieu of, or in combination with, a monetary fee. The director has to be convinced that this is in the best public interest. In major developments, it is often cost efficient for the development company to provide land and construct a park rather than for the company to pay impact fees for others to do the work.

This example is based on Ordinance #90-59 administered by Metropolitan Dade County Park and Recreation Department. The ordinance has been adapted here for illustrative purposes. The author has omitted and changed some details in order to facilitate an easier understanding of the general procedure that was used.

addition to impact fees. These require new developments to buy into existing facilities so the community can recoup its investment in the excess capacity.

A recoupment impact fee is calculated so that the cost of providing park and recreational facilities for new development in advance of need is apportioned to the new development in proportion to its use of each facility. When calculating recoupment fees, credit has to be given for tax received from the new development that will go to servicing debt associated with the excess capacity of facilities. If this credit is not given, then new homeowners would be paying twice for the same amenity.

Legal Challenges

Many developers resent being required to pay exactions for parks and have challenged their legality in state courts. They have claimed that exactions are unconstitutional because they violate the Fifth Amendment to the U.S. Constitution in which the last twelve words state: "nor shall private property be taken for public use, without just compensation." State courts generally have upheld the legality of exactions. A typical finding was issued in *Hollywood Inc. vs. Broward County* in which the court declared: "Open space, green parks and adequate recreational areas are vital to a community's mental and physical well-being" and as such an ordinance ensuring park and recreational facilities "falls squarely within the state's police powers."[15]

Given the court's general approval of the principle of exactions for parks, the focus of most legal challenges has now shifted to questions relating to what constitutes a reasonable dedication requirement. Several tests of reasonableness have been propounded by the courts, but the prevailing standard throughout the country is now the rational nexus test. This test requires the following:

Table 10.2 Average Cost of Acquiring an Acre of Land in Each Benefit District

Park benefit district	Average park land value per acre
1	$518,988
2	$518,988
3	$111, 750
4	$260,780
5	$139,533
6	$128,668
7	$ 64,090
8	$ 58,000
9	$109,364

Table 10.3 Persons Per Dwelling Unit by Type in Each Park Benefit District

Park benefit district	PPU single-family detached house	PPU single-family attached house	PPU multi-family unit structures
1	2.651	2.415	1.614
2	2.710	1.740	1.790
3	2.907	2.483	1.817
4	3.175	2.830	2.460
5	3.285	2.369	2.143
6	3.244	2.333	2.227
7	3.160	2.770	2.502
8	2.892	3.046	2.204
9	2.570	2.560	2.840

1. A connection between demand enacted by a development and the park facilities being developed with exaction resources from it.

2. Identification of the cost of the park facilities needed to accommodate the new demand. This establishes the burden to the public of providing the new facilities and the rational basis on which to hold new development accountable for such costs.

3. Appropriate apportionment of that cost to the new development in relation to benefits it receives. This establishes the nexus between the fees being paid to finance new parks to accommodate the new demand and the benefit that the new development receives from the new facilities.

Using this test, the courts have required that dedications bear a reasonable relationship to the park needs that can be attributed to the development, and they have required that what is dedicated be used to provide facilities to benefit the development. These guidelines do not preclude using exactions to finance park facilities that benefit several developments as long as the relative financial participation of each development is in proportion to its attributed need.

A refinement to the rational nexus test emerged in a U.S. Supreme Court ruling in *Dolan v. City of Tigard*.[15] Ms. Dolan owned a 9,700 sq ft store in Tigard's central business district. She wanted to double the size of the store and pave a 39-space parking lot. Tigard's land-use plan required new development to dedicate a permanent easement of land for biking and hiking pathways. However, the court was not satisfied that the city had demonstrated the additional vehicle and bicycle trips that Dolan's development generated reasonably related to the city's requirement for dedication of the easement. It ruled that the impact of the proposed development did not create a need for the path. In effect, the city was exercising leverage, without just cause, over a building permit application to expand its urban greenway system over private property without spending public funds.[16] The court stated: "The city must make some sort of individualized determination that the required dedication is related both in nature and extent to the impact of the proposed development" (p. 2319).[16] Thus, the court established a rough proportionality as the standard required for the relationship between dedication requirements imposed on a developer and the increased demands

on existing infrastructure attributable to the development.[17]

The courts consistently have ruled that facility standards for new and existing residents should be the same; for example, new residents should not be required by an exaction ordinance to pay for parks on the basis of five acres per 1,000 people when the existing community standard is less. Thus, deficiencies in facilities arising from demand generated by earlier development cannot be funded by exactions on new developments. By limiting the amount that can be exacted from a developer to that which is needed to serve the development's occupants, local governments are prohibited from using new development as a source of financing for facilities beyond those attributable to the development. Most challenges from developers, thus, revolve around determination of the existing level of service. For example, in "Calculating a Park Impact Fee," the existing level of service was 2.75 acres. That statistic is central to determining the impact fee of $1,641. If developers could demonstrate that it was too high, then their impact fee payments would be reduced. "Calculating an Impact Fee Using the Rational Nexus Test" on page 272 gives an illustration of how an impact fee may be determined using guidelines of the rational nexus test.

The analyses undertaken to refute or affirm this reasonable relationship are becoming increasingly sophisticated. The less sophisticated forms of dedication, such as ordinances using the fixed-percentage formula, may fail to convince a court that the development is only paying its fair share of facility costs. Developers have argued that such a formula does not relate needs to benefits and, as such, is not a reasonable measure to determine the dedication requirement. In contrast, challenges to the population-density formula, which is based on the number of people, generally have been refuted in the courts, suggesting that this approach is superior in the eyes of the courts to the flat-percentage approach.

Legal challenges to fees in lieu and impact fee provisions generally have turned on the question of where the fees were to be spent. An ordinance that allows cash to be spent anywhere in a jurisdiction for any type of park is likely to be challenged. An agency should have a parks master plan that divides the jurisdiction into geographical districts. Each district should have a separate fund in which to credit all dedication fees in lieu or recreation impact payments originating from that district. This fund will enable it to meet the courts' general

Calculating an Impact Fee Using the Rational Nexus Test

If the average amount of park land in a community is three acres per 1,000 residents, then planners would project future park land needs using this standard. Hence, a projected increase in population of 30,000 people over 10 years would mean that the community would have to provide an additional 90 acres of improved parks within 10 years. New development may be assessed impact fees for this cost.

Suppose a community decides that its existing park standard is not adequate and establishes a standard of five acres of improved park land per 1,000 residents. If the community has 100,000 residents but only 300 acres of improved park, it falls 200 acres short of meeting its adopted planning standards. If the community projects that it will have 30,000 more residents within 10 years, its plan must provide for a total of 650 acres of improved park land. Can new development make up the existing shortage? Not directly. The plan and its capital improvements component must first show how the community will eliminate the current deficiency without assessments on new development; perhaps the elimination will be through taxes that only current development will pay. Such taxation would equalize the burden of paying for existing deficiencies. In such a situation, new development could be held responsible only for the cost of providing the additional 150 acres of park land, which is the amount attributable to it. That is the approach to determining impact fees using the rational nexus test.

The courts will probably require that deficiencies be cleared up as quickly as possible. In this example, the community should make up its 200-acre deficiency within a reasonable time (usually above five years).

Suppose planners have determined that the present value of the community's expenditures for improved park land over the past 10 years is $30,000 per acre. At five acres per 1,000 residents, the cost per capita of new parks is $150, which would be the per-capita impact fee charged to new residential development for new parks. Assessing fees as new residents are added to a community would be cumbersome; it is more reasonable to assess them on a per-unit-of-housing basis. If the average household size is 2.5 persons, then the impact fee is $375 for each new home. Cost adjustments have to be made for homes built for different sizes of families, however, and many impact fee schedules base the fee on number of bedrooms and on unit type.

Adapted from James C. Nicholas and Arthur C. Nelson. The Rational Nexus Test and Appropriate Development Impact Fees. In Development Impact Fees. Edited by Arthur C. Nelson. Planners Press, American Planning Association: Chicago Illinois. 1988, pages 172-173.

requirement that expenditure of funds be directed to the acquisition and development of park and recreational facilities that serve the people who occupy the land being subdivided. These revenues should be spent primarily within the originating district, as shown in figure 10.2.

The size of these districts is determined by the distance that residents are likely to travel to visit a park. The rational nexus test requires that there must be a reasonable relationship between a development and the park and recreational sites that impact fees will fund. Thus, as the distance between the development and the amenities becomes greater, it is more likely that an ordinance will lose a legal challenge based on rational nexus. On the other hand, if the geographical districts are made relatively small so that they are more defensible to a legal challenge, then it will take

much longer for sufficient funds to accrue to enable park and recreation amenities to be developed. The size of the districts should be based on information from empirical studies measuring how far people in a community travel to parks. It may be a relatively long distance. For example, the ordinance in Broward County, Florida, required that impact fees be invested within 15 mi of the development from which they were collected. Because the 15 mi distance had been determined by a study and was not an arbitrary number, it was supported by the courts as being a reasonable standard.[15] In addition to geographic districts, there also should be a documented capital improvements plan showing where and when future park improvements are planned. The plan will demonstrate to those paying the fee that they can expect to see the park and recreation benefits for

Figure 10.2 Dedication fees in lieu or recreation impact payments should be spent within the originating district.

which they are paying within a reasonable time period.

The monies received from fee-in-lieu payments or impact fees must be expended within a reasonable time after the contributions and development take place. Exaction ordinances must make provision for refunding to the fee payer the payments with interest if the expected park and recreation amenities are not developed within a specified time frame. Typically, the time period is six years, "which is based on the normal five year capital improvement cycle plus one year to integrate the revenues into the capital improvement program" (p. 143).[8]

Perceptions of Exactions by Stakeholder Groups

A decision to impose an exaction ordinance affects four main groups of stakeholders: local government officials, developers, new residents moving into a community, and existing residents in a community. The four groups are unlikely to have any consensus of views regarding exactions. Indeed, there are often differences of opinion within each of the groups. However, an effective response to controversy, which exactions frequently provoke, requires an understanding of the perceptions and values of the stakeholders. This section articulates the major arguments that may be advanced either in support of or in opposition to exactions by each of the four groups that they impact. The relative weight of these concerns is likely to be influenced by the fiscal strength of the local government and the economic health of the area. The potential arguments attributed to each group are not necessarily exclusive to those in it, but they are the group to whom those arguments are likely to be most salient. To simplify the exposition, arguments cited in the context of one group are not reiterated in the discussion related to other stakeholder groups.

Perspectives of Local Government Officials: The Case for Support

A basic and long-held principle of land-use planning and growth management is that development must be supported by adequate public facilities and services and that, in achieving that objective, private and public investment must be coordinated. Park and recreation exactions are intended to ensure that park facilities are available when homeowners purchase their new homes.

> By requiring that facilities needed to serve new developments be constructed and paid for at the time of development, this approach seeks to avoid the chronic congestion of facilities resulting from development approvals issued without regard to the availability of facility or service capacity. The support for this viewpoint is apt to come from those elements of the community interested in sound management of the municipal enterprise (p. 33).[18]

The alternative approach to avoiding such congestion would be for the government jurisdiction to purchase land after development had been launched. The purchase price on the open market at that time is likely to be much higher than at the predevelopment stage.

Exactions provide land or raise revenues for capital development without increasing taxes. In communities where the growth issue is controversial, the enforcement of exactions enables officials to claim that they have protected the interest of current residents and that they are managing growth rather than caving in to either developers or antigrowth groups.[5] Exactions enable elected officials to provide amenities that appear to voters to be free because no one receives a tax bill or an explicit fee increase for them except for those few involved in land development.[5] This is especially important when local government's ability to raise taxes to increase revenue, assuming the political will to do so exists, is constrained severely by state constitutional provisions and legislation restricting the taxing powers of government. Some local governments needing capital facilities are already taxing at or close to the limits of their authority. In such situations, exactions may be one of few alternatives available for acquiring and developing park and recreational facilities.

There are obvious advantages to developing parks and schools on adjacent sites. However, it is often difficult for school districts and municipalities to synchronize bond issues and capital budgets in the timely fashion necessary to acquire land in the dynamic market place. Exaction requirements for schools and parks in large developments makes possible their physical juxtaposition.

A widespread perception (which later in the chapter is shown to be sometimes inaccurate) is that the new homeowner ultimately bears the costs of exactions. It is frequently believed that these people will be new community residents who are unlikely to be in a position to vociferously object to the extra costs. Thus, it is reasoned that revenues raised or facilities provided in this way are less likely to stimulate political protests from residents. However, new developments and newcomers to the community are not necessarily synonymous. For example, the results of a market survey commissioned by a developer in Colorado Springs indicated:

> Eighty percent of new houses are sold to people who already live in the community. So these dedication fees are charged not exclusively to newcomers to the community, but primarily to our brothers and sisters and our sons and daughters (p. 249).[9]

Finally, in some situations, commentators have argued that local government officials in upper-income communities may impose very high exaction requirements as a mechanism through which exclusiveness or cultural homogeneity may be maintained or achieved. It may be hypothesized, for example, that this may be one of the effects in Seal Beach, California, which imposed a fee of more than $22,000 per dwelling.[18] However, local officials in communities with especially stringent exactions typically characterize their policies as preserving the community's quality of life and argue that the high exactions reflect the total costs associated with the development.

Perspectives of Local Government Officials: The Case for Opposition

Development exactions are likely to create additional costs for a jurisdiction. If the exaction merely provides unimproved land or the money to purchase such land, the agency will be required to invest additional capital funds to develop the land for park and recreational purposes. In addition, an increase in operating funds will be needed to maintain the developed facility when it is completed. Whenever land is dedicated to a public agency, there is an opportunity cost involved because such an action removes it from the tax rolls. Thus, the city gives up the annual property tax revenue that the site would have yielded if it had remained in private ownership. However, it may be argued that the increase in property values in the area attributable to the proximity of park land compensates for this loss.

There may be concern that exactions will cause developers to take their projects elsewhere and that this will damage the long-term economic health of a community. A major worry of elected officials is that exactions will drive away development, particularly office developments and retail complexes, as sources of tax revenues. "Developers tell us that if we get too sticky about impact mitigation they won't be able to get financing for their projects," a Concord, California, council member said. "They option the land, and can go elsewhere if we won't go along with them. The worst situation is that they'll simply move one town over. We'll get the traffic and housing demand but not the taxes" (p. 105).[19] Indeed, cities that have weak economies make little use of exactions despite their financial difficulties because their leaders fear exactions could undermine economic development efforts.

The implementation of exactions may lead to complacency by tempting local government officials to discontinue their efforts to seek out additional resources and their pursuit of other land acquisition or development procedures and to redirect these energies to resolving other problems. Many exaction ordinances are still limited to providing primarily for acquisition of neighborhood park land, and additional funding frequently is needed to develop this land and to provide for other types of park and recreational opportunities in a jurisdiction.

Local government staff may express concerns about the difficulties of administering exaction programs and of developing the analyses to justify exactions that are becoming increasingly complex. Elected officials who commit to the principle of exactions often fail to recognize the considerable staff work that is required to set up, monitor, and enforce them, especially exactions relating to impact fees.

Mandating dedication of private resources through exactions is likely to create friction and animosity with at least some members of the development and business fraternity. These people then tend to view the public agency entity as an antagonist rather than as a partner. Such animosity militates against these powerful groups voluntarily cooperating and forming partnerships, which the agency may wish to encourage and facilitate in a variety of other contexts. Further, when resources are contributed as part of an exaction requirement, they cannot be used as part of an agency's share for matching grants from programs such as the federal Land and Water Conservation Fund or similar state grant aid programs. (These are discussed in chapter 11.) Only voluntary contributions are eligible to be used as matching contributions.

Summary of Possible Perspectives of Local Government Officials

Pros

— Park land will be available in the neighborhood soon after new homes are constructed.

— Acquisition occurs without additional tax funds.

— Joint provision of facilities with schools is expedited.

— Many new homeowners may be nonresidents and, therefore, unable to object to exactions.

— A community's quality of life is preserved.

Cons

— Jurisdiction usually has to pay costs of improvements on the land.

— Land is removed from the tax rolls.

— Cost of exactions may cause developers to move projects elsewhere.

— Community may become complacent about obtaining other resources to acquire park land.

— Some exaction ordinances are difficult and costly to administer.

— May lead to antagonistic relationship with developers.

In some contexts, animosity from developers may endanger the personal political aspirations of local elected officials because developers and real-estate interests are influential in many communities and are major contributors to local election campaigns. Indeed, many elected officials are involved in real estate or associated professions. However, in other jurisdictions, the citizenry is a more powerful force. For example, a Montgomery County, Maryland, official stated: "Here, politicians who don't insist that developers satisfy public concerns are at risk of getting voted out of office and replaced by people who'll say no to a development that isn't what people want" (p. 106).[19]

Perspectives of Developers: The Case for Support

Developers may support an exaction ordinance because they recognize that it protects a jurisdiction from poorer quality development. They may rationalize that ensuring a given level of park provision and recreational opportunities throughout the area may contribute to encouraging businesses to expand or relocate in the area and, thus, enhance their own long-term sales prospects.

Exactions make available strategically located neighborhood park and recreational facilities that enhance the ability to sell the property. Many real-estate projects feature recreation amenities prominently in their promotional campaigns because they have determined these are assets that new home buyers seek. Hence, the requirement to provide recreation amenities often is consistent with the developer's own inclinations and might be provided by the developer even if they were not required. However, developers probably would prefer to decide for themselves what facilities should be provided rather than to be mandated to give resources to a park and recreation agency and to have its officials make that decision for them.

Support from developers is more likely to be forthcoming if an exaction ordinance makes allowances for in-kind recreation amenities provided by developers and is flexible enough to permit the agency and a developer to agree to an alternative exaction to that specified in the ordinance (if it is in their mutual interest to do so). Thus, developers often will incorporate open space or facilities, such as tennis courts and golf courses, into a development because they believe such amenities will assist sales. Because the existence of such amenities eases the service burden placed on the park and recreation agency, it seems equitable

that the exaction requirements imposed should be reduced accordingly. Jurisdictions that have incorporated this flexibility generally give up to 50% credit for private recreation amenities. However, if credit is given for these amenities, then it should incorporate legal language that ensures a degree of permanency for these recreation amenities. Otherwise, the developer at some future date may change them to an alternative use.

However, after many years of giving this type of credit in Metropolitan Dade County, Florida, officials found that 47% of all neighborhood and community space was privately owned by homeowner associations, and there was a dearth of public open space. In addition, because this private park and open space could not be considered part of the public agency's existing level of service, it had a marked adverse effect on impact fee payments. In "Calculating a Park Impact Fee" on page 269, the existing level of service was 2.75 acres per 1,000 residents, and this statistic was central to determining the amount of impact fees. If all private space was included, then level of service may approach five acres per 1,000 residents. This, in effect, would almost double the required impact fee payment. For these reasons, Dade County removed in-kind credit for park and recreation amenities, and no credit is provided now.

If flexibility is designed into an exaction ordinance, it may facilitate securing maximal park and recreation benefits. For example, where waterfront adjoins a community, a waterfront docking area may be more desirable than more land to both the park and recreation agency and the developer. Similarly, it may be more desirable to all concerned for a developer to give less land but to make more recreation improvements on the property. The total package could be designed so that the dollar value is equal to what would have been received if only land had been obtained.

In many jurisdictions, claims that growth is a positive outcome for the community are viewed with skepticism. It is now widely assumed that, in the absence of exactions, development will result in local tax increases or service cutbacks.[5] Hence, the burden of fiscal proof has shifted away from those opposed to growth to its advocates. Their challenge is to demonstrate that their projects will not have an adverse fiscal impact on the community. Their support of exactions is one strategy that they may use to make this case. If the community refuses to approve tax and fee increases for park and other infrastructure improvements in new areas, then developers are unable to proceed. From the developer's perspective, this is clearly an inferior alternative to exactions. Some communities in which the residents' skepticism has led to an explicit goal to limit growth have found developers willing to offer substantial voluntary exactions.

A few communities, such as San Francisco and Petaluma, California, and Boulder, Colorado, have adopted explicit policies of growth limitation, forcing developers into competition for a limited number of development slots. The result, when markets are strong, is to encourage a bidding war of voluntary exaction commitments by developers, calibrated to win community support rather than merely to finance investments clearly attributable to their projects.[5]

Developers are frequently viewed with distrust and suspicion by at least some factions in a community. Enthusiastic endorsement of an exaction ordinance may contribute to alleviating this negative image by suggesting to residents that developers have a social conscience, are concerned for the general welfare as well as the bottom line, and are prepared to invest in community facilities. Thus, developers' support for exactions may be viewed as an investment in good public relations and as a means of winning public support.

Perspectives of Developers: The Case for Opposition

The medieval torture connotations of the term exactions are indicative of the unpopularity of this practice among many developers, who regard them as a kind of extortion. A typical reaction to exactions is to term them blackmail fees because "You have to pay or you don't work" (p. 27).[20] This is perhaps an unfair characterization because little coercion actually is involved. Developers are free to choose other localities in which to build if they find the rules unacceptable.

The developer as owner of the land is very conscious of the Fifth Amendment taking issue. Although the courts have ruled that an exaction that meets a reasonableness standard is a legitimate requirement of municipalities under their police powers authority and does not constitute a taking of private land without adequate compensation, many developers resent the courts' interpretations. They view it as an intrusion of their right to use all of their land as they see fit and find the principle of park land exaction to be repulsive and an anathema. It is this perspective that results in discussions of dedication issues with developers often being highly emotional.

Ostensibly, it appears that developers will be required to pay the cost of the exactions. There has been little empirical evaluation of how the market responds to exactions, but in a vibrant economy, it is unlikely that a developer will absorb the exaction costs in the long term. Rather, these costs are likely to be passed on either to the new homeowners or tenants or to the landowner from whom the land was bought.

Because the number of lots that may be developed is reduced, the developer may pass the exaction costs along to new homeowners either by reducing the size of each lot or by raising the price. Developers sometimes argue that this erodes their competitive position in the market place because developers in neighboring jurisdictions may not be subjected to these fees.

An alternative is that exaction costs may be passed back to the initial landowners, from whom a developer purchases the land, in the form of a lower sale price for their land. This is explained in the following scenario. Suppose a builder is about to purchase a piece of land when the city announces the adoption of a dedication or impact fee ordinance. Before the ordinance, the builder could build 100 units on the land and sell them for $100,000 each. Based upon the cost of construction and required profit, she was willing to pay $2 million for the land. As a result of the new ordinance, the builder must now charge $105,000 per unit due to the increased cost. However, if the developer can now sell the houses for $105,000 each, why did she not charge that price before the imposition of the fee? In fact, the market for comparable housing in surrounding communities that do not have such an ordinance limits her to selling the houses for $100,000 each; thus, she will not be able to sell them for $105,000. As a result, the builder is only willing to pay $1.5 million for the land, so she is able to recover costs and maintain her profit margin (p. 155).[21]

One observer noted, for example, that one or two years before Atlanta metropolitan local governments adopted impact fees, developers routinely were inserting a new paragraph in their land purchase option agreements requiring landowners to reduce their sales prices by the impact fee charged.[12]

However, those developers who have already acquired land for development at the time that the community decides to approve a dedication requirement will be unable to shift these costs back to the landowner. In such situations, the developers have to absorb this cost, or they have to accept some erosion of their competitive position and try to shift the costs forward to the homebuyer. Further, the ability to pass exaction costs through to new homeowners assumes a vibrant economy. In an economic recession when house prices and rents drop precipitously, exaction costs cannot be passed through to new homeowners and tenants. To address this concern, it is usual practice today for exactions to be phased in over a period of two years so developers can adjust to them.

Thus, there is no generalizable answer to the question: "Who bears the cost of the exactions?" Costs do not set prices; market forces of supply and demand set prices. When sellers substantially outnumber buyers, there is little opportunity to pass any cost increase on to the buyer. When buyers outnumber sellers, however, costs may be shifted to the buyer. Hence, depending on the prevailing elasticity of demand for new housing, some or all of the burden may be borne by new homeowners, by the original landowner, or by the developer. The empirical research on the issue of who pays has been summarized in the following terms:

> Early research on exactions suggests that the ultimate burden of developer exactions falls upon the user/buyer. These studies were undertaken, however, in regions with rapid growth and at a time of high inflation. It is possible that the ability to shift costs forward may be more related to the growing demand for housing and to general inflation than to any other factor. Studies have not yet tested impact-fee systems during periods of lower inflation and across communities with varying rates of growth. A recent survey of builders, however, indicates that they continue to pass fees forward to the buyers rather than backward to the property owners (p. 139).[22]

Developers can justifiably point out that it is more expensive for them to provide park and recreation amenities through exactions than it would be for a park and recreation agency to provide them using conventional government financing. The developer has to borrow money at private market rates to purchase his or her land. In contrast, if the agency were to provide these facilities, it could finance them at much lower rates using its tax-exempt bonds prerogative.

Enforcing dedication of the exaction when a subdivision plat is approved usually means a de-

veloper must provide cash well ahead of any income from sales of land. That cash may sit in an earmarked fund for months or years, earning interest for the jurisdiction but costing interest and opportunity to the developer. To defuse this situation, a jurisdiction could consider delaying payment of the exaction fee until the project is occupied or allowing payment of that fee over a five-year period at public sector interest rates.

Developers sometimes express concern that if land is dedicated, there is no guarantee that the agency will develop it. Similarly, if fees are set too low, there may be insufficient funds to deliver the planned project, which damages the credibility of the developer as well as the agency. Even if a dedicated site is developed, the long-term resources necessary to maintain it at a standard that enhances the subdivision may not be forthcoming. The exaction does not improve subdivision amenities unless the municipality makes a commitment to develop and maintain improvements on that land. In some instances, city representatives have instituted an exaction ordinance but at the same time have refused to increase, and in some cases have even reduced, the operating budget of the agency. Thus, the end result may be unsightly, debilitating areas that become overrun with vegetation, garbage, and vermin.

To prevent this situation from occurring, developers and agencies sometimes have cooperated to establish special assessment districts for parks in new subdivisions. This strategy has been particularly prominent in California where local jurisdictions frequently are unable to maintain new park lands because of the limits on collection and spending of property taxes that have been imposed upon them. The land is deeded to the city, but the new residents decide the level of amenities and improvements incorporated into it and the level to which it will be maintained. Typically, they vote to select from different options related to improvements and maintenance that will result in an annual tax payment to the special district of between $10 and $100, depending on the option selected. This strategy assures the developer and the residents that the land will incorporate the amenities that they want and will be maintained at the level that they desire.

Dedication or fee exactions usually amount to a relatively small percentage of total development costs, and they generally represent an irritant, rather than a fatal blow, to a development project. Opposition to them from the development fraternity stems from a belief that they add costs that will affect the bottom lines of projects in the pipeline when the exactions are imposed and that in principle they are unnecessary, inequitable, and subject to limitless extension once introduced. However, the strength of the opposition that developers mount to a particular ordinance in a given jurisdiction is likely to be a function of the prevailing popular and political climate toward development. For example, if there is widespread resistance to growth or if a community is unable to finance any park and recreation acquisition and development from conventional sources, then developers may be the primary advocates for exactions, citing all of the advantages of adopting them as a means of eroding opposition to development. Indeed, the National Association of Home Builders, which is the national trade association representing developers and builders, stated: "Developers and builders are acknowledging that impact fee payments may mean the difference between undertaking a residential development project or not. For in the absence of needed infrastructure, residential development cannot occur" (p. 146).[13]

Given this level of acceptance, opposition from developers increasingly revolves around what constitutes an equitable exaction. In this context, the focus of the debate shifts to the issues of double payment and differential exactions.

The double payment issue relates to the way in which existing facilities were financed. It may be argued that if property taxes were used to finance most existing facilities, then the land on which new development occurs has already paid for part of those facilities. Thus, as a quid pro quo, existing residents should contribute some proportion of the costs attributable to the new park and recreation developments, rather than impact fees being set to recover total costs. On the other hand, if existing park and recreation amenities were financed primarily from state sales and excise tax rebates, state and federal grants, or fees and charges, then the vacant land before development contributed nothing, and impact fees could justifiably be set to recover total costs.[23] An extension of this argument is that the magnitude of an exaction must be adjusted to reflect the value of state, federal, and other non-local government funds involved in financing the facilities that fees support. These external contributions effectively serve to reduce the resources needed from exactions.

In some contexts, differential impact fees may be imposed to reflect the different impact made by residents and outsiders. Where this is not done, developers may protest. For example, in San Clemente, California, the city wanted to raise $6 million through fees of $1,250 on each new home to help pay for new beachside parking structures. The parking was to be used by current residents and tourists as well as buyers of new homes, but builders thought the fees were out of proportion to the additional demand for parking likely to be created by new residents.[11]

To counter such charges of inequity, Manatee County, Florida, used a survey to ascertain how much use of specific park and recreational facilities was attributable to residents and how much was accounted for by tourists. The county found, for example, that residents accounted for only 18% of the use of beach facilities but for more than 90% of the use of swimming pools and baseball fields. Using these data, the county established an impact fee for new residential units and a different impact fee for hotel and motel rooms and for recreational vehicle spaces.[24]

A final irritation of developers is that frequently it is financially expedient for them to accept exactions, even when they believe the requirements to be inequitable, because the cost of a challenge often outweighs that of simply acceding to the exaction demand. A developer in California's Napa Valley illustrated this point. "I could have appealed this requirement, but it would have taken four to six months just to exhaust my administrative remedies," he said. "Had I then had to go to court, we'd be looking at a year to two years. I probably would have won, but by then my project would have been dead." He claimed that the local staff members were well aware that the payment for which they were asking was about the same as the cost of a six-month delay in the project (p. 106).[19]

However, a ruling in *First English Evangelical Church vs. Los Angeles County* may contribute to rectifying this situation. In this case, the court recognized the right to compensation for a temporary regulatory taking, which was defined as the period between enactment of the exaction and its invalidation.[25] Before this ruling, the remedy was limited to declaring an exaction invalid with the victorious developer having nothing but a sense of inner satisfaction to show for several years of land-use restraint by an invalid regulation. If the developer now sees that the courts can award compensation for economic losses incurred while proving an unfair exaction suit, then this becomes a more feasible course of action.

Summary of Possible Perspectives of Developers

Pros

— Enhances community quality of life so encourages future development in the area.

— Enhances the ability to sell property.

— Counters skepticism that existing taxpayers will be subsidizing new growth.

— Improves developers' image with the general community.

Cons

— Perceive exactions to be a taking.

— May be required to absorb some of the exaction costs when a new ordinance is passed.

— Erodes competitive position in relation to developments in nearby communities with no exaction ordinance.

— Is more costly for developers than for public agencies to provide recreation amenities.

— Adversely impacts a developer's cash flow.

— No guarantee is made that land will be improved after it has been provided or that it will be well maintained.

— Inequitable exactions because of double-payment issues and differential terms.

Perspectives of New Residents: The Case for Support

Exactions are designed to ensure that park and recreational opportunities are available at the time, or soon after, a new resident moves into the area. The alternatives may be to wait many years before the jurisdiction invests in such amenities in the neighborhood or to accept that those amenities may never be developed nearby. Their availability is likely to enhance the area's quality of life and will probably lead to an increase in the property value of the new home. As park facilities mature, they generally become more attractive, and their presence is likely to facilitate easier resale of a home.

Perspectives of New Residents: The Case for Opposition

If the value of property is raised because of the increased amenity value of the dedicated facilities, then property taxes also will be higher. At the same time, some new residents may not regard park and recreation amenities in close proximity as being positive attributes. They may not want a park or recreational facility close to their property because of concerns that it may be accompanied by noise, trash, and increased vehicular traffic, and it may attract undesirable elements from other neighborhoods that do not have satisfactory facilities of their own.

New residents may also cite opposition that developers may also identify pertaining to increasing the cost of homes and the risk that dedicated land would not be developed or maintained well, which were discussed earlier. If the exaction costs are passed on to the new homeowner, their magnitude may be just great enough to push the selling price of a new home beyond the financial reach of some individuals who could otherwise afford it. This situation may be of particular concern in the context of low-income housing. It could be addressed partially by designing flexibility into an exaction ordinance based on ability to pay so that low-income housing would be exempt from, or subject to reduced, exactions.

If exactions lead to an increase in the absolute cost of a home purchase, then impact fees are also likely to drive up the cost of home financing. If the fee amounts are incorporated into the selling price of a new home, then homeowners must bear the cost of amortizing the fee amounts over the life of the mortgage. A comparison between an impact fee of $1,100 and a fee of $3,476 over the life of a 30-year mortgage financed at 12.5% illustrated that the $2,376 fee difference resulted in a total cost to the homeowner of $13,878 over the lifetime of the mortgage—almost six times the difference in the original fee amounts.[13]

New residents may consider it inequitable that they be required to pay the full price of acquiring and developing their recreation amenities for two reasons. First, if residents of new subdivisions must finance new parks for which they generate a need, then they should not have to help retrieve outstanding debt for development of existing neighborhood parks, which frequently they are required to do because it is incorporated into their ad valorem tax. If the rest of the community does not share the cost of their parks, residents of new developments should not have to pay for the rest of the community's parks. In the past, this concern has not been prominent because the exaction requirement usually has been intended to finance only the land acquisition cost; the whole community paid for development costs. However, with the trend moving toward use of impact fees, which in some communities are set at a level intended also to recover all development costs, this equity concern is likely to emerge.

Second, most development in the past, particularly residential development, has not paid its own way. Rather, there has been a traditional pattern of one generation of residents providing for the park and recreational opportunities of the next generation. Hence, new homeowners may legitimately ask: Why do we have a primary responsibility to provide these new facilities when most of the facilities used by existing residents were inherited by them from previous generations? Do they not have an obligation to provide for us as others previously provided for them?

This sense of inequity and injustice may be exacerbated by the realization that new residents who will be most effected by an exaction ordinance are excluded from having any impact into decisions related to that ordinance. Purchasers of new housing are typically a geographically dispersed, and thus unorganized, constituency. For this reason, they are unable to voice their objections to such exactions. Three responses have been suggested to counter this line of argument.[26] The first concerns free choice. Although the locality sets up the exactions system, the homeowner chooses to assume the encumbrance of buying the new home. Second, it can be argued that the interests of future residents are already being represented by proxies in the community through the activism of the real-estate and development industries. However, it seems unreasonable to assume that the interests of real estate and future residents are always identical. The third response is that once they are part of the community, new homeowners can engage in retrospective voting and evaluation to remove elected officials and change ordinances.

Perspectives of Existing Residents: The Case for Support

If there were no exactions, then developers might reap a windfall gain at the expense of the general public, which must bear the service need costs generated by the new development. Exactions mean that existing residents will pay lower taxes

Summary of Possible Perspectives of New Residents

Pros

— Makes recreation amenities available in the neighborhood soon after new homes are constructed.

— Increases the property value of new homes.

Cons

— May have higher property taxes.

— May attract undesirables to the neighborhood.

— May pass costs on to new homeowners.

— Unfair that they also should have to contribute to retire debt for existing parks elsewhere in the community.

— Unfair when previous new residents were not required to provide their own park land.

— Are excluded from decisions related to exaction ordinances being passed.

than they would otherwise need to pay in order to acquire park and recreational resources in newly developed areas of a jurisdiction. Further, the provision of these facilities may forestall overcrowding of existing park and recreational facilities, which might otherwise occur if new residents went to existing amenities because such amenities were not available in their area of a jurisdiction.

Although the rational nexus test requires that exactions bear a reasonable relationship to the facility needs that can be attributed to a development, the courts do allow existing development to benefit incidentally from exactions assessed against new development. Hence, it is possible that existing residents in areas with deficient park and recreation amenities may benefit from exactions.

When an exaction ordinance is introduced or when the terms of an existing ordinance are made more onerous, there is likely to be a ripple effect throughout the entire housing market. All existing owners of comparable real estate in the jurisdiction are likely to receive a windfall benefit (and existing tenants are likely to pay higher rents).

> If, on one hand, exactions deter some developers from proceeding, the supply of property on the market will be less than it would have been otherwise, enhancing the value of existing property. If, on the other hand, developers go forward but raise prices to cover their exaction costs, the value of existing property is likely to rise in tandem because new and existing properties compete in the same marketplace (p. 49).[5]

Perspectives of Existing Residents: The Case for Opposition

It has been argued that the higher cost of new development will increase the taxable value of all property because assessments of new construction are the basis for assessing existing buildings.[22] However, if the tax base of all properties increases, then a lower tax rate can be imposed to generate the same amount of revenue from property taxes, so individuals' tax bills are unlikely to be impacted by across-the-board increases on taxable value.

Higher property taxes may be required in order to support the costs of developing facilities if the exaction does not cover total acquisition and development costs and the costs associated with operating and maintaining a developed facility.

However, when a subdivision is fully developed, this may be offset by the additional taxes that residences in the new subdivision bring in to a jurisdiction.

The existing business community may oppose exactions because of a fear that they will stymie growth and, thereby, restrict business expansion. This fear rests on the assumption that exactions will increase the cost of housing, which, as it was pointed out earlier, may be fallacious.

Finally, reliance on exactions may contribute to perceptions of private ownership of public recreational and park resources in subdivisions and may disrupt the sense of community in a jurisdiction. If an impact fee, which pays for the park land and its improvements in their subdivision, is imposed on the homes of new residents, then those residents may perceive that they have exclusive ownership of those facilities and resentfully regard as intruders other residents from outside the subdivision who use these public resources. This feeling is likely to be exacerbated if they pay taxes to a special assessment district established specifically to pay for the maintenance of those subdivision facilities.

Negotiated Planning Gains

A negotiated approach describes arrangements whereby developers agree to provide desired public benefits as part of their application for obtaining regulatory approval for projects. This approach is an alternative to a formal exaction ordinance and differs from it because the agreed public benefits are not mandated through a formal ordinance. Rather, the benefits emerge from negotiation between the developer and local government without the guidance of an ordinance specifying the form and magnitude of the public benefits. Thus, technically, the benefits that developers offer are voluntary donations rather than mandatory requirements. However, if sufficient gain in amenities to the community is not forthcoming, then planning permission for a project may not be granted.

The conceptual justification for this negotiated mechanism rests on the same philosophical bases as the justification for exactions, which were discussed at the beginning of this chapter. Acquisition through these agreements depends on the aggressiveness and skill of a community's planning staff and on the economics of a development. The approach may allow a city to secure significant public benefits without spending tax dollars or imposing exactions.

Summary of Possible Perspectives of Existing Residents

Pros

— Do not have to fully finance all park and recreation amenities in new developments.

— Forestalls overcrowding of existing parks.

— Improves selling price or rentals of existing property.

Cons

— Pay higher taxes to partially support development and fully support maintenance of facilities.

— New residents may resent existing residents if they use the new parks acquired from exactions in the new areas.

The following examples illustrate the type of park and recreation benefits that may be negotiated in this way. The author was involved in negotiating an agreement by which a developer was given permission to develop an office block above the height level normally permitted by the city zoning ordinance on condition that the ground floor incorporate a swimming pool and racquetball courts, which would be vested in the city to operate as a public facility.

In return for granting developers the right to develop the 11.2-acre California Plaza project in Los Angeles, the city council required that the developers construct a new $20 million Museum of Contemporary Art as part of the project and donate it to the city. The museum was part of a $1.9 billion development that included office space, hotels, apartments, and retail space to be built over the course of a decade.[27]

Some local governments, especially those that historically have enjoyed good relationships with developers, view formal exaction ordinances as being unnecessary and counterproductive. For example, the city of Dallas opted not to pass an exaction ordinance because officials believed that they could achieve more through negotiation.

> The city has in the past received gifts of park land from developers which offers good public relations and serves as a tax write-off for the developer. The city primarily tries to work with developers on a case-by-case basis. Negotiations between the developers and the city have proven to be effective (p. 82).[4]

Some jurisdictions have adopted an official policy toward dedication rather than a formal exaction ordinance. For example, in Galveston County, Texas, the official policy of the county was to request developers to donate either a portion of their land or a monetary contribution to be used for park and recreational purposes. The county found developers to be much more receptive to the requests and suggestions of county officials than they probably would have been to a legal requirement based on a mandatory exaction ordinance. As a result of this negotiated process, officials believe that developers donated more land than they would have been required to dedicate under a formal ordinance. Although this official policy was ostensibly voluntary, developers were aware that the county had the ability to be uncooperative and delay a development if it wanted. Because delays are expensive, developers had an additional incentive to concur with the official policy request. The following vignette illustrates how a negotiated exaction may emerge:

> The Rancho Solano project in Fairfield, California, illustrates how bargaining for exactions can produce a "win/win" solution. The developer initially proposed an 850-unit single-family luxury subdivision on 2,284 acres. The city bargained for dedication of a public golf course as part of the project's development agreement. The developer argued that such a major dedication would require increased project sales, so the parties agreed to increase the project to 1,200 units. The developer then agreed to dedicate the land for an eighteen-hole municipal golf course and to pay one-half the grading costs. But the city went a step further, calculating the increased land values resulting from the golf course and bargained for the capture of that value. The developer made additional

contributions to the city based on those calculations. The negotiations, then, led to increased housing in Fairfield, increased land values, creation of a public golf course, and substantial contributions to the city's infrastructure accounts (p. 227).[28]

Advocates of negotiated agreements suggest that they have three advantages compared with formal exactions; they are flexible, voluntary, and legally secure. Their flexibility means that exaction requirements can be matched closely to needs and that adjustments can be made to be responsive to the peculiarities of a development project's unique circumstances. Moreover, because the agreements are voluntary, they are not constrained by the legal bases, such as the rational nexus standard discussed earlier in the chapter, that mandatory exactions have to meet. However, from an ethical perspective, as the amenity gain becomes less related to possible impacts that a development causes, it becomes more difficult to justify imposing this cost solely on the developer.

The voluntary nature of negotiated planning gains means that the involved parties can agree upon exactions that would be open to legal and political attack if they were imposed on unwilling developers. Another important advantage to both the jurisdiction and the developer is that guidelines for administering a number of federal and state matching-grant funds prohibit mandatory dedicated resources from being used as a local government's matching contribution for securing a grant. However, voluntarily donated resources are eligible for use as a match, so the effective value of a park amenity gain emerging from a negotiated agreement can then be doubled.

Disadvantages associated with a negotiated approach when compared with a formal exaction ordinance include the additional time and expense involved; the introduction of uncertainty into the development process; the likelihood that negotiations involving similarly situated developers may result in differing outcomes, giving rise to charges of unfairness or special treatment; and the expertise needed to negotiate effectively.

Time costs may be substantial. For example, one study found that governmental costs associated with a planning gain negotiation were four times higher than the costs associated with administering an impact fee exaction ordinance.[29]

Although some see that an advantage of the negotiated approach is its potential for ameliorating friction with developers, the advantage may also be a source of such friction. Developers sometimes point out that the uncertainties inherent in negotiated planning gains make it difficult to predict project costs and secure project financing, and that there is potential for inequitable treatment and abuse. Negotiated agreements mean that exaction provisions are determined on a case-by-case basis through negotiation and compromise, which may result in substantially different levels of exactions for similarly situated developers. This inherent level of uncertainty and potential for arbitrary actions by government officials leads many developers to prefer the certainty of formula-driven exaction ordinances.

Public officials engaged in these negotiations may not have the time, knowledge, experience, or inclination to analyze fully the trade-offs involved. Thus, residents may be suspicious that developers are able to manipulate negotiated agreements to their advantage. Some staff members report that they are outgunned by developers in negotiations: "You find yourself in meetings with three city staff members—somebody from planning, somebody from public works, and one of the attorneys—facing a roomful of the top lawyers and consultants in the state, all working for the developer." One city planner said: "They can do studies we can only dream about and we just don't have the resources to refute their arguments" (p. 107).[19]

When planning gains are negotiated, the public agency has to weigh trade-offs of the costs and benefits that are likely to accrue. Clearly, decisions relating to planning gain must take place within a coherent planning framework. While the incentives and trade-offs depend upon compromise, the compromise must not be of such sufficient magnitude that it poses a threat to the locale's integrity. An argument has been made that the amenities available from a given project may become so attractive to decision makers that the prospect of receiving the amenities can divert attention from the merits of the project itself.[30] Thus, the integrity of zoning and land regulation is eroded. The type of issues that arise are illustrated in the following scenario.

Two development alternatives are presented for a given site. For one, the developer proposes a 100,000 sq ft commercial project. For the other, the developer proposes a 150,000 sq ft project and a cash contribution for the construction of a recreational center several miles away. The additional 50,000 sq ft of the second alternative will cause traffic problems for the immediate area surrounding the site. The public agency must weigh the two possibilities and decide which most advances the public interest. In simplistic terms, the agency is balancing the costs of the extra traffic against the benefits of the community center.

When considering the trade-offs inherent in negotiated planning gain agreements, ethical questions emerge concerning how fairly the resulting public costs are distributed. Thus, in the above illustration, it is the residents of a particular neighborhood who will bear the costs of increased traffic congestion, air pollution, noise, visual blight, and other adverse impacts from the larger project, while benefits from the gained amenities accrue to a different part of the community. This suggests that the elements in the agreement should be required to meet the same rational nexus tests that have evolved for measuring the legitimacy of more formal forms of development exaction.

Criticisms leveled at negotiated planning gains tend to focus on uncertainty and inconsistency associated with their application and on the time and expertise needed from public officials. In response to these criticisms, two mechanisms have emerged that attempt to retain the principles of planning gain but establish objective standards to guide its implementation. They are incentive zoning and the concept of linkage.

Incentive Zoning

In an incentive-zoning program, the items of the trade-off between the developer and public agency are stated in detail in the ordinance. Beginning in Chicago in the late 1950s, urban planners have used incentive, or bonus, zoning to encourage private developers to make cities more attractive and to provide increased public amenities.[31] Thus, some communities offer bonuses to developers in the form of increased building heights or square footage beyond what is permitted by a site's zoning in return for a developer providing public plazas, open space, or public recreational facilities on the site.

Incentive zoning differs from exactions in that it usually benefits the landowner or developer because the value of the bonus has to equal or exceed the cost to the developer of supplying the public benefit before the incentive becomes appealing. In contrast, an exaction ordinance may result in economic loss to developers by requiring them to provide land or various facilities as a condition of project approval.

The city of New York has the most comprehensive and complex system of incentive zoning in the United States. It has more than 30 special-development districts in which specific incentive ordinances apply to relatively small geographic areas deemed to be of special character. A typical incentive plan covers the theater district. Theaters were not a good economic investment. They had become jeopardized by the influx of high-rise office buildings, which were replacing the old and uneconomic two- and three-story theater buildings. New York without theaters would be a much less attractive place in which to live, work, or visit. There were compelling findings linking New York's pre-eminence as a national corporate headquarters to its theaters around which so many related activities, such as radio and television, shopping, dining, and tourism, clustered. Hence, this ordinance permitted developers to increase the size of any building development in the area by up to 44% of floor area in return for providing a legitimate theater that met the planning commission's specifications. Five legitimate theaters, which otherwise would not have come into being, were built under this innovative provision, and all five are currently in active use.[32]

In other New York incentive ordinances, developers were permitted to increase floor area by up to 20% in certain high-density commercial and residential districts if a public plaza that met the qualifications specified in the ordinance was provided at ground level. The intent was to generate more open space in the canyons of Manhattan. In Denver, a similar incentive ordinance offered developers a premium of 12 sq ft of floor area for each square foot of public plaza that they contributed at street level.

Incentive zoning has received three types of criticism. First, planners who are concerned with integrity of the cityscape point out that incentive zoning permits developers to circumvent design guidelines for building height and size. Second, it has been calculated that the value of bonuses granted to developers far exceeds the value of public amenities provided. Third, there is no guarantee that public amenities will emerge because, unlike exactions, participation in the program is at the developer's discretion.

Concept of Linkage

Exactions are becoming more substantial in magnitude and broader in purpose. This chapter has focused on land dedication, fees in lieu, and impact fees because these are the three types of exactions that have been used most commonly to acquire park and recreational resources. However, in some jurisdictions, the role of impact fees has been extended to embrace a wider range of social services through the concept of linkage. While exactions require developers to supply or finance public facilities or amenities made necessary by their development, the concept of linkage extends this responsibility to provide for other public needs, such as social services.

A growing number of cities are adopting downtown development policies aimed at linking large-scale commercial development (office and mixed-use buildings and hotels) to their effects on local social needs and amenities. Proponents of linkage recognize that such large-scale developments may produce jobs and additional tax revenues, but they point out that the new workers need things, such as places to live, transit systems, and child-care facilities. Supporters believe that developers who profit from constructing a new development logically should help pay for increases in municipal services and facilities that it creates. From a developer's perspective, provision of these amenities is likely to assist in gaining endorsement of neighborhood groups for a project, and these groups are the traditional opponents of new commercial development.[33]

This type of linkage can only be enacted by a city if the real-estate market is strong and if existing fees, taxes, and the like have not already eroded the incentive to build in the area. Without these conditions, developers will simply move their projects elsewhere.

In the broad context of parks and recreation, linkage ordinances have required developers to construct child-care facilities in or near their development sites or to pay an impact fee into a community fund for public child-care centers. A successful linkage requirement must pass the rational nexus test and demonstrate that the need for the child-care space is created by the residents or workers who will occupy the property being built.

The amount of linkage space or payment required usually varies according to the demands for a particular project. Boston's ordinance required commercial projects of 100,000 sq ft or more to contribute between 2% and 12% of gross floor area, or its monetary equivalent, to child-care facilities. In San Francisco developers of large office and hotel projects of more than 50,000 sq ft either had to set aside floor space (minimum of 3,000 sq ft) free of rent and utility charges for a nonprofit child-care provider or had to contribute

$1 per square foot of space to the citywide child-care fund.[34] In Berkeley, California, the child-care fee was calculated in the following way:

> We estimate the cost per child to construct a child-care facility and multiply it by the total number of children needing care to establish a lump sum mitigation. We also analyze the difference between what lower income households could pay annually for child care (using state of California program guidelines) and the Berkeley market rate. We multiply this difference by the number of child-care-impacted lower income households for a given project to determine a permanent annual child care subsidy.[35]

The developer can be required either to pay a linkage fee or to carry out mitigatory actions instead of paying fees either on site or at an approved off-site location. From the developer's perspective, it is often advantageous in leasing the property if mitigation components, such as public art or child care, are included as part of the overall project. As one developer commented: "We'd much rather invest the money in an enhanced project than turn it over to the city."[35]

This type of linkage has been embraced in other countries. For example, in Sheffield (a major English city) a city council official policy states:

> The City Council will, where appropriate, use its planning powers to encourage the provision of a wide range of community benefits. These will include:
>
> — Childcare facilities
> — Community facilities and meeting places
> — Recreation and play facilities
> — Landscaping and nature parks
> — Pedestrian and cycle facilities
> — Works of art
> — Street furniture

These linkages will be paid for "by the increase of the value of the land as a result of the grant of planning permission."[36]

Summary

Exactions provide local governments with at least a partial solution to their park and recreation capital-funding problems. They represent one of the safest political options for paying for new

Infrastructure because, in general, they tax builders and new residents, neither of whom, in many cases, are existing local voters. The alternative to exactions is property or sales taxes; from a political perspective, these taxes are more difficult to impose and are likely to be more controversial than exactions.

The continuum shown in figure 10.3 illustrates the array of approaches used to exact resources from developers in order to provide public park and recreation amenities. The continuum reflects the general sequence of evolution of exactions and their conceptual magnitude. They range from no obligation, through negotiated agreements and incentive zoning, to the statutory requirements represented by mandatory dedication, fees in lieu, and impact fees. Some people perceive recoupment fees and the concept of linkage (stages 7 and 8 in figure 10.3) to be the likely next stages in the evolution of exactions. They have the potential to exert even greater demands on developers, but at this time, ordinances of this type have been enacted in only a handful of communities.

The three most common forms of exaction, which are land, fees in lieu, and impact fees, have tended to follow a common pattern of evolution. First, a city begins to feel the adverse fiscal effects of rapid growth, higher borrowing costs, reduced federal and state grant aid, and higher construction and development costs. Second, as a result of these pressures, the city shifts responsibility for acquisition of land for neighborhood parks from the general taxpayer to the developer by introducing mandatory land dedication and fees in lieu. Third, as the use of dedication is expanded, the city and developers find it to be administratively cumbersome. Finally, the city simplifies and expands the magnitude of the exactions process by adopting a system of impact fees.[9]

The amount of land to be dedicated may be determined by using either a population-density formula or by specifying a fixed percentage of the total land area. Fees in lieu may be assessed either on the fair market value of the land, which otherwise would have been dedicated using the population-density approach, or as a percentage of the total fair market value of the land being developed. Impact fees may be imposed as a fixed dollar amount per lot or per dwelling unit or may be based on the number of bedrooms proposed in the dwelling units.

The principle of exactions has been upheld by the courts. Litigation is concerned primarily with issues revolving around the issue of fairness in terms of who benefits and who pays. Legal challenges increasingly revolve around what constitutes a reasonable exaction requirement. The most widely adopted standard is the rational nexus test that prohibits government from requiring more money or land than is necessary to serve the park and recreational needs attributable to that development and that requires the exaction resources to be used to provide facilities that will proportionately benefit the paying development.

Exaction policies exhibit wide differences in their degree of compulsion, uniformity of treatment, and predictability of requirements. These variations reflect differences between local jurisdictions in philosophy, politics, and economic status. Nevertheless, all stakeholder groups appear to be increasingly willing to accept them philosophically, and they are well entrenched in law. Future legal challenges are likely to revolve around the equitability of terms specified in an exaction rather than around the principle of exaction. For this reason, their formulation is becoming increasingly crucial, and the courts and exaction opponents are becoming more sophisticated and demanding in their scrutiny of an exaction's equitability.

Four main groups of stakeholders are impacted by exaction requirements. They are local government officials, developers, new residents moving into a community, and existing residents. The complexity of the issue militates against predictable outcomes from the relative political pressures exerted by these groups, for there are no right or wrong perspectives; there are only different perspectives. Indeed, antithetical views often emerge from within the same stakeholder group because for every argument offered, there is a counterargument. The potential support and

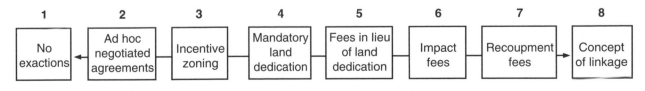

Figure 10.3 A continuum showing an evolution of approaches to exactions for park and recreation amenities.

opposition perspectives of each of the four stakeholder groups were discussed. The relative weight of these concerns within each group is likely to be influenced by the fiscal strength of the local government and the economic health of the area.

Some jurisdictions have opted to forego formal exactions in favor of a negotiated approach. Advocates of negotiated exaction agreements suggest that they may avoid the acrimony with developers (often associated with formal exactions), that they are more flexible, and that they can be used to attract matching grants. However, this approach requires a substantial investment of time, contains inherent uncertainties for the developer, and has potential for encouraging arbitrary actions by agency officials.

In response to these criticisms, two mechanisms have emerged that attempt to retain the principles of planning gain but establish objective standards to guide its implementation. Incentive zoning offers bonus increases in floor area to developers in return for providing public plazas, open space, or public recreational facilities on the site. Exactions are designed to meet physical facility needs associated with new development, but the concept of linkage extends this principle to embrace social needs generated by it.

References

1. Weir, L.H. 1928. *Parks: A manual of municipal and county parks*. New York: Barnes

2. Rohan, Patrick J. 1994. *Zoning and land use controls*, Volume 2. New York: Matthew Bender, 9-3.

3. Alterman, Rachelle and Jerold S. Kayden. 1988. Developer provisions of public benefits: Toward a consensus vocabulary. *New York Affairs* 10(2,3): 22-32.

4. Kaiser, Ronald A., James E. Fletcher and Susan Groger. 1992. Exacting land and fees from land developers for park purposes: A profile of municipal practices. *Journal of Park and Recreation Administration* 10(1): 12-30.

5. Altshuler, Alan A. and José A. Gomez-Ibáñez. 1993. *Regulation for revenue: The political economy of land use exactions*. Washington, DC: The Brookings Institution.

6. Kaiser, Ronald A. and James D. Mertes. 1986. *Acquiring parks and recreation facilities through mandatory dedication*. State College, PA: Venture Publishing.

7. Juergensmeyer, Julian C. 1988. The development of impact fees: The legal issues. In *Development impact fees*, edited by Arthur C. Nelson. Chicago: Planners Press, 96-112.

8. Nelson, Arthur C., James C. Nicholas and J.C. Juergensmeyer. 1989. Development impact fee policy and administration. Unpublished manuscript prepared for Metropolitan Dade County Parks and Recreation, Miami, Florida.

9. Snyder, Thomas P. and Michael A. Stegman. 1986. *Paying for growth: Using development fees to finance infrastructure*. Chapel Hill, NC: University of North Carolina.

10. Nelson, Arthur C. 1988. Development impact fees. *Journal of the American Planning Association* 54(1): 3.

11. Stevenson, Richard W. 1989. Debate grows on development fees. *New York Times*, February 16, section L, 25.

12. Nelson, Arthur C. 1994. Development of impact fees: The next generation. *The Urban Lawyer* 26(3): 541-562.

13. Soble, Carol E. 1988. Developers' perspectives on impact fees. *New York Affairs*, 10(2,3): 145-152.

14. Juergensmeyer, Julian C. and James C. Nicholas. 1988. A model impact fee authorization statute. In *Development impact fees*, edited by Arthur C. Nelson. Chicago: Planners Press.

15. *Hollywood Inc. vs. Broward County*, 431 So.2d 606 (Florida 1983).

16. *Dolan v. City of Tigard*, No. 93-518. U.S. S.Ct. (1994) 2309–2322.

17. Kozlowski, James C. 1994. Constitutional greenway dedication requires "rough proportionality" to development's impact. *Parks and Recreation* 29(9): 29-35.

18. Weschler, Louis F., Alvin H. Mushkatel and James E. Frank. 1987. Politics and administration of development exactions. In *Development exactions*, edited by James E. Frank and Robert M. Rhodes. Chicago: Planners Press.

19. Deakin, E. 1984. The politics of exactions. *New York Affairs* 10(283): 96-110.

20. Baca, Mickey. 1989. Impact fees: "Blackmail" or a fair sharing of costs? *New York Times*, January 15, section 10, 27.

21. Bland, Robert L. 1986. *Financing city government in Texas: A revenue manual for city officials*. Austin, TX: Texas Municipal League.

22. Nicholas, James C. 1988. Designing proportionate-share impact fees. *New York Affairs* 10(2,3): 127-144.

23. Nicholas, James C. and Arthur C. Nelson. 1988. Determining the appropriate development impact fee using the rational nexus test. *Journal of the American Planning Association* 54(1): 58.

24. Barneby, Mark P., Rom MacRostie, Gary J. Schoennauer, George T. Simpson and Jan Winters. 1988. Paying for growth: Community approaches to development impact fees. *Journal of the American Planning Association* 54(1): 26.

25. Marcus, Norman. 1988. Development exactions: The emerging law of New York State. *New York Affairs* 10(2,3): 80.

26. Beattey, Timothy. 1988. Development exactions and social justice. *New York Affairs* 10(2,3): 83-95.

27. Guenther, Robert. 1984. Novel links with developers gives arts institutions a boost. *Wall Street Journal*, April 18, section 2, 33.

28. Cowart, Richard H. 1988. Negotiating exactions through development agreements. *New York Affairs* 10(2,3): 227.

29. Nelson, Arthur C. 1993. *Development impact fee feasibility analysis for Cobb County, Georgia.* Atlanta, GA: City Planning Program, Georgia Institute of Technology.

30. Getzels, Judith and Martin Jaffe. 1988. *Zoning bonuses in central cities.* Chicago: Planners Press.

31. Rohan, Patrick J. 1994. *Zoning and land use controls*, Volume 2. New York: Matthew Bender, 8-3.

32. Marcus, Norman. 1992. New York City zoning—1961-1991: Turning back the clock—but with an up-to-the minute social agenda. *The Fordham Urban Law Journal* 18: 707-714.

33. Keating, W. Dennis. 1986. Linking downtown development to broader community goals. *Journal of American Planning Association* 52: 133-141.

34. Eichman, Caroline and Barbara Reisman. 1991. Enlisting developers as partners in child care. *Urban Land* 50(4): 2-6.

35. Mayer, Neil S. and Bill Lambert. 1988. Flexible linkage in Berkeley: Development mitigation fees. In *Development impact fees*, edited by Arthur C. Nelson. Chicago: Planners Press.

36. Elson, Martin J. and David Payne. 1994. *Planning obligations for sport and recreation: A Guide for negotiation and action.* London: The Sports Council.

CHAPTER 11

INTER-GOVERNMENTAL COOPERATION

Intergovernmental cooperation may take two forms. The first part of the chapter discusses joint working arrangements between different entities that pool their resources. Park and recreation departments most frequently implement partnerships with school districts. However, opportunities for joint acquisition and financing of amenities also exist with other departments in the same political jurisdiction; with other local government jurisdictions; and with other public institutions sited within a community, such as colleges or military installations. Beyond the local level, opportunities may exist to cooperate with state or federal agencies that own lands in the area.

The second part of the chapter addresses the type of intergovernmental cooperation that takes the form of grants given by federal and state agencies to local jurisdictions. The role of federal and state agencies in this context is to select projects that best meet criteria established by the enabling legislation for awarding the grants. In this case, these agencies are not involved directly in the acquisition of amenities or enhanced service delivery, but rather they facilitate local and state jurisdictions' efforts by assisting with funding.

The primary types of federal grant programs for parks and recreation that are available to state and local agencies are described. In addition to the federal opportunities, most states also have grant programs intended to assist local political entities to acquire and develop park and recreation amenities. The principles associated with distributing these state funds are similar to those articulated in the discussion of federal grant programs. This similarity, together with the differentiating nuances that characterize each state's program, would make any discussion of state grant programs tedious, redundant, and lengthy. Hence, no attempt is made in this chapter to describe the specific features of state-local intergovernmental cooperation. However, the major sources of funds that states use to develop their grant-funding opportunities were discussed in chapter 2.

Partnerships With Schools

The potential for using a common physical plant to provide for a community's education and recreation needs has long been recognized. For example, several schools in New York were opened in 1898 as evening recreational centers with leaders who were responsible for recreational programming. In 1907, Rochester, New York, funded a school–civic center demonstration project, and its success stimulated other cities to make wider use of their school facilities for community recreation. In 1911, the National Educational Association first passed a resolution approving the wider use of schools for recreational activities. In 1911, Wisconsin also passed legislation authorizing education agencies to levy a tax for community recreation. This led to Milwaukee establishing its school recreational center program, which today is perhaps the most extensive national example of a school board being involved in the direct delivery of recreation services.[1]

These early protestations of support for community use of school facilities were reinforced periodically. Thus, for example, in 1940 the National Education Association again gave support:

> An immediate step leading toward more complete provision of community recreation is to make available for leisure use all suitable school facilities in the community outside of school hours and during vacation periods. This is perhaps the most important single step any community can take in coordinating its recreation and education programs. In planning ahead for community use of schools, the plant must be designed to meet the requirements of the new programs (p. 7).[1]

Today, the involvement of schools in the delivery of community recreation services may take several forms. Most prominent among these are 1) the school board having primary responsibility for delivery of recreation as well as educational services in a community and, in effect, acting as the community's recreation department; 2) community educational programs, whereby school boards operate classes, usually in the evenings, in school facilities; and 3) joint-use or joint-provision of facilities, which involves school boards cooperating with recreation agencies to jointly use or provide recreational facilities. The discussion here is confined to this latter joint-use or joint-provision role because it is the only form of school involvement with recreation that requires inter-agency cooperation.

Cooperation between a park and recreation agency and a school district may take the form of joint provision or joint use. These two terms differentiate the time at which cooperation was initiated. Joint provision indicates cooperation was instigated at the outset before a facility was constructed. It implies that both agencies had input into its design in the planning stages, negotiated details of their respective roles in its management and in funding its operations before it was constructed, and contributed resources to its capital development. Joint use refers to shared use by agencies that was negotiated after a facility was built, so it was not purposefully designed for both their clienteles. Most commonly it relates to use of school facilities by park and recreation agencies. These relationships are illustrated in figure 11.1.

Benefits of Joint Provision

Joint provision is a superior option to joint use because it affords the opportunity to provide appropriate and well-designed facilities at the outset. For example, facilities designed for community recreational use could be grouped at one end of the school building in a special wing or in a separate building. Such a functional arrangement limits access to other parts of the building, making possible efficient control and economical operation and maintenance.

Figure 11.2 on page 294 schematically illustrates the case for joint provision. The section marked "School priority" in figure 11.2 shows that the potential use of recreational facilities built and exclusively used by a school district is likely to represent a very small proportion of their potential overall use. Such facilities may be used for only 180 days each year for a limited number of hours each day. Community-built recreational facilities are likely to be used extensively on weekends, in the evenings, and during school vacations. However, such facilities may experience much less intensive use on weekdays during the hours when people are at work or at school. Hence, the facility-use requirements of a school district and public agency are reasonably complementary.

The calculations in "Potential Use of School Plant" suggest that if use of the school plant is limited to school hours, including an allowance for extra-curricular activities (from 3:30 P.M. to 5:00 P.M. daily), then it will be used for only 18% of its potential capacity. In contrast, if the school is opened for community use during evenings, weekends, and school vacations, then usage of the recreation elements in the plant could increase to 61% of potential capacity. These calculations show that community use of recreational facilities in the plant is likely to be more than double the school's use if it is designed to facilitate community access.

In some communities, the real problem in terms of meeting recreation needs is simply one of harnessing the existing school resources and exploiting their full potential to meet the needs of the wider community. Indeed, the recreational facility needs of many communities would be met if all the new American schools and school extensions in the next 10 years were designed with recreational components suitable for community use. This would require relatively modest injections of capital and would be much more cost efficient than building facilities independent of schools.

In many school districts, the standard specifications for schools, especially junior high and high schools, incorporate a recreational complex. In terms of capital costs, probably 80% of the investment for a community recreational center has been made already. In these cases, implementing joint provision means modifying and extending the standard school facilities to provide a full range of community facilities upgraded to meet adult specifications.

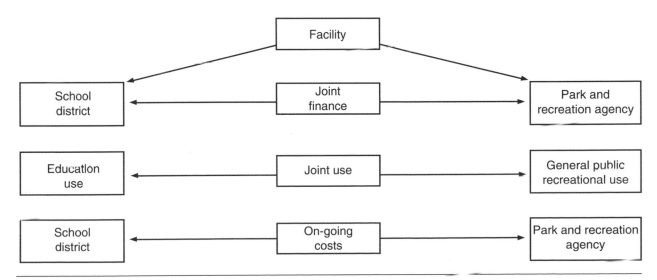

Figure 11.1　The responsibilities associated with joint provision.

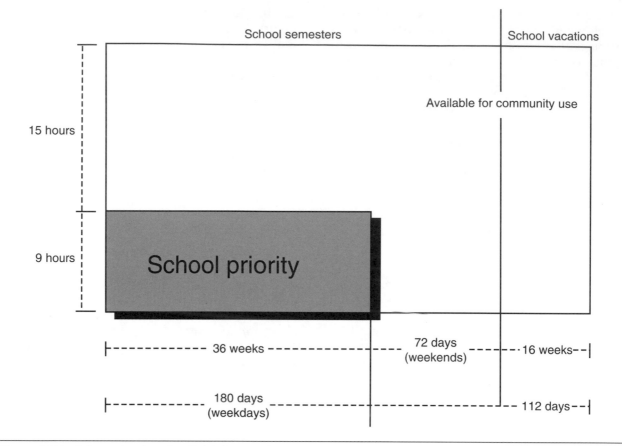

Figure 11.2 Schematic of a school's likely use of its physical plant.

Potential Use of School Plant

Total School Plant Annual Capacity

24 h per day × 365 days = 8,760 h

Total Annual School Use

9 h per day (8 A.M. to 5 P.M.) × 180 school days = 1,620 h

School use of potential capacity = 18%

Total Annual Community Use

[7 h per day (5 P.M. to 12 A.M.) × 180 school days] +
[24 h × 52 weekends (Saturday 9 A.M. to 11 P.M. and Sunday 12 P.M. to 10 P.M.)]
+ (16 h per day × 81 school vacation days) = 3,804 h

Community use of potential capacity = 43%

Total school and community use of potential capacity = 61%

Indianapolis Parks and Recreation Department conveyed 30 acres of real estate that it owned to Warren School District, on which the district constructed a new middle school. The standard recreational facilities associated with the district's middle schools were included, but the department paid to upgrade and extend them so that they met the needs and requirements of adult leagues: a football field, four soccer fields, a four-field softball complex, a track, outdoor basketball courts, and a gymnasium. The department also paid for an indoor aquatic center— Indy Island— to be added onto the school and to be operated by the department. The department receives free use of the school's facilities when they are not in use by the school, and the school receives free access to the pool for physical education lessons.

The economic case for a city and school district cooperating to provide recreational facilities is compelling. Providing these amenities is expensive and the same taxpayers pay the bill for both school and city facilities. Both school boards and city officials are under pressure from taxpayers to do more with less. Providing one set of facilities that both school and community constituencies can share is in essence using the same tax dollar twice. Certainly, it is more cost efficient than each agency building a separate set of recreational facilities for the exclusive use of its own clientele. Joint provision is likely to result in savings from reduced land acquisition costs, capital development costs, and operating expenses. The savings in land costs may be substantial.

In Plano, Texas, the parks and recreation department set a minimal acreage standard of 7.5 acres for park sites. The school district required a minimum of 10 acres for an elementary school site. However, both agencies recognized that when the two were combined into a park-school site, less land was required, and they adopted a combined-site standard of 15 acres. At $40,000 per acre, this 2.5-acre savings translated into $100,000 per site. Eight combined park-school sites existed among the 18 elementary schools throughout the city, representing a saving of approximately $800,000.

The savings accruing from sharing with junior high and high schools were more substantial because these facilities required larger acreages. The city's long-range land-use plan allocated land sufficient for a population of 350,000 using a standard of 15 acres of park land for each 1,000 people. Without joint use, 5,250 acres of park land would have been required for that population level. As a result of sharing, the requirement for land was reduced to 3,300 acres, representing a savings of 1,950 acres of land. At $40,000 per acre, the costs saved by not purchasing the land would be $78 million.[2]

Savings in the capital cost of developing facilities derive from one facility shared by two agencies needing a smaller area than the summation of areas from two separate recreational facilities. In addition to reductions in total area of recreational activity space needed, capital development savings come from reductions in external walls, site works, circulation areas, refreshment areas, meeting rooms, social spaces, and car parking lots.

In a school district bond election, Corpus Christi voters approved funding for an indoor swimming facility. A gymnasium operated by the city of Corpus Christi had already been approved in a prior city bond election. Both groups agreed to combine the projects. The swimming facility contained a shallow 25 yd, six-lane pool for instructional purposes and a 50 m, eight-lane pool for competition. After scheduling its programs at the facility, the school district made available all unscheduled space to the city parks and recreation department. The school district used the gymnasium when extra space was needed during large swim meets.

Common areas, such as locker rooms, public spaces, mechanical equipment, land costs, landscaping, and other public facilities, were shared, saving a substantial amount of money. The city enjoyed immediate savings in construction costs, as well as long-term savings in the use of larger, more efficient heating and air-conditioning systems and shared personnel for operating and maintaining the facility.

Responsibilities for staffing, utilities, programming, and maintenance of the facility were divided between the school district and the city, making the shared management work. While the school system provided maintenance of the swimming facility, the city paid the school district for its use of the facility.[3]

Throughout the city of Plano, more than 1,000 car parking spaces are available at school facilities for recreational users of those facilities. Construction of these at separate recreational centers, excluding land and maintenance costs, is likely to have exceeded $500 per space, resulting in a total savings of more than $500,000.[2]

Operating savings derive from economies associated with a smaller net area to service with utilities, landscaping, and cleaning and from the need for fewer janitorial, maintenance, and other support staff.

Joint provision is more common in the United Kingdom than in the United States. A study was undertaken in the United Kingdom to assess empirically the relative cost efficiency of jointly provided facilities and city-only provided recreational facilities. The researchers selected a sample of 44 recreational centers, which was representative of different areas of the country, varying sizes of centers, and different mixes of facilities within the centers. Cost efficiency ratios were obtained by dividing the annual operating costs of a facility by the number of admissions per year. The ratio showed the number of admissions per £1 of operating cost. The study concluded:

> The results leave no doubt as to which form of provision is the more cost effective. The average joint provision center generates 2.7 admissions for every £1 spent, while at the average separate center the ratio is 1.5 admissions. Larger centers tend to be less cost effective than smaller, because although they generate greater usage they have higher operating costs. But this is less apparent with joint centers, where large and small scale facilities are almost equally cost-effective. The range or mix of activities had no significant effect on cost effectiveness.[4]

The case for joint provision may be enhanced if one entity has spare capacity to manage a specialized facility, which the other would have to acquire. For example, in College Station, Texas, voters approved a school district bond referendum to construct an indoor pool at a new middle school. The school board and administrators were reluctant to place it on the ballot but ultimately yielded to community pressure to do so. The school district had no personnel with knowledge of pools and did not want the responsibility of operating it. The city had an aquatic staff who operated three existing pools. Hence, the city agreed to operate the pool. It provided lifeguards and swim instruction for the school during the day, for which it was reimbursed. The city operated and programmed the pool for community use outside school hours. The school district paid all of the pool's utility and chemical costs, and the city paid for all of the staff costs outside school hours.

In addition to economic efficiencies, there are other potential benefits from cooperation. A jointly provided recreational complex may serve as a social focus for the surrounding community. In some neighborhoods, the school buildings are the largest public space, and it is grossly underutilized.

Intensive programming of the facilities outside school hours could help foster a sense of community in neighborhoods that have no such identity. Some people believe that vandalism could decrease at a school site because of the facility's more extensive use, an increased integration in the life of the community, and an enhanced sense of neighborhood associated with the school plant. In many instances, the city's involvement in enhancing athletic field provision results in more aesthetically attractive school sites.

A major constraint on many children taking advantage of after-school programs offered by park and recreation agencies is their difficulty in getting from their school to a recreational center. With the growth of two-parent and single-parent working families, many children have no one available to transport them to these programs. This constraint is removed if public facilities are built on the school campus.

Some people who do not have children in the school system see no reason why they should support school bond issues that will result in their paying higher taxes because they do not perceive that any direct benefits will accrue to them. Others are offended at the duplication of facilities stemming from lack of cooperation in facility provision. Positioning a school as a community center through joint provision offers school administrators a vehicle for expanding their school system's base of support.

Difficulties Arising From Joint Provision

The major economies associated with joint provision are self-evident. However, there are a number of potential economic, morale, and managerial costs that are not so obvious and should be recognized. Additional economic costs may be incurred when facilities are managed by two agencies or used by two clientele groups. These may be illustrated by an analogy. It is generally accepted that a vehicle in an agency motor pool used by multiple drivers has a considerably shorter life expectancy than a single-driver vehicle. Drivers take less care of motor pool vehicles because they are not held exclusively accountable for their condition. If a similar mind-set prevails in a jointly provided facility, then costs of operation will be higher. Further, if a car is driven 20,000 mi each year, it will cost more to maintain and will wear out sooner than if it is driven 10,000 mi each year. It will not be twice as expensive, but the savings per mile are likely to be 20% to 30% rather than 100%. If the facilities and equipment in a jointly provided recreational area are used so much more, then their repair, renovation, and replacement will be required much more frequently.

Morale costs are incurred when individuals become frustrated by actions of others that adversely affect them. For example, frustration may arise if teachers arrive in the morning to find that a lathe, pottery wheel, basketball net, tennis serving machine, or computer was broken the previous evening when the community used the facility. Through necessity, many teachers have husbanded their resources carefully over the years with the result that they sometimes adopt a proprietary attitude toward the equipment. It is likely to require considerable diplomacy to remind such conscientious teachers that the damaged equipment is not their private possession—it belongs to the community whose members are entitled to use it—without taking away their obvious pride in maintaining it in first-class condition. Such incidents are likely to disrupt teaching plans, engender resentment, and lower morale. Hence, resources must be available to replace or repair damaged equipment quickly and to care and maintain it.

Joint provision inherently implies compromises that, in some instances, may also cause resentment and adversely affect the morale of teachers and recreation personnel. Inevitably, there are occasions when both parties want to use the same facilities at the same time and it is not possible for them to do so. From a community perspective, for example, the nonavailability of facilities during the school day is likely to exclude some clientele groups, such as evening shift workers, lunch-time enthusiasts, and homemakers, from using the facility at the time that is most convenient for them. Similarly, teachers and coaches may be frustrated by an inability to schedule varsity volleyball or basketball games at their convenience if they intrude into the community's time. In these situations, teachers and coaches may resent being restricted by community use, and recreation professionals may be frustrated by the school demands inhibiting full development of their programs.

There are additional managerial costs that reflect incremental increases in effort that managers need to make joint provision successful. The extra problems begin in the planning phase, which will be more protracted, because the needs and budget contributions of the school district and city have to be ascertained and synchronized. Input has to be solicited from both entities, and compromises have to be negotiated to resolve conflicting requirements. Management of the construction program is more difficult because there is more than one client, so any cost overruns or design changes cause greater problems. For example, if a construction bid exceeds the budgeted amount, then the facility cuts or budget increases needed have to be negotiated with two elected bodies, which are likely to bring different perspectives to the problem.

In joint-provision projects, managers have to remember that although a school district and a city are funded by the same taxpayers, they do not necessarily have the same active constituencies or the same historic methods of solving problems. In short, they have different political realities. From the outset, there should be a written agreement describing the respective roles of the two entities in a facility's operation, a facility's management structure, a facility's operational objectives, the budgetary responsibilities of each body in meeting operational costs, and a mechanism for resolving subsequent disputes.

Vision: The Key Ingredient

The public schools and park and recreation amenities belong to taxpayers. Thus, there is no excuse in any community for school facilities not to be planned and constructed so that they effectively serve the requirements not only of the school program but also of the people in the neighborhood and community for recreational opportunities. Indeed, no community should undertake the planning or construction of new facilities until all present public facilities are optimally used.

If an agency is considering an investment of $2 million in new facilities, then instead of building a new pool, gymnasium, or athletic fields it should consider spending those funds on making relatively minor adaptations to existing school facilities. Investing the money on small adaptations, such as changing accommodation, making separate facility entrances, creating storage facilities, or upgrading playing surfaces, may result in many more opportunities for community use than may result from building a single new facility. There should be a careful survey of all existing school facilities to see if this would be a superior investment for capital funds.

A number of potential problems that may impede cooperation efforts have been identified. These include problems of planning and construction, lack of maintenance funds needed for the heavier usage, adverse impact on staff morale, fear of vandalism and theft of school equipment, conflicts in liability and maintenance responsibility, and conflicts in scheduling. However, the major obstacle is the parochial, departmentalized thinking and lack of broad vision of senior administrators and elected officials. It is easier for managers and elected officials to develop and operate facilities that are fully under their control without the added complexities brought by cooperative ventures. A recreation manager experienced in partnerships with school systems observed:

> The difficult part of getting these partnerships going is there is a lot of hostility because everyone is looking out for their own best interests. It is hard to step back and look at what is best for the community. And what is best for the community, particularly in these times of very difficult funding, is to combine your efforts and work together (p. 38).[5]

There is a need for senior officials to broaden their vision so that it embraces the principle that facilities belong not to their agency but to the public at large. Despite the overwhelming logical case for joint provision and joint use, this will only occur when officials are sufficiently enlightened to pursue such a vision or when they are forced to do so by public opinion.

Partnerships With Other Public Agencies

In every community, there are opportunities for a park and recreation agency to cooperate with other public agencies to create additional amenities. This section discusses partnerships with other local agencies and with agencies at the state and federal levels of government. In joint provision projects with school districts, the school and community priority times and needs are reasonably consistent across jurisdictions, are well defined, and are generally complementary. In partnerships with other agencies, however, there is no such consistent theme or pattern. Although the principles needed to facilitate cooperation (which were discussed in chapter 6) apply, the nature of each of these cooperative ventures is guided by the special circumstances of each opportunity. Hence, this section consists primarily of a number of examples that are intended to illustrate the breadth of entrepreneurial thinking of park and recreation managers who have created partnerships with other public sector agencies.

Cooperative Ventures With Other Local Agencies

The definition of other local agencies includes other departments in the same political jurisdiction, counties and communities within them, and military installations and colleges that are located in the community. Examples of each of these types of local partnerships are included in this section.

Some park and recreation agencies enter into agreements with other public entities to maintain and operate their facilities at a profit to the agency. Thus, they effectively serve as contractors. This is particularly common in Illinois where most park and recreation agencies are special districts. State law provides that units of local government can negotiate agreements between themselves that are mutually beneficial or that are of ultimate benefit to the taxpayers. This has resulted in many park districts contracting with local cities, counties, and nonprofit organizations to maintain boulevards, civic grounds, street trees, and similar facilities.

In all major cities, the city owns numerous parcels of land under the jurisdiction of many different city departments that have no plans for their use. Searching through this inventory for potential park sites can be rewarding. This approach was pioneered by Robert Moses, the legendary figure who was commissioner of New York's parks for more than 50 years. When he was first appointed commissioner in the 1930s, he was flatly told by Mayor Fiorello La Guardia that there was no money with which to acquire playgrounds or parks. Moses responded by assigning a staff member to comb through the records of every publicly owned piece of land in New York that was controlled by agencies ranging from the board of education to the transportation department. As a result of this effort, Moses increased the number of city playgrounds from 119 to 179 in his first six months on the job.[6] Similar opportunities exist today.

In 1995, the city of New York acquired 416 acres of park land even though no tax funds for acquisition were available. Much of this land was obtained by reviewing the real-estate holdings of other city agencies, especially those of the Department of General Services and the Economic Development Corporation, and cooperating with them to take over vacant lots, parking lots, and properties forfeited to the city when owners failed to pay property taxes. The focus was on acquiring parcels adjacent to existing parks and playgrounds. After they were acquired, the parcels were fenced in so that when the existing areas were next renovated, they could be enlarged to incorporate the additional parcels.

These scavenging efforts were supplemented with resources obtained in legal settlements with polluters. More than $18 million won in law suits from companies involved in oil spills and illegal dumping were directed by courts to be expended on park acquisition or the city's inventory of remote natural lands, which were usually wetlands with interesting bird populations, on the fringes of the city. This land is relatively inexpensive to purchase because federal and state laws so limit the use of wetlands that wildlife sanctuaries are often the only possible alternatives.[6]

In Kansas, Johnson County Park and Recreation District's partnerships with the city of Roeland Park offers examples of partnerships between county government entities and incorporated communities within them.

In the first example, Johnson County agreed to construct and operate a $2.6 million aquatic center for the city. The city was unable to undertake the project itself because it had reached the legal limit of its debt ceiling, which prevented it from issuing further bonds. The city transferred title of the pool site to the county. The county issued revenue bonds to construct the facility. They were redeemed by annual lease payments appropriated by the city from its sales tax revenues. The city leased the facility from the county for a 20-year period, which was the length of the bond issue, at a rate sufficient to meet the annual bond payments. At the end of 20 years, ownership of the site and the facility were to be transferred to the city. During the 20-year period, the aquatic facility was to be operated and managed by the county, but any annual net deficits were the responsibility of the city. If the project generated net revenues, then they were shared equally by the city and county.

In a second agreement between the two entities, the city built a senior citizen center but requested the county to develop recreational programs and services in it because the county had existing personnel with those skills. The county paid rental for use of the facility and accepted responsibility for operation and maintenance costs, but it recovered these expenses by charging users to participate.

There are many occasions when collaboration between multiple local agencies is essential if a neighborhood is to be resuscitated. The breadth and depth of problems confronting some neighborhoods are beyond the scope of any single agency to resolve. These collaborations are especially characteristic of efforts to alleviate problems with at-risk youth. In these situations, park and recreation personnel work as part of an integrated team that pools its diverse expertise and resources to ameliorate the problems. The guiding principle and philosophy in the context of at-risk youth is rooted in the old African proverb: It takes a whole village to raise a child. One of the park and recreation field's foremost city directors has observed:

> While retaining our uniqueness and autonomy, we in the field of recreation, who share the same values and goals, can accomplish more by working together than we can on our own. This is the chance for us to demonstrate the full value of who we are and what we can do… Society needs help with its youth, and we have a piece of the solution (p. 19).[7]

A case study describing such a collaboration in Anaheim is described in "Neighborhood Revitalization in Anaheim" on page 300.

"Partnership Between the Community of Radcliff, Kentucky, and Fort Knox Military Installation" on page 302 describes a partnership between a military installation and a local community. Such ventures are likely to increase as more military Morale, Welfare, and Recreation programs are required to break-even at the same time that troop downsizing is reducing their customer base. One way for Morale, Welfare, and Recreation managers to address this conundrum is to enter into joint arrangements with civilian agencies outside the military installations' gates.

The Fort McPherson army post in Georgia joined with the adjacent city of East Point to form a program called Partnership. The on-post population at Fort McPherson was relatively small. By offering their programs to children from East Point, they were able to expand the number of program options available to both military dependents and city children. East Point had similar problems of not having the threshold numbers needed to support some programs. For both entities, programs that were not previously economically viable became viable. The post also provided facilities and management expertise in some special areas that were not previously available to the city, and post children were able to get involved in existing athletic leagues that the city ran.[8]

Colleges and universities are another type of public institution located in communities with which local agencies may cooperate. Iowa City Parks and Recreation Department signed an agreement with the University of Iowa that provided for

Neighborhood Revitalization in Anaheim

The Jeffrey/Lynne neighborhood in Anaheim was characterized by overcrowding, high crime, sanitation problems, landlords who deferred maintenance on their rental properties, illegal street vendors, and parking problems. The problems were complex and impossible to solve by functional, single-agency, service delivery systems. Hence, a task force was formed with representatives from the city manager's office; city attorney; community development; public works and engineering; fire; maintenance; planning; police; parks, recreation, and community services; and public utilities. The Parks, Recreation, and Community Services director chaired it. The task force had six main objectives:

1. To reduce incidents of crime and increase police presence in the area
2. To reduce code enforcement violations stemming from deteriorating property and over-crowding
3. To establish a temporary neighborhood center, which would allow residents to access social services, and to replace the temporary center with permanent quarters as soon as possible (within two years)
4. To provide a permanent site for youth to access recreational programs
5. To facilitate citizen participation in the development of solutions to neighborhood problems
6. To develop better cooperation between landlords and tenants to solve neighborhood problems

Initially, a concerted effort was expended in the law and code enforcement areas to gain a beachhead before human services and recreational programs could be introduced successfully. The following paragraphs summarize the processes used to revitalize the Jeffrey/Lynne neighborhood.

• Code enforcement. The task force expended an extensive number of work hours in the Jeffrey/Lynne area to address code violations relating to housing, health and safety, parking, and street vendors. The most common code violations included overcrowded houses and apartments, people living illegally in unconverted garages, cars parked on lawns, abandoned and stripped cars in the streets, and landlords who refused to repair damaged apartments. After gaining the confidence of the tenants and the attention of the landlords, the code enforcement officer's role switched to facilitative efforts that emphasized cooperation between a tenants' association and an apartment owners and managers group.

• Policing. The task force developed a community-based policing program to address problems of crime in the area. This effort involved the temporary assignment of an officer who lived in the neighborhood and patrolled on foot, made numerous arrests, and established personal contact with law-abiding citizens and children. After initial resistance, the police department facilitated the establishment of neighborhood watch units in the area. Many residents had a natural distrust for uniformed officers that, for some, was based on personal experiences with corrupt South and Central American police systems. Hence, it took time to firmly establish this relationship and to gain the trust of most neighborhood residents.

• Street and security lighting. The public utilities department improved street lighting in the area within the first six months of the neighborhood revitalization effort. Since then, the code enforcement officer has sparked interest among property owners to install outdoor security lighting on buildings in order to light courtyards, alleys, and landscaped areas that could hide illegal activity. The utilities department provided the lights at no cost to residents. Payback was based on increased electrical use for the lights and would occur in approximately five years after installation.

- Recreational programs. The parks, recreation, and community services department began serving the neighborhood through weekly visits by two mobile recreation units (step vans). One van, dubbed Fun on Wheels, provided a variety of recreational and sports equipment and board games. The second van, the Art Mobile, provided crafts-related activities. Weekly visits, one by each van on different days, generally would draw 200 or more children. Recreation staff reported that the vans had the same effect as ice cream wagons for drawing children into the streets. Three bilingual staff members accompanied each van. The staff assigned to the van units blocked a section of street with traffic control equipment and conducted games and art activities. With the opening of the new neighborhood park, a recreational program operated five days per week and provided a wide range of activities. The program incorporated activities that raised participants' self-esteem, discouraged drug and gang activity, and installed neighborhood pride.

- Community center establishment. A rental apartment was secured as a mini-community center for Jeffrey/Lynne. A community services outreach worker staffed the apartment and provided bilingual assistance, social service advocacy, and information and referral services. Later, it was extensively remodeled to accommodate typical neighborhood center uses. With the improved facilities, the outreach worker could facilitate the delivery of additional human services, such as English-as-a-second-language classes, nutrition classes, and a children's meals program.

- Gang outreach. The parks, recreation, and community services department provided gang outreach workers who contacted at-risk youth in the neighborhood in danger of using drugs, of joining (or already involved in) gangs, or of dropping out of school. Gang outreach services were provided both in the neighborhood's community center and at nearby junior and senior high schools. The gang outreach worker's office was located at the neighborhood center.

- Park development. Before initiation of the Jeffrey/Lynne project, no city park land existed in the neighborhood. Although the nearest park was only 0.5 mi away, two major barriers existed to Jeffrey/Lynne residents: a major city street that ran between the neighborhood and the park and a largely Caucasian neighborhood that the residents had to cross and which proved an intimidating prospect for many potential young recreationists. Thus, the task force explored the concept of closing part of a major neighborhood street, Audre Drive, in order to accommodate a street park. The concept required close study by, and in coordination with, several departments. Audre Plaza was developed, consisting of a 1.5-acre recreational area adjoining the neighborhood center. It resulted from closing Audre Drive and installing recreational equipment and landscaping on what was once the street. Daily attendance averaged nearly 1,500 people, which was a substantial number for a neighborhood community of approximately 6,000 residents.

From Mark Deven. Neighborhood Revitalization in Anaheim, California. In Models of Change in Municipal Parks and Recreation. *Edited by Mark E. Havitz. Venture Publishing: State College, PA. 1995. Copyright ©Venture Publishing, Inc. Used by permission.*

the city's long-term use of the university's three-field Hawkeye Softball Complex. In exchange, the city paid to purchase and install lighting on the fields, resulting in public availability for this first-class facility. To save time and money, the city contracted with the university's electrical services division to install the lights on a time and material basis.

Prince William County, Virginia; the city of Manassas; and George Mason University pooled their resources to construct a major complex on the university's Prince William Institute campus. It comprised a 50 m pool with spectator seating for 500, a leisure pool, two basketball courts, racquetball courts, an elevated track, large aerobics areas, large weight and cardiovascular areas, a day-care center, and meeting rooms. The county's assistant public works director observed: "We felt that having an indoor center that was twice as large as one we could build 10 years from now at a price at least 50 percent cheaper than if we built our own made up for the disadvantages of not controlling the center." Approximately 60% of users were county residents; 30%, city residents; and 10%, staff and

Partnership Between the Community of Radcliff, Kentucky, and Fort Knox Military Installation

Radcliff, Kentucky, is located in Hardin County between Louisville and Mammoth Cave National Park. Its population of 22,000 was the largest in the county. The community had a full-time convention and tourism commission staff but lacked a large meeting space and convention facilities. The city explored the feasibility of building these facilities but concluded that the cost of construction and maintenance was too high.

The neighboring military installation of Fort Knox was faced with the challenge of generating funds for maintaining its existing Morale, Welfare, and Recreation operations including the military clubs. The clubs previously were supported by tax funds but now were expected to be self-supporting. Military downsizing reduced the number of personnel on the post and made self-sufficiency of the clubs more difficult.

The result was a partnership by which Radcliff was able to promote the convention facilities located in the clubs on the military post. Regulations prohibited Fort Knox from marketing to the outside community, and the post had limited accommodation options. Radcliff could promote the facilities along with the many other attractions in the area both on post, such as the U.S. Bullion Depository (the Gold Vault), the Patton Museum, and the Armor Unit Memorial Park, and off post. Radcliff also had accommodations.

The potential economic impact of tourists on Radcliff substantially increased as a result of acquiring access to this additional facility. The post received revenues from charging for its meeting spaces, for its catering services, and from alcohol sales, which it was able to do in what was an otherwise dry city and county.

From Steve Spencer and Shannon Moman. A "golden" partnership. Parks and Recreation. *November 1996, pages 36-41. Copyright ©The National Recreation and Park Association. Used by permission.*

students of George Mason University. The university borrowed the money for the facility, which it owns and operates. The three partners pay a share of the operating and capital budget that is commensurate with the proportionate use of the center by their constituents. A group with representatives from each of the three entities oversees operation of the center.[5]

Cooperative Ventures With Federal and State Agencies

The most frequent partnerships between local jurisdictions and federal agencies to create park and recreation amenities have involved the U.S. Army Corps of Engineers. The corps has approximately 450 water resource development projects in the lower 48 states, and many of their reservoirs have multiple park sites adjacent to them. The terms of the federal Water Project Recreation Act of 1965 mandate that in any recreational facility development of water resource projects authorized after 1965, a nonfederal public agency must agree to bear not less than one-half the initial cost of the facilities and must agree to operate, maintain, and replace them thereafter. Hence, the Corps

actively promotes the availability of these opportunities to local and state jurisdictions, and it leases approximately 1,000 areas to states, counties, municipalities, and other qualified public entities.

Joint management with state agencies tends to occur most often when state and local agencies have adjacent resources or lands that are in close proximity. In these situations, it may be more efficient for one agency to operate both areas.

Lover's Key State Recreation Area was managed by Florida State Parks, and Carl Johnson Park was operated by Lee County. The parks were islands immediately south of Estero Island. The county leased Carl Johnson Park together with a portion of Hickory Island, which was contiguous to the other two islands, to the state for 50 years. The Lee County Parks and Recreation director observed that the parks "are contiguous with each other. We have both state and local bureaucracy working to align an area that should be one park with one bureaucracy" (p. 12).[9]

The 31 Boston Harbor Islands were designated a national park in the mid-1990s. However, responsibility for the park was divided among the city, the state, and local nonprofit groups. The park comprised 13 state-owned islands and 18 islands owned by Boston and an assortment of private organizations. For the first time in its history, the National Park Service committed to spending federal funds on land it did not own. The National Park Service agreed to contribute 25% of the park's operating funds; the remaining 75% came from state sales tax revenues and local donations. The functions and finances of the park were managed by an 18-member advisory council and a 13-member governing board. These groups included federal appointees, local advocacy groups, and a Native American heritage organization.[10]

Federal Grant Support

At any point in time, there are a variety of federal programs from which park and recreation departments solicit grant aid. Most of them are enacted with the goal of alleviating specific problems, such as juvenile crime, unemployment, or traffic congestion. It was noted in chapter 5 that park and recreation agencies may contribute to alleviating these kinds of problems. Hence, agencies developing programs whose objectives are compatible with those of the grant program are eligible to acquire these federal funds. These grant programs are authorized because there are political pressures for elected representatives to address a particular problem. They tend to be authorized for limited periods of time and are allowed to lapse when the political pressure on that issue has dissipated or when there is widespread belief that they have not been effective.

Only one federal program that was designed exclusively to provide grant aid for park and recreation amenities received consistent funding support over a prolonged period of time. That program is the Land and Water Conservation Fund. Its role is now much more limited than it was in the past. However, its contribution to stimulating park and recreational facility development for more than 25 years was so great that it is reviewed in some depth in this section. The program demonstrates the importance of ongoing efforts to secure a dedicated fund at the federal level for park and recreation land acquisition and facility development.

The discussion of the Land and Water Conservation Fund is followed by subsections that define dedicated funds, examine the conceptual basis for a dedicated fund in this field, and suggest alternative ways in which it might be formulated. Finally, some of the other, more ephemeral types of federal grant opportunities relevant to parks and

recreation, which periodically emerge, are described.

The Land and Water Conservation Fund

Spurred by serious recreational resource problems and deficiencies identified in the 1962 Outdoor Recreation Resources Review Commission reports, Congress enacted Public Law 88-578, the Land and Water Conservancy Fund, to become effective on January 1, 1965. The fund was created for the purpose of assisting all levels of government in the acquisition and development of outdoor recreational resources. More specifically, the fund provided

1. a funding source for the National Park Service, U.S. Fish and Wildlife Service, U.S. Forest Service, and (to a lesser extent) the Bureau of Land Management to acquire lands for their systems and
2. grants-in-aid to states and, through them to local jurisdictions, for the planning, land acquisition, and development of outdoor recreational facilities.

The Land and Water Conservation Fund was meant to provide a continuing, assured source of money that would allow for expansion of the nation's outdoor recreational estate. The intent was to provide a predictable floor of earmarked funds that would be insulated from the year-to-year competition for Congressional appropriations. Indeed, some members of Congress apparently believed that the fund would be a true trust fund with revenues that could not be used for other purposes (although Congress would have to appropriate money from the fund before it could be spent).

In fact, the fund was neither defined nor operated as a true trust fund in the same way, for example, as the federal Highway Trust Fund. Rather, the Land and Water Conservation Fund is what federal budgeteers term a special fund. In such funds, federal receipts are earmarked for specific purposes. However, the receipts are not required to be used for that purpose, and funds must be appropriated by Congress each year.

Initially, three sources of revenue for the fund were designated: proceeds from the sales of surplus federal real property, motor boat fuel taxes, and fees from recreational use of federal lands. Revenue from these sources between 1966 and 1968 reached about $100 million per year, which was far short of Congress' early expectations. To remedy this, Congress authorized adding $200 million each year to the fund and using outer continental shelf mineral leasing and royalty receipts to cover the difference between the authorized level and receipts from other sources. Subsequently, the fund's authorization was raised to $900 million in 1976. The use of outer continental shelf receipts for park land acquisition and development was a rational way of recycling the value of one natural resource back to public use in the form of another natural resource.

The legislation required that at least 40% of the annual Land and Water Conservation Fund appropriation be expended on federal projects and that up to 60% of it be distributed to state governments. The states, in turn, determined how much of their share would be available to county, special district, and municipal park and recreation agencies. During the life of the program, approximately 75% of states' allocations were passed through to local jurisdictions. In the early years of the program, the state-side appropriations exceeded those for federal land acquisition, but in recent years, the state-side funds have been reduced to nominal amounts.

A state or local agency's access to the funds is contingent upon them matching the funds on a 50-50 basis. In effect, the federal government pledges to match the state or local agency's contribution to produce resources for up to one-half of the total project's cost. The local matching share of a project's cost can be provided from several sources. Most often, the local contribution comes from a jurisdiction's general or capital development fund. However, Land and Water Conservation Fund regulations allow in-kind contributions of labor, equipment, materials, or land to be used as the matching share. In these cases, the fair market value of these resources is acceptable as the local agency's contribution. For example, if donated land is appraised at $300,000, then the agency could apply for a matching $300,000 grant from the fund. If approved, the fund money obtained could be applied toward the development of this land into a park. The net result could be the acquisition and development of a new recreational resource valued at $600,000 without any expenditure of local tax dollars.

The acceptance of in-kind resources as the matching share is a powerful incentive in acquiring land donations because donors see the value of their gifts doubled by the leveraging potential of grants from the Land and Water Conservation Fund. The matching program is also popular with local elected officials because it enables them to propose a bond issue of, for example, $500,000 for a new park and to inform voters that if it is approved, they are likely to receive a facility valued at $1 million. Further, it enables even the poorest communities that are unable to raise tax money for the match to organize in-kind labor, equipment, and materials in lieu of money and to use them to acquire the federal funds.

The Land and Water Conservation Fund is administered by the National Park Service. Most states have vested authority for the distribution of funds from the Land and Water Conservation Fund in their state park and recreation agency. The designated state agency is responsible for setting priorities for funding projects and for evaluating the relative merit of fund applications received from local jurisdictions. Projects acquired with Land and Water Conservation Fund assistance are required to remain in perpetuity for public recreation. On those rare occasions when use of this land for another essential purpose has been demonstrated to be unavoidable, it has to be replaced with property of equal market value and equivalent recreational usefulness.

The stimulus provided by the Land and Water Conservation Fund has been central to park and outdoor recreation development in this country for more than 30 years. Since it was enacted, the state side of the fund has awarded more than 37,000 matching grants totaling more than $3.2 billion. States and localities have matched this amount dollar for dollar to acquire 2.4 million acres of park land and open space and to develop more than 25,000 recreational sites. However, there has never been one year in which annual appropriations of Congress reached the authorized spending level of $900 million. The highest appropriations were made in 1978 and 1979 and amounted to $805 and $737 million, respectively. Of these totals, $315 and $370 million were allocated as grants to the states and $490 and $367 to the federal agencies.

In recent years, the state-side funding of the Land and Water Conservation Fund has been minimal. Its demise has resulted in a search for an alternative, more reliable source of federal funds that would be dedicated for the exclusive purpose of acquiring land and recreational facilities and that would make it less vulnerable to the political vagaries of the appropriations process.

The Dedication of Funds

The dedication or earmarking of funds refers to statutory restrictions on how the proceeds from specified taxes and revenue sources may be spent.

Dedicated revenues go directly into a designated account from which expenditures are tied to a specified program. Dedicated funds may be derived from annual income streams that are committed exclusively to park and recreational projects, or they may accrue from creation of a relatively large endowment or trust from which the annual interest is used to fund projects.

The strength of dedicated funds varies widely. The weakest of them, such as the Land and Water Conservation Fund, consist of earmarked funds that are deposited in a separate account and that cannot be appropriated without annual legislative action. The strongest are funds enacted by constitutional amendments that tightly define the purposes for which the funds can be used. Changing these purposes requires passage of another constitutional amendment. This removes the possibility of elected officials choosing not to appropriate the earmarked funds or choosing to pass legislation that diverts them elsewhere.

There are ongoing efforts to establish dedicated funds for park and recreation acquisition and development at both the federal and state levels. For example, the President's Commission on Americans Outdoors in 1987 recommended that Congress should create an endowed, dedicated trust that would provide a minimum of $1 billion each year to help pay for federal, state, and local land acquisition and for state and local facility development and rehabilitation.

The following subsection of this chapter examines the alternative approaches that have been used to this point in the unsuccessful effort to establish a stronger federal dedicated fund than the Land and Water Conservation Fund. However, dedicated funds have been established in a number of states, and in many cases these provide funds for states' matching grant programs with local jurisdictions. "The Michigan Natural Resources Trust Fund" describes the fund in Michigan; similar strong trust funds approved by constitutional amendment or voter initiative have been established in Missouri, Minnesota, Colorado, and Arizona. In the latter three states, all of the funds are financed by a constitutionally dedicated portion of the net proceeds from lotteries. As well as being financially viable, income streams used to support dedicated funds have to be politically acceptable. The antagonism of some groups to government-sponsored lotteries encouraged elected officials who supported lotteries to be sympathetic to proposals that at least some of the profits should be dedicated to meaningful social ends, such as conservation or park provision, rather than to the general treasury to be used at legislators' discretion. This clear public purpose effectively muted some of the opposition to lotteries. Examples of other types of revenues that have been used to support relatively weak dedicated funds in other states include the manufacturers' excise tax on selected sporting goods, the real-estate transfer tax, mitigation funds, lease revenues or severance taxes on mineral extraction, and sales taxes.

The merits of dedicated funds are controversial. The following arguments have been used against establishing dedicated funds:

The Michigan Natural Resources Trust Fund

The Michigan Natural Resources Trust Fund was established following a constitutional amendment approved in a statewide referendum. It required that revenues from oil, gas, and other mineral leases on state-owned lands be placed in a trust fund, from which the proceeds were used for acquiring and protecting lands of scenic, recreational, and environmental importance.

Each year, the amount available for project grants is derived by combining one-third of the annual leasing revenues with interest from the trust account. The trust account is capped at $200 million and was established in its early years by deposits of the remaining two-thirds of annual leasing revenues.

Not less than 75% of the annual funds had to be used to acquire land and no more than 25% could be used to develop recreational facilities. Projects were selected through a competitive process from those submitted by the state's natural resource agency, local governments, and nonprofit organizations. Annual allocations from the trust were approximately $25 million. Since 1976, the fund bought more than 136,000 state and local acres with these resources.

From Phyllis Myers. The varied landscape of park and conservation finance. Greensense. 1997, 3(1), pages 1-2.

- Hinders effective budgetary control by legislators.
- Leads to misallocation of funds, giving excess revenue to some programs while slighting others.
- Leads to an inflexible revenue structure—adjustment is difficult over time as conditions change.
- Statutes remain in force long after the need has passed.
- Removes a portion of government activities from periodic review and control.

In summary, these points emphasize that dedicated funds limit the ability of legislators to set annual priorities, and for this reason they often meet with resistance. For example, because of trust funds and other entitlement programs, only about 30% of the total federal budget is controllable. This is a matter of particular concern in times of fiscal constraint and leads to such questions as: Why should park acquisitions be immune from budgetary cutbacks when aid to the poor and pollution control activities, for example, are not?

The following arguments have been made in favor of dedicated funds:

- Makes it possible for those who receive the benefits of a government program to pay for it (for example, federal gasoline taxes fund interstate highway improvement programs).
- Guarantees a minimal level of expenditure for a specific program.
- Assures program continuity and allows for long-range planning.
- Can induce public support for new or increased taxes.

Most lawmakers and government officials who have no vested interest in the recipient program are likely to oppose creation of a new dedicated fund. Such funds limit their flexibility to adjust to changing priorities. They are likely to argue that if a program is worthy of funding, it should be able to compete successfully with other programs in the legislative battle for tax dollars. However, one effective justification for a dedicated fund is the benefit principle, which states that beneficiaries of a program should pay for it. A typical example of the benefit principle at the state level occurs in Oregon.

The owners of recreational vehicles, including motor homes, campers, and travel trailers, are among the principle users of state natural areas and parks, and many of the campsites constructed and maintained at state parks are for the exclusive use of recreational vehicle users. Thus, an annual recreational vehicle fee, which finances approximately 25% of Oregon's annual state parks operating budget, is levied on these vehicles.

This principle is apparent in some of the alternative dedicated-fund proposals and the federal grant opportunities discussed in the remainder of this chapter.

Thus, the case for a federal dedicated fund rests mainly on the source of its revenues. The next section suggests that this money could accrue either from mitigation severance payments made as compensation by extractors who diminish the country's natural resources or by users of recreational facilities. In this context, the federal government simply becomes an efficient conduit for expediting the logical financial relationship between extractors and users and the resources that they use rather than a subsidizer or provider of funds for recreation.

Alternative Approaches to Establishing a Dedicated Federal Trust Fund

The case for federal assistance to state and local jurisdictions was stated succinctly in the report of the Committee on Interior and Insular Affairs, which accompanied the House of Representatives' original Land and Water Conservation Fund bill proposal:

> Federal assistance to the states, the committee believes, is justified by three considerations. The first is that pointed out by the Commission; namely, the health and welfare of U.S. citizens all over the country. A second is the relief that such assistance will afford the Federal Government from increasing pressure to acquire and develop, on its own, areas of less than national significance. The third is the fact that we are becoming a more and more mobile people and that, regardless of our state of origin, we expect to take advantage of state and local park systems wherever they may be, just as we expect people from other states to do the same in our home territory.[11]

However, there has been skepticism in Congress about appropriating tax funds for this purpose at a time when the federal government is in a much worse financial condition than state and local governments. Indeed, the interest on the national debt exceeds $1 billion per day, which is greater than the highest level of annual grant funding ever made available from Land and Water Conservation Fund appropriations. This leads to the conundrum that there is rationale for federal support to the states and localities and that its positive impact has been demonstrated for more than 30 years; however, the magnitude of the federal government's fiscal crisis makes it unlikely that consistent, substantive, annual appropriations from federal tax revenues will be forthcoming for the Land and Water Conservation Fund in the future.

This has led advocates to seek a dedicated trust fund based on the benefit principle. It could take one of two forms. First, an initial corpus of, for example, $10 billion could be directed to the fund over a period of, for example, 5 years, and the interest from this endowment would finance future annual allocations. Second, an ongoing revenue stream could be dedicated and would generate sufficient funds annually to finance the program. The establishment of a true dedicated fund would create genuine capital resources for park and recreational projects that many mistakenly believed the Land and Water Conservation Fund would provide.

The fund's revenues would accrue from sources other than general tax monies, and its resources would be used exclusively for the acquisition and development of park and recreation amenities. Three approaches to financing such a true trust fund are discussed in the following paragraphs: extraction taxes and leases, a real-estate transfer tax, and a manufacturers' excise tax on recreational equipment. For the purpose of exposition, they are discussed separately, but some combination of the three mechanisms also could be used. For example, one of the early bills advocating a dedicated trust fund introduced in the Senate by Senator John Chafee proposed that resources would come primarily from a national real-estate transfer tax of up to 2.5% on transactions of $5 million or more and from offshore oil and gas leases.

The first approach is the use of extraction taxes and leases. It has been argued that America's natural resources located on public lands belong to all Americans of all generations. Current citizens are stewards of these resources for generations of Americans yet to come. The federal government annually receives more than $2.5 billion from oil leases, severance taxes, and mineral sales on its public lands. However, with the improvements that are emerging in deep-water drilling technol-ogy, the annual lease fees from offshore oil drilling in the outer continental shelf alone are projected to reach $4 billion in the near future. Most of the dollars go directly into the general fund of the U.S. Treasury to pay for programs and services that benefit only people living now. Some believe that this is an abrogation of the government's stewardship responsibility.

The case for financing a true trust fund with revenues received from extraction taxes and leases has been summarized in the following terms:

> Federal resource exploitation diminishes our natural estate and frequently precludes alternate uses of the land or water, at least during exploitation. Often, permanent degradation results. Thus, it makes sense that some of the federal revenues from using the nation's natural resources, including those on the outer Continental Shelf, should be used to preserve other natural resources (p. 288).[12]

It has been proposed that a trust fund be established by obligating a substantial portion of outer continental shelf oil and gas revenues for a period of four or five years. This source of funds is currently earmarked for the Land and Water Conservation Fund, so a conceptual linkage has been established legislatively. As an alternative or supplement to these funds, leases or royalties could be levied on onshore, nonrenewable resource extraction and production activities that occur on federal lands. Historically, the federal government has kept charges for onshore mineral extraction low. To give an indication of the potential from this source, revenues from a 1% severance tax imposed on oil, gas, and geothermal leases on federal lands would generate more than $20 million, so a 5% tax would yield more than $100 million. Similarly, an annual $25 claim renewal fee for Bureau of Land Management mining would yield approximately $33 million on the Bureau's $1.3 million hard rock mineral claims alone.[13]

The feasibility of extraction taxes and leases as the source of a dedicated fund is enhanced by the existing Land and Water Conservation Fund precedent because it usually is easier politically to build upon precedent than to enact legislation authorizing an entirely new revenue source. However, given the federal budget deficit, it seems politically unlikely that Congress will sanction taking receipts that are currently going into the general treasury and reassigning them to a dedicated fund for recreation.

A second alternative for financing a true trust fund is a real-estate transfer tax. A real-estate transfer tax, which sometimes is called a documentary stamp tax, is a tax imposed on transfers of real property. It is levied whenever property is sold, granted, assigned, transferred, or otherwise conveyed from one person to another. This tax was first introduced at the federal level in the Revenue Act of 1921, but it was repealed in 1965. Although this tax is no longer levied at the federal level, it was noted in chapter 2 that a number of state and local governments are using it to fund park and recreation developments and that their success demonstrates its potential.

However, the likelihood of a real-estate transfer tax emerging as a revenue source for a federal dedicated recreation fund appears low. A prime philosophical argument for repeal of the original federal real-estate transfer tax was that real-estate taxes should be the exclusive prerogative of local and state governments and not of the federal government. Because many state and local governments adopted this tax after it was repealed at the federal level, it seems unlikely that Congress would reinstate it.

One of the unsuccessful federal dedicated-fund bills (mentioned earlier in this section) that incorporated it recognized and sought to avoid this problem by imposing the real-estate transfer tax only on transactions valued at more than $5 million. Thus, it would not affect homeowners or small businesses but rather large developers of shopping malls, subdivisions, industrial complexes, and others who are now using up open space at a rapid rate. However, state and local governments would probably protest the usurping of their traditional property-tax base.

A third approach to financing a true federal trust fund is a manufacturers' excise tax on recreational equipment, which links the producers of recreational equipment with the provision of opportunities needed to use that equipment. In chapter 2, it was noted that two classes of recreational products are now subject to a federal excise tax: 1) guns and related equipment and bows and arrows (Pittman-Robertson) and 2) fishing equipment and gasoline used in pleasure boats (Wallop-Breaux). In both cases, the programs have succeeded because of support from the industries involved and very specific direction regarding use of the funds.

The manufacturers' excise tax seems to be a more feasible revenue source for a recreation dedicated fund than the other two alternatives for several reasons. First, its conceptual basis is strong because it generally adheres to the benefit principle. It proposes that those who use recreational resources should pay for them, which is consistent with the prevailing user-pay political sentiment. Second, existence of the hunting and fishing precedents gives it a degree of credibility. Third, it is a new tax and will not divert receipts currently going into the U.S. Treasury's general fund.

Challenges in implementing this tax relating to equity and public-private competition were elucidated in chapter 2. If implementation is forthcoming at the national level, an additional issue to be resolved is how to allocate resources from such a fund to the states equitably. The Pittman-Robertson and Wallop-Breaux apportionments to the states are based partially on the number of hunting and fishing licenses sold in each state. However, licenses are not required of bikers, skaters, or ballplayers, so allocations to the states from a recreation trust fund may not be consistent with the number of bicycles, skates, or baseballs sold in each state. In other words, most tennis rackets may be bought in Texas, but there is no guarantee that Texas would get more of the tax money from tennis rackets than any other state.

Like the existing two federal models of this type, any broader application of the excise tax to other recreational products would be an invisible tax, making it politically more palatable than other alternatives. Because it would be levied at the manufacturer level and built into the price, most consumers would not be aware that they were paying a tax and, thus, would be unlikely to protest. This invisible dimension may help minimize consumer opposition, but it also may hinder efforts to build constituency support for the program. If consumers are unaware of the tax and its positive contributions to their recreational opportunities, they are unlikely to respond with the vigor that would be necessary to protect it from future political threats.

Other Federal Grant Opportunities

In addition to the Land and Water Conservation Fund, other grant opportunities for local and state agencies to enhance their offerings periodically emerge at the federal level. Most of those that are of central interest to park and recreation agencies can be classified into four categories: surplus property transfers, greenways and trails development, public employment programs, and crime-prevention programs. These categories are discussed in this section.

Many of the federal acts that create these grant opportunities tend to authorize funding for a limited number of years. However, after a lapse of time, statutes that have slightly different eligibility and grant conditions but address similar issues tend to re-emerge. Hence, the goal of this section is to create an awareness of the types of opportunities that arise and the kinds of criteria and federal grant aid that become available rather than to emphasize the details of specific statutes.

Surplus Property Transfers[12]

In 1949, Congress passed the Property and Administrative Services Act that authorized the transfer of federal surplus real-estate property to state and local governments, and in certain cases to non-profit organizations, for specific public purposes. Those purposes included parks and recreation, wildlife conservation, and historic preservation. The disposal process used for this property is termed *public benefit conveyance*. The act authorizes public benefit conveyances to be made without monetary consideration in return for the public benefit that is derived.

The National Park Service has taken an active lead role in facilitating transfer of some of these lands through its Federal Lands to Parks program. Since 1949, 1,274 properties totaling more than 142,000 acres have been transferred for park and recreational use. These properties were conveyed with perpetual deed restrictions, which permanently preserve the land for public park and recreational purposes. This program has been particularly active in recent years because military downsizing has resulted in the closing of more than 100 big installations and numerous smaller ones, with their properties declared surplus.

The procedure for acquiring property through the Federal Lands to Parks program begins when the disposal agency, typically a military department or the General Services Administration, issues a notice announcing the availability of federal property. After other federal agencies are given the opportunity to acquire the property, the disposal agency designates the property as surplus to federal government needs and makes it available for state or local government use. The National Park Service monitors these announcements and alerts state and local agencies to opportunities for acquiring lands with unique environmental or recreational values or for acquiring parcels adjacent to existing park areas. The National Park Service staff help local partners with their applications to the disposal agency, which decides whether the property will be offered for disposal through a park and recreation public benefit conveyance.

When Chanute Air Force Base was closed, the village of Rantoul, Illinois, effectively converted the 2,000-acre base to private commercial and residential use. In addition, the town requested 147 acres for park and recreational use through a public benefit conveyance. The property included a youth activity center, athletic forum, swimming pool, arts and crafts building, open space, and lake.[14]

The closing of Myrtle Beach Air Force Base in Myrtle Beach, South Carolina, in the early 1990s created concerns in surrounding communities about loss of jobs and adverse economic impacts. When the city acquired at no cost the base golf course, named Whispering Pines, this alleviated some of the criticism. Approximately, 50,000 individual rounds of golf are now played annually on the course. It provides golfing opportunities for residents who may be unable to afford memberships in the area's many private clubs.

When Fort Benjamin Harrison, an army training camp, was closed in Indianapolis in the mid-1990s, the army left behind nearly 1,500 acres of pristine wilderness and a 230-acre golf course. Soldiers had been practicing their job in one of the largest tracts of hardwood forest in central Indiana. The land was conveyed to the state parks system and became Benjamin Harrison State Park, which is accessible by public transportation from downtown Indianapolis. It takes advantage of this strategic urban location by providing environmental education opportunities for all students in the city and county school system, as well as for teachers, hunters, forest and wildlife mangers, and other park visitors.[15]

Bernard Township, New Jersey, built its first swimming pool and community recreational center from surplus hospital grounds. A park-deficient area of west Los Angeles turned surplus Veterans Administration lands valued at $6.5 million into a 19-acre park of ball courts, picnic sites, and jogging trails. In Biloxi, Mississippi, a National Guard training site now houses a seafood industry museum, demonstrating the industry's significant impact on the community. A U.S. Army Corps of Engineers lockkeeper's house on land along the Green River was converted into a museum and restaurant that explains how the river shaped the Central Kentucky economy. A Civil War redoubt in Chattanooga became a 70-acre soccer complex hosting national tournaments. Near Santa Rosa, New Mexico, a 60-acre water treatment facility became a premier scuba diving center, attracting international visitors.[16]

Greenways and Trails Development

Concerns relating to automobile pollution and traffic congestion, to recognition of the advantages of encouraging development of an integrated transportation network, and to interest in highway beautification resulted in political pressures to authorize expenditures for trails from the nation's Transportation Trust Fund. Revenues for this dedicated fund are derived from gasoline taxes, and their use for purposes other than highway development was a departure from tradition. This revolutionary change was enacted by the Intermodal Surface Transportation Efficiency Act of 1991. The passing of this act coincided with the emphasis on greenways that emerged in the late 1980s and provided economic stimulus to fuel the growing greenways movement.

The legislators who drafted the Intermodal Surface Transportation Efficiency Act recognized that it is not possible for the nation to build its way out of the problem of increasingly congested highways and escalating levels of air pollution simply by pouring more concrete and rolling out more asphalt. Their solution was to redirect federal funding to an intermodal approach, which supplements the highway system with investments in mass transit, bicycling, and pedestrian facilities. Part of what motivated this shift was a growing awareness among legislators that while Americans enjoy the best highway system in the world, the downside of their love affair with automobiles is increasingly hard to ignore.

Travel by car is dangerous. In the mid-1990s, more than 40,000 vehicular fatalities occurred each year. Less well known is that cars and trucks are responsible for at least half of the country's air pollution (65% of carbon monoxide and 47% of nitrogen oxide), which contributes heavily to a problem that kills an estimated 60,000 people each year. Add to this the soaring rates of asthma and respiratory disease particularly among children in heavily congested areas, such as Los Angeles, and it becomes clear that while travel by car is convenient, it nevertheless exacts a heavy toll in terms of human life.[17]

Part of the Intermodal Surface Transportation Efficiency Act legislation related to transportation-enhancement activities, and at least 10% of expenditures from the Transportation Trust Fund were required to be allocated to these activities. The act identified 10 types of activities that quali-

fied for these funds, and among them were provision of facilities for pedestrians and bicycles, acquisition of scenic easements and scenic or historic byways, preservation of abandoned railway corridors (including their conversion and use for pedestrian and bicycle trails), and historic preservation. In the first six years for which the program was authorized, more than 7,000 projects in these categories were funded.

The 10% requirement made available more than $400 million each year for these enhancement projects. In the 18 years before the Intermodal Surface Transportation Efficiency Act, the federal government spent $40 million on bicycle and pedestrian facilities; however, in the first six years the act was authorized, $1 billion was invested in the facilities. This investment appears sound given that 40% of automobile trips are less than 2 mi and that many of these trips could be made on foot or bicycle if adequate and safe facilities were available.[17] The funds were allocated to states on a formula basis, and state departments of transportation were responsible for distributing them. The local community was required to commit at least 20% of the funds for a project, so the Intermodal Surface Transportation Efficiency Act grant could pay up to 80% of total costs.

Purchase of the 270-acre Rank Island in California to protect the San Joaquin River Parkway scenic viewshed was assisted by $3.4 million in Intermodal Surface Transportation Efficiency Act funds. The island, which is rich in biodiversity, was a recognized resource of statewide importance.

The city of College Station, Texas, received an Intermodal Surface Transportation Efficiency Act grant of $1.2 million to develop a 7 mi bicycle loop. It connected Texas A&M University, numerous apartments and neighborhoods, a regional mall, eight city parks, and an amphitheater. The loop included seven new bridges for creek crossings and a bicycle path crossing under three of the city's largest thoroughfares.

In the first six years of its authorization, the act directed $306 million and stimulated an additional $113 million in matching state and local funds to 814 rails-to-trails projects.[17]

On a much smaller scale, another section of the Intermodal Surface Transportation Efficiency Act authorized up to $30 million per year for the National Recreation Trails Fund. This fund was based on the benefit principle: the concept that people using motor fuel for off-road recreational purposes were taxed when they purchased fuel but received no commensurate benefits from that tax when the funds subsequently were used for highway purposes. The fund was intended to return benefits to recreational trail users for the gasoline taxes that they paid. Although it was authorized at $30 million and it was calculated that more than $150 million in taxes went into the fund from off-road motorized vehicle users (e.g., dirt bikes, all-terrain vehicles, snowmobiles, etc.) appropriations from the fund rarely exceeded $15 million. Like the Land and Water Conservation Fund, it was a 50% matching grant program, but the match could be provided by in-kind services, materials, and labor.

In 1998, the Intramodal Surface Transportation Efficiency Act was renewed by Congress with some amendments. The new legislation, titled the Transportation Equity Act for the 21st Century, was called TEA-21 for short. It substantially increased the money available for transportation enhancements by 20%, including investment in bicycle and pedestrian modes of transportation. It expanded the enhancement categories to include transportation museums. Significantly, funds authorized by a Democratic Congress and a Republican President were reaffirmed several years later by a Republican Congress and a Democratic President.

Public Employment Programs

On those occasions when the nation's economy has reached a point in its cycle that results in relatively high levels of unemployment, the federal government frequently has responded by providing funds for some form of job-creation program. Park and recreation agencies are extraordinarily well positioned to create meaningful construction, renovation, repair, and maintenance projects that can absorb relatively large numbers of people. Conservation and the provision of park and recreational opportunities are areas in which government entities can employ much labor with relatively little controversy because they are widely recognized as legitimate concerns of government. Thus, park and recreation agencies traditionally have been primary beneficiaries of federal job creation programs.

In 1996, Congress passed the Personal Responsibility and Work Opportunity Reconciliation Act, which was a major attempt to reform how federal welfare support was provided. A central element was that after 24 months on assistance, welfare recipients were required to engage in work or community service. Park and recreation agencies anticipated that this would create a substantial reservoir of potential labor for park maintenance and support positions.

The model for these programs that exemplified their potential value to society was the Civilian Conservation Corps, established in response to massive unemployment emanating from the Great Depression of the early 1930s. The Corps was managed by the National Park Service. In 1935, more than 100 Civilian Conservation Corps camps operated in the National Park Service, and almost 500 camps operated in the state parks.[18] The Corps enrollees worked on thousands of state and federal park-development projects. Between 1933 and 1942, more than 6 million young men were involved in the program. Their legacy is evident in many of these parks today and often is denoted by a plaque recognizing their work.

In recent years, federal employment programs have tended to focus on creating opportunities for youth. At least partially in response to the stimulus of federal funds, a national network of more than 120 youth corps operating in more than two-thirds of the states had emerged by the mid-1990s as heirs to the impressive legacy of the Civilian Conservation Corps. As mentioned, the federal government initiated strong incentives in the mid-1990s to move people off the welfare rolls into gainful employment. It seems likely that this will stimulate additional interest in the youth corps movement.

Some youth corps are community-based nonprofit organizations, while others are formed by state or local agencies. Typically, they seek to move young people from unemployment into full-time work and a better future. Corps organize young people from 16 to 25 years of age into crews, with each crew working under the supervision of an adult leader. The corps members generally receive stipends of around the minimum wage and may remain in the program for three months (in the case of summer programs) or 12 months or more (in the case of year-round programs). Because many members are educationally or economically disadvantaged, they are required to participate in classes in basic education, life skills, and job preparation.[19]

Each crew of 8 to 12 members undertakes highly visible projects, such as streambank stabilization, trail building, facility construction, tree planting, and community environmental education, that have inherent opportunities for learning. They do not engage in regular maintenance projects or in projects that would displace full-time adult workers or recently laid-off workers.

The Vermont Youth Conservation Corps helped staff heavily toured state parks each summer. The Pennsylvania Conservation Corps built a revenue-generating tourist cabin in a state park. The Wisconsin Conservation Corps fielded an elite crew for jobs on a three-week state parks tour. The San Francisco Conservation Corps installed numerous neighborhood play structures in the city.[18]

Youth Crime Prevention Programs

It was noted in chapter 5 that in the late 1980s and early 1990s, youth crime re-emerged as a prominent issue on the political agenda. The primary federal legislation in this area in the 1990s was the Juvenile Justice and Delinquency Prevention Act. Most of the federal response emphasized providing incentives for local governments to hire more law enforcement officers and equipment, to mandate more severe penalties for youth crime, to try more and younger juveniles as adults, and to authorize and fund more juvenile detention facilities. However, some funds, albeit relatively small amounts, were authorized for recreation-as-prevention actions.

In an era of fiscal constraint, local government funds for new programs often are not available. In these situations, internal funds can only be acquired by redesigning or terminating existing services. This is difficult to do and may take a period of years to accomplish. Thus, when park and recreation agencies were directed by elected officials to do something quickly to prevent youth crime, they looked for external resources from federal and state grant programs to fund the desired new services. The limitations and danger of this strategy were pointed out by the executive director of the Minneapolis Park and Recreation Board. He suggested that agencies actually might be contributing to the problems of youth by building expectations through short-term, one-time recreational programs, and then failing to follow through with long-term, ongoing services:

> We will undertake a disservice to our clients, who already are beset by part-time parents and part-time education, by offering part-time programs. To be effective, programs must be consistent, constant and sustainable. Otherwise I believe we simply feed the loop of failing to fulfill our promises (p. 24).[7]

Thus, federal funds may be a useful stimulus to launch these services, but if there is not a commitment to continue them beyond the grant period with local tax funds, then there are unlikely to be lasting positive impacts.

Summary

The economic case for a city and school district cooperating to provide park and recreational facilities is compelling. The same taxpayers fund the facilities that both entities develop, and joint provision is likely to result in savings from reduced land-acquisition costs, capital development costs, and operating expenses. The times at which school and community clienteles use recreational facilities are reasonably complementary. A school's physical plant is likely to contain many of the elements found in community recreational systems, but without community access, it is likely to be used for only 18% of its potential capacity. If community access is designed into the school plant from the outset, then use of its recreation elements may exceed 60% of potential capacity.

There are a number of potential economic, morale, and managerial costs that may be associated with joint-provision projects. These may arise from heavy use of the facilities, from frustration of managers and clienteles created by the need to compromise over equipment use and facility scheduling, and from problems in the planning and construction of facilities. To minimize such problems, there should be a written agreement between the school district and the city describing the respective roles and responsibilities of each body. A more significant obstacle to joint provision than these pragmatic issues is the parochial, departmentalized thinking and lack of broad vision among senior administrators and elected officials. Their vision should embrace the principle that facilities belong not to their agency but to the public at large.

In every community there are opportunities for a park and recreation agency to cooperate with other public agencies to create additional amenities. Cooperation may be with other local agencies, such as departments in the same political jurisdiction, counties and communities within the jurisdiction, and military installations and colleges in the community. The most frequent partnerships between local and federal agencies have been with the U.S. Army Corps of Engineers, which leases approximately 1,000 of its recreational areas to state and local jurisdictions. Joint management with state agencies tends to occur most often when state and local agencies have adjacent properties and, therefore, it is more efficient for one agency to operate both areas.

The Land and Water Conservation Fund is the only federal grant aid program designed exclusively for parks and recreation that has received funding support over a prolonged period of time. Even though its future role appears likely to be more restricted, its past success demonstrates the importance of securing a dedicated fund at the federal level for land acquisition and facility development. There are ongoing efforts to establish dedicated funds for park and recreation acquisition and development at both state and federal levels. They have been established by legislation, constitutional amendment, or voter initiative in a number of states, but efforts at the federal level have been unsuccessful to this point. Three sources of finance for funding a federal dedicated fund that have been suggested are extraction taxes and leases, a real-estate transfer tax, and a manufacturers' excise tax on recreational equipment.

In addition to the Land and Water Conservation Fund, there are other federal grant programs for which park and recreation agencies are likely to be eligible. Elected representatives enact these periodically in response to political pressures to address a particular social problem. Although they tend to be authorized for limited time periods, they often re-emerge in a different form in response to the ebb and flow of the magnitude of the social problem. Four categories of these types of programs are likely to be of most interest to park and recreation agencies: surplus property transfers, greenway and trail development, public employment programs, and youth crime prevention programs.

References

1. Artz, Robert M. 1970. *School-community recreation and park cooperation: Management aids bulletin #82.* Washington, DC: National Recreation and Park Association.

2. Bever, Thomas D. 1979. *Recreation and the tax dollar. Stretching limited resources: A case study of Plano, Texas.* Washington, DC: U.S. Department of Interior, Heritage Conservation and Recreation Service.

3. Trumble, Frank. 1995. Cooperation builds a pool: Texas children get a natatorium, thanks to the school district and city. *Aquatics International.* September/October: 17–19.

4. Coopers & Lybrand Associates Ltd. 1981. *Sharing does work: The economic & social costs & benefits of joint & direct sports provision. Sports council study #21.* London, England: Sports Council.

5. Schmid, Sue. 1995. Partners in recreation. *Athletic Business* 19(10): 31-38.

6. Martin, Douglas. 1995. The grabbing of the greens: Acquisitive parks department is wiley scavenger for bits of land. *New York Times,* February 12, section 1, 37, 41.

7. Witt, Peter A. and John L. Crompton. 1996. *Recreation programs that work for at-risk youth.* State College, PA: Venture Publications.

8. Sheman, Rachel M. 1997. Equal partners: A city-military partnership grows youth sports programs. *Athletic Business* 21(1): 20.

9. Slack, Lou. 1995. Negotiations move forward on proposed park merger. *Daily Breeze* January 27, A12.

10. Paul, Noel C. 1997. Nation's newest park is island unto itself. *The Christian Science Monitor,* June 30, 4.

11. U.S. Congress. House Committee on Interior and Insular Affairs. 1963. *Land and water conservation fund act. Report to accompany H.R. 3846. House Report No. 900 88th Congress, 1st Session.* Washington, DC: Government Printing Office.

12. Conservation Foundation. 1985. National parks for a new generation. *Visions, realities, prospects.* Washington, DC: The Conservation Foundation.

13. President's Commission on Americans Outdoors. 1986. Meeting funding needs. Unpublished discussion document: 11.

14. Kelly, John T., Curt Cornelssen and Margaret Bailey. 1996. Military base closure can change lands to parks. *Parks and Recreation* 31(1): 70-76.

15. *The Economist* 343(8022). 1997. From boots to electronics. Editorial, 28-30.

16. Szwak, Laura. 1990. From boot camps to ball fields. *Courier* May: 24-27.

17. Lerner, Steve. 1997. Unpaving the way. *Land and People* 9(2): 9-15.

18. Foresta, Ronald A. 1984. *America's national parks and their keepers.* Washington, DC: Resources for the Future.

19. Moore, Andrew. 1997. Youth corps serve parks. *Parks and Recreation* 32(3): 70-76.

CHAPTER 12

FACILITATION AND COPRODUCTION

In recent years, the range of recreational activities and interests that people pursue has expanded widely, resulting in a large number of fragmented interest segments. Many park and recreation agencies responded to these new demands by increasing both the diversity and quantity of their offerings. However, their limited resources meant that this only could be done by shifting away from direct delivery of services and leveraging their resources. One way of doing this was to adopt a facilitation strategy characterized by opportunity referral, technical assistance, brokering, and coproduction. This broadened service approach emphasizes the agency's role as a facilitator of park and recreational opportunities, which are at least partially created by others, rather than as an exclusive provider of ready-made packaged offerings. Implicit in the movement toward this role is a recognition that a park and recreation agency lacks the resources to accommodate the entire citizenry's demands alone.

However, as noted in chapter 6, the case for agencies' moving toward a facilitation approach extends beyond the issue of pragmatic expediency. It is a manifestation of the populist rationale for supporting privatization. It embraces a philosophical position which argues that a facilitative approach to park and recreation service delivery is a potentially powerful vehicle for community empowerment and for enhancing community development. The United Nations defines community development as:

> A process of social action in which the people of a community organize themselves for planning and action; define their common and individual needs and solve their problems; execute their plans with a maximum reliance upon community resources and supplement these resources when necessary with services and materials from governmental and non-governmental agencies outside of the community.[1]

Concern is not only with supplying benefits that citizens seek from particular service offerings but also with the contribution that these services can make as a vehicle for developing social networks and a sense of community identity and belonging. In the old days, people may not have had much leisure time, but they spent it in one another's company. Economic change, redevelopment, suburban sprawl, traffic, and patterns of migration have altered much of that. In order to re-create a sense of identity and community spirit people have to get together in new ways and in new places. Park and recreation services can play a role in this.

The creation of a working partnership with local residents means that the public agency does not provide services for community organizations to use; rather, it means that the community organization itself identifies needs, collectively makes decisions, and takes responsibility for at least part of a service's development, operation, and maintenance. It has been found that benefits emerge from the process of development itself: the stimuli, the debates on priorities, and the making of tough decisions by a community organization. Out of this process common goals emerge including active interaction among local citizens, and personal growth of the individuals involved.

Forms of Facilitation

Figure 12.1 shows that the facilitation role can take a variety of forms that can be expressed along a continuum ranging from minimal agency invest-

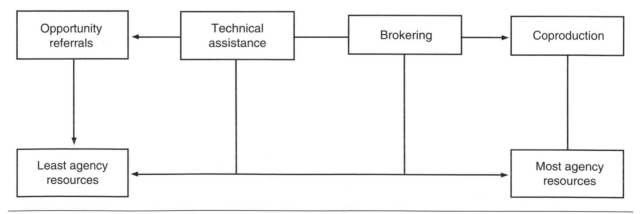

Figure 12.1 The facilitation continuum.

ment (opportunity referrals) to relatively substantial agency investment (coproduction). These forms are not mutually exclusive. Indeed, it is likely that some agencies will embrace all of them as part of their delivery strategy.

At a minimalist level, the park and recreation agency can act as a central source of referrals by providing comprehensive information about opportunities in the area. This requires relatively few resources. For example, a user may go to the public library, schools, recreational centers, or other convenient sites, and he or she may access a computer database that the agency establishes and regularly updates which lists both commercial and nonprofit suppliers and the sites of all recreational activity opportunities in the area. The Kitchener Parks and Recreation Department in Ontario provides free space to local organizations in its *Leisure Guide*, which is issued quarterly and widely distributed to the city's 180,000 residents. Figure 12.2 on page 319 shows a sample page from that *Leisure Guide*.

Technical assistance involves helping community groups to define their needs, establish effective administrative procedures, address legal issues, design programs, and suggest promotional and fundraising strategies. The model for such a role is analogous to the role that agricultural extension agents in the farming community undertake. The agency may offer leadership training for community groups, but the assistance is confined to advice and consultation and does not extend to providing tangible resource assistance. Delivery of the service remains the exclusive responsibility of the community organization.

Brokering positions the agency as a proactive middleman who uses a network of contacts in the community to link individuals with organizations that can meet their recreation needs. An example of how this may be implemented is given in "Brokering to a Corporate Constituency." This illustration involves corporations, but it could be adapted to other institutions, such as apartment or condominium complexes, colleges, or military installations.

Brokering to a Corporate Constituency

Johnson County Park and Recreation District, which serves suburbs in the greater Kansas City area, had a brokering agreement with almost 100 corporations in the area whereby it sought out or created recreational opportunities for 15,000 employees. After a company indicated a desire to be part of the program, the district undertook two surveys. First, the corporation's plant was inspected to identify possible areas for conducting classes and programs at the work site. All spaces, including work areas, were inventoried and their potential for recreational use was recorded. Second, the district conducted a needs assessment. If company policy permitted, questionnaires were distributed with employee paychecks. The alternative was to leave them with the personnel office, which distributed them at the workplace.

Employees returned completed surveys to boxes located at convenient and prominent places in the plant. The survey consisted of a single sheet with questions on both sides. Survey instructions stated:

> Recreation has been defined as "what anyone likes to do in his or her leisure time." In order that our recreation program will fully reflect your interests, this questionnaire offers you an opportunity to indicate those recreation activities in which you are interested—the things that you would like to do in your spare time. Although not all of these activities are now part of our program, a definite attempt will be made to add activities in which a substantial interest is expressed. If you have a favorite hobby or interest that is not listed, add it in the blanks provided.

The questionnaire listed a total of 120 recreational activities classified in five major categories: 1) sports activities; 2) social activities, subdivided into a) card and table games and b) other social activities; 3) outing activities; 4) cultural activities, subdivided into a) theatricals, b) out-of-town visits to concerts, opera, lectures, etc., c) fine arts, d) handicrafts, e) movies in the plant, f) music, and g) other cultural activities; and 5) miscellaneous activities, such as fashion shows and first-aid programs.

The district served as a broker to bring together employees desiring specified recreation services with the necessary facilities and qualified instructors. A recreation committee was established within each corporation to suggest service improvements to the district.

The county used four operational alternatives to provide programs and services to these employees. The preferred approach was to offer programs on site. The initial corporate facility inventory revealed spaces in the plant or on the grounds that could serve as areas for fitness classes, instructional programs, leagues, and special events. However, in many instances in-house facilities were inadequate for accommodating all employee interests.

A second alternative was to offer corporate employee programs at public facilities. Johnson County's recreation division did not own any tax-supported recreational facilities, but it leased space on a short-term basis at almost 100 locations in the county, mainly from the six school districts. The leasing policy had at least one advantage; because the agency was not tied to specific facilities, it could be flexible and could better adapt its offerings to shifts in population and interest.

School districts are reluctant to lease their facilities directly to a private corporation. Typically, they assign a business low priority in any competition for space and charge substantially higher rates than those that public entities pay. Because school districts were very willing to lease facilities to the district, however, Johnson County was able to act as broker and make them available for corporate use through this program.

A third service approach was to integrate corporate programs with those offered to the general public. In all general class programs, leagues, or tournaments, the district reserved 25% of the places for its corporate constituents. Thus, in a class with a maximal enrollment of 20, 15 places were allocated to the general public, and five were allocated to corporate employees. If either group did not use its entire allocation, the remaining spaces were offered to members of the other group on the waiting list. This provision made it possible to cater to employee interest groups that were too small to make it financially feasible to run programs at the plant site.

A fourth alternative was to organize classes for employees at private facilities. Staff negotiated agreements with managers of facilities, such as bowling alleys, ice rinks, tennis centers, racquetball clubs, and fitness centers.

Organizing employee excursions emerged as a major service. Trips that featured skiing, floating, rafting, fishing, hunting, and visits to football and baseball games proved popular. Again, the district was a broker. Its staff found out what employees wanted, developed a package tailored to satisfy those wants, and then invited local travel agents to bid on the package or organized it in-house.

The major focus of this chapter is on coproduction because it is likely to require most agency resources, is the closest form of facilitation to direct delivery, and is the option that agencies are most likely to adopt when they move away from direct delivery. Coproduction involves the agency in coordination and cooperation with a community organization to deliver a service jointly. The magnitude of resources invested by each party in the agreement will vary widely, but coproduction moves an agency away from a policy of responsible for and toward a policy of assistance to. It may involve both parties contributing funds for the capital development of a facility as well as to its operation and maintenance. Dallas' cultural arts policy offered an example of this.

The city of Dallas assisted qualified arts organizations in providing needed facilities in accordance with a carefully conceived and approved plan. Facilities developed under this program were constructed, owned, and maintained by the city. The cost of acquisition of sites was shared 75% by the city of Dallas and 25% by the cultural arts institutions. The cost of facilities was shared 60% by the city and 40% by the cultural arts institutions. The city determined program support for each organization each year as a part of the general budget process.

The Concept of Coproduction

Although coproduction has a long heritage, its prominence as a strategic policy dates to the late 1970s when it emerged as one of the responses to governments' fiscal stress. Conceptually, it challenges the traditional direct delivery service model

Alzheimer Society of Kitchener-Waterloo

The Alzheimer Society of Kitchener-Waterloo provides education and support to people with Alzheimer Disease or a related dementia, and to their family and friends. Services available include a resource library, supportive counselling, wandering registry, support groups, education meetings, speakers bureau, and referral to helpful community agencies. Please call 742-1422 or visit 501-151 Frederick Street, Kitchener.

Asahi Judo Club

Asahi is the largest Judo Club in Canada with classes for males and females ages 4 to 50+. Judo is an Olympic sport that features throws, holds, and other defensive techniques. All senior instructors have their National Coaching certification. Information: see ad on page 34 or call 743-4998.

Beaux and Belles Square Dance Club

The Beaux and Belles Square Dance Club offers three nights of dancing. Basic at 8:00 pm on Fridays at Highland Baptist Church and mainstream dancing at 8:00 pm on Thursdays at Highland Baptist Church. Plus level dancing takes place every Saturday at 8:00 pm at Mill-Courtland Centre. For more information call 570-9208 or 745-7014.

Canadian Mental Health Association
Waterloo Regional Branch

CMHA supports people who experience mental health issues and works with the community to reduce barriers that limit full participation. We assist with leisure planning by providing information, brochures, and support. Support is also provided for education, housing, employment, and all mental health concerns. Community Access Centre, 67 King Street, East, Kitchener. 744-2049.

Canadian Red Cross Society
Waterloo Regional Homemaker Service

Waterloo Regional Red Cross Homemaker Service provides 24 hour, seven days a week flexible services to people in times of illness, convalescence, disability and family crisis. Services include personal care, home management, ambulation, caregiver relief and child care. New Program: Household Support providing cleaning, errands, shopping, yardwork, etc. Fee for service. Call 746-6600.

Concordia Toastmasters

Toastmasters can help you improve your oral communication and leadership skills in a friendly, supportive atmosphere. Concordia Toastmasters meets at Resurrection High School, 455 University Avenue, West, Wednesday's from 7:00 pm to 9:00 pm. Come to our meetings or contact Roel Vis 570-2271, or Gordon Wray 745-1922.

Christkindlsmarkt (Christ Child Market)

The Joseph Schneider Haus Museum located at 466 Queen Street, South recreates the sights, sounds and smells of a traditional German Christmas Market and opportunities to purchase craft items daily December 6–24. Special theme weekends in the historic house. Please call (519) 742-7752 for information.

JM Drama

JM Drama is a community theatre group that actively supports the development of the arts in the Waterloo Region. We're a charitable organization that gives back to our community through staging quality, entertaining productions, and providing educational workshops and training. We also rent costumes and equipment. Join the fun! Call 741-0642.

Kitchener-Waterloo Field Naturalists

We have nature hikes and educational outings, half-day to whole weekend plus special projects such as tree-planting and habitat restoration. Also, club meetings provide informative, entertaining programs, on the fourth Monday of each month, September to May, 7:30 pm at Wing 404/Rotary Centre, Dutton Drive, Waterloo. Everyone welcome. Call Julie, 579-8871 or Cecile, 744-2369 for more information.

Kitchener-Waterloo Friendship Group for Seniors

The K-W Friendship Group for Seniors is looking for dedicated, caring volunteer visitors to share their time with a lonely senior or person with a disability living in the community. If you are 18 or older and can spare 2–3 hours per week to befriend someone in need, please call us at 742-6502.

Figure 12.2 Referrals to other organizations in an agency's leisure guide.

---

in which a park and recreation agency has exclusive responsibility for designing and producing services for a largely passive, consuming citizenry. It is based on a recognition that citizens need not always be passive recipients of park and recre- ation services. Frequently, there are opportunities for them to participate so extensively in their provision that they can be viewed as coproducers of services along with public agency personnel. Coproduction is a means of expanding the scope of park and recreation services that an agency can deliver, and it represents a willingness on the part of an agency to work with residents to develop their capacities as potential service coproducers.

Various definitions of coproduction have been proposed, but the central tenet in all of them is involvement of citizens in production of a public service. In the context of parks and recreation, coproduction is defined most usefully as a process in which individuals or community groups participate jointly with a public agency in the production of park and recreation services of which they or their families are primary beneficiaries. The intent is to move toward supported self-help; this is the idea that, with a little encouragement and some resources from the agency, people can produce many park and recreation services for themselves. Ideally, there needs to be enough assistance from the agency to ensure that the service is offered at the desired level but not so much that it is primarily an agency offering.

While individuals' contributions to coproduction are voluntary, their role is differentiated from that of volunteers in that volunteers personally do not receive direct benefits from the service output. It has been suggested that people volunteer for either expressive or instrumental reasons.[2] Those motivated by expressive reasons volunteer because a direct benefit accrues to them from doing so. The discussion of coproduction in this chapter focuses on them. In contrast, those people whose motives are instrumental volunteer because they believe that their efforts will result in the betterment of society. Their contributions to providing park and recreation amenities are discussed in chapter 13.

Frequently, coproduction is organized through a nonprofit community group, and it is likely to involve a formal agreement between the agency and the organization. The group performs two primary functions. First, it brings together those desiring a particular service, and it is a vehicle through which they can articulate their needs to an agency. Second, it pools its resources with those of an agency to deliver the desired service. The extent of the group's contribution is likely to vary according to the resources it has available (e.g., time, money, knowledge) and its demographic characteristics (e.g., age, income level, education).

Most commonly in this field, coproduction takes the form of an agency providing a facility, equipment, or a financial subsidy and of the group's resources producing a programmatic element. Typical coproducers include athletic clubs (e.g.,

Little League, swimming, soccer, softball), arts societies, senior citizen clubs, and neighborhood associations. The effectiveness of coproduction resides in the complementarity of the resources brought by citizens and the agency to production of a service. Their combined efforts determine the quality and quantity of it that is ultimately delivered. These principles are illustrated in the following example.

An undeveloped two-acre parksite in the community of North Douglas in Springfield, Oregon, had become an eyesore, covered with debris, weeds, and rocks. The community signed a contract with Williamalane Park and Recreation District to make the park clean and green through volunteer labor and fundraising efforts. A local contractor provided earth-moving equipment to bulldoze away the weeds, rocks, and debris. The park district hauled the unwanted material from the site. The city maintenance department leveled the park with grading equipment. The neighborhood residents organized several weekend work parties to pick up rocks and chunks of concrete and to hoist them into a dump truck. The volunteers then prepared the site for grass seed. Youngsters who had been troubling the neighborhood were among the most hardworking volunteers in cleaning up the park.[3]

The park district seeded the park and, with the neighborhood, sponsored a community Arbor Day to plant several trees. A nearby resident offered to help establish the trees by providing water from his well. The neighborhood then decided to raise funds for a basketball court. The park district provided shovels and wheelbarrows so neighborhood families could excavate a site for a basketball court. The city maintenance department provided base material and asphalt to surface the court, and the park district installed the basketball equipment.

The more formal the structure of a community organization is, the more stable it is likely to be and the more confident an agency will be that coproduction with it will be successful. Many organizations involved in coproduction officially have incorporated as 501 (c)(iii) nonprofit corporations and conduct their business as operating foundations. (These terms are explained in chapter 18.) Indeed, some agencies will only engage in coproduction with nonprofit organizations that are able to produce a copy of the IRS's letter of determination confirming their 501 (c)(iii) status because this implies a relatively high level of stability and continuity.

Occasionally, the opportunity to coproduce may be created by offering residents some form of direct material gain. For example, a severe ice storm in Dallas inflicted extensive damage on trees and shrubs in the city's parks. The cost of cutting and collecting the large number of damaged tree limbs was high. To reduce the cost, the city invited residents to pick up the wood after the city had cut down the damaged limbs. In this way the city saved the substantial collection expense. Local citizens were motivated to come and pick up the branches because they viewed these as a source of free firewood.

A park and recreation agency is likely to be involved more in coproduction than any other department of local government for four reasons. First, the necessary technical or specialized expertise is often available from individuals in the community who gain satisfaction from volunteering it, and these enthusiasts may be able to deliver elements of a given service as well as agency personnel. Second, there is less agreement in parks and recreation than in other areas of government as to the appropriate level of service that should be provided. Expectations in the community may differ, especially in fast-growing communities comprising large numbers of people who have moved in from elsewhere. If park and recreation services are relatively underdeveloped compared with those in jurisdictions from which people came, then these people are likely to seek ways to expand the range of opportunities. Third, the link between benefits accruing from enhanced park and recreation services and voluntary efforts that produce those services is relatively direct, so individuals can see that their investment of resources will result in obvious returns to them. Fourth, parks and recreation is one of the areas most likely to experience cutbacks in times of financial stress, which lead to a reduction in services that an agency is able to directly deliver. As one manager noted: "We would have argued the philosophy of coproduction forever, but it was the fact that there were no funds for the fall that really precipitated our move into it" (p. 12).[4]

Ostensibly coproduction may be viewed as a form of contracting out because park and recreation agencies shift some of their service responsibilities to private individuals, groups, and institutions who use their resources for this purpose. However, there are three distinctions between contracting out with commercial entities and coproduction. First, the latter involves volunteers who are motivated by self-help, whereas contracting out is targeted at other professionals whose raison d'être is monetary remuneration. Thus, in contracting out, the citizens' role is that of consumers of the service, consuming just as they would any other private good or service. In contrast, coproduction requires a commitment from citizens that they participate in service delivery. Coproduction supplements the agency's role in delivering a service, whereas contracting out supplants it.

A second distinction is that the park and recreation agency's ongoing involvement in coproduction as a joint working partner means that it is likely to be better able to retain control of the service output than if a service is contracted out to an entrepreneur. Finally, resources available to a program may be greater if coproduction, rather than contracting out, is adopted. In coproduction, all revenues can be reinvested in the program and dedicated to public use, but in contracting out, entrepreneurs retain a proportion of the revenues to reimburse them for their investment of resources.

Advantages of Coproduction

Six advantages have been identified that support the case for pursuing a strategy of coproduction rather than direct delivery. The first two, which are somewhat philosophical in nature and relatively difficult to verify empirically, are rebuilding an ethos and rebuilding empathy for government. In contrast, the last four are relatively pragmatic: cost reductions, enhanced responsiveness, use of citizens' talents, and enhanced opportunities to socialize.

Rebuilding an Ethos

There is a body of opinion in the United States that argues that self-reliance is a key feature of the American way. This is the populists' case for privatization. Its advocates believe that self-reliance is part of the country's heritage and cultural tradition and that the municipalization of everything represents a threat to the country's character. Such populists support privatization in the form of coproduction because "provision of direct recreation services by public and private agencies has emerged as a crutch, often limiting the individual's self-confidence and ability to act as his or her own best leisure resource" (p. 6).[5] There is a sense that direct delivery by public agencies undermines the confidence and competence of citizens and communities and creates dependency. Citizens lose an opportunity to help themselves learn about their own capacities to cope and grow. It has been suggested: "Too often we create programs designed to collect clients rather than to empower communities of citizens" (p. 51).[4] Two quotations from Abraham Lincoln help explain this patriotic advocacy for co-production: "You cannot build character and courage by taking away man's initiative and independence" and "You cannot help people permanently by doing for them what they could and should do for themselves."[6]

In more recent times, this perspective was invoked consistently by President Reagan throughout his term in office in the 1980s, which was the time when interest in coproduction accelerated as a proactive public agency delivery strategy. His views are illustrated as follows: "We're not advocating private initiative and voluntary activities as a half-hearted replacement for budget cuts. We advocate them because they're right in their own regard. They're a part of what we can proudly call the American personality. . . . We have let government take away many things we once considered were really ours to do voluntarily out of the goodness of our hearts and a sense of community pride and neighborliness. I believe many of you want to do these things again" (p. 15).[7]

From this perspective, an important advantage of coproduction is that it restores voluntary action to its rightful place in the American ethos. Despite the high-minded intentions of public agencies, their actions are sometimes socially regressive in that programs that are directly delivered are invariably regarded as the city's rather than as ours. The sense of ownership, belonging, commitment, pride, camaraderie, community spirit, and common purpose engendered by members of community organizations who coproduce services generally far exceeds that which is exhibited by users of directly delivered park and recreation services.

Rebuilding Empathy for Government

Coproduction has the potential to provide a bridge from disaffected citizens to their governments, reducing the distance between them. It offers one action that agencies can take to counter pervasive citizen apathy and indifference to government. There has been substantial decline in trust and support for public agencies during the last two or three decades, and this continues. As the park and recreation movement has become more professional, it has tended to pre-empt responsibility for opportunity-related decisions from citizens. Some citizens regard public agencies as being distant, impersonal, and dictatorial, and they are resentful of their inability to influence agencies' actions. Others perceive public employees generally to be lazy, untrustworthy, wasteful, and power hungry. These perceptions have attained the status of accepted myths and have become facts, even though the paradox of this situation is that when citizens are asked to evaluate their concrete experiences with public agencies and public employees, they do so in a much more favorable light.[8]

Working jointly with a park and recreation agency is likely to give citizens a broader perspective and meaningful insights into the agency's work. This may result in a heightened appreciation of the quality both of the services delivered and the effort invested by employees and in a greater awareness of the content, costs, and limitations of an agency's service capacity. In addition, the joint working and decision making are likely to cement personal relationships between an agency's employees and citizens. This may increase citizens' self-confidence in becoming involved with government and make them aware of their own and their organization's potential political potency. From the agency's perspective, as individuals invest more commitment, energy, and sweat equity in supporting the work of a park and recreation agency, the agency's political base grows stronger because people who are heavily involved tend to become active advocates.

Cost Reductions

Like other partnership arrangements discussed in earlier chapters of the text, the most obvious advantage of coproduction is that it either reduces an agency's costs or enhances the quality of service that can be delivered. An illustration is given in "An Illustration of Cost-Saving Coproduction Ventures in a Seattle-Area Park." The agency is able to leverage its resources to bring forth additional resources from the community, so the amount of service delivered per tax dollar is maximized. Indeed, it is likely that the potential return from resources invested in organizing coproduction arrangements will be higher than the return forthcoming from a similar amount of resources expended on additional equipment, facilities, or agency personnel.

The magnitude of the cost savings will vary widely, depending on how much of the capital and operating expenses are borne by the agency. Part of the cost savings is likely to be attributed to the

An Illustration of Cost-Saving Coproduction Ventures in a Seattle-Area Park

King County Parks Division operated Marymoor Park in Redmond, Washington. It was a large, multi-use area that relied heavily on coproduction. For example, the 12 soccer fields were scheduled by the parks division, but the programs were operated by the 6,000-member Lake Washington Youth Soccer Association. The county lacked funds to maintain these grass fields, so the association maintained them. The velodrome, which was used for the 1990 Goodwill Games, was coordinated by the Marymoor Velodrome Association, which offered classes as well as a racing series.

The Pea Patch was an area of 200, 10 ft × 40 ft plots of land that were rented to gardeners for $32 a season. A cooperative-use agreement was established between the model airplane club and the parks division, whereby the club mowed the runways and the parks division took care of the surrounding area. The popular climbing structure, which at 45 ft tall was one of the tallest freestanding climbing structures in the country, was built after a group of climbing enthusiasts approached the council and was operated by the climbers.

The recreation coordinator for the King County Department of Parks and Recreation said: "What we're having to do is have some of the groups who use our facilities take care of their own area of the park. With ever-shrinking budgets, we can't do everything we want to do. We need that kind of help."

Adapted from Sue Schmid. Park Partners: A variety of partnerships make a Seattle-area park a true cooperative venture. Athletic Business. March 1997, page 20.

agency's employing fewer people. In some cases, the responsibility for employing personnel may be shifted to the community organization, which is much better equipped to hire and lay-off staff according to fluctuation in demand than a public agency constrained by civil service procedures is. Other savings may be attributable to the greater flexibility of community organizations to raise revenues. For example, the subsidy to operate a program that a public agency directly delivers may be offset at least partially in a coproduction arrangement by the organization's ability to raise revenues from sources, such as private lotteries, raffles, or club alcohol sales, that are not available to public agencies. In addition, community organizations are sometimes able to qualify for funds from sources, such as foundations, that are not accessible to a public agency.

Enhanced Responsiveness

It seems reasonable to conjecture that services delivered through coproduction are likely to be more responsive to the needs and preferences of client groups than those directly delivered because decisions are made by, or closer to, the user group. Even when the intentions are good, the inertia of the status quo combined with the expediency of administrative convenience often re-sults in inflexibility and a lack of responsiveness to the needs of particular neighborhoods or user groups. Sometimes there is a tendency for professionals to assume that they know the needs of their clientele and to proceed with delivering a service without regularly soliciting feedback from the target group. Because the two entities are active partners in service delivery, coproduction forces an agency to directly communicate with the user organization in an ongoing dialog.

There is a tendency sometimes for agency personnel to become facility bound and view their mission as filling the agency's facilities rather than responding to a community's needs. Responsive management does not stop at a facility's front door! Coproduction helps keep the focus of attention on people's needs rather than on the facilities.

Use of Citizens' Talents

Every community has enthusiasts whose specialized expertise, knowledge, and skills in particular recreational activities exceed those of any agency personnel. Indeed, individuals champion many successful park and recreational programs. A person with a dream or vision often is the catalyst that makes something happen. This is especially true in creative areas, such as the arts, where it long has been recognized that public agencies cannot manufacture successful arts programs. There is a maxim that states: If you don't have a staff member who is really interested and knowledgeable about an activity, hire someone or recruit a volunteer who is. An enthusiast is likely to generate much better results than is a staff member who is merely performing an assigned duty.

Traditionally, agencies have used their resources to directly service the largest interest groups. However, coproduction encourages the emergence of program champions and initiatives from the community, which enables agencies to leverage their resources to assist smaller, nontraditional, specialized clienteles. This has the useful corollary of gaining support from a new constituency. "Coproduction of a Climbing Program" provides an illustration of how such initiatives may be fostered.

There are dangers in generalizing, but the competence level of many community organizations is sufficiently high that any suggestion of a patronizing attitude by public agency personnel is unjustified. Indeed, the commitment level of people in community organizations involved in co-

Coproduction of a Climbing Program

I read a small announcement in *USA Today* that Recreation Equipment Inc. (REI), the Seattle-based retailer of outdoor equipment, was inviting proposals from nonprofit organizations involved with climbing programs that encouraged instruction in safe climbing and mountaineering. The department was not involved at that point in rock climbing, but the mountains were only 30 mi away. A letter requesting various climbing equipment was sent to REI with the idea that we would offer climbing classes to the general public. After several communications, the large box of climbing gear arrived at the office. After playing with all the gear like kids, the programming staff realized that no one on the staff knew how to use it or had any climbing experience.

Using the REI equipment, the department vans, and the help of a local sporting goods store, the department offered our first series of classes. Two experienced local climbers were hired as instructors. Participants had to be turned away. After offering the series of classes for two years and always having more participants than could be accommodated, our instructors approached the department with the idea of installing a sport climbing wall in a public gymnasium and organizing the UpState Climbing Club.

After visiting the Chapel Hill, North Carolina, public sport climbing facility and discussing the operation with the staff, the department sent out public service announcements to the local media and installed flyers in all the local sporting good stores announcing the organization meeting for the UpState Climbing Club. At the meeting, we surveyed more than 80 interested people and gathered their input about operation hours, fees, and instruction class needs.

With the membership fees of the first 50 club members, $2,000 in department funding, and the volunteer labor of the club members at night and on weekends, the first four climbing routes were built, and operation hours and procedures were developed.

Frankly, I anticipated that no more than 100 members would be involved. However, now more than 600 members are in the club, and I am still surprised at its success. Not only has the membership grown, but with the membership and user fees, the gymnasium also has expanded to 12 climbing routes and numerous other strength and skill development amenities. No department funding is needed for the operation or continued development.

As with the UpState Climbing Club, most sport clubs and special event organizations have become 501 (c)(iii) nonprofit entities with their own employees that we supervise. The organizations have bylaws and officers. Depending on the clubs' needs, the park and recreation department provides various services, such as organizing their board meetings, hosting their meetings in our buildings, using our postage meter, marketing the activities, and designing the flyers and newsletters.

production is frequently higher than that of agency personnel. Typically, organizations have a turnover of officers each year. Turnover tends to avoid the burnout that sometimes afflicts agency staff who have had long-term responsibility for a particular program. Each year a high level of vigor and energy and of new ideas and creativity may be injected into the program because the organization's leadership knows it is only a one-year commitment. The energy is released because the group has ownership in the service and its leaders have been empowered with authority to direct the service for this relatively short period. Individuals may derive a deep sense of satisfaction from this leadership opportunity and from engaging in consensus decision making for the common good. The group's ownership through coproduction has the added potential benefit of reducing vandalism, littering, and other avoidable maintenance costs for which the organization may be financially responsible.

Enhanced Opportunities to Socialize

Census data show greater atomization of the population: smaller families, more unmarried people, fewer marriages, more divorces, and extended families that geographically are widely dispersed. These data suggest that the number of people seeking social opportunities is growing, and recreation is a primary medium through which this benefit can be derived. For many people, socializing is the primary benefit that they seek from participation in park and recreational activities.

This type of partnership has the potential for moving citizens away from "cafeteria" recreation, in which they participate in an activity offered and forget about it until the next visit, toward committed recreation, in which participants take on responsibility for organizing, financing, and programming. Experience has shown that extra involvement, identity, and the sense of belonging that committed recreation engenders generally leads to much greater levels of personal satisfaction with the park and recreation experience for many citizens.

Friendships are made through engaging jointly with others in projects in either a work or leisure milieu. Coproduction means that individuals are required to work with others to plan, organize, fundraise, lead, and deliver a service. This requires social interaction. When an agency directly delivers a service, individuals may derive some social benefit from using it. However, they are deprived of the opportunity to experience the deeper, intense relationships that may evolve from the interaction that coproduction necessitates. From this perspective, a policy of direct service delivery may be counterproductive.

If a youth soccer program is coproduced, some proportion of the children's parents will be involved in the complex task of delivering it. They will work jointly with others to do this. It is likely to involve regular meetings and telephone calls. From these contacts, some lasting friendships may emerge. In contrast, these opportunities are lost if the city is exclusively responsible for the program. In that case, parents are likely to appear for their child's game on Saturday morning and to drop them off at practices. At those times, they probably will not interact with other parents whom they do not know.

Concern should be not only with participation at facilities and in programs but also with beneficial personal and community development resulting from people being involved fully in the development of opportunities.

Limitations of Coproduction

Before deciding to pursue a more aggressive approach toward coproduction, an agency has to address three concerns. These relate to loss of political support, equity issues of who will and who will not be served, and quality of service.

Loss of Political Support

Earlier it was noted that coproduction could assist in reaching new constituencies and in building political support through forging closer links with citizens by involving them more centrally in decision making and leadership. However, while these links are being constructed, the initial movement away from direct service to the more nebulous facilitation and coproduction roles may result in some loss of political support. This may occur because it is more challenging for an agency to demonstrate accountability for facilitation and coproduction to elected officials. A corollary of this is that elected officials have more difficulty collecting political kudos for supplying resources to such a program if it is not directly delivered. Results from facilitation and coproduction are less directly attributable to agency personnel and less tangible than results from directly delivered services. Without being able to show that a given number of people have been served, it is difficult for an agency to convince elected officials that it is using its tax resources responsibly. For this reason, resources invested in facilitation and coproduction may be prime candidates for cutbacks in tight budget situations.

Another potential cause of loss of political support is loss of revenue. Coproduction requires that a user group be able to accrue a threshold amount of resources to make it viable. Hence, the programs most suited for coproduction are likely to be those that generate the most revenue, largest numbers, and strong constituency support. If primary responsibility for these programs is transferred to community or user groups and they require relatively little resource support from the agency, then the agency's contribution to the coproduction partnership is relatively small, and it may lose much of this constituency's political support. At the same time, the loss of this revenue from the agency's own budget is relatively large, which may reduce its flexibility and its credibility with elected officials. Ultimately, the agency's role may be confined to serving dependent populations that lack the capacity to engage in coproduction. Such programs are unlikely to generate revenue, and these populations are likely to be expensive to service. This may be philosophically desirable, but to avoid loss of political support, both the agency and its coproducers have to communicate effectively to elected officials the positive nature of the agency's contributions.

Equity Issues

Exclusive reliance on facilitation or coproduction for service delivery is likely to result in some segments of the community being excluded from access to these services. The exclusion may stem from several sources. First, some may lack the ability to pay fees associated with participating in the community organization. This is resolved frequently by the organization making arrangements to waive its fees or by the agency, United Way or other charity, or a commercial sponsor making a payment.

A second cause of exclusion may be that, at some point, leadership in the community organization becomes controlled by an idiosyncratic clique of individuals, who in subtle ways discourage those who are not their kind of people from participating in the organization's activities and who develop a sense of proprietary ownership. Such groups are then just as inaccessible, unresponsive, and undemocratic as the worst public agencies. Even if such a policy is not deliberately implemented, few community organizations are designed to provide a comprehensive, evenly distributed service for the whole community. Whether based on common interest in a recreational activity, locality, or ethnicity, most voluntary community organizations are generally rather narrow and selective service providers.

There is an African proverb that states, "If you have your hand in another man's pocket, then you must move when he moves." If the community organization partner produces most of the resources, it may feel entitled to chart the program's direction. This may be inconsistent with the comprehensive service program for the community that an agency is responsible for enacting. As a coproduction partner, a park and recreation department must retain some control of a program's general direction as part of its required mandate as a public agency. These issues of the public's right of access, nonexclusion, and program direction need to be specified in an initial written partnership agreement between the two entities to avoid subsequent misunderstandings and conflicts.

A final cause of inequity, and perhaps the most difficult to rectify, is that some segments of the community are ill equipped to operate in this way. It is likely that wealthier and better-educated groups will be most capable and willing to engage in coproduction, while poorer citizens and neighborhoods may be less able to respond to this service model. This suggests that exclusive reliance on coproduction may result in uneven distribution of park and recreation services and may exacerbate the gap between advantaged and disadvantaged sections of a community. To counter this limitation, it seems likely that the public agency would have to retain its advocacy role for programs for these segments and to continue with a direct delivery approach to them.

Quality of Service

The capacity of people to fulfill the responsibilities assigned to their organization in a coproduction agreement is central to its success. There are inherent difficulties in community organizations consistently maintaining desired quality standards for service delivery, particularly if they employ no professional staff and rely exclusively on volunteers. These difficulties arise because leadership and membership in organizations changes. Unfortunately, many members of community organizations are apathetic in the sense that they are not prepared to devote much time and energy to conducting the organization's business, and that they assume it will continue to be run by a relatively small core group of active enthusiasts. Thus, while much of the leadership will be competent, there are likely to be times when leadership may deteriorate and become incompetent. If the park and recreation agency is to intervene effectively at that point, the initial agreement should specify the desired standards, should specify how they are to be monitored, and should authorize the agency to take corrective action when necessary.

Transitioning From Direct Delivery to Coproduction

A major factor inhibiting the wider use of coproduction is the existence of an extensive range of services that public agencies directly operate. Before citizens will engage in coproduction, there has to be an environment that requires their involvement. As long as opportunities are provided at the desired level by an agency, there is no incentive for citizens to invest effort in coproduction. If public agencies withdraw from direct delivery, then a vacuum is created. Those who desire the service then have a reason to step forward and explore alternative ways of securing it.

Agencies that traditionally have relied predominantly on direct service delivery are likely to experience difficulty in transitioning both their clientele groups and their employees to coproduction. The expectations of both groups have to be readjusted, which is likely to lead to some initial disappointment and frustration. A period of consciousness raising is needed to address these concerns before attempting a transition. This would involve articulating reasons for the shift from direct delivery and identifying its implications for both community organizations and employees.

A decision regarding whether coproduction is a superior option to direct delivery should be evaluated against four criteria:

1. Are net costs substantially lower? Savings are likely because citizens would do tasks that were previously the responsibility of agency personnel, but there may be offsetting costs associated with things such as subsidies, technical assistance, and promotion.
2. Will quality of service be maintained when citizens, who may lack professional training, take responsibility? The organization's effectiveness may be especially compromised if key leaders burn out.
3. Will some sectors of the community be excluded?
4. Will the opportunity increase the depth and quality of participants' experiences?

It is likely to be easier for an agency to acquire resources to extend services through joint provision with community groups than it is to persuade elected officials to provide additional staff for direct delivery of services. The latter is a more permanent cost commitment than the former. Supporting coproduction, rather than hiring permanent staff, gives an agency more flexibility to shift, initiate, or terminate resources.

The impetus for citizens to engage in coproduction is likely to come from one of four sources:

- A desire to replace services reduced or terminated because the agency lacked resources to continue with direct delivery
- A desire to initiate a new service for which the park and recreation agency has no budgeted funds
- A desire to enhance the quality of services beyond the level that the park and recreation agency has the capacity to deliver
- A desire by a community group to raise funds for its cause through the sweat equity of its members

The first three of these stimuli are self-evident, but the last stimulus may need further explanation. A common example is the involvement of community groups in the maintenance of small neighborhood parks. In many communities, there are numerous open space areas of two acres or less that park and recreation agencies have to maintain. They frequently require hand maintenance and the use of small-scale equipment that homeowners likely possess. It is often inefficient for agency personnel to travel from a central or regional point to maintain them. Indeed, the time spent in traveling and in loading and unloading equipment may be greater than the time expended on maintaining the park! Thus, coproduction with community groups is a rational solution. An agency can negotiate or solicit bids from community groups, and if they are lower than the city's costs, the group can be authorized to do the work.

Seven churches in Indianapolis had contracts with Indianapolis Parks and Recreation Department for grounds maintenance, such as mowing, edging, trimming, and keeping clean, on 24 small parks in close proximity to them. The contracts ran from early May through the end of October each year. They mowed the parks weekly, collected trash three times each week, and received an annual fee of between $1,000 and $12,000 for this work, which was done voluntarily by church members. It raised funds for the churches and connected them more intimately with the neighborhoods. It also raised the standard of service beyond that which the department was capable of delivering because the grounds were close to the church, the members lived in the area, and they took pride in doing the work.

Seattle's parks and recreation department contracted with 20 community groups to provide maintenance in a number of the city's smaller neighborhood parks. Participating groups either approached the city directly or were recruited by the department. The program dispensed monthly amounts that ranged from $300 to $500, for a total annual cost to the city of $60,000. For the most part, payments were retained by the community organization itself; however, in a few cases, these organizations did pay the persons—usually neighborhood women—who did the actual work. The amount of payments was based on pre-established estimates of how long certain maintenance tasks should take. Work performance was monitored by district crew chiefs. Although holding down maintenance outlays was a consideration, officials emphasized that a more important motive was stimulating pride and concern. Among the indirect benefits was a considerable reduction in vandalism.

The success of coproduction will depend not only on the strength of potential community organization partners but also on the responsiveness of park and recreation personnel to the concept and on their ability to embrace the different types of managerial skills it requires. Some tension and friction may occur in partnerships between agency personnel, whose pay raises may depend upon performance quality, and community volunteers, who make a part-time contribution for the good of the community. Personnel may be resistant to coproduction if they 1) see it as a threat to their position or professional standing or as a usurpation of their power or authority, 2) regard the organization's people as being inadequately trained, 3) perceive the personal effort required of them as being substantially greater than the effort required if the service were directly delivered, or 4) perceive the community organization as having a different value culture from that which prevails in the public agency. A transition to coproduction

will require retraining employees. The management skills required for direct delivery where employees have exclusive control, such as administration, fiscal management, and operational procedures, will need to be replaced by skills that emphasize interactions, brokering, mediation, negotiation, networking, and entrepreneurship.

Demonstrating Accountability

In the past, coproduction arrangements typically have been relatively informal without a written contract or formal evaluation. This is changing as agencies increasingly are required to demonstrate responsible stewardship of the public resources with which they are entrusted. More emphasis is being placed on documenting the leveraging impact of their coproduction investments.

For example, as one of its criteria in evaluating coproduction opportunities, Indianapolis Parks and Recreation Department required the resources provided by the community organization be equal in value to those that the department expended. The department developed a standard Understanding-of-Agreement form to document the relative contributions. An illustration of how it is used is given in figure 12.3. This was not a formal contract, but it clearly established the expectations and responsibilities of both entities. It assisted in ensuring accountability by forming the basis for a joint evaluation of the resource contributions of both entities after the event. Figure 12.3 shows that the community organization's investment in the special garden show event totaled approximately $11,000, including an $8,000 contribution to Friends of Holliday Park, the support group for the park at which the event was held. The department matched this amount. Much of its investment was in in-kind rather than in cash resources. Each entity kept a detailed tracking log of all of its contributions to the project. When the project was completed, actual investments were compared with those that were specified in the original Understanding-of-Agreement document, and adjustments were made if necessary.

Agency Conduits for Investing in Coproduction

There are a number of different conduits through which agencies may contribute resources to community organizations in coproduction agreements. The most common arrangement is for an agency to provide and maintain facilities and for the public

Event name: Orchard in Bloom Garden Show

Event description: The Orchard Country Day School Parents' Association, in conjunction with Indy Parks and the Friends of Holliday Park, organize the Orchard Bloom Garden Show at Holliday Park. This event is a fundraiser for Orchard Country Day School and the Friends of Holliday Park.

Project type: Alliance

Target market: Families, persons interested in gardening, multi-state region draw

Event location: Holliday Park

Dates of event: April 29, 30, and May 1

Goal of Orchard in Bloom Committee: To organize a garden show event through volunteer efforts, partnering with Indy Parks resources, that serves as a fundraiser to Orchard Country Day School and the Friends of Holliday Park.

Orchard in Bloom contributions/responsibilities	Dollar value	Orchard in Bloom contributions/responsibilities	Dollar value
Repairing event damage on grass and road sides	$ 628.00	20 passes to event	$ 160.00
Two truckloads of topsoil		Mulch	$ 288.00
Aerator rental		Used on Rock Garden, % of total amount brought	
Fertilizer		Pansy plantings	$ 30.50
Grass seed		Two flats @ $12 + 1 hour ($6.50)	
High school youth labor		Tree prunings	$ 475.00
Symposium: Children/plants/gardens scholarships	$ 330.00	Judd Scott	
Six IP staff ($55/person)		Cash contribution to Friends of Holliday Park	$ 8,000.00
Table at opening night party	$ 480.00	(15% of net profits, not to exceed $8,000)	
(Pansy Passion Preview Party)		**Total contribution of Orchard in Bloom (contributions + cash)**	**$10,966.50**
Recognition of Indy Parks in Pansy Passion Program		Orchard in Bloom expected net revenue (excluding cash contribution to Friends of Holliday Park)	$46,000.00
Full page ad in program	$ 575.00		

Orchard in Bloom promotional contributions (that included Indy Parks)

Landscapers tent sponsor sign	TV/radio spots	Showbook program
IPR name on sign at sponsorship tent entrance	IPR name on contributor board	IBJ article
Indianapolis Register insert (20,000 distribution)	Posters, flyers, yard signs	Invitations
Sponsor recognition signage	Indianapolis news article	Indianapolis Star article

Total expenditure in these areas by Orchard in Bloom totaled approximately $20,000. This total is not listed in the main contribution, because these are indirect benefits to Indy Parks.

Goals of Indy Parks: To partner with neighborhood groups to share responsibilities and expenses in organizing events that maximize the use of parks, and create activities that could not exist if each party tried to do it alone.

Indy Parks contributions/responsibilities	Dollar value	Indy Parks contributions/responsibilities	Dollar value
Holliday Park rental		Disposal of sawdust	$ 774.32
Wedding Circle, 3.5 weekdays		Electrical use—outdoor outlet	$ 35.00
($225/day) . . . Wed, Thurs, Fri, 1/2 Mon	$ 787.50	IPR staff time (John and Janice)	
Ruins, 9 weekdays ($225/day)	$ 2,025.00	(Wed, Thurs, Fri, meetings) 64 total hours	$ 1,000.00
Wedding Circle, 2 weekend days		Volunteer hours ($6.50/hour)	
($510/day)	$ 1,020.00	40 hours	$ 260.00
Ruins, 4 weekend days ($510/day)	$ 2,040.00	Indy Parks cash contribution	$ 0.00
Holliday House, 3.5 weekdays		**Total Indy Parks contribution**	
($425/day) . . . Wed, Thurs, Fri, 1/2 Mon	$ 1,487.50	**(contributions + cash)**	**$11,157.45**
Holliday House, 2 weekend days		Expected revenue	
($830/day)	$ 1,660.00	Donation from OCDSPA to Friends of Holliday Park (15% of net profits,	
Rolling of ground	$ 61.13	not to exceed $8,000)	$ 8,000.00
Removal of bollards	$ 7.00		

Contact persons: Indy Parks, John Schaust, 327-7180:W
Orchard in Bloom, Patti Halloran, 259-1515:H

Figure 12.3 A sample Understanding of Agreement between Orchard Bloom Garden Show and Indianapolis Parks and Recreation Department.

Source: Jeff Coates, Indianapolis Parks and Recreation Department.

organization to be responsible for programs that use them. Many agencies offer in-kind and technical assistance to organizations, often on an informal ad hoc basis. Some have moved into rental programs that offer groups and individuals the opportunity to rent recreational and hand-maintenance equipment. For example, portable scoreboards and field line markers may be rented to softball leagues for their games; timing equipment, to competitive swimming, running, or triathlon groups; or shovels, trash barrels, and hand-maintenance equipment to groups that want to improve their local parks.

A few jurisdictions have established low- or no-interest loan programs that make it easier for public organizations to become involved in capital projects. For example, Calvert County, Maryland, set up a revolving loan fund to help nonprofit organizations buy recreational and natural land, park buffers, and historic sites. The fund was the first in Maryland. It was created by special state legislation and seeded with $1 million from Calvert County. The fund offered interest-free loans. Nonprofit organizations owned and managed the land, which also was protected with county-held conservation easements.[9]

A growing number of agencies are establishing grant programs to aid community organizations. Some use a standard proposal or application format and process, and they incorporate the organizations' grant requests into their formal budget preparation procedure. Organizations usually are invited to seek assistance from agency staff in developing and submitting their proposals so that they are represented and presented as favorably as possible.

Grant applications may be evaluated by staff, by a community advisory board, or by some combination of both. Often the grants are restricted to cost of materials or equipment, and the organization is expected to volunteer or pay for the labor component of a project or program. Further, organizations usually are required to accept responsibility for maintenance of any facilities or equipment funded with the grant.

The city of Aurora, Colorado, made grants to neighborhood-based organizations to undertake public improvement projects in their neighborhoods. These included tree and shrub plantings and park and playground improvements. Organizations or groups of neighbors applied for grants of up to $5,000. A group was required to provide at least a 25% local match for the grant, usually in the form of labor or donated resources. All improvements had to be on public land or right-of-way and, in most cases, had to be maintained by the community. The funds could be used for materials, rental of equipment, specialized labor, or construction management. The city provided technical assistance in project design and implementation.[10]

Hartford Parks and Recreation Department annually distributed announcements inviting neighborhood residents and groups to contract with it to operate recreational programs using grant funds from the city. Recreation staff helped in planning the programs, preparing budgets, and writing proposals. Advisory councils comprising neighborhood residents reviewed the proposals and decided which would be funded with their fixed neighborhood allocation. Between 100 and 150 contracts were written each year. These contracts ranged in size from $500 to $8,000 and were monitored by recreation staff. While many of the programs were conventional, others might not have occurred to even the most imaginative recreation director.

Vouchers

A major challenge associated with implementing a grants program is making decisions about which programs and community organizations should receive the limited funds and about what portion of the available money should be awarded to each group. Vouchers offer a way to resolve this conundrum by putting emphasis on citizens' judgment rather than on the expertise and good intentions of agency personnel. Vouchers are subsidies to participants, and these are invariably more efficient than grants, which are subsidies to service suppliers, because they enhance citizen choice. To this point, vouchers have received little attention from park and recreation agencies, but the author believes that they have the potential to be used in a variety of situations.

The basic idea of vouchers is to give resources to citizens so that they can purchase the services of their choice from authorized suppliers. A public agency issues vouchers to citizens. Citizens exchange their vouchers for services that their preferred supplier delivers. The provider of the services then returns them to the agency and receives cash for the vouchers acquired. Vouchers are a way of increasing an agency's responsiveness to citizens' needs and demands. They give citizens choice and control of service delivery.

Medicare, the food stamp program, some public housing assistance programs, and the GI Bill are all examples of voucher systems that the federal government administers. For example, under the terms of the GI Bill, former military personnel receive a funding allocation for their education. These individuals select where to spend this allocation from among a wide range of authorized tertiary educational institutions. The federal government then reimburses the educational institution, making the allocation in effect a voucher.

The only extended voucher program in the park and recreation field of which the author is aware was undertaken some years ago in the city of South Barwon in Australia. A description of its operation is included in the following paragraphs because it offers useful insights into the opportunities and challenges associated with its implementation in this field.

Located about 50 mi from Melbourne, the city of South Barwon had a population of 40,000 and operated a recreation voucher program for approximately 15 years. The voucher scheme was only discontinued when the city of South Barwon was merged in the mid-1990s with eight other local jurisdictions to form a single new political entity called Greater Geelong.

The city of South Barwon budgeted $570,000 for park and recreation services, which constituted 17% of its total tax revenues. Of this total, $70,000 covered its recreation voucher scheme and $500,000 was allocated to park and recreation services in the traditional manner. All recognized, private, nonprofit, and community recreation organizations in South Barwon that did not receive any services for parks and recreation from the $500,000 annual appropriation by the city council were eligible to receive funds from the voucher program. Organizations could use these funds for either capital or operating purposes because the city council placed no restriction on their use. Recipients of voucher funds were required to describe the benefits that accrued from using these funds. The city then considered these responses and ruled upon each organization's eligibility in its annual application for inclusion in the voucher scheme.

Guidelines for administering the voucher scheme in South Barwon are shown in "City of South Barwon Guidelines for Recreation Voucher Grants" on page 332. When each taxpayer received his or her tax bill, a recreation voucher was included with a list of recreation organizations that had been approved by the council to receive grants. The value of each voucher was printed on it. Two different organizations could be nominated on each voucher, but the full amount could also be committed to a single organization. A voucher was issued for each taxable property in the city, so owners of more than one property received a corresponding multiple number of vouchers. By completing a voucher and returning it to the city, a taxpayer effectively was saying: "Take $20 (if that was the voucher's value) of my tax payment and give it to recreation body X," or, "Divide it and give $10 each to recreation organizations Y and Z."

Each returned voucher was numbered, and taxpayers were required to include their name, address, signature, and tax assessment number on it. This information authenticated the vouchers and further safeguarded against possible forgery. The individual taxpayer's nominated organization or organizations were confidential. Finally, the city distributed taxpayers' votes to organizations in the form of checks for the value of the total vouchers that taxpayers allocated to each group.

Any genuinely nonprofit community recreation groups were eligible for admission to the scheme. An organization simply submitted an application to the city each year. This application required information relating to the location of the organization, its activities, and its membership fees. One person on the city staff served as liaison for the voucher program and made recommendations on eligibility to the council. Groups from outside the city limits were permitted to participate in the scheme if they provided services to city residents. This provision recognized that some specialized activities may not be available within the city's boundaries. However, for an external organization to qualify, there had to be no providers of similar services within the city.

Expenses associated with administering the scheme were low. Approximately 300 staff-hours were required to distribute and collate the vouchers. Additional personnel and supply costs were limited to printing vouchers and application forms, buying postage, recording lists of organizations and vouchers received, processing checks, considering groups for approval, and addressing correspondence related to this task.

Expectations of the South Barwon Voucher Scheme

The city hoped that the recreation vouchers would achieve four results: provide recreation services that were more responsive to citizen desires, offer seed funds that would encourage the creation of new recreational opportunities, better meet the recreation needs of disadvantaged groups, and

City of South Barwon Guidelines for Recreation Voucher Grants

1. All clubs and organizations must be first approved by council before being eligible to receive a grant.

2. To qualify, clubs must be noncommercial, recreation or sporting organizations operating, or about to operate, within the city of South Barwon. If outside the city of South Barwon, the club must not duplicate recreation services offered by any club or sporting organization within the city of South Barwon.

3. Recreation vouchers are valid in the municipal year of issue only.

4. Canvassing of support for the return of vouchers from the general taxpaying community will not be permitted and could cause council to immediately disqualify that club from receiving further grants.

5. Vouchers must be returned to the city offices with tax payments. The name of the chosen club must be designated clearly on the voucher.

6. Clubs must submit an application each year for registration to qualify for a further grant. These applications must be accompanied by details of current officebearers, etc., as requested.

7. The payment of the grant will be forwarded to the club's address as shown on the application for registration unless written notification is given to the contrary.

8. Vouchers are not transferable.

9. Vouchers not directly assigned by ratepayers will not be redeemed.

10. Vouchers assigned to non-approved clubs or clubs that do not qualify will not be redeemed.

11. The identity of taxpayers designating vouchers for any particular club will be retained by council as confidential information. However, the total number of vouchers received by any club may be publicized.

12. Where the amount of vouchers allocated by taxpayers in any year is less than the funds set aside by council for this purpose, the balance of funds will not be distributed among the clubs receiving grants.

13. Council reserves the right to withhold payment of a grant to a club.

14. Approval of a club as an organization qualified to receive a grant under one year does not necessarily pre-qualify that club for subsequent years.

15. Where a club based outside the municipality qualifies for a grant, this may be withdrawn in writing by council when a club with similar activities commences operation within the municipality and becomes qualified.

16. Organizations that presently are provided for or operated with substantial council support, such as libraries and elderly citizens clubs, do not qualify for a grant.

17. Organizations, such as political or religious organizations, do not qualify for a grant. However, bona fide recreational clubs that are part of such organizations may be approved by council.

resolve the council's annual difficulty of deciding which nonprofit recreation groups should be supported with public funds. These issues are elaborated on in the following paragraphs.

There was a concern that the city had become unresponsive in its allocation of resources for recreation services by supporting the same groups year after year even though priorities had changed. The city had always subsidized the traditional, male-dominated, major Australian sports of football, cricket, and field hockey by developing capital facilities (e.g., playing fields) and changing accommodations and by accepting responsibility for general maintenance of these areas. These facilities were rented to private, nonprofit clubs at nominal rates and typically were leased for approximately 10% of their maintenance cost. In most cases, clubs that rented them had exclusive use for the relevant season. Such financial arrangements meant that the city subsidized each active participant group member with approximately $23 per year.

However, other minor sport and recreation groups, such as those offering track and field, netball, badminton, baseball, surf lifesaving, lawn bowls, tennis, creative arts, and many others, received virtually no public support even though they provided similar recreational opportunities. Indeed, in total, these minor clubs that received no assistance from public funds had a clientele similar in size to that of the substantially subsidized traditional sport clubs.

The voucher scheme was intended to alleviate this imbalance by enabling taxpayers to become active selectors instead of passive receivers of recreation services. With this plan, citizens could direct their allocation for the recreation subsidy to their chosen pursuit and not pay to subsidize someone else's recreation. Because they had more control over the delivery of recreation services, the system was perceived to be more responsive to citizens' wishes. The intent was that offerings effectively meeting people's perceived needs would prosper, and those that did not would be either redesigned or discontinued. Organizations received public funds only to the extent that they could attract support from citizens.

It was hoped that vouchers would introduce dynamism and encourage diversity in the recreation system by spreading the recreation dollar more evenly to meet the many interests that were not being served. There was a specific expectation that new recreational organizations would emerge. An internal city document stated: "We could see new community organizations being formed and different recreational activities started. We could see families coming together to form Family Fitness Groups or participate in Family New Games. The money redeemed for the vouchers could be used by new groups to purchase equipment or hire a venue in which to stage their activities. A whole host of new recreation activities could be created."

The South Barwon Council was conscious that too often the very young, the aged, the physically handicapped, and the socially and economically deprived were being neglected in favor of physically active people. The voucher scheme was conceived as "a possible stimulant to the 'recreationally inactive' to start them exploring the many lesser-known opportunities now available throughout the community." The city recognized that it could justifiably be accused of an elitist approach to providing recreation services if it continued to subsidize opportunities solely for the existing active population.

The final expected effect of recreation vouchers was that the council would no longer have to select which nonprofit recreation groups should receive public subsidies. These decisions often aroused controversy because some interest groups inevitably were passed over in favor of others. Using vouchers transferred the selection decision from the council to the citizens. With a voucher scheme, it was expected that recreation organizations would no longer try to exert pressure on council members but instead would recognize that public resources could only be obtained by offering services that people wanted. The voucher scheme enabled elected officials to say to all groups soliciting funds: "If your service is valuable, then the citizens will demonstrate their support by committing their vouchers to it." The scheme also permitted the subsidizing of groups that had a substantial constituency but were politically controversial.

Finally, the city recognized that one of the most difficult tasks facing any government is how to terminate a service that it has supported traditionally. Vouchers enabled citizens to make this decision; therefore, city officials would not be subjected to the pressure that inevitably arises from terminating support of a special interest.

Lessons and Limitations of the South Barwon Voucher Scheme

The simplicity of the voucher scheme implemented in South Barwon may be somewhat deceptive. While it was an exciting innovation, it had several limitations, and in the years that they operated this system, city officials learned many lessons. These limitations and lessons are discussed here under six headings: opposition from entrenched interests, monitoring the scheme, ambiguity in defining recreation, the nonreturned decision, imperfect communication, and the equity issue.

• *Opposition from Entrenched Interests*: It was anticipated that if the voucher scheme was funded by taking money from the existing recreation services budget, then traditional beneficiaries would vigorously oppose vouchers and make the scheme politically unfeasible. Therefore, a supplementary appropriation was added to the recreation budget to fund the voucher scheme.

The original intent was that the ratio of voucher funding to traditional funding gradually would move toward an equal division of the two financing methods over a period of years. This intent was not realized because vigorous opposition emerged from those who saw that their share would decrease if this shift occurred, particularly in the major sports of cricket, football, and field hockey. Indeed, councilors who were involved personally with these major sports sought to abolish the voucher scheme or to reduce, rather than to increase, its role. They perceived it as a threat to the financial support that these major sports traditionally received from the city.

Some of the council who were not fully supportive of vouchers challenged their usefulness in reflecting the preferences of taxpayers. They suggested that while the vouchers gave some indication of general support for particular recreational activities in the community, they should be interpreted with great care because people are capable of taking a benevolent attitude and can issue vouchers to clubs that need the most help, rather than to their first choice of recreational activity.

• *Monitoring the Scheme*: For a voucher scheme to work, it must be monitored from the outset. Groups that attempt abuses must be sanctioned in order to establish the legitimacy of the scheme. The city issued guidelines, but while carefully following the written rules, some groups sought to abrogate the intent of the voucher program.

A perceived danger was that recreation organizations would be tempted to spend great amounts of time, energy, and money on public relations and propaganda activities. The general canvassing of taxpayers to request them to assign their vouchers to a particular organization was prohibited because of possible adverse reactions to solicitations or junk mail deliveries.

Vouchers were only accepted directly from taxpayers so that they could not be collected and handed in by a beneficiary group. This prevented the possibility of fellow members harassing individuals who belonged to several organizations. It also precluded the possibility of an organization soliciting vouchers through raffles or similar methods. Before this rule was implemented, one imaginative organization announced a raffle for a vacation to the Fiji Islands. The entry ticket for the raffle was a completed recreation voucher assigned to that group!

The city believed that extra emphasis on promotion had some positive dimensions, particularly in increasing citizens' awareness of the recreational opportunities available in South Barwon. The simple act of providing a list of organizations to citizens and asking them to select one or two to support had the spin-off benefit of improving awareness.

• *Ambiguity in Defining Recreation*: When it was first introduced, a significant limitation of the South Barwon scheme was its failure to define recreation precisely and clearly. Initially, the city did not recognize the importance of this issue. Consequently, the criteria for admission to the voucher scheme were fuzzy. This created a continuing problem because, after criteria were established, efforts to amend them became controversial and had to be abandoned. The criteria were set out in item 2 of the guidelines. They were generic rather than specific, requiring only that an organization be "non-commercial and recreational and/or sporting."

Lack of specificity in these criteria caused the interpretation of what constituted recreation to be broadened incrementally each year. It resulted in the inclusion of a number of community service groups whose involvement with recreation was relatively peripheral. These groups often had a long-established tradition of voluntary community service and of receipt of donations from citizens. Their name recognition was high, so they received substantial support, which detracted from one of the original intents of the voucher program: to encourage more responsive offerings and a greater diversity of recreational opportunities.

• *The Nonreturned Decision*: Typically, there was a 50% return rate for the vouchers. The redemption rate is likely to be influenced by what happens to the $20 if taxpayers do not complete and return their vouchers. Under the GI Bill, for example, servicemen and servicewomen forfeit their vouchers if they choose not to use the educational opportunity. The same rule was adopted in South Barwon. If the voucher was not returned, then the city did not spend the $20. Effectively, this nonresponse reduced the annual tax bill, so it may appear that there was incentive for non-users not to return the vouchers. However, the individual taxpayer does not receive the $20 as credit. This savings must be shared with those who do return their vouchers. Therefore, nonreturners forego the opportunity to allocate $20 but, assuming that 50% of the vouchers are returned, only receive $10 in tax savings. Individuals who assign their vouchers allocate $20 and also receive the benefit of a $10 tax saving because 50% of the citizens did not assign their vouchers.

Other decision rules that could be considered include returning the unredeemed voucher money to the general fund and disbursing it for other uses, returning it to the traditional budget for recreation services, or distributing the unassigned dollars pro rata among the organizations receiving support from those citizens who did assign their vouchers.

• *Imperfect Communication*: The communication issue consists of three dimensions. The first dimension concerns the need to know how other citizens assign their vouchers. In South Barwon, people redeemed their vouchers within a single time period. The city made no interim announcements about the amount of money accruing to each organization, and this lack of information could lead to undesirable results. For example, assume that a group of taxpayers wanted to encourage the development of four organizations, but they were able to assign dollars to only two of them. If they all voted for numbers one and two, then organizations three and four would be left without support. However, if they had better information about how other taxpayers were assigning their vouchers, some might have switched their dollars to organizations three and four in an attempt to ensure that they received a minimal level of support.

The evidence suggests that a second source of imperfect communication was the difficulty in explaining the concept of recreation vouchers to citizens in the early years. Although response rates built up to 50%, only 16% of taxpayers returned their vouchers in the first year. The proportion increased as understanding of the program improved.

The third dimension of imperfect communication concerns the need for citizens to be familiar with the groups seeking their vouchers. Imperfect information causes inequities and inefficiency. When citizens do not possess sufficient knowledge to make intelligent choices among organizations, they become vulnerable to hucksterism. This concern is particularly important for poorer citizens who notoriously are hard to reach through printed material.

One of the expectations of the recreation-voucher scheme was that it would place financial resources directly into the hands of the economically disadvantaged, enabling them to select recreation services most relevant to their needs.

While this goal is laudable, its attainment may be chimerical because of the information access inequities that may accompany a voucher scheme. Theoretically, affirmative dissemination efforts could be designed and undertaken with special attention to the informational needs of the economically disadvantaged. However, this task is likely to be too difficult and expensive to be practical.

• *The Equity Issue*: Perhaps the most obvious limitation of the South Barwon scheme involved the weighting and distribution of the vouchers. To receive a voucher, residents had to pay real property taxes directly. This created two kinds of inequities. First, there were inequities among those who paid property taxes. Only residential property—not commercial property—was included in the scheme. Further, the absentee landowner, single-family homeowner, and 100-unit apartment owner each received the same one-voucher allocation.

Second, inequities existed because some citizens did not pay property taxes directly. An initial expectation of the voucher scheme was that it might better serve disadvantaged citizens. However, there was no evidence indicating that this group benefited. Because the disadvantaged were more likely to live in rental units, landlords, in fact, assumed more control. This had the pernicious effect of successfully disenfranchising the poor from choosing the types and extent of recreational activities entitled to public financial assistance.

Usefulness of Vouchers and Future Directions

The usefulness of vouchers in the delivery of public services has generated substantial discussion over a relatively long period of time; however, there have been few opportunities to gain insights from their application at the local government level. Generalizations and implications from the South Barwon experience can be suggested only with caution because it was limited in scope and funding amounts. Obvious dangers also are presented by generalizing from a single experience in a specific jurisdiction with a high per-capita income and a highly educated population that is located in a country with different traditions from those prevailing in North America. Nevertheless, it does illuminate several points of interest. Like many Australian cities, South Barwon did not employ many recreation professionals. Community recreation traditionally was facilitated with seed money or in-kind maintenance assistance to nonprofit organizations. Thus, there was no opportunity to observe how an established professional staff would react to a voucher scheme. However, resistance emerged from those representing traditional entrenched interests and prevented expansion of the plan that officials originally had envisioned.

Vouchers give citizens direct control over resource allocation decisions and, thus, offer intriguing possibilities for demonstrating responsiveness and accountability to citizens' demands. Implementation is likely to be more difficult in a larger jurisdiction because of increased logistical problems and greater difficulty in monitoring the procedure to minimize abuse. Success depends on a willingness to monitor the marketplace vigorously. If vouchers were used on a large scale, such regulatory efforts might be uneven.

The voucher concept is flexible enough to support a wide variety of specific applications. Indeed, although the scheme that South Barwon operated was an exciting innovation, it represented a rather tentative application of the voucher principle. Other applications could lead to much more radical changes in the structure and type of service delivery. For example, instead of limiting a voucher scheme to providing funds that encourage production by nonprofit organizations, cities could broaden it to incorporate recreational offerings, such as swimming pools and recreational centers, directly operated by a municipality. In this situation, citizens would control the total recreation budget.

Citizens could retain vouchers and use them as directly redeemable coupons or certificates instead of returning them to the city. With this mechanism, citizens could directly contract for the services they desired. Vouchers could be used to purchase specific types of recreation services from authorized public and private suppliers. The supplier would then return the voucher to the city for redemption at its face value. Redeemable vouchers could be used to remove the monopolistic impact of service delivery and deliberately stimulate competition both within the public and nonprofit sectors and among public, nonprofit, and private agencies. This may streamline the system and lead to increased accountability, greater cost efficiency, and more-relevant service delivery.

Clearly, there is a danger that resources may be allocated to the most persuasive, rather than to the most responsive, organizations. In South Barwon, traditional volunteer agencies that had substantial name identification gained a disproportionately large share of the voucher resources without making any noticeable efforts to be more responsive. This suggests that image may be more important than substance. Thus, organizations may decide to divert considerable time, energy, and dollars to promotion rather than to focusing these resources on service.

The method of disseminating information is a crucial consideration. In South Barwon, this method was limited to providing taxpayers with a list of eligible organizations, and naturally, citizens had a higher awareness of long-established agencies. A substantial commitment to disseminating more-detailed information as part of the voucher system is required if new organizations are to be encouraged. This is particularly important if groups with relatively low educational levels are to be reached. Reliance on traditional approaches to transmitting information to these groups is unlikely to succeed. Unless everyone has equal access to information, including an equal ability to understand it, it cannot be said that all citizens have free choice, which is a fundamental premise of voucher schemes.

The South Barwon experience demonstrated the feasibility of using vouchers in the recreation field and identified a number of ways that this approach could be improved. The next step would appear to be for some recreation agencies in North America to implement voucher use on a small scale, incorporating the suggested improvements from the South Barwon scheme. This would enable professionals to further refine the principle and to test its appropriateness in the North American context.

Summary

Facilitation can take a variety of forms that can be arranged along a continuum ranging from opportunity referrals requiring minimal agency investment, to technical assistance and brokering, to coproduction that may involve substantial agency investment. Coproduction is the closest form of facilitation to direct delivery and is defined as a process in which individuals or community organizations participate jointly with a public agency in the production of park and recreation services of which they or their families are the primary beneficiaries.

Six advantages that support the case for agencies pursuing a strategy of coproduction rather than direct delivery have been identified. They are rebuilding an ethos of self-reliance in communities rather than municipalizing everything, rebuilding empathy for government by involving citizens in working more closely with it, reducing service cost or enhancing quality so that the amount of service delivered per tax dollar is leveraged, enhancing responsiveness because more decisions are made by user groups, using citizens' talents and enthusiasm, and enhancing socialization opportunities that emerge from jointly engaging in projects with others.

Three concerns have to be addressed before moving to a coproduction approach. They are loss of political support potentially arising from the greater difficulty of demonstrating accountability and results to elected officials; equity issues arising from the potential exclusion of some segments of the community who are unable to pay fees, provide leadership, or organize themselves; and reduced quality of service resulting from turnover in volunteer leadership.

As long as agencies directly deliver services at the desired level of quality, there is no incentive for citizens to invest effort in coproduction. Thus, transitioning to coproduction from direct delivery is likely to occur only if an agency reduces the quality level or terminates a service, if an agency does not provide resources for either a new service or a higher level of existing service that users desire, or if a community organization perceives coproduction as a means of raising funds for its cause through the sweat equity of its members. It is likely to be easier for an agency to acquire resources to extend services through joint provision with community groups than for it to persuade elected officials to hire additional staff for direct delivery of services. The success of coproduction will depend not only on the strength of the community organization partners but also on the responsiveness of park and recreation personnel to the concept and on their ability to embrace the different types of managerial skills it requires. Agencies increasingly are required to demonstrate responsible stewardship of public resources, which has led to more emphasis being placed on documenting the leveraging impact of their coproduction investments.

Agencies' investments in coproduction may take many forms including provision and maintenance of facilities, in-kind and technical assistance, equipment rental, and low- or no-interest loans. A growing number are establishing grant programs and inviting community organizations to apply for funds on a competitive basis.

Vouchers potentially offer a responsive way for agencies to allocate grant funds for coproduction. Vouchers enable citizens to purchase the recreation service of their choice from a list of authorized nonprofit suppliers, who redeem the vouchers from the agency for cash. Recreation vouchers are perceived to have the potential to achieve four results: provide recreation services that are more responsive to citizen desires, offer seed funds that will encourage the creation of new recreational opportunities, better meet the recreation needs of disadvantaged groups, and resolve the difficulty of deciding which nonprofit community groups should be supported with public funds and how much should be given to each.

References

1. Crompton, John L. 1982. Save service delivery costs by giving responsibility for neighborhood public recreation services back to the citizens. *Spirit* 2(2): 26-29.

2. Caldwell, Linda L. and Kathleen L. Anderek. 1994. Motives for initiating and continuing membership in a recreation-related voluntary association. *Leisure Sciences* 16: 33-44.

3. Reed, David J. 1997. Community partnership transforms neighborhood. *Friends of Parks and Recreation* 6(1): 18.

4. Osborne, David and Ted Gaebler. 1992. *Reinventing government*. Reading, MA: Addison-Wesley.

5. Envisaged by a group of concerned recreationists. Interpreted by Ken Balmer. *The Elora prescription: A future for recreation*. 1978. Ottawa, ON: Ministry of Culture and Recreation.

6. Buller, Cynthia. 1983. Yesterday's idea meets today's needs. *Recreation Alberta* April: 12-13.

7. Brudney, Jeffrey L. 1987. Coproduction and privatization: Exploring the relationship and its implications. *Journal of Voluntary Action Research* 16(3): 11-21.

8. Levine, Charles H. 1984. Citizenship and service delivery: The promise of coproduction. *Public Administration Review* 44: 178-187.

9. Myers, Phyllis. 1996. New deals. *Greensense* 2(2): 4.

10. Valente, Carl F. and Lydia D. Manchester. 1984. *Rethinking local services: Examining alternative delivery approaches. Special report #12*. Washington, DC: International City Management Association.

PART III

SUPPORT
FROM
EXTERNAL
SOURCES

CHAPTER 13

SUPPORT FROM VOLUNTEERS

The three keys to American democracy are involvement, civic spirit, and volunteerism.

Alexis de Tocqueville 1835

The oldest military wisdom advises: Never volunteer for anything. Americans have traditionally ignored this advice. The involvement of citizens on an unpaid basis in a wide variety of park and recreation functions has a long tradition. Indeed, the organized recreation movement began with volunteer leadership, and many park and recreation systems evolved from volunteer organizations and efforts.

Volunteering differs from coproduction, which was discussed in chapter 12. In coproduction, residents' contributions are voluntary, but they participate in producing a service because they or their family directly benefit from its output. Volunteers, as defined in this chapter, personally do not gain material benefits from the service output; it is others who do so.

Many park and recreation agencies are able to recruit individuals from court-ordered restitution programs that require them to spend time working on civic projects. This may include people convicted of driving while intoxicated, parolees, individuals in half-way houses, or long-term prisoners who are gradually introduced to the world outside of prison before they are released. While these people are a useful source of external resources, there is an element of coercion in their recruitment, which means that they do not qualify as volunteers and are outside the scope of this chapter.

By definition, volunteers are not paid for their labor. Indeed, some volunteers even pay for the privilege of volunteering. For example, members of the Volunteer Conservation Corps take working vacations each summer in national forests and parks. They agree to provide their own transportation to their work areas. They also provide their own equipment, pay a registration fee, and sometimes buy their own food! However, on occasion agencies may reimburse volunteers for out-of-pocket expenses, such as transportation, meals, and uniforms.

Volunteers should be made aware that they are entitled to a number of tax benefits under the charitable contribution provisions of the Internal Revenue Code. They may deduct expenses incurred when servicing a government agency or certain private nonprofit groups. Examples of deductible expenses include transportation, special uniforms, telephone calls, meals, and lodging.

However, they may not deduct the value of the time they contribute.

Volunteers have changed. They used to be primarily homemakers, but today they are as likely to be senior citizens, young adults, or middle managers. A volunteer today may come from a variety of backgrounds and may even be someone who in former years would have received help from volunteers. The potential of the handicapped, welfare recipient, and mentally retarded for assisting a park and recreation agency may be substantial, but it is rarely recognized. To invite them to serve as volunteers may be paying them a compliment. It may say to them, "We want you," and may provide them with a feeling of self-worth. Many senior citizens who could be actively involved are not asked to help simply because the people who do the asking are used to relying on young people or housewives as volunteers, and the habit is slow to change.

The changing patterns of work and family have transformed the world of the volunteer. Agencies are arranging programs after regular working hours and on weekends so that working people can volunteer. A volunteer coordinator in Houston noted:

> We take jobs to volunteers, and not the other way around. We've got executives doing volunteer work downtown between five and six-thirty in the afternoon so they can do something while they're waiting for the traffic to clear besides go sit in a bar. We've been recruiting people who like to jog to come over to Hermann Park and jog with the blind (p.5).[1]

This chapter begins with a review of the potential benefits that may accrue to a park and recreation agency from using volunteers, a discussion of what motivates volunteers to offer their services, and a description of the differentiating attributes of corporate volunteers. The discussion then focuses on the actions that agencies need to take so their organizations attain a state of readiness to receive volunteers. The remainder of the chapter considers how to recruit volunteers and then how to retain them.

Benefits That Volunteers Bring to an Agency

The most obvious benefit from recruiting volunteers is the additional labor that they supply. Volunteers offer an agency a means of leveraging its resources to derive more productivity from its existing funds and personnel. Without them, the level and range of park and recreation services offered would decline substantially in many agencies. It is important that volunteer labor is viewed as a means of improving an agency's type, level, and quality of services and not as a cost-saving device. Volunteers are unlikely to offer their services if they sense that they are regarded as a means of cheap labor. Further, for cost savings to occur, volunteers would have to replace paid personnel, which is likely to be counterproductive. If this occurs, "the results are lamentable and predictable in the form of resentments and antagonisms that have repeatedly subverted volunteer initiatives" (p. 45).[2]

The range of activities that volunteers may undertake is extensive. "Mobilizing Volunteers Through a Neighborhood Park Enhancement Program" describes an extensive citywide volunteer program whose goal was to improve the mainte-

nance of neighborhood parks. "99 Ways Volunteers Can Help in National Parks" on page 344 provides an indication of the wide array of tasks that volunteers can undertake. This list was derived from a survey of superintendents at selected national parks. However, volunteer tasks can be classified into three categories:

- Administrative volunteers who contribute as members of boards, commissions, advisory groups, or in other policy-related or fundraising functions
- Program volunteers who help to plan, carry out, or support program activities including direct leadership, coaching, transportation, providing entertainment, or similar roles
- Staff volunteers who assist in clerical, maintenance, or other related roles[3]

Mobilizing Volunteers
Through a Neighborhood Park Enhancement Program

Indianapolis Parks and Recreation Department recognized that the key to renovating and maintaining the city's neighborhood parks was to mobilize neighborhood volunteers. Each neighborhood park was provided with a park department staff member who was designated an ambassador. Ambassadors were responsible for introducing the Neighborhood Park Enhancement program to the community at each site. The intent was to organize neighborhood volunteers to be responsible for keeping the facility free of trash, discouraging vandalism, and contributing labor to periodic beautification efforts at the facility. The ambassadors communicated the department's standards of maintenance to the community and the community's concerns about maintenance needs to the park maintenance staff.

Each ambassador made a weekly inspection of the park, noting comments on a standard 70-item check list and reporting quality concerns to park maintenance staff and neighborhood leaders. Each ambassador was required to dedicate a minimum of 3 h each month to communicating with neighborhood leaders. The neighborhood group could comprise neighborhood associations, churches, businesses, schools, service organizations, and others. In some instances, ambassadors trained and contracted with neighborhood groups to do the routine weekly inspections of neighborhood parks. This enhanced their sense of ownership in the park as well as freeing up staff time.

Each year, at least one major cleanup and beautification project in each park was organized. Typically, this involved large numbers of local people volunteering labor for one day. The first of these workdays was launched at a neighborhood park on 61st Street and Broadway. The park department developed a plan of what park staff would do and what volunteers would do. Indianapolis Parks and Recreation Department did preparation concrete work, put in sidewalks, and put up a shelter. Next, in one day, the volunteers put up a playground, repainted the tennis complex, refurbished picnic tables, relandscaped the park, and resodded areas of the park. They raised the money to do this from local sources, and the staff of the parks department directed the work. More than 125 people volunteered their labor on that day. This model was then adopted widely throughout the Indianapolis Parks and Recreation Department system of 95 neighborhood parks.

99 Ways Volunteers Can Help in National Parks

■ Cataloging and cleaning the museum ■ Manning gate for passes ■ Maintaining park herbarium ■ Compiling a bird list ■ Performing Indian tribal dances ■ Identifying cultural resource sites ■ Doing office work ■ Providing environmental education programs ■ Staffing desk at visitors' center ■ Re-establishing natural vegetation ■ Controlling and ushering the crowd ■ Preparing multimedia programs ■ Acting as campground hosts ■ Preparing orientation manual ■ Removing graffiti from statues ■ Writing pamphlets for foreigners ■ Obliterating and rehabilitating trails ■ Surveying caves ■ Participating in ornithology studies of eagles and falcons ■ Providing photographic and graphics work ■ Recruiting other volunteers ■ Mapping ■ Arranging for site concerts ■ Taking air quality readings ■ Rebuilding backcountry bridges ■ Participating in speakers bureau ■ Manning contact station outside park ■ Issuing permits and put-in points ■ Providing cannon firings—black powder ■ Providing archeological excavation ■ Participating in paleo-entomological research ■ Operating traveling library ■ Taking an animal census ■ Gardening (produce, herbs, and flowers) ■ Doing cabinetmaking for interpretation ■ Painting ships and structures ■ Hosting for special events ■ Stabilizing and preserving roads ■ Grooming horses and cleaning stables ■ Leading overnight backpack trips ■ Producing publications ■ Taking invertebrate animal surveys ■ Gathering fire behavior data ■ Setting up pest management program ■ Rehabilitating overused campsites ■ Scheduling, loading, and unloading heliport ■ Collecting and transcribing oral history ■ Signing for deaf visitors ■ Leading snorkeling tours ■ Planning facilities ■ Leading star walks ■ Doing prescribed burns ■ Managing the wildlife ■ Building a jail facility ■ Providing entomology identification ■ Doing search and rescue work ■ Giving bus and train tours ■ Living as artists-in-residence ■ Manning first aid station ■ Compiling catalogues ■ Providing small mammal studies ■ Checking climbing routes ■ Giving group talks to children ■ Writing and producing skits ■ Doing park cleanups ■ Manning fire tower ■ Building diversion dams ■ Giving first aid courses ■ Writing trail guides ■ Guiding raft trips ■ Conducting campground checks ■ Patrolling the trail ■ Giving guided walks and talks ■ Working with mounted assistance unit ■ Creating exhibits ■ Working as roving park contact ■ Marking boundaries ■ Leading canyon climbs ■ Sewing historic clothing ■ Leading site tours ■ Providing trail measurement ■ Working as courier ■ Working with cross-country ski patrol ■ Being specialized lecturers ■ Monitoring visitation ■ Taking fish creel census ■ Reducing feral animal population ■ Aiding handicapped visitors ■ Giving campfire talks ■ Working with backcountry patrol ■ Leading snowshoe walks ■ Working as librarian ■ Giving choir concerts ■ Working in fisheries management ■ Picking up and dropping off mail ■ Conducting field study projects ■ Conducting marine life research ■ Leading nature hikes ■ Doing telemetry and trapping of endangered species

From Lorraine Hororst. Volunteers in the Parks: Getting the Most Out of Your Volunteer Program. *National Park Service: Washington, DC. 1982.*

Volunteers may provide the extra resources needed for an agency to undertake a pilot or demonstration project. Often elected officials are reluctant to fund new services because they are not convinced of their value. If a new project can be launched with volunteers and its value can be demonstrated, then it subsequently may receive funding support in the agency's core budget.

In areas where agencies are servicing dependent populations, volunteers are sometimes more effective than professionals in building caring client relationships characterized by acceptance, approval, empathy, respect, understanding, and trust.[4] Care is different from service, as the following anecdote illustrates:

Over 6,000 people in our community of 100,000 perform volunteer work. One hundred participate in the "Meals on Wheels" Program, donating a few hours a week and driving expenses to take hot meals to elderly people who cannot cook for themselves. This program is the perfect example of the kind of in-kind redistribution program economists typically attack. The charge would go something like this: "Why have a separate bureaucracy charged with one small thing—delivering hot meals to the elderly? What is so special about a hot meal anyway? Why not give the poor the money we spend on the program to do with as they wish?"

This analysis misses something. The most important thing that the volunteers bring the elderly is not the hot meal, but the human contact and the sense that someone cares. Volunteers can do this more convincingly than bureaucrats (p. 68).[5]

Through direct contact with service recipients, volunteers can help to humanize the delivery of park and recreation services. They also often possess closer ties to neighborhoods in a community and have greater knowledge about them than an agency's personnel do. Hence, they may strengthen an agency's communication links with the community and provide feedback on perceptions of the agency's existing performance, neighborhood expectations, and unmet wants and desires.

As volunteers, individual community members experience firsthand the problems and rewards of working in a park and recreation agency. They may gain an appreciation for the creative problem-solving that is required to work within the constraints imposed upon the agency. Certainly, volunteer familiarity appears to breed respect rather than contempt.

Their exposure can quickly erode negative political rhetoric indicting "the bureaucracy" to reveal the valuable work typically performed, often under trying conditions of budget cutbacks, escalating demands, and popular apathy, if not outright hostility. Through participation in these organizations, volunteers develop greater insight and appreciation for public agencies and their employees that can generate support in the larger community (p. 70).[4]

Volunteers can become credible advocates for an agency. Indeed, one director commented to the author: "It's not what volunteers do for you that is important, it is the political base they build." They can both mobilize public opinion and lobby elected officials, which paid employees are not permitted to do. In these roles, they may be effective advocates for an agency's programs and services and

may be effective in achieving increased appropriations that preserve or enhance budgets and employee positions. A study of volunteers in Maryland, for example, concluded:

In Maryland volunteers function as lobbyists to protect the recreation budget from expenditure cuts and in many instances exert pressure for increased expenditures ... Although recreation is not considered a vital service, it fared no worse than other services [in the annual state budget]. The role of volunteers at budget time appears to be important in the process of allocating public resources (p. 71).[4]

Although the benefits of using volunteers are likely to outweigh the costs, there should be an awareness of those costs. Volunteers have to be recruited, screened, interviewed, trained, fitted into positions, coordinated so that their part-time schedules meet the agency's needs, supervised, evaluated, and recognized by an awards program. All of these tasks consume the time of paid employees and, hence, are costs to the agency. If an agency fails to recognize and prepare for the additional demands on its resources that accompany the use of volunteers, then the unexpected increase in staff workloads could result in reduced, rather than improved, levels of service.

Motives of Volunteers

This section is concerned with what motivates people to invest their time, emotional energy, and sometimes their personal resources to volunteer. Identifying volunteers' motives is key to understanding why they start volunteering; how to energize them and sustain their enthusiasm; how to supervise, place, and reward them; and why they quit. These motives define and circumscribe the benefits that individuals seek from volunteering. It has been observed:

People never volunteer without expectations. They have certain ideas and perceptions about what they hope to gain from the experience. The supervisor of volunteers must try to help the volunteers ascertain what the goals and expectations are and then help volunteers attain them (p. 61).[6]

Many times, people are unsure or are unable to articulate what motivates them. They do not analyze their motives. However, they usually do have a feel for what they want, and a good interviewer is likely to elicit what benefits they are seeking.

Alternatively, a questionnaire may be given to volunteers to ascertain the benefits they want. These benefits are their compensation in lieu of a salary, so ensuring their volunteer experience yields these benefits is the key to retaining them. If they are not well paid in benefits, then they are unlikely to continue volunteering. Hence, an agency's challenge is to assign tasks to the volunteers, supervise their work, and recognize and reward their performance in ways that yield the benefits sought.

It has been assumed frequently that people are motivated to volunteer by altruism. Altruism is defined by Webster as "the principle or practice of unselfish concern for or devotion to the welfare of others."[7] Explaining a volunteer's behavior by altruism stems from the classical tradition exemplified, for example, by the ancient Roman philosopher Seneca who wrote: "He that does good to another, does good also to himself, not only in the consequences but in the very act; for the consciousness of well-doing is, in itself, ample reward."

However, in most cases this is an oversimplified and incomplete explanation of why people volunteer because, while concern for the welfare of others is likely to be prominent, this concern is not wholly unselfish. This idea was articulated by a volunteer teacher of recreational skills to disabled children: "Don't get me wrong. I don't teach these classes as a charity. I'm basically a very selfish person. I teach them because I get tremendous gratification." Thus, the altruism is not unconditional. Often, something is expected in return, and prospective volunteers are likely to ask themselves, What is in it for me? The do-good feeling may be a necessary but is usually not a sufficient condition to explain why people volunteer. Altruism should be viewed as a generic primary motivator common to most people who volunteer. Hence, the extent to which an agency is perceived to be helping dependent groups or contributing to community well-being is likely to be critical to its ability to recruit and retain volunteers. However, the identification and understanding of the other more selfish motives is likely to be of at least equal importance to this effort.

The benefits sought by volunteers beyond altruism may be classified as the desire for social interaction, status, personal growth, and self-image enhancement.

The needs of volunteers seeking social interaction, affiliation, and belonging have been described in the following terms:

An affiliation motivated volunteer is most concerned about relationships with others. This person is concerned about the quality of personal relationships, seeks the company of others as much as possible, enjoys social interactions, wants to be liked, wishes to avoid conflict, dislikes playing or working alone, goes out of the way to meet people and make friends, and enjoys stable relationships. This person usually wants to help people and develop warm and friendly relationships (p. 62).[6]

The park host volunteer program operated by the National Park Service and many other federal and state parks agencies appeals to many retirees who seek social interaction. It is briefly described in "Campground Host Programs."

The desire for status, prestige, and power has been described as follows:

Satisfying the need for power should not be equated with granting dictatorial rights, but rather with the opportunity to act in an influential manner, and often to do this with others, who are also positively power-oriented . . . For people whose lives do not provide adequate opportunity to act in leadership roles, participating in voluntary activities may well provide needed opportunities (p. 235).[8]

Hence, these needs are usually met through leadership opportunities. These types of volunteers have a concern for reputation and position, want to give advice, want their ideas to dominate, want authority and control, and are often assertive and outspoken.[6] They seek recognition in a visible, meaningful way for playing an important role in the community and contributing to its well-being.

Volunteers with a desire for personal growth, achievement, and sense of accomplishment want to be challenged and take pleasure from striving to excel. They tend to stick to a task, want feedback about how they are doing, like setting their own pace, eagerly accept responsibility, show concern for excellence, try to be efficient, set moderate goals, and take calculated risks.[6] The acquisition of new skills and new experiences may be sought in order to enhance career goals and to build a more impressive resume. The volunteer experience may be seen as a way of accessing the park and recreation field and as a first step to future part-time or full-time employment in the field.

Campground Host Programs

Campground Host programs involve using volunteers who can furnish their own lodging (e.g., tent, camper, trailer, or motor home) and can contribute a specific amount of time to serve as resident hosts at federal or state park campgrounds. Individuals, couples, or even families can serve as hosts. Often, retired couples find it the ideal way to spend a few months. Some hosts live in town and stay in the campground only on weekends.

Campground hosts provide information to visitors on things to do and see, help visitors register and find campsites, distribute maps and brochures, clean restrooms and campsites, perform emergency repairs, provide emergency assistance for visitors in need, reduce litter and vandalism through low-key incentive programs, gather useful information, keep agency personnel informed on conditions and problems in the campground, and perform other duties as appropriate.

Hosts are provided a free campsite, usually near the main entryway to the campground or in a conspicuous location so that they are readily noticeable and available to campground visitors. The normal camping time limit also is waived. If available, utility hookups can be furnished at no cost to the hosts.

Campground hosts usually work under a specific agreement and job description just like any other volunteer. They also must receive enough orientation and training to be able to adequately perform their job. Some parks supply their hosts with portable radios for emergencies; others use citizens band radios (CBs) or cell phones for this purpose.

The desire to enhance self-image or to feel useful relates to the observation in chapter 5 that an increasing proportion of the population is working in menial, low-paying, nonchallenging jobs as a result of the transition to a service economy. Work provides them with a paycheck but with little sense of self-worth. This type of work experience may also extend to some people who are in well-paying positions. One volunteer coordinator observed: "Many people don't feel completely fulfilled at their job. They work for money, and they do volunteer work for a sense of worth and value. We see engineers and accountants, for example, who are tired of numbers and want to work with people" (p. 5).[1] Volunteering offers rejuvenation opportunities to those whose work leaves them with a feeling of emptiness, a feeling of not being fulfilled, and a sense of uselessness. Similar sentiments about not feeling useful are expressed by some retirees. As the baby boomers move into retirement, which increasingly means when they attain the age of 55 or 60 years rather than 62 or 65 years, large numbers of them are likely to seek volunteering opportunities that enable them to feel useful.

Traditionally, park and recreation agencies have viewed volunteers as an external resource that enables them to extend, supplement, and enhance their range of services. This is a myopic perspective because, for some people, volunteering is a recreational activity. If the benefits that individuals seek from participating in park and recreational programs were solicited, it is likely that they would resemble the four categories of benefits that volunteers seek, which were discussed in the previous paragraphs. Thus, park and recreation agencies should view the creation of meaningful opportunities for volunteering as a recreational program that they offer. There remains a distinction between the two; volunteers are usually driven by altruistic intentions as well as self-interested motives. However, people engaging in recreational programs typically do not seek this helping benefit.

The implication of this recreation perspective of volunteering is that if park and recreation agencies want to retain their volunteers, the agencies must facilitate these recreational experiences for them. A volunteer's first work experience is particularly critical in ensuring that he or she will continue to volunteer. In the past, for example, some park and recreation agencies have recruited volunteers primarily to undertake mundane administrative office chores or for relatively menial work that professional staff members did not want to do. However, these types of tasks are not conducive to delivering the benefits and rewards that many volunteers are seeking. A better approach may be to hire people to perform these tedious tasks and reward them with a paycheck and to recruit volunteers to do the more challenging work that offers nonmonetary rewards, which volunteers seek.

Corporate Volunteers

Corporate volunteerism is defined as volunteerism that is supported in a visible, active way by the company itself. The company plays some role in how or why an employee becomes a volunteer. It may take the following forms, which are listed in declining order of commitment from a company:

- A small number of companies, such as Xerox, IBM, and Wells Fargo Bank, instituted "social-service leave," which is a corporate equivalent of the sabbaticals granted to professors. Employees were able to work with full salary and benefits for as long as one year on a particular project.

- "Time-release" during business hours for 3 h each week, for example, to accommodate volunteer activities, as long as the employee's workload can accommodate that level of outside involvement.

- Occasional full days when a large number of employees engage in renovation or construction of a facility.

- Encouraging employees to do volunteer work in their own time by establishing a volunteer coordinator in the company's public relations department who coordinates and encourages their involvement.

- Setting up a mechanism through which employees can become informed about a park and recreation agency's volunteer opportunities. This may take the form of a fair held in the company cafeteria, regular electronic-mail announcements, or announcements in company newsletters.

Corporations are not philanthropic institutions. Shareholders are likely to be unhappy if they believe that employees' talents and energies are being directed away from a company's primary mission, which is to maximize return on investment for shareholders. Thus, there have to be good business reasons underpinning a decision to encourage corporate volunteerism. Advocates believe that it boosts employee morale and promotes team work, camaraderie, and loyalty, which lead to increases in productivity. Employees bond with, and feel more committed to, a company because of its caring value system. Companies also believe that it improves their image as model corporate citizens. They want to be perceived as organizations with integrity, strong values, and genuine concern for the community. There is a belief that these attributes secure the trust of residents for a company, translating into a preference to engage in business transactions with it rather than with competitors.

It is noted later in chapter 14 that group projects are likely to be especially appealing to corporate volunteer coordinators because they are conducive to fostering team work and camaraderie. A park and recreation agency needs to identify companies likely to have employees with the skills they are seeking, then it needs to contact the public affairs division of the company to explore the possibility of securing volunteer assistance.

The benefits to a park and recreation agency extend beyond the volunteer assistance it obtains. By being involved with park and recreation agencies, companies gain a much better understanding of how these agencies operate and of how important their services are to a community. Businesses may become advocates for them.

Preparing an Agency for Volunteers

When an agency makes a decision to expand its volunteer efforts, the temptation often is to plunge ahead with recruitment. However, recruitment of volunteers is step 2! Step 1 is to lay the groundwork for their acceptance into the organization and for their sustained involvement. For a volunteer program to succeed, an agency's operating environment must adapt to accommodate it. If an agency fails to make sufficient preparation to retain them, then the energy and costs incurred in recruiting volunteers largely is wasted. The challenge is to integrate volunteers seamlessly into the existing organization.

This section discusses four primary tasks involved in creating agency readiness for volunteers. The first task is to secure employee support. At least some employees may feel some insecurity because they view volunteers as a threat to paid staff positions. The second challenge is to agree on the organizational arrangements for managing the program. The third task is to ensure that there is insurance coverage for volunteers. The fourth task is to define the niches that volunteers will occupy and to develop job descriptions for them.

Securing Employee Support

The anticipated improvements in service resulting from recruiting volunteers are contingent on employees enthusiastically embracing their involvement as partners in service delivery. Without a positive organizational mandate, it is unlikely that volunteers will secure the benefits that they seek. The parks and recreation field has a long-standing tradition both of working with nonprofit groups in coproducing services and in involving pure volunteers as partners. However, some agencies have not welcomed volunteers:

> Without question, the most serious impediment to a successful volunteer program is the likely indifference or, worse, outright opposition of regular personnel to volunteers. Perceived threats to job security fuel the natural apprehensions of employees and give rise to feelings of demoralization and hostility (p. 33).[5]

This antagonism is often manifested by listing the potential liabilities of volunteers: uncertain reliability in fulfilling their work commitments; lacking relevant training, skills, and experience for the tasks assigned; requiring excessive supervisory time, especially in relation to the assistance that they might provide; and encroaching on employee prerogatives.[4]

Suspicion of volunteers is likely to be especially strong if an agency's employees are members of a labor union. Labor unions may view volunteers as doing jobs that could be done by new full-time employees who would become union members. At a minimum, union officials are likely to require a written policy stating that the agency will not replace paid employees with volunteers. The long-term view of volunteers as a source of support for legislation, advocates with the general public, and resources for better-serving residents is often lost on unions, even though these positive outcomes are in the unions' long-term self-interest.

Volunteers are likely to embrace as a moral issue the tenet that they should not fill the positions of paid staff. They do not invest their time and talents to help keep taxes down; rather they do it for altruistic reasons and for certain benefits that they seek from it. Indeed, the evidence suggests that volunteers are actually less likely to be involved in delivering services in jurisdictions that have enacted limitations on taxing authority as part of the tax revolt movement than in other communities.[4]

To ameliorate the possibility of employees being suspicious or antagonistic toward volunteers, they should be extensively involved in planning for how volunteers will be integrated into the agency. Those employees that volunteers are most likely to impact should be encouraged to detail how the volunteers can be used most effectively to improve service delivery. This approach is likely to inculcate a sense of ownership and commitment that is key to gaining acceptance. This can be reinforced by recognition and reward programs that highlight not only the contribution made by a volunteer but also the role played by his or her employee supervisors and colleagues in facilitating that contribution.

Organizational Arrangements for Managing Volunteer Programs

The management of volunteer programs may be classified in three ways: as being ad hoc or ongoing, centralized or decentralized, and employee or volunteer coordinated. The ad hoc, or episodic, approach means that an agency or its sub-units solicit volunteers on a spontaneous, short-term basis to help with major one-time projects or to address specific problems when they arise. This contrasts with recruiting them on a sustained basis to assist with ongoing work. The ongoing approach requires a much stronger support structure and essentially institutionalizes volunteers as part of an agency's organizational culture.

Centralized programs are designed and operated by a single office in the park and recreation agency. The responsibilities of the manager of this office are to guide the paid staff in the development and design of volunteer roles and in the preparation of job descriptions for volunteers. He or she then recruits and interviews volunteers, arranges for a second interview or a meeting between new volunteers and the paid staff with whom they will work, conducts the final screening process as needed, and provides new volunteers with an orientation to the organization (p. 15).[9]

The volunteers are then deployed and supervised by sub-units within an agency. This approach facilitates a coordinated approach; avoids duplication of effort; and makes a more aggressive, systematic thrust possible by focusing an agency's resources in one place. The effort is likely to be more visible to senior managers who may increase their support for it. Centralization may also make it more feasible to shift volunteers to more suitable positions in the agency if their initial placement proves unsatisfying or to appraise them of job enrichment opportunities that may arise elsewhere in the agency.

A decentralized approach is characterized by individual sub-units within an agency taking responsibility for their own volunteers. More people become involved in planning and managing the volunteer effort, which implies that a stronger commitment to it is likely. This strategy becomes increasingly compelling as the diversity and geographic jurisdiction of an agency increase. However, it does have an inherent danger.

In the public sector, lamentably, the decentralized approach can unwittingly generate disincentives for managers to introduce volunteers. Top agency officials mistakenly may equate nonpaid work with unimportant activities to the detriment of a department's (and a manager's) standing in the organization, or they may seize upon the willingness to enlist volunteers as an excuse to deny a unit essential increases in budget and paid personnel. One purpose of involving top management, employees, and volunteers in designing and implementing the volunteer program is to avoid such misunderstandings (p. 50).[2]

Irrespective of whether the effort is ad hoc or ongoing or is centralized or decentralized, it needs to be staffed. Staffing may be done by either a paid employee or a volunteer. This individual or office is the focal point for contact with the volunteer operation within the sub-unit or agency for those inside and outside of the agency. If the position is the major responsibility of a paid employee, then it communicates agency commitment to both volunteers and employees. It suggests that volunteers are recognized as an important external resource that the agency is committed to using. The more senior the manager responsible for volunteers is, the stronger this commitment will appear. An alternative is to appoint an experienced and committed volunteer to this position so that the volunteer effort almost becomes self-managed. Such an individual is likely to be particularly credible when recruiting new volunteers.

Liability Risk

The willingness of volunteers to contribute their talents may be deterred by potential personal liability for simple mistakes that they may make in the course of their volunteer service. Volunteers in the National Park Service or other federal agencies are protected under the federal Tort Claims Act. This act provides protection against personal liability as long as they are acting within the scope of their assigned responsibilities. Some states have similar statutes that typically include the following types of clauses:

Any volunteer of a nonprofit organization or governmental entity shall incur no personal financial liability for any tort claim alleging damage or injury from any act or omission of the volunteer on behalf of the organization or entity if—(1) such volunteer was acting in good faith and within the scope of such volunteer's official functions and duties with the organization or entity; and (2) such damage or injury was not caused by willful and wanton misconduct by such volunteer (p. 34).[10]

Many agencies also carry insurance that covers their volunteers. When an agency does not carry it, the agency usually can add a rider, which protects volunteers, to cover them at minimal cost to its existing liability policy. Unfortunately, however, protection by these statutes and insurance policies against liability is not synonymous with protection against being sued, which is a threat that may concern some potential volunteers. The financial and emotional costs of defending themselves in a law suit may be sufficiently daunting to dissuade them from volunteering. Real liability insurance should also insulate volunteers from the costs associated with defending a lawsuit.[10]

In chapter 7, it was noted that in contracting-out situations, agencies often seek relief not only from any liability responsibility, but they also require indemnification of costs incurred from having to defend any lawsuits that arise. Similar indemnification guaranteeing legal assistance and legal costs should be extended to volunteers in the unlikely event that they are subjected to a lawsuit alleging negligent acts. It was hoped that the federal Volunteers Protection Act passed in 1997 would do this. However, it merely provided individuals with a defense in case of legal actions and offered weaker protection than already existed in many of the state statutes.

From an agency's perspective, liability risk associated with volunteers will be increased if it fails to train them fully. Volunteers are likely to be classified by the courts in the same category as paid employees, viewed as agents of the agency. Thus, the agency is obligated to ensure that their training in the task to which they are assigned is as thorough as that given to employees. Volunteers should be required to take a risk management training course just as regular employees are required to do.

Developing Job Descriptions

An agency should have a specific objective in mind when it recruits volunteers. Too often volunteers find an agency that says it wants help, but the agency really does not know what kind of help it wants. The formulation of job descriptions can help avoid the frustration that both volunteer and agency experience when this occurs.

The first stage in developing job descriptions is for senior managers to work with employees to conduct a needs assessment to identify jobs that volunteers could undertake. The work must fit a part-time situation. Either the work must be small enough in scope to be approached productively in a few hours each week, or it must be designed to be shared among a group of volunteers. It is essential that staff participate in the program's design in order to help decide where volunteers could be used. The most effective recruitment mechanism is the availability of positions that appeal to the motivations of volunteers. Hence, the most important criterion in this identification of jobs process is that the positions provide opportunities that deliver the social interaction, status, personal growth, and self-image enhancement needs of volunteers, which were discussed earlier in the chapter. Many of these needs are likely to be best met by positions that entail direct contact with the park and recreation agency's clientele. However, the identified positions should cater to a wide range of aspirations, and every volunteer's job need not provide close contact with clientele.

Like employees, volunteers are richly diverse in their needs and goals. As a consequence, public organizations will enjoy success in recruiting them to the degree that agencies offer a range of jobs that appeal to a diversity of motivations. An organization should no more allocate exclusively routine, repetitive tasks to volunteers than it should place them solely in highly ambitious work assignments (p. 55).[2]

The needs assessment may involve reassessing the job descriptions of existing employees to see if some of their responsibilities could be performed by volunteers, thus freeing them to develop new or to expand other existing services. Prime candidates for delegation to volunteers are tasks with the following characteristics:

- Those performed periodically, such as once each week, rather than on a daily or inflexible basis
- Those that do not require the specialized training or expertise of paid personnel
- Those that might be done more effectively by someone with special training in that skill

- Those for which the position's occupant feels uncomfortable or unprepared
- Those for which the agency lacks in-house expertise.[11]

Job descriptions for volunteers are no different from those developed for paid personnel. Their basic purpose is communication, and volunteers need the same information as paid employees to determine whether they are interested in the position. The job description should include

- job title;
- specific description of the work to be accomplished;
- benefits of the position to the volunteer;
- authority invested in the position;
- job site, location, and working conditions (e.g., office, outdoors, etc.);
- time commitment (e.g., hours per week);
- knowledge and skills required;
- training required and to be provided;
- supervision or guidance to be provided and reporting relationships; and
- evaluation schedule.

A job description addressing most of these items, which was developed by the Corps of Engineers, is shown in "Sample Volunteer Job Description" on page 352.

From a park and recreation agency's perspective, job description preparation is a planning tool. It focuses attention on the adaptations needed within the agency to accommodate the volunteer, and it provides the criteria for subsequent evaluations of a volunteer's performance. The job description also establishes parameters of a volunteer's authority and responsibility, which alleviates the likelihood of tensions and misunderstandings with paid employees or other volunteers.

Recruitment of Volunteers

Elected officials sometimes speak confidently and platitudinously about the existence of a large number of volunteers who are waiting to be asked to help. This is illusory. Recruitment is not easy. The reality is that the pool of volunteers is likely to be small and competition for their services from nonprofit organizations and other public agencies is likely to be substantial. Few park and recreation agencies can boast of a waiting list of volunteers. The difficulties are likely to be particularly acute

Sample Volunteer Job Description

Position title

Visitor Center Assistant

Job description and duties

- Answer visitor's questions and provide any needed assistance.
- Maintain appropriate records of visitation as well as report equipment breakdowns or other unusual occurrences.
- Operate audiovisual equipment in the presentation of films, slide shows, and videos to the visiting public.
- Maintain displays in a clean and operational manner.
- Present short interpretive talks to groups of visitors as required.
- Perform all duties safely.

Desired skills and abilities

The individual needs to be able to meet and work well with people. His or her appearance should be neat and a positive reflection of the organization. The individual should have the ability to remain calm in busy situations. Public speaking skills are desirable but not mandatory.

Training and orientation needed

Necessary training will be provided in service effectiveness, audiovisual equipment operation, cardiopulmonary resuscitation, and first aid. A thorough orientation regarding the Corps of Engineers and the project will be provided.

Materials and equipment used

Slide projectors, public address system, tape players, video cassette recorders, and video monitors

Schedule

Anytime between 10:00 A.M. and 6:00 P.M. daily

Benefits

- Opportunity to develop programs and special events
- Opportunity to meet new people and interact with the public
- Work in a clean, safe, and professional atmosphere
- Opportunity for additional training and skill development
- Growth in natural, cultural, and human resources

From William Dzombak. Volunteer coordinator's handbook. #EP1130-2-429. U.S. Army Corps of Engineers: Washington, DC. 1993.

at rural units of state and federal park agencies where the local population base is very small. Consider the difficulties confronting park managers at locations, such as the following. The nearest town to Badlands National Park is Interior, South Dakota, which has a population of 62. The next closest town, Wall, is 30 mi from the park and has a population of only 542. Cape Hatteras National Seashore, which is located near Manteo, North Carolina, has a population of about 600 and has difficulty finding volunteers even in a heavily visited tourist area. Most of the local residents work, and the seasonal population is very transient.

Volunteer recruitment efforts may take two different forms: generic and targeted.[12] They may be regarded as opposite poles of a continuum. Most recruitment strategies are likely to adopt features from both of these extreme strategies. Generic approaches are general invitations to the public to get involved with the park and recreation agency on a broad scale. These approaches usually are adopted when the agency needs a large number of volunteers to assist with an event and the tasks do not require any special skill. The case described in "Clearing Exotic Plants From a Nature Preserve" is this type of approach. Generic approaches typically communicate the agency's needs through a wide array of promotional tools, such as agency newsletters, newspapers, letters to the editor, public announcements on radio and television, posted notices in stores and on bulletin boards, and slide shows to service groups.

In contrast, targeted volunteer recruitment occurs when a park and recreation agency seeks to fill a specific need with a qualified volunteer. Suppose that an organization needs a photographer to shoot a special event but does not have the budget to pay a professional. The volunteer manager then seeks to network and recruit volunteers from a select pool of people who may be able to assist. There may be a professional organization of photographers or a fine arts school in the community, or the volunteer manager may simply approach a local newspaper and ask for an in-kind donation of a photographer for the day (p. 162).[13] In this situation, the generic Volunteers Wanted approach was unlikely to work because specific skills were needed.[12]

Recruitment is an ongoing process. Through personal contact, most individuals learn about opportunities for volunteering that interest them. The contact may be with existing volunteers, someone associated with the agency, or a family member or friend. Relatively few people seek out the volunteer opportunity on their own. This suggests that the park and recreation agency and existing volunteers are likely to be the most effective sources of new recruits. The logical place for agency personnel to look for volunteers is in the pool of regular or previous users of the agency's services. The strength of the personal approach is illustrated in "Use the Personal Approach" on page 354.

Through the recruitment process, attention should focus on meeting the needs of volunteers as well as those of the agency. If only the agency's needs are considered, many volunteers will quickly become dissatisfied with the lack of a good fit. Starting with the development of recruitment strategy, the successful volunteer recruiter tries to match the needs of the program with the needs of the volunteer. Questions the recruiter must keep in mind continuously include the following: What can a volunteer get out of the volunteer experience? Who are the people most likely to find satisfaction in the opportunity? How can the program give them a motivational paycheck that will keep them interested?[12]

Interviewing

After individuals have expressed interest in a position as a result of an agency's recruitment process, they should be interviewed. Just as a park and recreation agency would not consider hiring

---

Clearing Exotic Plants From a Nature Preserve

California's Coachella Valley was invaded by alien tamarisk, which had taken over the reserve's Thousand Palms Oasis. It was thought it would be impossible to remove the thousands of trees and their innumerable sprouts. "People just said it would be useless to try; we'd never get the job done" said the park manager. (Tamarisk aggressively displaces native trees and shrubs, and by extending its roots down to the water table, it extracts water at such a high rate that it desiccates springs, drains pools, and even dries up perennial streams.)

Nonetheless, volunteers began removing the alien species patch by patch, cutting the large trees and pulling sprouts while on their hands and knees. "The work was satisfying," reported one volunteer who was recognized as the head tamarisk basher, "especially when the water began to flow again in the springs that tamarisk had totally dried up." Today, the Coachella Valley Ecological Reserve is essentially free of tamarisk, and the willows, palms, and salt-tolerant shrubs are returning.

From Mary Huffman. Volunteering: It's a connecting thing. The Nature Conservancy Annual Report, page 16. Copyright ©1990 The Nature Conservancy. All rights reserved.

Use the Personal Approach

"I put a sign-up sheet in the back of the room but nobody signed up." People like to be recognized and appreciated for who they are. A sign-up sheet says, in effect, "I'll take anybody." Who wants to be thought of as just anybody?

When you approach people on a one-to-one basis and show that you've taken some interest in them, they'll be more responsive. Using your job description and volunteer profile, let them know that you recognize they have the qualifications you're looking for, and that you've noticed and admired certain qualities they have. Make them feel wanted and needed for who they are. Do not say, "Mary, I can't get anybody else to do this. Will you help me?" Say, "Mary, I've watched you at meetings and noticed you're really comfortable talking with new people. We need someone like you to serve as a hostess for our fundraising event. Are you available?" However, do not say it unless it is true.

If Mary is like most people, she is likely to ask, "What's in it for me?" Even if she does not say it, she is probably thinking it. Be prepared to point out certain benefits of the position. Maybe Mary is chairman of another committee. By serving as hostess, she can spot potential committee members. While the spirit of service is an important motivating factor for any volunteer, it helps to give the volunteer a reason for taking on this particular assignment. You will need to learn enough about Mary to know what benefits are of interest to her.

You will probably be turned down now and then. When this happens, listen to what the person has to say. If there is good reason, be gracious and leave open the possibility of some future position. If the person is just showing reluctance, ask again at another time. Sometimes it takes a person a while to warm up to the idea of volunteering or to be made to feel confident. You may have to provide encouragement by saying, "Will you think about it?" Follow up sometime soon. Be sure to have a list of several candidates so that if one says no, you can go to the next.

From the American Association of Retired People. Recruiting Volunteers. Highlights. April 1987, page 11.

paid employees without interviewing them, they should not hire volunteers without similar screenings. Both some agency personnel and volunteers may believe that this is too formal and contrary to the spirit of volunteering, but interviewing offers both the agency and the volunteer an opportunity to understand each other's needs better before any commitment is made.

The first responsibility of a public agency is to its clients, who can hardly be expected to benefit from misplaced or deficient volunteer assistance . . . Prospective volunteers deserve an interview to elucidate their motivations and desires for government service, and to have the organization take them seriously. The interview should clarify the expectations not only of the volunteer but also the sponsoring agency. Inadequate screening can result in misassignments to positions that underutilize applicants' talents and energies, or conversely, that demand too much of particular incumbents. In either case, volunteer burnout and attrition are likely outcomes (p. 105, 106).[5]

Some agencies use a volunteer job portfolio, which is a file of job descriptions for all volunteer positions available in the agency. During an interview, agency representatives, together with the volunteer, seek to match interests, skills, and needs with these opportunities. The goal is to help volunteers reach the best decision for themselves. If, at the end of the interview, it is apparent that there is not a good match, then it is important to confront this reality and decline the offer of assistance.

Retention of Volunteers

Retention of volunteers is dependent upon the agency providing a positive work experience. Volunteers have two major complaints. The first complaint is: "There is not enough work to get my teeth into. . . . It is not sufficiently interesting or challenging." The second complaint is: "I am taken for granted." Like paid employees, volunteers should be made to feel a part of the organization. They need to feel that what they are doing is important. This means investing in their orientation, training, supervision, and evaluation to a similar extent as if they were paid personnel.

An agency's first actions are critical to reinforcing the positive attitude that volunteers are likely to bring when they report for work. This means that the agency should have prepared a work space, furnished it with supplies and equipment, planned a schedule of the first day's tasks, and ensured that the volunteers' supervisors are present when they arrive. The challenge for supervisors is to make volunteers feel welcome and a necessary part of the agency's team from the outset.

Like paid employees, volunteers represent the park and recreation agency to the public. To enable them to do this effectively, agencies must provide volunteers with an initial orientation. The intent of the orientation is to give them a better understanding of the agency's history, mission, tradition, policies, and values; its organization, operating rules, and procedures; the range of services offered; and the name, roles, and positions of people within the agency with whom volunteers are likely to interact. The orientation may be given by supervising employees, but it should be standardized and structured, otherwise it is likely that some volunteers will receive inadequate information.

If troops are sent into battle without training, they probably will be defeated. Hence, the general orientation should be followed by specific training for the jobs that volunteers are to perform so that they are equipped to fulfill their tasks. A volunteer who receives training that improves understanding of the job and strengthens the skills needed to do it is more likely to experience job satisfaction, is better equipped to work independently of supervisors, and is more likely to provide better service to clients. Volunteers usually appreciate training and assistance because it builds self-confidence in their ability to do the job. The amount and types of training needed depend on the skill that is required to perform the assignments and on the expertise that volunteers already possess. Individuals such as specialists, professors, or professionals from other fields may not require additional training and may be integrated into the program immediately following an orientation.

Effective supervision is essential to ensuring quality performance and the effectiveness of volunteers. Without it, volunteers may reduce, rather than enhance, the level of an agency's service delivery. When the library in Virginia Beach, Virginia, began to expand its use of volunteer personnel in response to the creation of the citywide volunteer program, library employees were not trained initially and were not expected to manage volunteers as closely as paid employees. As a result, some volunteers were not performing up to the standards expected of department employees. Some volunteers were disrupting the routine operations of the department and lowering productivity of paid employees. Department supervisors were encouraged to evaluate the performance of volunteers as they would evaluate paid employees. Subsequently, volunteers were disciplined and even fired using procedures similar to those used for paid employees. Performance of volunteers improved so that volunteers became considered an integral part of the library operation (p. 144).[14]

As they gain experience in their job, volunteers should be encouraged to offer input on how their efficiency and effectiveness could be improved. The advantages of this strategy were identified by one writer in the following terms:

> Just as for paid staff, citizens are more likely to accept and endorse organizational policies and programs, and to generate useful input regarding them, if they enjoy ready access to the decision-making process. Participation is key to empowerment of volunteers. The term connotes a genuine sharing of responsibility for the volunteer program with citizen participants; more attentive listening to volunteer ideas and preferences; and greater recognition of the time, skills, and value provided to organizations through this approach. Empowerment is thought to result in increased feelings of personal commitment and loyalty to the volunteer program by participants and hence greater retention and effectiveness (p. 48).[2]

One measure of the effectiveness of a volunteer program is the extent of turnover. Just as with paid staff, some volunteer turnover should be expected as time availability and motives change. However, if most volunteers turn over frequently, then there is probably something wrong with the agency's volunteer program. The temptation may be to dismiss this as evidence of the unreliability of volunteers, but it is usually evidence of an agency's inadequacies in recruiting or managing volunteers.

Exit interviews with volunteers who leave are essential in order to gather information that might identify problems in the existing system. People are most likely to give frank feedback on their experiences when they are leaving. A telephone call inviting their renewed participation may be appropriate if volunteers who are used on specific projects rather than on an ongoing basis have not offered their services in the previous 12 months.

Evaluation

An evaluation of each volunteer's performance should be scheduled. It need not be lengthy, complicated or complex; however, it should be conducted formally at least annually, and the agency and volunteer should make a mutually agreed upon, written record of it. Evaluation is a joint responsibility and equally important to both parties. Sometimes agencies are reluctant to conduct performance evaluations because they are concerned that volunteers may interpret them as questioning the quality of their contribution. However, volunteers' feedback to the agency regarding the quality of their experience, support, training, and opportunities for personal growth is as important as the agency's comments to volunteers on the adequacy of their performance. The purpose of an evaluation is "to ascertain the degree to which the needs and expectations of the volunteer and the agency are met, so that job assignments can be continued, amended, or redefined as necessary" (p. 58).[2] It is a mechanism through which volunteers can improve their contribution. The benefits to volunteers from evaluation have been expressed in the following terms:

> No citizen contributes her or his time to have his or her labor wasted in misdirected activity or to repeat easily remedied mistakes and misjudgments. That an organization might take one's work so lightly as to allow such inappropriate behavior to continue is an insult to the volunteer and an affront to standards of professional conduct underlying effectiveness on the job. For many who contribute their time, moreover, volunteering presents an opportunity to acquire or hone desirable job skills and/or to build an attractive resume for purposes of paid employment. To deny constructive feedback to those who give their time for organizational purposes, and who could benefit from this knowledge and hope to do so, is a disservice to the volunteer (p. 58).[2]

Sometimes poor performance is the result of misunderstanding what is required, and this misunderstanding may be discovered only through a joint evaluation and appraisal of the job. Occasionally, the evaluation discussion may result in the agency finding another position for a volunteer that is more suited to meeting his or her needs!

Big Bend National Park in Texas had a trial period for new campground hosts. During the first few weeks of their 90-day commitment, these volunteers were assessed by the district ranger. At the same time, the volunteers decided if their expectations for the job were being met.

Independence National Historical Park in Philadelphia was able to reassign a volunteer who was no longer able to meet the demands of rigorous tours. The volunteer became the park's official greeter, which was a job limited to just one building.

Recognition and Rewards

There is an adage that states: Nobody works for nothing. Volunteers receive nonmonetary compensation so unless they receive the rewards that they seek, their continued commitment to an agency is unlikely. Satisfying their motive for volunteering is a key to their retention, and it is much easier to retain volunteers than it is to recruit them. The agency's challenge is to provide this recognition in a way that is most meaningful to the volunteer; that is, the rewards should be related to their motivations for volunteering.

Recognition and reward can take four different forms. At a basic level, it should occur daily. It should involve making volunteers feel welcome and a part of the team and should consist of showing appreciation with a smile and a thank you. Sincere acknowledgment of an individual's contribution is the least expensive recognition, but it is too often forgotten.

At another level, it is usual for agencies to host a formal event, such as an annual recognition banquet, at which all volunteers are acknowledged. This is frequently scheduled in the third or fourth week of April to coincide with National Volunteer Week. Formal recognition at this occasion may include the presentation of service pins, patches, certificates, plaques, or small gifts. These may reflect length of service or number of hours of service contributed during the year. Other types of formal events, such as an investment seminar or health-care counseling, may be offered periodically during the year. Some agencies have developed a menu of these kinds of programs and have invited the volunteers to pick the type of reward event that they would like. Some agencies are not authorized to spend tax funds on these types of recognition gifts, so they rely on their associated nonprofit foundation, local merchants, or other private sources to provide resources for this event. Other formal mechanisms may include volunteer-of-the-month awards or posting an honor roll of volunteers In public areas of the facilities in which they work.

The purpose of reward and recognition efforts is not only to say thank you but also to meet each volunteer's needs. Thus, the third type of reward links recognition to the motives for volunteering. In order to do this, supervisors have to communicate frequently with their volunteers and listen carefully to what they identify as their motives. Relating this to the four categories of volunteer motives that were identified earlier in the chapter, some of the following actions may be effective rewards:

- Meaningful recognition for volunteers motivated by personal growth, achievement, and a sense of accomplishment may include

  — giving them more responsible and meaningful work;

  — tangible rewards that can be displayed and that acknowledge their achievements;

  — a letter from a senior manager listing the accomplishments in terms that may be useful in securing a paid position in the future;

  — assigning them to projects with clearly stated goals, clearly defined parameters, and frequent check marks that indicate success; and

  — providing training opportunities that encourage personal growth.

- For volunteers motivated by affiliation, social opportunities, and a sense of belonging, consider

  — assigning them to organize social activities or to participate in them,

  — assigning them to meet and greet participants and visitors,

  — requesting suggestions and input for improving the atmosphere of the workplace and personnel-related issues and decisions, and

  — organizing periodic social events for volunteers and staff to become better acquainted.

- Volunteers motivated by status, prestige, and power may respond most positively to

  — opportunities to train, supervise, and provide direction to other volunteers;

  — an impressive job title;

  — opportunities to interact with senior managers; and

  — publicity in agency publications that inform others of their impact on people and programs.

- Volunteers seeking to enhance self-esteem or to feel useful may respond to

  — opportunities to help others on a one-to-one or small-group level in which they win the trust and respect of clients and

  — frequent gestures of appreciation from supervisors.

A final type of reward that may be used is giving volunteers free access to the agency's services, programs, and facilities. In some agencies, these perks include, for example, making available complimentary spaces in all recreational classes for volunteers. An agency does not incur any direct cost from this policy; however, there may be a small amount of opportunity cost, such as by a free volunteer occupying a class space that could have been filled by a paying participant. It is important that these rewards are positioned as a gesture of appreciation and not as an incentive program. Many volunteers are likely to be insulted and unresponsive to any suggestion that they contribute their services for tangible rewards.

Usually, some type of points system is established by which volunteers are credited with points for each hour they contribute, and they can redeem their points at various levels for admission to the agency's programs and facilities. These types of rewards also serve as a means for introducing volunteers to new activities, which may lead to them subsequently becoming regular participants in those activities. For example, units of the National Park Service offer their volunteers rewards, such as free recreational vehicle parking and camping privileges; open access to library facilities at historic sites; extended trail rides or camping trips in the backcountry; or special instruction by staff members on a topic of interest.

Summary

Volunteer support differs from coproduction in that volunteers personally do not benefit materially from the service output; it is others who do so. Although they are not paid, they are permitted to deduct expenses directly incurred as part of their service on their income tax returns.

Volunteers are a means by which an agency can leverage its resources to derive more productivity from its existing funds and personnel. However, in addition to providing another pair of hands, volunteers may help humanize the delivery of park and recreation services because of their intimate knowledge of people at the neighborhood level; may provide feedback to the agency on its performance as perceived by residents in their neighborhood; may gain respect for an agency's work as they acquire insights into the challenges and constraints with which it is confronted; and may become advocates for it in the community and with elected officials. Recruiting and managing volunteers does exact a cost from the agency because substantial amounts of personnel time may be required to fulfill these tasks.

Identifying volunteers' motives is key to understanding why they start volunteering; how to energize them and to sustain their enthusiasm; how to supervise, place, and reward them; and why they quit. If volunteers are not well paid in benefits, then they are unlikely to continue volunteering because this is their compensation in lieu of a salary. Altruism is a necessary, but not a sufficient, condition to explain why people volunteer. It is a generic primary motivator, but it is invariably accompanied by other, more selfish motives. These can be subsumed into four main categories: socialization and affiliation, whereby volunteers are concerned about establishing quality relationships with others; status, prestige, and power needs, which may be met through leadership opportunities; desire for personal growth, achievement, and sense of accomplishment, which is likely to be forthcoming only from challenging tasks; and desire to enhance self-image or to feel useful, which often is sought by individuals who find that their paid work offers them little satisfaction and fulfillment.

If the benefits that individuals seek from participating in park and recreational programs were solicited, they likely would resemble these four categories of benefits. Thus, agencies should view the creation of meaningful opportunities for volunteering as a type of recreational program that they offer and not merely as an external resource that enables them to extend, supplement, or enhance their range of services.

Corporate volunteerism refers to volunteerism that is supported in a visible, active way by a company that plays some role in how or why an employee becomes a volunteer. Its advocates argue that companies receive benefits because it is a vehicle for boosting employee morale and for promoting team work, camaraderie, and loyalty, which lead to increases in productivity. It also may improve their image as good corporate citizens.

Before starting to recruit volunteers, an agency has to ensure that it is in a state of readiness to receive them. Four primary tasks are involved in creating agency readiness. First, employee support must be secured. If personnel believe that volunteers ultimately may be used to replace them as a cost-saving strategy by the agency or that they will usurp their status or authority, then they are likely to oppose or to be indifferent toward volunteers. Success depends on agency personnel enthusiastically embracing volunteers as partners in service delivery, so personnel suspicions have to be removed.

The second readiness challenge is to establish organizational arrangements for managing the volunteer programs. Three sets of decisions have to be made relating to whether the program should be ad hoc or ongoing, centralized or decentralized, or employee or volunteer coordinated.

The third factor for agencies to review is the extent to which their existing liability insurance covers volunteers. Usually, this coverage can be acquired at minimal cost. However, such coverage does not protect volunteers from being sued, and the financial and emotional costs associated with that possibility may deter some individuals from volunteering.

The fourth readiness task is to develop job descriptions. These should emerge from an assessment of the agency's needs and offer details of what the job entails.

Recruitment efforts for volunteers may be either generic or targeted. Generic approaches are general invitations to the public to become involved with the park and recreation agency in tasks that do not require any special skills and for which large numbers of individuals may be required. Targeted efforts are used when an agency seeks to fill a specific need with a qualified volunteer. Most volunteers become involved only after personal contact from existing volunteers, agency personnel, or a family member or friend. Relatively few seek out the volunteer opportunity on their own. After initial interest has been expressed, there should be an interview. The interview will enable both the agency and the volunteer to have an opportunity to understand each other's needs better before any commitment is made.

When volunteers commence work, the challenge for supervisors is to make them feel wanted and to assign work that will yield the benefits that they seek. Like paid employees, volunteers are agency representatives and should be given an initial, structured orientation followed by training specifically related to the jobs that they are to perform.

Formal evaluations are useful sources of feedback for both the agency and the volunteer. They enable volunteers to communicate their feelings about the quality of their experience, the extent to which it is providing them with the benefits they seek, and the adequacy of the support and training they are receiving. In return, volunteers receive the agency's comments on its perceptions of their level of performance.

Volunteers receive nonmonetary compensation, so the agency's challenge is to recognize and reward their contributions in a way that is most meaningful to them. Recognition and rewards can take four different forms: ongoing, daily gestures

Why I Am Not a Volunteer

Somehow, I get the feeling that not to be a volunteer in someone's program today is to be uncivilized. However, like many of my fellow sitter-outers, I have reasons for letting opportunities pass me by. You, the program operator and the professional, have supplied me with them. Do you really want to know why I am not a volunteer?

1. For a long time, I never knew you wanted me. You communicated quite well, "I'd rather do it myself, mother." You are articulate in expressing your needs in dollars and decimals. Your silence on service, I figured, was your last word.

2. Once you did call for help, and I stepped forward. However, you never told me how to get started. I later thought that maybe what you actually said was, "Why don't we have lunch . . . sometime?"

3. I persevered, however, I reported for duty. You turned me over to a department head, and he, in turn, sent me down to the section chief. He was out, and the secretary did not know what to do with so rare a species as a volunteer, so she suggested that I get in touch next Tuesday. I called, but my message got lost.

4. I might have overlooked the run-around. People cannot be blamed for doing the best they can, and the worst and best are hard to distinguish in the emptiness of a vacuum. For some reason, I thought you, as their leader, would have given a bit of thought beforehand to what you would do with me, a volunteer, or you would have at least let someone else know I was coming and given them the worry of organizing the situation.

5. At the time of the spring mail-out, my neighbor and I appeared on the scene. We worked; for two days we licked stamps and envelope flaps until the steak at supper tasted like tongue. Then I learned from the slip of a clerk that before our coming you had turned off the postage machine. I really cannot blame you. If you had not gone out of your way to make work for us, what could a couple of volunteers have done for two whole days?

6. I tried again a number of times. However, you really did not expect much from me. You never trained me or insisted that my work be to a standard. A particularly tough day was coming up for the crew, and I cut out—it was a perfect day for golf. On my return, you said nothing about my absence, except to ask about my score. I never learned if my truancy made any difference.

7. In spite of all, I think I did make a contribution. However, the only real thanks I got was a letter from you—a form letter. I know how "demanding" this letter was on you. My neighbor had typed the master copy, I had copied it, and together we had forged your name, stuffed the envelopes, sealed, stamped, and mailed them.

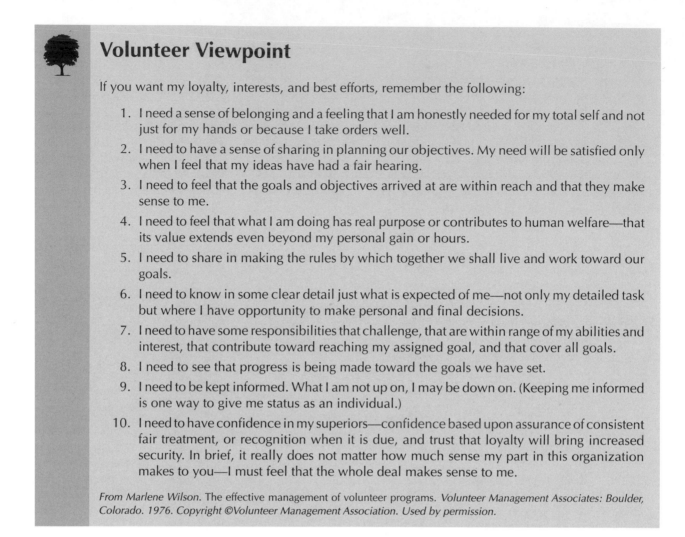

Volunteer Viewpoint

If you want my loyalty, interests, and best efforts, remember the following:

1. I need a sense of belonging and a feeling that I am honestly needed for my total self and not just for my hands or because I take orders well.

2. I need to have a sense of sharing in planning our objectives. My need will be satisfied only when I feel that my ideas have had a fair hearing.

3. I need to feel that the goals and objectives arrived at are within reach and that they make sense to me.

4. I need to feel that what I am doing has real purpose or contributes to human welfare—that its value extends even beyond my personal gain or hours.

5. I need to share in making the rules by which together we shall live and work toward our goals.

6. I need to know in some clear detail just what is expected of me—not only my detailed task but where I have opportunity to make personal and final decisions.

7. I need to have some responsibilities that challenge, that are within range of my abilities and interest, that contribute toward reaching my assigned goal, and that cover all goals.

8. I need to see that progress is being made toward the goals we have set.

9. I need to be kept informed. What I am not up on, I may be down on. (Keeping me informed is one way to give me status as an individual.)

10. I need to have confidence in my superiors—confidence based upon assurance of consistent fair treatment, or recognition when it is due, and trust that loyalty will bring increased security. In brief, it really does not matter how much sense my part in this organization makes to you—I must feel that the whole deal makes sense to me.

From Marlene Wilson. The effective management of volunteer programs. *Volunteer Management Associates: Boulder, Colorado. 1976. Copyright ©Volunteer Management Association. Used by permission.*

of appreciation; an annual formal event; specific rewards governed by each volunteer's motives for contributing; and providing complimentary access to the agency's services, programs, and facilities.

The not so tongue-in-cheek confession of a former volunteer reported in "Why I Am Not a Volunteer" alludes to many of the issues discussed in this chapter and offers a salutary lesson in how not to manage volunteers. In contrast, "Volunteer Viewpoint" gives insights into how to successfully manage volunteers.

References

1. Broyles, William. 1980. Behind the lines. *Texas Monthly* 8(6): 5-6.

2. Brudney, Jeffrey L. 1995. Preparing the organization for volunteers. In *The volunteer management handbook*, edited by Tracy Daniel Connors. New York: Wiley, 36-60.

3. Temple University Department of Recreation and Leisure Studies. 1986. *Philadelphia recreation volunteerism project*. Champaign, IL: Sagamore.

4. Brudney, Jeffrey L. 1990. *Fostering Volunteer Programs in the public sector: planning, initiating and managing voluntary activities*. San Francisco: Jossey-Bass.

5. Osborne, David and Ted Gaebler. 1992. *Reinventing government*. Reading, MA: Addison-Wesley.

6. Henderson, Karla A. 1980. Programming volunteerism for happy volunteers. *Parks and Recreation* 15(9): 61-63.

7. *Webster's encyclopedic unabridged dictionary of the English language*. 1989. New York: Gramercy Books.

8. Peach, E. Brian. 1995. Reward and recognition systems for volunteers. In *The volunteer man-*

agement handbook, edited by Tracy Daniel Connors. New York: Wiley, 222-243.

9. Fisher, James C. and Kathleen M. Cole. 1993. *Leadership and management of volunteer programs*. San Francisco: Jossey-Bass.

10. Kozlowski, James C. 1997. Volunteer protection bills offer "carrot and stick" to states to enact federal "feel good" tort reform. *Parks and Recreation* 32(6): 34-40.

11. Ellis, Susan J. 1986. *From the top down: The executive role in volunteer program success*. Philadelphia: Energize Associates.

12. Bradner, Jeanne H. 1995. Recruitment, orientation and retention. In *The volunteer management handbook*, edited by Tracy Daniel Connors. New York: Wiley, 61-81.

13. Stepputat, Arlene. 1995. Administration of volunteer programs. In *The volunteer management handbook*, edited by Tracy Daniel Connors. New York: Wiley, 156-186.

14. International City Management Association. 1989. *Service delivery in the 90s: alternative approaches for local governments*. Washington, DC: International City Management Association.

CHAPTER 14

SUPPORT FROM DONATIONS

The discussion in this chapter and chapter 15 focuses on acquiring support from donations, and the discussion shifts to sponsorship in chapter 16. The terms donation and sponsorship often are used interchangeably and are considered to be synonyms, but this is a mistake. Even though the notion of voluntary exchange underlies both donations and sponsorships, the two are conceptually different. The notion of voluntary exchange requires that something of value be offered in exchange for something else of value. Before a donation or sponsorship investment is made, the contributor is likely to ask two questions: "What is in it for me?" and "How much will it cost me?" The trade-off is weighed between what will be gained and what will be given up. Both donations and sponsorships offer funds, resources, or in-kind services to park and recreation agencies, but contributors differ in the nature of what they seek in exchange.

The key motive underlying donations is philanthropy, which literally means affection for mankind. Thus, the only value that is supposed to accrue to the donor is the satisfaction of knowing that good is being done with the donated resources. Philanthropic donations are considered to be altruistic rather than commercial because they focus on humanistic or community concerns rather than on a commercial return on the investment.

Although sponsors may offer similar types and amounts of support to those provided by donors, the benefits they seek in return for their contributions are different. Sponsorship is defined as a business relationship between a provider of funds, resources, or services and a park and recreational program or organization that offers in return some rights and an association that may be used for commercial advantage.[1] The distinctive terms in this definition that differentiate sponsorship from philanthropy are business relationship and commercial advantage.

While these conceptual distinctions are clear, they are sometimes difficult to ascertain in a specific context. The effective, operational determination of whether a resource contributed by an individual or company to a park and recreation agency is classified as a donation or a sponsorship is made by the IRS. If the IRS rules that a giver receives a tangible, measurable, economic benefit from the contribution, then it is classified as a sponsorship investment undertaken for commercial advantage and is not eligible for a tax deduction. In contrast, if the benefits are perceived to be intangible, emotional, and not measurable, then the contribution qualifies as disinterested generosity and is eligible for a tax deduction.

Total philanthropic giving by individuals, corporations, and foundations exceeds $130 billion.[2] The contribution of foundations is discussed in chapters 18 and 19, which point out that, for a variety of reasons, many donations are made to foundations associated with park and recreation agencies rather than directly to a department. This chapter focuses on donations from individuals and business enterprises made either directly to an agency or to its support foundation. Although there are some areas of overlap, the motives and tax incentives associated with individuals and businesses are different, and, hence, they are discussed separately.

Almost 90% of total philanthropy comes from living individuals or individuals' bequests, and 45% of the total is given to religious organizations. Corporations contribute about $6 billion in direct funds to philanthropic causes, but these statistics do not record in-kind donations or donations from cause-related marketing (which is discussed in chapter 15). These two types of corporate donations have increased substantially in recent years and have replaced traditional cash donations at many companies.

The importance of donations to the parks and recreation field is illustrated in Minnesota, which has kept donation records since 1840. Minnesota residents have gifted 3,700 parcels of land totaling more than 78,000 acres for parks, wildlife management areas, scientific and natural areas, and other management units of the Minnesota Department of Natural Resources, with most being donated by private donors.[3]

There is a long tradition of donation support for public park and recreation services in the United States. In 1929, the National Recreation Association published a report resulting from a survey of 1,000 towns and cities that stated:

> The total area of the donated parks was approximately 75,000 acres, which was estimated to represent nearly one-third of the total municipal park acreage in 1925-26. Although no valuation was available for many of the parks, the total reported value of those for which estimates were given exceeded $100 million. The study proved that gifts were a very important factor in the acquisition of municipal park systems in American cities (p. 43).[4]

The author of one of the earliest texts, which was published in 1935, in the park and recreation field noted:

Private initiative and generosity have always played an important part in furthering the progress of municipal recreation. In the earlier period, private philanthropy in this field found it necessary not only to provide areas but also the means for their operation. Now that cities are assuming the responsibility for recreation needs and can generally be counted on for maintenance funds, the field remains open for the financially more significant, and personally more appealing gifts of lands, buildings, swimming pools and other specialized projects. The size and numbers of these gifts within recent years show how attractive this means of expression is to wealthy and civic-minded persons (p. 43).[4]

As the field evolved to become a service that residents expected government to provide, there was a decline in the perceived civic imperative for donors to contribute. In more recent years, the two factors that have been most influential in encouraging major donations to park and recreation agencies have been the availability of matching grants to multiply the value of a donation and the structure of the tax laws that are sympathetic to those who donate appreciated property.

The face value of donations can be multiplied when they can be used as a jurisdiction's matching contribution for a state or federal grant. The ability to leverage donations in this way is appealing to donors because it dramatically magnifies the impact and value of their donations. For example, grants that local agencies receive from the federal Land and Water Conservation Fund and the federal Intermodal Surface Transportation Efficiency Act, which were discussed in chapter 11, required the local jurisdiction to contribute 50% and 20%, respectively, of the total cost. However, a donation of cash, volunteer services, materials, real property, or equipment to the jurisdiction could be used as a jurisdiction's share of the match in lieu of cash and could qualify it for the federal grant.

The town of Hamden, Connecticut, was seeking a federal TEA-21 grant for a hiking and biking greenway project but was having difficulty raising the 20% local contribution that was required. The town solicited a donation of $20,000 from the owners of a new supermarket that was under construction. This donation enabled the town to apply for $80,000 from the TEA-21 grant program. Thus, the supermarket owners could see their $20,000 donation yield a $100,000 project.[5]

Many major donations involve appreciated property. Reasons for this are discussed later in the chapter, but at this point, it is important to dispel the myth that a donated piece of land is free to the agency. There is no such thing as a free piece of land. Land donations are a source not of free amenity but of free capital assets. Donated land does have a cost. Land donated to a park and recreation agency or nonprofit organization is removed from the tax roll, and any loss of tax revenue is an indirect cost. Furthermore, park development, maintenance, and operations all have a cost.

Reduced tax support has made maintaining and operating the parks that park and recreation agencies currently possess increasingly difficult. For this reason, it has become common practice for agencies to reject offers of donated property because they lack the operational funds to subsequently manage it. For example, an 81-year-old lawyer, conservationist, and former state official wanted to donate a 2,000-acre wildlife prairie park located 10 mi from Peoria, Illinois, to a public agency. The park was a former strip-mining site appraised at $19 million. It was inhabited by bison, bobcats, otters, eagles, badgers, and other animals; had trails for hiking and viewing; and had lodging and banquet accommodations. The park attracted about 250,000 paying visitors each year but ran at an annual deficit of about $300,000. Because of this deficit, no public agency would accept the property as a donation. The spokesman of the Illinois Department of Natural Resources stated: "It is a very generous offer, but we have declined it. It would take 300,000 bucks that we just don't have. Our land management people need more money for the sites we already have."[6]

Similarly, in Texas the governing commission of the state parks system placed a moratorium on future acquisitions unless they were accompanied by an endowment to pay for their operations. The largest land gift to the Texas state park system was a donation of 40,000 acres of rugged west Texas ranch land. It became the second largest component in the state's park system. However, the 62 sq mi of canyons, bluffs, and woodland plateaus were only accepted because they included a private endowment to maintain the property and to offset the loss of approximately $7,600 per year in property tax revenue to the county and local school districts. The state park director said: "This signals a threshold change in how we go about land acquisition. At a time when states are giving local governments more and more responsibilities, we shouldn't be damaging their ability to pay for services."

A related concern is that jurisdictions receiving land donations may lack the resources and commitment to develop the land so that it is useable as a park. Failure to improve it may result in the land becoming an eyesore and liability rather than an asset to the community. A donor adopted the following strategy to ensure that this failure to improve the land did not occur. In Washoe County, Nevada, the developer of a 300-unit subdivision wanted to donate six acres of land to the county for an active recreational neighborhood park. To ensure that the county developed the land in this way, the developer sold it to the county at its fair market value of $80,000 and then donated the $80,000 to the county. The county agreed to put these proceeds into a separate account that could be used only for development of the park property. To ensure that the money was not used for other purposes, bank officials controlled the disbursement of funds. When the park was completed, it was open to all members of the public, but the subdivision's homeowners' association was solely responsible for maintenance of the park at standards specified by the county's parks department.

Donations From Individuals

At the age of 83 years, Dorolou Swirsky deeded her entire estate, which was worth $500,000, to the Sunnyvale Parks and Recreation Department: "I have neither an immediate family nor an extended family to leave my possessions to. Witnessing first-hand the struggles and frustrations of limited governmental funding across the country to provide proper guidance for our young people, I wanted to ensure that my modest estate might become a 'beacon' used for the good of many to help finance those youth programs that might not otherwise be available." The intent of her gift was "to leave a means to provide a positive and constructive influence on the lives of the young people in our community. My gift is to be a gentle reminder year after year that our youth are our future."[7]

Individual donors to park and recreation agencies are likely to be characterized by a wide spectrum of attitudes, motives, and styles. Some desire anonymity, while others crave recognition. Some people are motivated by guilt; others, simply by a desire to do good; and some, by a desire to leave a mark. Some people have special emotional reasons for wanting to contribute to public park and recreation services, for example, contributing a memorial to a deceased parent.

Tax breaks are an important incentive for encouraging individual donations, and they are explained in some detail in this chapter. However, the substantial amount of donations to the park and recreation field that are made by people for whom there is no substantial tax benefit indicates that other, less selfish motives also are involved. Indeed, even where donors do receive a substantial tax incentive, they rarely get back in value what they donate.

Occasionally, a donation of land may be made because of a concern about the donor's exposure to liability, particularly if the property contains a lake or some other feature that may be considered an attractive nuisance. The absentee landowner is especially vulnerable in this respect, for if fences or signs are torn down and not immediately replaced, the landowner may be subject to a liability suit for any injuries that subsequently may occur.

In general, the attraction of park and recreation agencies to donors appears to be three-fold:

- People associate parks with permanence. They are forever, unlike buildings that have a more finite life. A gift of a park is a lasting legacy, which will benefit a donor's descendants along with other future visitors.

- Some of the donor's finest life experiences may have taken place in parks. These moments become cherished memories that many people would like to sustain.

- Park and recreation agencies generally have a positive public image. People believe that they are accountable and will deal honorably with their donations.

It is much more difficult to secure donations for operational and maintenance purposes than for capital facilities. The greatest potential for major capital donations from individuals to park and recreation agencies is probably through gifts of land. Experience has indicated that those most likely to donate land have the following characteristics:

- They are good stewards of their property, are concerned for its welfare, and seek perpetuation of its existing state. Usually they have lived on it for many years.

- They have philanthropic capability; that is, they have enough money to take advantage of the tax advantages afforded to donors of gifts to a public agency or tax-exempt organization.

- No significant heir or heirs are interested in acquiring the property.

- A substantial time period has elapsed since the property was purchased, so its value has appreciated substantially from what the landowner paid for it. Given this condition, a landowner is likely to receive substantial tax benefits for donating the property. These are explained in the following section.

Tax Considerations

For some potential donors, tax considerations are the primary reason for contemplating a major land donation to a park and recreation agency or foundation. Even donors whose primary motives are altruistic usually will (and should) seek to derive the maximal tax benefit from their donations. Hence, taxes are a factor that park and recreation agency managers cannot ignore responsibly. The purpose of this section is to discuss and illustrate the tax consequences inherent in various types of donations. The central principle of this discussion of tax structure is the notion of net cost of a donation. This notion recognizes that the amount of money in which a seller of property is interested is not the selling price but rather the amount that he or she will realize from a sale after expenses and taxes.

It is beyond the scope of this text to discuss the tax structure in great detail because, while park and recreation managers should be well informed on the issue, they do not need to be experts. Their task is to identify potential donors and then to alert them to some of the tax principles that may make it advantageous for them to donate. If interest is aroused, the donor should be counseled to retain a tax expert to recommend how the donation should be structured to the donor's best advantage. Thus, what is presented here is a simplified discussion of tax laws, which are complex and constantly changing.

The tax rules deny tax deductions to a donor if there is a quid pro quo; that is, the donation must not result in personal benefit measurable in money to the donor. Even where they are substantial, psychological benefits are permitted. For example, if a park is named after the donor, the personal satisfaction received from the donation may be very high; however, because the benefit is not measurable in money or money's worth by the IRS, a tax deduction would be permitted. In contrast, if a developer made a donation of park land to a jurisdiction in order to secure a change in zoning, approval of a subdivision, or some other act that financially benefited him or her in a tangible way or in order to enhance the value of his or her remaining property, then tax deductions would not be permitted because there was a quid pro quo.

From a tax perspective, it is useful to differentiate between present donations and deferred, or planned, donations. A present donation requires the donor to make an outright gift, transferring immediate possession and use of it to the agency. With a deferred donation, the donation itself is not deferred because the agency does receive an immediate gift. However, the agency's actual possession and use of the donated property is deferred to some future time. The future time may be a specified number of years or a specified future event, such as the death of the donor or someone designated by the donor. Planned gifts do not weaken the financial security of donors in their lifetime, and they tend to be relatively large. Both types of donations normally yield a current tax deduction (income or estate tax) to the donor, but the deductions from a present donation are likely to be significantly larger.

The first part of this section on tax considerations addresses present donations. The consequences for estate taxes were discussed previously in chapter 4, so the discussion here primarily is confined to the income tax and capital-gain tax implications of donations. The latter part of this section offers a brief review of five fairly common types of deferred, or planned, donations and suggests a strategy for soliciting them.

Influence of the Tax Structure on Encouraging Individual Present Donations

The tax laws offer incentives for individuals to make donations. The amount of money in which a potential donor is interested is not the fair market selling price of a piece of property; rather, it is a comparison between the amount that will be realized from the sale after expenses and taxes have been paid and the tax savings that may accrue from donating the property. This constitutes the net cost of the donation. In effect the tax laws offer government subsidies to agencies and nonprofit organizations that are equal to the income, capital-gain, or estate taxes that federal and state governments forego when donations are made to these entities.

Two tax laws are particularly relevant. First, donations made by individuals to a public park and recreation agency or to a nonprofit organization are fully deductible up to 30% per year of an individual's adjusted gross income. *Adjusted gross income* is a federal income tax term that is defined as a taxpayer's annual gross income from all sources minus certain allowable deductions. One of the allowable deductions is for gifts made to government or qualified nonprofit organizations. The deduction permitted for a gift is equal to the full fair market value of the donation. If the value of the donation exceeds 30% of adjusted gross income, the excess may be carried over and deducted over the next five years until it is used up.

The value of a donation deduction to an individual will depend upon the magnitude of his or her annual adjusted gross income. The federal income tax rates and adjusted gross incomes to which they are applied that prevailed at the time this book was written are shown in table 14.1. The gross income ranges are adjusted upwards annually as they are indexed to inflation. By amending the adjusted gross income ranges in this way, people are not pushed into a higher tax bracket merely by inflation. They only move into a higher range and pay a higher level of tax when the real purchasing power of their income has increased.

Table 14.1 indicates that a single person whose adjusted gross income was $70,000 would be taxed at a rate of 15% on the first $24,000, 28% on the amount between $24,000 and $58,150, and 31% on the income between $58,150 and $70,000. If this individual made a donation valued at $20,000, then he or she would pay less tax because the donation deduction would reduce the adjusted gross income from $70,000 to $50,000. Table 14.2 illustrates the tax benefits from this donation. Without the donation, the individual's federal income tax bill is $16,835. However, when the $20,000 donation is deducted from the $70,000 adjusted gross income, the tax bill is $10,880. Thus, the tax deduction of $20,000 results in a tax saving of $5,955 (from $16,835 to $10,880). The net cost to the taxpayer of the $20,000 donation, therefore, would be $14,045 (from $20,000 to $5,955). Table 14.1 indicates that tax rates increase with adjusted income growth. Thus, at the highest rate (39.6%), a $20,000 donation made by those with an adjusted gross income of more than $263,750 would receive a tax deduction of $7,880, so the net cost to an individual of making the donation would be $12,120.

The second tax relevant to individual donors is the long-term capital-gain tax. This tax is applied to the sale of any capital asset that has been held for a period of more than 18 months. Such assets may include stocks, mutual funds, bonds, and, of particular interest to park and recreation professionals, real estate other than the primary house of residence. Long-term capital gain is defined as the difference between the cost associated with acquiring the asset and the income accruing from its sale. If an asset has been held for a period of 18 months or less (i.e., short term) then the income is considered to be part of an individual's

Table 14.1 Federal Income Tax Rates

Tax rate	Single person income ($'s)		Joint return income ($'s)	
	Increment	Cumulative	Increment	Cumulative
15%	< 24,000	—	< 40,100	—
28%	34,150	58,150	56,900	96,900
31%	63,150	121,300	50,800	147,700
36%	142,450	263,750	116,050	263,750
39.6%		> 263,750		> 263, 750

The federal government adjusts both the tax rates and the incremental ranges of adjusted gross incomes to which they apply. The ranges are indexed to inflation so they increase annually. The reader should check those that prevail at the current time.

Table 14.2 Federal Income Tax Implications of a $20,000 Donation for a Single Individual With a $70,000 Adjusted Gross Income

Tax rate	Tax paid if a donation of $20,000 is made		Tax paid if no donation is made	
	Tax bracket	Taxes paid	Tax bracket	Taxes paid
15%	< $24,000	$3,600	< $24,000	$3,600
28%	$24,000-$50,000	$7,280	$24,000-$58,150	$9,562
31%	—	—	$58,150-$70,000	$3,673
Total taxes paid		$10,880	—	$16,835

annual ordinary gross income and is taxed at the regular income tax rate.

The maximal rate of capital-gain tax for an individual is 20% (compared with the maximal income tax rate of 39.6% on ordinary income). Beginning in 2001, the top rate of capital-gain tax will be 18% for assets purchased after 2000 and held for at least five years. Investors in the lowest income tax bracket who pay a federal income tax of 15% (see table 14.1) pay a capital-gain tax of 10%. Gains on investments bought after 2000 by these individuals and held five years will be taxed at only 8%.

Unlike the tax ranges associated with income tax, the capital-gain tax is not indexed to inflation. Thus, if a parcel of land was purchased 30 years ago for $10,000 and is now sold for $30,000, the capital gain is $20,000 even though most of this gain may be attributed to inflation rather than to an increase in real value. In real-income terms (real income is defined as income adjusted for inflation), the asset may be worth no more (and possibly even less) than it was 30 years ago. Some argue that this is unfair and advocate that the proportion of a capital gain that results from inflation should be deducted from the nominal capital gain. Nevertheless, periodic proposals to index the capital-gain tax have been rejected primarily because it would reduce income to the federal treasury and, hence, worsen the federal deficit.

If a landowner wants to dispose of a property in fee simple in the near future, there are three alternative strategies he or she could pursue. The financial implications of each of these strategies are summarized in the hypothetical case shown in "Implications of an Individual Selling Land at Fair Market Value, Negotiating a Bargain Sale, or Making an Outright Donation" on page 370.

First, the land could be sold at fair market value. The market price is anticipated to be $750,000, but to sell the property, the landowner would hire a real-estate broker who would claim 10% commission on the sale. Long-term capital-gain tax is levied on the difference between the cost paid for the asset and the net sales price realized, which is $525,000 in this illustration. After federal and state long-term capital-gain taxes have been applied, the landowner retains $393,750 from the profit on the land sale. In addition, he or she retains the cost basis amount that was deducted to calculate the capital gain. Thus, the landowner's after-tax overall proceeds from the sale are $543,750.

A bargain sale is a sale of property in which the amount of the sale proceeds is less than the property's fair market value. When a bargain sale is made to a government agency or a qualified nonprofit organization, the excess of the fair market value of the property over the sale price represents a donation to the organization.[8] Each part of a bargain sale is reported separately according to its tax consequences. Thus, the donor reports both a sale and a contribution.

The bargain sale illustration in "Implications of an Individual Selling Land at Fair Market Value, Negotiating a Bargain Sale, or Making an Outright Donation" assumes a selling price that is 60% of fair market value. Often land is donated or offered as a bargain sale because its owners are good stewards of the land and want to see it retained for conservation purposes. In other instances, the bargain sale approach is used because it offers tax advantages. For tax purposes, the property is assumed to be divided into two sections. In this illustration, the first section of 180 acres (60% of 300 acres) is treated as if it were being sold at fair

Implications of an Individual Selling Land at Fair Market Value, Negotiating a Bargain Sale, or Making an Outright Donation

The following illustrations are based on four assumptions:

1. The landowner is in the highest income tax bracket.

2. The landowner is committed to disposing of 300 acres of potentially attractive park land that has appreciated in value from $500 per acre to $2,500 per acre since it was purchased 20 years ago.

3. The federal long-term capital-gain tax is 20%, and there is also a state long-term capital-gain tax of 5%.

4. $1 in year one is worth more than $1 in years two and three, but to simplify the exposition, these calculations do not consider the net present value of money.

Sale at Fair Market Value

Selling price (300 acres × $2,500)	$750,000
Less broker's commission at 10%	75,000
Net selling price	675,000
Less cost basis (300 acres × $500 original purchase price)	150,000
Long-term capital gain	525,000
Federal and state long-term capital-gain taxes at 25%	131,250
Amount remaining after levying the tax	393,750
Plus cost basis	150,000
Overall proceeds	**543,750**

Bargain Sale (Sell at 60% of Fair Market Value and Donate 40%)

The 60% Sale

Selling price (180 acres × $2,500)	$450,000
Less cost basis (180 acres × $500)	90,000
Long-term capital gain	360,000
Federal and state long-term capital-gain taxes at 25%	90,000
Amount remaining after levying the tax	270,000
Plus cost basis	90,000
Proceeds from 60% sale	360,000

The 40% Donation (120 Acres Valued at $300,000)

Adjusted gross income of the landowner	$860,000
Maximal donation deduction permitted in year one ($860,000 × 30%)	258,000
Value of year one income tax deduction (federal income tax at 39.6% and state income tax at, for example, 5.4% = $258,000 × 45%)	116,100
Remaining deduction applied to taxable income in year two ($300,000 value of the 40% donation – $258,000 applied on year one)	42,000
Value of year two income tax deduction ($42,000 × 45%)	18,900
Overall proceeds ($360,000 + $116,100 + $18,900)	**495,000**

Outright Donation

$750,000 × 45% $337,500

Given an adjusted gross income of $860,000 and the 30% rule, this deduction would accrue over a three-year period.

Adapted from William T. Hutton. Primer: Understanding and illustrating tax benefits. The Back Forty: A Newsletter of Land Conservation Law. *Hastings College of the Law: San Francisco. 1995.*

market value, while the second section of 120 acres is treated as a donation. The sale price of the 180 acres is $450,000. Because it is really the whole 300 acres that is being sold for this price, no real-estate broker is needed and no commission is paid. The law requires that the cost basis of bargain sale property must be allocated between the sale and donation elements of the transaction.[6] Thus, only the cost basis of 180 acres can be used in calculating the long-term capital gain in the illustration, "Implications of an Individual Selling Land at Fair Market Value, Negotiating a Bargain Sale, or Making an Outright Donation." After the long-term capital-gain tax has been paid and the cost basis has been added back into the proceeds, $360,000 accrues from the 60% sale of the property.

The donation segment of the bargain sale was valued at $300,000 (40% of $750,000). However only 30% of the adjusted gross income can be deducted in a year ($258,000), so some of the deduction has to be carried forward to year two. With an adjusted gross income of $860,000, the landowner is in the highest federal income tax bracket of 39.6%. Most states also levy a state income tax, and the rates for this tax vary widely among states. To simplify the arithmetic used in the illustration, a state income tax of 5.4% has been assumed. By being permitted to deduct the $258,000, the landowner pays the 45% total income tax only on $602,000 of income instead of the

$860,000, resulting in a savings of $116,100 in year one. A similar deduction process in year two using the remainder of the $300,000 donation results in savings for that year of $18,900. Thus, after-tax overall proceeds accruing to the landowner from both the sale and donation components of the bargain sale are $495,000.

A bargain sale transaction is likely to be expedited quickly; perhaps, it will be expedited several years sooner than it would be if the sale were at fair market value. The delay in waiting for a fair-market-value sale may mean that the landowner forgoes interest on the cash in hand, which he or she would have from a bargain sale, and continues to pay taxes on the property. Thus, at least some of the $48,750 difference between the net proceeds from the fair market value and bargain sale may be discounted by the element of time.

It should be noted that although the tax laws authorize tax deductions for bargain sales negotiated with park and recreation agencies, this opportunity is not always available to those agencies. In some cases, the agencies are required to conform with state or federal legislation that mandates them to offer landowners the full fair market value for property. For these situations, a non-profit organization has to be used as an intermediary. The details of this strategy are described in chapter 18.

The third strategy that a landowner could use is to make an outright donation. Given the landowner's adjusted gross income, the most that can be donated in any one year is $258,000, so the deduction for a $750,000 donation would have to be spread over three years. At the end of that period, the landowner would be able to retain $337,500, which would have been paid in income tax if a donation had not been made.

The difference between a sale at fair market value and the overall proceeds that would accrue to the landowner from the other two strategies should be viewed as the real cost of making the donation.[9] The illustrations in "Implications of an Individual Selling Land at Fair Market Value, Negotiating a Bargain Sale, or Making an Outright Donation" indicate that if the landowner proceeded with an outright gift, then the income forgone compared with the bargain sale and fair market value sale options is $157,500 and $206,250, respectively. However, if the landowner elected to receive these additional financial amounts, then it would cost the agency or the nonprofit organization $450,000 and $750,000, respectively, to acquire this park land. These large amounts to be paid by the agency are likely to be acquired only after great effort from sources such as public bond referenda, foundation grants, and fundraising. Given this situation and the landowner's relatively high adjusted gross income, he or she may be persuaded to offer the outright donation even though it entails loss of income. In addition, a strong emotional appeal may be made to the landowner on the following basis. If he or she pays capital-gain and income taxes, they go to Washington, DC; however, if a donation is made, then the public in the local area will be the beneficiaries.

Friendly condemnation is another strategy that a park and recreation agency could use.[10] It may enable landowners to avoid paying capital-gain tax and, hence, may enable the agency to purchase the land for less than market value. The power of condemnation (also called eminent domain) enables a government jurisdiction legally to acquire land at its appraised value even when a landowner does not want to sell it. It is used most commonly to acquire rights-of-way for new highway projects. Using these dictatorial powers usually arouses passionate opposition and angst, so governments rarely resort to it. However, if condemnation acquisitions are forced upon landowners, they do not have to pay capital-gain tax on the land that they are required to sell. For a friendly condemnation, landowners encourage an agency to write them a letter indicating their intention to acquire property by eminent domain so that the land can be sold without paying capital-gain tax.

It is possible to defer capital-gain tax and to reduce the amount that has to be paid by heirs through engaging in a tax-deferred exchange.[10] This involves a landowner swapping property held for a particular purpose (most often investment) for another piece of property that must be used for the same purpose. The tax advantage is that the capital-gain tax that the landowner would have paid if the first property had been sold is deferred until the property obtained in the swap is sold.

The owner of a property in Rhode Island, which the Nature Conservancy was eager to acquire, was reluctant to sell because it had been bought in the 1960s and, hence, there was a low cost basis and the likelihood of a large capital-gain tax payment. She preferred to leave the property to her children to sell, giving them the benefit of the so-called stepped-up basis. (The children would pay taxes only on the difference between their selling price and the property's value at their mother's death). The solution was to buy a property that the children wanted, so the Nature Conservancy bought farmland in Kansas and swapped it with the mother for the Rhode Island natural area. The children will inherit it after her death, and if they decide to sell, their gain will be determined by the value of the farmland in the mother's estate, i.e., it becomes the cost basis. Thus, the large capital gain in the Rhode Island property will escape federal taxation.[10]

Tax structures are created by federal and state legislatures and, thus, are subject to frequent adjustments. These adjustments may substantially impact the incentive to donate. For example, the highest federal income tax rate shown in table 14.1 is 39.6%, but in 1980, the highest federal rate was 70%. Similarly, until 1997, the maximal federal capital-gain tax was 28% instead of the current 20% tax rate used in "Implications of an Individual Selling Land at Fair Market Value, Negotiating a Bargain Sale, or Making an Outright Donation." If the 70% federal rate, 5% state income tax rate, and the 28% capital-gain tax rate had been used in the bargain sale and outright donation illustrations given in "Implications of an Individual Selling Land at Fair Market Value, Negotiating a Bargain Sale, or Making an Outright Donation," then the overall proceeds from these options would have been $525,000 and $562,500, respectively. At these rates, it would be financially more advantageous to the landowner to make an outright donation of the property than to try to sell it in whole or in part.

When tax rates fall, the financial incentive to donate land or other capital assets is reduced, whereas when they are raised, the incentive to donate is increased. This maxim applies equally to both the income tax and the long-term capital-gain tax. However, while the incentive is reduced, tax reductions do increase available disposable income, which enhances the capacity of individuals to donate.

If a decision has been made to make a donation of property that has appreciated highly and is subject to long-term capital-gain tax, then the donor should donate the property rather than donate the proceeds from its sale. If it is sold, then the owner is required to pay the long-term capital-gain tax. Thus, the remaining proceeds, when donated, will be reduced by this amount, which means that the magnitude of the income tax donation is reduced by that amount. In contrast, if the property itself is donated, the owner does not have to pay long-term capital-gain tax, so the net value of the donation is higher, as is the consequent tax deduction for which the donor is eligible.

Two limitations associated with the income tax deduction should be noted.[11] First, such deductions are only useful if an individual has income to shelter with them; if he or she does not, the deductions have no value. Thus, for example, the donation of attractive ranch land appropriate for park use often may not be feasible because many ranchers have little or no taxable income to shelter with the donation deduction. Second, an inequity of the deductions is that the U.S. Treasury (or federal taxpayers), in essence, pays more (through the deductions offered) for a piece of land that is owned by an affluent landowner than it would if the same piece of land were in the hands of a lower-bracket landowner. There is no rational reason why there should be different payments by taxpayers for the same piece of land.

In addition to the income tax benefits that accrue to a landowner, a donation in fee or a less-than-fee donation, such as a conservation easement, would have the effect of reducing inheritance taxes. Like the income tax, the estate tax is progressive and cumulative. The impacts of inheritance taxes were discussed in chapter 4 and, thus, are not reiterated here. Finally, in relation to the effects of the tax structure on incentives to donate, it should be noted that the landowner is no longer responsible for paying property taxes on the donated land. Similarly, if a less-than-fee donation is made, then the landowner's property taxes will be reduced commensurate with the reduced value of the land.

Phased Acquisition of Property

Many purchases or bargain sales of property are completed through phased payments. These phased payments enable a public agency to spread the purchase price over a number of years and may serve to accommodate the landowner's tax requirements. The phasing may be achieved either through an installment sale or through a lease-purchase arrangement.

An installment sale is based upon an agreement between the landowner and the purchaser specifying that the park and recreation agency either pays for the land in annual installments or buys a portion of the land each year. Local agencies may be authorized by their ordinances or state law to use the former approach, but state and federal agencies must use the latter approach because they cannot pledge the credit of government. The two parties negotiate the use of the land during the period in which installments are being made and the responsibility for property taxes.[12]

The lease-purchase arrangement is a variation of installment purchasing whereby an agency leases the entire property from a landowner at a nominal rent, which is a procedure that takes it off the property tax rolls and removes liability from the owner. Each year, the agency pays a portion of the total purchase price and, in exchange, receives title to a commensurate piece of the land, converting that piece from lease to ownership. There must be exchange of land title for installment payments so, if for any reason the agency is unable to complete the full amount of the payments, the public secures ownership of the proportion of land for which the agency has paid.

The county commissioners in Washington County, Minnesota, wanted to purchase a 579-acre tract in the St. Croix River Valley, which subsequently became the St. Croix Bluffs Regional Park. They lacked time to organize the referendum necessary to authorize general obligation bonds. Hence, they opted to use a combination of outright purchase and a lease-purchase agreement. The county first acquired a 208-acre parcel outright for $1.13 million. The remaining 371 acres were subject to a lease-purchase arrangement. An initial lease payment of $137,000 was made, which was to be followed by 10 annual lease payments of $500,000. After 10 years, the county would own the property obtained at a cost of $6.26 million. Its appraised value, based on its maximal development value, was $11 million.[3]

Five Types of Planned Donations

This section offers a brief review of five fairly common types of deferred, or planned, donations: life-estate and remainder-interest donations; bequests; charitable-remainder bequests; gift annuities; and donations of life insurance.

Life-Estate and Remainder-Interest Donations

The life-estate and remainder-interest donation involves making a donation of a personal residence or of a farm or open space to a public agency or qualified nonprofit organization but reserving the landowner's right to live on the property until he or she dies or, if he or she chooses, until the spouse, children, or both die. The right to remain on the property is called life estate or life tenancy. The act of donating the property now to take effect at the landowner's death is called the gift of a remainder interest.[13]

This approach ensures preservation of the land for future generations while the landowners continue to live on their property and to receive a federal income tax deduction. During their lifetimes, the donors remain responsible for maintenance costs and other expenses (usually including property taxes) but also retain any income that the property generates.

If a park and recreation agency is given $2.5 million in cash today, it is certainly worth more in purchasing power than if it is given the same amount in 10 years. Thus, because the recipient agency will actually take possession of the donation at some time in the future, the value of the gift is reduced for income tax purposes. The value of the deduction is determined by actuarial tables that the IRS publishes and depends primarily on the ages of the designated life tenants. Thus, if the life tenant is relatively young, then the value of the donated property will be low relative to its present fair market value.

If the married landowners are aged 65 and 62 years and the property is worth $2.5 million, then the IRS tables value the remainder interest in the property at $889,400. Alternatively, if the landowner is aged 65 years and widowed, then the remainder interest value of the property is $991,400. As with other donations, the deduction in any single year is limited to 30% of the donor's income, and the balance of the deduction can be carried forward for five years.[13]

A superior alternative for the property owner who is interested in preserving the land's conservation qualities is to donate both a conservation easement and a remainder interest. This is essentially the same as making a donation of only a remainder interest, but it results in much greater tax benefits.

If the landowner is aged 65 years and widowed and donates a conservation easement on the $2.5 million property that is valued at $1.5 million, then this donation is immediately deductible. The remaining $1 million remainder interest is valued by the IRS tables at $396,560. Thus, the total income tax deduction is $1,896,560. (Compare this amount with the $991,400 amount shown in the earlier example in which only a remainder interest was donated.)[13]

The use of life-estate donation has been proven to be valuable in securing individual land donations or bargain sales for park and recreation agencies. Many property owners are land poor; that is, they own property on which they have to pay heavy taxes, but they have no cash flow with which to pay those taxes. In these cases, the life-estate arrangement is particularly attractive. They receive a cash payment that can be enjoyed while they are living, and at the same time, they are able to stay on the land and continue living as if the property were still their own.

In effect, the landowner's assets have been liquified. The public is not permitted to use the property during the landowner's lifetime; however, in some instances, the landowner may want to retain only a small part of the total that can be maintained relatively easily, and the public can be given immediate access to the remaining portion. The landowners would continue to pay real-estate taxes on the land while they have use of the property.

Bequests

Bequests can be made by a will, which is a legal document giving instructions for distribution of assets after death. A donation in this form ensures that the deceased's wishes for the property to remain as open space will be carried out without the fear that heirs will be forced to sell the land to a developer in order to pay the estate taxes.

Bequests to park and recreation agencies and qualified nonprofit organizations are allowed as deductions in determining the net value of an estate on which the federal estate tax is imposed. (This was discussed in chapter 4). Thus, on a bequest of $100,000 from an estate on which the highest marginal tax rate of 55% is payable (estates valued in excess of $3,000,000, see table 4.2), the net cost to the estate will be $45,000. (This disregards any additional state estate tax that may also be payable and that would have the effect of further reducing the net cost). If the bequest had not been made, the remaining $55,000 would have been paid in tax to the federal government.

However, if donations are made by bequest, then the donors cannot take advantage of any income tax deductions to which they would be entitled if they were living. For this reason, it is advantageous for a present or a remainder-interest donation to be made while the donor is living.

If the $100,000 had been donated while the taxpayers were still living, the tax saving would have been

income tax savings (39.6% $\times$ $100,000) = $39,600

estate tax savings (55% $\times$ $100,000) = $55,000

total tax savings $39,600 + $55,000 = $94,600

Money in an Individual Retirement Account that is included as part of a bequest is particularly prone to high taxation. Unlike other assets, if the Individual Retirement Account money is bequeathed to individuals other than a spouse, then it is subject not only to estate tax but also to income tax when it is distributed to the designee. These two taxes combined may consume more than 70% of the Individual Retirement Account assets. If the Individual Retirement Account funds are bequeathed to a public agency or qualified nonprofit organization, then all taxes generally are avoided.

Charitable-Remainder Funds

These types of funds enable donors to place property into a trust account on behalf of a public agency or nonprofit organization. Although control of the property is given up, donors retain a life income for either themselves or others whom they may nominate from the trust until they are deceased. At that time, the remainder of the trust's assets go to the designated organization. The length of the period over which life-income payments are made is limited to the life of the donors or to 20 years if others are nominated.

The life income is paid annually. A trust that pays a fixed-dollar annuity is called a charitable-remainder annuity trust, and the annuity amount must be set at no less than 5% of the initial value of the trust assets. If a percentage of payout is chosen, the trust is called a charitable-remainder unitrust, and the annual payout to income beneficiaries

must not be less than 5% of the value of the trust assets valued annually.[9] The income from the unitrust will rise and fall based on the value of the assets place in the trust.

Generally, the remainder donation qualifies for both income tax and estate tax deductions. Like remainder-interest donations, the value of the deductions will depend on the conditions placed on the trust and the age of the donor and other beneficiaries: "The amount of the charitable income or estate tax deduction obtainable upon the creation of the trust is determined with reference both to actuarial expectancy and the prescribed payout. The higher the income payout, the smaller the charitable income or estate tax deduction" (p. 11).[9]

Most large cities and most states have community foundations that are willing to serve as the trust manager for park and recreation agencies or their support organizations. Local banks and other financial institutions also have trust departments that can work with agencies and the donor to establish a charitable trust to benefit the agency.

Gift Annuities

Gift annuities enable a donor to transfer property to a park and recreation agency or qualified nonprofit organization in exchange for a commitment by the agency to pay the donor a specified amount each year during the remainder of the donor's life. The transfer, however, is not wholly a quid pro quo because the value of the property transferred to the park and recreation agency or nonprofit organization exceeds the value of the annuity guaranteed to the donor. The donor intends to make a contribution in the amount of the excess, and the amount so contributed is an allowable deduction.[8]

The Maryland National Capitol Park and Planning Commission was attempting to acquire 170 acres of land, which was appraised at $350,000. The owners, who were married to each other, wanted to retire in the near future. They had no children, wanted this land to stay as a park, and wanted an income of $1,000 per month from this transaction to help them in their retirement years. It was determined that by depositing $200,000 in a trust escrow account at 7% interest, they could be guaranteed $1,000 per month for the rest of their lives. The difference in value entitled them to a $150,000 federal tax deduction, and donation of the land meant that it was not subject to estate taxes. The commission acquired the land valued at $350,000 and received the $200,000 escrow back after these people died, so its net cost was the interest on the $200,000.[14]

Gifts of Life Insurance

Life insurance is purchased by individuals to provide for the security of their families. However, if that security over time becomes adequately provided from other sources, then an individual may elect to designate a park and recreation agency or its support group as sole beneficiary of the policy. If no premiums remain to be paid on the policy, then an individual can claim an income tax deduction equal to the replacement value of the policy for the donation. If premiums remain to be paid on the policy, then the deduction is approximately equal to the cash surrender value of the policy. If the annual premiums continue to be paid by the donor, they are tax deductible as a contribution.

Donations From Businesses

The average size of donations that businesses make is likely to be substantially greater than those derived from individuals because corporations are likely to have more resources. If donations are needed urgently, then businesses become especially prominent because they can often make quick decisions and forward funds within a few days. Further, the human effort and associated expenses required to secure a relatively large contribution from a business is likely to be less than that required to obtain an equivalent amount from many individual donors.

Companies may make donations directly, may make them through a corporate foundation, or may use both of these mechanisms. Although philanthropic donations from corporations amount to more than $6 billion, they do not include in-kind donations or donations derived from cause-related marketing, which have increased dramatically in recent years, and their value probably far exceeds the value that traditional corporate philanthropy provides. Bartering and in-kind arrangements can be quite complex.

The San Diego Mozart Festival did not have the funds to rent the Cathedral Church of St. Paul for some of its concerts. However, the festival manager learned that La Scada Italian Shoes in Del Mar was drastically reducing some of its stock and also needed a charitable tax deduction. Therefore, the festival manager accepted the shoes and traded them to the cathedral's thrift shop in lieu of the concert rent.[15]

Sometimes it is easier for companies to make in-kind donations of equipment, materials, or personnel expertise because they can be hidden from shareholders or employees who may be skeptical of the value of the donations in improving the company's profitability. It is difficult for a company to explain to employees receiving no pay raises or to shareholders receiving low dividends why it can afford to make monetary donations! Thus, for example, in the Department of Recreation in Philadelphia, Gerrard Roofing Technology provided the materials and work for a new roof for a dilapidated community center building (estimated at $30,000); Asplendh, a tree-cutting company, made its trucks equipped with high ladders available to the department to fix the lights in all the open baseball and basketball courts (estimated at $6,000); and the *Daily News*, a local newspaper, provided ongoing publicity for the department's annual fundraising run and its pool campaign (estimated at $57,000).[16]

Nine of 10 businesses do not make a donation of any kind. Among those who do, the percentage of domestic pre-tax income allocated to donations averages approximately 1%; the tax laws encourage companies to make annual donations of up to 10% of their net income before taxes. Because most giving is done by few firms, these firms should probably be the first to be approached by park and recreation personnel.

An asset that companies can donate and that costs them nothing in physical resources is their corporate reputation. That is, the institutional clout conferred on a park and recreation agency by the reputation of a company aligned with it. If a business backer in the community lobbies for a particular park or recreation investment and if the business is highly visible and well respected, then it adds considerable credibility to the agency's advocacy for the project.

> One of the most helpful things you may be able to give your nonprofit partner is clout; that is, your corporate weight applied to its cause. Most nonprofit organizations work hard to effect change in a particular area, but they often lack the contacts or pull with officials that can readily promote change. As a business, you may be better positioned to get legislators, other businesses, or community leaders to take action (p. 194).[17]

Motives for Business Donations

Corporate philanthropy is an oxymoron. Even though some corporate contributions may be technically accepted by the IRS as donations, they are

A Shareholder Challenge to Corporate Donations

At an annual meeting of shareholders of the Potomac Electric Power Company, a shareholder presented the following proposal to be voted on at the meeting:

> Resolved: that the shareholders recommend that the Board take the steps necessary to amend the Corporation's Certificate of Incorporation by adding thereto; 'No corporate funds of this corporation shall be given to any charitable, educational or other similar organization, except for purposes in direct furtherance of the business interests of this corporation and subject to the further provision that aggregate amount of such contributions shall be reported to the shareholders not later than the date of the annual meeting.'

The shareholder submitting the proposal stated: "Over the years your company has given away hundreds of thousands of dollars of your money to charitable and educational institutions, money which belongs to you. Last year the total amount was $225,406."

The board of directors and the management of the company recommended a vote against the proposal's adoption.

> The Company, as a responsible corporate citizen, recognizes the need to meet its civic and social responsibilities. Among those responsibilities is the financial support of local organizations and institutions whose purpose is to improve the economic and social health of the community and otherwise to aid in the solution of community problems.
>
> The Company, therefore, makes limited contributions for charitable, social and community purposes where, in its judgment, such support is reasonable and contributes to the improvement of the community and the general environment in which the Company operates.

From the Potomac Electric Power Company. Summary of the Proceedings, Annual Meeting of Shareholders. *Washington, DC. Copyright ©1980 Potomac Electric Power Company. Used by permission.*

Figure 14.1 A business executive sees a donation as an "investment" from which some form of benefits will be returned to the business at some future time.

not altruistic. Corporations do not exist to give resources to public agencies or nonprofit organizations; rather, as the shareholder motion in "A Shareholder Challenge to Corporate Donations" indicates, their purpose is to produce and sell goods and services. Thus, the motives stimulating donations reflect enlightened self-interest in which companies seek to enhance their positions in the marketplace and their profitability through donations that they make.[18] The director of Philanthropic Administration at General Motors Corporation said: "We view philanthropy as an investment, a strategic asset that requires the same level of disciplined processes and evaluation as any other aspects of the business" (p. 19).[19]

The officers of a corporation have no mandate to give away their stockholders' money. Their charge is to invest company resources in a way that optimizes the return to stockholders on their investment. It is the prerogative of the individual stockholders to make donations out of dividends received from the company if they wish to do so, but the corporation has no right to make donations on their behalf. A business should only make donations when it believes that it is in its selfish interest to do so (see figure 14.1). This guiding principle dates back to the 19th century when railroads made major donations to the YMCA, which provided cheap lodging for workers and, later, for crew members who often ended the workday far from home.

Although they are viewed by companies as investments, donations must be for exclusive public purposes in order for the IRS to accept them as tax deductible. The deduction will not be allowed if the company cannot receive tangible economic benefit in return for a donation.

Park and recreation personnel seeking to induce more donation support from corporate entities should focus on the potential benefits of their services to business. The key is to find the quid pro quo, that is, to answer the question, "What is in it for the business?" This section identifies five primary motives that undergird corporate donations to park and recreation agencies. They offer insight into the types of appeals to which corporations are likely to be most responsive. For the purpose of exposition, the motives are discussed separately, but any given donation is likely to be stimulated by some combination of these motives.

Tax Deductions for Surplus Property and Inventory

The nature of capital-gain tax deductions associated with donations of appreciated real estate is described after this discussion of motives. However, there are at least four situations in which developers may want to donate park land or recreational facilities but in which the capital-gain tax and appreciated property may not be the primary motive.

First, legislation may have been passed that rendered the property useless for the purpose for which it was purchased originally. For example, with the passing of the Flood Plains Act, which limited federal insurance protection in those areas and on lands subjected to protective wetlands legislation, some developers could no longer pursue their intent to build. In some cases, developers recognized that a donation would relieve them of having to pay property taxes and would provide tax relief on their other income. Hence, they approached public park and recreation agencies and offered the land as a donation.

In other cases, land may be surplus to a company's requirements, but commercial development of it may be nonfeasible or controversial. In Indianapolis, WISH TV (Channel 8) purchased a 40-acre site to build a new transmission tower. Only 12 acres of this site were required for the tower, but the seller would not divide the property. Therefore, the company had to acquire 28 acres that were surplus to its needs. The site was a prime area for development because it had a creek flowing through it and was close to an existing park. Thus, property taxes on the land were high. Despite these assets, development of the site would have been difficult for two reasons. First, many people are reluctant to live close to a transmission tower. Second, local residents wanted the attractive site to remain open space and would have contested its development. WISH TV did not want to be associated with controversy and did not want to pay the property taxes; therefore, the 28-acre site, which was valued at $450,000, was donated to Indianapolis Parks and Recreation Department.

Sometimes the donation may occur after completion of a development. Often a developer uses recreation amenities, such as a golf course, marina, or ski slope, as a central loss-leader attraction. This serves to increase surrounding land values and provide a distinctive marketing theme around which to promote the development. After completion, the recreation component may be donated to a public agency because the donation relieves the developer of property taxes and maintenance responsibilities. However, agencies increasingly are resistant to these types of donations, arguing that the property should stay on the tax rolls and that maintenance should be the responsibility of a homeowners' association.

Finally, if corporations donate equipment from current unsold inventory, then they are permitted to deduct more than its cost. They can take a stepped-up deduction, which equals the cost of making the product plus half of the difference between its retail price and its cost. For example, if they donate an item that cost $50 to manufacture and sells for $100, they can deduct $75.[17] In addition, there are inventory control benefits. Donating products to a park and recreation agency can save a company warehousing costs as well as inventory carrying costs and can help a company dispose of out-of-date products without destroying them.[17]

Product Trial

Before organizations or individuals purchase a product or service, they like to try it. If a company can induce such a trial through donations, then that is a major step toward securing a sale. Consider the following examples.

Mower manufacturers, golf cart companies, and other suppliers of equipment to agencies frequently are willing to donate equipment, especially new models, in the hope that an agency will either be impressed sufficiently to place a major order or at least that its managers will be comfortable endorsing it to their peers.

Prospective food concessionaires seeking to service special events or functions that the agency operates may donate their services to a function to demonstrate their competency.

Wilson Racquet Sports developed a nationwide tennis racquet donation program. It required all of Wilson's promotional players and advisory staff members to return their previous supply of promotional tennis rackets to Wilson at the beginning of their new contract year. This resulted in 15,000 rackets being redistributed annually. After inspection, they were donated to tennis organizations that did not have the resources to provide new players with equipment. The intent was to strengthen Wilson's brand recognition at the grassroots level and to recruit additional new players to the sport of tennis.[20]

Rollerblade Inc. donated 2,000 pairs of in-line skates for free use in parks in New York and a comparable amount of safety equipment for a three-year period. This represented a $1 million investment by the company. As part of the agreement, the city offered free instruction on the basics of skating and the proper use of equipment in 15 six-week training courses, provided vans that stopped at parks throughout the city to offer free skating in a program specifically aimed at attracting younger skaters, and conducted regular hockey clinics. Rollerblade made the donation because it wanted a test market for a new strategy intended to increase interest in in-line skating and its products. The company's president stated: "Last year the industry was pretty slow in the domestic market. When we looked at what we needed to do with our marketing, we concluded that what we needed to do was return to grass-roots marketing, but on a broader level."[21]

Livingston and Company was a small advertising agency in Seattle with a long-standing commitment to doing pro bono work for local nonprofit and public organizations, such as Seattle's Museum of Flight, zoo, and aquarium. The agency believed that the best way to generate paying work was to do high-visibility advertisements for these organizations. With donated work, their creative staff were freed from client constraints and could indulge in dramatic advertisements that appeared on high-visibility, donated billboards in the city. They aimed to make people stop and ask, Who did that? A senior manager stated: "We love pro bono work. It's the best way we could advertise the agency" (p. 138).[17]

A company that donated a roof to a community center required, in return, a ceremonial opening with the mayor present and newspaper coverage because it wanted to show off its advanced technology. The company also requested that the facility be made available to them for prospective clients to view.[16]

Public Relations

Some business executives believe that donations made by a commercial enterprise are a tax imposed upon them for doing business, and failure to make donations would damage their public image. They view donations as a response to critics who suggest that business serves no social good and does not distribute its resources equitably among those who generate those resources.

They recognize that donations to a park and recreation agency can help visibility and can help them gain respect in a community with considerable value to a company. This was exemplified by Saturn Corporation in their Build a Kingdom for Kids program described on page 380. The public relations function and corporate image, which the program was designed to create, cannot replace substance in a business operation, but Saturn believed that without them the company would not always obtain full commercial advantage from its achievements.

Build a Kingdom for Kids

The credo of Saturn Corporation is: "We're a different kind of car company," and its operating philosophy is "Building together." The Build a Kingdom for Kids program was designed to exemplify and strengthen these Saturn brand images. It resulted in the construction of more than 60 playgrounds on sites designated by park and recreation agencies. The program was organized and paid for by Saturn regional dealer associations. Each playground was constructed by volunteers in one day.

Building together was achieved by volunteers drawn from the staff and families of regional Saturn retailers, Saturn Corporation senior managers who flew in, and Saturn car owners and their families who were invited to participate. The main purpose was to build relationships between these groups and to demonstrate their credo by giving back to the community. Still, Saturn harvested substantial media and community goodwill from the projects. The written goals were:

- generate customer enthusiasm;
- create positive word-of-mouth advertising;
- demonstrate the Saturn difference;
- show the retailers' commitments to the community; and
- build a better community for retailers, customers, and their families.

Saturn had been positioned as a high-quality product, and to ensure that the playgrounds reflected the product, a core group of four or five individuals from Saturn Corporation were responsible for the planning, preparation, and supervision of on-site construction and for offering technical expertise to the regional Saturn retailers. Often this involved site clearing and some cement work done in advance of the building day.

Media interest was stimulated by press releases, such as that shown in figure 14.2. Giving back to the community was a generous positive action likely to generate media interest. The projects were visually appealing for television and generated feature and human-interest stories including interviews with volunteers, agency and elected officials, and Saturn executives and retailers. Media and public relations appeal was enhanced by a celebratory dedication event at the completion of each project, for which the dealers typically invested $5,000 to $10,000 on food, drinks, entertainment, give-aways, contests, and prizes.

In some segments of the community, Dow Chemical company acquired a negative image through its manufacture of pesticides and other chemical products for agricultural use. The company was subjected to allegations from some conservationists that these products damaged the environment. It also encountered resistance from communities that were reluctant hosts for the company's chemical production facilities. To counter such charges, Dow invested in conservation projects intended to bolster the bottom line indirectly by demonstrating a good neighbor policy. It pledged $3 million to a wetlands initiative organized by the Nature Conservancy and Ducks Unlimited to acquire and restore endangered wetland on and near company property. The company's gift sparked an equal matching grant from the National Fish and Wildlife Foundation. The program encompassed seven major projects involving more than 380,000 acres in the United States and Canada.[22]

Northwest Airlines donated more than $100,000 to the Memphis Arts Council. The gift comprised cash, airline tickets for guest artists who flew to Memphis to participate with the city's cultural groups, and free companion airline tickets for individuals who donated to the arts. The airline had an advertising campaign based on the theme "Northwest for Memphis." Their spokesman said: "We want to substantiate our advertising claim that 'Northwest is for Memphis.' We can't advertise it unless we are. We are trying to be a viable corporate citizen in Memphis, and, hopefully, we are proving ourself."[23]

Donations enhance a company's autonomy by giving it more freedom in addressing issues of public concern. "United Airlines' Neighbor Woods" shows how United Airlines used a donation to shift

New York and New Jersey Saturn Retailers to Build "Kids' Kingdoms"

New York, NY—Saturn Retailers in New York and New Jersey will be building 12 new playground sites throughout the New York City metro area this weekend. Materials and labor have been donated by the 25 participating Saturn Retailers. The project, called "Build a Kingdom for Kids," involves construction of each playground site in one day through the efforts of Saturn Retail and customer volunteers. Over 1,000,000 children each year are expected to enjoy the swings, bars and slides at their new "Kids' Kingdoms."

Saturn Corporation President Skip LeFauve praised the participating Saturn Retailers' contribution. "A part of Saturn's business philosophy is to meet the needs of our neighbors, the communities in which we live and operate," said LeFauve. "The 'Build a Kingdom for Kids' project demonstrates that our Retailers enthusiastically share this philosophy."

The "Build a Kingdom for Kids" project was inspired by a similar project involving Saturn Retailers throughout the country who built a children's park in Saturn's Spring Hill, Tennessee, backyard about two years ago.

"This is a powerful event," remembers John Burns, principal owner of Saturn of Hempstead, New York. Burns explained, "All these different people are coming together as a team to give something back to the community. The Saturn Retailers in the New York metro area wanted to recapture that spirit with the 'Build a Kingdom for Kids' project."

Five playground sites will be built on Saturday, June 3, with the remaining sites constructed on Sunday. Each build day will begin early in the morning, concluding with a site dedication in the evening with the "Kids' Kingdoms" ready for play the next day.

"Kids' Kingdom" equipment, materials, site preparation and supervision are being supplied by Kompan/Big Toys, Northeast, Inc. based in Marathon, New York. Each site is accessible to the physically challenged and meets the requirements of the Americans with Disabilities Act.

Figure 14.2   Sample press release.

United Airlines' Neighbor Woods

When United Airlines established a major new maintenance base at Indianapolis, they were given substantial financial incentives to move there. The airline planned to move 6,500 people during a five-year period to the $300 million maintenance facility in Indianapolis. They wanted to convey an image that they were good corporate citizens and that they would give back to the community and not just take resources from it.

They wanted a high-visibility project. Initially, the Indianapolis Parks and Recreation Department approached United about refurbishing the city's 120 playgrounds, especially those in the inner-city. However, United's employees and their flying customers did not live in the inner-city. They were relatively affluent and lived in the suburbs, so they were not likely to identify well with a playground renovation program.

The airline was responsive to the park department's next suggestion, which was a tree-planting program. Trees have connotations of clean air, filtration, and beauty, which counter the negative image associated with airlines on the pollution issue, with which their environmentally conscious, middle-class employees and customers could identify.

Thus, United agreed to plant a tree every year for every employee who was working in Indianapolis for the next 10 years. The program was called "United's Neighbor Woods." In the first year, 450 trees were planted, but by the fifth year when full capacity was reached, United was planting 6,500 trees per year. This donation fully funded the city's urban forestry program. The trees had a 3 in diameter, were seven to eight years of age, and cost approximately $150 each.

United Airlines received high visibility for the donation. Each year, there are four or five editorial articles in the Indianapolis media. Indianapolis Parks and Recreation Department ensures that United employees are involved in ceremonial plantings to generate publicity, and they stage plantings to create photograph opportunities for the media.

its image in Indianapolis from that of a taker to a giver.

Similar public relations motives possibly accounted for Canon USA giving the National Park Service $1.2 million to conduct natural resources research and restoration work in the national parks. The donation funded a program called "Expedition into the Parks: Preserving America's National Treasures," which sent volunteers into 20 parks to help researchers inventory and monitor plants and animals and their habitats. The donation was used to restore habitats that these species needed for survival. Canon also provided the volunteers with equipment, such as laptop computers, cameras, and binoculars, that helped researchers perform their work. Canon was a major producer of camcorders and photocopiers. Many people used camcorders to preserve their memories of visits to parks. This was a way in which Canon could establish or strengthen the nexus in people's minds between the company's camcorder and park visitation. The photocopiers used large volumes of paper. Through this donation, Canon sought to reinforce its position as an environmentally aware and sensitive company rather than as an exploiter of natural resources.

One business executive expressed the value of donations in the following terms: "We believe we win dividends most responsibly and consistently—in recruitment in the marketplace, in access to research, in our strong association with community service, and in fostering a reputation for excellence" (p. 366).[18] The dividends of image, respect, and commitment to the community become particularly important in times of crisis for a company. For example, in a corporate down-sizing or a plant-closing situation, corporations are likely to be granted more goodwill if they have demonstrated good corporate citizenship through donations to the community over the years.

Another dividend from making donations to a park and recreation agency is that it may create opportunities for senior managers to establish closer contacts with a jurisdiction's political leadership or to call on support from influential organizations in the community to assist the company. Consider the situation described in "Seeking Influence Through Donations."

An example of how the city of New York created a donation opportunity in its park system that yielded positive public relations is given in "The Donation of Cellular Phones to Deter Crime in New York's Parks." This program received widespread media coverage not only in New York but also nationally. In addition to the corporate public relations value, the two companies were demon-

Seeking Influence Through Donations

Philip Morris Corporation was a major producer of cigarettes and beer. For several decades it had also been one of New York's and the nation's largest sponsors of the arts. In addition to the many millions of dollars in cash it donated to arts groups in the city of New York, the company offered other kinds of support, such as assistance with audience development and advertising. It often paid for lavish opening-night parties at which the Philip Morris cigarettes at every table were the only obvious signs of their support.

When the city of New York proposed strong public anti-smoking legislation, the company's executives contacted arts institutions that had benefited from their donations and asked them to lobby the city council to reject their legislation. The dilemma for the arts groups was whether they should stand aside and risk offending their most generous benefactor or whether they should participate in lobbying and perhaps offend many of their individual patrons. The company had established long-term relationships with many of the groups to which it gave money. An arts organization spokeswoman said: "I don't smoke and I hate people smoking, but Philip Morris is a great supporter. They are our largest corporate supporter. I say thank God for sinners; they are the only people to support the arts."

Her remark underscores the clearest benefit Philip Morris received from its arts philanthropy—a positive image among people who would normally have few kind things to say about a cigarette and beer maker. Through the arts, it created a positive and influential constituency from people who were unlikely to think positively about the company's Marlboro advertisements.

Adapted from Paul Goldberger. Philip Morris calls in I.O.U.'s in the arts. New York Times. October 5, 1994, page A1.

The Donation of Cellular Phones to Deter Crime in New York's Parks

Cellular telephones and bright blue vests marked "Safe Parks" were passed out to hundreds of regular park user volunteers in Prospect Park in Brooklyn and Marcus Garvey Park in Harlem. The phones were programmed to reach only 911, the emergency number. A city of New York spokesman said: "We don't need knives, guns and mace. We need a way to call for help."

The intent was to distribute the 2 oz telephones to volunteers in every city park, including 1,000 in Central Park. The volunteer force was assembled by officers patrolling the parks who approached people whom they recognized as regular visitors. The goal was to have 20 to 30 volunteers in the parks for each hour from 5 A.M. to 9 P.M. It enables regular users to combine crime-fighting with their regular activities.

A spokesman noted that not only do the telephone carriers feel safer, but their presence also reduces the anxiety of people not carrying the telephones. "The most important use is to reassure people in the parks that other people in there are their friends and neighbors," he said. "The truth about this city is that people will help other people."

The 500 telephones were donated by Nynex and Motorola, neither of which charged for calls made on the telephones.

Adapted from Douglas Martin. Police enlist park users in safety drive: Hundreds of volunteers to get cellular phones. The New York Times. August 21, 1994, volume 143, section 1, page 45(L).

strating to millions of individuals through the media that cellular phones were a personal safety device that they should consider having on their person. Bearing in mind that these phones were probably eligible for a stepped-up tax deduction, the net cost of the donation to the companies was relatively small, especially when compared with the value of the extensive media coverage that they received.

An example of a smaller agency initiating public relations opportunities comes from Champaign Park District in Illinois. The park district wrote all the businesses in Champaign suggesting that instead of sending out Christmas cards to their customers this year, they should donate that money for the park district to plant trees in the parks. Three days before Christmas, the park district arranged for a major advertisement in the local newspaper acknowledging their contribution and noting the donations were a Christmas present given by the businesses to the residents of Champaign.

Healthy Community Context

A company is a component of the community in which it is located physically. To some extent, its well-being depends on the social and physical well-being of that community. Hence, enlightened self-interest by companies extends to recognizing that if a community is healthy, then its industry and business is more likely to be healthy.

Tokyo Electronics was located on the south side of Austin. The company wanted to invest in its neighborhood to demonstrate its intent to be a good neighbor. The city was constructing a new sports facility in the area. Tokyo Electronics agreed to donate $25,000 for the purchase of equipment for it. Using a list that the city developed, the company selected the equipment to be provided through the donation. It chose relatively permanent equipment, such as exercise machines, scoreboards, and weight-training equipment, that would carry its name for several years to maximize visibility from the contribution.

It was noted in chapter 5 that quality-of-life elements, such as parks and recreation, are becoming increasingly important in the decisions of senior employees who are choosing where they want to work. Companies recruiting them are sensitive to this.

When Motorola, which is a major electronics company, recruited executives for its Austin plant, a central focus of the recruitment appeal was the high quality of life available in the city. The company invariably lodged the potential recruits at hotels that faced the Town Lake, the city's most distinctive park feature and asset. The hotels abutted onto a hike-and-bike trail that stretched around the lake's perimeter for 15 mi. It offered a delightful aesthetic experience for hotel visitors who strolled along it and for the large number of residents who walked, jogged, and biked it. Keeping the trail clean was difficult because of its heavy use. Motorola donated $10,000 each year to support cleanups, gravel for the trail, bridge repair, and trail repair. In return, the city arranged a media event at which Motorola presented their outsized check and ensured that the company received recognition from the council.

Urban customer service firms, such as retailers and financial institutions, are sensitive to the opportunities for social and physical investment in maintaining or improving their market areas. Their need for an ordered, growing local economy encourages them to spur economic development by supporting park, recreational, cultural, and artistic opportunities that draw people and their money. If the neighborhood or service area in which they are located deteriorates, then the financial health of these businesses is also likely to deteriorate. Improvement in the infrastructure, beautification, and desirability of the local community is likely to mean, in the long term, improvement in the profits of businesses located there.

Employee Development and Morale

Companies can contribute donations by making the expertise of their employees available to park and recreation agencies. Such donations are likely to be relatively substantial because employees' time is expensive, especially if specialized or management staff are involved. Shared managerial expertise may be forthcoming in computing, legal, financing, engineering, human resource, or any other technical area in which a park and recreation agency has a need. Companies benefit from the enhanced skills and broader perspectives that employees gain from working in a different context.

A vice president at Arco Chemical Company in Philadelphia planned the move of the city's Please Touch Museum to a $1 million building and called on the experience he gained by working on $1 billion worth of plant construction during his career. He noted: "Meeting people outside my industry and learning to deal with them really sharpened my interpersonal skills" (p. 1).[24]

Compos-It Inc. was a 30-person graphic design and typesetting firm in Montgomery, Alabama, that made partnerships with local arts groups a key component of its business strategy. Each year, the company donated $20,000 in in-kind services to local arts organizations. The company's owner helped found Jubilee, an annual three-day arts festival. She and other Compos-It employees sat on boards of several arts organizations. "Nobody knew who we were until we became involved with the arts," said the owner. "Now we are viewed as the quality place in town for graphic design and typesetting work" (p. 15).[17]

IBM loaned employees to public and nonprofit organizations, and in its policy statement, it identified the benefits to the organization, the employee, and the company. It believed the employee gained an opportunity to

- practice and test business skills in an alternative environment;
- develop previously unused skills;
- develop a lasting interest in social problems; and
- encounter different concepts, ideals, priorities, values, cultures, and ways of life.

The receiving organization gained

- expertise and experience that it could not otherwise afford to buy,
- a fresh approach to a problem, and
- a contact in a different field of work that may be helpful in the future.

The company gained from

- the increased experience and broadened approach of its employees,
- the easing of promotional log-jams and manpower imbalances,
- an opportunity to influence realistic community planning,
- general approval that employees give to such enlightened company initiatives, and
- keeping its goals and values in step with those of the rest of the community.[25]

The artisan skills needed in park maintenance and construction make parks prime sites for attracting artisan training programs. Consider the following examples.

Military Reserve Component Units are groups of inactive military personnel who participate in training exercises one weekend each month and two weeks each summer. The National Guard, Army Reserves, and Navy Construction Battalions (Seabees) are three units that most often undertake community projects. They can respond with personnel, skills, and equipment, not normally available, free of charge to civilian agencies. For example, an engineer unit can build a playground or community athletic field while engaging in training appropriate to the unit's military responsibilities. Grading, hauling, dumping, demolition, and construction tasks are other examples of compatible work often performed by Military Reserve Component Units.

In some communities there are iron workers, bricklayers, operating engineers, cement masons, roofers, painters, electricians, plumbers, or other craftsmen who are affiliated with unions that participate in apprenticeship training programs. Generally, these unions offer classroom and on-the-job training nine months each year for their students. Alternatively, there may be vocational high school or college classes in the community. Their instructors are seeking continually worthwhile work projects to increase students' skills and education.

Finally, it should be noted that supporting public park and recreational programs may be perceived as a means of building employee morale. Shell Oil Company alludes to this concern in its donations policy statement:

> Our programs of charitable giving are related to the civic responsibilities of employees of the sponsoring Shell companies. In a sense, the Company regards itself as their partner in citizenship. For this reason, most charitable support is made on a local basis where Shell people live and work.

Rationales for Businesses Not Making Donations

Because 9 of 10 firms do not make donations, it is important that the park and recreation manager should be informed of the arguments that these businesses are likely to put forward in support of their stand. Before donations will be forthcoming from these firms, strategies to refute these negative arguments must be developed:

- If it is seen to make a donation, a firm opens itself to pressures and demands that it cannot effectively control. It lays itself open to new conflicts, stresses, and strains.
- It does not have the right to give away stockholders' money. The stockholders should be given all income, and they can make gifts as they prefer, supporting those

activities that most appeal to them or none at all.
- Business sticking to business will provide increasing ability for individuals to finance philanthropy. Corporations sticking to their job will provide rising real income to permit individuals to enlarge their donations.
- The total program may produce results, but the particular business could not give enough to make any appreciable difference.
- Other companies that are comparable in size are not contributing so why should we?

Influence of the Tax Structure on Corporate Donation Decisions

Like individuals, corporations are required to pay federal income taxes on their net income. This tax is also levied by some states. However, the tax implications vary according to whether the corporate entity is an S corporation or a C corporation. S corporations are limited to having no more than 75 shareholders, and these corporations do not directly pay income taxes. Rather, the income gains or losses and taxes are computed at the corporate level, but they are passed through to the shareholders and reported by the shareholders as individuals according to their proportional share ownership. Thus, any deduction from a charitable donation would be passed through to the shareholders.

This section focuses on the tax implications for C corporations because they do pay income taxes directly. For individuals, the maximal tax rate on capital gain is almost half the top rate of income tax on ordinary income (20% compared with 39.6%); however, the long-term capital gains of corporations are taxable at the same rates as ordinary income. The rates range from 15% on taxable income less than $50,000, to 34% on amounts more than $75,000, to 35% on income more than $10 million. Like the rates for individuals discussed earlier in the chapter, these corporate rates are substantially lower than those prevailing in 1980, so the tax incentives for major corporations to donate appreciated land for park use have been reduced during the past two decades. A corporation can deduct the value of donations up to 10% of its taxable income (before the dividends received and the charitable contribution deductions). Amounts exceeding this can be carried forward for five years.

The example in "Implications of a Corporation Selling Land at Fair Market Value, Negotiating a

Implications of a Corporation Selling Land at Fair Market Value, Negotiating a Bargain Sale, or Making an Outright Donation

The following illustrations are based on three assumptions:

1. The corporation is a C, not an S, corporation.
2. The corporation is in the highest federal income tax bracket (35%) and is also in a state that levies a corporate income tax of 5%.
3. The corporation is committed to disposing of 100 acres of potentially attractive park land that has appreciated in value from $2,000 per acre to $12,000 per acre since it was purchased 30 years ago.

Sale at Fair Market Value

Selling price		$1,200,000
Less broker commission at 10%		120,000
		1,080,000
Less cost basis		200,000
		880,000
Long-term capital gain at 35% federal rate	$308,000	
Long-term capital gain at 5% state rate	44,000	
Remainder after paying long-term capital-gain tax		528,000
Plus cost basis		200,000
Overall proceeds		**728,000**

Bargain Sale (Sell at 50% of Fair Market Value and Donate 50%)

The 50% Sale

Selling price (50 acres × $12,000)	$600,000	
Less cost basis (50 acres × $2,000)	100,000	
Long-term capital gain	500,000	
Federal and state capital-gain taxes at 40%	200,000	
Amount remaining after long-term capital-gain tax	300,000	
Plus cost basis	100,000	
Proceeds from the 50% sale		$400,000

The 50% Donation

$600,000 × 40% income tax deduction	$240,000
Overall proceeds	**640,000**

Outright Donation

$1,200,000 × 40%	$480,000

Adapted from William T. Hutton. Introduction to the Problem of Accruing Properties From Partnerships, Corporations, Estates and Trusts. The Back Forty. 1996.

Bargain Sale, or Making an Outright Donation" on page 386 illustrates the different outcomes to a C corporation of selling an appreciated property at fair market value, negotiating a bargain sale, or making an outright donation.[7] The overall proceeds from each of the three scenarios suggest that it is most advantageous for the company to proceed with a fair market sale. However, there are three factors that may persuade the company to pursue one of the other two options.

First, the differences in overall proceeds between the fair market price and the bargain sale and outright donation are $88,000 and $248,000, respectively. On a property valued at $1.2 million, a major company may regard the potential positive public relations value to be worth the income foregone. For example, St. Joe Mineral Corporation, which is a large mining company listed on the New York Stock Exchange, donated a 9,000-acre strip-mined area valued at $1.8 million to Missouri State Parks. Although the calculations showed that donation of the land compared with a sale at fair market value cost St. Joe a little more than $170,000, the company considered this a reasonable price to pay for the considerable amount of favorable publicity that the donation yielded.[26]

Second, opting for the bargain sale alternative costs the company only $88,000, but it saves the public agency $600,000. Similarly, the $248,000 donation cost to the company is relatively small compared with the $1.2 million price that the agency would have to pay for a fair market purchase. The cost to the company is so much lower than the burden that the community's taxpayers would have to incur to acquire this property that the company may be persuaded that this is a situation in which it should demonstrate its commitment to being a good corporate citizen in the community.[9]

Third, as part of the company's income, the $728,000 overall proceeds from the fair market value sale presumably will be distributed in the form of dividends to the company's shareholders. If these shareholders are themselves in the highest individual income tax bracket (39.6% federal income tax and 5.4%, for example, state income tax), then a further $327,000 will be paid in income taxes, leaving only $401,000 in the shareholder's pockets from this $1.2 million property sale. (Of course, this amount will be higher if the shareholders are in a lower marginal income tax bracket and if the state does not levy an income tax). The corporation may regard this so-called double-tax effect as confiscatory and opt instead for the

donation because the net return is now less than would accrue from an outright donation.[9]

Chevron Corporation sold the Santa Monica Mountains Conservancy 3,035 acres of "drop-dead beautiful countryside" on the northern slope of the Santa Susana Mountains in California. The property was combined with nearby holdings to form a nearly 6,000-acre chain of public wildlands, which were to be given to the state of California for management. The corporation had owned the property for more than one century, so the capital-gain tax was potentially substantial. The property's appraised value was $7.3 million, but a bargain sale was negotiated for $4.4 million. The transaction was packaged as a gift of 851 acres in one of the canyons, Pico Canyon, and sale of 2,184 acres for $4.9 million.[27]

Summary

Donations are conceptually different from sponsorships in that they are altruistic and offer no tangible financial gain or measurable personal benefit to the giver. They have played a central role in the evolution of many park and recreation systems. In recent decades, it has been possible in some situations to use donations to leverage additional grants from state or federal governments. However, some jurisdictions have had to reject offers of donated property because they lack the resources to operate additional facilities. Individuals who make major capital donations to public park and recreation agencies are likely to be good stewards of their property, be relatively wealthy, have no heirs, and own property with a value that has appreciated substantially since they purchased it.

The tax structure encourages donations. For individuals, the value of a donation is fully deductible from taxes paid on their annual adjusted gross income. If property held for more than 18 months has appreciated in value, then it is subject to long-term capital-gain tax when it is sold. However, if the property is donated, then the landowner avoids paying capital-gain tax and receives an income tax deduction. In some situations, these tax conditions may result in an individual's net return from a donation being sufficiently comparable with the return from a fair market or bargain sale; the landowner may be persuaded to proceed with the donation.

Deferred, or planned, donation means that actual possession and use of a gift made to an agency is deferred to some future time. There are five fairly common types of deferred donations: life-estate and remainder-interest donations; bequests; charitable-remainder trusts; gift annuities; and donations of life insurance.

Donations from businesses include not only cash but also in-kind materials, equipment, and labor. The officers of a corporation have no mandate to give away their stockholders' money. Rather, their charge is to invest it in a way that optimizes shareholders' return on investment. Five primary motives underlying these donation investment decisions have been identified: tax deductions for surplus property and inventory, product trial, public relations, healthy community context, and employee development and morale.

Like individuals, corporations can deduct the value of donations from their taxable income, and sale of appreciated property is subject to a long-term capital-gain tax. The incentive to donate is increased because when shareholders receive their share of the proceeds from an asset sale in the form of dividends, their net return is decreased because those dividends are also taxed. Again, the impact of the tax laws is to make a donation of appreciated property an attractive alternative to selling it at fair market value in some situations.

References

1. Sleight, Steve. 1989. *Sponsorship: What it is and how to use it*. Maidenhead, Berkshire, England: McGraw-Hill.

2. McIlquham, John. 1995. Giving flattened by inflation. *Non-Profit Times* July: 1, 6, 8.

3. Allmann, Laurie. 1997. *Natural areas: Protecting a vital community asset*. Minneapolis: Minnesota Department of Natural Resources.

4. Huus, Randolph O. 1935. *Financing municipal recreation*. Menasha, WI: George Banta Publishing.

5. DeMatteo, Ann. 1994. Food store grant will underwrite bridge on trail. *New Haven Register*, December 12, section B, 1.

6. Johnson, Dirk. 1996. A park worth millions, and he can't give it away. *New York Times*, January 6, section L, 6.

7. Friends of Parks & Recreation. 1995. A gift of action for youth of today and tomorrow. *Friends of Park & Recreation* 5(1): 9.

8. Abbin, Byrle M., Diane Cornwell, Marvin J. Dickman, Richard A. Helfand, Ross W. Wagner, Joseph P. Toce and Mark L. Vorratz (editors). 1995. *Tax economics of charitable giving*. Twelfth edition. Washington, DC: Arthur Anderson.

9. Hutton, William T. 1996. The back forty. Unpublished manuscript handed out at a workshop on maintaining private lands with conservation easements. Austin, TX, April 11-12, 1996.

10. Endicott, Eve. 1993. Preserving natural areas: The Nature Conservancy and its partners. In *Land conservation through public-private partnerships*, edited by Eve Endicott. Washington, DC: Island Press, 17-42.

11. Browne, Kingsbury. 1984. Taxes as a form of public financing: Treasury's open space protection program. In *Land saving action*, edited by Russell L. Brenneman and Sarah M. Bates. Covelo, CA: Island Press.

12. Milne, Janet E. 1984. The landowner's options. In *Land saving action*, edited by Russell L. Brenneman and Sarah M. Bates. Covelo, CA: Island Press, 22.

13. Small, Stephen J. 1992. *Preserving family lands*. Revised Second edition. Boston, MA: Landowner Planning Center.

14. Kerslow, Warren W. 1981. Statement at workshop on public land acquisition and alternatives. The U.S. Senate Committee on Energy and Natural Resources, Subcommittee on Public Lands and Reserved Water. Washington, DC: Superintendent of Documents, 472.

15. Willett, John. 1994. Profiting from a partnership with the arts. *San Diego Daily Transcript*, May 13, A1.

16. Perlmutter, Felice D. and Ram A. Cnaan. 1995. Entrepreneurship in the public sector: The horns of a dilemma. *Public Administration Review* 55(1): 29-36.

17. Steckel, Richard and Robin Simons. 1992. *Doing best by doing good*. New York: Penguin Books.

18. Kelly, Kathleen S. 1991. *Fund raising and public relations: A critical analysis*. Hillsdale, NJ: Erlbaum.

19. Alperson, Myra. 1995. *Corporate giving strategies that add business value*. New York: The Conference Board.

20. Schmid, Sue. 1995. What a racquet. *Athletic Business* 19(4): 24.

21. Canedy, Dana. 1997. Program to provide in-line skates at parks. *New York Times*, March 19, B7.

22. O'Donnell, Frank. 1993. Corporate America turns on to the environment. *Nature Conservancy* 43(1): 27-32.

23. Romine, Linda. 1995. Northwest Airlines pledges $100,000 to Arts Council. *Memphis Business Journal* 16(43): 7.

24. Dann, Donald H. 1985. Support the arts with your time and talent. *Business Week*, July 22, 145.

25. Clutterbuck, David. 1981. *How to be a good corporate citizen.* Maidenhead, Berkshire, England: McGraw-Hill, 28, 37.

26. Howard, Dennis R. and John L. Crompton. 1980. *Financing, managing and marketing recreation and park resources.* Dubuque, IA: Brown, 82.

27. Levin, Myron. 1995. Chevron to sell state 3,000 acres in heart of woodlands. *Los Angeles Times*, April 6, B1.

CHAPTER 15

POPULAR DONATION VEHICLES

Detailed discussion of a recommended approach for soliciting both donations and sponsorships is forthcoming in chapter 17. The material in this chapter reviews vehicles that park and recreation agencies have used effectively as part of their solicitation efforts to acquire donations. They are unique to donations and are not likely to be used in the context of sponsorship. However, these vehicles alone will not generate donations. To be effective, the vehicles depend on agency personnel implementing the principles of solicitation discussed in chapter 17.

The seven vehicles discussed in this chapter are planned donation workshops, gift catalogs, donating personal bricks, donation boxes and fountains, check-off donations, adopt-a-facility programs, and cause-related marketing.

Planned Donation Workshops

The most efficient way for a park and recreation agency to launch a planned giving program is to initiate a series of workshops. These provide a network of contacts and prospects that serve as a starting point. Subsequently, staff can develop individually targeted and personally tailored approaches to each prospect. People attending the workshops also may assist in identifying additional prospects.

The planned giving workshops are designed for people who are interested in setting up their own planned giving instrument or will but are uncertain as to how to proceed. Many are apprehensive about the legalese involved, may not understand the range of possibilities, and do not know where to turn for help. A workshop provides the opportunity for these people to gain understanding and to be referred to reliable sources for assistance.

To conduct a workshop, the agency could enlist an instructor from a local law firm, law school, bank, or community foundation to provide an overview of the process of establishing a will and to discuss the many options possible. Attendees leave with a better understanding of wills and potential beneficiary options. They also know where to turn for services. The event could be scheduled and publicized as a community service. A fee may be charged to cover expenses for the workshops, and park and recreation projects may be suggested as potential beneficiaries.

A variation on this theme is to bring in several lawyers who provide free legal services, including drafting of wills, for senior citizens in the community. Lawyers may be willing to participate in order to gain exposure to potential clients whom they can serve as executors. The park-giving option can be presented and explained by the park and recreation agency, friends of the park, or the lawyers themselves.

A further variation is to orchestrate a more prestigious event in which the invitations come from a top-flight presenter, that is, a highly respected individual known to be a philanthropist who is willing to speak on behalf of the park and recreation agency's needs. The presenter sets the tone for the seminar in the keynote speech, explaining the giving needs and opportunities of the agency along with his or her own personal commitment. The presenter then introduces three panelists recruited from the community's leading law, bank, and accounting firms. Top firms may want to participate because it represents good business and favorable exposure for them. Usually it is possible to find sponsors willing to pay for invitations, refreshments, and meeting space for such a prestigious event.

An alternative type of planned giving workshop serves professionals who deal with wills, for example, lawyers, bank trust officers, and tax consultants. These people are gatekeepers who manage the affairs of relatively wealthy people. They can open the gate and provide access to, or directly influence, their wealthy clients.

The leisure services department in St. Petersburg, Florida, believed that influencing this group of wealthy people was the most efficient way to launch its planned giving program. Accordingly, the department approached the chamber of commerce and the local bar association with a proposal to host a seminar on recent major changes in tax laws affecting planned giving. The chamber and bar association enthusiastically agreed to co-sponsor the seminar. The small business council of the chamber was so impressed that a public agency was aggressively seeking outside support that it made a small grant to help underwrite the seminar. The co-sponsors and other professional organizations in St. Petersburg provided their membership mailing lists to help publicize the event.

The city's leisure services director was very candid in welcoming the 110 participants to the seminar. He said that the goal of the city in hosting the session was to acquaint the delegates with the benefits of charitable trusts set up to benefit parks and recreation in St. Petersburg. Participants at the seminar viewed it as an opportunity to broaden their knowledge and skills at a bargain price.

The seminar was presented by a nationally recognized expert in planned giving from Washington, DC. Participants were charged a small fee. The seminar was held at the St. Petersburg Yacht Club. As an added inducement to participate, the co-sponsors arranged 5 hours of continuing education credit for the lawyers and certified public accountants who attended. As an awareness exercise, it was successful. One lawyer stated that he had never thought of the city as a potential beneficiary; the scouts and hospitals, yes, but not the city!

The leisure services director and his staff each had a goal of establishing a working dialogue with at least 10 of the seminar participants so that they could be made aware of the donation opportunities (or needs) that the park and recreation agency afforded. These contacts were made at the workshop. They continued to be nurtured over time so that the professionals were reminded continuously of park and recreation giving options that they could suggest to their clients.

The followup was the real payoff. Periodically, a lawyer or accountant asked the park and recreation director to sit in on a meeting with a client interested in a charitable trust. The director listened as the donor explained his or her desires for the trust and followed the meeting promptly with a one-page proposal tailored to the needs of the donor. Typically, one or two additional meetings with the donor were needed to complete the arrangement. In the first three years after this seminar launched the program, more than $2 million had been pledged in planned giving to the city of St. Petersburg.

Key Features of Successful Planned Donation Workshops

Make the planned donation workshop a classy event. Planned giving seminars should be imbued with quality. They should be held in attractive and dignified surroundings, such as yacht clubs, country clubs, corporate conference rooms, or museum board rooms. In addition, to attract top professionals or potential major donors, presenters must have name recognition.

Build and follow up on contacts. Planned giving is a process that depends on nurturing personal relationships both with financial advisors and with donors themselves. At the seminar, agency personnel should circulate and meet people and subsequently should stay in touch with the financial advisors whom they meet there. This will involve calling seminar attendees occasionally to remind them of the opportunities available to give to park and recreation projects.

The director should attend all follow-up meetings with potential donors. This demonstrates the park and recreation agency's genuine interest in and need for obtaining a contribution. Major donors typically want to deal directly with the top manager.

One or more respected co-sponsors should be involved. Co-sponsors lend credibility and help persuade people to attend planned giving seminars.

For professional wills seminars, continuing education credit should be arranged. Many professionals, such as lawyers and accountants, are required to continuously upgrade their skills by attending educational seminars. A planned giving seminar can meet that need. Local professional organizations can arrange the credit for attendees.

Thinking should focus on the long-term, not the short-term, return. If the seminar loses money it should be regarded as an investment in acquiring long-term resources.

Gifts Catalogs

A gifts catalog illustrates, describes, itemizes, and prices specific park and recreation needs. Individuals, neighborhood organizations, school groups, service clubs, businesses, and corporations can select items from the catalog's list of projects and programs. Cash, materials, equipment, labor, expertise, and professional services can be given to an agency for the specific project or program that the donor wants to support.

A gifts catalog is a fundraising adaptation of the retail sales catalog concept. The catalog can be viewed as a Sears catalog of community giving. Just as the Sears catalog offers a variety of items covering a wide price range, the gifts catalog describes needs that can appeal to potential donors of many income levels or funding preferences. Catalogs can suggest a variety of options. In addition to cash donations, the agencies seek equipment, skills, and services, because some donors may find these items easier to give than cash. An illustration of a page in a typical gifts catalog is shown in figure 15.1. Gifts catalogs have been produced as booklets, brochures, posters, portfolios, letters, newspaper or magazine articles, and even as videos. The key feature is a listing of needs from which a prospective donor may select.

Compared with the donations that it can attract, the gifts catalog is an inexpensive, fast, and

Sacramento History Museum

REBUILD THE ARBOR

The Sacramento History Museum is an authentic reproduction of Sacramento's original city hall and waterworks (circa 1854). Shortly after completion of the original structure, the police chief rounded up local prisoners and had a large wooden arbor constructed that spanned the building's large facade. Upon completion in 1860, passion vines were planted to cover the arbor and provide shade from the hot summer sun.

A replication of the original arbor, together with an outdoor seating area, would create a cool, inviting entrance. A bronze plaque and public recognition will accompany your generous gift. *$25,000*

No. 401
BRING THE PAST TO LIFE
FOR ALL TO ENJOY

The California Gallery is the site for a continuing series of exhibitions showcasing our recent past. Your sponsorship of a future exhibition will include artifact selection, preparation, installation, and signage. A reception will be held in your honor for this unique gift. *$5,000 - $30,000*

No. 402
FROM RAGS TO RICHES

Sponsor the conservation of dresses worn by famous and not-so-famous Sacramento women. Pick a vintage or favorite style, and we'll find a dress which you can bring back to life for exhibition at the Museum. Quilts and linens are in need of conservation as well. *$200 - $6,000*

No. 403
ELIMINATE THE FOXING

"Foxing" is a term used to describe the deterioration process which will eventually destroy old documents and photographs. With your contribution, specialists can halt this process and restore gold rush maps and historic documents from our rich past. *$50 - $4,000*

No. 404
SACRAMENTO HISTORY MUSEUM
ASSOCIATION MEMBERSHIP

You can help bring color and life to the rich history of the Sacramento Valley. Special benefits of membership include free admission, a monthly newsletter, discounts at the gift shop, invitations to receptions for new exhibitions, and discounts on special events.

Please specify membership category on order form: Pioneer $25; Settler $40; Prospector $50; Pathfinder $100; Argonaut $250

Figure 15.1   Sample page from a gifts catalog.

easy method of raising funds. Many park and recreation agencies that have used gifts catalogs report that the catalog has paid for itself many times over. Frequently, they are able to solicit sponsorship for production of the catalog.

A partnership between the Lutheran Brotherhood, a fraternal life-insurance association, and Florida State Parks resulted in the publication of 80,000 copies of the Florida State Parks Gifts Catalog. The Lutheran Brotherhood provided the printing for the catalog, counter publicity, cards, posters, award certificates, and stationery for the project. The program generated more than $200,000 in donated goods and services.[1]

Advantages of Gifts Catalogs

Gifts catalogs have four major advantages. First, they increase the opportunity for public investment. A greater sense of involvement with the park and recreation system is likely to result in higher participation and interest. The gifts catalog approach can foster an understanding of the problems and costs of providing park and recreation services by communicating these realities directly to the public. Donors who pay directly for the project or program that they select out of the gifts catalog have an investment in their park and recreation system. People tend to follow their investments closely. The city of Sacramento Department of Parks and Community Services in California noted:

> We've found that many residents would never think to give to parks and recreation, to a government agency. However, once they've seen the catalog, it changes their outlook. They're looking at your agency in a different frame of mind and feel confident that their gift will make a difference. We've seen residents become involved in their neighborhood park once they've donated to it through the catalog program (by planting a tree, installing a bench, etc.). They may have taken the presence of the park for granted before, as a passive amenity, but now the park is something to be cared for, and a wonderful sense of community pride emerges (p. 26).[2]

Second, they provide a service to potential donors. Most people make contributions of some kind each year. At the beginning of the year many do not know to which cause or service they will give. Putting a gifts catalog in their hands gives them an opportunity to fulfill their basic motivations to do good. The catalog offers a service by helping them find a need to support. There are often occasions when people seeking a gift for a friend may appreciate suggestions provided in a gifts catalog.

A handful of typical responses logged by Santa Monica Mountains National Recreation Area in response to its first gifts catalog demonstrated some reasons why people appreciated its availability:

- "I have a wealthy friend who is difficult to find a present for. The gifts catalog helped me find the perfect gift."
- "I have had many fine experiences over the years in national parks. I'm glad to have a chance to return the favor."
- "I'm affiliated with a small environmental group which is looking for just such an opportunity to help out."
- "A loved one died recently and I've been looking for a lasting memorial in his memory. When I heard about the gifts catalog, I knew I'd find a suitable project and now I have."

Third, gifts catalogs increase awareness of an agency's needs among prospective donors. They provide residents with specific information about short- and long-term goals of the park and recreation agency. Even though a specific gift, such as the construction of a new softball field, may not be donated, the fact that it is listed in the gifts catalog may reinforce the agency's commitment in residents' minds to provide a facility that softball players desire.

Fourth, a major advantage of the gifts catalog is that nearly all of the offerings in it are likely to be tangible. Thus, such gifts are visible not only at the time that they are given, but also in subsequent years. Tree items in gifts catalogs are particularly successful because of their high visibility and beauty; because of the powerful symbolism of growth, future development, and long life associated with trees; and because the cost to an individual is relatively affordable. Agencies have used a variety of approaches in gifts catalogs to capitalize on these attributes:

- Local nurseries may sell Christmas trees with roots and pot to individuals for their use over Christmas, but the trees are then donated to the park and recreation agency. It alleviates the guilt of wasting trees. The nursery provides written instructions on how to care for the tree. If individuals are unable to deliver their trees to the agency, then pick-ups can be arranged. The agency retains the trees in a greenhouse until the best season for planting arrives. In essence, individuals temporarily rent the trees, then in the spirit of Christmas, they donate them to the community.

- Trees may be planted in memory of an individual. They may be requested in lieu of flowers at a funeral.

- A tree may be planted to honor an individual's retirement as a symbol that celebrates a successful career and a new phase of life.

- Births at local hospitals are followed up in some communities with a letter suggesting a tree be planted so that the child and tree can grow together. To promote the program, a flyer may be distributed at prenatal classes.

Certificates can be given to individuals recognizing their trees. Existing planting patterns can be shown to donors, and a ledger of honor recording their donation of a tree can be displayed. Some believe that identifying individual trees with individual owners is not advisable because of the danger that a particular tree may be vandalized or die. However, others have reported that such identification encourages people to care for their tree and even to replace it if it is vandalized.

Many taxpayers are frustrated that they cannot see the direct benefits of their taxes. They do not know precisely where their tax dollars are spent and often wish they could direct their payments to projects that they support. Donors to some charities often feel the same frustration. The gifts catalog allows a person to determine where the donation goes and to point with pride to something that he or she helped provide for the community. It provides an avenue for direct expression of public support, pride, and spirit.

Developing a Gifts Catalog

The inventory of an agency's needs to be displayed in the catalog should be comprehensive. The idea is to portray a full range of gifts from which donors can choose. A brief narrative describing the need and the estimated price should be included alongside each item. It is difficult to predict the response to a specific item in a gifts catalog. Analyses have shown that donors are interested in contributing to a wide variety of park and recreation needs.

Gifts catalog programs should be designed to attract contributions of differing size. An individual or corporation may donate $100,000 for the renovation of a park, but a class of fifth graders may also contribute $10 to the purchase of bird seed for a nature center. Recognition of the importance of both gifts is fundamental to a successful long-term campaign. The local media may focus a human interest story on the fifth graders' contribution, providing free promotion for the project and the gifts catalog program.

The gifts catalog could include some novelty fundraising ideas that would attract valuable publicity to the project. For example, a professional golfer, a rafting operation, or a hang-gliding instructor could donate a lesson or an outing to be listed in the gifts catalog. These lessons or outings could then be purchased by members of the community, with the proceeds benefiting the agency. Perhaps the local professional baseball team could be persuaded to donate an open challenge to any group of 9 or 10 individuals in the community who would pay a few thousand dollars for a chance to take on the pros. Alternatively, a city council person may be persuaded to give up an evening for $200, and donors could contribute $200 to take out a council person and give him or her a piece of their mind.

The size should be kept manageable. Many gifts catalogs designed for general distribution are small enough to fit into a regular-sized envelope. The design and format of the gifts catalog must be of high quality. A gifts catalog is really an advertising print piece; therefore, copy must be interesting to read and accompanied by engaging photographs or graphic imagery. If at all possible, the agency should consult a professional design firm that has produced sales catalogs or similar print pieces. They may consider donating their services for this project.[2] However, if the catalogs are multicolored or overly glossy, there is a danger of offending people who may believe that some of their gift funds are used to pay for the catalog.

Identifying the target audience is a prerequisite to developing a gifts catalog. Some cities have developed separate catalogs for different target markets. For example, Anaheim developed three different catalogs for corporations; civic groups, school groups, neighborhood organizations, and foundations; and individual citizens. Even this approach did not enable the Anaheim department to target and tailor its gift solicitation as specifically as the staff wished. Hence, the permanent catalog was replaced with a portfolio that could be quickly adapted to solicit gifts for particular projects from more specifically defined target groups. The portfolio approach incurred lower production costs, permitted narrower targeting, and allowed updating to be done quickly at minimal cost.

The timing of a gifts catalog is especially important. Special holidays, such as the Christmas giving seasons, have proven to be ideal times. Holidays also offer an opportunity to provide updates and reminders about the gifts catalog's availability. A gift of a tree to the park system may be an attractive alternative to an individual who has previously given flowers on that occasion. Many people would be happier to have a gift donated to the community in their name than to receive a bottle of perfume or a new tie. Other gift-giving holidays, such as Mother's or Father's Day, also offer opportunities for promoting a gifts catalog.

The theme and title of a gifts catalog need to capture the attention of the reader. In California, the city of Sacramento Department of Parks and Community Services entitled their catalog *Gifts to Share*, which evoked a positive spirit among donors. It reinforced the notion that the donor had given a gift to be enjoyed and shared by all people in Sacramento. Other themes and titles that have evoked thoughts of pride, caring, improving, and building toward the future include the following:

Visions

Excellence Through Giving

Imagination

Tell Sacramento You Care

Share in the Future

Garden of Giving

Traditions

Share in a Living Treasure

Legacies[2]

It is important to be creative in developing a catalog. If there are facilities that need renovation or expansion, there are several ways to categorize construction-related items, such as buy a brick. The alternative is to ask for contributions to expand our community center, which does not sound very interesting. Similarly, a gifts catalog must offer something besides drinking fountains and trees. If there is a need to plant new trees, ask someone to give a living gift. If donations are being sought to conserve Victorian clothing exhibited in

the city's museum, the phrase "from rags to riches" may catch the reader's attention. Although pictures are an effective communication technique, words are also important.[2]

Finally, promotional effort is essential. A gifts catalog is only a tool. It facilitates donations, but it will not be effective unless there is a coordinated effort to get it into the hands of potential donors and to motivate them to give. Untargeted mass mailings are not likely to be productive. Personal followup should be an integral part of the promotional plan. Agencies report that a high percentage of prospective donors who are approached personally with the gifts catalog respond with a donation.

Donating Personal Bricks

Donating personal bricks is a grass roots strategy that offers residents the ego gratification of having their names immortalized in brick on a project with which they want to be associated.

Fair Park in Dallas is managed by Dallas Parks and Recreation Department. The Friends of Fair Park, which is a 501(c)(iii) organization (a type of nonprofit organization that is explained in detail in chapter 18), sold personalized bricks to be placed in a special walkway of the park called the Texas Promenade, which is located between the Music Hall and the Science Place in the park. In return for a donation of $37, a brick was engraved with the donor's name. Special bricks were also available. For $250, a donor could receive a halo brick, which was a personalized brick surrounded by plain bricks so it would stand out.

It is likely that most people would like to be immortal. Failing that, they might settle for having their names live forever or at least for as long as an engraved brick might endure on a project. The case study described in "Solicitation of Personal Bricks to Develop Pioneer Square in Portland" on page 398 illustrates the magnitude of the organizational challenge needed to bring this type of program to a successful conclusion.

A similar concept was used by the author in soliciting donations from visitors to York Minster, one of England's greatest cathedrals. Visitors were sold minutes of time. The cost per minute of maintaining and operating the Minster was calculated, and visitors were invited to purchase as many minutes as they wished. Donors received an artistic scroll, incorporating a sketch of the Minster and recognizing that their generosity kept the cathedral open for a particular number of minutes.

Solicitation of Personal Bricks to Develop Pioneer Square in Portland

To complete the redevelopment of Pioneer Square, which is a public plaza in the heart of Portland's central retail district, a campaign to raise $500,000 by selling the opportunity to donate a personal brick was launched. A steering committee was chaired by two city commissioners. A $20,000 grant in seed money was obtained to rent and equip office space, hire individuals to direct the campaign, and retain a public relations and advertising firm to define the campaign and to produce materials.

To make the program as egalitarian as possible, all bricks were placed randomly and sold for the same amount. After estimating the costs of the program to be $5 per brick (including imprinting bricks), a price of $15 was established. In addition to equality, the random placement made possible the low price.

The advertisements were stunning; they were evocative, witty, humorous, and effective. Good organization, excellent materials, a popular cause, and a novel idea made the campaign a natural for helpful media coverage. The campaign broke with a full page advertisement in the daily newspaper. Well-done public service announcements followed on radio and television. The campaign lasted almost one year and made major pushes at the beginning, Christmas ("Jingle Bricks"), and Valentines Day ("Don't Brick My Heart").

The most visible part of the campaign was the sales booth. Open from 10 A.M. to 6 P.M. weekdays and from 11 A.M. to 5 P.M. on Saturdays, this volunteer effort was maintained for almost one year! Working in pairs and in shifts lasting from 2 h to 3 h, volunteers explained the parameters for imprints, supervised the completion of forms, handed out brick buttons and identification cards, and collected money.

The sales booth was located on the construction site—a central downtown spot—in a trailer loaned by a bank that had used it as a temporary branch office. An attractive area evolved around the booth with a patio of demonstration-imprinted bricks, outdoor furniture with umbrellas, and flower-filled planters. With donations of labor and materials including the bricklayers union, a masonry contractor, and several nurseries, this landscaping cost virtually nothing.

While the question of how a person would eventually find his or her brick in the completed square rarely came up, campaigners believed that by the time construction was completed, an enterprising individual or group would take on the job of mapping the imprinted bricks as a way of making money. This did happen. However, some purchasers resented having to pay another fee for finding their brick, and in future campaigns, it is recommended that the cost of a brick finder be included in the purchase price of the brick.

Orders arrived by mail. All newspaper advertisements, mailers, handouts, and forms picked up from the booth prominently displayed order forms that carried a post office box address. These orders and all check orders from the sales booth went directly to a donated bank lockbox service that processed the checks and returned copies of them attached to the orders. Because the checks usually had the purchaser's address printed on them, these copies helped immeasurably when the purchaser's handwriting was illegible.

Telephone orders made with charge cards accounted for a significant proportion of the total purchases. This was a particularly popular way for both the elderly purchaser and the busy executive to place orders. The telephone number was 22-BRICK.

Processing the brick orders to ensure accuracy, completeness, and timeliness is complex—and very important! A brick number, ranging from 000 001 to 048 657 in this case, followed it until placement in the square. Staff used this number for things, such as filing, owner inquiries, and tracking. After checking the brick order for suitability, completeness, readability, and error, staff assigned the number and then entered the order into the computer.

The computer was programmed to print a brick certificate, which was an ornate document including the imprint, brick number, and date of computer entry. Mailing labels addressed to brick purchasers were produced in alphabetical order in the same batch. For each day's input, the computer generated an alphabetized list of purchasers showing their address, total dollar amount of purchase, and corresponding brick numbers.

With a daily batch of brick certificates, frequently from 200 to 700 at a time, volunteers put labels on certificate envelopes, which they kept in order; organized the certificates to go into the envelopes; and stuffed them. An accompanying note explained that the imprint on the certificate was exactly as it would appear on the brick and that any errors had to be reported within two weeks.

The biggest challenge for the masonry contractor was to maintain accuracy control when faced with a book of 835 pages with 57 names per page. The masonry contractor separated the imprinted bricks into lots of 500. Each lot was tagged with the pages of the book represented by the imprints it contained. The lots were then transferred to wooden pallets of 1,500 for shipping to the construction site. The pallets also had to be tagged in the same manner. As masons installed named bricks, they noted the imprint of any broken or deficient bricks on the check-off sheet of imprints so that it could be remade and installed at a later time.

The sale of nearly 50,000 bricks at $15 each raised approximately $500,000 after expenses. Beyond the actual financial gain, however, the tremendous public support for the project ensured its completion and brought a sense of broad ownership to this unique block in downtown Portland. Each person whose name appears on a brick has a feeling that the square is partially his or hers. This may also have been the first fundraiser in history that people were sad to see end because they wanted to buy more bricks in the future. Indeed, the manager of the square later had no trouble selling another 12,000 bricks at $30 each to replace some unnamed bricks and to provide a start-up administrative resource.

From John L. Crompton. Doing more with less. *Venture Publishing: State College, PA. Pages 70-74. 1987. Copyright ©Venture Publishing, Inc. Used by permission.*

Art students were hired to produce distinctive medieval calligraphy on the ancient scrolls.

Donation Boxes and Fountains[3]

On-site collection devices may be used to enable visitors to make a donation toward maintaining a facility. These are likely to be especially effective at facilities at which there is no admission charge. The need for these opportunities was articulated by a National Park Service ranger:

> People have always wanted to give us money, especially if they enjoyed our ferry ride and interpretive talk. Until we were able to set up our donation box, we had no way to accept these cash contributions from visitors. Now, we're collecting a little extra, enough to run this ferry a few additional weeks this year. But perhaps the best part is that we no longer have to refuse their offers of help. Now they give a little and walk away feeling better knowing they've helped.

It has been found that people are more likely to donate generously if they can visualize how their donations are being used. Thus, a specific project may be illustrated alongside the donations box showing pictures and sketches of what needs to be done.

At Alcatraz National Monument in San Francisco, the metal collection canister was set into a cell door with an interpretive panel alongside. Photographs showed the kinds of maintenance tasks and restoration projects that were underway. The sign stated: "Your donation is appreciated. It will be used to fund maintenance projects and enhance interpretive activities on Alcatraz." The park averaged $1,000 per month in donations.

When visitors can see that others have contributed, they are more likely to give themselves. Thus, it is important that the receptacles be made of a translucent material. An empty box rarely attracts donations. Salting the donation box with a few visible dollars or even with $5 and $10 bills often prompts the next visitor to contribute like amounts. People are more apt to give when they know that others have contributed. Staff at Lyndon B. Johnson National Historic Site had three donation boxes in different locations. The park frequently collected more than $7,000 in contributions in a summer season. At Hawaii Volcanoes National Park, the park's donation box attracted more than $50 per day, which was enough to employ a seasonal interpreter.

Fountains, pools, and wishing wells are natural collection devices. Few can resist the urge to toss coins into bodies of water while making a wish. The fountain pools in the center courtyard of the U.S.S. Arizona Memorial Visitor Center in Hawaii have long been used by visitors unable to resist the urge. Discreet signs were placed around the pools indicating that monies collected would be used to help operate and maintain the memorial. An average of $57 per day was collected for park maintenance.

Check-Off Donations

Some jurisdictions have provided opportunities for residents to add a voluntary donation for a park and recreation project to their state income tax return or their utility bill. Funding for state nongame activities has been acquired from this source in several states.

In New Jersey, residents could check a box on their state income tax form, voluntarily donating $10, $5, or $2 to the Endangered and Nongame Species of Wildlife Conservation Fund. The fund was used to hire additional staff for nongame management and enforcement, create more and better facilities to care for injured wildlife, and to develop teaching aids relating to endangered and nongame wildlife.

A similar program in Ohio was intended to raise funds to help protect the state's nature preserves and scenic rivers and to help protect the more than 1,000 species of wildlife not taken for sport or commercial purposes. It was based on state income tax refunds. Individuals receiving a refund on their state income taxes had the option of donating portions of it or all of it by checking a box on their income tax form.

Several cities in Texas established a check-off donation opportunity on their city utility bills. On each water bill in Irving, Texas, a citizen or organization was given the opportunity to make a donation to assist the park and recreation department with land purchases and development. In Bedford, Texas, 50¢ was automatically added into each water bill. Every resident had the right to subtract out the 50¢ if he or she preferred not to make the donation. Approximately $2,275 per month, which accrued to $120,000 over four years, was raised from this community of 25,000 residents, and participation in the program was close to 70%.

The success of check-off opportunities is likely to depend on the relative appeal of the designated projects to residents. However, some evidence suggests that while check-off programs are reasonably well supported initially when they are widely promoted and the cause is fresh in residents' minds, over time this donation support declines as initial supporters gradually lose their initial enthusiasm and withdraw.

A more recent variation of check-off donations has been associated with the use of license plate funds. When renewing their license plates, drivers are offered a check-off option to purchase special plates, which indicate their support for an environmental cause, for a premium price. The premium is used to fund the cause. Examples include the following:

- Massachusetts sells an environmental license plate, and revenues benefit the state's environmental trust fund.

- Virginia sells a "Friend of the Chesapeake" license plate, and $15 from each $25 plate is designated for the Chesapeake Bay Restoration Fund, which is targeted to environmental education and restoration projects.

- Maryland also has a Chesapeake Bay plate, and $12 of the $20 cost goes into the Chesapeake Bay Restoration Fund. It annually awards $750,000 from this fund in small grants for environmental projects including land restoration and shoreline improvements.[4]

Adopt-a-Facility Programs

Adopt-a-facility programs require a business, service club, youth organization, church group, or group of friends to make a sustained commitment to support a facility's operation. The adoption is a formal contract between an adopting group and a park and recreation agency. In some cases, the adoption commitment may be limited to volunteer activities, but in others, donations of cash or equipment supplement the volunteering. Some businesses that become involved contract with a service group to undertake the litter pickup, mowing, planting, or light maintenance that the agreement requires.

The Board of Recreation Commissioners in Monmouth County, New Jersey, launched an adopt-a-trail program. Fourteen groups adopted a designated section of the 9 mi Henry Hudson Trail. They signed a formal agreement to do litter pickups at least four times each year. After consulting with the park system program coordinator, adopting groups can also do light maintenance tasks, such as brush clearing, pruning, and graffiti removal.

Groups designate leaders who ensure that safety is a priority.[5]

Within one year of launching its adopt-a-park program, the city of Pampa, Texas, reported that 24 of its 31 parks had been adopted and that park maintenance expenses had been reduced by 30%. The most substantial donation was made by Cabot Corporation, which adopted a park in an economically depressed area. Donating more than $50,000 to the project, they renovated it by building a basketball court; purchasing picnic tables, fire grills, park benches, and playground equipment; and building a hike-and-bike asphalt trail throughout the park. This type of program works best when local neighborhood groups commit to it. If the adoption is limited to people from elsewhere periodically scheduling visits to maintain the park, much of their work is likely to be undone quickly.

Many zoological facilities offer adoption packages. As their value increases, so do the range of benefits offered. In Texas, for example, the Fort Worth Zoo packages ranged in value from $35 to $1,000. For a $35 contribution, the adopter received an adoption certificate, photograph of the animal, and bumper sticker. Other benefits, such as T-shirts, subscription to the quarterly magazine, and free passes, were added at different incremental values. The $1,000 package included the parent's name being placed on the zoo's "Walls of the Wild" honor roll, a presentation to the parents at the zoo informing them of their animal's characteristics, periodic updates on its status, and an invitation to a gala reception called "The Zoo Parents Family Reunion."

In the city of New York, 20 public monuments were offered for private adoption because they needed restoring and the city lacked the resources to do it. Restoration costs for each monument ranged from $3,500 to $275,000. In addition to contacts by cash donors, the city was contacted by artisans who offered to donate their expertise to the restoration effort.[6] A similar adoption program was initiated at Gettysburg National Battlefield in Pennsylvania for its 1,000 monuments and 410 artillery pieces.

The adopting party often is recognized by a sign that states: "This Facility is Adopted By . . ." (see figure 15.2 on page 402). As well as recognizing an organization's contribution, this sign provides incentive for it to perform the agreed tasks well. Adoption programs encourage resident ownership in a facility as people come to view it as their facility. Vandalism is likely to be reduced because more eyes are now critically watching the facility.

Cause-Related Marketing

If there is such a thing as a win-win-win proposition, cause-related marketing is it. Corporations earn money and goodwill. Nonprofit organizations gain money and exposure. Consumers spend money and feel good about it. In cause-related marketing, capitalism has actually become a philanthropic tool.[7]

Cause-related marketing strives to achieve two objectives—to improve corporate performance and to help worthy causes—by linking donations to a cause with the purchase of the company's products or services. Discussion of it has been deferred until the end of this chapter because it is a hybrid that incorporates attributes of both donations and sponsorships (which are discussed in chapter 16). It aligns the direct financial objective of increasing sales with corporate social responsibility. Cause-related marketing qualifies as sponsorship because it is a business relationship that is undertaken for commercial advantage. However, it meets the donation criterion of making contributions to alleviate social and community concerns or creating public benefits because corporations position their motive as being social consciousness. Although the benefits to donors do exceed their costs in cause-related marketing campaigns, corporations, nevertheless, proclaim their donations to be acts of altruism and seek to deduct their donations.

Cause-related marketing may be formally defined as the process of formulating and implementing marketing activities that are characterized by an offer from a business to donate a specified amount to a designated cause or organization when customers purchase a given product or service.[8] Most often this is done through the use of cents-off coupons; for each coupon redeemed, the business donates a fixed amount, frequently up to a pre-established ceiling, to the agency.

American Express coined and copyrighted the phrase cause-related marketing to differentiate campaigns that tie charitable contributions directly to product promotions from standard corporate donations in which dollars are given outright to a charitable cause. Every time somebody used its products, the company made a cash contribution to its nonprofit partner. The nonprofit partner received not only the cash contribution but also extensive publicity. The company's promotional effort typically included an extensive advertising campaign that stressed the programs and community benefits that the nonprofit agency

Figure 15.2 Facility adoption recognition sign.
City of Fort Worth Park and Recreation Department.

delivered together with ways in which the public could assist this organization. A typical advertisement for a cause-related marketing campaign is shown in figure 15.3.

This technique is particularly effective with affluent target markets. It is based on an appeal to Americans' social consciousness, the decline of the "me" generation, and an awareness that government is less willing or able to finance these causes now than in the past. The rationale of American Express for using cause-related marketing was that local civic pride was a powerful stimulant to the sale and use of the company's products and services. At the same time, American Express gained the goodwill of a grateful community. In the words of their chairman: "cause-related marketing is our way of doing well by doing good."

Everyone in Madison can become a philanthropist with Universal Business

Many Madison citizens support the arts. But now, everyone has a chance to get into the act.

Through August 31, every time anyone in Madison uses a Universal Business service, Universal Business will make a donation to the Madison Community Theater and the Madison Arts Council.

When you use your Universal Business charge card, the contribution will be a modest ten cents. But multiply that ten cents by the thousands of purchases made in Madison and the Madison Community Theater and Arts Council will have an amount no one has to feel modest about. Last March alone, Madison citizens charged more than 15,000 purchases.

Universal Business will also donate $2 for every new Universal Business card member. To apply, simply call (800) 555-8888 and we'll send you an application or take your information over the phone.

Use the Universal Business card to purchase a travel package worth $500 or more (including cruises, car rentals, airplane tickets, and hotels) at one of the Universal Business travel agencies in

Madison, and we'll donate $5 to the Madison Community Theater and the Arts Council.

When you travel, use your Universal Business phone card to call home. Universal Business will donate five cents for every call a Madison citizen makes on a Universal Business phone card.

Finally, for every transaction made at a Universal Business ATM, we'll donate $1. Apply for a new ATM card, and we'll donate $5 to the Madison Community

Theater and the Madison Arts Council.

Of course, we stand to benefit from this philanthropy. That's the great thing about the free enterprise system. Only now, it's working both ways. Because every time you do something good for yourself, we'll do something good for theater and art in Madison.

Each time you shop, eat out, or travel, you can support the cause of art and theater in Madison. It's a small but important way for all of us to applaud.

Why the Madison Community Theater Deserves a Hand

More than 200 productions have graced the stage of the Madison Community Theater. Founded in 1952 under the leadership of Charles Russel, the theater has emerged as an arts leader in the Madison area.

Today, the Madison Community Theater, under the direction of Ella Malloy, provides opportunities for new talent as well as seasoned veterans of the stage.

Besides producing the Shakespeare Festival every

summer, the Madison Community Theater also provides educational opportunities for high school students, conducts acting and directing workshops, and co-sponsors the annual Arts Brigade with the Madison Arts Council.

The Madison Arts Council works to preserve and promote art in the Madison area. The Art Council sponsors productions at Madison High School, finances exhibits of local artists at the Madison Art Museum, and

coordinates the Arts Brigade in cooperation with the Madison Community Theater.

This spring, the Madison Community Theater invites you to enjoy the works of George Bernard Shaw with productions of two of his greatest plays.

Arms and the Man: April 3, 5, 8, 11, and 14.

Pygmalion: May 22, 24-26, 28, and 30.

For showtimes and tickets, call the Madison Community Theater at 555-8927.

Figure 15.3 A typical advertisement for a cause-related campaign.

Sales of Nabisco Inc.'s Animal Cracker cookies doubled in the first week of a tie-in that donated to the World Wildlife Fund 5¢ of each package sold. A promotional campaign ran concurrently and focused on the 93-year-old brand's unprecedented change in packaging and cracker shapes to emphasize endangered species.[9]

The Nature Conservancy (whose work is discussed in chapters 18 and 19) had cause-related links with many products. They included

- a percentage of revenues from sales of High Birches Mountain Spring Water;
- a contribution from Canon USA for each toner cartridge returned for recycling;

- $1 per package sold of Aromatique fragrance;
- a percentage of business customers' telephone bills from MCI Telecommunications;
- 5% of sales from The Nature Company, a California-based retailer; and
- 10% of wholesale revenues from Vancouver-based Second Nature Software.[10]

American Express was the most visible advocate of this approach; however, the principles that American Express used have been applied on a smaller scale to local businesses in all sizes of communities and can be adapted readily to meet

First Constitution Bank Cause-Related Marketing Program With Mystic Marine Aquarium

The First Constitution Bank was approached by the Mystic Marine Aquarium in Mystic, Connecticut, to help it fund a whale study center. Interested in whales and sensing a marketing opportunity, the bank's new chief executive officer agreed. Rather than just writing out a check, he decided to get the community involved. After all, whales were Connecticut's state mammal. People rarely resisted a chance to help them. Suppose the bank linked its donation to the opening of new accounts? It would give the public a chance to help and would give the bank a popular cause with which to associate and build business.

In partnership with the aquarium, the bank launched Operation Whale Save, a two-part cause-related marketing campaign to raise money for the new whale study center. The bank advertised that each time someone opened a qualifying account, the depositor would get a free toy whale, and the bank would donate money to the center. The same would happen when someone applied to the bank for a loan. At the same time, all 25 bank branches were equipped with a television and a video cassette recorder so that they could show a program developed by the bank about the aquarium and narrated by television star William Conrad.

The campaign was extremely successful. Besides boosting business for the bank and raising funds for the aquarium, Operation Whale Save generated tremendous public recognition. Newspaper reporters, writers in environmental journals, and public officials acclaimed the environmental action.

Buoyed by this success, First Constitution decided to expand its environmental marketing efforts the following year by launching a program called Help Save Our Sound. The social goal of Help Save Our Sound was to generate public awareness of and support for the restoration and preservation of Long Island Sound, which was one of Connecticut's most valuable, but polluted, resources. The program's marketing goal was to strengthen the bank's image and business in its home state. Its nonprofit partners were the Nature Conservancy and the Long Island Soundkeepers Fund, which were two reputable environmental groups working to protect the sound.

Help Save Our Sound was structured much like Operation Whale Save. With a cause-related marketing campaign at its core, the program made donations to the two organizations each time someone opened a new account or applied for a loan. However, the program branched out. As an added inducement and an added educational opportunity, the bank gave a *Recycling Handbook* to each new depositor. The 20-page booklet opened with a letter from the bank's chief executive officer explaining the bank's commitment to Long Island Sound and the Help Save Our Sound program, and it offered tips on how to conserve, reuse, and recycle household items.

The Connecticut Fund for the Environment produced the *Recycling Handbook* for the bank. The last page bore a full-page advertisement for the organization, describing its work and soliciting memberships.

A bank mailer and lobby brochure described the Help Save Our Sound campaign and gave tips for saving water. It also included full-page descriptions and a mail-in form for making donations or becoming a volunteer for the two organizations.

The effect of these sponsored advertisements was not only to raise awareness and donations for the organization but also to reinforce the bank's commitment to the cause and to strengthen its image as a good public corporate citizen.

The bank used special events to expand the campaign's reach, sponsoring numerous beach cleanups during the summer as well as a children's art contest. These events drew people whom the bank otherwise might not have reached and attracted media coverage. They also provided numerous opportunities for the bank to reinforce its association with the cause.

The bank also used a special event to reach another important audience: legislators. It held the first State of the Sound Address, which was a public event well covered by the media, that provided a forum in which state and national lawmakers could talk about their actions to protect the environment. It announced its own in-house recycling program and its decision to stop using

Styrofoam, balloons, and other nonrecyclable products that could harm Long Island Sound. The bank also challenged businesses across the state to examine the impact of their own operations on the environment and to begin recycling efforts and other environmental programs of their own. Essentially, the bank used the event to position itself as part of the solution to environmental problems rather than as part of the problem.

The results of the Help Save Our Sound campaign were extremely positive. A survey of First Constitution's customers indicated that most new accounts had been opened because of the Help Save Our Sound program and that the bank's name and image were associated positively with the environmental program.

The cause-related marketing campaigns raised $50,000 for the Nature Conservancy and the Long Island Soundkeepers Fund. Additional money came from other, independent fundraising events that Help Save Our Sound prompted. Teenagers, local environmental groups, and other companies in New Haven called the bank to ask whether they could hold their own fundraisers and give the money to Help Save Our Sound. Several bank customers also wrote the cause into their wills—possibly the first unsolicited bequests in bank history!

Finally, as a result of First Constitution's efforts, the U.S. Environmental Protection Agency announced that it would open a New Haven office to oversee the cleanup of Long Island Sound, giving the bank more publicity and more acclaim.

From Doing Best by Doing Good *by Richard Steckel and Robin Simons. Copyright ©1992 by Richard Steckel and Robin Simons. Used by permission of Dutton, a division of Penguin Putnam Inc. Pages 40-44.*

the needs of park and recreation agencies. An illustration of their use by a local business is given in "First Constitution Bank Cause-Related Marketing Program With Mystic Marine Aquarium."

The chief executive officer of American Express stated:

The program works. At first, we didn't know whether we'd found a new way to help business or just an interesting formula for giving money away. It's both. The increase in business we've seen in our cause-related markets proves the concept is as successful as any marketing program we've ever tried. We're doing good deeds, and we're also pleased with the commercial results (p. 1).[11]

Each cause-related marketing program initiated by American Express began with an announcement that the company would donate a small sum to the cause each time one of its clients in the area

- used the American Express card,
- purchased American Express Travelers Checks,
- purchased a travel package of $500 or more (excluding air fare) at an American Express vacation store, or
- applied for and received a new American Express card.

Thus, the size of donation to the selected cause depended on business done by the company in a specific geographic area during a set time period, which was typically three months.

However, it was the program's most distinctive feature—a tailor-made advertising campaign that described both the cause and the way in which American Express clients could help it—that most dramatically linked the two. Most park and recreation agencies or nonprofit organizations cannot afford either expert creative talent to write and design first-rate advertising or the money for placing advertisements that reach the target audience. When a cause-related program was implemented, the same talent and experience that went into other advertising efforts of American Express were harnessed to explain both the cause and program to clients. A case study illustrating how the relationship worked is given in "An American Express Cause-Related Marketing Program With the Chicago Lincoln Park Zoo" on page 406.

In addition to generating a wealth of goodwill, cause-related promotions have had powerful catalytic effects. Local donations to causes frequently increased, sometimes dramatically, even after the promotion ended. Examples include the following:

- In California, the program resulted in a $25,000 increase in ticket revenues for the San Jose Symphony, but the symphony also received $107,000 in additional corporate

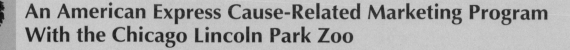

An American Express Cause-Related Marketing Program With the Chicago Lincoln Park Zoo

Lincoln Park Zoo is owned and operated by the Lincoln Park Zoological Society, a nonprofit organization that provides funds and services to enhance the zoo beyond the allocation of funds it receives from the Chicago Park District's budget.

American Express elected to link with the zoo because it had widespread name recognition; was the oldest, most-visited zoo in the country; had positive connotations in Chicago; and had a visitor profile consistent with the American Express target market. The company agreed to make a small cash contribution to the zoo's renovation program each time American Express services were used in 12 counties in the Chicago area. Terms of the commitment were

- 1¢ for each purchase charged to the American Express Card,
- $1 for each approved American Express application,
- 15¢ for each purchase of American Express Travelers Checks, and
- $5 for each travel package of $500 or more (excluding air fare) purchased at an American Express Vacation Store.

This arrangement was widely promoted for the three months in which it operated. The zoo received $152,000 in cash from the arrangement. However, perhaps more importantly, American Express invested heavily in an advertising program in Chicago, promoting the arrangement and giving the zoo considerable exposure. The company ran television, radio, and print advertisements that explained the program and described the zoo's unique features, animals, and current needs. Point-of-sale advertising was displayed in restaurants, hotels, retail shops, and department stores. The zoo's own promotional budget was minimal, and this program created a level of awareness in the community about zoo activities that otherwise could not have been achieved.

grants as a direct result of American Express involvement.

- Several prominent Pittsburgh business leaders who first heard of the organization through the American Express campaign eventually served on the board of the Pittsburgh Center for the Arts.

The approach is particularly effective if other businesses also cooperate in the effort. An executive of American Express, commenting on the success of the whole cause-related marketing program, stated:

One of the most gratifying aspects of the whole program was the way our business partners rallied around. Banks that were selling other brands of travelers checks began to prefer ours. Restaurants and retailers that never accepted any cards began accepting the American Express card. And hundreds of these businesses in many markets not only displayed point-of-purchase material but often participated by making marketing donations of their own.

An extensive number of partnerships have emerged between banks that issue credit cards and nonprofit conservation organizations. Again, the banks are seeking to capitalize on the goodwill of people for the social-cause group with which they identify. The Sierra Club linked with a subsidiary bank of Chase Manhattan Corporation. The bank offered a Visa card featuring the Sierra Club logo and a quotation from John Muir: "When we try to pick out anything by itself, we find it hitched to everything else in the universe." Each time someone used the card, the Sierra Club received a donation from the bank that ranged from 0.5% to 5% of the amount charged. The Sierra Club typically received $20 to $40 per year from each cardholder so that 20,000 cardholders generated from $400,000 to $800,000 per year.

Promoters of these cards challenge consumers to answer the question: "Why use a bank card that just gives money to the bank, when you can use

NeighborWoods Street Tree Planting Project

NeighborWoods was a cooperative project between the Austin Parks and Recreation Department, residents, and businesses that planted thousands of street trees each year in Austin. The city council set a goal of planting 300,000 trees on public property, such as street sides, medians, and parks, in a 12-year period from 1989 to 2000. Before this program, very few trees were planted, so as aging trees died, they were not being replaced. Most funding for the program came from donations.

The program was coordinated by the Austin Parks and Recreation Department, which used aerial photographs to identify neighborhoods with too few trees. Forestry staff then went into those neighborhoods and posted signs in the right-of-way in front of houses that needed trees. At each house, staff left a door hanger with a postage-paid return card. Residents filled out the cards by marking the type of tree or trees they wanted and signed an agreement to plant and water the tree or trees for two years. This was a key element because watering was the most expensive task in the tree planting project. (Austin had an average of 33 in of rain and 100 days per year with a temperature of more than 90°.) After the cards were mailed back, the trees were ordered and delivered to the residents.

Austin Parks and Recreation Department purchased trees with funds donated through a check-off on residents' utility statement for the tree planting program or donated by businesses, of which the most responsive was the Jack Brown Cleaners Hanger Recycling Program. Jack Brown Cleaners had multiple outlets in the city. To encourage people to return hangers when they brought in clothes to be cleaned, the stores contributed 1¢ to the tree planting program for each recycled hanger. This donation amounted to approximately $30,000 per year.

Residents in Austin exhibited unusually high levels of environmental sensitivity. Hence, this cause-related program positioned Jack Brown Cleaners favorably, providing residents with a reason to prefer that business to its competitors and at the same time saving the cleaners the expense of purchasing new hangers. The Austin Parks and Recreation Department ensured that Jack Brown received high visibility from the program.

one that gives money to a group you support?" By tapping people's loyalty to causes this way, banks have an opportunity to encourage card-switching and to increase their market share. The cost to the banks is relatively small because these payments reflect a small portion of what they earn from annual fees and the interest that they charge card holders. It is also a small part of the percentage of each transaction, which ranges from 1.5% to 6%, that they charge their participating merchants.

"NeighborWoods Street Tree Planting Project" and the following examples illustrate the potential of using the principles of cause-related marketing in the specific context of a park and recreation agency.

First National Bank of Denver committed to pay for planting a tree on the South Platte River corridor in the name of each depositor who put $500 or more in a new or existing account within a given time period. The program was advertised extensively, giving substantial exposure to the South Platte reclamation project. It raised $30,000 for the project.

Frito-Lay initiated a friendship playground program in Houston, Miami, and San Antonio aimed at the Hispanic market. The program promoted the snack food company's five top-selling brands: Lay's, Ruffles, Fritos, Doritos, and Cheetos. Frito-Lay made a donation toward the building of a neighborhood playground for each empty bag of the snacks returned to local stores. The playground program ran for six months in each city and included television and radio advertising.[12]

American Express donated 5¢ to the San Francisco Arts Festival each time customers used their card and $2 for each new card member signed. The company exceeded its marketing goals because the program greatly stimulated card use. The festival received a contribution of more than $100,000.

The optimal length of a cause-related campaign is difficult to assess. A fine line exists between maximal exposure and customer fatigue. The most common time frame is three months. That is long enough to generate sufficient publicity, establish a strong presence in consumers' minds, and give them time to buy. It is short enough that the campaign does not lose its novelty. It also corresponds with a calendar quarter, making it easy to track results.[7]

Some campaigns, such as the one operated by First Constitution Bank and described in "First Constitution Bank Cause-Related Marketing Program With Mystic Marine Aquarium," last much longer. However, in these cases the campaign structure is often amended and extended to retain the customer's attention. Another strategy is for companies to link with annual events so that they reinforce previous campaigns in customers' minds. For example, Proctor and Gamble has carried out a cause-related marketing campaign with the Special Olympics annually and has raised millions of dollars for the cause. The repetition of the campaign has cemented the association between the company and the Special Olympics and has produced residual benefit to the company even at other times of the year.[7]

Cause-related marketing has opened an entirely new channel of monetary support for park and recreation agencies. The power of tying into a park and recreation cause was illustrated by Thrifty Car Rental Company. Thrifty Car Rental tested different sales incentives on older adults. When they offered a 10% discount, only 11% of the older adults said that it would be a major motivation for renting a Thrifty car. However, when they offered to use a portion of the car charges to buy vans for senior citizens' centers, 40% of the older adults said that it would make them choose Thrifty.[13]

At the same time, and perhaps more importantly, cause-related marketing also harnesses the creative promotional talents of private companies, improving awareness levels and heightening interest in the agency's projects.

Summary

The most efficient way for a park and recreation agency to launch a planned giving program is to initiate a series of workshops. These can be directed either at people interested in setting up their own planned giving instruments or wills or at professionals who deal with these types of programs. The workshops will provide agencies with a network of initial contacts and raise awareness of the opportunities and advantages of considering park and recreation projects as part of a planned giving program.

Gifts catalogs are fund raising adaptations of the retail sales catalog concept. They create a greater sense of involvement with the park and recreation system in the community, enable people to make meaningful presents to friends by purchasing something from the catalog on their behalf, and provide residents with specific information about the agency's needs.

Donating personal bricks is a grassroots strategy that offers residents the ego gratification of having their names immortalized in brick on a project with which they want to be associated. Donation boxes and fountains often are used at facilities at which there is no admission charge. Some jurisdictions have provided check-off donation opportunities for residents on income tax returns or utility statements. Adopt-a-facility programs require an entity in the community to make a substantial commitment to support a facility's operation.

Cause-related marketing links donations to an agency project with the purchase of a company's products or services. It embraces some characteristics of philanthropy and some characteristics of sponsorship. In addition to direct donations, cause-related marketing also harnesses the creative promotional talents of private companies that improve awareness levels and heighten interest in the selected park or recreation project.

References

1. La Page, Wilbur F. 1994. *Partnerships for parks*. Tallahassee, FL: National Association of State Parks.

2. Harder, Lori and Bill Moskin. 1988. *Gifts to share: A gifts catalog how-to manual for public agencies*. Sacramento, CA: Department of Parks and Community Services.

3. National Park Service. 1984. *Donation boxes and fountains*. San Francisco: National Park Service.

4. Myers, Phyllis. 1995. License plates raise funds. *Greensense* 1(2): 3.

5. Hauenstein, David. 1996. Make a difference, adopt a trail. *Green Heritage* 29(6), 2.

6. Dunlap, David W. 1987. Monumental generosity from all over. *New York Times*, March 15, section 4, 6E.

7. Steckel, Richard and Robin Simons. 1992. *Doing best by doing good*. New York: Penguin Books, 194.

8. Varadarajan, P. Rajan and Anil Menon. 1988. Cause-related marketing: A coalignment of market-

ing strategy and corporate philanthropy. *Journal of Marketing* 52: 58-74.

9. International Event Group. 1995. Nabisco cookie brands find sponsorship sells. *Sponsorship Report* 14(15): 1.

10. International Event Group. 1996. Nature Conservancy ties top $3 million. *Sponsorship Report* 15(15): 1.

11. Higgins, Kevin T. 1986. Cause-related marketing: Does it pass the bottom-line tests? *Marketing News* 20(10): 1,18.

12. *Special Events Report* 7(19). 1988. Frito-Lay chips in for playgrounds. Editorial, 3.

13. *American Demographics* 14(1). 1992. Cause-related reasoning. 2.

CHAPTER 16

SUPPORT FROM SPONSORSHIPS

The previous two chapters were concerned with support from donations, and it was emphasized that the distinguishing feature of donations is that they are made for altruistic reasons. The donor receives no tangible, net economic benefit from the contribution. In contrast, sponsorship is defined as a business relationship between a provider of funds, resources, or services and a park and recreational program or organization that offers in return some rights and an association that may be used for commercial advantage.[1] The distinctive terms in this definition that differentiate sponsorship from philanthropy are business relationship and commercial advantage.

The conceptual distinction between the two types of support is clear; however, in practice, the classification of a given contribution as being a donation or a sponsorship depends on a company's success in persuading the IRS that it receives no financial gain from the partnership. Companies often distinguish between the two sources of support based on the company budget line from which the support originated. If resources come out of the marketing and promotion budget, then they classify it as a sponsorship. However, if its source is the community relations budget, then it is considered a donation.

Until recently, park and recreation departments showed little interest in sponsorship. Three factors have resulted in sponsorship now being viewed as a major and growing source of financial support for park and recreation programs. First, sponsorship revenue has been crucial to the ability of departments to operate some programs, events, or facilities that could not be afforded without this source of funds. Second, the growth in the number and scale of festivals and special events the departments stage has been extraordinary. These events have proved to be appealing vehicles for sponsors. Third, a better understanding of the role of sponsorship has evolved. Some managers were reluctant to beg for money from local businesses to support a department's offerings. Managers tended to view sponsorships as guilt money that a local business felt pressured into contributing to a department program because it was located within the city. Now, more park and recreation managers recognize that they are brokers who can provide companies with valuable vehicles that enable the companies to communicate more effectively with their customers. Indeed, it has become fashionable for agencies to talk of business partnerships with companies rather than sponsorships.

Reservations about the appropriateness of sponsorship in some contexts still exist, especially when an agency faces a difficult balance between the sanctity of public spaces and the clear need to generate revenue. For example, in the mid-1990s, there was legislation in Congress that would have authorized the National Park Service to name corporate official sponsors. The intent was that 8 to 10 selected companies would be permitted to pay approximately $15 million each to the National Park Service. In return, these select companies could use in their advertising a special symbol to promote themselves as an official sponsor of the national parks system, similar to the use of the Olympic rings. It was anticipated the program would raise from $100 to $150 million a year.

Critics feared that the plan would give the Secretary of Interior and National Park Service officials too much discretion in determining when to accept corporate contributions and when to repel them, leaving open the possibility that corporate dollars could improperly tilt department policy. A critic suggested that a company seeking government permission to develop federal land, for example, "could become a major sponsor of the Park Service. If the Park Service becomes too dependent on the contribution, the Department of Interior could try to keep their corporate sponsors happy with decisions that conflict with broader conservation goals."[2]

The magnitude of the growth in corporate interest in sponsoring can be gauged by comparing the $4 million cost of being an official corporate sponsor of the 1984 Los Angeles Olympic Games with the $40 million paid by each of the eight primary corporate sponsors of the 1996 Atlanta Olympic Games. The extraordinary amount of corporate investment in sponsoring professional and elite amateur sports suggests that there are opportunities for park and recreation agencies to make quantum gains in the resources that they currently are acquiring from these corporate sources.

A park and recreation agency offers a variety of potential opportunities that businesses may perceive to be of value. The benefits include increased public awareness, image enhancement, product trial or sales opportunities, and hospitality opportunities (see figure 16.1). Companies in return may offer support through investments of money, media exposure, and in-kind services.

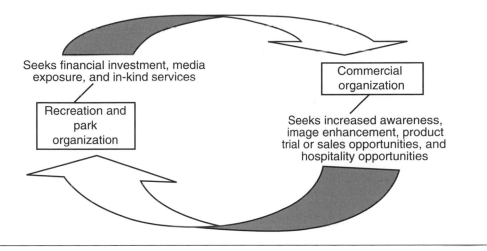

Figure 16.1 The sponsorship exchange relationship.

Benefits Business Organizations Seek From Sponsorships

The marketing mix consists of four components: product, price, distribution, and promotion. Promotion is fundamentally an exercise in communication. Its role is to facilitate exchange with present and potential clients by informing, educating, persuading, or reminding them of the benefits offered by a company, its products, or services. Traditionally, messages have been communicated through some combination of four vehicles: personal selling, advertising, publicity, and incentives (sometimes termed sales promotions). Sponsorship offers a fifth vehicle that can contribute to the total communication effort of a company. It complements the other four vehicles rather than supplanting any of them.

The question, "Which of these five vehicles is the best to use?," is the wrong question to ask. The correct question is, "How can each of these vehicles link with the others to achieve our communication objectives?" Sponsorship offers a way to attract the attention of a specific target market, which can then be accessed by the full range of a company's communication tools. It is likely to be most effective when its use is integrated with the other four vehicles.

Sponsorship has two special strengths. First, positioning has become a central concept in marketing strategy, and corporate and brand image development are key factors in positioning. Image is used to differentiate and position products that are essentially similar. Sponsorship is particularly suited to image enhancement. Second, in many situations sponsorship may offer opportunities for a company to establish a more intimate and emotionally involved relationship with its target audience than the relationship feasible with the other four communication vehicles. A company's relationship with most of its audiences is usually rather distant and obviously commercial, but sponsorship enables a target market to be approached through activities in which they are personally interested. The intent is to communicate with audiences through their interests and lifestyle activities. In the context of parks and recreation, sponsorship allows a company to deliver its message to consumers who are in a relaxed state of mind and in an environment that makes it likely that they will be receptive. It may facilitate potential customers spending quality time with a company and its products: "When you reach prospects who are interested in or are attending an event, they are yours. They are there because they want to be. They're part of the event and in a receptive mood" (p. 4).[3]

Sponsorship's potential contributions are not limited to these two special strengths. Indeed, its role in a company's total communications effort is likely to vary widely in different industries.

When used by tobacco companies, its function is similar to that of advertising. In the case of building companies using sponsorship for guest hospitality purposes, it can be regarded as related to personal selling. When used by the large multinational oil and banking groups, its function lies broadly within the realms of public relations, and its usage in motor sport by oil companies and car manufacturers may be regarded as promoting sales (p. 7).[4]

Companies seek to communicate with groups other than their customers. Other groups that sponsorship decisions may affect include employees, shareholders, and financial institutions. For example, a particular sponsorship may create a sense of pride and unity among employees. However, in this chapter the discussion is focused primarily on how businesses use sponsorship to communicate with customer publics because this is likely to be the predominant concern when sponsorship decisions are made.

It is important to both the park and recreation agency and to a sponsoring business that the company's objectives are clearly prioritized and that they are stated in terms that are specific and measurable. Specific means that they should delineate target markets, quantity of impact, and timing. It has been noted: "There is no such thing as a generally effective sponsorship in an abstract sense" (p. 226).[1] The types of benefits that a sponsorship could offer may be discussed in general terms, but those sought should then be specified in measurable terms.

Measurable objectives achieve two things. First, they facilitate evaluation and accountability because only if objectives are measurable can the outcome from a sponsorship be evaluated. Second, they serve to crystallize executive thinking because managers are forced to consider the limitations of a recreation sponsorship and examine carefully whether it is the best vehicle to achieve the specified objective. From the park and recreation agency's perspective, the careful development of written objectives at the outset offers guidance as to what benefits the agency should focus on facilitating. It also protects against unrealistic expectations on the part of the business, possibly leading to subsequent recriminations if they are not met. These sponsorship objectives will fit within the broader goals of a company's overall communications strategy. At Cadillac, for example, a particular recreation sponsorship investment's objectives had to specifically contribute to one of two broad goals:

> Two goals dominate our marketing strategy at Cadillac. A recreation sponsorship investment's objectives must specifically contribute to one of these broad goals. One is to impact our narrow and demographically specific target market with direct product exposure that will result in immediate sales. The second goal, though more abstract, is equally important—to reinforce and enhance

Cadillac's image among the general public—to use our name as a metaphor for excellence: "The Cadillac of its class" (p. 4).[5]

There is a general consensus that for sponsorship to be effective, there should be a relatively long-term commitment. If the sponsorship is for an annual event, then from three to five years usually is advocated as the optimal time period. Short-term commitments do not provide adequate time to exploit a sponsorship. It usually takes longer to establish a linkage between the recreational event and a sponsor's product in the target market's mind, and this linkage is key to achieving the awareness and image benefits being sought. If a company is not prepared to commit for more than one year, the agency should at least persuade it to consider committing for the next two years to first right of refusal, which is a potential step towards recognizing the relationship as an ongoing partnership. A one-time sponsorship may generate some short-term awareness, but there is unlikely to be any positive image benefit. Further, once the event is over, awareness is likely to dissipate quickly. One experienced executive suggested to companies that the following sequence is likely to occur:

> The first year will be spent learning about the event or activity, making contacts (and probably quite a few mistakes) and finding your way in this new area. The second will start to show the potential you are hoping for, while the third should, if you have done your work correctly, see the benefits accrue, the audience accept your presence and motives, and the media to be comfortable with linking you with the activity (p. 124).[1]

An alternative approach to extending the time period of a sponsorship so that it has long enough to establish linkage in people's minds is to expand from a single event to multiple events spread over several months.

EDS is one of the nation's primary computer companies. They sponsored the national cycling championships, which were held in Indianapolis. As part of this arrangement, they also agreed to sponsor a series of local cycling events organized by the Indianapolis Parks and Recreation Department. This model of integrating major event sponsorship with sponsorship of related local events has been replicated frequently in Indianapolis. This strengthens the sponsor's bonding with the local community, increases local interest in the national event, and provides the repetitive exposure and longevity needed to establish linkage in the target market's minds.

A similar approach was adopted by the city of Myrtle Beach, South Carolina, which sold a series of events as a package to a number of different sponsors. Twenty companies paid $5,000 each to sponsor an entire summer season of 10 special events in Myrtle Beach. The city's leisure services manager said: "It is a lot easier to get several companies to sponsor a group of events than trying to get 10 sponsors for one event, 15 sponsors for another and 15 more for yet another . . . If you sell a series of events to a large group of sponsors, what they are participating in is the cumulative effect of all the events" (p. 30).[6]

Businesses may seek a large number of narrowly focused benefits from sponsorship, but the benefits can be classified into four broad categories: increased awareness, enhanced image, product trial or sales opportunities, and hospitality opportunities. It is assumed in this discussion that businesses are seeking product benefits from their sponsorship. The profusion of multiple-product companies has caused many corporations to recognize a need to raise their corporate profile with financial institutions, shareholders, and other key publics. This has led some businesses to seek to communicate messages through sponsorship about the corporation as well as its products. Hence, the benefits listed in "Benefits That May Be Sought by Businesses From Sponsorship" may be applied to corporate entities as well as to their products.

A sponsorship is likely to have the potential to yield multiple benefits involving all, or some combination, of the four categories. For example, sponsorship of a single major recreational event

Benefits That May Be Sought by Businesses From Sponsorship

Increased Awareness

- Create awareness of a new product.
- Increase awareness of an existing product in new target markets.
- By-pass legal prohibition on television advertising imposed upon tobacco and liquor products.

Image Enhancement

- Create an image for a new product.
- Reinforce the image of an existing product.
- Change public perceptions of an existing product.
- Counter negative or adverse publicity.
- Counter behavior that is detrimental to the company's interests.
- Build pride among employees and distributors for the product.
- Assist employee recruitment.

Product Trial or Sales Opportunities

- Offer product trial to potential new customers.
- Induce incremental sales increases through promotional give-aways, coupon tie-ins, sweepstakes, and point-of-purchase displays.
- Create on-site sales opportunities.
- Promote a different use of an existing product.
- Reinforce the image of an existing product.

Hospitality Opportunities

- Develop bonding with key customers, distributors, and employees.
- Develop in-house incentive opportunities.

may lead to increased awareness of the sponsor's product; stronger bonding by extending hospitality to existing key clients, potential clients, distributors, and decision makers; using hospitality privileges to create staff and dealer incentives; and inducing product trial by potential new customers. A corporate sponsor is likely to devise as many benefit opportunities as possible from a sponsorship in order to optimize return on the investment.

The Relationship Between Sponsorship Benefits and the Consumer's Purchase Decision Process

A variety of decision-making paradigms that model the stages through which potential consumers pass before purchasing a product or service have been proposed. The most widely accepted of these models is the awareness-interest-desire-action (AIDA) concept. In the model of the product-adoption process shown in figure 16.2, an addi-

tional stage, reinforcement, has been added to the end of the AIDA sequence. It has been noted that what the company does to nurture the relationship with the customer, to build it, and to strengthen it is crucial to the company's marketing effectiveness and efficiency. To work hard to attract new customers and then to be complacent in strengthening the relationship makes little sense.[7]

Hence, customer retention as well as attraction of new customers is likely to be a primary objective of some businesses sponsoring recreation. This involves reinforcing, reassuring, and confirming to customers that they made a wise decision in purchasing the company's product.

The product-adoption model shown on the left side of figure 16.2 suggests that potential purchasers of a product pass through a process comprising five stages from initial awareness to committed loyalty. They are defined as follows:

- Awareness. An individual becomes aware of the existence of a particular product and acquires some limited knowledge of its attributes.

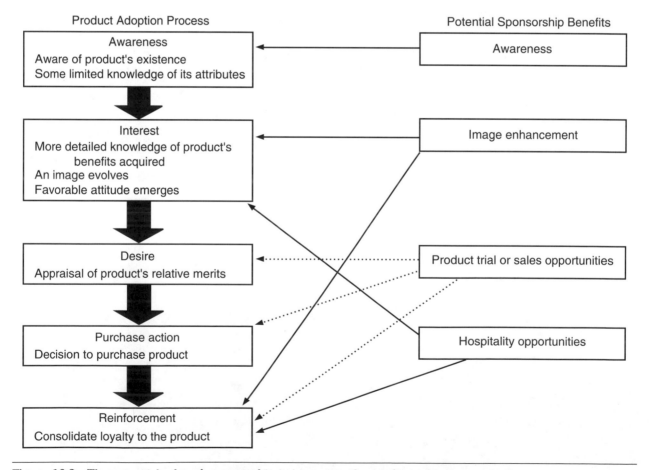

Figure 16.2 The potential roles of sponsorship in impacting the product-adoption process.

- Interest. More detailed knowledge of the product's benefits is acquired. Interest in it and a preference for it develop as a favorable attitude emerges. A distinctive image of it evolves.

- Desire. An appraisal of the product's merits is made. If it is perceived to meet an individual's needs better than alternative offerings, then there is a desire or intent to purchase.

- Purchase action. This is the culmination of all that has gone before, and the product is purchased or rejected.

- Reinforcement. To reassure and confirm to purchasers that a wise decision was made and to consolidate loyalty to the product.

The product-adoption model emphasizes that a purchase decision is usually the culmination of a process that starts long before an actual purchase takes place and continues long after an initial purchase is made. A company's challenge is to design sponsorship benefits that will move potential customers from their present stage in the adoption process to the next stage toward committed loyalty. Figure 16.2 illustrates how the four main benefit categories available to businesses from sponsorship may be used to facilitate the product-adoption process. The broken and continuous lines in figure 16.2 indicate the stage in the adoption process at which each of the sponsorship benefits may be targeted. For example, the two solid lines emanating from hospitality opportunities indicate that this benefit may be targeted at two groups: existing customers and suppliers to reinforce and consolidate links and potential customers and suppliers to nurture interest in the company and its products. In the following

Target Stores Built Awareness of Their New Gardening Centers Through Sponsorships

Each year, Indianapolis Parks and Recreation Department collaborated with one of their support groups, the Friends of Holliday Park, and with the Orchard Country Day School Parents' Association to produce an annual "Orchard in Bloom Garden Show." This was held in the 80-acre Holliday Park and was a fundraiser for both the friends group and the parents association.

The event has become a springtime tradition incorporating not only landscaped gardens, garden exhibits, retail booths, and educational displays but also an educational symposium, fashion show, and musical performances by children.

In the mid-1990s, Target Stores expanded its scope to include outdoor gardening centers and wanted to generate awareness of this expansion. These centers were intended to be superior to those that had been opened by competitors, such as K-Mart and WalMart. The Orchard event organizers were able to supply Target with details of visitor numbers and profiles based on market research that they had undertaken at previous years' events. Target Stores agreed to be the major sponsor for the event. They invested $15,000 and in return received the following benefits:

— Name and logo on tickets and prominent mention in publicity

— Name and logo on program front cover

— Name and logo on posters, fliers, and signage

— Name on contributor board posted at show entrance

— Complementary four-color advertisement on first page of program

— Program listing of contributors

— One table of 10 to patron's party

— 50 passes to the show

In addition, Target had the opportunity to showcase its new venture into the bedding plant, tree, and shrub market, which substantially increased the awareness of gardening enthusiasts that Target was now able to meet gardeners' needs. Target used coupons, permit promotion, and cooperative radio advertising to support their direct sponsorship investment.

subsections, the potential role of each of the four categories of sponsorship benefits in facilitating the product-adoption process is described and illustrated.

Increased Awareness

Sponsors who seek awareness benefits are trying to move potential consumers on to the first stage of the adoption process. Thus, if a sponsor is a well-known company whose products already have high levels of awareness, then this benefit will not be sought because sponsorship could only marginally increase awareness. For this reason, most major sponsors who have a high profile with their target markets tend to use sponsorship to effect other stages of the product-adoption process. However, when the awareness level is low or a new product line is being introduced, sponsorship can have an impact in expanding the number of potential customers. (See "Target Stores Built Awareness of Their New Gardening Centers Through Sponsorships.") This then provides a broader base at which to target communication strategies aimed at more advanced stages of the adoption process.

Trailhead Outfitters is an outdoor specialty store located in Chesterton, Indiana. It serves as a jumping-off spot for visitors traveling to Indiana Dunes State Park. The store coordinated a National Trails Day event that involved restoring 26 mi of trail in the Knobstone area of southern Indiana in a two-day period. The store manager was surprised at the interest in the event from the local community and the traffic it ultimately brought into the store: "We received coverage in the local paper, and many first-time shoppers said this coverage is what brought them into the store. The event itself wasn't expensive, and the return has been immense. . . . Protecting the land and getting involved on a grass roots level with trail conservation is something that goes hand-in-hand with our store . . . Outdoor specialty stores are supposed to provide quality service, and this includes service outside the walls of the store. It's a great equalizer with the megastores, and if you do it right, it isn't expensive to initiate" (p. 58).[8]

Leather accessories manufacturer and retailer Mark Cross of New York sponsored the Boston Ballet because it wanted to increase visibility for its new store in Boston. The company's public relations manager noted: "Many people who attend Boston Ballet are the same people who appreciate fine leather goods" (p. 6). In return for its sponsorship, Mark Cross' benefit package included one-time use of the ballet's mailing list to invite about 1,000 of the 15,000 subscribers to an in-store reception with the artistic director and dancers. Mark Cross also received tickets to productions that they used as employee incentives and in customer raffles; ballet costumes for store window display; and identification in the ballet's radio and newspaper advertisements, program, and newsletter.[9]

Image Enhancement

Image is the sum of beliefs, ideas, and impressions that a person has of a business or its products. It may be defined formally as the mental construct developed by an individual on the basis of a relatively few selected impressions. Images are ordered wholes built from scraps of information, much of which may be inferred rather than directly observed or experienced, and these inferences may have only a tenuous and indirect relationship to fact.

The importance of corporate and brand images to companies is well documented. Sponsorship enables a company to link its products immediately to a known set of image qualities, such as public service orientation (community events), environmental responsibility (preservation causes), world-class performance (top sports events), artistic excellence (cultural institutions), or durability (long-distance running or triathlon events).[10] Advertising does not have to work so hard to create desired image qualities for the product because they are acquired by association with the park or recreation service. Thus, image benefits are sought most frequently by companies that are striving to create interest and a favorable attitude toward their products by borrowing the image of a recreational program or event and using it to enhance the product's image with its target audience.

> In crude terms the company says, "We want to be known as a company that recognizes and pays tribute to excellence. We do so publicly in this exhibition." The institution says, "We will lend our prestige to X company and help it to get the recognition it deserves for bringing this exhibition or concert to the public." It's a lot cheaper than taking out ads saying how great we are. (p. 15)[11]

An explanation of how companies anticipate that this association will work is given in "Balance Theory: An Explanation of Why Corporations Seek To Associate With the Positive Image of Conservation Efforts."

Balance Theory: An Explanation of Why Corporations Seek To Associate With the Positive Image of Conservation Efforts

Conoco Inc., a major oil company, sponsored the Jane Goodall Institute, which supports the work of the internationally recognized chimpanzee researcher, Dr. Jane Goodall. Environmentalists strongly criticized Dr. Goodall for accepting their support. She reported: "They said, 'How can you, with your stated concern for the environment, dirty yourself by accepting money from the filthy petroleum industry?'"

Goodall defended her decision by saying that Conoco was at least trying to eradicate past misdeeds and should not be persecuted still: "It is more environmentally friendly than its competitors."

The oil company was later sold to DuPont Company, which was known to use animals in testing and to emit chlorofluorocarbons into the atmosphere. Dr. Goodall expressed her concerns to senior DuPont managers:

> If we can make some change with a company as large as DuPont leading the way, then everybody wins. The animals will benefit, and hopefully, because we endorse the corporation, DuPont will benefit too, and more money will become available for it to do even more to make the environment a better place.

An industry commentator, reacting to Dr. Goodall's rationalization for accepting the sponsorship, was skeptical that she understood the magnitude of the value that the company would derive from it. He explained the likely outcome in terms of balance theory:

> The logic is simple: If I like the idea of preserving the natural habitat of chimpanzees and your company makes that possible, then I like your company. If a brand I'm not fond of is supporting a cause I'm very fond of, my mental calculus is out of balance. If I think all oil companies are irresponsible scumbags, and I think Jane Goodall is a wonderful person who does heroic work, and I learn that Conoco and Jane Goodall are closely associated, my mental calculus is off balance.
>
> My mind will want to reestablish the balance, and there are two ways to do it. I can either raise my impression of Conoco or I can lower my impression of Jane Goodall and her work. Because our perceptions of causes and other highly-valued objects in our environment are related to our deeply-felt values, they are much less likely to change. Our attitudes toward brands are a lot more flexible and more likely to change to bring our mental calculus back into balance.

This association is likely to be particularly effective when a relatively new product or a product or company with low awareness is involved. Because few or no competing impressions of the product currently exist, the company hopes that by associating with a program, the program's image attributes will be associated with its product. Consider the image-enhancement products gained from the following linkages.

Nissan provided the Los Angeles County Department of Beaches and Harbors 37 new lifeguard trucks valued at $280,000 in return for the right to advertise the Nissan line as the official vehicles of the beach for a five-year period. Nissan incorporated its official status in its television and print advertisements in the Los Angeles area. Nissan's truck merchandising manager said that the arrangement fit the company's advertising campaign for its hard body pickups. "Hard bodies" is West coast slang for the lean and tawny among beach visitors.[12]

Outdoor retailer Eddie Bauer Inc. sponsored the American Forests' Global ReLeaf program. Consumers were invited to add $1 or more to their catalog or store purchases toward the planting of a tree, and Bauer matched the donation. A company spokesman said: "Customers always thought of us as an environmental company because of our product, and our brand identity and image solidify with a program like this. Also, there always has been concern over our using a lot of paper for our catalog. What better way to overcome that than reforestation? It shows consumers we recognize our use of paper and want to make an effort to rectify it. The response has been tremendous" (p. 6).[13]

In Phoenix and Indianapolis, the water companies, which are private utilities, sponsored the Kool Kids program. Whenever the heat index rose to more than 90°, then the children in the inner-city were allowed to use the city swimming pools in those areas at no charge. Announcements were made in the media when these conditions arose to alert residents that this opportunity was available. The pools stayed open until the heat index dropped below 90°. Sometimes it meant the pools remained open until 11 P.M. When it gets that hot, people become irritated and short tempered. This opportunity was intended to alleviate those reactions. The water companies paid the entrance fees for these children. This sponsorship positioned the water utilities as caring companies in the community. However, they also invested in it because, on hot days, inner-city children are tempted to turn on fire hydrants in the streets, lowering the pressure and wasting water. The Kool Kids program was a constructive alternative.

Professional sports players and teams have an image of being overpaid, spoiled, and exploitive of communities among a section of the public. To improve that image, many professional teams and players have sponsored public recreational programs in their communities. In Philadelphia, the professional baseball franchise was asked to assist in maintaining a baseball league and purchased 14 pitching machines to enrich the local youth baseball league. As well as demonstrating good citizenship, the Philadelphia Phillies also were assuring increased present and future interest in the game.[14]

Through a partnership with the city of Oakland, California, the Golden State Warriors basketball franchise created Nite Hoops to provide a place for young men to play organized basketball from 9 P.M. to 2 A.M. The program incorporated a mandatory component for participants' attendance in educational and employment training sessions.[15]

Although image association with a park and recreation agency or program is a primary reason why sponsors invest in it, the reciprocal potential for positive association with a company may be equally important to an agency. If the agency links to a sponsor with a strong, positive public image, then this institutional clout may help enhance its status in the community and improve its public persona.

Image is not static. It is amended by information that individuals receive from a multitude of sources. However, it is unlikely to change easily. If people have developed a set of beliefs and impressions about a product, it is difficult to change them. This relative permanency exists because once people have a certain image of a product or company, they tend to be selective perceivers of further data. Their perceptions are oriented toward seeing what they expect to see. Hence, it is likely to be difficult for sponsorship to be effective in changing image. In addition to impacting the interest stage of the adoption process by borrowing a recreational program's image, many companies use image enhancement to reinforce existing product image, to give existing purchasers good feelings about purchasing it, and to encourage their loyalty towards it. Cadillac, for example, has an established image, and the company's sponsorship objective is "to reinforce and enhance Cadillac's image among the general public—to use our name as a metaphor for excellence: 'The Cadillac of its class.' "[5]

Product Trial or Sales Opportunities

Product trial or sales opportunities may be used to impact the desire, purchase action, or reinforcement stages of the adoption process. Product trial opportunities are particularly valuable because moving people from interest in a product to the desire stage, which involves seriously evaluating its merits to determine whether a purchase should be made, is a difficult communications task. There are likely to be many products in which individuals may have an interest and are disposed favorably toward but that they have never tried, especially products for which the cost of trial is high in terms of money, time, or potential embarrassment. Sponsorship offers a vehicle for encouraging trial, which frequently is the most effective method by which potential customers can assess a product's merits.

The makers of Ultra Fuel high-carbohydrate energy drink and Hydra Fuel fluid replacement drink sponsored 75 multisport and 6 cycling events soon after they launched the drinks. A spokesman observed: "We're not like Gatorade, with a big ad budget that allows us to go after everybody. Our objective is to get our drinks into the hands of premier athletes and the people who follow the sports in which they compete. Brand identity for the two drinks is not there right now. Fewer than 10 percent of triathletes and biathletes have tried the products. Our goal is to sample 50,000 people this year" (p. 6). At each event, the drinks were poured at all aid stations on the course, at a booth, and at the finish line, and the company received signage and the right to display an inflatable sign.[16]

Times Mirror publishing corporation made a $750,000 sponsorship investment in a multimedia exhibit called Ocean Planet at the Smithsonian Institution. As a tie-in, the premier issue of its *Pop Sci for Kids* focused on the exhibit. It also sold an exhibition catalog ($39.95), souvenir magazine ($5.95), and CD-ROM cartridge ($39.95). The company received the profits from producing the items; the Smithsonian received a mark-up, a 5% royalty, and a 50% royalty on T-shirts and other souvenirs.[17]

Converse launched a new tennis shoe, the Converse Classic, by sponsoring the Converse Classic Tennis Tournaments, comprising the largest U.S. Tennis Association–sanctioned series for local players. The series involved 3,500 players from 37 American cities. The players represented the top level of tennis at the grassroots level. All of them received a free pair of Converse Classic shoes. Thus, the tournaments provided Converse with trial opportunities for a new product with a targeted group of opinion leaders across the country. An executive commented: "We decided to take the shoe to the consumer who is the toughest critic—the local player. We wanted to put shoes on the feet of players to see if we could create an implied endorsement from the enormous player pool. What these players wear is very important to their peers at the club level" (p. 20).[18]

An example of a comprehensive investment that the Tennis Industry Association made when it sponsored an initiative with park and recreation agencies is described in "Inducing Product Trial: The Tennis Industry Association's Program" on page 422. It was designed to induce people to try the game of tennis and to expand the tennis market because suppliers of tennis equipment recognized that expanding their future sales depended upon their expanding the number of tennis players.

The San Jose Sharks, a National Hockey League team, developed a similar strategy. When the National Hockey League expanded its horizons by awarding a hockey franchise to a team called the Sharks in San Jose, California, many skeptics laughed. They wondered how hockey would succeed in a traditional nonhockey community that had lost its predecessor hockey team, the California Golden Seals, to Cleveland 20 years earlier. The Sharks were successful, and their success was based on a community development program that nurtured fan attendance and interest. The Sharks focused on youth between the ages of 6 and 16 years by developing a street hockey program called Sharks & Parks. It started in 30 community centers and expanded to 200 locations with more than 20,000 children participating. The program extended beyond San Jose to neighboring cities. The Sharks also involved two of their sponsors in the program: Pepsi and Franklin Sports. Each participating center was given goalie sticks, adult sticks, youth sticks, nets, a complete set of goalie equipment, rubber pucks, no-bounce balls, administrative manuals, stickers, buttons, and posters. The Sharks also provided each center with a 2 h training program that reviewed rules and regulations and included demonstrations and scrimmages.[19]

Examples in the following paragraphs illustrate events that may be used to identify prospects for product trial. In such cases, subsequent tailored packages can be developed to induce the trial.

Bell Cellular Inc.'s primary sponsorship goal was sales, so it used its on-site presence at events to generate targeted leads. These were followed up with tailored pitches. For example, the entry form to win a car included questions on earnings and other key demographics.[20]

The Rihgu Royal Hotel in Manhattan was a relatively new hotel that sponsored receptions for arts groups appearing in the city. For example, it hosted a black-tie opening night reception for the San Francisco Ballet for 350 people. The Rihgu was able to present its facilities to the correct clientele, and its marketing staff made potential business contacts while the up-market crowd celebrated late into the night. The staff members were looking for leads for potential Christmas party business.[21]

Mercedes-Benz Canada Inc. paid $200,000 (Canadian) to be primary sponsor for the Montreal Museum of Fine Arts exhibit entitled "Moving Beauty: A Century of Automobile Design." The exhibit contained five historic Mercedes, and the museum also displayed the marque's current SL320 model in the lobby during the exhibit. The museum mailed 1,500 of its top patrons an offer to purchase a raffle ticket for $1,000 to win the vehicle. The 200 patron responses, which liquidated

Inducing Product Trial: The Tennis Industry Association's Program

The Tennis Industry Association is a 130-member organization comprising tennis equipment, footwear, and apparel manufacturers and marketers; accessories companies; court products companies; management firms; publications; the governing bodies of tennis; and the professional tours. The organization's mission is to promote the game of tennis. Its members recognize that their businesses can only thrive if the game itself thrives.

In the mid-1990s, tennis was slumping badly with fewer new players coming into the game. It had declined from being the tenth most popular activity in the United States at the peak of its popularity in 1978 to being ranked twenty-sixth among recreational activities. The industry was faced with declining sales and an image crisis.

The Tennis Industry Association's research found that more than 70% of tennis played in the United States occurred on public courts and concluded that linking with public park and recreation agencies was key to reviving interest in the game. Accordingly, the Tennis Industry Association developed a three-year initiative and invested $15 million in sponsoring it with park and recreation departments. The initiative was intended to bring the industry together behind a sustained long-term effort to make tennis more popular. This would result in sales boosts for the association's manufacturers and marketers and in more fans and supporters for the professional tours and governing bodies.

The goal of the initiative was to bring 500,000 new players into the game by attracting first-time tennis players and by quickly moving them to a reasonable level of proficiency. The program was called Play Tennis America. Park and recreation agencies were offered a turnkey-packaged program at no cost to them. The Tennis Industry Association supplied free materials, such as program guides, training videos, and instructional handouts. The association trained instructors in the Play Tennis America format.

Play Tennis America operated at more than 1,000 sites in more than 100 cities. In each city, it was launched with heavy promotion using materials that the Tennis Industry Association provided. The association awarded a $20,000 grant, which was spent mainly on newspaper and radio advertisements, to each city for this purpose. The design of the advertisements made tennis appear cool and relevant to young people. Each site offered free lessons and use of equipment to all applicants aged eight years or more for a 7- to 10-day period in the summer. The Tennis Industry Association reimbursed local tennis professionals, who taught these lessons, for each participant in the program. These new players were then funneled into Play Tennis America's three-phase program that comprised 9 h of group lessons, 9 h of supervised play, and an introduction to league play. The program's emphasis was recreational and social rather than competitive. It was intended to provide players with a structure commensurate with their skill development and ability level in order to encourage them to continue playing regularly.

Mercedes' sponsorship fee (resulting in the sponsorship not costing the company), created a mailing list of interested potential customers for the company.[22]

Manufacturers Hanover Bank sponsored Corporate Challenge races in 12 American cities; in Oslo, Norway; and in Stockholm, Sweden. The runners' release form asked entrants if they owned or rented their homes and if they would consider switching banks. This enabled the bank to target prospective new customers with tailored follow-up actions.[23]

Product trial may also be used to reinforce the favorable feelings that existing users have toward the product. When a beverage company or its distributors sponsor races, the availability of complementary beverages at the end is intended to remind runners of their refreshing, recuperative qualities and to consolidate loyalty toward them.

Hospitality Opportunities

Hospitality opportunities may be used either to interest targeted individuals in a product or to strengthen bonds with existing customers and reinforce their commitment to the company and its products. "Guest hospitality refers to those opportunities whereby the company can make face-to-face contact with select publics in a prestigious social context, thereby strengthening and personalizing relationships with decision-makers, trade channels and business associates" (p. 37).[4] Hospitality is a key element in many companies' relationship marketing strategy.

Philip Morris Corporation sponsored the Vatican Collection, an exhibition at the Art Institute of Chicago that presented papal acquisitions from several centuries. Before the exhibition opened to the public, the company held preview receptions for selected guests, including government officials, religious and business leaders, and other people important to its tobacco and alcohol businesses. The receptions gave Philip Morris executives a chance to interact with these individuals in a positive setting.[24]

GTE Southwest Telephone Company sponsors Yule Fest, which is organized by the city of Austin Parks and Recreation Department in Zilker Park. On the night before the official opening, the festival is opened for GTE's preferred customers and city council members. This offers GTE's officials the opportunity to interact socially with two groups who are critically important to the company's business success. GTE has an ongoing need to use city right-of-ways, so the city council's cooperation is important. GTE's officials are part of the ribbon-cutting party who open the festival and consequently are featured in media coverage of the event. Their sponsorship is recognized with the lead-in phrase, "GTE brings to you," and is supported by extensive advertising in local media.

Relationship marketing is concerned with attracting, developing, and retaining customer relationships. Its central tenet is

the creation of true customers, which are customers who are glad they selected a firm, who perceive that they are receiving value and feel valued, who are likely to buy additional services from the firm, and who are unlikely to defect to a competitor. True customers are the most profitable of all customers. They spend more money with the firm on a yearly basis, and they stay with the firm for more years. They spread favorable word-of-mouth information about the firm, and they may even be willing to pay a premium price for the benefits that the service offers (p. 133).[7]

Establishing this kind of relationship requires the building of social bonds with customers, "staying in touch with them, learning about their wants and needs, customizing the relationships based on what is learned, and continually reselling the benefits of the relationship" (p. 138).[7] The objective of offering hospitality at a recreational event to existing or prospective customers is not to conduct business but rather to use a relaxed, informal context outside the normal business environment to create a personal interactive chemistry that will be conducive to doing business later. The role of hospitality opportunities in facilitating sales at the interest stage of the product-adoption process was well articulated by the observer who noted:

An invitation to discuss trade is often counterproductive because the target audience is wary that acceptance of the invitation to discuss trade will be interpreted as a commitment to actually trade. Moreover, in the case of a meeting which has as its sole objective the investigation of opportunities for trade, embarrassment is the only result where one party wishes to trade but the other does not. This contrasts with a situation where any non-professional common interest—stamp collecting, social drinking or recreation event—is either the pretext for a meeting, the real object of which is to investigate opportunities for trade, or is the main attraction where trade is discussed only incidentally. In these cases both parties can avoid loss of dignity in the event that they are unable to reach agreement about prospects for trade, and can meet again in the future to discuss other projects without rancor (p. 176).[25]

Consider the experience of Citibank when it made a major sponsorship investment in underwriting the New York Philharmonic Orchestra on a tour of Europe. Top bank management and local staff entertained at preconcert cocktail parties, sit-down dinners, buffet suppers, and post-concert receptions in the cities that the orchestra visited. Their guests included current and potential clients, local elected officials and other dignitaries, and leaders from the business community. Citibank credited the tour and its related events with having bolstered relations with current customers, developed future prospects, and improved the bank's international standing.[26]

Citibank equated the cost of this sponsorship to six, 30-second network television commercials, and they believed that the sponsorship investment was much more cost effective in enabling them to reach and impact their selected target audience.

Recognizing the importance of hospitality to sponsors, the Indianapolis Parks and Recreation Department established a hospitality division and offered hospitality services to sponsors as an option in its contractual agreements with them. This service relieved sponsors of the responsibility for making the hospitality arrangements for their event. The division organized tents; tables; furnishings; decorations; food and beverages; transportation of guests to and from the site; name tags; and, in the words of the director of the park department, "anything else that will make the sponsor feel good." The department solicited bids for these services from a short list of companies in the city who met their standards. Caterers offered an array of different menus from which sponsors could select, and contracted companies provided the beer or liquor license if needed.

The Media's Key Role in Enhancing Sponsor Benefits

One of the central issues in negotiations between a sponsor and a park and recreation manager is likely to be the probable extent of the program's media coverage. A park and recreation manager is likely to solicit three types of sponsorship benefits: financial, media, and in-kind. It is often best to secure media sponsorship first. Having print and air sponsors commit to the dollar value of their support and agree to promote other major sponsors is likely to make securing financial and in-kind sponsorships easier. Alternatively, the agency can ask the major sponsor with which media the company would prefer to be associated or with whom it has worked effectively in the past, and then it can approach those media. Often, the first question asked from a potential financial sponsor relates to how much media promotion will be forthcoming. It is possible to have more than one media sponsor, but they must not be competitors. Sponsorship by one newspaper, one radio, or one television station is likely to result in its competitors in the same medium avoiding significant coverage of the event.

If a sponsor is seeking increased awareness or image enhancement benefits, then a key to receiving them is the extent of visibility and the quality of that visibility (in terms of its compatibility with the intended projected product image) that can be achieved with the target audience. As one major company president who sponsored an art exhibit at the Metropolitan Museum of Art in New York observed:

> The visibility we're after can take several forms. Not only are we careful to see that as many attendees as possible recognize our part in the exhibition, but we are very interested in getting media coverage to extend that recognition. I can't overstate the importance of this to us, or to any other company that sponsors an exhibition or other cultural event.[11]

A sponsor likely will require a projection of the extent of media coverage before committing to an investment. In addition to extending the audience, media coverage has a second important dimension; it takes the form of news, which engenders greater credibility than exposure gained through advertising.

Park and recreation agencies often have access to celebrities, such as professional sport personalities, performing artists, and television newscasters. Delivering these celebrities as part of a sponsorship agreement adds value for the sponsor. It is also likely to substantially increase the quantity of press coverage provided and to enhance the quality of the event in the public's eyes.

Sponsors may seek two types of media exposure. The first is a trade-out in which the media provide promotional air time or space in exchange for recognition as the presenting sponsor. Ideally, these partnerships would be negotiated with a television station, radio station, newspaper, and outdoor billboard company. The benefits associated with this title may include rights to transmit the program and a number of program tickets or program merchandise that the media sponsor can give away as prizes to its audience.

The second type of media exposure is of an editorial nature. Many sponsors think of the media only as a conduit to a wider target audience. However, in an editorial context, benefits are not exchanged, and the media are interested in satisfying their audiences and not sponsors. Sponsor visibility may be important to the sponsor, but it is not important to the media. To achieve exposure, the sponsor and recreation manager have to start from a position of satisfying the media's needs by providing interesting and informative stories.

The media frequently are reluctant to accept and acknowledge the role of sponsors at a recreational event. Many newspapers and television stations believe that crediting sponsors of recreational events in editorial coverage could potentially harm their advertising revenue because companies are spending their communications money on the sponsorship rather than on advertising. A media executive noted: "When you are in the business of selling air time, you don't want to give away air time" (p. 33).[27] This explains why one company received so little television news coverage in its sponsorship of a major marathon.

> In more than three hours of coverage, our logo never appeared recognizable, even though it was on the runner's bibs, start and finish line banners, and signs along the route. In fact, although pre-race interviews were conducted beneath the starting banner, shots were kept tight to frame our logo out of the picture (p. 4).[28]

Sponsorship of Recreation by Tobacco and Alcohol Companies

Tobacco and alcohol companies have been major sponsors of recreational events and programs. To many people, it appears incongruous that recreation, which exemplifies a healthy, fit lifestyle, should be used as a promotional vehicle for products that appear to be the antithesis of this lifestyle. In short, these linkages that are consummated for financial purposes seem to defeat the broader raison d'être for recreation.

Momentum is growing to prohibit tobacco companies' sponsorship of park and recreational programs. The controversy over permitting tobacco companies to link with these activities by sponsoring them revolves around three central issues.[29] First, the linkage obscures the connection between tobacco products and disease. Tobacco products physiologically are damaging even when used as they are supposed to be used. The Centers for Disease Control links almost 450,000 deaths each year in the United States to tobacco-related illnesses, which constitutes about one-sixth of deaths from all causes.[30] This fact makes their association with recreation objectionable to many.

The success of tobacco companies in using sport and recreation to obscure the substantial hazards of their products is illustrated by the following exercise: "Quick speak the words 'Virginia Slims' and what do you see? A) Chris Evert or B) the cancer ward? If you answered A)— and most people do—then Philip Morris has you right where it wants you."[31] There is a link between the word slim and the activity of tennis as a means of becoming slim. Tennis champions are in peak physical condition, and because endurance is important, their hearts and lungs are particularly strong and healthy. The obvious implications of the linkage are that tennis and smoking are both acceptable activities and that smoking is not harmful and is even desirable for women.

A second central issue in the tobacco sponsorship controversy is the belief that the recreation linkage enables tobacco companies to penetrate the youth market. When Louis Sullivan was secretary of Health and Human Services, he noted that 80% of smokers start when they are teenagers. Thus, "tobacco companies are faced with a business problem. Either they get children to start smoking or they go out of business."[32] Because tobacco kills almost 450,000 people each year and because other smokers die from other causes or quit, replenishing the pool of long-term customers at a rate of almost 1,200 per day has to be a primary goal of the industry. Indeed, according to the commissioner of the U.S. Food and Drug Administration, each day 3,000 children and adolescents start smoking—one-third of whom will die as a result.[30] The failure of a generation of young people to start smoking would devastate the tobacco industry!

Tobacco companies deny that they target children with their advertising promotion on which the industry spends more than $6 billion each year, but a document subpoenaed by the U.S. Federal Trade Commission suggests that the denial is merely a public relations stance.[33] It reports advice that the industry received from its research agencies about the approach it should take with children:

> Thus, an attempt to reach young smokers, starters, should be based . . . on the following major parameters:
>
> - Present the cigarette as one of a few initiations into the adult world.
>
> - Present the cigarette as part of the illicit pleasure category of products and activities.
>
> - In your ads create a situation taken from the day-to-day life of the young smoker, but in an elegant manner have this

situation touch on the basic symbols of the growing-up, maturity process.

- To the best of your ability (considering some legal restraints) relate the cigarette to 'pot', wine, beer, sex, etc.
- DON'T communicate health or health-related points.

A third central issue in the controversy over tobacco companies sponsoring park and recreational activities is the contention that such sponsorship circumvents the ban on cigarette advertising and promotion in broadcast media. Critics argue that the inclusion of brand names and logos in broadcasts of events is a blatant breach of the spirit of the legislation against cigarette advertising. Indeed recreation sponsorship may offer one feature not available to tobacco companies in their advertising. That is, it enables cigarette brand names to be shown or mentioned on television and radio without being accompanied by the surgeon general's health warnings that are required on print advertisements.

The magnitude of sponsorship of park and recreation agency programs and events by beer companies is substantially greater than the investment of tobacco companies. As the magnitude of their investment in recreation sponsorship has increased, it has been accompanied by a com-

mensurate increase in criticism from people concerned about alcohol abuse. Awareness has been heightened in recent years that alcohol is a drug with the potential to become addictive. The concern is that about 13 million people are alcoholics in the United States, and beer companies promote that it is natural for this intoxicating drug to be consumed while watching or participating in a pleasant, recreational activity. Sponsorship and advertising by beer companies promotes the image that beer is not very different from soft drinks, and its negative consequences, such as traffic deaths, domestic violence, physical deterioration, and pregnancy risks, are ignored. It has been noted: "Beer comes to share the luster of healthy athleticism. . . . It's really paradoxic that alcohol and all it stands for should be associated with excellent athletic performance. You cannot have one and the other at the same time. If you're going to perform as a top-grade athlete, you have to cut out alcohol" (p. 78).[34] Many cities have felt uncomfortable with this contradiction and have enacted bans on alcohol company sponsorship. A typical perspective is offered in "Rationale for Enacting a Ban on Sponsorship by Beer Companies."

In response to their social critics, the beer companies assert that their sponsorship and advertising activities have no effect beyond brand

Rationale for Enacting a Ban on Sponsorship by Beer Companies

Huntington Beach, California, has been described as the quintessential Surfin' USA town. It had been host for many years to professional events that the Professional Surfing Association of America organized. A primary sponsor of these events was Budweiser. However, the city of Huntington Beach expanded its long-time ban on alcohol consumption at the beach with a new ban on alcohol advertising. Similar bans were subsequently enacted at the neighboring city of Seal Beach, which had hosted the Women's Professional Volleyball Association Tournaments (sponsored by Coors Lite Beer) on the beach for the previous five years.

A spokesperson for the Huntington Beach city administrator's office said that because the city took a stand against drug use and alcohol misuse and banned alcohol on the beaches, it would be inconsistent to allow alcohol advertisements. "We have the image of being a surfing beach," she said. "We wanted to give a strong message to the young population who frequent our beach that alcohol use is not for them."

A spokesperson for Seal Beach said: "Some of our residents were concerned about a rowdier element being attracted to this type of event. Some people express concern over the mixed message our city might be sending its youth, supporting drug awareness programs and at the same time hosting events sponsored by a beer company."

Adapted from Kathy Brown. Beer ban darkens beach: California move threatens professional surfing. Marketing. May 20, 1991. 96(26), page 26.

shifting among current drinkers. Further, they point out that when used in moderation, beer has not been shown to be a danger to health. Thus, cardiologist George Sheehan, who served as the philosophic guru of runners, summarized the evidence:

> There are numbers that suggest good things about alcohol. The happy, healthy, productive, long-lived people studied by sociologists in a famous Alameda County, California, project turned out to be moderate drinkers. They averaged a drink or two a day. And subsequent studies have confirmed the protection alcohol gives against coronary disease. A landmark study at the Kaiser Permanente in Los Angeles found a 50 percent decrease in coronary disease admissions for those who took two drinks a day. Researchers have gone so far as to suggest alcohol deficiency is a risk factor (p. 93).[35]

Two factors make the decision confronting park and recreation managers about whether they should solicit or accept sponsorship from beer companies much more difficult than the decision associated with tobacco companies. First, the magnitude of sponsorship dollars that would be forfeited is substantially larger. Second, unlike tobacco, the problem is not the consumption of beer but rather the abuse of beer. In contrast to tobacco, beer has not been shown to be harmful when imbibed in moderation. Further, the existing evidence suggests that recreation sponsorship is not likely to induce consumption increases.[29]

These two factors make it tempting for park and recreation managers to rationalize that there does not appear to be a strong enough case to ban beer companies from sponsorship opportunities. Certainly, the case for a ban ostensibly appears to be much less compelling than the case that can be made to ban sponsorship by tobacco companies. However, the alcohol dilemma is compounded by the widespread abuse of alcohol and the consequences of that abuse. Clearly, there are contradictions with recreation being associated with tobacco or alcohol products. Many park and recreation managers are confronted with a dilemma: balancing a moral, ethical obligation to discourage tobacco use and alcohol abuse with the reality of surrendering substantial economic resources.

Integrating Sponsorship With Other Communication Vehicles

Association with a program or event per se is of limited value to a company. Satisfactory returns on investment depend on extensive leveraging of this association. To sustain an ongoing relationship with a sponsor, a park and recreation agency has to be receptive to a sponsor's requests to cooperate in facilitating this leveraging.

The 1-800-Flowers company focused its sponsorship efforts on flower shows. The 150-store retailer sponsored the nine-day New York Flower Show where it operated a 1,500 sq ft store and conducted demonstrations, seminars, and sweepstakes. Additional promotional efforts leveraging the sponsorship included national sweepstakes that awarded trips to the event and that consumers entered in its stores or online, show-themed displays in all company-owned stores, in-store ticket sales including a $3 discount on $12 admission with a $29.99 purchase, announcements in the company's 1.5 million-person circulation newsletter, show-themed bouquets, drawings for tickets in the company's New York stores, and radio giveaways of tickets and bouquets.[36]

There are two attributes of sponsorship that suggest it is likely to be most effective if it is integrated with other communication vehicles. First, increased awareness and enhanced image benefits of recreation sponsorship accrue by providing implicit messages generated by the linkage between a company and the park and recreational program. Unlike advertising or sales promotions, sponsorship does not offer direct messages indicating why a product should be purchased. If the target audience is aware of the name but has no idea what the product is or does, then awareness and image benefits are not delivered. It has been noted: "There is absolutely no point in using sponsorship to create name awareness and to develop an image based on association with an event, if supporting explicit information is not available to the audience of the sponsorship" (p. 43).[1] If the other communication vehicles are not used in conjunction with a sponsorship, the effort may end in a result such as that used to promote name awareness of the brandy Metaxa: "Major television exposure gained from a linkage with international soccer tournaments left millions of people around the world aware of the name but totally unaware of what it meant" (p. 43).[1]

A second integrative attribute of sponsorship is that it provides a theme that can be incorporated

The Xerox Marathon Campaign: An Example of Integrating Other Communications Vehicles With Sponsorship

This campaign was created to support the launch of a new line of photocopiers designed to re-establish Xerox's position in the Copier market. The marketing strategy was for the new product line to be introduced internationally with a common theme and the decision was to use sponsorship to link in with the product advertising campaign. The company and its agencies undertook extensive research to determine the attributes purchasers of copiers wanted in the product. This research showed that the most important attribute was that the machine did not break down—it should have the ability to run indefinitely.

Because of the international introduction the company had to develop a common marketing strategy with a universal message. Once again research was used to determine that the name 'Marathon' produced the same perceptions in all markets, perceptions of endurance and strength. The advertising campaign used to launch the product used the marathon runner theme in print and television advertising in the US, Europe and Latin America.

The objectives for Xerox's use of sponsorship were to get increased exposure for the new product launch on an international basis, to attract media attention, to provide a means to inform the sales force, and to attract existing and new customers. Alongside these objectives was the determination to integrate the Xerox advertising campaign with the sponsorship of events. Every element used in the advertising was incorporated into the sponsorship and associated promotions.

Fortunately for Xerox a major boom in running coincided with the launch of the new product line, so the company, since it was prepared to react quickly, became a major sponsor of international marathon events under the Marathon label. Also, the company discovered that the demographics of marathon participants were the same as the Xerox target audience so they were easily able to target the business audience they were looking for. Most of the marathon events Xerox sponsored achieved television coverage. Among the events the company sponsored was the Rotterdam Marathon which brought together for the first time the two best marathon runners of the day and achieved significant television exposure. Xerox also sponsored the New York City Marathon along with many regional events that were tied in to local Xerox offices and their customers. The company sponsored the World Cross-Country Championship, held for the first time in the United States, as well as the US Men's Olympic Marathon Trials and the Los Angeles Olympic Games. All of these events achieved significant television exposure that included corporate branding.

At all these events the company and its agencies worked hard to get the Xerox name across to both on-site and television viewers. Xerox branding was placed on every conceivable object that would be viewed on-site and by the television cameras. Finish line tape, blankets to wrap competitors in as they finished, runners' bibs, signage and banners all had Xerox identification. With event sponsorship in place the company created their own team. Team Xerox comprised a team of top-class marathon runners who competed in most of the events the company sponsored, dressed, of course, in a Team Xerox uniform. Finally, the company organized a promotion called the Xerox Corporate Marathon Relay aimed at bringing together the company's sales force and their customers.

This event was unique in that entry was by invitation only and that invitation for a team entry had to come from a Xerox representative. Invited corporate teams comprised ten runners, at least two of whom had to be women, and each team member had to run just over two and a half miles. The top three teams won an award and the winning team received a trip to the Xerox National Championship held in a different location each year.

This newly-created sponsorship provided the Xerox salesforce with the golden opportunity to go directly to its customers and invite them to enter the company's event. All invitational packages were sent to the Xerox district offices and the salesforce then took on the job of inviting their top 100 customers.

At the event the sales team were able to meet once again with the customers or potential customers and mix with them in a social and sporting environment. After the race the sales team would return with results and photographs for all the teams. At just one of their events Xerox had the opportunity of bringing together over 1,500 customers—the sort of opportunity that most companies would dearly love to have. In 1984 the winning team in each of the Corporate Relay events was given a trip to the Xerox Relay Championship held just three days before the Olympic Trials. The winning team was also given a trip to the Olympic Games at Xerox's expense. According to Xerox, these promotions had very beneficial results. Not only did extensive publicity impinge directly on their target audience, but the promotions aimed at the corporate clients reached that audience and impacted on the company's sales force who were very enthusiastic about the campaign. In addition to the tremendous amount of goodwill the promotion generated among existing and potential clients, the company also sold 400,000 Marathon copiers in the first 21 months of the campaign—an effect that is directly measurable on the bottom line and amounts to a very successful new product launch.

From Steve Sleight. Sponsorship: What it is and how to use it. *McGraw-Hill: London. Pages 102-104. 1989. Copyright ©Steve Sleight. Used by permission.*

into the messages of the other communication vehicles: personal selling, advertising, publicity, and incentives. It offers a hook (i.e., a focus or unifying theme) to which the other communication vehicles can relate. The importance of this hook was emphasized by the marketer who noted that the Sunday newspaper may contain 50 advertising inserts, that the average household watches more than 1 h of commercials during prime time each day, and that the average consumer receives approximately three pieces of unsolicited mail each day. Given the extent of this clutter she concluded:

> That's why theme marketing events which can synergistically unite all aspects of the communications mix, make sense to Maxwell House. They create a point of difference for our brands and let us build our franchise with both the grocery trade and the consumer, without incurring exorbitant advertising expenses (p. 4).[37]

The Xerox Marathon case is an excellent example of integrating sponsorship with other communications vehicles by using a common theme: the ability to run indefinitely. An advertising campaign in both print and television media was linked directly into the sponsorship. Publicity was forthcoming from the substantial coverage that the events received both on television and in other media. This was reinforced by the formation of Team Xerox, comprising top-class marathon runners who competed in the races. The sales force was provided with a platform from which to engage in personal selling because only teams that a Xerox representative invited could enter. Thus, the sales force in each district office invited their top 100 customers, interacted with them in a social and sporting environment at the event, and subsequently presented them with results and photographs.

A commonly used strategy for obtaining integrated advertising support is for a sponsor to give cosponsoring media event tickets, event merchandise, sponsor's products, or the opportunity to meet a celebrity in exchange for media time. This type of arrangement is particularly prevalent with radio stations, and the ratio of air-time value to merchandise value with radio station tradeouts usually approximates five to one.

Integration has cost implications. The direct sponsorship investment represents only part of a company's total investment. The associated indirect costs incurred in using other communication vehicles in concert to optimize a sponsorship's impact may include those associated with a company's own media promotion highlighting tie-ins; advertising related to the event, such as air time or program inserts; merchandising; hospitality; video coverage; and dealer or customer tie-ins.

The indirect costs are likely to be at least equal to those of the direct investment and often range up to three times the direct costs. For example, a senior executive of American Express observed that sponsors rarely spend enough money promoting their activities. He stated that American Express normally spends $3 on promotion for every $1 invested directly in the sponsorship.[38] A list of items that should be costed to identify total costs associated with a sponsorship is given in table 16.1. One experienced executive advises companies: "A promotional spend of less than an equal amount to the sponsorship fee suggests that you are not spending enough to secure the proper level of benefits for you—as opposed to the event" (p. 119).[1] Park and recreation managers seeking sponsorship may fail to consider these indirect costs and try to convince potential buyers of a sponsorship's potential return on investment based only on the direct cost.

Measuring the Impact of Sponsorship

Evaluation answers the question: "What did the sponsoring company achieve in relation to what it said it wanted to accomplish in its objectives?" Its primary purpose is to discover, and act on if necessary, deviations from a sponsorship's desired outcome. Evaluation identifies sponsorships that are not meeting their objectives. In these cases there needs to be a reappraisal of what could be done to improve the results. Thus, evaluation guides and reduces influence of the emotional dimension of decision making.

From the perspective of a park and recreation agency selling a sponsorship, it is important that measurement audits are included in the sponsorship package that is presented to prospective sponsor companies. The type of measurement used to evaluate sponsorship should be governed by its objectives. If these objectives are clearly specified, then it facilitates easier selection of the best measure to assess the extent to which they were met. This emphasizes the importance of establishing objectives in terms that can be measured before the sponsored event occurs instead of after it is over. Even if this is done, however, there are several factors that make assessing the impact of sponsorship investments challenging:

1. The simultaneous use of other communications mix variables. Because sponsor-

Table 16.1 Items Contributing to the Total Cost of a Sponsorship Fee

Item	Cost
Sponsorship fee	
Advertising costs:	
Print	
Radio	
Point-of-purchase	
TV	
Printed materials	
Signage/banners	
Staffing/van	
Apparel	
Hardware/airtime costs	
PR opportunities	
Ticket purchases	
Other	
Total cost	

Bell Cellular Inc. cited in *IEG Sponsorship Report* (1991). July 1, p. 5. Copyright © IEG, Inc. Used by permission.

ship is usually used in conjunction with other components of promotion, it is difficult to isolate its unique impact. Even if other promotional tools are not being used simultaneously, there is likely to be some carry-over effect from previous marketing communications' efforts that make isolating the impact of sponsorship difficult.

2. Uncontrollable environmental factors. Changes in sales levels may be attributable to environmental changes (e.g., an increase or reduction in the intensity of competitive effort or varying levels of discretionary income as a result of changes in economic conditions) rather than the sponsorship.

3. The pursuit of multiple objectives. Sponsors often seek multiple benefits from their investment, which means that a variety of measurement methods may be required to assess effectiveness of the sponsorship.[4]

Linking Sponsorship to the Communication Process

The process through which companies seek to communicate a message to individuals in their target market through sponsorship is shown in figure 16.3. The sponsor codes messages into a transmittable form (or arranges and locates those messages so that the media incidentally will transmit them). The form may include written captions, company or brand name, logo, or verbal material. The coded message is transmitted by print media, broadcast media, or personal contact. For communication to occur, individuals in the target market must absorb, receive, and interpret the message. The ultimate goal of a total communication strategy is to generate sales. A company's expectation is that its sponsorship investment ultimately will contribute to that end.

An intervening variable shown as jagged lines in figure 16.3 is noise. Noise consists of other stimuli or communications that compete for the intended receiver's attention. A message from a sponsoring

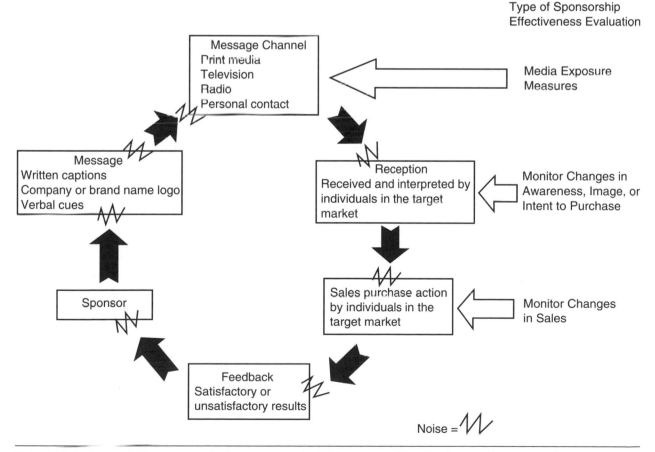

Figure 16.3 Stages in the communication process at which sponsorship effectiveness is measured.

organization to its target market is subject to the influence of extraneous noise and distracting stimuli that interfere with communication of the message. This noise may distort or distract attention from the transmission or reception of the message at any stage in the process. It may prevent members of the target market from receiving the message, or it may lead to them interpreting it differently from the way in which the sponsor intended. In the context of sponsorship in which the message is incidental to the main event, there is likely to be substantial noise that may cause the message to appear inconsequential and to be ignored.

Figure 16.3 shows the stages in the communication process at which the effectiveness of sponsorship can be measured. The further through the process that an evaluation takes place, the stronger the evidence of a sponsorship's contribution to increasing sales is. Most frequently, sponsorship objectives relate to creating a climate conducive to the development of sales in the future rather than to stimulating immediate sales. For this reason, most evaluations are undertaken earlier in the communications process. If sales are not measured, then the next most convincing measures for demonstrating economic return from a sponsorship (i.e., the probability that a desired increase in level of sales will result) are those that are completed at the reception stage of the process because this stage is only one step removed from the sales purchase action.

It was noted earlier in this chapter that individuals pass through a series of stages from first becoming aware of a product or company to finally making a purchase decision. The three stages in this process that precede purchase action and that are encapsulated in the reception stage of the communication process are awareness, interest, and intent to purchase. These stages emphasize that a decision to participate is usually the culmination of a process that may have started long before an actual purchase takes place. Thus, sponsorship of a recreational program contributes to ultimate sales impact if it succeeds in moving individuals from their present stage in the adoption process on to the next stage toward making a purchase decision.

Measuring Message Exposure

The most frequently used type of sponsorship-effectiveness measure is taken at the message channel stage. This approach assesses the extent and value of media coverage that the product or company receives. It usually involves quantifying

- duration of television coverage, including both verbal and visual mentions;
- duration of radio mentions; and
- extent of press coverage as measured in single column inches.

Typically, these media mentions are tracked, and each is assigned a dollar value based on the paid advertising rate. For example, one year Volvo calculated that it received $7 in value for every $1 spent on its sponsorship of tennis. This resulted from 2.26 billion impressions including television, print, radio, event attendance, and promotions. These impressions were calculated to translate to $32.8 million in equivalent value, and Volvo spent less than $5 million on its sponsorship.[39]

Measures of media coverage frequently inflate its real value. This inflation may occur in three ways. First, article length is measured and equated with advertising space, even though the sponsor's name may only be mentioned a couple of times in the article. Second, typically, the maximal rate card value is assumed when quantifying the cost of equivalent advertising space, and few companies in fact pay these full rates.

The third and most fundamental source of inflation is the assumption that 2 s here and 4 s there of background signage or logo, when summated, are equal to a television spot that gives an advertiser 30 s in which to sell. Thus, an editorial in *Sponsorship Report* commenting on these procedures being used by the John Hancock Company stated: "Ad equivalencies are bunk. If Hancock management thinks 30 seconds of ID has the same value as a 30 second ad spot, that's its problem" (p. 2).[40] A defender of these procedures responded: "Is it better to interrupt a broadcast with your message? Is it better to upset viewers? Of course you usually won't upset them because they are probably in the kitchen or the bathroom."[41] This type of defense is not convincing. Sponsorship lacks the direct impact possibilities normally associated with direct advertising. This is widely recognized and explains why the rule of thumb adopted by sponsors who do use media coverage measures as their primary evaluation tool is that total exposure received should be worth at least three to four times the cost of their sponsorship.

In addition to the pragmatic limitations of the media exposure approach discussed in the previous paragraphs, there is a fundamental conceptual flaw in considering it as a proxy measure of a sponsorship's impact on awareness. Measurements of media exposure are taken at the message channel point in the communications process. That is, they purport to assess the extent of media output of the company's message that has occurred. Media output, however, does not equate to awareness in the target market, which occurs at the subsequent reception stage.

> While you can certainly get a guide to the visibility of your sponsorship and the potential for awareness among your target audience, you certainly cannot tell by measuring media mentions how many of your target audience saw and registered the mentions, nor how the viewers' attitude to you or your product has been influenced by the sponsorship (p. 227).[1]

For awareness to occur, members of the target market have to interpret the message and then absorb it. There is a substantial probability that this will not occur because individuals are exposed to many more communications than they can possibly accept or decode. If a name, picture, cue, logo, banner, or other advertisement does not appeal or if there seems to be no good reason why it should be noted, then an individual is unlikely to open his or her senses to it, and, therefore, it will not be received. Hence, communication is not a one-way process from the sponsor organization to its target market, which use of the media exposure measure implies. Rather, it is a two-way process that depends on the intended recipients being interested sufficiently to interpret and absorb the communication.

Despite the substantial limitations associated with using media exposure and advertising equivalency visibility measures to evaluate the impact of sponsorship, these measures continue to be widely used for three practical reasons. First, they are easy for management to understand. Second, this type of data is relatively easy to collect. Third, they offer quantifiable statistics that give the appearance that sponsorship decisions are being based on supportive data and, thus, offer peace of mind to the people responsible for making those decisions. Park and recreation managers who want to include a measure of their event's potential in sponsorship proposal packages also can relatively easily adopt this measure. Indeed, media exposure is the only evaluative measure that they can undertake with-

out intruding into the sponsors' business. Other measures (which are discussed in the following sections) requiring, for example, pre- and post-tests of awareness levels of a sponsor's product or sales performance are likely to be outside the agency's realm of access.

Measuring Impact on Awareness and Image

Research designs seeking to measure the impact of sponsoring a park and recreational program on awareness and image are likely to incorporate a control group whose members have not been exposed to the sponsorship. The control group can be measured and used to discount the effects of other simultaneous communication efforts in which a company may be investing. A two-part survey conducted before and after the event can be used to measure and compare response of the control group and the sponsorship-impacted group. This approach will enable measurement of changes in awareness and image in the target audience.

Research results reported in the NutraSweet case (presented in "Awareness Research at Nutra-Sweet" on page 435) emphasize the importance of getting visitors involved in tie-in activities associated with the sponsorship to maximize increases in awareness levels rather than relying only on name exposure. It compares levels of awareness between two samples: one that participated in the tie-in activity and one that did not.

The data reported in table 16.2 on page 434 emphasize the importance of measuring changes in image attributable to sponsorship some time after an event has finished rather than on the site. These data were collected by the author in an attempt to measure the impact of sponsorship on image. Six major sponsors of the festival event (shown in bold type) were each paired with a nonsponsoring company in the same industry. One additional pair of companies, both of which delivered phone services, were included to serve as controls even though neither of them was a sponsor.

The pairs of companies were presented to a probability sample of respondents as they entered the site. They were asked to express how they felt about them on a seven-point scale ranging from very poor (1) to very good (7). In a follow-up mail survey that the same respondents completed from one to five weeks after the event, they were asked the same question. The results are reported in the columns entitled "Before" and "After" of table 16.2.

Table 16.2 Results of an Attempt to Measure Changes in Image Resulting From Sponsorship

Name of company	Before	After	Difference score
Pepsi Cola	4.69	4.47	−.22
Coca Cola	5.54	5.66	+.12
Miller Beer	4.58	4.15	−.43
Budweiser Beer	4.24	3.82	−.42
Lone Star Factory Outlet	4.29	4.03	−.26
Mall of the Mainland	4.31	3.66	−.65
Continental Airlines	4.67	4.51	−.16
Delta Airlines	4.74	4.45	−.29
Randall's Food Markets	5.52	5.16	−.36
Kroger Food Stores	5.02	4.95	−.07
Kodak Photographic Services	5.80	5.70	−.10
Fuji Photo Film, U.S.A.	4.81	4.36	−.45
AT&T Phone Services	5.54	5.35	−.19
MCI Phone Services	4.29	3.88	−.41

Source: Lisa L. Love and John L. Crompton. 1992. Visitor profile, evaluations and economic impacts of the Dickens on the Strand Festival. College Station, TX: Department of Recreation, Park and Tourism Sciences, p. 24.

It was anticipated that sponsoring companies' scores would be higher after the event as a result of their investment. Contrary to these expectations, the results show that in 13 of the 14 cases, image score declined in the follow-up survey. This suggests that awareness surveys conducted at, or immediately after, an event are likely to yield optimistic results. This may be attributable to the excitement, high level of arousal, and positive expectation or experience that the attendees enjoy at that time extending to their perceptions of the companies' images. However, at a subsequent time when the immediacy of a program or event has passed, excitement about the sponsoring companies may also dissipate.

Measuring Impact on Intent to Purchase

The product-adoption process suggests that potential purchasers move from awareness, to interest, to desire or intent to purchase before investing in a sales action. Hence, intent-to-purchase studies are perhaps the most useful indicators of the impact of sponsorship on future sales. Bassing America is a membership organization of 55,000 fishermen. A key to the organization's success in attracting and retaining sponsors is the research that Bassing does each year concerning its members' purchases and intentions to purchase. It is an approach that park and recreation agencies could emulate.

Bassing tries to find out what members own by brand, what they have purchased by brand, their intent to purchase by brand, and when they anticipate buying. The information is compared with previous years' results (looking back three or four years) to determine if sponsors' products are being supported. Findings are especially helpful when contract renewals are near. The results show sponsors how involvement with Bassing has increased their sales. For example, in 1986, 15% of members owned a Ranger boat and another 21% said that they intended to purchase one. By 1989, 27% owned and 43% intended to buy a Ranger boat.[42]

Measuring Impact on Sales

The most desirable measure from a sponsor's perspective is the impact that a sponsorship

Awareness Research at NutraSweet

NutraSweet sponsored state games in Massachusetts, Illinois, Florida, New York, Indiana, Texas, and North Carolina. The company matched each sponsored dollar with a minimum of $1 in promotional spending. A research firm was commissioned to evaluate the effectiveness of their sponsorships.

The sponsorship goals for NutraSweet were to establish a link between the sweetener and good health (the sweetener is positioned as a nutrient) and to promote awareness and favorable opinions of NutraSweet on a grassroots level. The research was designed to measure consumers' reactions to the brand's participation in each state's games. Specifically, the research was designed to measure

- awareness of NutraSweet sponsorship and what the sponsorship said about NutraSweet and
- visitor reaction to NutraSweet Place.

NutraSweet tested two groups of people at the games: people who had been exposed to NutraSweet Place (an activities center) and people who attended the games but did not visit the activities center. The first group of names was collected at NutraSweet Place by means of entry blanks for a prize drawing. The second group of names was collected in the field from attendees who passed an initial screening question, again by means of an entry blank for a prize drawing.

Telephone interviews were conducted in the two weeks following the games with open-ended questions designed to elicit recall and reactions to sponsors in general followed by questions specific to NutraSweet's on-site activities. On a combined aided and unaided basis, virtually all survey respondents were aware that NutraSweet sponsored the games. Visitors to NutraSweet Place were significantly more aware of NutraSweet's sponsorship due to their exposure to the center's activities. On an unaided basis, 86% of people who attended the activities center and 50% of people who did not visit the center recalled the sponsorship.

Attendees' attitudes were more favorable toward NutraSweet after attending the games, and a significantly larger percentage of visitors than nonvisitors to NutraSweet Place felt more favorably toward the company. No one felt less favorably toward it.

Of the sponsors included in the study, NutraSweet received the highest overall rating: excellent or very good. Again, the company was rated higher by visitors to NutraSweet Place than by nonvisitors. Eight of ten visitors and seven of ten nonvisitors rated NutraSweet excellent or very good.

Nearly all respondents (98%) considered NutraSweet to be an appropriate sponsor of the games specifically because of its health and fitness positioning. Of the visitors to NutraSweet Place, nearly 60% learned something about the product. About two-thirds of the visitors took product samples, brochures, or coupons with them, and among those, about 75% reported having read them.

In summary, research indicated that NutraSweet's active presence and promotional activities on site, i.e., the extensive support activities for the sponsorship, made a significant difference in how well the brand attained its goals of increased awareness and favorable image. From the research, it was determined that sponsorship opportunities must offer NutraSweet

- an exclusive or dominant sponsorship identity in all media and promotion,
- the ability to play an active role on site,
- sales promotion opportunities for their customers in the food and beverage industry, and
- first-class entertainment in conjunction with the event.

investment has on sales. Often this is a long-term, rather than an immediate, objective of sponsorship and, thus, is not an immediate concern. When it is an immediate concern, direct impact on sales can most easily be measured where there are tie-in promotions with the event.

Burroughs Wellcome Company experimented with a women's tennis sponsorship to market a new sunscreen lotion. By distributing coupons at the venue and tracking how many were redeemed, the company found that the tennis events effectively reached the target audience of upscale women aged 30 years and over. In the following year, the company expanded its sponsorship to 12 major tournaments based on those results.

Bell Cellular Inc. spent $500,000 (Canadian) on sponsorships each year and a similar amount promoting those ties. They co-sponsored events, such as the Cadillac Golf Classic. To prompt attendees to subscribe on site, Bell Cellular offered coupons worth $110 (Canadian) off the first year's bill. In one year, they signed up 1,675 new subscribers accounting for nearly $1 million (Canadian).[20]

General Nutrition Centers sponsored numerous events connected with their 2,500 stores. Typically in return for sponsorship, they offered a 20% discount on event entry fees that brought people into the stores. A computerized tracking system in the cash registers of all company-owned stores measured traffic before, during, and after an event and tracked increases over the same-period same-store levels from the previous year. For example, General Nutrition Centers provided $2,000 sponsorship to the Los Angeles Marathon Bike Tour. The discount entry opportunity brought in approximately 200 incremental customers, which, given an average purchase of $20 per visit, provided a two-to-one return on investment.[43]

Summary

The distinctive conceptual features that differentiate sponsorships from donations are that a sponsorship is a business relationship and is seen by companies as a means by which they can secure a commercial advantage. In practice, companies differentiate the two sources of support based on whether the IRS is likely to rule that a measurable financial gain has accrued to the company and whether the resources come from the company's marketing budget or its community relations budget.

Sponsorship offers a fifth communication vehicle that complements personal selling, advertising, publicity, and incentives. It has two special strengths. First, it contributes to establishing a position in consumers' minds that differentiates one product from another through its role in image enhancement. Second, it facilitates opportunities for a company to establish a more intimate relationship with its target audience than the relationship feasible with the other communication vehicles.

It is desirable that a park and recreation agency work with its business partner to formulate a set of specific, measurable, prioritized objectives for its sponsorship investment. This will assist both partners in crystallizing thinking about how the sponsorship opportunity can be best exploited and in evaluating the level of success that the investment delivered. If an annual event is involved, then from three to five years generally is recognized to be an optimal time period for a sponsorship commitment.

Businesses may seek a large number of narrowly focused benefits from sponsorship, but they can be classified into four broad categories: increased awareness, enhanced image, product trial or sales opportunities, and hospitality opportunities. These benefits are linked to the five stages of the customer's product-adoption process: awareness, interest, evaluation, decision, and reinforcement. A company's challenge is to design sponsorship benefits that will move customers from their present stage in the adoption process on to the next stage toward committed loyalty.

If products already have high levels of awareness, as most major sponsors' products do, then this benefit will not be sought because sponsorship could only marginally increase awareness. Image enhancement is sought more commonly. Sponsorship is unlikely to be effective in changing image because once people develop a set of beliefs and impressions about a product, it is difficult to change them. Thus, emphasis tends to be on reinforcing existing product or company image and giving current purchasers good feelings about it. Sponsorship offers a vehicle for product trial at a recreational event. This is particularly valuable because, until individuals try a product, they are unlikely to purchase it, especially if it is a relatively expensive product.

A sponsor's objective in creating hospitality opportunities is not likely to be to conduct business. Rather, the likely intent is to use a relaxed informal atmosphere to create a personal interactive chemistry that will be conducive to doing business later. Hospitality can be used to foster closer links not only with customers but also with other important publics, such as distributors, retailers, and political leaders.

It is likely that a sponsor will require a projection of media coverage, which will extend the benefits sought beyond those in attendance at an event. In addition to extending the audience, media coverage has a second important dimension: it takes the form of news, through which it engenders greater credibility than through advertising exposure. Media exposure may be obtained either through trade-outs or through editorial coverage. Media are often reluctant to acknowledge the role of sponsors in editorial coverage because companies are spending their communications money on sponsoring the event rather than on advertising their products in the media.

Tobacco and alcohol companies are major investors in sponsoring recreational activities. Tobacco companies derive three major benefits from this association. First, the sponsorship confers upon them a positive image and an aura of respectability, which obscures their role in causing an array of fatal diseases. Second, it enables them to penetrate the youth market. Third, sponsorship of sport offers a means by which the tobacco companies can circumvent the ban on cigarette advertising and promotion in broadcast media.

Breweries have a long history of associating with recreation because the ages of maximal beer consumption and maximal recreational involvement are the same for both men and women. However, as the magnitude of recreation sponsorship by breweries has increased, it has been accompanied by a commensurate increase in criticism from those concerned about alcohol abuse. Public sentiment to inhibit beer company sponsorship has been less strident than feelings toward tobacco sponsorship. The most likely reason for this is that unlike tobacco, which causes disease and illness even if it is used as intended, the problem with beer is not its consumption per se, but abuse of the level at which it can be safely consumed.

A company should integrate sponsorship with its other communication vehicles. Sponsorship only can offer implicit messages and cannot indicate why a product should be purchased. Other vehicles have to be coordinated with it to provide explicit support information. It offers a hook, or a unifying theme, that can be incorporated into the messages of the other communication vehicles to provide a coherent promotional focus. Integration has cost implications. The indirect costs associated with using other promotional vehicles in concert to optimize a sponsorship's impact are likely to be at least equal to those of the direct investment and often range up to three times the direct costs. Park and recreation managers may fail to consider these indirect costs and try to convince companies of a sponsorship's potential return on investment based only on the direct cost.

The effectiveness of sponsorship can be measured at various stages in the communication process, but an evaluation taken further through the process yields stronger evidence of a sponsorship's contribution to increasing sales. The most frequently used measure is to assess the extent and value of media coverage that the product or company receives. These equivalency measures have a tendency to inflate the real value of the media coverage. In addition, this approach is flawed conceptually because it measures only the extent of media output and offers no insight as to whether consumers received, interpreted, and absorbed the message. Communication is a two-way process that depends on the intended recipient absorbing the communication, and media output measures fail to consider this.

Measuring changes in consumers' levels of awareness and image attributable to sponsorship involves comparing responses of those exposed to the sponsorship with those of a control group whose members were not exposed to it. The most useful indication of the impact on future sales are intent-to-purchase studies because they are the stage in the process immediately preceding a purchase action. Direct impact on sales is measured most easily when there are tie-in promotions associated with the sponsorship.

References

1. Sleight, Steve. 1989. *Sponsorship: What it is and how to use it.* Maidenhead, Berkshire, England: McGraw-Hill.

2. Gerstanzang, James. 1996. Administration park plan is setting off sparks. *Los Angeles Times,* September 16, A12.

3. McCabe, Logan J. 1989. Integrating sponsorship into the advertising and marketing mix. *Special Events Report* 8(7): 4-5.

4. Meenaghan, John A. 1983. Commercial sponsorship. *European Journal of Marketing* 17(7): 5-73.

5. Perelli, Sherri and Peter Levin. 1988. Getting results from sponsorship. *Special Events Report* 7(22): 4-5.

6. Sherman, Rachel M. 1997. Package deal: How a city turned a whole year of special events into a lucrative fund-raiser. *Athletic Business* 21(5): 28-32.

7. Berry, Leonard L. and A. Parasuraman. 1991. *Marketing services: competing through quality*. New York: Free Press, 132.

8. O'Brien, Sean. 1995. The new trailhead. *Sporting Goods Business* 28(4): 558-559.

9. International Events Group. 1995. Mark Cross sponsors ballet to reach upscale women. *Sponsorship Report* 14(21): 3.

10. International Events Group. 1995. Sponsorship vs advertising: Comparing return. *Sponsorship Report* 14(21): 4-5.

11. Elicker, Paul H. 1978. Why corporations give money to the arts. *Wall Street Journal*, March 31, 15.

12. Pringle, Paul. 1986. Selling sand: Los Angeles seeking corporate sponsors for beaches. *The Tampa Tribune*, September 22, AA1 and AA8.

13. International Events Group. 1995. Eddie Bauer uses first national cause to reinforce image. *Sponsorship Report* 14(22): 6.

14. Perlmutter, Felice D. and Ram A. Cnaan. 1995. Entrepreneurship in the public sector: The horns of a dilemma. *Public Administration Review* 55(1): 34.

15. Witt, Peter A. and John L. Crompton. 1996. *Recreation programs that work for at-risk youth*. State College, PA: Venture Publishing, 278.

16. International Events Group. 1992. Twin Laboratories pumps up sponsorship for sports drinks. *Sponsorship Report* 11(16): 6.

17. Dunham, Richard S. 1995. The Spirit of St. Louis brought to you by Ford. *Business Week* 34(23): 38.

18. Moritz, Jeffrey. 1980. Sports marketing: Grass roots action. *Marketing Communications* 5(11): 19-21.

19. Corwin, Michael. 1997. Sharks adopt California parks. *Friends of Parks and Recreation* 6(1): 15.

20. Lavelle, Bob. 1991. How Bell Cellular boosted its return from events. *Special Events Report* 10(12): 4-5.

21. Sebastian, Pamela. 1992. Arts groups go after corporate sponsors with all the brashness of the big top. *Wall Street Journal*, February 19, B1.

22. International Events Group. 1996. Museum draws sponsors through product tie-ins to exhibit content. *Sponsorship Report* 15(6): 6-7.

23. Bleakley, Fred. 1991. For Manny Hanny sponsoring races is good business. *Wall Street Journal*, May 24, A7B.

24. Steckel, Richard and Robin Simons. 1992. *Doing best by doing good*. New York: Penguin Books, 23.

25. Bentick, Brian L. 1986. The role of the Grand Prix in promoting South Australian entrepreneurship; Exports and the terms of trade. In *The Adelaide Grand Prix: The impact of a special event*, edited by J.P.A. Burns, J.H. Hatch and T.J. Mules. Adelaide, Australia: The Centre for South Australian Economic Studies, 176.

26. Goodman, Suzanne K. 1981. *Partners: A practical guide to corporate support of the arts*. New York: Cultural Assistance Center Inc., 14.

27. Lowenstein, Roger and Hal Lancaster. 1986. Nation's businesses are scrambling to sponsor the nation's pastimes. *Wall Street Journal*, June 25, section 2, 33.

28. Eaton, Rod. 1991. Inside Target stores' sponsorship philosophy. *Special Events Report* 10(17): 4-5.

29. Crompton, John L. 1993. Sponsorship of sport by tobacco and alcohol companies: A review of the issues. *Journal of Sport and Social Issues* 17(3): 148-167.

30. Feingold, Eugene. 1996. CREF must get rid of its tobacco-related investments. *The Chronicle of Higher Education*, October 11, B5.

31. DeParle, Jason. 1989. Warning: Sports stars may be hazardous to your health. *The Washington Monthly* 21(8): 34-48.

32. Muscatine, Alison. 1991. Where there's smoke there's ire: Tobacco sponsorship sparks debate. *Washington Post*, April 24, F3.

33. Chapman, Simon. 1986. Advertising and smoking: A review of the evidence. In *Smoking out the barons: The campaign against the tobacco industry*, edited by the British Medical Association. New York: Wiley.

34. Johnson, W.O. 1988. Sports and suds. *Sports Illustrated* 69(6): 68-82.

35. Sheehan, George. 1989. *Personal best*. Emmaus, PA: Rodale Press.

36. International Events Group. 1996. 1-800-Flowers revamps event portfolio. *Sponsorship Report* 15(1): 5.

37. Klein, Judy. 1988. Using events to increase sales at General Foods and Maxwell House. *Special Events Report* 7(11): 4-5.

38. Graham, Judith. 1988. Warner Canto: AmEx exec. on prowl for special events. *Advertising Age* July 31: 13.

39. Schlossberg, Howard. 1991. Volvo proves marketing through sport pays. *Marketing News* (1): 19.

40. International Events Group. 1992. Editorial associations. *Sponsorship Report* 11(9): 2.

41. Cited in Urbanski, Al. 1992. Fast track: Strategies for business success. What's a sponsorship worth? Supplement in *Newsweek* November 9.

42. *Special Events Report* 9(7). 1990. Evaluation: Measuring return on investment. Editorial, 3, 6-7.

43. International Events Group. 1995. General Nutrition Centers sees sales increase, seeks deals. *Sponsorship Report* 14(23): 5.

CHAPTER 17

SOLICITING SPONSORSHIP AND DONATION INVESTMENTS

Private support for public park and recreation services is not new. However, in the past, contributions often were forthcoming on the initiative of the donors, whereas what has now evolved is an organized effort by agencies to solicit funds to counter budget cuts. The onus is on the park and recreation manager to assume the entrepreneurial posture that traditionally has been associated with leadership in the commercial sector. Contributions used to enter the field randomly like leaves falling off a tree. Today the park and recreation manager has to shake the tree and try to direct the contributions to fall into this field rather than into another.

Both individuals and businesses are likely to be solicited for contributions. However, most effort is likely to focus on businesses because they have greater capacity to provide support resources and are more likely to make such investments on a regular basis. How corporations make sponsorship and donation investment decisions and the implications of these decision processes for park and recreation agencies apply equally to soliciting contributions from individuals.

In the past, decisions to support an agency program frequently reflected the personal interests of senior management rather than a careful assessment of the benefits likely to accrue to the company from its investment. Today, this type of decision is unusual. Accountability for an investment has to be shown by demonstrating its potential for increasing a company's profitability.

The efficiency and effectiveness of efforts to solicit sponsorships and donations are likely to be a function of the philosophy that underlies a park and recreation agency's approach and a function of the extent to which the approach is systematically organized. Park and recreation managers are most likely to succeed in soliciting resources if they adopt a marketing approach, which means that they look at their sponsorship and donation opportunities through the eyes of the business or individual from which they seek to attract investment. This approach is illustrated by the well-known marketing aphorism, "To sell Jack Jones what Jack Jones buys, you have to see Jack Jones through Jack Jones' eyes."

A marketing approach to corporate solicitation involves carefully targeting specific companies or types of companies, identifying their motivations for investing, and designing proposals that will bring about mutually satisfying exchanges over an extended period of time. Park and recreation managers who accept this philosophy and use it to guide their actions are likely to view themselves as brokers who are concerned with furthering the welfare of potential corporate investors by encouraging them to buy into the agency's services. They seek situations in which both the business and the agency win.

Soliciting contributions is not only about raising resources but is also a primary means of building a constituency. Indeed, it has been suggested that effective fundraising should be compatible with friend raising; that is, it enhances the number of stakeholders who are supportive of the agency.

The extent to which managers are able to see their opportunities through the eyes of potential investors and tailor a proposal to meet the needs of donors and sponsors is likely to determine their success. A marketing approach requires a park and recreation agency to identify what companies are likely to want in return for investing their resources. This information forms the basis for developing a presentation for each prospect. Too often, agencies spend too much time thinking about their own needs and not enough time considering what their potential investor wants.

Primary reasons for companies rejecting what appear to be good investment opportunities relate to budget cycles and amount of lead time. Budgets are planning documents that make operational what a company is committed to doing for the next 3, 6, or 12 months, depending on the length of budget cycle used. If an investment is not included as part of that plan, then it is unlikely that either money or manpower will be available to support it. Thus, it is important that park and recreation agencies are familiar with their target companies' budget cycles and are able to bring a corporate investment opportunity to their attention in advance of the budget being formulated so that it has a chance of being included.

Other possible constraints reinforce the need for a long lead time. After there is agreement in principle, detailed contract negotiations will take time. A company is likely to support its investment with related promotions and advertising that must be included in the budget. Integrating sponsorship or donation investments with promotional efforts to maximize the return on them, as discussed in chapter 16, requires company manpower that has to be planned and allocated so it is available at the time it is needed. An experienced executive observed: "Advertising is one of the major determinants of lead-time, due to the time required to prepare and place advertising in the media. For these reasons, it is unlikely that companies will consider sponsorship proposals which cannot be included as part of their regular budgetary planning process" (p. 123).[1]

It has been noted: "Every company is a potential sponsor for some event but not every company is a potential sponsor for every event" (p. 46).[2] The initial discussion in this chapter focuses on what constitutes a good fit between a company and a park and recreation agency program, event, or facility because considerable effort is wasted if the companies approached do not offer a good match. This discussion is followed by suggestions on how to identify and nurture a set of companies whose images and target markets are compatible with those of the program or event.

Before approaching targeted companies, a proposal has to be developed, followed by preparation of proposals and the packaging and pricing of the benefit packages included in them. Communicating the proposal involves finding out who in a company should be contacted, delivering the presentation, addressing objections to points included in it, and facilitating the closing stage during which a specific investment is requested. The chapter concludes with discussions of how to screen proposals, address rejections, formulate a contract, and foster a close, joint, working relationship between a park and recreation agency and its investors.

Matching a Recreation Service With a Potential Corporate Investor

This section focuses on two key conditions that characterize a good fit between a park and recreation service and a corporate investor. First, the desired image of the company and the image of the service must match. The second condition, which is discussed later in this section, is that the target market of the company and the target market of the recreation service must match.

Matching Images

Sponsorship and donation investments transmit implicit, rather than explicit, messages, so image association is of central importance. By linking their product with a recreation service through an investment, a business hopes to borrow the image of the recreational event and use it to enhance the product's image with its target audience.

Strength of image linkages between a product and a recreation service can be conceptualized along a continuum (see figure 17.1). If there is no obvious link between a company and the recreation service it is supporting in the target audience's mind, then it is unlikely that the company will receive commensurate return on its investment. For example, Southland Corporation, the former owner of 4,000 7-Eleven convenience stores, sponsored cycling. However, there was no obvious link between the stores and cycling. "They never figured out a way to use it to get people in the stores" (p. 33).[3] The lack of a natural link between sponsor and the event means a target audience is likely to filter out subconsciously the relationship as being irrelevant.

There are examples of successes in which no obvious linkage exists. Cigarette brands that have forged strong image links with particular recreational activities fall into this category. The magnitude of investment in direct and indirect expenditures needed to achieve such successes is likely to be relatively high (see figure 17.1). However, the benefits accruing to sponsors in image terms also are likely to be relatively high because the product will have borrowed more added value from the recreational activity.

In some cases, there may be no obvious product link, but there may be existing image compatibility. Thus, Alka-Seltzer Plus sponsored the U.S. Ski Team because "the team has the same needs as the product's customers. Neither can let a cold stop them" (p. 6).[4] Similarly, Proctor & Gamble's Old Spice line of men's toiletries sponsored stops on

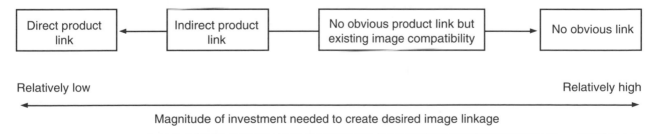

Figure 17.1 Continuum of linkage strengths between a product or service and a recreation event, program, or facility.

the professional beach volleyball tour because "Beach Volleyball builds on Old Spice's long-standing sea imagery. Plus the sport is synonymous with young men and that is our target" (p. 3).[5]

Coors supported river cleanup programs in many communities. For example, in Indianapolis, the company invested $40,000 each year in supporting about 15 river cleanup efforts. The company provided gloves, bags, equipment, and food and beverages for the volunteers. The program reinforced the image conveyed by the company's promotion emphasizing that their beer was brewed using pure mountain-stream water from Colorado. It also positioned the company as being environmentally concerned, countering the image that discarded beer cans lying in river valleys created. The projects were often highly visible to passing motorists and tended to receive high exposure in the media because the settings were photogenic and had human interest appeal.

The S.C. Johnson Company, makers of Deep Woods Off!, entered into a partnership agreement with Florida State Parks to undertake a joint advertising campaign to promote state parks. This project was a summer campaign centered on floor displays of the company's insect repellent with an advertising display featuring the slogan "Take Off! to a Florida State Park." The display included 100,000 rack cards with a complete guide to state parks, along with local radio advertising and display advertising using the same theme. The campaign provided more than $200,000 in free advertising annually for state parks. In addition, the S.C. Johnson Company donated $40,000 in cash to state parks to support special projects and needs.[6]

When the National Association of Stock Car Auto Racing (NASCAR) race car circuit staged a race at the Indianapolis Speedway for the first time, they partnered in two programs with the Indianapolis Parks and Recreation Department. Most of the race cars were made by Chevrolet, so the Chevrolet dealers in the Indianapolis area agreed to host an event for children called Race Back to School. This was held during the week before school started. It was an open house involving an educational program with the car drivers. Each child received a lunch box, pail, coloring book, and crayons that NASCAR put together.

The second program committed NASCAR and the Chevrolet dealers to contribute 400 large trees costing $500 each to the city's urban tree program. The number was dictated by the name of the race,

The Brickyard 400. This donation was intended to emphasize their concern for clean air and the environment and to counter their gasoline pollution image.

This type of image matching may be facilitated by park and recreation managers listing a set of descriptors that best describe their service and then seeking products whose existing or desired image fits with those descriptors.[7] Typical words may include accuracy, health, masculinity, strength, aggression, uniqueness, perseverance, thirst, reliability, speed, femininity, softness, risk, excellence, creativity, danger, cooperation, versatility, and problem solving.

It has been noted that

the "natural" image of park lands makes them prime partners for various natural food products. The heritage image of parks is a perfect fit for corporations that may be selling "tradition" and "permanence." The family fun connection to parks is easy to capitalize on, as is clear mountain air, sparkling waters, and refreshment! (p. 11)[6]

For image transfer from a recreation service to a product to be effective, a target audience must perceive that there is a natural and comfortable relationship between them. Indirect product link (see figure 17.1) means that a logical link exists between using a product and spectating or participating but that the product is not essential for those activities to take place. The most pervasive park and recreation sponsors of this type are the beverage and food suppliers. However, as the following two cases illustrate, the potential is much broader than that.

Subaru was the dominant sponsor of American skiing. The company's initial sponsorship coincided with its introduction of the first four-wheel-drive passenger car into the United States. It was recognized that the car would appeal to skiers and mountain residents. Sponsorship of skiing was a natural fit. After the first year of ski-team sponsorship Subaru sold twice as many cars in the United States as it had originally projected.[8]

Canon USA committed to a three-year, seven-figure sponsorship to be the official camcorder of Little League Baseball. The sponsorship was the result of a survey that revealed primary buyers of camcorders were parents of children from 6 to 12 years of age who earned average and above-average incomes. A central theme of the promotional campaign that Canon used to support the sponsorship was that parents tape their children in action as a way to "preserve vivid memories" and "enhance your child's enjoyment of the game by serving as an instructional tool for hitting, fielding, base running, etc." (p.7)[9]

Shoe, clothing, and equipment products are the most visible sponsors classified as having direct product links with physical recreation because their products are essential for participating or spectating (see figure 17.1). These companies include

- those that make and distribute retail and service recreational equipment, e.g., the balls, sticks, bats, pucks, nets, gloves, uniforms, etc.;
- those that benefit from recreational events that bring visitors to the community, e.g., hotels, motels, restaurants, bus lines, and travel agencies;
- those that make and sell T-shirts, sweatshirts, and souvenir items;
- those that develop, fabricate, and install recreational area lighting systems indoors and outdoors; and
- those that design and print tickets, programs, and other visual materials.[10]

Matching Target Markets

After image compatibility has been explored, the second key condition that characterizes a good fit is that the target market of the company and target market of the recreation service must be compatible. It is important to be able to say to a company, "Your clients are our clients." The most common type of match is on the basis of geography and socio-demographics, especially income.

Nestlé Foods Corporation signed a six-figure sponsorship agreement with the city of Los Angeles to help refurbish seven city attractions, including the Los Angeles Zoo. "We jumped at the program because it's not a rehash; it's not being done down the street," said Nestlé's Los Angeles regional sales manager. The company, which does 10% of its American business in the Los Angeles area, offered free admission to the zoo in the summer with proof of purchase and supported the promotion with full-page newspaper advertisements. "The stores are looking for relevant consumer promotions; their initial reaction has been outstanding" (p.3).[11]

Chrysler Corporation sponsored the Boston Symphony Orchestra on a five-city, seven-concert tour across the United States. Attendance at each performance averaged 2,500. Although this was not a large number, the demographic profile was appealing to Chrysler: equal number of men and women, 90% college educated, average age of 54 years, and average income of $80,000. A Chrysler spokesman said: "To reach these types of people we have to go where they recreate and have fun." The new luxury Chrysler LHS and New Yorker automobiles were parked at the entrances to the concert halls. "Whenever we launch a new product we try to maximize our exposure to its target market. Not only is it an opportunity to expose the audience, but there is the ancillary benefit of them talking to other people," the spokesman said. In addition, Chrysler was given access to 150,000 qualified names from the mailing lists of the various host organizations. At each performance, Chrysler promotional materials were on each patron's seat; a message was included in the concert program about Chrysler's commitment to supporting the arts; and a few days later, each patron received a video tape in the mail explaining Chrysler's new auto line.[12]

An alternative to using socio-demographics for matching the markets targeted by a park and recreation agency and a business is compatibility of their lifestyles. Nabisco Inc.'s Cream of Wheat hot cereal agreed to a $75,000 sponsorship arrangement with the National Park Service. An insert in each cereal package offered consumers an environmental how-to brochure, *30 Things Your Family Can Do to Save the Earth*, for $1 and three proofs of purchase. Respondents also received a free parks guide. If the offer moved more than 35,000 brochures, Nabisco agreed to increase its sponsorship payment by $25,000. Their promotion manager said: "We want Cream of Wheat to be perceived as all-natural, nutritious, and healthy; we found our target audience hikes, camps, and does outdoorsy things" (p. 10).[13]

Callard C. Bowser invested $500,000 in sponsorship of 44 performing arts and music events in 14 cities to promote its Altoids mint candy. Their project manager observed: "Our 18 to 49 year old college-educated target market uses the product in this genre." Many singers, opera performers, and actors, particularly those with more intimate scenes, use the product. Theater attendees use the product to avoid coughing during performances. Altoids sampling and trial were offered to audiences on site.[14]

Silhouette Vodka sponsored skiing and sailing following the findings of a study showing that these two groups exhibited relatively high vodka consumption. Sponsorship of these sports could be effective for several reasons. First, people consumed the product either immediately before, sometimes during, or after the event without violating any athletic rules. Second, there were alcohol retail outlets, such as ski lodges and yacht clubs, that provided on-site sampling opportunities. Third, the sports were perceived as upscale, image building, and lifestyle oriented.[15]

The emphasis placed on compatibility of target audiences makes it imperative for park and recreation managers to initiate research that delineates the audience profile of their event. A detailed example of the benefits of this approach that accrued to Bassing America Corporation is given in "How Bassing America Identified Potential Sponsors for Its Amateur Fishing Tournaments." Sponsors are unlikely to invest if these types of research data are not available.

Developing a Set of Potential Company Investors

The effective development and nurturing of sponsors requires that a computerized system be established to facilitate networking and scheduling. The system should enable an agency to scan corporate interests and characteristics then quickly to compile a list of prospective corporations or service organizations likely to invest in a particular service or project. Thus, the agency can make the right contact with the right potential sponsor at the right time.

The geographic scope of a service's audience, including any media audience, will dictate whether the search for sponsors should be limited to companies located within the community or should be extended to regional companies and regional offices of larger companies. This decision guides the types of reference sources that will be used to

How Bassing America Identified Potential Sponsors for Its Amateur Fishing Tournaments

Drawing from its 55,000 members, Bassing America conducted an annual survey at its spring events. Seventy-five percent of participants in its amateur fishing tournaments completed the four-page survey that included questions about product usage. Bassing used the results to target new sponsors.

They discovered, for example, that 67% drank liquor and that of those people, 61% cited bourbon as their liquor of choice. After analyzing brand preference and researching the industry, Bassing targeted two bourbons for proposals. Neither brand was a category leader; they were brands that Bassing felt could gain market share by sponsoring their events.

Within a few weeks, favorable responses were received from both. Bassing met with one and held the other on the sidelines. After two successful meetings, they were thrown a curve. The company's management wanted to use the tournaments to promote their rye brand. Bassing reminded them that the research showed only 8% of their liquor drinking members chose rye, but the company was determined. Bassing declined the offer and broke off talks because they believed the sponsorship was doomed to fail. They contracted the other bourbon brand, George Dickel Tennessee Sippin' Whiskey, and signed a contract and promotional package at the first meeting.

Another question on the survey that helped Bassing obtain a sponsor was: "Do you eat while fishing?" It was followed by: "If yes, what?" Seventy-eight percent of respondents said that they ate while fishing, and 38% wrote that they ate Vienna sausages. Bassing researched Vienna sausage makers and found that only one brand had ample distribution within their tournament territory. They made a presentation to that brand, Armour Star Canned Meats, but were turned down because they missed the company's budget cycle. The following year an agreement was signed.

This type of survey could be conducted by all park and recreation agencies. They could conduct on-site interviews themselves or hire a research firm. After two or three surveys, a definite mainstream customer lifestyle is likely to emerge. The agency is then in a strong position to approach systematically a prospective sponsor with a niche or target for its product or service.

Adapted from Lesa Ukman. Evaluation: Measuring return on investment. Special Events Report. IEG Sponsorship Report, Chicago. April 16, 1990. 9(7), pages 3-6. Copyright ©IEG, Inc. Used by permission.

develop an initial list of potential sponsors whose images and target markets are compatible with those of the recreation service. Such reference sources exist at all geographic levels. At the local level, all area businesses, professional and civic organizations, and social clubs deemed to be potential candidates should be identified by using such sources as the Yellow Pages, local chamber of commerce business listings, libraries, and local business magazines.

Once a list of prospective companies has been developed based on their compatibility with the selected program's image and patron demographics and lifestyles, three criteria can be used to prioritize this list of prospects: size of a business, its image in the community, and its past proclivity for working with public agencies.

Larger businesses usually have greatest potential for investing resources in park and recreation services. In addition to the greater magnitude of resources that they have available, their senior managers are more likely to be big people with a broader view of the world and a more sensitive community conscience.

Businesses that have a negative image may be responsive because of their need for good publicity. Park and recreation agencies generally have a wholesome, positive image, and linkage with them may help a business redeem its public image. However, an agency has to be careful that support from such sources does not tarnish its own image. The debate over the appropriateness of public agencies accepting sponsorship of their events by manufacturers of adult products such as beer, liquor, and cigarettes is an example of this dilemma.

If a company has worked with a public agency in the past, even if it was not the parks and recreation department, then it is likely to be a prime prospect. Such businesses are aware of the benefits to be gained from supporting public agency programs, so park and recreation personnel have only to persuade them that they will receive a better return on their investment in this field than the return from other agencies that they have supported in the past.

When a short list of companies to approach has been defined, then the agency should identify people in the community who have contacts at each of the companies or organizations on that list and who support the agency's park and recreational programs. All of the agency's staff also should be requested to name contacts that they have at these businesses. Members of advisory interest groups (e.g., soccer associations, Little League organizations, historic groups, etc.) with whom the agency works should be inventoried, and their company contacts should be identified. Finally, the list should be shared with civic and political leaders in the community who support the agency's programs.

The role of these contact people is to open the door and help an agency secure an interview for a staff person with the key individual who can make the investment decision at each business. The ideal outcome of this process is that these contacts can identify an internal supporter within a company who will champion a proposed solicitation before the formal proposal is submitted. An investment is more likely to come to fruition if it is championed by a senior-level decision maker. The champion's commitment may be stimulated by personal interest. One company executive responsible for sponsorship decisions observed:

> There certainly must be corporate interest. It may be employee interest that precipitates the event interest. It may of course be a key executive, an agency recommendation, or the outcome of a marketing plan. To make the event work there must be a champion. The champion must have the interest, authority, and single-minded vision to make the event work (p. 212).[16]

An alternative approach to building a personal contact network is to initiate a contributions feasibility study. This involves the park and recreation manager contacting key business leaders in the community and asking them for ideas about how to solicit investments for the agency's programs. Because they are being asked for ideas and not resources, they are likely to assist. These initial contacts can be asked for referrals to other influential people whose input should be sought. In addition to providing ideas about how best to proceed, this approach provides the agency with insights into the key corporate players and the decision process involved, raises awareness of the agency's needs, and builds a corporate base of interest in the agency's investment opportunities, which, in time, may be responsive to solicitations.

A similar strategy that some agencies adopt is to establish a public relations advisory board comprising people who are public relations professionals in radio, television, newspapers, sales, advertising, and graphics. These people are able to serve as gatekeepers because they have an extensive range of business contacts and can assist the department in accessing targeted companies.

This board can provide a steady flow of information on corporations' promotional needs. It can assist in analyzing which company may be the best target for supporting an event or program and which media are most likely to be interested in cosponsoring it or in providing trade-outs.

New companies moving into a community are likely to be particularly responsive. Frequently, the chamber of commerce compiles and disseminates a weekly list of such companies. These companies are often looking for vehicles that give them a positive image, rapid visibility, name recognition, and maybe even product-trial opportunities. They may be especially appropriate targets for a new service with which a company can be associated at the outset and can grow as the program develops.

To test the efficacy of the initial set of prospective companies, one experienced manager advised: "Put yourself in the shoes of the CEO or marketing director of the prospective sponsor, and if you can't see why she/he would become excited about being a partner in your event, don't waste your time, or theirs" (p. 55).[17] If the shoe does not fit, the park and recreation agency might succeed in attracting a sponsor initially; however, the sponsor is then likely to withdraw with some level of bad feeling, and the organization has to replicate the effort to attract another company.

Each identified potential corporate investor and information relating to it should be entered into a system that facilitates easy access and retrieval. A typical system, which was developed by Jackson County Park and Recreation Department in the Kansas City area, is described in "A Sample Sponsorship Tracking System." Each potential sponsor was issued an account code of 0 through 6 using the following classification:

0: less than 100 employees

1: from 101 to 250 employees

2: from 251 to 500 employees

3: from 501 to 1,000 employees

4: National headquarters (regardless of size)

5: more than 1,000 employees

6: Civic, social, and service organizations

Each record contained the account number; the company name; address; telephone number; contact person and title; type of company product or service provided; advertising budget; budget cycle; advertising media; and space to record any investment that a company has made.

The budget cycle for each company's promotion budget was identified. Each week the computer printed out a list of corporations whose promotional budget cycle was due to begin in eight weeks. This eight-week lead period gave staff the time to re-establish contact with the corporation's decision makers and to prepare a proposal for possible inclusion in next year's promotion budget. Many times opportunities for sponsorship or donations are missed because, although a corporation is interested, it cannot offer support, for the project is not included in the current budget.

Each management person in the agency should be assigned as the agency's liaison with a number of businesses and with responsibility for identifying who controls the spending for promotion and for establishing a relationship with that individual. In making these assignments, the agency should attempt to match the personalities and interests of each staff member with those of the corporation's decision maker. Being liaison person with a corporation does not mean that a staff person is necessarily responsible for implementing a program that is sponsored.

A second, follow-up file maintained a record of all contacts made with prospective sponsors or contributors by telephone, mail, or in person. (See "A Sample Follow-Up File" on page 450.) Each record contained the company name, the person contacted, and the project with which the contact was concerned. Files were provided for the dates and descriptions of contacts, their decisions to accept or decline a proposition, and comments that they made about the association that might be helpful at a later date. In this file, staff also kept a log of the companies to which a proposal was sent, the date it was mailed, and all follow-up contacts concerning that project. This type of system is valuable in preventing duplication so that companies are not invited by different people from the park and recreation agency to support different programs without internal coordination of these requests.

Preparation of Proposals

Company managers are unlikely to review anything extensive initially. They are more likely to scan quickly rather than to read the material, so the first two paragraphs are particularly critical. Hence, the first approach should be limited either to one or two pages or should comprise a full proposal with a brief executive overview at the front. The central concern should be to specify the

A Sample Sponsorship Tracking System

Account type:	4
Prospect corporation:	Jones Manufacturing
Mailing address:	P.O. Box 1000
Mailing city:	Kansas City
Mailing state:	Missouri
Mailing zip code:	64141
Location:	31st and Southwest Trafficway
Location city:	Kansas City
Location state:	Missouri
Location zip:	64141
Telephone:	(816) 968-1234
I. Contact and title:	Frank Jones, chief executive officer
II. Contact and title:	Bill East, president
Type of company:	Headquarters of building systems manufacturing
Number of employees:	500
Product service:	1) Engineering, manufacturing, marketing of building systems for nonresidential construction, grain-storage bins, and farm buildings and 2) under-the-floor electrical distribution systems, agricultural products, and energy-management systems.
Budget month:	October
Advertising budget:	$3,000,000
Advertising media:	Newspapers, consumer magazines, business publications, direct mail to consumers and business establishments, and network and spot radio
Investment A:	
Date A:	00/00/00
Project A:	
Investment B:	
Date B:	00/00/00
Project B:	
Investment C:	
Date C:	00/00/00
Project C:	
Reason declined:	

potential benefits to the company. Too often, proposals make the mistake of describing the merits of a program, its level of excellence, or its economic impact. Sponsors do not buy programs; they buy the expectation of benefits. They buy promotional platforms that help them sell products or services. Hence, proposals should address the sponsor's need, not those of the agency.

The Portland Bureau of Parks and Recreation in Oregon enclosed its proposals in a softback folder entitled "Prospectus." The inside cover contained the impressive, arresting general statement of philosophy shown in figure 17.2. This was written in corporate language designed to capture the attention of senior managers to whom proposals were sent.

A Sample Follow-Up File

Company:	Jones Manufacturing
Contact:	Bill East
Project:	Missouri Town educational poster for youth
Date:	07/09/98
Explain:	Mailed past-years' Missouri Town educational poster and youth sponsor proposal.
Date:	07/17/98
Explain:	Received letter asking to set up time for a presentation. Set meeting for August 1, 9:00 A.M.
Date:	08/01/98
Explain:	Had meeting with Mr. East and Mr. Jones. Explained the restoration project and the poster concepts. They will be in touch with us after they make a decision.
Date:	09/01/98
Explain:	Mr. Smith telephoned. Jones Manufacturing accepted our proposal.
Conclusion:	
Comment:	Contribution of $25,000 for poster project

A brief proposal is shown in "Sample Short Proposal Seeking Corporate Sponsorship." Testimonials and references are powerful, so if letters of support from existing sponsors of this or other agency programs describing the benefits that companies have received are available, then they should be included. If interest is forthcoming after receiving the one- or two-page proposal, then the remaining material and perhaps a short video can be used to offer more details. Alternatively, if a company is interested, it may respond by sending the park and recreation agency a standard questionnaire to complete, which it uses to evaluate the investment's potential against the company's objectives and other investment opportunities available to it.

A complete proposal should incorporate the elements shown in "Elements to Include in a Proposal" on page 453. The proposal specifies benefits that can be made available to the company, and a list of those most frequently offered is given in "Possible Sponsor Benefits" on page 454.

Experienced sponsors will request that the park and recreation agency provide a detailed budget of the service's costs. This will allow companies to understand the role of their investment in the context of the overall total budget and to reassure them that the event is adequately funded. Companies may also be able to identify various ele-

ments for which they can assist in reducing costs. For example, companies can often obtain better prices on printing, advertising, or other items than park and recreation agencies can.

At the end of the short proposal, the agency should indicate an intention to call in one week to 10 days to find out if the company is interested and, if so, to arrange a meeting. This prevents the problem of companies taking weeks to respond and means that, if the response is negative, the agency can focus its efforts on more likely prospects.

Developing and Pricing Benefit Packages

There are a variety of different ways and levels at which companies can become associated with a park and recreation service. Thus, it is normal practice to create different levels of benefit packages so that a wide range of investment opportunities can be offered. The number of levels is likely to vary with the size of the program, but the standard structure that has emerged in recent years consists of four categories of sponsorship: title sponsorship, presenting sponsorship, official sponsorship, and official supplier status. Each higher level of sponsorship builds on the benefits package offered at the previous level. It has been

Prospectus

The Portland Bureau of Parks and Recreation is making its first public offering to a limited number of local firms to participate in high-yield joint ventures.

The Park Bureau is a glamour subsidiary of the City of Portland, a municipal corporation. We are a vertically integrated organization which markets a broad range of recreational facilities and programs. Our bottom line is assuring equitable provision of recreation opportunities while serving as a steward for the public interest.

With a small investment your firm can share credit for such projects as:

- a new river-oriented park in the Sellwood neighborhood;
- concerts in downtown parks and plazas;
- Leach Botanical Park;
- handicapped access improvements.

The kind of credit might range from permanent signing to widespread publicity attached to the sponsorship of major concert series.

Your firm will realize a high long-term return on such an investment. A joint venture with our firm will:

- produce greater public awareness of your company and its commitment to the local area;
- verify your company's fulfillment of its social responsibility;
- associate your company with the public image of our highly visible, publicly acclaimed recreation activities and parks.

We know you work hard to get your message across. But we also know communication is more of an art than a science. Our programs and facilities enjoy a positive image with your target publics. You can take advantage of this well-established image through joint sponsorship.

The inserts suggest several projects which may be of particular interest to your firm.

Figure 17.2   Prospectus from the Portland Bureau of Parks and Recreation.
Portland Bureau of Parks and Recreation.

Sample Short Proposal Seeking Corporate Sponsorship

Introduction

The Jackson County Parks and Recreation Department has undertaken a project at Missouri Town 1855 to restore the original Colonel's House. The house has been sitting in a shell state for 18 years and has been the centerpiece of the town's development since it was moved from Bates City, Missouri. The total number of dollars needed to restore the house is $250,000. The Jackson County Parks and Recreation Department has invested $50,000 to develop all architectural plans and specifications. This will ensure that the home is restored to its original state. Jackson County Parks and Recreation has contracted with John Muller & Co. to assist in the development of a poster that can be used as an educational tool for the 80,000 students and teachers who visit Missouri Town 1855 each year.

The colorful poster is unique; there are 100 questions about life in 1855 that is presently portrayed at Missouri Town. Each student is provided with a poster and an invisible-ink pen. As they reach each question, they color the area directly below it, and the correct answer to the question emerges from invisible ink, helping the student learn about Missouri Town and its heritage. This visual learning aid will be given to each student who visits the town and will be paid for by the group tour fee. All proceeds from the poster will be used in the restoration of the Colonel's House.

Sponsorships are needed to fund the poster. The following proposal outlines the benefits of participating in the poster project.

Goals for the Missouri Town 1855 Educational Poster for Youth

- Through a colorful educational poster, create an awareness among the youth, teachers, and parents who visit Missouri Town each year of the heritage and history of what life was like in 1855.

- Create a poster that generates positive public awareness for individual sponsors through pre- and post-poster publicity and on-site impressions.

- Create a poster within a limited budget that returns the profits to the restoration of the Colonel's House to ensure that future generations have the opportunity to view what life was like in 1855.

- Ensure attractive demographics that match a sponsor's targeted demographics in developing the poster.

Pre- and Post-Poster Publicity

The Jackson County Parks and Recreation Department will mail programs to approximately 10,000 teachers in the Kansas City area promoting the poster for fall educational school trips to Missouri Town.

Jackson County will host a press conference announcing the poster concept and a sponsor's participation in the development of the poster.

Jackson County will provide a promotional advertisement in the county parks and recreation tabloids that are distributed to 100,000 homes each quarter in Jackson County and surrounding counties for the next five quarters.

Jackson County will display the poster on activity bulletin boards in Jackson County schools. Jackson County will promote the poster and sponsor at the Missouri Town Festival, a two-day celebration that annually draws 50,000 people.

Jackson County will submit (through public service announcements and written articles) the concept and usage of the educational poster to the following prominent publications: teachers' magazines, *Grandview Advocate*, *KC Times*, children's magazines, *KC Star*, historic magazines, *USA Today*, *Heritage Programs & Museums* newsletter, *Raystown Post*, *KC Magazine*, *Friends of Missouri Town* newsletter, *Corporate Report*, scholastic magazines, *Kansas City Business*, *Independence Examiner*, *Journal*, *Blue Springs Examiner*, and *Lee's Summit Journal*.

Jackson County will encourage electronic media coverage through special news reports inviting stations to visit Missouri Town 1855 and look at the restoration project and the youth poster concept. This will include channels 4, 5, 9, 41, and 62.

Reports to Sponsors

During the next year, Jackson County will ensure that the sponsor receives accurate demographic breakdowns of who received the poster by age, sex, race, and the area of the city in which they live. This will help to assure the sponsor that the posters were used as envisioned in the original plan and provide an account of both parents' and youths' reactions to the poster.

Benefits to the Community

The primary goal of the poster is to raise money for the Colonel's House through generous sponsor donations to development of the educational poster. The program will accomplish two things: demonstrate that learning about history can be fun and beneficial to students and complete the Colonel's House, which will restore a major piece of the total master plan of Missouri Town that the 150,000 visitors each year can appreciate.

Elements to Include in a Proposal

Profile of the Park and Recreation Agency
— Brief description of the activity or event
— Brief history
— Mission goals and objectives of the park and recreation agency

Description of the Event or Program
— Date, day, time, and location
— Past attendance figures and target audience description
— Content and theme
— Agency's capabilities and experience in presenting the event or program

Compatibility With Potential Sponsor's Image and Target Market
— How is the event compatible with the sponsor's image?
— Why would the sponsor be willing to associate with the event?

Sponsorship Benefits
— Clearly outline all sponsor opportunities and benefits. Try to provide information on exactly what the sponsor could derive from the partnership, for example:
  - public awareness of this similar sponsorship reached x percent compared with only y percent for z;
  - it would have a television audience of x million viewers of which about y percent are in your target market;
  - in terms of interest, x rank above every other recreational activity in the community among your target markets;
  - each year, the event has received x column inches in the local papers, whose circulation is x thousand; and
  - list the opportunities for exposure of the sponsor's involvement.

Media and Promotion Plan
— State the proposed (or approved) media coverage
— Explanation of how the event will be promoted

Sponsorship Investment
— The range of opportunities for investment
— The magnitude of those opportunities

Impact Measurement
— How the sponsor's benefits will be measured
— How the sponsor's benefits will be evaluated

Addenda Support Materials
— Newspaper clippings, photographs, and letters from satisfied sponsors at previous events
— Past event programs or brochures
— Video material

Possible Sponsor Benefits

Sponsor's Name Exposure

— Inclusion in the event or program title

— Banners and signage

— Participants' clothing

— Advertisements in program, press guide, and score cards

— Scoreboard and public announcement exposure

— Product display areas, branded merchandise, and give-aways

— Logo on award trophies and certificates

— Press release and broadcast promotion exposure

— Expected media attendance, budget for promotions, and advertising

— Involvement of personnel, such as master of ceremonies, officials, or presenters of awards

— Production of sponsor boards recording highlights with color photographs for display in the sponsor's place of business

— The right to record the event for the company's own purposes and have unlimited right to use those recordings to extend its involvement with the event

Hospitality

— Availability of free tickets

— Facilities for hospitality

— Availability of celebrities for sponsor promotion

— Parking passes

— Product sampling opportunities and coupons

— Co-sponsorship benefits

---

noted that there is no established list of rights for each of the categories. In fact, these sponsorship categories have no legal meaning other than what is agreed upon when the sponsorship package is designed. There is, however, a general pattern that distinguishes the four sponsorship categories from each other.[18]

Title sponsorship means that the sponsor's name becomes integrated into the program title or facility name. This is the highest form of association with a program and offers a sponsor maximal leverage for borrowing the image of the recreational program to improve its product's (or corporate) image. An example of a title sponsorship opportunity offered by Indianapolis Parks and Recreation Department at its velodrome is given in "Indianapolis Department of Parks and Recreation Corporate Sponsorship Opportunity." The major risk is that, if unexpected costs occur, then the title sponsor company may have to increase its financial commitment in order to avoid the risk of being closely linked to an inferior program. The title

sponsor is likely to insist on the right to veto unsuitable co-sponsors.

When Citicorp became the official sponsor of the Tampa Orchestra's pops concert series, it was renamed the Citicorp Super Pops. Similarly, when Merrill Lynch sponsored the Pittsburgh Symphony's great-performer series, the series was renamed the Merrill Lynch Great Performers series. Again in Tampa, NCNB made a sizable contribution to a performing arts center, which was renamed as the NCNB Performing Arts Center.[19]

Presenting sponsors of a major recreational program generally pay about one-half to one-fourth of what the title sponsor pays. They are given exclusive rights to associate with a program within a product category. Because this association is not available to competitive products, it can be exploited as a positioning factor in the product's marketing strategy.

Official sponsors typically are charged about 10% of the title fee. Their benefit package is substantially smaller than that of presentation spon-

Indianapolis Department of Parks and Recreation Corporate Sponsorship Opportunity

Title:

Annual Title Sponsor, Major Taylor Velodrome

Description:

Encompasses title sponsorship for each of the velodrome events in the 1993 season on a negotiable basis in addition to associated print and electronic media exposure. Yearlong balustrade signage included.

Location:

Major Taylor Velodrome

Timetable:

Late April through September per negotiations

Target market:

Metropolitan Indianapolis and local areas and national cycling associated audiences

Cost:

$10,000, which varies with timetable and desired exposure

Benefits:

Included in all promotional-media, sponsor-radio spots throughout the season. Valued at $20,000.

- One 23 in $\times$ 2.5 ft billboard-style balustrade advertisement for one calendar year
- Your company's name and logo incorporated into the season's velodrome racing program
- Placement on the velodrome's message board facing Interstate 65 and exposure to 74,000 vehicles each day
- Public announcements during each night of racing
- Your company's name in press releases
- Distribution opportunities for samples and literature either as door prizes or racing prizes (primes)
- Prominent recognition on the season schedule
- Free race admission for all corporate employees
- Opportunities throughout the season for your own promotional projects

Contacts:

Joe Smith or Jean Sponsor at (999) 666-3333

---

sors. It is unlikely that they will be permitted to invest if presenting sponsors in the same product category have committed to the program. This low level offers smaller companies an opportunity to associate with relatively little financial risk, but given the commensurably small benefit package, they are likely to have to work hard to obtain their promotional objectives.

Official suppliers are not directly linked to the recreational program itself. Rather, they offer their goods or services to the park and recreation agency that is staging it or to the participants or spectators who are part of it. Food and beverage suppliers and equipment suppliers are typical.

Two variations of this standard approach are illustrated in "Kinder Fest at the Movies Sponsorship Levels" and "Coconut Grove Arts Festival Price and Benefit Sponsorship Packages." The former shows how the approach was adapted by an agency seeking relatively small amounts of

Kinder Fest at the Movies Sponsorship Levels

Sponsoring companies or organizations would receive the following incentives for their support:

Theater Sponsor Level: Up to $100

- Mention on all flyers (e.g., schools, businesses, radio remotes)
- Limited radio spots (e.g., radio remotes prior to event and at event)
- Framed Kinder Fest poster

Character Sponsor Level: From $100 to $200

- Mention on all flyers (e.g., schools, businesses, radio remotes)
- Limited radio spots (e.g., radio remotes prior to event and at event)
- Framed Kinder Fest poster
- Sponsor a movie character at the event (e.g., could hand out promotional items, etc.)
- Waiver on booth space if used

Front-Row Sponsor Level: From $200 to $400

- Mention on all flyers (e.g., schools, businesses, radio remotes)
- Limited radio spots (e.g., radio remotes prior to event and at event)
- Framed Kinder Fest poster
- Sponsor a movie character at the event (e.g., could hand out promotional items, etc.)
- Waiver on booth space if used
- Advertising on radio and print advertisements for the event
- Banner space at the event

Major-Ticket-Holder Sponsor Level: From $400

- Mention on all flyers (e.g., schools, businesses, radio remotes)
- Limited radio spots (e.g., radio remotes prior to event and at event)
- Framed Kinder Fest poster
- Sponsor a movie character at the event (e.g., could hand out promotional items, etc.)
- Waiver on booth space if used
- Advertising on radio and print advertisements for the event
- Banner space at the event
- Inclusion on the Kinder Fest T-shirts (used for promotional items and sold at the event)
- Inclusion in all advertising space on radio, in print, and on television cable

sponsorship for a young children's summer film festival it was organizing in a park. The latter offers an example at the other end of the size scale when the basic four-category model was expanded to seven categories. The title and presenting sponsorship categories were retained, but the official sponsor and official supplier titles were replaced by five levels of opportunity.

The use of different sponsorship levels allows sponsors who may not be able to afford the investment if only one level were offered to choose a lower level of sponsorship. If this is not done, a park and recreation manager may offer a $30,000 proposal to a company that has only $10,000 to invest and, therefore, may lose the opportunity to secure $10,000 of support. However, an agency should probably start by presenting the top-level package that contains all of the benefit components and also by letting the prospect know that smaller packages are available because, if the agency starts at a low level, it is rare for the sponsor to suggest increasing it. The importance

Coconut Grove Arts Festival
Price and Benefit Sponsorship Packages

Title Sponsorship ($250,000)

Incorporation of sponsor's name and color logo into the event name in all print and electronic promotions and publicity including front cover of 50,000 brochures; front cover of 500,000 copies of special section in *The Miami Herald*; front cover of 15,000 program books; 10,000 pieces of office stationery, envelopes, and business cards; 50,000 poster order forms; front of 1,000 volunteer T-shirts; 1,000 volunteer hats; 1,500 invitations; 2,500 newsletters; sponsor boards (5 placards at each entrance); and three street banners.

> Executive rights: category and main stage exclusivity
>
> First rights: first choice of promotional opportunities and booth, sign, and inflatable locations (size to be decided)
>
> General rights: logo use; four display, sampling, and sales locations (size to be decided); 10 banners or inflatables (locations to be decided); full-page advertisement in *The Miami Herald* special section; full-page editorial in program book; identification atop sponsor boards at festival entrances; hospitality for 100 near main stage; 100 each of souvenir T-shirts, hats, posters, and programs; 10 invitations to poster unveiling and Collector's Circle breakfast; and six parking passes

Presenting Sponsorship ($175,000) (To Be Sold Only if Title Is Vacant)

Identical to title sponsorship except sponsor's name is not incorporated into event name; three display, sampling, and sales locations; six banners; 75 of each souvenir; six invitations; four parking passes; and smaller advertisement in *The Miami Herald* special section.

Platinum Sponsorship ($75,000)

Identical to title and presenting sponsorships except identification is not incorporated into festival logo; location of identification in program and *The Miami Herald* special section; first rights revert to this level only in the absence of title and presenting sponsor; and fewer general rights benefits, i.e., only two display, sampling, and sales locations.

Gold Sponsorship ($50,000)

Identical to platinum sponsorship except no first rights revert to this level, and there are fewer general rights benefits.

Silver Sponsorship ($35,000)

Identical to gold sponsorship except there is only one display, sampling, and sales location, and there are fewer general rights benefits.

Bronze Sponsorship ($20,000)

Identical to silver sponsorship except identification does not appear in print and electronic advertisements and publicity.

Patron ($10,000)

Receives identification only in brochure, *The Miami Herald* special section, and sponsor page of program book. Booth location allows displays only.

of this kind of flexibility is that it enables managers to work with a company to customize a package.

However levels of sponsorship are defined, a single price should not be attached to each component in a package that is developed. If components of packages are individually priced, then a sponsor is likely to look for items to cut. If sponsors want to negotiate certain elements to reduce the price, then they will raise the issue. The park and recreation manager should not invite this action by individually pricing components in the initial proposal.

Many businesses may prefer to support a program with in-kind services rather than with cash, and this is equally valuable if the services are budget relieving. See the example in "Mainly Mozart Festival Bartering Arrangements." To ascertain the level of benefits that a sponsor should receive in exchange for in-kind services, a valuation of the services has to be made. This is likely to be challenging. For example, if a company provides computing systems software and advice, in-house printing, or courier service, how is the real value of these services determined? The following procedure has been suggested.

Treat in-kind deals the same as cash deals if they are substitutes for line items in your budget. For example, if you have no need for a car, do not let an auto company offset its

Mainly Mozart Festival Bartering Arrangements

San Diego's Mainly Mozart Festival had a continuing barter agreement with Doubletree Hotel at Horton Plaza. From this arrangement the festival receives

- approximately 450 rooms each night for guest artists during the festival and accommodations for recitalists presented as fundraisers throughout the year,
- underwriting for the annual black-tie recital and dinner including all pre- and post-concert food and drink and for the opening-night VIP (very important persons) party,
- hosting of annual meetings and other business and support events,
- significant donations to the festival's annual fundraising radiothon, and
- the chairs that the festival orchestra uses on stage.

In return, the hotel receives

- a box at the Spreckles Theater for the entire festival and additional first-class seating as requested;
- free balcony seating for all Doubletree employees;
- complementary attendance at all other festival events throughout the year;
- inclusion in all print advertising on display banners downtown, on festival posters, in the festival program, and in 70,000 subscription brochures promoting hotel packages or special airline packages; and
- inclusion in all radio and marquee advertising.

The festival manager observed: "If it were not for such a trade agreement, the Mozart Festival would possibly not exist. It has been calculated we would have to raise an additional $75,000 each season to pay for the services offered by the Doubletree."

The Doubletree manager noted: "We had just taken over the hotel from Omni. Our original reasoning behind the partnership was to get the Omni image out of everybody's mind and the Doubletree image in. Now, of course, we get networking. As a result of people coming here in connection with festival events, we see a definite spin-off in catering and food and beverage—a bank day meeting, a wedding rehearsal dinner and the like. We also notice a rise in hotel overnight business during the festival, folks who don't want to drive home at night."

Adapted from John Willet. Profiting from a partnership with the arts. San Diego Daily Transcript. May 13, 1994, section A, page 1.

cash payment by throwing in a car. However, if you require air travel, treat the airline as a cash sponsor. Clarify how you will calculate the value of its payment. For example, is it based on the value of the lowest discounted air fare or the retail rate?[20]

The bulk of a sponsorship fee (at least 65%) should be paid when contracts are signed because costs associated with obligations to the sponsor, such as exposure in collateral materials, are likely to be incurred before the event takes place. A park and recreation agency should offer discounts for multiyear commitments because they save time, labor, and legal fees that an equivalent number of one-year contracts would require.

There is a growing trend for major sponsors to seek to self-liquidate the cost of their sponsorship by involving many of their suppliers in the event. A park and recreation agency may approach a grocery chain and offer it title sponsorship of a golf tournament for $18,000. The agency may suggest to the chain that it offer $1,000-per-hole packages to 18 of its vendors. In return for their sponsorship, the vendors may be offered special in-store promotions and the highly sought-after end-aisle location for a given period of time. Each hole on the course would have the sponsor's banner on it. This enables the grocery chain to receive all the visibility, image, and goodwill benefits associated with title sponsorship at no direct cost to itself.

Communicating the Proposal

There are four elements to consider in communicating a proposal. First is the preparation effort that requires an agency to determine who in the targeted company should be approached with the sponsorship proposal and then to seek out information about these contact people that will aid communication with them. The presentation element itself incorporates two other considerations: handling negative reactions and closing.

Preparation

After a list of the most probable corporate investors has been derived, the next stage is to prepare an approach tailored to each of these prospects. The preparation commitment is time consuming, but it is essential. Success in soliciting support is more likely to result from good preparation than from good presentation techniques. Key questions in the preparation phase are: "Who in the company should be contacted?" and "What is their role?"

In companies that are extensively involved in sponsorships and donations, these functions are likely to be the responsibility of specialized executives or departments. If the business is relatively small, however, investment decisions may be made by the chief executive. When an agency solicits product, rather than corporate, sponsorship from large companies with multiple brands, it is likely to find that the relevant contacts are brand managers rather than senior corporate officials. Finally, sales managers of regional offices should not be overlooked because an increasing number of companies are decentralizing marketing functions and funds.

The worst approach is to send a proposal to the attention of the vice-president of marketing or the chief executive officer. It should be addressed personally to the contact person. The relevant individual can be tracked by phoning the company's public relations or press office, the company's receptionist, or the secretary or assistant of the vice-president of marketing and community relations.

Proposals should be directed at the highest level to which the park and recreation agency has access. This recognizes the adage that top level managers are paid to say yes, while middle managers are paid to say no. Too often there is a mistaken tendency to contact employees at a lower level and hope that the request will filter up to the key decision makers because park and recreation managers feel less intimidated and more comfortable with them. Despite all that has been said about companies objectively evaluating proposals, there are still instances in which, if all else is approximately equal, the egos and personal interests of senior executives or marketing directors may be a consideration in the decision.

Once the contact person has been identified, that individual's role in the decision-making process has to be ascertained. Several corporate actors probably play a role in the decision-making process, and they fall into three categories: gatekeepers, influencers, and decision makers. However, one person may fill more than one of the roles.

It is most probable that the contact person in a large company will be a gatekeeper. This person may simply receive the proposal and forward it to others who make the decisions. Alternatively, the gatekeeper may be assigned the role of a first screener who eliminates some proposals and forwards a selective list to the decision makers. A rule of thumb is that the gatekeeper can say no, but he or she cannot say yes. The manner in which a gatekeeper passes along a request may be critical. If he or she is not personally supportive, the information may be relayed less accurately and with fairly evident disapproval. Thus, gatekeepers are key people in determining the success of a proposal, and their support must be won. Park and recreation managers should try to persuade gatekeepers to permit the presentation of their case directly to the decision makers. This will ensure that the proposal is presented in its best light and that there is an opportunity to answer any questions or objections the decision makers may have.

An influencer is a person whose views or advice help shape the attitudes of decision makers and, thus, who exerts some influence on the final decisions. The third type of actor is the decision maker who decides whether to support the proposal. In this preparation stage, it is important to identify who will have final decision authority.

For these reasons, it is useful to ask who will be representing the company at the meeting and what is their position, status, and role in the decision process. This will influence who attends from the park and recreation agency. One park and recreation manager who is experienced in sponsorship solicitations suggests always taking one more person to the meeting than the sponsor will have there. One additional nodding head is always an advantage in any sales situation. Certainly, it is important to have more than one person present because others can often catch verbal and nonverbal cues from the prospective contributor that one person working alone may miss.

An important adage in soliciting contributions is that people invest in people first and organizations second. This is true of corporate executives. A valid aphorism in soliciting support is: "It is not what you know, but who you know." Park and recreation managers are not only selling investments but also are selling relationships. Success is likely to be as attributable to positive personal chemistry as to the worthiness of the investment. The optimal scenario for a park and recreation manager is to have a well-known track record of successful sponsorship partnerships and a network that enables him or her to personally call the decision maker in a targeted company, brief the individual on the proposal, and then follow up with a comprehensive document.

The importance of personal chemistry makes it imperative that a park and recreation agency search for linkages between its personnel and the gatekeepers, influencers, and decision makers in a targeted company. The key questions are: "Who in the agency knows any of the key corporate actors?" and "Who can we enlist as an ally?" The best type of linkages are personal acquaintances, but if these links are weak, then it becomes important to seek referrals. Are there any mutual contacts who could introduce agency personnel to key company officials?

The park and recreation manager's task is to learn as much as possible about the individuals who are gatekeepers, influencers, and decision makers and to match their backgrounds with senior personnel from the agency who have similar backgrounds. A substantial body of empirical research demonstrates that positive interaction between the potential corporate investors and agency representatives is likely to be facilitated greatly if their backgrounds, personalities, interests, and lifestyles are compatible. Greater perceived similarities result in stronger mutual attraction or affinity between them. This matching process necessitates finding out background information, such as interests, hobbies, families, and goals. The contact person's secretary or receptionist may be willing to give this type of information.

Presentation

An effective presentation explains all aspects of the agency's proposition as it relates to benefits that the prospective sponsor or donor seeks. The first minute of a presentation can be the most critical part of it even though it represents only a minuscule percentage of the total presentation time. The first impression often determines receptivity in the mind of the potential corporate investors to the central substance of the presentation.

Although there are many ways of making a presentation, the best approach is facilitating interaction with the prospect's representatives and encouraging them to be active participants in the communication. Rather than talking to the prospective contributors, strive to enter into a dialogue with them. This approach begins by exploring the company's needs: What benefits do you want to see from a project in which you invest? and What criteria are most important in your evaluation of proposals? The primary task of the park and recreation manager during this stage is to listen and to suppress premature tendencies to talk about what the agency has to offer. The key is to build a sponsorship proposal around the company's priorities, which means asking questions to derive this information and not guessing. When the company personnel hear the proposal, they should believe that they are listening to an echo of their views. During the listening phase, the park and recreation manager should be considering the features, advantages, and benefits of the agency's program that are relevant to the company's needs.

After the company's representatives have explained their needs, the agency manager is in a position to organize and tailor the presentation to show how the program is able to meet them. The presentation should be careful not to promise more than can be delivered. In the interests of developing a long-term, ongoing relationship with a company, it is always better to under-promise and deliver more. Indeed, if it becomes apparent after listening to the company's expectations that the programs cannot deliver them, then the agency, in the interest of a long-term relationship, should articulate that view and gracefully withdraw.

Using the features, advantages, and benefits approach, the park and recreation manager begins by explaining the agency's credentials and the outstanding and unique features of the program. The advantages portion of the presentation addresses ways in which the opportunity is superior to other investment options available to the company. The benefits section translates features and advantages into benefits and addresses the central question of how the event can help the company achieve its objectives. For example, if the company's primary aim is to increase sales in a market that the program can reach, then the presentation may concentrate on packaging trade incentives that can be presented to dealers, retailers, franchisees, or wholesalers to encourage them to sell more products. Alternatively, if awareness is the major objective, then the presentation will identify ways that the program could extend the product's audience reach, gain more publicity, and link with a media co-sponsor. The benefit packages that the park and recreation manager has in mind will need to be customized and amended to obtain the best fit with a company's objectives.

Throughout the presentation, the focus should be on a contribution to, for example, the park, the park's wildlife and plant communities, or the enrichment of visitors' experiences. It should not be on the agency. People prefer to contribute to meet the programmatic needs of citizens rather than the needs of an agency.

By the end of the presentation, company executives must feel comfortable with the park and recreation manager's attitude toward the proposed arrangement and with the agency as a partner. They must believe that the agency is willing and able to fulfill its commitments and that it has an understanding of the company's commercial needs.

Handling Negative Reactions

If the presentation is to yield the anticipated result, it is necessary to elicit any negative reactions that the company may have. These should not be dreaded; they should be welcomed. They provide valuable feedback and are the prospect's way of communicating how to make the presentation successful. Responding to negative reactions removes barriers, and the objections provide clues as to the best track for the remainder of the presentation. Guidelines for dealing with negative reactions include the following:

- Never argue.
- Respond with facts.
- Avoid inflating the objection (i.e., if it is weak, try to ignore it).
- Show respect for honest objections.
- Find some common ground (e.g., "I know what you mean. I agree.").
- Turn the objection into a reason for contributing (e.g., "Actually, this is exactly why this contribution is needed so badly").
- Address it as a positive addition to the dialogue (e.g., "I'm glad you brought that up").
- Remember, the prospective contributor is always right.

Quiet prospects who hold questions and reservations in their minds and give few clues about their inward resistance are likely to be least influenced by the presentation. If no objections are raised, then it suggests either that the company was prepared to respond positively at the start or that the company representatives were not interested sufficiently to raise an objection.

Over a period of time, a park and recreation manager is likely to hear all of the various objections that can be raised and will not be surprised by them. The manager should keep track of flack, documenting the objections received and determining the best way to handle them so that he or she is prepared to respond when they arise.

Closing

At the closing stage, the park and recreation manager typically summarizes the major benefits on which there has been agreement, addresses anticipated objections or reservations concerning the investment, and requests that the company take specific affirmative action. Many people find closing to be the most difficult part of a presentation. They feel guilty or lack the self-confidence to ask for a commitment, or they have not thought through ahead of time to how they will orchestrate the closing to obtain a commitment from the company.

There are many approaches to closing that could be used. Three of the most common are illustrated as follows:

- Obtain agreement on a major benefit and then build upon it. "If I understand you correctly, Mr. Smith, you are most interested in increased visibility from your investments." "Yes." "An investment of $30,000 would enable us to . . ."

- Ask an open question and pause. "Mr. Smith, you have seen the benefits this investment could provide. What are your reactions?" or "How should we now move ahead?"

- Use the based-on technique that refers to a major point that was agreed previously and build upon it. "Based on your desire for maximal visibility, I would like to suggest an investment of $30,000, which would give you high visibility with the new target market you are trying to reach."

Often, when the question is asked at closing, a company may not be prepared to invest in a project at the level that the agency seeks. However, there may be a willingness to invest at a lower level. This reaffirms the desirability of the agency's having more than one investment level in mind, so if the main investment opportunity is rejected, other options can be presented. In addition to asking for money, be prepared to seek contributions of in-kind materials; volunteer time; names of other potential contributors; and, perhaps, a commitment to solicit others on behalf of the program.

At the end of the meeting, the park and recreation manager should have a clear idea of what happens next. The company representatives should be asked whether they require any further information from the agency or whether a more comprehensive proposal for presentation to a committee or board should be prepared. Finally, there should be clarification of who will contact whom and when.

Criteria Used by Companies to Screen Proposals

The number of sponsorship opportunities offered to companies known to use this communication medium can be overwhelming. As sponsorship has grown, companies have developed approaches for sifting through the multiple opportunities that they are offered to identify those likely to yield the highest return on their investment. The criteria and screening procedures that they use are intended to ensure that the benefits specified in a company's sponsorship and donation objectives are delivered.

The screening criteria likely to be most pertinent to businesses engaged in sponsorship and donations can be summarized under eight headings from which the mnemonic acronym CEDAR PEP is derived: customer audience, exposure potential, distribution channel support, advantage over competitors, resource investment level required,

Screening Criteria Used by Business Organizations To Determine Which Park and Recreation Sponsorship Opportunities Will Be Supported

Customer Audience
- Is the demographic, attitude, and lifestyle profile of the target audience congruent with the product's target market?
- What is the on-site audience?
- Is sponsorship of this park and recreation service or event the best way to communicate about the product to this target audience?

Exposure Reach

— What is the inherent news value of the event?

— What extended print and broadcast coverage of the sponsorship is likely?

— Will the extended coverage be local, regional, or national? Is the geographic scope of this media audience consistent with the product's sales area?

— Can the program be tied into other media advertising?

— Can the sponsorship be used to create consumer and trade promotions?

— Will concession areas at the site cooperate in selling the company's product and logo items?

— What opportunity does the program offer for a sustained presence? That is, what is its future growth potential, and how long is the sponsorship usable before and after the program?

— Are banners and signage included in the sponsorship? How many? What size? Where will they be placed? Will they be visible during telecasts?

— Will the product's name or logo be identified on promotional materials for the activity?

— Are program posters included? How many? What size? Where will they be placed?

— Are press releases included? How many?

— Are tickets or ticket order forms included? How many?

— Are point-of-purchase displays included? Where?

— Will there be television advertisements? How many spots? Which stations?

— Will there be radio advertisements? How many? Which stations?

— Will there be print advertisements? How many? Which publications?

— Where will the product name appear in the program? Will it appear on the front or back cover? How many and what are the size of program advertisements? How many programs are to be printed?

— Will the product's name be mentioned on the public address system? How many times?

— Can the sponsor have display booths? Where will they be located? Will they be visible during telecasts?

Distribution Channel Support

— Are the sponsorship's advantages apparent to wholesalers, retailers, or franchisees?

— Will they participate in promotions associated with the sponsorship?

Competitive Advantage

— Is the program unique or distinctive?

— Has the program previously had sponsors? If so, how successful has it been in delivering desired benefits to them? Is it strongly associated with other sponsors? Will clutter be a problem?

— Does the program need co-sponsors? Are other sponsors of the event compatible with the company's product? Does the company want to be associated with them? Will the product stand out and be recognized among them?

— If there is co-sponsorship, will the product have category and advertising exclusivity?

— Will competitors have access to signage, hospitality, or event advertising? Will competitors be allowed to sell their product on site?

— If the company does not sponsor the event, is it likely that a competitor will? Is that of concern to the company?

Level of Resource Investment Required

— How much is the total sponsorship cost including items such as related promotional investments, staff time and administrative and implementation effort, and in-kind resources, as well as the sponsorship fee?

— Will it be unwieldy and difficult to manage the sponsorship investment?

— What are the levels of barter, in-kind, and cash investments?

— Does the park and recreation agency guarantee a minimal level of benefits to the company?

Park and Recreation Agency's Reputation

— Does the park and recreation agency have a proven track record in staging this or comparable programs? Does it have the expertise to help the product achieve its sponsorship goals?

— Does the agency have a reputation and image with which the company desires to be associated?

— Does it have a history of honoring its obligations?

— Has the company worked with this park and recreation agency before? Was it a positive experience?

— Does the agency have undisputed authority and control over the activities that it sanctions?

— How close to its initial projections have the park and recreation agency's previous performances been in delivering benefits to sponsors?

— How responsive are the agency's staff to sponsors' requests? Are they readily accessible?

— Is there insurance? What are the company's potential liabilities?

Entertainment and Hospitality Opportunities

— Are there opportunities for direct sales of the product and related merchandise or for inducing product trial?

— Will celebrities be available to serve as spokespeople for the product? Will they make personal appearances on its behalf at the event, in other markets, or in the media? At what cost?

— Are tickets to the event included in the sponsorship? How many? Where are the seats located?

— Will there be access to first-class hospitality areas for the company's guests? How many will be authorized?

— Will there be clinics, parties, or playing opportunities at which the company's guests will be able to interact with celebrities?

Project Characteristics

— What is the perceived stature of the event? Is it the best of its kind? Is it prestigious? Will involvement with it enhance the product's image?

— Does it have a clean image? Is there any probability that it will be controversial?

— Does it have continuity or is it a one-time event?

park and recreation agency's reputation, entertainment and hospitality, and project's characteristics. A set of screening criteria that make these eight major concerns operational are shown in "Screening Criteria Used by Business Organizations To Determine Which Park and Recreation Sponsorship Opportunities Will Be Supported."

They are derived from a synthesis of screening criteria that have been reported by a variety of authors.[1, 21-26]

A company is unlikely to consider all of the criteria listed in "Screening Criteria Used by Business Organizations To Determine Which Park and Recreation Sponsorship Opportunities Will Be

Supported" in its screening process. To do so would create an unwieldy and unmanageable system that would defeat the objective of clarifying the process. Further, a common set is unlikely to be appropriate for all companies because the benefits sought from sponsorship are different. Rather, each company is likely to select from this comprehensive list the 12 to 15 criteria that are deemed to be most salient to meeting its objectives.

Handling Rejections

Sponsorship and donation support may be conceptualized as a program that a park and recreation agency is selling. From this perspective, it is reasonable to anticipate that development of a corporate investment program may follow a typical program life-cycle curve that progresses from introduction to take-off through maturation to saturation. The introduction stage may last two or three years before the corporate investment product gathers momentum and enters the take-off stage. During this period, a park and recreation agency may experience a large number of rejections to its proposals.

The success or failure of an initial personal communication interaction with a prospect should not be viewed in the immediate context of whether support was forthcoming. Rather, the contact should be regarded as the beginning of a long-term relationship. A period of time may be needed to consolidate the personal relationships that have been established before corporate support emerges. Early efforts may yield relatively little, but they are made in the anticipation of increased return in the future as personal relationships and confidence in the park and recreation agency are nurtured.

When a targeted company rejects a sponsorship proposal, there should always be an effort to find out why. This involves asking questions, such as: "Was the package wrong?" "Did we fail to deliver enough benefits?" "Was the return on the company's projected investment inadequate?" "Did we ask for too much of an investment?" "Did we misread the company's target market?" "Did we send the wrong person?" "Was the presentation ineffective?"

It is essential to follow up. The objective is not to challenge the decision but rather to ascertain why the proposal was not accepted and if the company would be interested in working with the park and recreation agency in the future. When proposals are turned down, it is often not because a business cannot benefit from them but rather because their timing is not right for the company. Polite persistence pays off. Thus, immediately after an unsuccessful effort, a letter of thanks should be sent to let a prospect know that the time spent visiting with the agency's representatives was appreciated. Contact should be maintained with the targeted company on the assumption that it may be a prime prospect for support in the future.

There are three major reasons why targeted corporations reject sponsorship opportunities offered by public park and recreation agencies that appear to be well suited to their needs. First, and most common, is the fundamental mistrust that some corporations have of a government agency. A corporation's dealings with government often are perceived to be negative because they tend to be associated with items such as property evaluation, taxation, inspections, exactions, and zoning. This general negativism is hard to overcome if decision makers in the business are not acquainted with the park and recreation agency's operations. Second, sponsoring companies often are required to insure an agency against liability associated with a special event or program as well as to insure themselves. Sometimes companies refuse to do this. Third, there are political nuances. For example, if an agency's elected officials are predominantly Democrats and a corporation's chief executive is Republican, it may preclude that company from investing in an agency service.

The Contract

The notion of an exchange relationship is the conceptual underpinning of all marketing transactions. However, in the context of corporate investments, a fluent exchange is especially challenging to transact because it involves a business relationship, at best, between organizations with vastly different aims and, at worst, between a commercial company and an inexperienced agency with different needs and expectations.[1] The two parties often operate in totally different environments, do not understand each others' businesses, have dissimilar reasons for their involvement, and seek different ends from the arrangement.

For these reasons, once general agreement has been reached with a company, some form of written document should be developed to ensure that both sides' interests are protected. Initially, this should be drafted by representatives from both sides without input from lawyers so that the issues are freely discussed. When a draft has been completed, then legal advisers may be used to ensure that the intent is expressed accurately.

Agreements may be documented by a letter of confirmation, a letter of agreement, or a formal contract. The magnitude of resources being exchanged and the expectations of the company will guide the appropriate format. A confirming letter is not a contract per se because it is not signed by both parties. The letter of agreement is a contract signed by both parties but is less formal, less expensive, and often less intimidating than a standard contract. The formal contract is no more enforceable than a letter of agreement, but it does commit the parties to giving greater attention to the details involved. It has been observed:

> Misunderstandings usually arise when the parties to the agreement have different views as to who will do what to exploit the sponsorship. The way to avoid this is to go through every possible element of the project beforehand and to agree the areas of responsibility. These details should be included in the contract so that in the event of any disagreements the original arrangement can be referred to (p. 192).[1]

Working Together to Make It Happen

When a partnership agreement is reached, this should not be regarded as the terminal consummation of a relationship. From the company's perspective, it may be a trial offer only from which the business will withdraw if returns are not satisfactory. The park and recreation agency also should view it from this perspective and recognize that the agreement offer is a tentative initial step. Sometimes all efforts are directed to securing a corporate investment, and little thought is given to servicing it. A long-term association and commitment will evolve only if a company's objectives are met.

Corporate investors add another dimension of responsibility for the park and recreation agency. It is required to make additional efforts to coordinate the company's desires, and they become a second audience who must be satisfied. A key to a successful, ongoing, resource support effort is the marketing adage: Your best customers are your best prospects. If investors are pleased with the results accruing from their expenditure, then they are likely to be receptive to future support requests. They are also likely to be valuable sources of testimonials and referrals to others. It is much less costly in time and effort to sustain an existing sponsorship arrangement than it is to find a new partner. This means that the short-term perspective, "We need the checks from sponsors so we can go about our business," (p. 55)[17] is likely to be very costly in the long term.

A key to nurturing a close working relationship and to building goodwill is constant communication between the parties and a total commitment to meeting the company's needs. The park and recreation agency should assign to each corporate investor a staff member as contact liaison who serves as a conduit through which all communications pass. This individual should be positioned as an advocate within the agency and charged with seeking to further the company's goals.

The more that executives and employees of an investing company can be involved and can feel ownership in planning and implementing the program that they are supporting, the more likely they are to make a long-term commitment. A good example of this type of close involvement is given in "Working Together To Make It Happen at Musikfest" where the main sponsor not only provided cash but also was involved energetically in planning the event (the infrastructure), providing public relations expertise for promoting it, making its advertising agency's design skills available, and providing a large number of enthusiastic employee volunteers.

Post-Event Followup

The way in which the followup is addressed will influence the likelihood of receiving future support from investing companies. The intent in the follow-up stage is to enhance relationships that have been established. A prime objective should be to make the individual in the company who made the decision to invest look good to senior management and throughout the entire organization. The followup should consist of three actions.

The agency's first responsibility is to make investors feel appreciated and to ensure that they are thanked and recognized in a way in which they deem appropriate. Some may not seek public recognition and visibility. They may prefer anonymity for many reasons, but primary among them is to avoid the barrage of requests that occur once their name gets placed on a donor or sponsorship list.

However, most businesses are likely to seek recognition. Therefore, an agency should have a recognition program. Such a program should be

Working Together To Make It Happen at Musikfest

Meridian Bancorp had assets of $6.8 billion and 150 offices in 12 Pennsylvania counties. Meridian was a $25,000 sponsor in the first year of Musikfest, which was held in Bethlehem, Pennsylvania, and took a leadership position in getting the festival off the ground. "Musikfest convinced us that a well-organized, outdoor event could impact a community's tourism and economic development. And the best place to have our banking operation is in a healthy community," said Jeffrey W. Gordon, vice president of marketing and communications for Meridian. "Before Musikfest, our event involvement was the standard night at the opera, day of distance running or the ubiquitous charitable golf tournament," said Gordon. These tie-ins ranged from $10,000 to $15,000. However, the sponsorship of Musikfest "did more for Meridian than the sum of a dozen smaller events," according to Gordon.

After four years, the nine-day celebration had grown into an $800,000 event that drew 410,000 people. The festival budget grew large enough to attract national artists, but Meridian was able to keep its sponsorship fee in the mid-five-figure range because of the number of festival co-sponsors. By the fourth year, more than 40 companies accounted for more than $400,000 in sponsorship.

The key to Meridian's success with Musikfest was the bank's involvement in the festival's infrastructure, according to Gordon. "By participating in the infrastructure, we have the opportunity to build social relationships with the corporate, government and educational leaders in the community. In the long run, these social relationships can lead to new business," said Gordon.

Meridian's first commitment to Musikfest was with public relations support. "Sponsorship is different than a traditional ad buy in that the extent of media coverage you get is an art in itself. We've learned it is essential to have our own PR people promote the event," said Gordon.

Gordon said that the bank's senior management looks for tangible evidence that the bank is getting its money's worth. "Management is especially interested in media recognition of our involvement and encourages us to help promote an event," he said.

Meridian also made its advertising agency available to Musikfest to design the festival logo and brochures and provided printing and other in-kind contributions. However, Gordon relayed that the bank's most impressive commitment was made by its employees, who volunteered from all areas of the company. For example, Meridian's security director took charge of Musikfest's security and audit operations.

Some of the bank's most successful Musikfest promotions included the production of a national television clip filmed for *Good Morning, America*; a press junket for travel writers during the first weekend of the festival; and cross-promotions with festival co-sponsors, such as the Coca-Cola Bottling Co. of Lehigh Valley, which tagged its six packs with festival promotions.

The bank also set up a Musikfest Media Center, which generated daily releases and photographs, arranged dozens of telephone interviews and daily radio updates, dispatched videotape to area television stations, and "garnered more media attention than any other event in the history of our region." Meridian has learned to market aggressively and merchandise its associations. Each year, it produces two or three souvenir items that bear the Meridian logo and that festival attendees can purchase. The bank also sends out notices with statements and produces point-of-purchase materials and posters for its branches. The events are included in some of its national advertising as well.

Adapted from Pennsylvania Bank Compounds Community Event Involvement. Special Events Report. IEG Sponsorship Report, Chicago. February 16, 1987. 6(4), pages 1-2. Copyright © IEG, Inc. Used by permission.

structured in the shape of a pyramid to increase the incentive to invest in order to receive more recognition. Figure 17.3 illustrates the pyramid principle and shows the types of donor recognition that was used by the city of Dallas.

Smaller agencies can use the same principle scaled down to their level. The director of parks and recreation in a small city developed the following recognition program. Everyone was recognized no matter how small the gift. Gifts of $15 or more

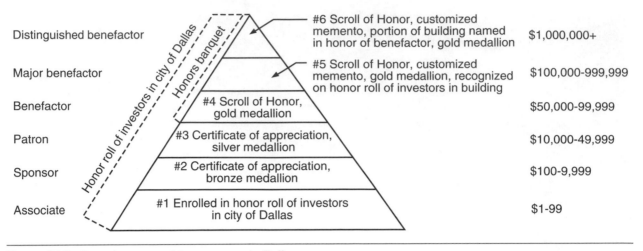

Figure 17.3 Donation recognition program in Dallas.

were acknowledged with a certificate of thanks and a paperweight with the park and recreation department logo. A paperweight was selected because it sits on top of a desk and is a very visible symbol of the donation. People who donated $100 or more received a personalized plaque etched in gold and presented by the mayor at a formal ceremony. Donations of $1,000 or more rated a presentation by the council, complete with media coverage. If the donor was a member of a local civic or business group, the presentation was made in front of the group by council members to maximize importance and to get others in the group excited about making a contribution. After the presentation ceremony, an 8 in × 10 in color photograph of each donor was posted for a month in the Hall of Fame, located in the lobby of City Hall.

One of the most important principles of contributor recognition is to do it promptly. Contributors generally give considerable thought to their decision and for them to suspect that an agency has not recognized or appreciated their contribution clearly jeopardizes a future relationship with them.

A second follow-up task is to evaluate (in association with, rather than for, the contributor) the extent to which a contributor's objectives were achieved to be sure it meets their needs. Evaluation measures relating to the impact of sponsorships were discussed in chapter 16. This evaluation is critical in soliciting business contributions because executives need a scorecard to justify to stockholders and superiors their investment of company resources. The evaluation material should include a portfolio that incorporates photographs, newspaper articles, copies of all promotional material mentioning the sponsor, and a short videotape showing highlights of the program and the company's role in it.

The final follow-up task is to initiate discussions about future investments in the program. These will be guided by the timespan and arrangements for renewing or canceling that were included in the contract. The discussions should be held soon after the program is completed so that maximal time is available to make changes in any future partnership or to find other sponsors if necessary.

A Concluding Example: The Importance of Flair and Imagination

This chapter has offered a systematic approach for soliciting sponsorships and donations. Although planning and strategies are key contributing ingredients to success, they are only tools. It is people who acquire these support resources. Success requires that the planning and strategies be implemented by individuals with personality, imagination, enthusiasm, and flair. The example reported in "William Penn Mott Tells How He Solicited a Major Donation for Children's Fairyland in Oakland" illustrates the importance of these ingredients. It is a vignette in which William Penn Mott tells how, at a relatively early stage in his career, he solicited a major donation for Children's Fairyland in Oakland. Mott was one of the great inspiring figures of the park and recreation field. His career spanned more than 60 years, and among the many positions he held were director of Oakland Parks and Recreation Department in California, director

William Penn Mott Tells How He Solicited a Major Donation for Children's Fairyland in Oakland

I want to make some points about how to solicit a donation by using an illustration which I think that you will enjoy. If you are going out to raise funds, whether you do it or somebody else does it, you have to know the person from whom you are going to raise the funds. You have got to do research in advance whether it is a person, a corporation, or whatever. You have to study that organization or individual and understand his background and his interests and identify his particular concerns.

In Oakland we built Children's Fairyland, and I think a lot of you are familiar with it. It is an animated three-dimensional interpretation of children's stories. I decided that one of the sets I would like to build would be Robinson Crusoe. I wondered where to get the funds because, in Children's Fairyland, the whole construction cost was donated, and all its operations costs came from the revenue it generated. That was the only way we could get it done.

The thought occurred to me that I would try to get the money from Trader Vic. Some of you may be familiar with the Trader Vic restaurants that expanded out of California around the country. Trader Vic is Victor Burgeron. He is quite a large man, has a limp leg, and is what you would visualize as an old gruff sea captain. That's the kind of person that he is. He had never up to that point made a contribution of any kind to the city of Oakland, even though he got his start in Oakland with his Trader Vic restaurant. So, I decided that is the man I am going to tackle for Robinson Crusoe because Trader Vic restaurants are built around a Polynesian theme and have some of the kinds of artifacts that were needed for a Robinson Crusoe set.

I researched his whole background and found that he went to the South Seas every year sailing and to collect artifacts, that he was very much interested in Polynesian art and that type of thing, and that his wife was particularly interested in children's hospitals and in children. I knew from Trader Vic's background that I couldn't get him to Children's Fairyland under any conditions. But, I thought I could get him there through his wife because she was interested in children and the children's hospital.

Although I didn't know either one of them, I decided to call Mrs. Burgeron, and I told her what I had in mind. I would like her to see Children's Fairyland. I knew she was interested in art. Children's Fairyland was done with an artistic flair, and it was designed and developed by an artist with whom she was familiar. I used his name and said: "I would appreciate it very much if you would visit Children's Fairyland and bring your husband so he could see what Children's Fairyland is like, and I could get some counsel from him in connection with the development of the Robinson Crusoe set." She agreed to do that.

I got to Children's Fairyland a little after they got there. To get into Children's Fairyland, you have to stoop down to go through the instep of the Old-Lady-Who-Lives-in-a-Shoe entrance. This is so that all adults are at the same level as children when they come into Children's Fairyland psychologically as well as physically. Trader Vic is quite a big man as I told you, both in height and width. He had to stoop down to go into Children's Fairyland. When I came through the gate, I introduced myself. He said to me—and I am going to use his language now—"What in the heck am I doing here?" and he has a gravelly, gruff voice that you can hear a mile away.

I said: "Well, I decided that I would like to develop a set to interpret Robinson Crusoe for the kids in Oakland. I know that you have a great deal of interest in the art forms of the South Pacific and have spent a great deal of time down there. I know that you sail down there. I need a dug-out canoe; I need some bamboo; I need some goat skins; and I need some parrots and alligators. I thought possibly you would be able to at least get for me a small dug-out canoe that would be in scale with what I'm doing here at Children's Fairyland."

He looked me straight in the eye and he said, "Young man, you don't know anything about the Robinson Crusoe story. Robinson Crusoe was in the Caribbean, not in the South Pacific, and I don't know anything about the Caribbean."

When he made that statement, I knew that he was on my side. He had corrected me. I knew Robinson Crusoe wasn't in the Caribbean all the time. He had corrected me so he was then trapped into assisting. You understand this: he was then ego-involved and became committed. We talked a little bit and then he said: "I have got to get out of this place, but I will get you the dug-out canoe. I'll do that much for you. I'm going to the South Seas next week."

As he was walking out, I said: "You have a tremendous artist that does the decor for your restaurants. Could he help me a little bit on the design of this?"

Victor Burgeron said: "Sure, talk to him. I'll tell him that you are coming."

Now that the project was moving, I had the man who made our models make a beautiful model of what the Robinson Crusoe set was going to look like.

When Victor Burgeron returned from his South Seas trip, he had a beautiful little dug-out canoe right to scale. He had some goat skins, which he had brought for me; some bamboo; and he had made arrangements for parrots to be sent. I showed him the model of the set, which was really beautifully done, and I said: "This is what we are going to do. There is your dug-out canoe. This is the way we are going to use the goat skins, the bamboo, and so forth."

He was quite pleased and said: "Well, that's a very nice model. You have done a nice job."

Then I said: "I'm going out to raise the money to finish this, and I appreciate very much what you have done for me in getting this dug-out canoe and the other materials."

He said: "Who in the heck are you going to get the money from?" I said: "Well, I don't know at this point. I'm going to talk to different people." He said: "I started this durn thing. I will finish it." That is exactly what he said. You could hear him all over the restaurant. I said: "Gee, that's great. If you are going to do that, I sure appreciate it." I didn't tell him how much it was going to cost. I said: "You want me to go ahead and finish this set?" He said: "Yes, go ahead and finish it."

I finished the set. I was scared to death as to how I was going to break the news to him of what this thing cost. At that time, in Oakland and throughout California there was a television series on which they talked about business and what it did for communities. The program had a tremendous rating—everybody was watching it. So I went to them and said: "How about doing Trader Vic's restaurant and his success and relating it to the Robinson Crusoe set in Children's Fairyland?" I took the producer over to the site and he got all excited about the photographic possibilities.

The opening of the set was scheduled so it could be covered by the show. Of course Trader Vic got tremendous publicity. A couple of weeks after the show was aired, I went down to Trader Vic's for lunch and said: "Well, the set is all finished. I hope you appreciated all that television publicity and promotion."

He said: "It was just tremendous. I am getting letters from all over the state about it. It was just great." I said: "Well, here is the bill for the set." It was $25,000. Children's Fairyland is small, and the Robinson Crusoe set is no bigger than a corner of an average sized room.

When he got the bill and looked at it, you could hear him bellow all the way to the City Hall in Oakland. He gave me a check for $25,000 right there and then and said: "Get out. I never want to see you again."

I have seen him since many times, and he always reminds me about this. He really is a great guy.

From a presentation given by William Penn Mott at the National Recreation and Park Association Annual Congress in Dallas, Texas, 1975. Published in Doing More With Less *by John Crompton. Venture Publishing: State College, PA. 1987. Copyright ©Venture Publishing, Inc. Used by permission.*

of the California Parks and Recreation Department, and director of the National Park Service.

In the author's view, the following points contributed to the success of Mott's solicitation effort:

- Mott targeted Victor Burgeron for this donation for two reasons. First, the Robinson Crusoe set reflected the atmosphere and public image of Trader Vic's restaurants. Second, the theme also tied in with Victor Burgeron's leisure interest of sailing around the South Sea Islands. Mott tailored his presentation to these two strong complementary approaches to arouse Victor Burgeron's interest.

- Mott prepared thoroughly by investing effort in researching Victor Burgeron's professional and leisure interests (and those of his immediate family) before making his approach. As a result of this research, the initial contact was made with Mrs. Burgeron because of her known interest in children. She served as the gatekeeper, and it was her influence that persuaded Victor Burgeron to view Children's Fairyland. Her presence at the initial site visit and her sympathy for the project presumably made it more difficult for her husband to reject Mott's initial request for artifacts.

- The approach was carefully timed to coincide with Victor Burgeron's departure on a South Seas vacation the following week. This was the ideal time to launch the project and gain momentum by persuading Victor Burgeron to commit himself to active assistance and involvement in acquiring artifacts.

- Mott cared deeply about Children's Fairyland. He was a product champion espousing his cause. His conviction, sincerity, and enthusiasm were conveyed to Victor Burgeron.

- Mott provided a clear idea of what was envisioned. The initial visit with Victor Burgeron was on site—not in an office—so he could see clearly the quality of the other sets and the context of the planned Robinson Crusoe attraction. A model of the set was built so its potential could be easily appreciated. As the artifacts were acquired, they were incorporated into the set. In this way, their visibility helped sustain momentum.

- Victor Burgeron gradually acquired ownership in the set, so eventually it became his project. Mott did not ask for the $25,000 at the outset. The link and emotional involvement were built slowly and progressively. Mott's initial request was for counsel and advice, then a few artifacts, then the use of the company's artist, and then the use of a model to illustrate how the initial artifacts fit in and what remained to be done. Finally, Burgeron identified so much with the project that he offered to finance the whole set.

- Extensive and extended media coverage emerged from the project, giving Trader Vic's restaurants enhanced image and visibility. The commercial value of this publicity far exceeded the $25,000 that Trader Vic invested in the project. Mott did not present the bill until after his establishments got this publicity, so Burgeron was able to place the cost in the context of the economic value of the media coverage to his business.

Summary

Adopting a marketing approach is a key to successfully soliciting corporate and individual resource support. This requires that proposals focus on potential for delivering what investors are likely to want in return for contributing their resources. Park and recreation managers should perceive themselves as brokers who are concerned with furthering the welfare of potential investors by offering opportunities in which both they and the agency win.

There are two key conditions that characterize a good fit between a park and recreation service and a corporate investor. First, the desired image of the company and the image of the service must match. Sponsorship activities transmit implicit, rather than explicit, messages, so image association is of central importance as a business hopes to borrow the image of the program and use it to enhance its product's image with its target audience. The second characteristic of a good fit is that the characteristics of the company's target markets must match those in the recreational program in socio-demographic, geographic, or lifestyle profiles. Using these two guidelines, a list of potential corporate investors and a profile of each company on the list can be developed and entered into an information retrieval system.

A one- or two-page proposal should be sent to the targeted companies, and a follow-up call should be made one week to 10 days later. Opportunities should be packaged to offer different levels of benefit packages so that a wide range of investment amounts can be accommodated. The most frequently used benefit structure consists of four categories: title sponsorship, presenting sponsorship, official sponsorship, and official supplier status. However, there are numerous variations from this basic structure.

There are four elements to consider in communicating a proposal. First is preparation, which involves identifying who in the targeted company should be approached with the proposal and seeking out information about him or her. This information includes determining whether the contact person is a gatekeeper, influencer, or decision maker; whether anyone in the park and recreation agency is acquainted with the individual; and background material, such as the person's interests, family, and lifestyle, that will help facilitate positive personal interaction between the individual and the park and recreation agency's representatives.

The second element is the presentation, which should be interactive. The park and recreation manager listens to the company's benefit needs and then explains the features, advantages, and benefits that the program is able to offer to address those needs. Third, negative reactions to the proposal should be solicited so that there is an opportunity to address and reverse them. The fourth element of the presentation is closing, which is the time when the company's representatives are asked to commit to an investment.

As recognition of the effectiveness of sponsorship and donations has grown, companies have developed criteria and screening procedures for sifting through the multiple opportunities that they are offered. They tend to focus on eight factors in their evaluation: customer audience, exposure potential, distribution channel support, advantage over competitors, resource investment level required, park and recreation agency's reputation, entertainment and hospitality opportunities, and the project's characteristics.

When a proposal is rejected, reasons for the negative outcome should be identified. If these can be rectified in the future, then the initial rejection may constitute the beginning of a long-term relationship. When a proposal is accepted, a written contractual document should be developed to ensure that both sides' interests are protected. To nurture a long-term relationship, the park and recreation agency has to view the corporate investor as a partner and work to help the company realize its objectives. This may be achieved by nominating a staff person to be liaison with the company and to be its advocate within the agency. If multiple investors are involved, facilitating interaction and networking between them may be productive. Follow-up actions involve ensuring investors receive appropriate recognition, helping the key decision makers in the company evaluate the extent to which their objectives were met, and initiating discussions about future investments in the event.

References

1. Sleight, Steve. 1989. *Sponsorship: What it is and how to use it.* Maidenhead, Berkshire, England: McGraw-Hill.

2. Decker, Jill. 1991. Seven steps to sponsorship. *Parks and Recreation* 26(12).

3. Lowenstein, Roger and Hal Lancaster. 1986. Nation's businesses are scrambling to sponsor the nation's pastimes. *Wall Street Journal*, June 25, section 2, 33.

4. *Special Events Report* 6(8). 1987. Alka-Seltzer Plus backs U.S. ski team. Editorial, 6.

5. International Events Group. 1992. Old Spice digs beach volleyball. *Sponsorship Report* 11(18): 3.

6. LaPage, Wilbur F. 1994. *Partnerships for parks.* Tallahassee, FL: National Association of State Parks.

7. Goslin, Anneliese. 1992. Preparing sponsorship proposals for recreation events. *Trends (SAART)* 7: 2.

8. Raabe, Steve. 1989. Sponsorship of ski events buys Subaru mountains of publicity. *Denver Post*, February 10, 1C.

9. *Special Events Report* 9(19). 1990. Little League catches big sponsor in Canon. Editorial, 1.

10. Meagher, John W. 1992. And now a word from our sponsor. *Athletic Business* 16(5): 14.

11. *Special Events Report* 7(16). 1988. L.A. lands sponsors for new music marketing program. 3.

12. Triplett, Tim. 1994. Corporate sponsors get artsy to find upscale consumers. *Marketing News* 28(10): 23.

13. *Special Events Report* 10(20). 1991. Cream of wheat warms up to National Parks. Editorial, 3.

14. International Events Group. 1996. Altoids mints new arts and music sponsorships. *Sponsorship Report* 15(11): 1-2.

15. Dixon, Don. 1987. How to package, price and sell your event to sponsors. *Special Events Report* 6(8): 4-5.

16. Copeland, Robert P. 1991. Sport sponsorship in Canada: A study of exchange between corporate sponsors and sport groups. Master's thesis, University of Waterloo.

17. Charney, Bill. 1993. Sponsor renewal: How to keep them coming back. *IFA's official guide to sponsorship.* Port Angeles, WA: International Festivals Association.

18. Brooks, Christine. 1990. Sponsorship by design. *Athletic Business* 14(12): 58-62.

19. Mescon, Timothy S. and Donn J. Tilson. 1987. Corporate philanthropy: A strategic approach to the bottom-line. *California Management Review* 29(2): 49-61.

20. McCally, John F. 1990. Corporate sponsorship and the U.S. Olympic Festival '90: A mutually beneficial marketing arrangement. Unpublished paper. Mankato, MN: Department of Marketing, Mankato State University.

21. Perelli, Sheri and Peter Levin. 1988. Getting results from sponsorship. *Special Events Report* 7(22): 4-5.

22. Riffner, Dick and Frederick G. Thompson. 1987. Special event programming—relative value assessment. *Special Events Report* 6(6):4-5.

23. Furst, Disson and Allen Furst. 1991. A method for scrutinizing sponsorship opportunities. *Special Events Report* 10(9): 4-5.

24. Frankel, Bud. 1988. Event marketing: Panacea or problems? *Marketing News* 22(24): 12.

25. Samson, Roger. 1989. Using evaluation to determine what's working and what's not. *Special Events Report* 8(8): 5.

26. Ensor, Richard J. 1987. The corporate view of sports sponsorship. *Athletic Business* 11(9): 40-43.

CHAPTER 18

SUPPORT ROLES OF FOUNDATIONS

During the past two decades, the role of foundations in the acquisition of land has shifted from a peripheral to a central one. The adverse financial environments in which many agencies have been required to operate in this period created vacuums that frequently were filled by foundations undertaking a myriad of different tasks. Whereas two decades ago it was difficult to find examples of park and recreation agencies working with foundations, today it is the exceptional agency that does not have experience working with them. The variety of tasks that they are requested to undertake has resulted in the emergence of foundations with widely different missions and the development of a host of innovative techniques and strategies for securing park and recreational resources.

Because of the growth in roles, techniques, types, and number of foundations involved with the field, the discussion of foundations is divided into two chapters. After an initial description of the technical legalities of foundations and how they are established, the bulk of this chapter is devoted to a review of the multifaceted ways in which they support the work of public agencies. These extend far beyond the notion of awarding grants, which is the popular conception of foundations' primary support role. Chapter 19, which follows, identifies the different types of foundations and the niches that they occupy.

Legal Status

Foundations are defined as nongovernment, nonprofit corporations that are organized and operated for the benefit of the general public. A foundation is created through articles of incorporation, is structured in accordance with state regulations, and is recognized by the state as an independent legal entity. Its articles of incorporation state the purposes, define its powers, and establish bylaws, which are the procedures governing its operations. The purposes may be defined narrowly or broadly, depending on its particular objectives.

Foundations that are set up for park, recreational, or conservation purposes basically exist in two forms. They include private foundations, which typically are established by a single donor, and public charities, which several major donors or the public at large fund. Almost all of the foundations in this field are public charities because of two major advantages. First, the federal income tax deduction is larger for donations to public charities than to private foundations. Second, a conservation easement donated to a public charity is a tax-deductible gift, whereas an easement donated to a private foundation is not deductible.

After incorporation, a foundation has to apply to the IRS for federal tax-exempt status under section 501(c)(iii) of the Internal Revenue Code. This explains why public foundations are sometimes referred to as 501(c)(iii) organizations. To achieve tax-exempt status, the corporation must assure the IRS that it has been organized to serve public purposes. The IRS will assume it is a private foundation, and the organization has to persuade the IRS that it is a public charity by demonstrating that it has a broad base of community support, particularly in regard to fundraising. The IRS has a public support test formula that disfavors large private contributions and large endowments and favors support from a broad base. In its evaluation, the IRS also will rely heavily upon the purposes and powers that the corporation defined in its articles of incorporation. Tax-exempt status is needed both to avoid having to pay income tax on the foundation's income and to permit tax-deductible donations and conservation easements to be made to it. Donations made to a 501(c)(iii) organization are fully deductible by the donor for income tax purposes as charitable contributions in the same way as donations to public agencies (which were discussed in chapter 14) are.

Tax-exempt status is granted to foundations because they are seen as a medium through which private wealth is channelled to public purposes. Originally, spheres of charitable activity were believed to be of such public interest that they justified the use of tax incentives to encourage development of foundations. Although government is now involved to some extent in virtually all of these areas of activity, foundations remain because they complement, rather than duplicate, the role of government.

A corporation is a legal entity comprised of individual members but legally recognized as an independent entity. The distinguishing feature of a nonprofit corporation is that it is organized for charitable or educational purposes rather than for private benefit. The corporate status protects individuals from personal liability for corporate debts and liabilities. Although they can be dissolved, corporations are typically perpetual, and for this reason, both public agencies and the business community view them as more stable and businesslike than unincorporated groups.

Foundations are governed by boards of directors whose mandate is to further the aims and purposes set forth in the articles of incorporation and in the bylaws. The board appoints the foundation's senior professional staff and supervises their actions. As tax-exempt organizations, they are prohibited by federal law from contributing to political campaigns and are restricted to an insubstantial amount of legislative lobbying activities.

The Roles of Foundations in Support of Public Agencies

A popular conception of foundations is that they are organizations that give out grants. However, in the past two decades in this field, they have been used extensively as vehicles to provide many other supporting functions for agencies. While foundation grant aid remains an important potential asset, relatively few park and recreation agencies have benefitted from this type of support. In contrast, a much larger number of agencies have benefitted from the other support roles of foundations, which constitute the focus of this chapter.

Figure 18.1 shows that foundations may support public agencies 1) by facilitating the acquisition of donations and grants that would not otherwise be forthcoming to the agency; 2) by being prepared to accept responsibility for, and address issues that involve, risk or controversy that it would be impolitic for a public agency to address; 3) by providing more agility in the market place than an agency's regulatory authority permits, enabling the foundation to act as an intermediary on the agency's behalf in negotiations with property sellers, to engage in real-estate trading, and to use a more extensive array of creative acquisition and financial mechanisms than are available to the agency; 4) by offering specialized expertise that an agency does not possess, is unable to release from other duties to focus on a particular project, or may need to mediate conflicts; and 5) by engaging in projects that extend beyond an agency's jurisdictional boundaries. Each of these potential support roles is discussed in this section.

Facilitate Donations and Grants

Many individuals and corporations will not donate to a public agency because it is an arm of government, but they will donate to a foundation because it is independent of political pressures. They are more comfortable donating to a foundation, even if the donation eventually supports a government project. This sentiment tends to be especially strong if the donation involves land. Those who have owned land for a long time frequently have an emotional attachment to it and passionately are concerned about its future use. Because government agencies are subject to political pressure and are expected to deliver a wide

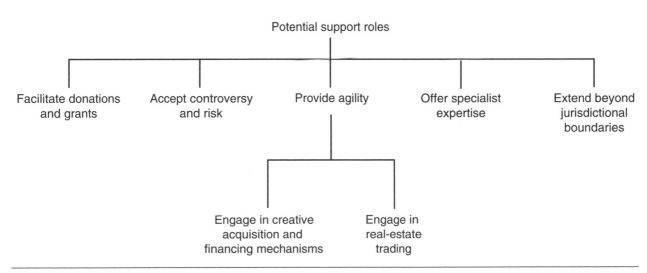

Figure 18.1 Ways in which foundations may support public agencies.

array of services, many people suspect that at some point in the future, agency officials may misuse the donated resources in some way. For example, if a donation of park land is made, the donor may be concerned that in the future, the park may be breached by a highway or may be converted for a school site or waste disposal plant. Lands that were thought to be protected because they were designated as parks have often been threatened and sometimes lost to development. Dams have filled wild canyons, and highways have been constructed through parks. A classic early example was the struggle over Hetch Hetchy Valley in Yosemite National Park. Thirty years after the park's establishment, in the face of substantial national public criticism, the valley was dammed to form a reservoir for the city of San Francisco.

Abuse of a donor's intent by public agencies could be avoided by inserting a revertionary clause indicating that if the donor's intent is abused, then the resources will revert to another specified organization that can be trusted to fulfill the original agreement.

There is a commercial airport inside the boundaries of Grand Teton National Park. It serves the park; the city of Jackson Hole, Wyoming; and the surrounding area. The airlines, ski resorts, tourism officials, and chamber of commerce wanted to extend the runway so larger jets could land there. Conservationists were outraged. They wanted to see the airport closed. The U.S. Department of Interior indicated support for the conservationist strategy and threatened not to renew the airport's lease when it expired.

Regional politicians were supportive of expansion and responded to the department's threat by seeking to have Congress change the park boundaries so that the airport would be outside the department's jurisdiction. They aborted this action, however, when they realized that the land was part of a major donation from John D. Rockefeller, which constituted a substantial proportion of the national park. The donation agreement contained a reverter clause stating that if any of the donated acreage ceased to be part of the national park, then the entire parcel of land would revert to the Jackson Hole Preserve, which is a preservation foundation that the Rockefellers also support.

Although the reverter clause safety mechanism is available, there are both pragmatic and philosophical reasons why donors generally prefer giving their resources to a foundation rather than to a government agency. There are two pragmatic concerns. First, the reverter process is cumbersome and is likely to be controversial. Second, significant tax advantages may accrue from donating resources. (These were discussed in chapter 14.) It is likely to be financially disadvantageous for donations to be returned through a reverter clause to the individual or corporation that donated them. Thus, if a donation is to be given to an agency, it is common for it initially to be made to a foundation, and then for the foundation to donate it to the agency with a reverter clause included. If the conditions of the donation are not honored, then the donation would revert to the foundation, as in the Grand Teton National Park example. This strategy has the added advantage of the foundation serving as a watchdog with legal teeth. It has the desire and the power to demand enforcement of the donation agreement beyond the life of the donor forever. At the same time, if it is impossible to carry out the original charitable intent of the donor, the foundation often has the power to modify the terms of the donation, providing it is in accordance with the general charitable purposes for which the donation was made.

Additionally, despite the safety mechanism of the reverter clause and the low incidence of actual bad faith by agencies, direct donations to an agency are unlikely because of the negative image of government that some people hold and because of the philosophical differences about its role that others hold. William Penn Mott stated:

> At the state level in the past 12 years, the state park foundation has raised $51 million, and contributed 20,000 acres of additional lands to the state park system. So I strongly support and recommend to you the establishment of a foundation. It should be made up of people of integrity, people who are not in government, because today, we have to remember that people are suspicious of government. I have had many people come to me, cuss out the governor of California, and cuss out state government backwards and forwards, then turn around and say to the foundation, we'll give $100,000 to a state park project. But they wouldn't give it to the state. That happens all the time.[1]

The lack of trust in government may relate not only to suspicion of bad faith and philosophical differences but also to a concern that although its intentions may be noble, a park and recreation agency is too cumbersome and subject to too many regulatory constraints to use donated resources efficiently on designated projects.

In Philadelphia, both of these concerns led the recreation commissioner to direct private resources intended for the department's programs through a foundation. A local nonprofit organization, Urban Affairs Coalition, was invited to administer the donations. Thus, it was clear that the money, which was earmarked for specific programs, would not become part of the general city budget. The nonprofit organization would guarantee that donations would only be used for the program designated by the donating party.[2]

Sometimes landowners or companies are resentful of a jurisdiction not authorizing actions that they want to undertake. As one commentator noted: "It is often hard to differentiate between the people you pay your taxes to or the agency official who has just served you with a wetlands violation order, and a new government representative who wants to help you protect your land" (p. 22).[3] Company officials or landowners find it difficult in these conflict situations to contemplate making donations to the jurisdiction. Similarly, the jurisdiction may feel uncomfortable accepting a donation from a company that is likely to be seeking its approval of a permit or zoning change. Again, a donation to a foundation removes any public perception of there being a quid pro quo involved.

In addition to facilitating donations from individuals and corporations, agencies supported by foundations that are seeking financing to launch agency-sponsored projects are sometimes eligible for grants from large grant-aiding foundations (which may have policies not to award grants directly to government agencies) or from state and federal grant programs targeted at support foundations.

The Florida legislature authorized the Partnership in Parks program that enables state funds to be provided directly to state park citizen support organizations and to be matched to private donations for facility development using a 60% (private) to 40% (public) ratio.

Accept Controversy and Risk

It has been observed that public agency officials "often feel that they are on the front line, encum-bered by bureaucracy, politics, the press, and insufficient resources. It is difficult to take risks in such an environment" (p. 164).[4] Foundations are able to invest in projects that may be too controversial for elected officials to support with public funds. This is especially germane in the arts. What constitutes good art or where the parameters of art are fixed are matters of subjective judgement rather than the result of evaluation against objective criteria. Thus, although a city council may be prepared to subsidize arts in the community, its members may be reluctant to select specific projects to support because of the potential for controversy. Is a modern sculpture, which is to be erected outside the city's new recreational center, an inspired piece of art or a heap of ugly metal? Are some of the pieces in a touring art exhibition that is brought to the community pornographic? These types of issues arise periodically. They typically arouse passionate, heated debate, making it inevitable that regardless of their decision, elected officials will be chastised by one side or the other.

An artist who was dying of acquired immunodeficiency syndrome (AIDS) photographed himself in the nude with a noose around his neck; the Nassau County Museum of Art in New York, where his work was displayed, censored the image. A board member noted that this incident demonstrated why "serious artists don't trust a museum run by politicians, any more than politicians trust a museum run by artists. Divorce with alimony is the only way to go if you want to avoid these SNAFUs."

Soon after, further artistic and financial acrimony persuaded the county to cede control of the museum to a private board of trustees. The county, which owned the Georgian-style Gold Coast mansion and its 145 acres of grounds, provided alimony comprising maintenance and $200,000 each year in financial support to the operating foundation compared with $700,000 when it was county operated. The board of trustees hired and paid for the staff. In a five-year period, attendance increased from 10,000 to more than 225,000 each year. The change in operating organizations was positive not only from a financial perspective but also culturally and educationally.[5]

These are the kind of no-win issues that elected officials usually seek to avoid. A strategy that facilitates avoidance is for them to appropriate an amount annually from the city budget to support the arts and to assign the funds to a local arts foundation. The board of this foundation should have wide representation from all community arts groups and should take responsibility for distribution of the public funds. When a controversy arises, elected officials who have adopted this strategy are able to distance themselves from the issue if they choose to do so and need not be directly involved.

At the federal level of government, this role is undertaken by the National Endowment for the Arts. The endowment is funded primarily by an annual appropriation from Congress. It was established in order to reduce the political risk of controversial decisions and to ensure that public funding for the arts would be on a nonpartisan basis. It removed the risk of controversial decisions from government and placed it in the hands of a body widely recognized as having expertise in this area. However, this approach is itself sometimes controversial because it authorizes the expenditure of tax dollars by an organization that does not have direct accountability to the voters.

A support foundation can invest resources and effort to mobilize projects for which it would sometimes be impolitic for an agency to use public funds or its employees' time. The Texas Parks and Wildlife Foundation was able to acquire and move on to its headquarters site a changing room and shower facility that was surplus from Bergstrom Air Force Base, located 5 mi from the headquarters. It was used by the agency's employees who liked to exercise during their lunch hour. Substantial logistical effort was involved in negotiating, site planning, and physically moving the facility, and it would have been controversial to use state funds or employees for the project.

Often a city council or state legislature is reluctant to support financially a new program because its members are skeptical that it will be as effective as its advocates anticipate. Hence, it does not rate high enough on their priority list to qualify for funding. However, a foundation may be prepared to provide funds to initiate such a project with the intent of demonstrating to the legislative body that it is worthy of public support. Frequently it is said that foundation funds represent the venture capital of philanthropy, for they often support new or unproven programs. Indeed, a primary reason that government, through the tax incentives it is able to offer, encourages the forma-

tion of foundations is that foundations can engage in imaginative, high-risk programs that others are unwilling to support.

In the communities of Longview and Kelso in Washington, a coalition of interest groups wanted to launch the Youth After-Hours program in high-crime, high-risk neighborhoods. The program operated in those neighborhoods' schools from the time classes finished until 5:30 P.M. each day and in vacation periods. An initial commitment from Weyerhaeuser Company Foundation to provide major funding for three years was key to the program's success because it provided funding for a time period sufficient for the program to demonstrate its viability.[6]

Provide Agility

The term agility embraces the attributes of speed and flexibility. It enables foundations to support public agencies by responding quickly to property acquisition opportunities that arise in the market place, which public agencies are ill equipped to do. It is rare for a property to enter the market at exactly the right price and exactly the right time for a public agency.[7] Foundations can serve as intermediaries and adjust the variables of time, price, and land configuration so that they are better able to meet the needs of both the landowner and the acquiring agency.

Property transactions often involve delicate timing, the dividing or aggregating of land parcels, and complex tax or legal circumstances. Governments at all levels do not have the flexibility to engage successfully in such transactions. Agencies usually have to solicit public input and await the outcome of a bond referendum or legislative authorization. They have to put appraisals and, sometimes, survey work out to bid, so months may pass before they can make an offer to a landowner. This is likely to result in opportunities being lost. At the federal level, it often takes five years to move a project through the planning, authorization, and appropriation stages to actual acquisition. The laws, regulations, and processes that lead to these delays have been put in place to protect the public interest. However, in some land acquisition situations they do not serve the public interest because such a long timeframe makes it difficult to react to trends or to respond to a willing seller.

To surmount these problems, an agency may invite a foundation to act as an intermediary by engaging in a pre-acquisition. In this role, the foundation acquires a specified property or an option on it with the understanding that the agency will purchase it from the foundation when anticipated funds become available for this purpose. For example, bonds may have been authorized but not yet sold. The following example is a typical, straight-forward illustration of pre-acquisition.

Patience Island in Narragansett Bay, Rhode Island, was a 200-acre undeveloped island that had been earmarked to become part of the Bay Islands Park System. The island was owned by a Narragansett real-estate partnership that had a number of other holdings, had financial difficulties, and was forced to sell. Backed by a letter from the state expressing its interest in purchasing the land, the Nature Conservancy stepped in and bought it for cash. The island was resold to the state a year later.[4]

The pre-acquisition role of foundations is extensive. For example, the U.S. Forest Service's land acquisition program relies heavily on foundations. In a five-year period more than 240 Forest Service acquisitions, involving more than 288,000 acres at a cost of almost $150 million, were purchased from foundations acting as intermediaries.[8]

It should be noted that if a donation for a capital project is made directly to a government agency, then construction of the project will have to go through the agency's formal bureaucratic bidding procedures. If it is made to a foundation and the project subsequently is transferred to the agency after completion, then the foundation can negotiate with preferred contractors to do the work without being restrained by the agency's requirement to accept the lowest bid.

Foundations often are able to buy land at a better price than public agencies can. Reasons for this may include foundations having more time to devote to landowner negotiations; landowners having different expectations when negotiating with foundations than with public agencies; foundations having more experience in negotiating tax-advantaged sales; foundations being unconstrained by government procedures; and foundations not being required to offer fair market value as many public agencies are, so they can negotiate a bargain sale or buy at auction.[9]

Acquisition costs to an agency may be reduced by a foundation holding the desired land until market rates are favorable for the issuance of bonds. It was noted in chapter 2 that a percentage-point difference in bond interest rates amounts to a substantial amount over the life of the bond.

Using a foundation to pre-acquire a property also may avoid escalations in cost. These may arise not only from natural market forces in rapidly appreciating markets and from inflation associated with a delay in the purchase but also from a government agency that is known to be interested in acquiring a specified property. The rise may be attributable to landowners believing that a government entity has deep pockets and, thus, can afford to pay high prices and believing that once a commitment has been made to citizens, elected officials are unlikely to retract it. Alternatively, the rise may be caused by speculators stepping in, purchasing part or all of the land in question, and realizing a profit at taxpayers' expense. Consider the following example.

When Point Reyes National Seashore, north of San Francisco, was authorized by Congress, the estimated cost of land acquisition was $14 million. However, appropriation of the land acquisition money took a number of years. Meanwhile, speculators subdivided properties, recognizing that this substantially increased property values. By the time the $14 million had been expended, the cost had risen astronomically. Although 12 years later nearly $58 million had been spent for acquisition, all of the land still had not been acquired.

In situations such as Point Reyes in which parcels of land owned by many different entities and individuals are to be acquired, a foundation's ability to proceed with discretion and maintain silence about the intended purchases until all have been effected is crucial to avoiding cost escalation. It contrasts with the public disclosure regulations to which park and recreation agencies have to adhere.

In many bond campaigns, the precise parcels of land to be acquired are not identified because of the potential for cost escalation. The uncertainty of how the bond money is to be used may negatively impact some voters. This problem can be surmounted by foundations acquiring options on desired property in advance of the bond issue so that parcels can be specifically identified without fear of cost escalation.

In Portland, a major open-space bond referendum failed, but three years later a $135 million bond for open space was passed. Supporters believe a key difference was that in the second referendum, some key target properties were designated specifically. They had been optioned for purchase by the Trust for Public Land. "The last bond effort was criticized because we weren't specific about which properties might be acquired," said the director of the Regional Parks and Greenspaces Department. "This time TPL's options told the public exactly what land might be protected" (p. 4).[10]

Sometimes using a foundation for pre-acquisition is needed in order to meet the terms of a grant program. Some state and federal grant programs specify that matching funds for a donation that an agency receives are available only during the remaining portion of the fiscal year in which the donation is made and for one additional financial year. (The federal Land and Water Conservation Fund discussed in chapter 11 was one such program.) If the grant funds for this period have already been allocated, then the opportunity for a matching grant is lost. However, an alternative is for the land to be donated to a foundation that, in its role as an intermediary, could hold it until the agency was assured of matching funds and at that time would pass it along to the agency.

Similarly, land frequently has to be acquired shortly after it becomes available either because the donor or seller needs the tax advantages at that time or because if it is not removed from the market, others will purchase it. However, the rules of many matching-grant programs prohibit applicants from negotiating a sale or accepting a donation being used as match until the grant is approved. Again, a foundation can act as an intermediary and acquire the land before selling or donating it to the agency after the matching grant has been obtained.

The Trust for Public Land acted as an intermediary for the city of Garland, Texas, in the purchase of 35 acres for Windsurfer Bay Park on Lake Ray Hubbard. Working in advance of the park department's application to the state for a matching grant, the Trust for Public Land negotiated an option contract with Sunbelt Savings Bank, which owned the property. This assured the city that the property would be available if, and when, it received a $600,000 acquisition matching grant from the state. The application, review, and approval process for the grant often took from 12 to 18 months. If the property had remained on the market during this time period, it was likely that Signal Bay would have been sold to a developer, and the opportunity for a new park would have been lost.[11]

Sources of Pre-Acquisition Finance

A key factor in determining the level of agility that foundations can offer is the extent of funds available to them. In order to be effective in a pre-acquisition role, they need access to a source of interim financing to bridge the period between purchasing property (or an option on it) and reselling it to a public agency. A variety of interim financing strategies are used, but the most common is establishment of a revolving fund. A revolving pre-acquisition fund is defined as a fund that provides loans to buy land with the understanding that the loan will be repaid from a government resale payment, a private fundraising effort, or a combination of the two. The loaned money can then revolve into a new project.[12]

This fund requires securing an initial pool of money from grant-aiding foundations, bequests, or supporters or from profits on previous transactions.

In their pre-acquisition role, foundations may make a profit on transactions by acquiring property at less than fair market value through donations or partial donations and by selling it to the public agency for an amount at, or closer to, fair market value. The profit may be used to create a revolving fund; to fund future acquisitions; to provide the resources that these organizations need to operate; or to cover costs incurred in attempting to negotiate transactions that are never finalized or costs arising from helping public agencies acquire property without the foundation actually being a party to the transactions.

The 3,200-acre Evans Ranch was the largest, most biologically significant undeveloped property remaining along the front range in Colorado. The landowners were in financial need and were forced to sell the property, but they had a desire to protect it from development. The market price was $4.5 million. The Colorado Open Lands foundation secured a one-year option and then brought in noted landscape architect Ian McHarg who created the Stewards of the Valleys concept for the land. The ranch was split into five smaller units of 640 acres each, with each unit containing a 35-acre building area. A conservation easement covered the remaining land. The five units were quickly sold for $1.5 million each, which raised $7.5 million. Colorado Open Lands paid off the $4.5 million cost of the property and generated $3 million to fund its future operations while saving most of the ranch.[13]

The Nature Conservancy sold a property to the U.S. Forest Service for more than $1 million that had been donated to it. The donor made this gift to the Nature Conservancy with the intention and understanding that the Nature Conservancy would sell this property and use the proceeds to acquire other high-priority conservation lands. After deducting its costs in this transaction. The Nature Conservancy realized a gain of more than $877,000.[8]

Some foundations and public agencies have institutionalized the level of profit accruing to the foundation from resale of the property by agreeing on a predetermined fee for this service.

The Alachua Conservation Trust bases its fee for this service on the notion of shared savings. When the total deal costs the government less, the fee to Alachua Conservation Trust to support its overall work will be higher. This arrangement, which Alachua Conservation Trust pioneered and other foundations in Florida adopted, provides an incentive to foundations to negotiate the best prices possible and to minimize transaction costs, both of which benefit taxpayers.[14]

There is concern, such as in the examples described, that government's total acquisition cost may exceed a property's value because tax benefits that donors receive represent a cost to the federal and state governments which forego that tax income. For example, if it is assumed in the Nature Conservancy illustration that the fair market value of the property was $1.5 million and that the donor claimed a 45% tax deduction (see table 14.1) when he or she gave the property to the Nature Conservancy, then the government's total cost was $1.675 million (i.e., $675,000 in taxes foregone and $1 million purchase price from the Nature Conservancy).[8]

It should be noted that foundations also may experience financial loss from these transactions because either they willingly sell land to an agency for a price below its acquisition cost, or its acquisition cost is greater than the appraised fair market value that a public agency legally is authorized to pay. The losses are willingly incurred because the transactions help to further the foundations' goals.

All federal, and many other, agencies do not have the authority to purchase land for more than its appraised value without having specific congressional approval, which may take a long time to obtain. This is frustrating when the difference between the appraised value and the selling price is relatively small. When this situation occurred in the National Park Service's attempt to buy a small additional tract at Petersburg Battlefield in Virginia, the Conservancy Fund purchased the land, absorbed the small amount of money that had blocked the agreement, and sold it to the National Park Service for the appraised value.[15]

Alternative interim financing sources include securing a bridging loan from a bank, from a national support foundation, or from a grant-aiding foundation (these types of foundations are described in chapter 19). Some states now have programs that authorize direct grants and access to loan funds for nonprofit organizations for planning, acquisition, or management of land protection projects. The California State Coastal Conservancy established the first of these programs in 1982. Others have subsequently been enacted in Rhode Island, Vermont, New Jersey, Iowa, Maryland, Wisconsin, Florida, and Connecticut.[9]

Wisconsin's Natural Areas Match program stipulates that donations of privately raised funds or qualified natural land to the state for conservation purposes (including donations of restrictions on private lands) generate a dollar-for-dollar match of state funds for buying natural areas.[3]

Foundations often limit their financial risk in this pre-acquisition role by obtaining purchase options on the land and exercising these options just before selling the land to a public agency or by negotiating a letter of intent with a public agency that guarantees the foundation's reimbursement if, and when, the agency purchases the property. Option arrangements grant the prospective buyer the exclusive right (but not the obligation) to purchase a property during the period that the agreement specifies. Before the option expires, the buyer must either exercise the right to purchase on the terms specified in the agreement or forego this right, in which case the seller is free to sell the property to another. The option binds the seller and not the buyer. By negotiating an option whereby the landowner accepts a small fraction of the property's value as a type of down payment, a foundation is able to reduce substantially the amount of time and money it must invest in holding the property. Indeed, a foundation is able to leverage millions of dollars in potential acquisitions through relatively small option commitments. Although the option amount usually is applied toward a property's purchase price, it is generally not refundable in the event of the transaction not being consummated.

Melrose was one of more than 30 outstanding antebellum homes that attracted visitors to Natchez, Mississippi. Economic conditions forced the owner to offer it for sale, and there was concern that its grounds would be subdivided. The owner wanted to protect it but could not wait for the lengthy period of time that the National Park Service needed to receive authority to purchase it. The Trust for Public Land purchased an option for one year and used the time to lobby Congress and to assist the National Park Service in acquiring funds for it. In this time period, the Trust for Public Land also paid for appraisals, surveys, inventories, and other tasks that had to be completed before a transaction could be consummated. When authorization was obtained, the Trust for Public Land assigned its option to the National Park Service.[15]

In addition to pre-acquisition, a foundation's agility facilitates two other support roles. They include the ability to acquire real estate using financial transactions with mechanisms not available to public agencies and the authorization to engage in a limited amount of real-estate trading.

Creative Acquisition and Financial Mechanisms

Agencies are constrained by the limiting nature of the legislation and regulations that authorize them to acquire property and finance transactions, so they lack flexibility in the method of payment and type of program terms that they are able to offer. For example, agencies are likely to lack the authority to bind land with options until donor or purchase funds can be arranged, to bid for land at auctions, to issue promissory notes or mortgages, or to pay for property in installments. In contrast, foundations specializing in acquiring property for park or recreational purposes are empowered to act in these ways.

The Enchanted Forest was a 235-acre remnant of old-growth oak woodland near Cape Canaveral, Florida, that harbored many rare birds and mammals. Local environmentalists had tried for years to protect the property that was to be developed as an industrial park, but they could not pay the $10 million price. The developer and owners had financial trouble and defaulted on their mortgage.

Financing a Park With a Lease Agreement

The city of Austin was interested in acquiring a 220-acre expanse of forest and pasture, which was located just 2 mi from downtown, known as College Park. It was scheduled to be developed, but when a depressed real-estate market forced the developer into bankruptcy, the land became available at a fire sale price of $1 million. However, the city lacked the cash to purchase it, and no bond issue was scheduled in the near future.

The Trust for Public Land worked with the city to formulate an acquisition strategy. The trust purchased the land and executed a lease-donation agreement with the city. The agreement provided for the city to make an initial lease payment of $250,000 and similar annual lease payments in the succeeding three years. At the end of the lease term, Austin would have the right to buy out the land's underlying fee title for a small additional cost or, at the discretion of the Trust for Public Land, receive it by donation.

By structuring the acquisition in this manner, the city council could pay for the park out of its annual budget appropriations and avoid committing itself beyond a term of one year for each lease payment (a legal constraint imposed in most municipalities in the United States). In addition, the lease-donation arrangement allowed Austin to apply for state matching funds to secure a park-development grant for the property.

Because the city's lease payments were subject to annual budget appropriations, the Trust for Public Land was at some risk in recovering its acquisition costs. However, given the city's credit worthiness and the benefits of providing a park to this area that was underserved with parks, the Trust for Public Land chose to accept the risk.

From Ted Harrison. Financing parks with leases. Land and people: Trust for Public Land annual report. *Trust for Public Land: San Francisco. Pages 14-15. 1993.*

The property was auctioned on the courthouse steps, and the Nature Conservancy purchased it for $3.9 million. Brevard County received a matching grant from the state, so when the county purchased the property from the Nature Conservancy for this price, it cost county taxpayers less than $2 million. This acquisition was only possible because the Nature Conservancy was able to act as intermediary and to buy the property at auction.[3]

Sometimes payments for land have to be made in installments over time, either because this is dictated by a landowner's tax situation or because an agency cannot accumulate all of the money at once. In these situations, a foundation may act as an intermediary. It can purchase the land in total or in annual installments in accordance with the landowner's wishes, and it can convey the land in total or fractional interests to the agency as funds become available.

The Pennsylvania Game Commission was eager to purchase a 3,835-acre, pristine glacial bog but needed to spread the project over two years to capture enough federal matching funds. The Nature Conservancy purchased the property and then conveyed it to the government agency in two separate installments as matching funds became available.[3]

Engage in Real-Estate Trading

Foundations are able to accept donations and make property purchases that may require engaging in real-estate trading practices, such as exchanging or selling property or commercially exploiting it. Statutory hurdles generally prohibit public agencies from engaging in such actions. These statutory constraints are appropriate because it is not desirable that property acquired for park and recreational purposes should be sold to the private sector without an extensive public debate of the issue and a subsequent vote of public or legislative approval. Thus, in contrast to a public agency, a foundation may accept a property donation that has relatively low utility for park and recreational purposes, but the foundation then may sell it on the open market and use the proceeds to acquire property that is more desirable for these uses.

In essence, this means that although legal restrictions exist, a foundation can use real-estate activity as a source of fundraising. If it engages in substantial development activities or otherwise acts as a real-estate dealer, the foundation will lose its tax-exempt status. Nevertheless, within these limitations, foundations may accept property that has no value for park or recreational purposes, and then they can either resell it in the market or trade it with a developer for land that is useful for these purposes.

The Santa Monica Mountains Conservancy in California negotiated a bargain sale of 3,035 acres owned by Chevron Corporation. The property combined with nearby holdings to form a nearly 6,000-acre chain of public wildlands on the northern slope of the Santa Susanna Mountains. The bargain sale price was $4.9 million. Half of the cost had to be paid immediately, and the other half had to be paid within the next five years. The Conservancy was able to raise the immediate $2.45 million by selling another 53-acre property in its inventory to the city of Santa Clarita. This sale made the acquisition possible. It planned to raise much of the remainder from state grants, anticipating that sometime during the next five years, voters would approve a state bond issue.[16]

When a government agency considers acquiring a large parcel of land from an owner, it may find that the area contains parcels that are of minimal use for its purposes. However, the owner typically will not be willing to divide the parcel; it is an all-or-nothing deal. A foundation can be used to resolve the conundrum. The foundation can purchase the entire tract and then resell the unneeded parcels, conveying to the public agency only the land it wants. Often, the land resold is important for uses, such as agriculture, housing, and economic development, and elements in the local community may oppose its removal from such uses and from the local tax rolls. Hence, the foundation's actions as an intermediary may resolve a political, as well as a management, problem.[3]

Property was donated to a foundation in San Diego with the proviso that it was to be used to support the parks department. An analysis indicated that rather than develop the relatively small piece of land into a park in an area that was quite well endowed with larger parks and rather than sell it, the foundation should lease it to commercial concerns for development. The returns on these leases in which escalator clauses were included were likely to yield a significant income stream that the foundation could use to support future park projects.

The Brandywine Conservancy formed a limited partnership to protect the 5,300-acre King Ranch

An Illustration of the Time and Expertise Needed to Bring Projects to Fruition

At 760 acres, Hatchet Ranch was the largest ranch in Wyoming's Buffalo Valley, an enclave of ranch land within the Bridger-Teton National Forest at the eastern gateway to Grand Teton National Park. The U.S. Forest Service wanted to protect the valley lands, including Hatchet Ranch, from development. A developer was prepared to pay $4.5 million for the property, and the Forest Service had only $2.8 million appropriated for the purchase.

The Jackson Hole Land Trust provided expertise and staff assistance to facilitate the transaction. As part of their protection strategy, they identified potential conservation buyers (see chapter 4) who were interested in buying the land as ranch land subject to conservation easements being imposed on it. When the four-party closing between the seller, the Forest Service, the land trust, and the conservation buyers finally took place, the 21 documents on the table and the 15 people around it only hinted at the complexity of the transaction. The land trust played a critical role by accomplishing the following:

- Negotiating a considerable reduction in the overall purchase price
- Putting up forfeitable earnest money to satisfy the sellers that the conservationists were serious
- Tracking down and contacting 14 separate owners of mineral rights and two owners of rights-of-way to clarify the title
- Addressing unexpected legalities and costs resulting from hazardous materials being found on the site
- Negotiating conservation easement language with three levels of the Forest Service and two levels of the Office of the General Counsel of the U.S. Department of Agriculture
- Working with three different potential conservation buyers
- Working with the state's U.S. Congressional delegation to obtain a special waiver to expedite congressional oversight

The project took 3,000 person-hours (50% of two people's time for one year). Much of this time was spent addressing emergencies: a problematic appraisal, problems with the title, and hazardous waste problems. The foundation had the expertise and personnel resources to bring the project to fruition, whereas with an extensive range of other duties to perform, government officials simply did not have the time.

From Eve Endicott. Local partnership with government. Granted with permission from Land Conservation Through Public-Private Partnerships, *edited by Eve Endicott, © Island Press 1993. Published by Island Press: Washington, DC, and Covelo, CA. Pages 199-200.*

in southeastern Pennsylvania. The partnership bought the property and donated an 800-acre natural area to the Brandywine Conservancy. It then placed the ranch under a conservation easement and resold large lots that were subject to the terms of the easement.

Offer Specialized Expertise

Foundations that specialize in park acquisition often have acquired substantial expertise in that area. Negotiation techniques, real-estate finance strategies, tax planning, and knowledge of property law are some of the tools that these organizations can offer to public agencies. Sometimes, a public agency needs a foundation simply to provide the staff to negotiate an acquisition; to advance the money for an option, appraisal, or survey; or to arrange a closing. Even if an agency has the expertise to do some of these things, its own staff may be too committed with other projects to handle a particular transaction. Some insight into the extent of the time commitment and expertise involved can be gauged from the experience of the Jackson Hole Land Trust in negotiating the protection of Hatchet Ranch, described in "An Illustration of the Time and Expertise needed to Bring Projects to Fruition."

As private organizations with essentially public purposes, foundations can be effective mediators in reducing or eliminating the polarization and antipathy that sometimes characterize relationships between public agencies and developers. They can create an atmosphere of possibility around a stalled or seemingly impossible project and can make it work.[3] Developers are often answerable to investors, which makes it difficult for them to accept willingly project modifications that adversely affect profitability. Park and recreation agencies are constrained by regulations. Their actions are subject to legislative, executive, and judicial approval and are subjected to both informed and uninformed public scrutiny. A foundation's independence, acceptance of risk, and agility gives it a degree of flexibility that may not be available to developers and agencies. Further, its expertise in structuring complex land transactions and innovative financing packages can be crucial to successful mediation.

The Balcones canyon lands of the Texas hill country was an oasis of hills and streams near Austin over which there had been repeated clashes between developers and conservationists. The Nature Conservancy helped organize and then chaired a planning committee of government officials, environmentalists, developers, and other business groups to develop a multipurpose resource protection and use plan.

There were federally listed endangered species in the area, so the key element in the plan was the habitat conservation plan required under the Endangered Species Act. Instead of requiring developers to fight for their projects individually and face costly individual federal reviews and possible litigation, the final conservation plan identified whole areas appropriate for development. At the same time, the final plan called for a preserve system of about 65,000 acres including several entire watersheds and large expanses of the oak and juniper habitat that the critically endangered golden cheeked warbler and black-capped vireo required. These species are much more likely to survive in large preserves than in the disconnected protected parcels that would have resulted from piecemeal negotiations with the developers.[3]

A foundation's expertise may also be used to lobby on behalf of an agency and rally public support. Agency personnel cannot lobby legisla-tors, but foundations can do this provided it is restricted to an "insubstantial" amount. They may assist agencies by planning and implementing a bond campaign. If a foundation invests substantial resources in such an effort, an agency indirectly may reimburse it by asking the foundation to act as the pre-acquisition agency's intermediary on some of the property transactions that are funded from the bond issue. The foundation could make a profit on its resale of land to the agency to recover its campaign costs.

Extend Beyond Jurisdictional Boundaries

Foundations are not confined by political boundaries as public agencies are. Therefore, they are free to operate across jurisdictions. When a resource extends beyond a local, county, or state boundary, as is often the case with wildlife habitat or watersheds, this a useful attribute.

A canal in Louisiana across from Vicksburg National Military Park was part of General Ulysses Grant's strategy to control the Mississippi River and split the Confederacy. The owner offered to donate it to the National Park Service, but the service was unable to accept the offer because the property was outside the park's authorized boundary. The land to be acquired fell within the territory of the National Park Service's Southwest regional office in Santa Fe, New Mexico, whereas the park in Mississippi reported to the regional office in Atlanta. The Conservation Fund was able to accept the donation and coordinate negotiations involving the two National Park Service regional offices. When Congress adopted the legislation authorizing a boundary adjustment, the foundation donated the land to the park.[14]

Summary

Foundations are defined as nongovernmental, nonprofit corporations that are organized and operated for the benefit of the general public. They are legally independent entities that have tax-exempt status, enabling tax-deductible donations to be made to them. While some agencies have benefitted from grants awarded by foundations, many more have benefitted from the other five support roles developed by foundations, which were discussed in this chapter.

Foundations facilitate donations and grants from individuals and corporations that will not donate to public agencies because they are an arm of government but will donate to foundations because they are independent and free of political pressure. A second support role is that they are able to accept controversy and risk that public agencies seek to avoid. This is especially useful in the arts because subjective judgments as to what constitutes good art frequently are controversial. Foundations are a potential source of support for innovative, high-risk, unproven programs that public officials are reluctant to fund because they are skeptical of their effectiveness.

Perhaps the major attribute of foundations is that they provide agility. This enables them to support public agencies, which do not have agility, by responding quickly to property acquisition opportunities that arise in the market place. They engage in pre-acquisition; this involves purchasing a specified property (or option on it) with the understanding that the agency will subsequently purchase it from the foundation when funds become available. Foundations are often able to acquire the land more cheaply than public agencies, and pre-acquisition avoids the probability of later escalations in cost.

Consistent support for pre-acquisitions requires a foundation to have the bridging financing capacity necessary to do this. Most achieve it by establishing a revolving fund, which initially may be built up with grants from grant-aiding foundations, bequests, or supporters; with profits from transactions that accrue when property is acquired at less than fair market value and resold to agencies at a price closer to market value; by bridging loans secured from a bank, a national support foundation, or a grant-aiding foundation; or with state grant or loan funds.

Extensive use of options gives foundations leverage to support public agencies by acquiring real estate and structuring financial transactions with mechanisms not available to agencies and by engaging in a limited amount of real-estate trading.

Specialized expertise is a support function available from foundations that focus on park acquisition. Negotiation techniques, real-estate finance strategies, tax planning, and knowledge of property law are some of the tools that these organizations can offer to public agencies. As private organizations with public purposes, foundations can be effective mediators in alleviating any polarization between public agencies and developers. Foundations also may be used to rally public support and to engage in some limited amount of legislative lobbying. Finally, foundations are able to operate across jurisdictions, which is particularly useful when acquisition of amenities that cross local, county, or state boundaries is being considered.

References

1. Mott, William Penn. 1981. Financing in the future. A presentation at Texas A&M University.

2. Perlmutter, Felice D. and Ram A. Cnann. 1995. Entrepreneurship in the public sector: The horns of a dilemma. *Public Administration Review* 55(1): 29-36.

3. Endicott, Eve. 1993. Preserving natural areas: The Nature Conservancy and its partners. In *Land conservation through public-private partnerships*, edited by Eve Endicott. Washington, DC: Island Press, 17-42.

4. Bendick, Robert L. 1993. State partnerships to preserve open space: Lessons from Rhode Island and New York. In *Land conservation through public-private partnerships*, edited by Eve Endicott. Washington, DC: Island Press, 149-171.

5. Parks, Steve. 1995. Portrait of a young museum: The Nassau County Museum of Art is thriving, five years after its separation from local politics. *Newsday*, February 6, B4.

6. Morehouse, Gloria and Kristin Renzema. 1996. Youth after-hours program. In *Recreation programs that work for at-risk youth*, edited by Peter A. Witt and John L. Crompton. State College, PA: Venture Publishing, 151-160.

7. Poole, William. 1993. Preserving urban and suburban gardens and parks: The Trust for Public Land and its partners. In *Land conservation through public-private partnerships*, edited by Eve Endicott. Washington, DC: Island Press, 61-82.

8. U.S. General Accounting Office. 1994. *Federal lands: Land acquisitions involving nonprofit conservation organizations*. Washington, DC: General Accounting Office. June, GAO/RCED-94-149.

9. Myers, Phyllis. 1992. *Lessons from the states*. Washington, DC: Land Trust Alliance.

10. Poole, William. 1995. Portland's choice. *Land and People* 7(1): 3-6.

11. Harrison, Ted. 1995. Resource protection partners: Expanding the capacity of open space acquisition programs. *Texas Recreation and Park Society Magazine* May/June: 10-13.

12. Endicott, Eve (editor). 1993. *Land conservation through public-private partnerships*. Washington, DC: Island Press.

13. Miller, Anita P. and John B. Wright. 1991. Report of the subcommittee on innovative growth management measures: Preservation of agricultural land and open space. *The Urban Lawyer* 23(4): 821-844.

14. Endicott, Eve and contributors. 1993. Local partnerships with government. In *Land conservation through public-private partnerships*, edited by Eve Endicott. Washington, DC: Island Press, 195-218.

15. Brown, Warren. 1993. Public-private land conservation partnerships in and around national parks. In *Land conservation through public-private partnerships*, edited by Eve Endicott. Washington, DC: Island Press, 104-128.

16. Levin, Myron. 1995. Chevron to sell 3000 acres in heart of woodlands. *Los Angeles Times*, April 6, B1.

CHAPTER 19

TYPES OF FOUNDATIONS

The previous chapter described the legal structure of foundations and the variety of ways that they can contribute to supporting the work of park and recreation agencies. This chapter identifies the various types of foundations, discusses their differentiating characteristics, and delineates their specific niches in supporting agencies' work.

The taxonomy of foundations shown in figure 19.1 forms the framework for the discussion in this chapter. It identifies three main types of foundations: operating foundations, which directly deliver services; support foundations, which solicit resources to assist agency delivery of services; and grant-aiding foundations, which are a potential source of funds for agencies and their support foundations. Hence, the continuum at the bottom of figure 19.1 indicates that operating foundations are closest to the ultimate user or visitor to an amenity and that grant-aiding foundations are farthest removed from the ultimate beneficiaries. The subcategories within each of the three main categories reflect differences in the mission or scope of foundations.

Operating Foundations

Public operating foundations are perhaps the most endemic type of foundation in the parks and recreation field. Almost every local system has recreational activity groups, especially youth sports organizations, such as Little League, soccer, softball, and swimming clubs, that use its facilities, and many of them are likely to be 501(c)(iii) organizations. The role of these groups in delivering recreation services was discussed in chapter 12. This section focuses on operating foundations with forms and origins different from those of recreational activity groups.

An operating foundation uses its resources to deliver a service directly. The IRS defines it as a foundation that spends substantially all of its net income directly for the active conduct of the activities constituting the purpose for which it is organized and operated. Thus, in contrast to grant-aiding or support foundations, an operating foundation's funds are expended on direct service delivery rather than on making grants or other-

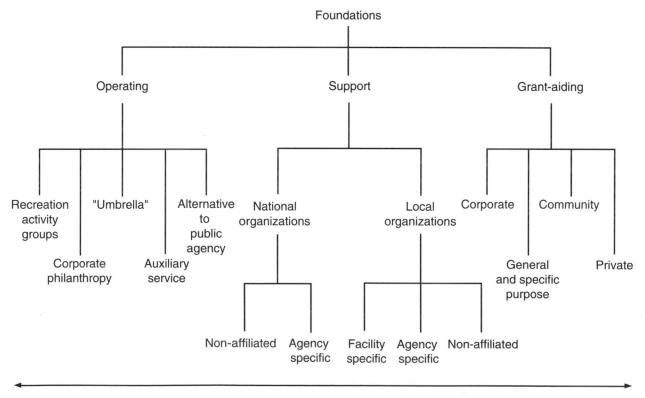

Figure 19.1 The different types of foundations available to assist park and recreation agencies.

wise facilitating the work of other organizations that then deliver the service. Most operating foundations are supported by membership dues, surplus operating revenues, or subsidy from a grant-aiding foundation.

With the exception of those operating foundations that are expressions of corporate philanthropy, almost all of them involve a joint arrangement with a public agency. Usually, the agency retains ownership of the land, structures, and improvements but is relieved of some managerial or programmatic responsibilities. Many agencies believe that they are able to exercise greater control by working with an operating foundation than by contracting with or leasing to a commercial entity. In many cases, an operating foundation may have better ties with the local community than will a commercial entity. This may translate into more donation and volunteer support and may engender a greater sense of identity, pride, and common purpose.

Operating foundations offer public agencies another tool with which they can respond to resource allocation problems and difficulties associated with required bureaucratic procedures. As jurisdictions continue to evolve from their direct provider role to being catalysts for service provision, it seems likely that operating foundations will become increasingly prominent. Peter Drucker has argued: "a well-managed nonprofit gets at least twice the bang out of each buck that a government agency does" (p. 19).[1] He also has suggested that a move into nonprofitization through the use of operating foundations will emerge as a natural extension of privatization. Drucker's views have credibility because he was the earliest popularizer of privatization in his 1969 book, *The Age of Discontinuity*, at a time when most ridiculed the concept.[2]

Beyond their utility for delivering youth sports (recreational activity groups), operating foundations appear to have emerged in response to four different sets of stimuli. First are those operating foundations that were expressions of corporate philanthropy. Second are umbrella operating foundations whose purpose is to serve as a vehicle for cooperative governance that enables a number of different partners to pool their resources to offer services. Third are those established primarily in national and state parks for the purpose of delivering auxiliary services, which complement the services that the public agency managing the facility offers. Fourth, interest is growing in the use of

operating foundations as alternatives to public agency management. In this context, they take responsibility for managing a whole entity rather than designated auxiliary services within it. Operating foundations that are organized to accomplish each of these four missions are discussed in this section.

Expression of Corporate Philanthropy

The most extensive operating foundation with this mission is the Leroy Springs Foundation, based in Lancaster, South Carolina. An overview of the scope of its operations is provided in "Leroy Springs & Company Operating Foundation" on page 494.

Another well-known example of an operating foundation is the James Foundation. The founder's family owned an ironworks in the area. She supplemented this by acquiring 1,500 acres of attractive land around it. Upon her death, ownership of this land passed to the operating foundation. The James Foundation employs from 50 to 55 people, including people hired for seasonal work. It is located in Meramec Village, Missouri, which has a population of approximately 3,000. The foundation was formed as a result of a substantial bequest of 1,800 acres of land, buildings, and cash. The original endowment was $2.5 million, and this has now grown to more than $40 million. However, there are other beneficiaries from the endowment, so the James Foundation receives approximately $250,000 per year. The land was developed into Meramec Spring Park, which is a highly used and diversified public-use area, offering trout fishing, playgrounds, shelters, historic structures, and trails in a natural setting. In the 1960s, there was a substantial increase in the endowment's value. This enabled the foundation to satisfy additional local needs by developing the 56-acre St. James Park in the center of the community, containing a swimming pool complex, playgrounds, tennis courts, and a fishing lake. The foundation developed and now operates the James Memorial Library, which is a regional library serving an eight-county region. Finally, it contracted with the city to operate a nine-hole municipal golf course and a cemetery (which includes the gravesite of the original benefactor).

Umbrella Foundations

When a coalition of public and nonprofit organizations decide to invest funds to develop a facility or deliver a service, the most efficient vehicle to

Leroy Springs & Company Operating Foundation

Leroy Springs & Company Inc. is an operating foundation that was established by the president of Springs Cotton Mills in 1938 with funding provided through the Springs Foundation (the Springs Mills' corporate foundation). The president strongly believed in supporting and unifying community life; he particularly believed in providing his workers with opportunities for scholarship and recreation that they otherwise might not obtain. Initially, Leroy Springs & Company's activity focused exclusively on creating scholarship opportunities, but in 1953 the operating foundation was given substantial funds from the Springs Foundation to purchase several recreational facilities.

Leroy Springs & Company's philosophy is to provide recreational activities not otherwise available in the communities it serves and to make its services as inexpensive as possible so that all members of the community can participate, especially the low-wage earner. Their facilities are open to all who reside or work in the towns of Fort Mill and Chester and in Lancaster County (all in South Carolina). The foundation avoids duplication of services that local governments provide unless communities demonstrate the need for expansion of programs. The foundation cooperates extensively with public agencies. For example, Leroy Springs & Company shares its baseball fields with city-supported teams, and local high schools offer their gymnasia for company-sponsored basketball programs.

By the mid-1990s, the operating foundation had recreational assets valued at $50 million and an annual budget for its programs of $12.5 million. Almost $11 million of the annual budget comprised income from its operations, while the balance was a subsidy that the Springs Foundation provided. Staffing consisted of 250 full-time and 100 seasonal employees who serviced approximately 1 million visitations to their facilities.

More than 86% of total income was derived from the foundation's Springmaid Beach resort operation, which was located on the ocean front at Myrtle Beach, South Carolina. This resort included a hotel with 432 rooms, a large campground, an outdoor pool, and a fishing pier. Springmaid Beach originally was conceived to provide Springs Mills' employees with affordable and easily available facilities for vacationing, particularly with families. That philosophy has been retained, and in the mid-1990s, it was still possible for the foundation's target population to stay at the hotel for less than $10 per room per night, even though the rooms were high quality and located on a prime beach-front site!

Leroy Springs & Company's other major complexes are located in Lancaster, Fort Mill, Chester, and Kershaw. These embrace three golf courses, extensive athletic fields, three swimming pools, three community centers, bowling lanes, and other amenities. In addition, the foundation purchased 280 acres of mountain property near the Blue Ridge Parkway and equipped it with cabins, a bunkhouse, campsites, shelters, and stables.

The foundation monitored the recreation needs of its target population on an ongoing basis and made recommendations to the Springs Foundation as to how to best meet those needs. The Springs Foundation provided the funds for all Leroy Springs & Company's capital improvements.

accomplish their goal may be an independent operating foundation with all of the partner organizations represented on its governing board. An example of this approach was the Long Center in Clearwater, Florida.

The Long Center was developed and subsequently operated by a foundation. The facility was established to provide a centrally located, accessible facility that met all of the community's youth sports needs. The outdoor facilities included athletic fields, a track, an outdoor swimming pool, and basketball and tennis courts. The indoor fa-

cilities included space for soccer and tennis, a three-court hardwood gymnasium, an adult fitness room, 75,000 sq ft of classrooms, and aquatic facilities. The capital cost of $15 million was far beyond the reach of any one entity but was achieved by an array of organizations serving multiple clienteles who pooled their resources. They included the Clearwater Parks and Recreation Department; YWCA of Clearwater; Upper Pinellas Association of Retarded Citizens; city of Safety Harbor Leisure Services; and Clearwater for Youth, which was a youth sports organization. The operation was funded from user fees, concessions, sponsorships, and donations, but any annual deficit was met by an assessment on the partners.[3]

Sometimes organizations within an area have recognized advantages in cooperating to promote their services and have formed an operating foundation for this purpose. The extended promotional effort emerging from several agencies and organizations cooperating may generate benefits to each that are greater than those that each entity could obtain from its own more-limited promotional budget.

Florida's First Coast of Golf was established by a group of Professional Golf Association tour executives, golf professionals, and marketing professionals in tourism to promote the First Coast as a golf destination. The area had built some of the best golf courses in the country, both public and private, but the courses had substantial excess capacity that the operators wanted to fill by attracting more nonresident golfers. The organization was modeled after Myrtle Beach Golf Holidays, which was a foundation that had been doing this work in Myrtle Beach, South Carolina, for many years. Florida's First Coast of Golf developed literature and disseminated it through media investments in golf publications. They purchased booths at consumer golf shows, and they sponsored familiarization tours for golf or travel writers so that the writers could become better acquainted with the area's opportunities by playing some of the courses.[4]

Deliver Auxiliary Services for Public Agencies

Many federal and natural resource agencies have established cooperative associations or friends groups to develop, provide, and sell auxiliary services. Agencies often are unable to deliver efficiently many auxiliary services that their visitors seek due to a host of government regulations pertaining to things such as the printing, publishing, and quality of publications; prohibition of on-site sales to visitors; and purchasing and personnel hiring procedures.

The role of cooperating associations is particularly prominent in the National Park Service. They were first recognized by Congress in 1946, and these associations now assist in more than 300 units of the system. In general, these nonprofit associations produce interpretive materials such as guide leaflets, pictures, crafts, maps, and books; acquire historic objects and develop displays;

install museums and other facilities; distribute educational and scientific materials produced by the Park Service; operate book stores and sales counters; furnish newsletters about park activities to visitors; conduct tours, interpretive lectures, and films; and operate living history sites at which craftsmen exhibit and demonstrate their handiwork with old crafts and answer visitors' questions.[5] They also identify gaps in the spectrum of educational materials and opportunities and seek to service those unmet needs by commissioning new resources, materials, or programs.

Cooperating associations sometimes assist the Park Service in less conventional ways. For example, one year in Crater Lake, the association printed and set up road signs around the park because park funds were low and because, according to a Park Service official: "It would have probably taken months to get formal approval, requisition, and printing when those signs were needed yesterday." Some cooperating associations, for example at Golden Gate National Recreation Area and at Jefferson National Expansion Memorial, have hired directors of development to lead in fundraising and friend-raising efforts.[5]

The Park Service strongly influences the organization and activities of the associations. A Park Service employee (typically the chief park interpreter or historian) works with the cooperating association. Most of the associations make extensive use of volunteers, but many also employ paid business managers and clerical staff. Their merchandise and pricing decisions are subject to the Park Service's approval. The Park Service has compiled a list of appropriate items that associations may sell and exercises complete editorial and design control over all publications.[5]

At the state level, similar nonprofit corporations function in a variety of roles ranging from control of concessions, to provision of an array of supplementary services within a park, to responsibility for operating a whole park. Advantages and benefits accruing to an agency from using nonprofit corporations to deliver these services include the following:

- The revenue and profits available to the agency are greater. All profits are dedicated to public use, whereas the agency receives only a percentage of gross receipts from traditional agreements with private entrepreneurs.

- Some concessions and services are fringe operations; that is, the potential for profit by private enterprise is small, so entrepreneurs are reluctant to participate. Nonprofit corporations are able to use volunteer labor, which reduces their operating costs and enables them to operate on a break-even basis; this option is not often available to commercial enterprises.

Alternative to Public Agency Management

In an increasing number of situations, the mandate of operating foundations has been extended beyond that of an auxiliary role to that of assuming responsibility for management of selected public facilities. In most cases, this has been stimulated by the withdrawal of public funds from a facility and the subsequent emergence of a group that is interested in maintaining or upgrading it, which forms an operating foundation to accomplish this goal. This is illustrated in the following three examples.

The National Park Service was responsible for the 128-acre Turkey Run Farm in northern Virginia, but major budget cuts forced the service to schedule its closure. Rather than see the park close, citizens and businessmen founded an operating foundation called Friends of Turkey Run Park. Supporters included some of the Washington, DC, area's largest businesses including Marriott, Mobil Oil, First American Bank of Virginia, and The Morris Foundation. Employees of the popular 18th century working farm became employees of the operating foundation. The Friends were able to operate the facility at a lower cost by using fewer employees and by providing compensation time rather than paying overtime.

The McDonald Park Youth Tennis Center of the New York Junior Tennis League, which was a 501(c)(iii) organization, operated a free tennis program for boys and girls from ages 6 to 18 years at an outdoor park in Brooklyn, New York. The seven-court tennis facility in the park had been neglected by the city because of budget cuts, and the courts were not playable. Therefore, the New York Junior Tennis League requested that the facility be turned over to them to operate. The parks department enthusiastically agreed, recognizing that an established program would discourage vandalism; would revive a deteriorating facility; and if things went as planned, would draw youngsters back into the park.

As the operating foundation, New York Junior Tennis League renovated the complex using funding from donations. Daily maintenance was the responsibility of the center's staff and the players. The league provided all equipment including rackets and balls. Because no fees were charged, all children could participate. With support and encouragement from the local school district and neighborhood association, the tennis center became the most popular and successful tennis site in Brooklyn. In a typical year it had 1,200 registered players.[6]

Asphalt Green was a 5-acre recreational complex on the east side of Manhattan in New York, containing a park, playing fields, and a youth sports and arts center. The city leased the site for $1 per year to a neighborhood foundation that took care of all buildings, operations, and programming with funds from government grants, foundations, and corporations. The foundation transformed the original concrete, vacant, unused city block into a heavily used park and recreational complex. It was used by more than 100 organized park groups including 55 schools.

In other cases in which operating foundations have assumed management of public facilities, the government perceived this to be a superior option to a public agency delivering the services. With federal funds, Garden Grove, California, built the Village Green Cultural Arts Complex, containing an art gallery, a performing arts theater, and an outdoor amphitheater. It formed a nonprofit organization to manage and operate the complex. The city's reasons for forming the organization were two-fold: to avoid the political problems of programming and to avoid operating a program believed to be far from a traditional city service and one in which cities inherently lack the flexibility to manage efficiently. (For example, if the costume person cannot finish the costumes before the opening of a performance, then management may need to purchase clothing at the last minute, which is a task that is likely to be difficult under city purchasing procedures.) The city retained ownership of the facility and was responsible for building alterations, renovations, and exterior maintenance of both the grounds and building, as well as for utilities. The city contributed approximately $50,000 each year to operating expenses and appointed a 17-member citizen board as trustees for the operating foundation. The foundation paid for direct operating costs of the programs, including janitorial services.[7]

The following example illustrates the frustration that bureaucratic procedures in large cumbersome organizations can cause. In these circumstances, an operating foundation is an appealing alternative. Madison Square Park, located in a commercial district of New York, had been neglected for decades. It had changed from being a focal point of neighborhood activity to a menace to the neighborhood's vitality. The park was picturesque on its large site with winding paths, towering trees, and handsome monuments. Major corporations located around it donated funds to the city parks department to renovate Madison Square Park. The agency failed to do the work effectively or in a timely manner. The donors concluded it was pointless to proceed with improvements through the hard-pressed city government, and a more effective mechanism for carrying out the corporations' objectives was an operating foundation funded by the companies that could coordinate all aspects of the park's operations (i.e., cutting the grass, staffing facilities, organizing and programming activities, providing security guards,

An Operating Foundation Established To Run Public Golf Courses in Baltimore

The city of Baltimore was losing more than $500,000 annually on the operation of its five municipal golf courses. The lack of profitability caused the city council to reduce the funds allocated to the golf courses, which led to deterioration in course and clubhouse conditions, declining patronage, and poor employee morale. The Professional Golf Association and Ladies Professional Golf Association relocated two tour events previously held on Baltimore courses to other cities. Baltimore's Pine Ridge Golf Course, which was one of the region's finest courses, was removed from *Golf Digest*'s listing of top 100 courses.

Reasons for the poor economic performance of the courses included the following:

— The city's golf professionals received 100% of the revenue from the pro shop, food service, lessons, and driving range. They also received 80% of the revenue from golf cart rentals but paid none of the expenses.

— The city employed too many full-time workers (120) and never used part-time workers, even though course use was seasonal.

— The benefits package for employees was 50% of wages, and leave and overtime policies were excessively generous compared with industry standards.

— Equipment repairs, conducted by the off-site, central maintenance department, were slow, unreliable, and expensive.

— Fee schedules were artificially low, and politicians, celebrities, and friends of employees routinely played for free.

— Crucial operating decisions required immediate action but were often held up by multiple park board and city council meetings. When decisions were made, they were motivated politically.

Recognizing the problem, the mayor formed a committee of prominent business leaders to assess the golf operation and make recommendations. They presented the mayor with four options:

1. Maintain the current management under the Department of Parks and Recreation.
2. Create a city-run golf course authority using an enterprise fund.
3. Lease the five municipal courses as a package to a private contractor through competitive bidding.
4. Create a nonprofit operating foundation.

Their recommendation was to create the operating foundation, even though it had never been tried before in the context of golf courses. They saw the following potential benefits from this option:

— By law, all of the profits were returned to support the golf courses. It created a system whereby golfers supported other golfers because revenue was not diverted to the general fund. In addition, the corporation was tax exempt.

— This option effectively removed politics from business decisions. Day-to-day management decisions were streamlined because they were separate from the normal municipal bureaucratic processes.

— Payroll problems were reduced because the nonprofit corporation operated separately from the existing city labor unions.

— Unlike their third option, this option would keep almost all revenues within the municipality because the corporation would be run by and for Baltimoreans.

In the first 10 years after the operating foundation took control, the number of rounds played at the five courses increased from 195,000 to more than 360,000. The city had been losing $500,000 annually, and there were no subsequent city losses; therefore, the city saved $5 million in the 10-year period. In addition, more than $4.2 million was invested in capital improvements without using tax dollars or bond issues. Funding for operational and capital purchases came from playing fees. Green fees remained the lowest in the mid-Atlantic states and increased at a level that was lower than the inflation rate.

Golf Digest magazine placed Pine Ridge Golf Course back onto its list of top 100 courses. Although Pine Ridge no longer holds this distinction in deference to the new courses that are being developed across the United States, it and its sister course, Mt. Pleasant, are rated as one of the top 10 public courses in the three-state area surrounding Baltimore (i.e., Maryland, Delaware, and Virginia).

From Lynnie Cook. An alternative approach to municipal golf course management: The private, not-for-profit corporation. Parks and Recreation. April 1996, pages 74-81; A.S. Lee. Baltimore's better idea. Golf World. March 5, 1993. 46(24), pages 16-20; and Lynnie Cook. Baltimore Municipal Golf Corporation: Not-for-profit golf course management. In Models of Change in Municipal Parks and Recreation. Edited by Mark E. Havitz. Venture Publishing: State College, PA. 1996.

and planning for the park's physical renewal). The companies projected that annual costs would be $80,000 and that they would incur an additional initial cost of $230,000 for renovating the park. They regarded this expenditure as an investment to increase the value of their existing real estate and working conditions and not as a philanthropic venture.[8]

The Baltimore golf courses case study illustrates the variety of efficiency benefits that may accrue from using an operating foundation. Many of these efficiencies are identical to those identified in chapter 9 in the context of contracting out with a commercial company. The trade-offs between these two options appear to revolve around the extent to which any efficiencies and superior technical expertise that a commercial contractor offers are offset by the profits that the contractor would take out of the program. The revenue surplus accruing to an operating foundation is likely to be higher than that accruing to an agency from a commercial contractor who would seek to retain a substantial portion of it as profit margin. Concern also may center on whether a commercial

contractor would put profitability ahead of the public's interest. For example, the contractor may have no desire to keep fees low for selected clienteles or to engage in unprofitable outreach activities to disadvantaged groups.

All of the illustrations in this section have related to selected facilities from within a public park and recreation system. Milton Keynes in England offers a vision of the future, in which an operating foundation may be used to operate a whole park system rather than selected entities within a system.

Milton Keynes is the largest new town in the United Kingdom. It is situated in a green fields site located about 80 mi from London. Early in the 1990s, the city's governing body established the Milton Keynes Parks Trust, which is the equivalent of an operating foundation in the United States. It manages one of the largest urban park systems in the country but is entirely independent of local government. It was created by endowment of a portfolio of commercial property, which had been owned by the city's governing body, worth approximately $30 million. This property comprised offices, local shopping centers, and industrial units. The income from this portfolio was used to both maintain and market the business properties and to provide the funds with which the trust manages the park lands. The trust's responsibilities extend to 4,000 acres of park land and a further 800 acres of greenways. These areas embrace lakes, athletic fields, natural resource areas, wildlife reserves, and major river valleys. The trust's board consists of 13 individuals recruited from local business, conservation, forestry, sporting, and local council groups. A chief executive leads the 21 employees, most of whom are in managerial or supervisory roles because the trust relies entirely on outside contractors for almost every aspect of its hard and soft landscape maintenance. The cost of this contracted-out work is approximately $3 million each year.[9]

Support Foundations

Support foundations are defined as 501(c)(iii) organizations whose mandate is to secure additional resources exclusively for enhancing park and recreation services. The taxonomy shown in table 19.1 differentiates support foundations by the geographic scope of their operation and by their institutional affiliation. This taxonomy is used as the framework for discussion in this section.

The horizontal axis of table 19.1 (geographic scope) categorizes support foundations as national organizations that are active in many regions across the country or as local organizations whose operations are confined to a single region, state, county, or city area. The vertical axis identifies a foundation's primary institutional affiliation. Some have no such affiliation. Rather, they may elect to support any institution that can assist in fulfilling the foundation's park or recreation mission. In contrast, some 501(c)(iii) organizations are established by agencies or their advocates specifically to further the agencies' agendas, and their efforts are concentrated on that affiliation; however, others are still more narrowly focused, limiting their support efforts to a single facility.

One of the six cells shown in table 19.1 is not functional. By the definition used here, it is not possible for a national organization to have an institutional affiliation that is facility specific. Hence, the discussion in this section recognizes five different types of support foundations: national non-affiliated, national agency–specific, local facility–specific, local agency–specific, and local non-affiliated foundations.

National Foundations

The National Park Foundation is the only foundation in this field that works exclusively with a single federal agency, and it is discussed at the end of this section. However, many 501(c)(iii) organizations that are involved in making additional park or recreational resources available operate at a national level in all regions of the country without affiliation to any specific agency. Among the most prominent is Ducks Unlimited, an organization

Table 19.1 A Taxonomy of Support Foundations

Institutional affiliation	Geographical scope	
	National organizations	Local organizations
Non-affiliated	e.g., The Nature Conservancy Trust for Public Land The Conservation Foundation Ducks Unlimited National Audubon Society	e.g., Alachua Conservation Trust, Florida
Agency specific	e.g., National Park Foundation	e.g., local park and recreation department foundations
Facility specific		e.g., Central Park Conservancy, New York City Friends of the park organizations

dedicated to the conservation of waterfowl, wetlands, and other wildlife. Ducks Unlimited works particularly closely with the U.S. Fish and Wildlife Service and its state-equivalent agencies to protect duck habitat; with the National Audubon Society, which operates approximately 100,000 acres of sanctuaries; with the National Wildlife Federation; and with the Sierra Club. Each of these organizations has more than 1 million members. They acquire and manage land and water areas and support a variety of public agencies in many of the ways noted in the previous chapter. However, their work is focused relatively narrowly on tightly defined aspects of parks, recreation, or conservation, e.g., duck habitat or bird sanctuaries.

In contrast, three 501(c)(iii) organizations operate at a national level with relatively broad mandates and include the Nature Conservancy, the Trust for Public Land, and the Conservation Fund. These organizations have pioneered many of the acquisition and financial mechanisms that are now widely adopted by foundations in this field. Examples of their work were cited extensively in chapter 18. The Conservation Fund is a nonmember foundation with 12 state and regional offices. It protected more than 1 million acres across the United States in the first 10 years after it was founded in 1985. Nevertheless, it is somewhat smaller in the scale of its operations than the Nature Conservancy and the Trust for Public Land, which are described in the following two subsections.

The Nature Conservancy

The mission of the Nature Conservancy is "to preserve plants, animals, and natural communities that represent the diversity of life on Earth by protecting the lands and water they need to survive." Its emphasis is on saving the last of the least (i.e., rare and endangered species) and the best of the rest (good examples of important American ecosystems and habitats).[10]

The Nature Conservancy was incorporated as a 501(c)(iii) organization in 1951. Two years later, a group that had purchased a scenic, unspoiled 60-acre tract in the Mianus River Gorge in the suburbs of New York asked if the newly formed conservancy would accept the tract as a gift. It agreed to do so. (The tract has since been expanded to 440 acres.) This serendipitous happening indicated to the group that its mission would be best served by acquiring and protecting its own natural sanctuaries. During its first 15 years, the Nature Conservancy remained a largely volunteer organization that acquired relatively small tracts of land as preserves by depending largely on gifts of money and land from its members.

In the second half of the 1960s, it set itself the task of transforming to a fully professional organization that was better equipped to meet growing needs. Its assets grew rapidly from $3 million in 1965 to $73 million in 1973. Growth in this period was assisted by large contributions from grant-aiding foundations. The Ford Foundation, for example, granted it $2.5 million in this period.

In 1975, the Nature Conservancy acted in a preacquisition role in protecting 60,000 acres of the Great Dismal Swamp in Virginia and North Carolina. At that time, this was the largest ever real-estate transaction involving a private conservation group. The Nature Conservancy worked with two large timber companies that owned the land and persuaded them that they would benefit more from the tax deductions and positive public relations, which would accrue from donating the land, than they would from selling it to developers. The Nature Conservancy then deeded the total acreage to the U.S. Fish and Wildlife Service. The size of this transaction caused the organization to think bigger. Since that time, emphasis has been on protecting sizable ecosystems rather than on obtaining unrelated, relatively small pieces of land. This emphasis means that much of the Nature Conservancy's work involves assisting public agencies in purchasing land because the cost of acquiring the large tracts of land necessary to protect ecosystems is often so high that government participation is essential. Acquisitions of this magnitude cannot be completed by relying only on creative application of the tax code and philanthropic capability.

Today, the Nature Conservancy has more than 800,000 members and 1,200 employees who operate out of more than 50 regional and field offices across the country. Its current assets exceed $500 million. It owns more than 1,500 nature preserves containing more than 800,000 acres, which is the largest system of private nature sanctuaries in the world. It has worked with all of the federal land-holding agencies, with all of the states, and with hundreds of municipal and county governments and special districts. Of the more than 8 million acres that the Nature Conservancy has been responsible for protecting to this point, approximately half (representing more than 3000 transactions) have been preserved in cooperation with public agencies.

The Nature Conservancy's more than 1,500 preserves are scattered throughout the country. The smallest is 0.5 acre on Scotia Lake Island near

Schenectady, New York. The largest is the 67,000-acre North Rosillos Mountains Preserve in Texas. Fewer than 50 of these sanctuaries are managed by full-time employees; volunteers of the local Nature Conservancy chapters care for the remainder. The Nature Conservancy would prefer to pass on ownership of most of these lands to public agencies because if its resources are tied up in managing land, it has fewer resources available for acquiring new property. However, the operating budgets of public agencies have made it difficult for them to maintain the properties that they currently own, so many of them refuse offers of new properties. If the budget situation of public agencies remains unchanged, then it seems likely that the Nature Conservancy's role in owning preserves will expand rather than contract.

The Nature Conservancy is unusual among environmental organizations because it is not an activist group; that is, it does not take public positions or become a vigorous advocate on key environmental issues. Unlike most other major conservation groups, it does not employ registered lobbyists. This approach has sometimes earned them the ire of other conservationists, who see its strategy of allying, rather than confronting, the corporate world as being akin to sleeping with the enemy. The president of the Conservancy observed:

> We are not in the conventional sense an issue-directed organization. On the other hand, we are not antagonistic to other groups which are more issue-directed. They have created a climate of public opinion generally favorable to environmental protection, and made it an important issue. But we have chosen another role. We are quite good at identifying, acquiring and managing natural areas that need protection. We are probably more knowledgeable than anyone else about real estate, and tax and zoning regulations which affect conservation. We think if we became more partisan on political and economic issues—say acid rain—we would be less effective in what might be called our niche (p. 90).[10]

The operative words for the Conservancy are partnership and bridge building. Companies feel more comfortable doing business with an environmental organization that is not strident and overly critical of the corporate world. Not surprisingly, the Nature Conservancy has the support of more companies than any other similar organization.

Indeed, it has more than 500 big corporations that pay an annual membership fee to be Nature Conservancy associates. The Conservancy's ability to forge partnerships with business also has been a key ingredient in its ability to secure extensive support from grant-aiding foundations.

The following examples of the Nature Conservancy's work are intended to convey the wide variety of tasks it undertakes. These six examples illustrate its traditional role in pre-acquisition, its ability to mediate disputes between environmental and business interests, its management of resources that others own, its program of acquiring and dispersing surplus property, the national inventory of flora and fauna, and its acquisition of a working ranch to experiment with new conservation strategies.

The Nature Conservancy played a role in pre-acquisition with the Lyons Falls Pulp and Paper Company, who owned substantial amounts of forest land in the western Adirondacks in New York. The company publicized that it would consider the sale of access and development rights easements over parts of its land as part of an effort to expand its overall timber holdings. At the same time, two tracts of forest land entered the market in the company's area: the 10,800-acre J.P. Lewis tract and the 3,200-acre Three Lakes tract. The Nature Conservancy purchased the two tracts. It then conveyed the underlying titles to both tracts, including timber rights but subject to access and development rights easements, to Lyons Falls in exchange for development rights and access easements over an additional 3,000 acres of Lyons Fall land along the Moose River. The Nature Conservancy then sold the easements on all 17,000 acres to the state of New York to preserve the entire area from incompatible development and to recover its costs. This forestalled the threat of the land being subdivided and being developed for second homes.[11]

The Nature Conservancy mediated disputes between environmental and business interests when developers and environmentalists squared off over a prime piece of real estate on the eastern outskirts of Palm Springs, California. The U.S. Fish and Wildlife Service discovered the endangered fringe-toed lizard lived in the Coachella Valley, so the agency shut down $19 billion worth of proposed real-estate development there. Developers and environmentalists were preparing to wage a lengthy and costly court battle when a Fish and Wildlife Service official contacted the Conservancy. Over the next year, a plan emerged in which developers agreed to pay $600 per acre for land developed within the lizard's habitat. Those funds would be used to purchase land for a preserve that environmentalists would manage.

Today, the Coachella Valley Preserve includes 18,000 acres, and it demonstrates how developers, environmentalists, and government agencies can work together to preserve a species. Developers were able to proceed with their projects, and the fringe-toed lizard continues to thrive.[12]

The Nature Conservancy managed resources that others own as part of a national agreement between the Nature Conservancy and the U.S. Department of Defense to identify, monitor, and manage significant habitat on military installations. The Department of Defense provided funding for the Conservancy to study the ecology of the Nipomo Dune system found partly on Vandenburg Air Force Base. The Department of Defense land is part of a patchwork of ownerships in this coastal dune and wetland system stretching 75 mi along the central California coast. The Nature Conservancy has agreements with the Department of Defense, Santa Barbara County, Pacific Gas and Electric, and even the state's Off-Highway Motor Vehicle Recreation Division to manage their lands under a coordinated scheme to protect more than 200,000 acres of this fragile habitat.[11]

The Nature Conservancy's Trade Lands program accepts donations of land from corporations, and to a lesser extent from individuals, that are surplus to their needs. A Conservancy spokesperson noted: "Through tax savings, corporations can release capital that had been previously locked up in real estate; and they can eliminate a lot of costs associated with ownership such as taxes, insurance, maintenance, security and administration. In addition to federal law, which encourages charitable donations of property, many corporations also want to be good, environmentally conscious citizens" (p. 44).[12] Many of these properties have no attributes that make them inherently interesting to the Conservancy. Hence, the Nature Conservancy sells them and uses the proceeds to acquire places that are ecologically significant. They have sold more than 1,200 of these properties, generating more than $160 million. These surplus properties have included urban convenience stores, warehouses, apartment complexes, single-family houses, obsolete factory sites, and parcels left over from development projects.

In the mid-1970s, the Ethyl Corporation, which produces a wide range of industrial chemicals, acquired 620 acres of titanium-rich land in western Tennessee. The land, most of which was wooded, included about 12 small lots for second homes.

Faced with a declining market for titanium years later, Ethyl lost interest in the mining operation. It donated the property to the Nature Conservancy, which in turn sold it in multiple parcels; two large parcels were purchased for the timber and several remaining platted lots were bought by the existing lot owners. The Conservancy then used the funds from these sales to support its conservation activities elsewhere.[13]

The Nature Conservancy has worked with each state to create the state's national heritage inventory, which systematically identifies habitats needed to protect rare and endangered plant and animal species. This is funded either by the states or by federal, foundation, or the Nature Conservancy's own funds. Support from grant-aiding foundations included grants of approximately $1 million each from the J.N. Pew Memorial Trust, the John D. and Catherine T. MacArthur Foundation, and the William and Flora Hewlett Foundation. Typically, the inventory initially is formulated by a four-person team: a botanist, zoologist, ecologist, and data-processing specialist. They begin by searching the existing records, texts, theses, museum, and herbarium collections to find the flora and fauna thought to exist in the state. Then, they do fieldwork to test reports against current knowledge. This inventory enables the Conservancy to set priorities for preserving habitats. In many cases, the states have now taken control of the inventory and responsibility for periodically updating it. These inventories have become the commonly accepted reference points on issues pertaining to land protection, environmental impact, resource management, and endangered species reviews.[10]

To experiment with new conservation strategies, the Nature Conservancy operated a working ranch. For more than one century, cattle and wildlife have lived side-by-side along the Yampa River in Colorado. While cows grazed on floodplain grasses, nearly 80 species of birds, such as greater sandhill cranes, great blue herons, and bald eagles, fed or rested on the river and its surrounding trees. The Nature Conservancy purchased the ranch for $850,000 from the Carpenter family and continued to operate it as a working ranch. The Conservancy owned a 315-acre preserve and a 400-acre development easement on adjacent properties. By keeping the ranch in production, the Nature Conservancy hoped to learn how conservation and agriculture can best work together. An education center was established to showcase the history and operations of the ranch and the ecological significance of the Yampa River.[14] Research and restoration projects test new conservation strategies and provide valuable information for land stewards elsewhere in the country.

Trust for Public Land

The mission of the Trust for Public Land is "to conserve land for people, to improve the quality of life in our communities, and to protect our national and historic resources for future generations." The foundation was started in San Francisco in 1972 and now has a national presence with more than 200 employees working out of 24 regional and field offices nationwide. Since its founding, the Trust for Public Land has completed more than 1,500 projects involving the protection of more than 1 million acres of land valued at more than $1.5 billion, and its current assets exceed $80 million. It now completes, on average, a land-saving transaction every other day. From the outset, the Trust for Public Land had four key goals that directed its activities:

- To acquire and preserve open space to serve human needs
- To operate a self-sustaining conservation organization
- To create a new profession of public-interest land specialists
- To pioneer new techniques of land preservation and funding[15]

Many of the skills, such as expertise in real estate, tax law, and structuring financial arrangements, that the Trust for Public Land offers are similar to those available from the Nature Conservancy. However, the Trust for Public Land differs from the Nature Conservancy in four major ways.

First, there is a different programmatic emphasis. Its founders acknowledged the importance of protecting environmentally sensitive areas and endangered habitats, but they saw that there was a need for an organization that could create recreational lands in the cities and suburbs similar to the way in which the Nature Conservancy operated in ecologically sensitive contexts. As part of its management creed, the trust adopted Aldo Leopold's observation: "Weeds in a city lot teach the same lessons as the redwoods" (p. 7).[15] The emphasis is on preserving land for people more than for animals or plants, although the land they preserve may contain these resources. While the Nature Conservancy focuses exclusively on ecologically important land, the Trust for Public Land's mandate is broader, aiming at saving open space for human use and enjoyment.

Although the Trust has helped to preserve a variety of wild and natural lands, a parcel need not be either large or environmentally pristine to warrant TPL's attention. TPL works to secure lands—and sometimes buildings—that serve a public benefit, such as lands of cultural, historical, recreational, environmental or open space value (p. 61).[16]

The Trust for Public Land's philosophy makes it clear that number of acres is not the criterion of success. One or two acres in a critical inner-city area may be of more value than 100 or 200 acres on the periphery. One implication of the trust's more generic mission is that it tends to operate in urban areas much more frequently than the Nature Conservancy does and is involved in projects such as neighborhood parks and community gardens.

A second differentiating characteristic is that the Trust for Public Land does not own or manage permanently any land. Its role is that of an independent pre-acquisition organization in land transactions for government agencies or that of an advisor on such transactions. Examples of the trust's third party intervention role were provided in chapter 18. As transaction facilitators, its project managers are able to do more than simply offer landowners the tax advantages of transferring land through a nonprofit partner. Completing a requirement involves studying the needs of the landowner and the agency, working out where funds might come from and how land might be managed, and trying different angles until the pieces click into place.[15]

Third, unlike the Nature Conservancy, the Trust for Public Land is not a membership organization. Approximately two-thirds of the trust's operating costs are recovered from profits on transactions. These are made by acquiring property at less than fair market value and selling it to the public agency for an amount closer to fair market value. The balance of its budget is generated by contributions, grants, and low-interest loans from foundations, corporations, and individuals. The Trust for Public Land perceives there to be two advantages from this strategy. First, the staff effort needed to sustain the organization's viability is reduced, so administrative overhead costs are kept to a minimum. Second, the trust's need to compete for philanthropic support with nonprofit groups that have similar agendas is minimized.

A fourth differentiating characteristic is the trust's greater emphasis on building capacity with other groups to do this work rather than on trying to do it all on its own. The trust must invest effort in training others on the techniques of acquiring land and must help them establish land trusts at the local level, which are the vehicles through which their aspirations can be brought to fruition. In this way, the trust leverages its effectiveness and frees its own staff to focus its direct efforts on the most significant projects. Two initial criteria are used to prioritize these. One is the "but for" test, which asks would it happen if the Trust for Public Land were not involved. The other is the value test, which establishes $1 million as an approximate minimal value to warrant the trust's direct involvement.

The Trust for Public Land has pursued a number of broad initiatives, several of which have capacity-building components. Three of these, which include the Urban Land program, assisting in the development of land trusts, and the Green Cities initiative, are briefly described in the following paragraphs to illustrate the variety of vehicles and contexts that the trust uses to fulfill its mission.

The intent of the Urban Land program was to revitalize abandoned vacant lots, which typically are overgrown with weeds, are littered with trash, and add to the blight in many inner-city areas, by transforming them into attractive miniparks and community gardens that may yield flowers and vegetables. In many large cities, tens of thousands of such vacant lots exist, and many are owned by banks that have obtained them through foreclosures. It has been suggested that these rubble-strewn lots represent "a collective sense of hopelessness and despair."[17] Transforming these eyesores into miniparks or community gardens can change the whole atmosphere of a neighborhood by giving its people a feeling of power, direction, and common purpose. Indeed, another founding tenet of the Trust for Public Land held that the very act of organizing such facilities could infuse a neighborhood with a much-needed sense of pride and community ownership that could mobilize residents for other social projects. The key to success is grassroots empowerment. Local people have to initiate, build, and operate the projects. They cannot be imposed from above.

The Trust for Public Land launched this program in the mid-1970s. The trust provided in-depth training and technical assistance to many hundreds of interested groups and completed a large number of demonstration projects in cities, such as New York, Newark, Boston, Miami, Denver, and Oakland. The early effort was intended to build capacity by creating a cadre of knowledgeable groups who could then, in turn, teach others. Thus, over the past 20 years, many local organizations that now foster minipark and community garden programs in their cities have been nurtured.

The Trust for Public Land remained involved in the program at a more macro level. For example, the trust created an endowment of $1 million to provide capital for the acquisition and protection of community gardens in New York's five boroughs and in other urban centers throughout the state.

The West Side Community Garden Inc. (a land trust) received a $28,000 interest-free loan from this endowment to complete a $150,000 campaign to finance its share of permanent garden improvements on a 0.5-acre Manhattan site. The garden was a joint venture among the land trust, the Trust for Public Land, and the developers of adjacent luxury housing.[16]

The extraordinary growth in land trusts over the last 20 years is discussed later in the chapter, but it constitutes the second example of a Trust for Public Land broad initiative. A primary factor that contributed to that growth was the nurturing of land trusts by the Trust for Public Land. Only a handful of land trusts existed outside of New England when the trust was founded. Again in the late 1970s, the trust recognized that its mission was too vast to accomplish alone and that its impact could be leveraged substantially if its knowledge and techniques were shared with people at the local level who could then form their own foundation to do this work. The organizers of land trusts have connections in the community, and they have a level of familiarity with the local land and political milieu to which the Trust for Public Land as a national organization could not hope to aspire.

The Trust for Public Land had a training program that helped land trusts to get started, promoted regional land-trust networks, taught land trusts how to acquire and protect open space, and linked the efforts of public agencies with those of land trusts. More than one-third of the nation's 1,200 land trusts were founded or trained with the Trust for Public Land's help, and the trust helped launch the Land Trust Alliance, which is a national group that has assumed responsibility for educating new land trusts. Often, the Trust for Public Land works in partnership with land trusts that it may have helped to establish.

Ulster County is only a 2 h drive northwest of the city of New York. The county's Rondout and Wallkill Valleys are within the Hudson River watershed, which is an intricate system of hills, woods, streams, lakes, and historic farms. Development pressures have increased dramatically in the county because of its proximity to New York. After hosting numerous presentations to local residents, the Trust for Public Land assisted in the selection of initial board members and helped two new land trusts to incorporate. The Trust for Public Land then helped the Rondout Valley Land Conservancy complete a number of projects, including their acquisition of land along the Rochester Creek Gorge. Similarly, in a co-venture with the Trust for Public Land, the Wallkill Valley Land Trust acquired a conservation easement to protect seven acres of the scenic Wallkill River waterfront. The Trust for Public Land also assisted the land trust and the town of New Paltz to acquire a 14 mi abandoned rail line for conversion into a public bikeway.[18]

The Green Cities initiative launched in 1991 is a third illustration of the Trust for Public Land's broad initiatives. It was a rallying point around which the trust addressed the park and open space needs of people in major cities. The urgency of the initiative was emphasized by the rioting in Los Angeles in May 1992. It was launched in response to the recognition that areas most in need often had the fewest park and recreational resources. Under this initiative, the trust's goal was to help generate $2.5 billion for urban open space and recreation and to assist in the acquisition of 250 properties that met high priority needs in the targeted cities by the year 2000. The primary effort was focused on 12 cities, but a secondary focus was extended to an additional 11 cities.

The initiative gained momentum from a grant to the Trust for Public Land of $6.5 million from the Lila Wallace–Reader's Digest Fund, which is the nation's largest private donor to arts and culture, to create, restore, and maintain parks in underserved neighborhoods in seven of the target cities. In all of these primary targeted cities, i.e., Austin, Oakland, Cleveland, Portland, Providence, Boston, and Baltimore, the trust made a long-term commitment to provide services, such as planning, organizing, and supporting new funding initiatives, in addition to engaging in its core real-estate acquisition services. Thus, the initiative took many forms: protecting open land around fast-growing metropolitan areas, acquiring vacant lots for conversion to neighborhood parks and gardens, planning new greenways, and developing new sources of funding. The common thread throughout the effort was strong community involvement.

National Park Foundation

The only organization that qualifies as a national agency–specific foundation (see table 19.1) is the National Park Foundation. It is unique because it was established in 1967 by an act of Congress to receive and administer gifts of real estate and personal property, including money, exclusively for the benefit of the National Park Service. At the time that the Congress created the National Park Foundation, it believed that the United States was losing potential private donations to further the Park Service's work because of legal restrictions on the secretary of the Interior's authority to accept and use such gifts. Therefore, to encourage private gifts for the benefit of the National Park Service, Congress established the foundation, giving it considerably broader authority than the secretary possessed to accept and use donations. Congress also anticipated that the foundation would use donated funds to buy real property for additions to the national park system. Its mission is to

- help conserve, preserve, and enhance the national parks for the benefit of the American people;
- support programs primarily for education and outreach, visitor information and interpretive facilities, volunteer activities, and National Park Service employees; and
- generate funds for grantmaking and assistance programs through gifts from private individuals, foundations and organizations, corporations, and a range of fundraising and marketing activities.

By congressional charter, the chairman of the foundation board is the secretary of the Interior and its secretary is the director of the National Park Service. All of its other 17 members are senior executives from major corporations.

When Congress created the National Park Foundation, it provided no financial assets for the organization. Thus, in its early days, the foundation relied directly on the U.S. Department of the Interior for a significant amount of its financial and operational support and almost entirely depended on the Park Service to conduct its negotiations and acquisition activities. Subsequently, it operated more independently, but it worked exclusively for the Park Service, enabling the service to accept gifts and undertake purchases without being subject to the restrictions ordinarily imposed on the secretary of the Interior. By the mid-1990s its assets totaled almost $40 million, and it was making annual grants to the Park Service totaling $5 million.[19]

The foundation engages in fundraising campaigns for both major high-visibility projects and a series of ongoing broad initiatives. The following two examples illustrate high-visibility campaigns.

The National Park Foundation spearheaded the campaign to raise $5 million to restore the Washington Monument. The restoration was needed to combat the effects of weathering, aging, and welcoming 2,500 visitors daily. It secured Target Stores as the lead partner, guaranteeing a minimal contribution of $1 million and a commitment to use its marketing talent to help the National Park Foundation raise the additional $4 million. Others engaged in the effort included 3M, Procter & Gamble, Visa, Neutrogena, EMI-Capitol Records, and Coca-Cola. The $5 million was raised in 18 months.

Floods in January 1996 caused millions of dollars in damage to the C&O Canal National Historic Park. Insufficient federal funds were available to repair all the damage. The Park Service requested the National Park Foundation to launch a major fundraising effort. The foundation rallied leading area corporations and foundations to contribute major gifts, established a toll-free line for individual contributors, and helped enlist thousands of volunteers to do some of the critical hands-on work. They raised more than $1.1 million in the next few months for the park.[19]

Three initiatives that illustrate the National Park Foundation's ongoing work in capacity building in the Park Service are its competitive grants, expeditions, and classroom programs. The competitive grants program is used to help fund innovative conservation, preservation, and education efforts in the national parks. Most grants range from $5,000 to $20,000 and are awarded to pilot new programs.

Biscayne National Park in Florida was awarded a $10,000 grant from the National Park Foundation to support transporting inner-city students to the park's reefs, islands, and Adams Key Environmental Education Center via a chartered, glass bottom boat. The program enabled fifth- and sixth-grade students to participate in a three-day, two-night stay on the island that included hands-on water activities and laboratory projects.

A $14,700 grant to Craters of the Moon National Monument in Idaho was used to fund development of a children's trail that taught young visitors about the park's resources. The trail had wayside exhibits that children had prepared and written and that discussed volcanic eruptions, explained lava formations, and described wildlife and animal activities where lava is prevalent.

A second foundation initiative is its Expeditions into the Parks program that brings Park Service staff, researchers, and volunteers together to collect critical scientific data. The program primarily was underwritten by a $1 million commitment from Canon USA, Inc.

Joshua Tree National Park in California received $40,000 to improve and better understand bighorn sheep habitat; manage tamarisk, which is a tree that is threatening water sources for sheep; revegetate; and continue scientific studies. An initial inventory of bighorn sheep was completed using remote video, still cameras, and binoculars; habitat protection was begun with curtailment of off-road vehicle entry to sensitive areas; and propagation of native plants and eradication of exotics, including the tamarisk, was undertaken. The Student Conservation Association and high school students volunteered many hours to the project.

The Parks as Classrooms is a third initiative. It was established in nine parks through a $1 million grant from the Pew Charitable Trusts, which was supplemented with another $4.6 million from other sources.

At Acadia National Park in Maine, for example, the National Park Foundation grants enabled more than 8,800 students and 346 teachers to participate in the program. Educational materials produced included *A Kid's Eye View—The Science Behind the Scenery of Acadia National Park*; a video and accompanying study guide highlighting the research efforts at the park; eight teacher guides for third- through sixth-grade children; ranger guides for individual programs; an environmental education staff training manual; a teacher resource library; and discovery kits on animals, geology, and the inter-tidal zone. Despite the close proximity of the schools to the park, students would have had little chance without this program to experience hiking a mountain, crouching by a tidepool, exploring the carriage roads, or traveling back in time to the 1800s. The grant made it possible for the park to offer college internships, to take on a more visible role in the community, and to highlight other aspects of the park, such as the research work undertaken to protect the park's resources.[19]

Local Foundations

During the past decade, there has been extraordinary growth in the number of support foundations working at the regional, state, county, and community level. Traditionally, the support role of these local organizations was passive. They were vehicles for receiving donations and gifts or for facilitating auxiliary fundraising or service functions for an agency, which bureaucratic restrictions prevented the agency from doing directly itself. Most of the recent growth, however, has occurred as a result of a surge in interest among individuals and groups wanting to adopt a more pro-active stance to acquiring resources. Many of these new foundations are widely known by the generic name *land trusts*. Given their emerging prominence, a review of their status is given in the following paragraphs before proceeding with discussion and illustrations of facility-specific, local agency-specific, and local non-affiliated foundations.

Land trust is a generic term for various types of conservation organizations. They usually are defined as those nonprofit conservation organizations that work within a local community, state, or (occasionally) regional area in the direct protection of lands for open space, recreational, or conservation purposes. The roots of land trusts can be traced to the village improvement societies that emerged across New England in the mid-1800s. They were formed for the purpose of improving quality of life and the environment. This was a fairly generic mandate, but part of it often included acquiring small parcels of land in their communities for public use and enjoyment. Founded in 1853, the Laurel Hill Association of Stockbridge, Massachusetts, was the first such organization and is still active today.

The first organization with a more narrowly focused mandate more like today's land trusts was the Trustees of Reservations in Massachusetts. Founded in 1891, it is now one of the largest land trusts, with approximately 20,000 acres owned in more than 70 reserves, conservation easements on more than 70 additional parcels of land, and more than 50 full-time and 100 part-time employees. The Society for the Protection of New Hampshire Forests was founded 10 years later in 1901, and it too has grown to be one of the largest land trusts.

By 1950, 53 land trusts existed nationwide, and most of them were in the New England area. By 1965, 132 trusts were operating in 26 states.[20] The impetus that the Trust for Public Land provided in the 1970s created momentum that led to exponential growth. Today, more than 1,200 land trusts exist, and their numbers are increasing rapidly. Given their responsiveness to local conditions and their entrepreneurial, but voluntary, approach, there is every reason to anticipate that this growth will continue. Land trusts offer local residents the means to become involved directly in defending ecologically sensitive land, open space, recreational lands, farmlands, and parks from development pressures and, in so doing, to shape the quality of life in their communities. Their total membership is close to 1 million, and they have helped to protect more than 3 million acres, which is an area about the size of Connecticut. The learning curve is relatively long for a group mastering real-estate law, tax consequences, negotiation, and constituency-building techniques. Thus, it seems likely that as growing numbers of people form and join these groups and acquire this knowledge, the effectiveness of land trusts will be enhanced dramatically in the future.

Land trusts have followed an evolutionary pattern similar to that of the Nature Conservancy, the Trust for Public Land, and other national organizations in that many of them have progressed from the passive acceptance of land to the more complex role of pre-identifying key parcels and forging partnerships with public agencies to protect them. However, because of their smaller size and more localized scope of operations, land trusts tend to have more difficulty than national foundations in raising financial resources to engage in acquisition transactions and to pay staff and operating costs. It has been noted:

> Although some land trusts may find that a volunteer work force is sufficient for their needs, it has been the experience of most land trusts that volunteers simply cannot give the long-term continuity of effort required by a sustained program of complex partnership projects. Each project is a learning experience, and it is important to have staffers who will be around long enough to apply the lessons they have learned (p. 201).[21]

To surmount their financial limitations, land trusts sometimes pool their resources with other similar organizations so that together they can acquire and share professional expertise that none of them could afford individually.

The Compact of Cape Cod Conservation Trusts is staffed by an experienced land conservationist who provides technical assistance to 16 land trusts. They pay annual dues ranging from $1,000 to $4,500 depending on the level of assistance desired and pay a share of the Compact's administrative costs. The 16 land trusts use their local contacts to secure gifts and easements, many of which would not come to the attention of a single, larger regional foundation.[21]

An alternative strategy for overcoming their financial limitations is for land trusts to work in partnership with national organizations. Many national organizations, which are aware of the strengths that land trusts bring to such partnerships, encourage this partnership. The land trust's local knowledge and role in building political support is crucial. No land in any community is likely to be protected without local support. Land trusts are much better equipped than national organizations to mobilize key constituencies and trusted opinion leaders in a community in support of a project. Landowners are likely to feel more comfortable making a donation or sale through a familiar local person or entity. Land trusts also enable local donors of land to have both very real participation in the formulation of policy and active involvement in the continued management of their now-protected land.

The growth in both number of land trusts and the complexity of tasks that they are undertaking generated the need for a national coordinating organization to facilitate the sharing of expertise among them. Thus, in 1982 the Land Trust Alliance was formed. Its mission is to provide information, training, policy advocacy, and networking in order to reduce any sense of isolation and to build the efforts of individual land trusts into a strong, effective national movement for volunteer land conservation.

Facility-Specific Foundations

Three different sets of circumstances may lead to the formation of a facility-specific foundation. First, the facility may be publicly operated, in which case the foundation's role is to enhance and expand the resources and amenities that the public agency provides. Second, as in the case of a land trust, the cost of acquiring a facility may be borne in part or in whole by a foundation before passing it through to a public agency, and the foundation then may or may not remain active in supporting the facility. Third, the foundation's mission may be to administer an endowment bestowed upon a facility, which has been bequeathed to a public agency, to be used for its perpetual maintenance.

Facility-specific foundations tend to be associated strongly with specialized facilities that attract interest from those with higher incomes, for example, zoological gardens, orchestras, ballet companies, and parks. Many examples of friends-of-the-park foundations exist to enhance a park's amenities. Typically, these organizations comprise individuals with a high level of appreciation for a park, with a sense of commitment to its well being, and for whom it is an important element in quality of life. Hence, these groups tend to be action oriented. Parks can be isolated islands in a community. They are tended by professionals and funded by agencies, and local people may not be connected to them. Friends groups are a voice for the parks, helping to counter their disengagement by communicating their importance and value. They become salespersons for a park's projects. Their role has been described in the following terms:

> Park appreciation is the lifeblood of any friends group; consequently they tend to focus their considerable energies on such activities as interpretation of the parks' natural and cultural history, beautification of park grounds and facilities, and restoration of park structures. Friends fund raising activities in support of their programs would normally be a prohibited activity if done by park employees. Their programs bring to the park a human dimension that would otherwise be absent, or at least significantly smaller. It has become almost axiomatic that the professional staff maintains the park, but it is the volunteer staff that gives meaning and life to the park! (p. 16).[22]

These qualities of friends groups are exemplified by the illustration given in "Friends of Pisgah State Park, New Hampshire."

Often the impetus for forming a friends foundation springs from a perceived external threat to a park's well-being. A former director of the New Hampshire state park system reported:

> Among the friends groups who were "self-starters" in the New Hampshire state parks system, one out of every two had "crisis" origins: either a threat of park closure or the potential loss of a park feature. And two-thirds of those having calmer origins were subsequently strengthened by a threat to the park's integrity or program (p. 16).[22]

Examples of the types of activities undertaken by friends foundations include the following:

- In Massachusetts, the Maudslay State Park Association rented a van and provided tour guide service for mobility-impaired visitors to enjoy the expansive former estate's spectacular rhododendron and azalea plantings.
- In Hawaii, the Friends of Iolani Palace operated, maintained, and provided guided tours of the only royal palace in the United States.

Friends of Pisgah State Park, New Hampshire

New Hampshire's largest state park, Pisgah, is a 13,500-acre primitive park with no interior development. The land was acquired between 1968 and 1972 with money from the federal Land and Water Conservation Fund. More than 24 homes and camps on its two impoundments were razed in an effort to restore the park to its natural condition. Laced with old roads, abandoned homes, and mill sites dating from the mid-1880s logging era, this lightly supervised backcountry became a mecca for off-highway recreational vehicle users. Local police, fire departments, and conservation officers were called upon to address the resulting problems, emergencies, and visitor conflicts.

Through the efforts of two successive park rangers and the state park planner, a trail network plan for diverse user groups was developed. An ad hoc citizen steering committee was formed in the mid-1980s with the encouragement of the director of parks. Comprising neighbors and a representative coalition of park users, this group evolved into the Friends of Pisgah Inc. In rapid succession, the friends developed articles of incorporation, a draft park management plan, and a capital fund legislative action strategy. In little less than one year, the friends succeeded in expanding Pisgah's staff to three full-time, equipped rangers and gave the park an orderly, zoned plan for shared use and appreciation of its many assets.

A history committee began to do research on the park's colorful past and to develop interpretive signs to tell the area's story. Other committees worked on the parks' forestry needs, field and orchard restoration, road repairs, naturalist-led hikes, and visitor center planning. In their second year, the friends blocked a development threat on the park's northern border by borrowing money to buy the land. The $80,000 loan, secured through a supportive local bank, saved the 177-acre tract, which later became part of Pisgah State Park.

Since their initial successes, the Friends of Pisgah have acquired and dismantled a historic house to be reassembled in the park as a visitor center, developed another visitor center and logging museum at a nearby wayside, created a wildlife habitat plan for the park, held several volunteer workdays at other nearby state park and forest lands, and developed a major greenway project to connect all of these lands.

In its first seven years, the Friends of the Pisgah generated more than 10,000 h of volunteer labor, tens of thousands of dollars of volunteer support, and an enormous amount of local pride and goodwill toward the park.

- In Connecticut, the Friends of Dinosaur Park Association provided funding and extensive volunteer support for programs, activities, events, and developments at Dinosaur State Park.
- In North Dakota, the Fort Abraham Lincoln Foundation spurred the reconstruction of General George Custer's former command and interpreted frontier military life at the state park.[22]

Perhaps the largest and highest profile friends-of-the-park group is the Central Park Conservancy, which has been responsible for the renaissance of New York's Central Park. Its role is described in "The Central Park Conservancy's Contribution to the Renaissance of New York's Central Park" on page 510.

Some facility-specific foundations are formed primarily to raise funds for an amenity that a group desires, but which they are unable to persuade a public agency to finance. For example, Crooked Creek Community Council was a nonprofit foundation established by residents in an area of Indianapolis' northwest side. A developer had planning permission to construct a 142-unit apartment complex on a 22-acre site adjacent to an existing park. It was a heavily wooded natural area, encompassing a segment of Crooked Creek, and was heavily populated by various species of wildlife. The surrounding residents regarded preservation of this site as important because they perceived it to be

The Central Park Conservancy's Contribution to the Renaissance of New York's Central Park

The Central Park Conservancy was established as a support foundation in 1980 with a mission to preserve and restore the 843-acre Central Park in the city of New York. The park was lauded as the outstanding achievement of its famous architects Frederick Law Olmsted and Calvert Vaux when it was created in the 1860s and 1870s, but by 1980 it had become notorious for its scruffiness, graffiti, broken equipment, dirty fields, crime, and noise.

By the mid-1990s, the Conservancy was providing two-thirds of the park department's operating budget for the park, as well as half of the money for its capital projects and more than 60% of its staff. It employed 172 of the park's 244 employees. One measure of the organization's importance to the park's well-being by that time was that although Central Park's chief of horticulture was paid by the parks department, his 40 gardeners were paid by the Conservancy. The Conservancy also marshaled more than 3,000 volunteers who served as guides, instructed student groups, planted and tended bushes and flowers, picked up litter, and gave money.

The Conservancy conducted a campaign of park renewal ranging from flower planting to building construction. This involved investing $165 million in the park. About 230 grant-aiding foundations contributed to the Conservancy, ranging from high profile New York foundations, such as the Astor Foundation, the Commonwealth Foundation, and the J.M. Kapland Foundation, to a host of less well-known organizations. The most visible projects in this campaign included Strawberry Fields, which is a grassy swath that honors the late John Lennon and is funded by a gift from his widow, Yoko Ono; the stately Conservatory Garden; the Dairy, which was once a place for city children to sample fresh milk and is now the park's visitor center; Bethesda Terrace, which boasts a large, majestic fountain and which had to be reclaimed from drug users and physically rebuilt; and the Dana Discovery Center, which was funded primarily by the Dana Foundation and served as an educational and program center on environmental matters, with a focus on the park itself. The renaissance of the park was accompanied by a steady fall in the annual number of reported crimes there.

Some of the Conservancy's members have argued that the city should step aside and let the private group manage the park. This proposal would require that the Conservancy receive all of the $4.3 million revenues from park concessions and accept responsibility for all park operations except police and electricity. The city's general fund currently receives the revenues.

Critics of this proposal, however, raise issues of who would be politically accountable for the parks. "We elect the politicians, not the Conservancy," one of them pointed out. "What if, at some future point, the Conservancy decided to charge admission?"

Adapted from Arlie Schardt. The Green(way)ing of America. Foundation News. September/October 1993, pages 22-23; and Douglas Martin. Benefactor wants private group to manage central park. New York Times. January 17, 1997. Page B3.

a centerpiece of their community. The city was unwilling to purchase it because the mayor and council were advocating a policy of renovating existing facilities before purchasing any additional resources. However, the city encouraged the Crooked Creek Community Council to purchase it and provided them with technical assistance and letters of support from the mayor, parks director, and others that the foundation used in soliciting grants and donations.

The property owner agreed to accept $350,000 for the 22 acres, and the Crooked Creek Community Council purchased an option on it. The Indianapolis Parks and Recreation Department agreed to

commit $100,000 to purchase it. The remaining funds were raised from the Indianapolis Foundation ($100,000); the Indiana Heritage Trust, a state grant program ($50,000); and donors in the local area ($100,000). The project would not have come to fruition without the advocacy role, persistence, and fundraising effort of the community organization.

The following two examples illustrate facility-specific foundations that were formed from bequests.

The Trexler Foundation was formed from the will of General Harry Trexler in Allentown, Pennsylvania. He left a portion of his Springwood Farm to the city to be used as a park and $250,000 as an endowment to pay for the perpetual maintenance of the park. In addition, interest from one-fourth of his remaining endowment was to be paid annually and perpetually to the city of Allentown for the improvements, extension, and maintenance of all of the parks.

Dr. W.W. Samuell, one of Dallas' leading physicians, left his real estate to the city he loved. His will was written on a prescription blank: "Real estate to City of Dallas Park Board for park purposes—not to be sold. Balance to Park Board as permanent foundation. First National Bank, administrator." He bequeathed 800 acres of farmland in close proximity to Dallas and a 100-acre tract within the city limits, which became some of the city's most prized parks. In addition, several downtown properties were kept as revenue-producing properties, and other properties were sold because they were unsuitable for either park lands or revenue properties. The money was deposited in the Samuell Foundation. The foundation money is used for improvement and maintenance of the Samuell parks.

Local Agency–Specific Foundations

The primary purpose of this type of foundation is to support the park and recreation services of its affiliated agency. Such foundations usually are initiated by public agency personnel, but occasionally the stimulus may come from concerned residents in the jurisdiction. Most foundations of this type operate at the community level. Directors or members of the foundation are likely to have a wide range of contacts in financial and business circles, who normally may not be available to park and recreation agencies.

If this type of foundation is able to attract a board of directors comprising outstanding community leaders, its very existence may be influential. Legislators or councilors may rationalize that if such eminent private citizens support the agency, then the city or state also should provide support. Thus, the foundation may assist not only by directly facilitating the acquisition of greater resources for parks and recreation but also by improving the credibility, stature, and political support of the agency.

Local Non-Affiliated Foundations

Local non-affiliated foundations pursue their mission without having exclusive allegiance to a single agency. Rather, they seek to cooperate with any institution that can assist in fulfilling their park and recreation goals.

The Alachua Conservation Trust in Gainesville, Florida, was formed with the help of the Trust for Public Land and had an initial goal of filling an empty niche in the community by helping public agencies, ranging from the city to the state to the regional water management district, buy land. All levels of government had monies to spend on land acquisition, but there was a shortage of staff to negotiate the acquisitions. Alachua Conservation Trust obtained appraisals for properties and, working in close cooperation with the government agency, negotiated options with landowners typically for six months. Once the government funds became available, Alachua Conservation Trust either assigned the option to the public agency for a predetermined fee or acquired the property and then immediately sold it to the agency, using the government check to pay the landowner.[21]

Grant-Aiding Foundations

Four different types of grant-aiding foundations are recognized in this text: corporate, general or special-purpose, community, and private. No attempt is made to give a detailed, in-depth treatment of the idiosyncrasies of each type, but some awareness of the differences between them is needed for park and recreation personnel to understand and use them successfully.

While corporate foundations are legally no different from the other three types, it should be noted that they do not have the same level of independence. Because of their close ties to a company, corporate foundations ultimately must answer to shareholders, so the projects that they support must be both in the public's interest and in the company's interest.

Whereas the mission of support foundations is to focus on park and recreation amenities, most grant-aiding foundations have multiple fields of interest. Hence, when seeking funds from these organizations, agencies in this field are usually in competition with applicants from other spheres of interest. In seeking these funds, the approach should embrace many of the principles for soliciting donations and sponsorships that were described in chapter 17. However, three additional guidelines are likely to be particularly important in applications to grant-aiding foundations.

First, grants made to governmental agencies are likely to be for projects that normally are not funded with tax resources. This field is a traditional area of governmental provision, and grant-aiding foundations are unlikely to support traditional services that they believe normally are financed by tax dollars. Agencies seeking grants for innovative programs, exploring different directions, or aiming to meet the wants of a new type of clientele are most likely to be successful.

Second, most grant-aiding foundations confine their philanthropy to specific geographical areas, usually a city, county, group of counties, or state. This is done for three reasons. First, the belief that because the money was earned in that region, it is appropriate that it should be used for the benefit of those people. Second, it enables trustees of the foundation to evaluate their efforts more effectively than they can if donations are made nationwide. Better decisions can be made when effort is concentrated on people and problems with which foundation administrators are familiar. Third, economy of administration is possible to a greater degree than would be the case if the staff were required to travel all over the country checking on institutions.

The third important principle that should be stressed is that foundations give to clearly defined fields of interest. Even those general purpose foundations that have very broad statements of purpose in fact do identify a number of fields within their terms of reference and restrict support to those fields.

These three factors should serve as guidelines before any applications are submitted. A shotgun approach ignoring these factors will cause considerable frustration both to the agency and to the foundations.

Grant-aiding foundations are sometimes described as a body of money surrounded by outstretched hands. Applications for grants are likely to be very competitive. An agency will always be competing against other organizations both from within the field and from other interest areas. Foundations receive requests for grants far in excess of their capability to respond. They necessarily have to reject most proposals they receive. "What Makes a Good Proposal?" provides guidelines for writing a grant proposal; however, before the proposal is written, the agency should examine critically the nature of the project using the three guidelines suggested above to determine whether a grant from a particular foundation is at all feasible.

The administration of major foundations is professionalized, and it follows specific criteria. These are listed in "What Criteria Do Foundations Use in Assessing Proposals" on page 514. Each foundation has its own philosophy and program interests and will evaluate proposals it receives differently. However, the following guidelines are illustrative of those used in evaluating proposals:

- The project must match the foundation's goals and interests. Each foundation has specific interests just as the park and recreation agency has a particular interest with its project. They must overlap. Most foundations have well-defined areas of interest in terms of geography, content, and the amount of money they distribute; these can be determined by reviewing *The Environmental Grantmakers Association Directory*; *The Foundation Directory*; *Foundation Reporter*; *Foundation News*, a bimonthly magazine; or other guides.

- The agency must have a sound reputation. It is mandatory that it have an image of being operated and managed efficiently. Prospective contributors will take into account an agency's past and present accomplishments before they will consider funding the proposal.

- Foundations usually prefer to support highly leveraged projects. This means that they provide seed money or give "challenge" grants, serving to arouse action, prime the pump, and perhaps attract relatively large amounts of public money for the project. Seed money helps break financial log jams. It involves small amounts of money used in imaginative ways to produce relatively big results. As one foundation director commented, it is amazing how much is 95% ready to happen, and the foundation's role is to provide the 5% needed to get the ball rolling! The challenge grant is perhaps harvest money rather than seed money, for it is reaped only if all financial goals stated in the challenge are reached.

- The projects should have a considerable degree of innate viability and capacity for self-help. Foundations usually do not like to be involved in a project for an extended period of time. If their funds are committed, it reduces their flexibility. For this reason also, many foundations prefer project giving to general support giving. The extent to which they are involved with general support giving is a measure of the degree to which their own potential to pursue new initiatives is tied up.

- The end should be greater than the means so that after the money has been spent, there are substantial benefits to show for it.
- Relativity of giving is an important consideration. Foundations often believe that if too much is given, it discourages spreading the base. It diminishes the initiative of the enter-

prise. At the same time, it is probably just as bad to ask for too little money as for too much, for then the foundation may feel its impact would be insignificant.

- Often foundations will give when there is no one else to give and hold back when there is a sufficiency of others.

What Makes a Good Proposal?

A good proposal will have most of the features and will address many of the questions listed below. Starred items often are addressed most conveniently in appendices.

Clear Summary of What Is To Be Accomplished

— Minimum of professional jargon

— Major features of the proposed plan set forth clearly and logically

— Objective assessment of the importance of the problem addressed

Defense of Why This Plan Is Needed

— Why are others not meeting this need now?

— Can they?

— Will they? Would they if funds were available?

— If a new organization is proposed, is it required? Are you sure?

— If others are performing a similar function or parts of the proposed function, how does the proposed function differ and why is the difference important? (Here, it may be sensible to include a short, state-of-the-art synopsis of related work done by others in the field addressed by the proposal.)

— Is this the right time for the proposed endeavor?

Description of the People To Be Involved

— Brief explanations of positions and corresponding duties

— Biography or curriculum vitae for each key individual proposed*

— Defense of the qualifications of the people responsible for the job to be done

Realistic Financing Scheme

— Annual budgets, including projected income (if any) by source, and projected expenditures accumulated in logical categories, usually natural expense object classifications (e.g., salaries, benefits, rent, travel, telephone, supplies, equipment, etc.)*

— Limited time horizon (Many foundations prefer two- or three-year projects and set an outside limit, e.g., five years.)

— Program for eventual self-support or support from sources other than the foundation

Appropriate Organizational Arrangements

— Funds administered by an existing or a new organization, frequently a tax-exempt educational or philanthropic "public charity"

— Appropriate guidance from a responsible board of trustees, directors, or advisors (A list of proposed board members and their duties or responsibilities is often helpful.*)

What Criteria Do Foundations Use in Assessing Proposals?

The criteria they use vary, but they include many of the following considerations:

Competence of Persons Involved

— Quality of references and of reference sources

— Opinions of members of the foundation's staff

— Opinions of outside proposal reviewers (professional or specialized consultants)

— Quality of project staff (Are they among the best of all possible people to undertake the venture?)

Feasibility and Realism of the Proposal

— Is the time right for the endeavor?

— Is the action proposed adequate to the problem addressed?

— Is the sponsoring agency or institution clearly enthusiastic about the substance of the proposal?

— Are the proposed facilities and staffing sufficient for the job?

Importance and Utility of the Venture to the Community or to Society

— Is there a demonstrable need for the project?

— Whom will the project benefit, and how will it do so?

— Is it based on ethical and moral premises?

— Will there be a measurable improvement if the venture is successful? Will harm be done if it fails?

Originality and Creativity of the Proposed Venture

— Is the project already a part of any other existing program?

— Does the project duplicate or overlap other existing or past programs?

— Is it new and innovative? Alternatively, does it help conserve beneficial programs that might otherwise atrophy or be lost?

— Could the project be carried out better elsewhere or by other persons?

Appropriateness of the Project to the Foundation's Policy and Program Focus

— Is the program consonant with the foundation's current program objectives?

— If so, does it address an area that should receive priority in consideration of proposals?

Prospects for Leverage and Pattern-Making Effects

— Will the project attract other financial support (if needed)?

— Will the project produce significant changes in a wide circle?

— Will the results be transferable to other projects and localities?

Need for Foundation Support

— Are public sources of funds available (i.e., federal, state, and local governments)?

— Are other private sources more appropriate (i.e., other foundations, other private institutions, or individuals more active in the field)?

Soundness of the Budget

— Is it adequate for the job to be accomplished but not so generous as to be wasteful?

— Is it evident that the project director (or principle support staff) is familiar with the administrative intricacies of conducting the proposed project and that he or she has planned carefully for contingencies?

Persistence, Dedication, and Commitment of the Proposers

— Have they persevered in efforts to secure needed funds?

— Have they devoted sufficient time to planning and launching the venture?

— Is the project one of their primary interests or a major professional preoccupation?

Provision of Objective Evaluation of Results, Where Feasible

— Will the project staff maintain adequate records to demonstrate success of the project?

— Where the project lends itself to statistical evaluation, has provision been made for recording and analyzing relevant data?

— Where necessary, has appropriate evaluation advice been sought?

- The agency needs to justify the gift and not to assume the justice of its case without analysis.
- Grants tend to flow toward challenging programs rather than to needy agencies in keeping with the foundation's role as the venture capitalist of philanthropy.

Corporate Foundations

The several avenues through which a business may provide support to park and recreation agencies are illustrated in figure 19.2. Occasionally, a business will seek to cooperate with a public agency in direct pursuit of tangible profits that is its raison d'être. This may involve direct partnerships, which were discussed in chapters 6 through 9, or sponsorship, which was the focus of chapter 16. On other occasions, a business may engage in enlightened philanthropy. This may come in the form of a donation directly from the company as described in chapter 14, through an operating foundation as discussed earlier in this chapter, or through a company's foundation, which is the focus of discussion in this section. These distinctions are made because each funding avenue that corporations use offers different types of opportunities requiring different solicitation strategies and makes different demands upon public agency managers seeking access to these resources.

An example of a corporate foundation established specifically to support the work of a park and recreation agency is given in "The Ackerley Youth Foundation Formed To Support the Seattle Parks and Recreation Department's Youth Programs." In addition to supporting special events, the Ackerley Foundation supported recreational programs and activities by purchasing vans to transport youth to and from community centers, refurbishing several basketball courts, and purchasing a variety of athletic equipment for recreational centers throughout Seattle. The foundation also supported 10 recreation leader positions to help develop and coordinate recreational activities for youth.

More than one century ago, Andrew Carnegie, who was the first great corporate philanthropist, observed: "It is more difficult to give money away intelligently than it is to earn it in the first place."[23] A primary reason for funneling philanthropy through a foundation is that it professionalizes responsibility for the corporation's philanthropic effort. Corporate foundations typically are staffed by experienced grant managers who design and implement a donations policy that is consistent with furthering the corporation's economic goals. They exude a level of professionalism and sophistication that may not always be present when donations are made directly by senior managers in a corporation.

The use of a corporate foundation takes the heat off senior company managers who are constantly pursued by impassioned fundraisers. The foundation vehicle creates organizational distance for managers, enabling them to respond legitimately that they have no access to a company's philanthropic budget and to deflect donation requests to the foundation.

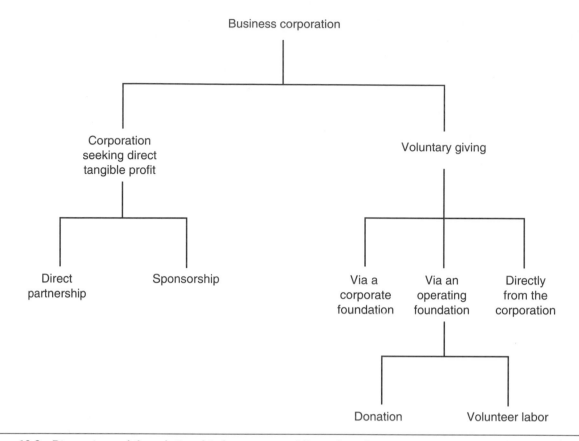

Figure 19.2 Dimensions of the relationship between a public park and recreation agency and a business.

The Ackerley Youth Foundation Formed To Support the Seattle Parks and Recreation Department's Youth Programs

The Ackerley Youth Foundation's mission statement is "to provide at-risk youths with positive influences and recreational activities as alternatives to violent actions."

The Ackerley Youth Foundation was formed by Barry and Ginger Ackerley in the fall of 1993 with the goal of supporting Seattle's at-risk youth through the resources of Ackerley Communications Inc. The Ackerleys owned the SuperSonics, which is the National Basketball Association franchise in Seattle.

The idea for the foundation grew out of a conversation the Ackerleys had with Seattle Mayor Norm Rice on ways to prevent youth violence in the city. The Ackerleys also drew upon the many positive experiences that they shared with children who participated in the Seattle SuperSonics' community relations programs. Children's enthusiasm for positive interaction could be seen in the success of the Sonics' basketball camps held each summer. The Hoops Camps provided children with the opportunity to learn basketball fundamentals and life skills from the SuperSonics' players and rewarded children who stayed off drugs and in school with Sonics tickets and give-aways. The success of this program, which after four years grew to 60,000 children participating statewide, prompted the formation of the Ackerley Youth Foundation.

The Ackerley Youth Foundation used the resources of all of the Ackerleys' local companies, which included Ackerley Communications Inc., Ackerley Outdoor Advertising, the Seattle SuperSonics, radio stations KJR-AM/KLTX-FM, and television station KVOS in Bellingham.

From Reco Bembry and Al Tufono. The real deal: The evolution of Seattle, Washington's At-Risk Youth Program. In Recreation programs that work for at-risk youth: The challenge of shaping the future. Edited by Peter A. Witt and John L. Crompton. Venture Publishing: State College, PA. 1996, page 93. Copyright ©Venture Publishing, Inc. Used by permission.

Corporate foundations are distinctively different from independent grant-aiding foundations, which are discussed in the following sections. Unlike independent foundations, the boards of trustees of corporate foundations are likely to consist principally of officers from the affiliated corporation who are interested in seeing that the grants awarded are aligned carefully to further the company's well being.

Many perceive the oil and automobile industries, for example, to be major sources of environmental pollution. This negative perception stimulates suspicion, controversy, and adverse reaction, which is manifested in pressure to create more-restrictive clean air and clean water laws. These negative reactions are likely to adversely affect the profitability of corporations in these industries. Hence, they use philanthropy through their foundations to counter such criticisms. ARCO's philosophy and mission is described in "Using a Foundation To Further a Company's Agenda: The ARCO Example." The General Motors Foundation has similar goals.

The General Motors Foundation "seeks opportunities to link GM's philanthropic activities with its business strategies." Its mission is "to ensure that we maintain our leadership position as a valued, responsible corporate citizen by enhancing the quality of life and our corporate reputation, consistent with our business goals and objectives." To deflect criticism alleging irresponsibility toward pollution, one of the foundation's areas of emphasis is the environment. Its investments in this area enabled the foundation's annual report to quote the president of the Nature Conservancy as saying: "The conservation work funded by General Motors is among our most urgent. This work includes completing the acquisition of the largest remaining remnant of Tallgrass Prairie in Oklahoma, helping us set up an office and acquire land in the Atlantic rainforest in Brazil, establishing a conservation program in Indonesia, and acquiring critical land along Lake Huron in Michigan. GM has also donated badly needed pick-up trucks so that our preserve managers can adequately take care of Conservancy properties. GM's financial commitment to our conservation work has exceeded that of any other corporation."[24]

Some foundations were established in response to a corporate philosophy that it was good for business to be perceived as reinvesting in the source from which corporate profits were dependent.

Using a Foundation To Further a Company's Agenda: The ARCO Example

ARCO is one of the largest oil companies in the United States. A former director of the ARCO Foundation stated: "As distrust and dislike of the oil industry spread, ARCO management sensed the need for bold action to improve our relations with the public and win its trust. The Foundation was seen increasingly as our 'good face' to the outside world, and ARCO made a very conscious effort to play a leadership role in philanthropy as well as in our communities."

The foundation's annual grant-making budget was pegged at a fixed share of ARCO's domestic pre-tax profits: 1.25% of a three-year average. The foundation implemented a decentralized approach to grantmaking that relied heavily on ARCO operating company recommendations on the best way to serve their communities. Grants were focused on five categories, one of which was the environment. In this area, "Grants are aimed at supporting programs that preserve our natural environment and further the use of sound science in dealing with environmental issues."

The major criterion was that grants were made to environmental organizations acknowledging the positive contributions that the oil industry made to the standard of living. Thus, grants were given to "balanced environmental organizations that support rational land-use and natural-resource policies," and the foundation explicitly did not support "adversarial environmental organizations." It was interested particularly in supporting "environmental education that develops curricula and programs in which the relationship between the economic cost and the public benefit of environmental decisions is articulated" and "land preservation efforts that assist in the ecological restoration of unique locations that have been environmentally damaged."

From The next 10,000 days. *ARCO Foundation Annual Report. 1993-94. Copyright ©ARCO. Used by permission.*

Patagonia, an outdoor-products manufacturer, committed 10% of its pre-tax profits or 1% of its sales, whichever was greater, to environmental causes through its corporate foundation. "Since 1984, our tithing program has distributed funds to over 500 different organizations. Rather than dilute the impact of our donations by spreading them thinly to a variety of causes, we have chosen to aim our dollars directly toward environmental issues. Patagonia products are designed for outdoor use and we feel a strong responsibility and commitment to keep the environment in its natural state for future generations. We are particularly interested in supporting environmental groups which operate at the most basic grassroots levels and which share our concern and sense of urgency about the state of the Earth" (p. 154).[25]

Similarly, Ben & Jerry's Homemade Ice Cream established a foundation in 1985 with a stock donation that now serves as its endowment. Each year the foundation receives a portion of Ben & Jerry's company philanthropic dollars, which is approximately 7.5% of pre-tax profits.

The foundation's mission is "to support and contribute to progressive social change in the United States—efforts to change the underlying conditions that create social problems such as racism, sexism, poverty, and environmental destruction. We primarily fund small grassroots organizations, and are willing to take risks funding new projects and small organizations struggling to survive" (p. 22).[25]

Earlier in this chapter, the examples of operating foundations emanating from corporate philanthropy emphasized that they were focused on communities in which the company's employees lived. This is also a distinctive feature of corporate foundations.

Monsanto Fund, the philanthropic arm of Monsanto Company, pledged $2 million in funds and services to help implement a master plan for the renovation of Forest Park in St. Louis. Monsanto's support primarily was directed toward a redesign of the lakes, ponds, and canals that make up the park's watershed system. A spokesperson for Monsanto said the company has "about 5000 employees in the metropolitan area. So our interest in the well-being of this region is intense and we believe a healthy, vibrant Forest Park is fundamental to this well-being."[26]

When large corporations leave a community, one of the net losses to the jurisdiction is donations to local agencies and organizations from corporate foundations. Thus, for example, when GTE North Inc. consolidated operations and closed its regional headquarters in Westfield, Indiana, donations were no longer forthcoming from the company's foundation to arts groups in the city, such as the opera, repertory theater, and international violin competition.[27]

Corporate foundations stabilize a company's donations program. Corporations typically make most funds available for philanthropy in years of good corporate profits. By using a foundation rather than direct giving, a company can contribute more in profitable years, enabling the foundation to place some of this money in a reserve fund and use it to supplement smaller contributions in leaner years. This permits more consistent levels of support to grant recipients and more long-term planning in grantmaking.

A particularly innovative strategy for stabilizing grantmaking was developed by Questar Corporation, a natural gas company based in Salt Lake City. It donated stock to organizations that the company committed to supporting on a long-term basis. Questar formed an endowment for the arts by using large blocks of Questar stock. It then designated a core group of organizations for regular, ongoing support from the dividends of the stock. The strategy worked for the company and the groups; it created a more-stable stockholder base for the company and gave these groups a perpetual source of funds. In addition, it saved fundraising time on both sides and gave the recipient groups a modicum of security. "Lots of nonprofits run hand-to-mouth. With the endowments, we want to help them run more like a business," said Questar's director of community affairs.

The endowment funneled annual grants averaging $20,000 to six major arts organizations in Utah. The endowment was worth $700,000, with annual dividends ranging from $100,000 to $120,000. This is not a large sum for major corporate donors with widespread operations, so the endowment strategy may be best-suited to a smaller regional company, such as Questar that had approximately 2,600 employees and principle operations in four states.[28]

A survey of major corporations revealed that 86% of them had a direct donation program and revealed that 46% of them had a corporate foundation (see figure 19.3).[28] In recent years, a trend among companies with foreign operations has been to set up foundations as a way to fund programs overseas. The foundation provides a structure that enables companies to make grants to

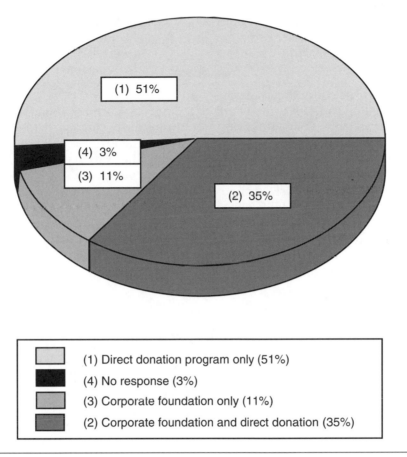

Figure 19.3 Profile of corporate voluntary donations.

Myra Alperson. *Corporate Giving Strategies that Add Business Value.* The Conference Board: New York. 1995. Reprinted by permission of The Conference Board, New York City.

nonprofit groups supporting overseas projects and to give them tax relief in the process. Smaller companies usually do not have foundations because the financial reporting rules and paperwork associated with them is too burdensome to justify, given their level of donated funds.

General or Special-Purpose Foundations

The terms of reference in the articles of incorporation of general foundations are phrased broadly. For example, the mission of the J.P. Morgan Charitable Trust is to "make grants to worthy causes for a variety of charitable purposes," and that of the Rockefeller Brothers Fund is to "improve the well-being of all people." However, in practice, both of these organizations, like almost all other general foundations, define specific program areas that they will support in pursuit of its broad mission. The J.P. Morgan Trust has six program areas: arts, education, environment, health and human ser-

vices, international affairs, and urban affairs. Similarly, the Rockefeller Brothers Fund has six program areas: sustainable resource use, world security, nonprofit sector, education, New York City, and special concerns (South Africa). Many projects that are outside of these program areas would improve the well-being of all people, but they will not be considered for funding. The goal of the sustainable resource use program is "to foster environmental stewardship." In this regard, the Rockefeller foundations have a distinguished history of contributions for the purchase of land for use as national parks. Their contributions at Grand Tetons, Acadia, Smoky Mountains, Colonial Williamsburg, Bull Creek, and the Virgin Islands were crucial to the establishment of those national parks.

The Richard King Mellon Foundation is a general purpose foundation, but land conservation is one of its defined program areas of interest. This program reflects the interests of Richard King Mellon who was a financier, industrialist, and ardent sportsman. Mellon prohibited the felling of trees on his vast estate, and the foundation's directors remain faithful to his conservation ethic. Examples of its work include the following:

- Ten separate gifts of land in a single package valued at $21 million to the National Park Service and the U.S. Fish and Wildlife Service. This was considered the largest single private gift of land ever given to the nation, encompassing more than 100,000 acres. The major portion of this gift comprised about 90,000 acres of wetlands for a wildlife refuge in North Carolina. The properties had been acquired over a period of years through the Conservation Fund, a foundation based in Virginia, on behalf of Mellon.[29]

- The Mellon Foundation donated 40,000 acres of woodlands, canyons, and granite bluffs in west Texas to the Texas Parks and Wildlife Department, which was the largest gift of land in the agency's history.

Special-purpose foundations support philanthropy in specifically defined fields that are specified in the articles of incorporation establishing them. The National Recreation Foundation, described below, and the National Fish and Wildlife Foundation are good examples. The National Fish and Wildlife Foundation was established by Congress in 1984. It is dedicated to the conservation of fish, wildlife, and plants and of the habitats on which they depend. Among its goals are species habitat protection, environmental education, pub-

The National Recreation Foundation

The National Recreation Foundation has an endowment of more than $30 million. Its mission is to "enhance the role of recreation as a positive force in promoting the mental, physical, social and spiritual health of the community at large." The National Recreation Foundation's initial funding base was established in 1918. The Playground and Recreation Association of America, one of the ancestor organizations of today's National Recreation and Park Association, was operating a highly successful program designed for "stimulating and aiding communities in the neighborhood of training camps to develop and organize their social and recreational resources in such a way as to be of the greatest possible value to the officers and soldiers in the camps." The association joined with six other national agencies to create the United War Work Campaign, which solicited funds to support their efforts. The funding campaign took place during the week of November 11 to 18, 1918, when the war in Europe suddenly ended. The campaign raised $190 million, of which the association was allocated more than $16 million.

The Playground and Recreation Association continued to deliver these services in the immediate period after the war and used most of the money doing this. However, when the need for these services ended, a surplus of almost $1.5 million remained. This was placed in an investment portfolio and formed the basis of the National Recreation Foundation's current endowment.

The National Recreation Foundation has always had a special relationship with the National Recreation and Park Association and its predecessor organizations. It has been a major donor to the association, but its grants have been made for special projects that were consistent with priority issues that the foundation identified and not for general operating expenses. However, it also considers proposals from other organizations.

It is the foundation's policy to identify periodically two or three critical issues facing society and to invite selected organizations to submit recreation-related proposals to address these issues. In the last half decade of the 1990s, the priority issues were at-risk youth and fostering healthy lifestyles. The goal of the latter project was to document and publicize the relationship between recreation participation and lower health-care costs and to encourage an aggressive campaign to increase the level of fitness among all segments of the population.

The National Recreation Foundation is administered by a board of 22 trustees who are responsible for soliciting creative and innovative proposals from organizations in their geographic area. It does not review proposals that members of the board have not invited.

llc policy development, natural resource management, habitat and ecosystem rehabilitation and restoration, and leadership training for conservation professionals.

The foundation is funded primarily by an annual appropriation of approximately $6 million from the federal government and supplemented by $3 million in donations primarily from major corporations. The federal funds may not be used for its operating expenses. In its first 12 years it awarded 1,834 challenge grants using $85 million in federal funds that leveraged an additional $237 million for conservation projects. In 1996, for example, the foundation made 213 grants totaling $8.9 million.[30]

Perhaps the most widely recognized special-purpose foundation to park and recreation agencies is the Joseph P. Kennedy Memorial Foundation. The Joseph P. Kennedy Foundation supports innovative programs for the mentally retarded. It has made contributions to local park and recreation agency programs in this area, but its major efforts have been in the creation and sponsoring of the Special Olympics program to serve as a model for greatly expanded sports and recreational programs for the mentally retarded. Fully sanctioned by the United States Olympic Committee and endorsed by all major professional organizations of recreators, special educators, coaches, and athletes, the Special Olympics has become the largest year-round sports organization for the mentally retarded in the world, involving more than 500,000 retarded youth, 150,000 volunteers, and organized chapters in each state and in a growing number of foreign countries.

The mission of the special-purpose Lila Wallace–Reader's Digest Fund is "to invest in programs that enhance the cultural life of communities and encourage people to make the arts and culture an active part of their everyday lives." The Fund's assets exceed $750 million, and it interprets its mission by focusing on three program areas: arts and culture, adult literary, and urban parks. The Fund launched its urban parks initiative in 1994 with a five-year program in which it invested $15.6 million to create, restore, or improve at least 20 parks in cities across the country. The inclusion of urban parks stemmed from a recognition that "Parks are important to the cultural life of cities. Centers of beauty, recreation and relaxation, they bring people together and promote a sense of community." In addition, the fund's founder, Lila Wallace, was a lover of parks and gardens during her life.

Over a five-year period, the Lila Wallace–Reader's Digest Fund made grants of $8.3 million for park improvements in the city of New York. The grants supported, among other projects, revitalization of 5,000 acres of woodland in the city's outer boroughs, the opening of the Urban Forest Ecology Center in the Bronx, and the restoration of the Harlem Meer in Central Park.

The Fund awarded $6.5 million in grants over four years to support foundations in seven mid-sized cities—Austin, Baltimore, Boston, Cleveland, Portland, Providence, and San Francisco—to enhance existing and to create new parks in underserved neighborhoods. The Trust for Public Land helped to acquire and develop park space. Local agencies and support foundations developed collaborations among community groups and residents for the design and programming of parks, giving all stakeholders a voice in the process.

The Fund made $7.5 million in challenge grants to five support foundations to restore sections of major parks in Chicago, Houston, New York, and San Francisco and to improve usage of them. Each group was required to match its grant from the fund.

Community Foundations

The first community foundation was established in Cleveland, Ohio, in 1918, but its early use was limited. However, changes in tax laws over the past three decades have resulted in community foundations becoming the fastest growing segment of philanthropy in the United States. Now, more than 400 such entities exist, and they are located in every major metropolitan area and state in the country. They hold more than $10 billion in assets, make annual grant awards of more than $800 million, and have attracted more than 15,000 donors who gave during their lifetime or through their estates.

A community foundation is a 501(c)(iii) grant-making organization that is structured as an amalgam of separate grant-making funds and accounts, all of which serve the needs of a local, regional, or statewide area. They meet the needs of donors who prefer to contribute to a field of service or to the general welfare of their community rather than to a specific organization. They provide assurance that the donor's charitable directions will be honored as long as they are beneficial. At the same time, they ensure that the charitable uses will not become obsolete because a responsible group of community leaders will be in a position to exercise their best judgment regarding the beneficial use of such funds in the event of changed conditions. History is full of examples of funds given for purposes that seemed good at the time but that later became outmoded. Community foundations can accomplish these changes without the delays, expense, and possible narrow limitations that would be involved if a court ruling had to be sought to amend the original terms of the gift. It permits charitable funds donated in the past to be reallocated among those charitable organizations that are able to perform the services most needed by the community at any particular time.

In addition to filling this niche for donors whose desires are community based but rather broad, community foundations have a second mission. In this role, they offer an alternative to establishing an independent, separate 501(c)(iii) agency that is a support, facility-specific, or private foundation; they inform donors that they can achieve their same goals by establishing a fund at the community foundation for these purposes. The community foundation serves as an umbrella foundation servicing the causes of a multitude of different donors. The advantages of depositing resources in a fund at a community foundation rather than establishing an independent support foundation for this purpose include the following:

- It alleviates the legal and financial burden associated with establishing and administering an independent foundation. For example, creating a fund at a community foundation can be done in one day, whereas the procedures for establishing an independent support foundation will require legal assistance and may involve six months or more of interaction with the IRS. An organization simply enters into an agreement with a community foundation to establish and maintain a fund, stipulates the specific purpose, and deposits an initial donation.

- It enables relatively small endowment funds to be pooled for investment purposes, which is likely to result in higher interest earnings.

- It facilitates management of assets, bequests, investments, and endowment funds by a staff or by professional external financial managers with expertise in this area.

- It gives access to professional foundation staff who can offer advice on attracting future donors.

These advantages have persuaded many groups who had established independent support foun-

dations to subsequently transfer their funds to a community foundation. Another factor contributing to the rapid recent growth in community foundations has been changes in the tax law. These have made it advantageous for private foundations (discussed in the next section) to transfer their endowments to a fund in a community foundation.

The number of separate funds administered by community foundations is likely to be extensive. For example, the California Community Fund manages more than 300 funds, and the Communities Foundation of Texas consists of more than 600 separate funds. The criterion for establishing a community foundation is that its service area should be large enough to attract a broad base of contributions that can be administered efficiently but should not be so large that the foundation is isolated from some of the people it serves. Community foundations charge an annual fee for managing the funds that, typically, equals from 1% to 2% of the fund's value. This is consistent with the fee range of private financial managers and is used to pay their administrative costs.

Grants are made from each fund in accordance with the instructions that a donor gives the community foundation when the fund is established. A variety of restrictions may be imposed on funds. The funds can be placed in one of five categories: 1) unrestricted, which means that the foundation has complete discretion as to their disbursement but must stay within a grant's defined geographic sphere of interest; 2) specified for general fields of interest so disbursements are restricted to use in these fields, one of which may be parks and recreation; 3) designated for specific organizations that the donor named at the time the contribution was made to the community foundation; 4) advised funds, which are popular alternatives to establishing a private foundation, meaning that the donor (or a person or committee designated by the donor) can advise the community foundation on their distribution; and 5) designated for use in specified local geographic areas. This latter category of area funds enables many smaller communities to establish funds with large community foundations instead of initiating their own community foundation. Some of these local area foundations are large enough for the community foundation to establish a local office in the area with full-time or part-time staff.

A community foundation will take responsibility for making grants from its unrestricted funds, but grant decisions for funds that are restricted will be made by disbursement committees whose composition is circumscribed in the original agreement with the community foundation. The community foundation and the local-area fund-distribution committees comprise members selected because of their broad knowledge of the needs and interests of their communities.

Examples of assistance to park and recreation agencies by community foundations include the following:

- The city of Ventura Parks and Recreation Department in California collaborated with the Ventura County Community Foundation to establish four endowment funds to benefit city programs: Senior Citizen Fund, Special Olympics Fund, Youth Scholarship Fund, and Ventura Pier Fund. The community foundation advised on raising funds for the endowments, used its professional financial manager to invest the funds, and distributed the interest income to the city, thereby alleviating the city of these administrative responsibilities. With the community foundation as a partner, donor confidence in the fundraising campaign was enhanced and issues relating to fund management were resolved.[31]

- The 66-acre Dallas Arboretum is located on the shores of White Rock Lake, an outstanding location for a public botanic garden. Funding from the Communities Foundation of Texas provided a new walkway with tadpole ponds on each side; sculptures; and, at the end of the walkway, four gigantic toads which project 20 ft jets of water.

- The Chicago Community Trust, with an endowment of $800 million, disburses approximately $30 million in grants each year. Among its grants for a typical year in the mid-1990s were $300,000 to the Chicago Zoological Society, $207,000 to the Chicago Horticultural Society, $180,000 to Lincoln Park Zoological Society, $130,000 to the city's open space project, and $50,000 to Friends of Ryerson Woods.

- On the local level, the Cleveland Foundation in Ohio has helped to foster neighborhood involvement; community park planning; and responsiveness to the needs of special populations, such as the Talking Garden for the Blind. At the regional level, it provided financial and leadership support for a strategic, long-range plan for Cleveland Metroparks called Metroparks 2000. Its ongoing support helped the Ohio Department of Natural Resources create an 8 mi stretch of green along Lake Erie and Cleveland's downtown, which received almost 12 million visits each year and was the most heavily used state park in Ohio. At the national level, it helped create the Cuyahoga Valley National Recreation Area, comprising 33,000 acres close to downtown Cleveland.

Private Foundations

Private foundations are established by an individual donor or family for the purpose of controlling, to the fullest extent possible, the use of the donor's philanthropic contributions. This vehicle enables a donor to contribute large amounts in high-income years and to retain some of those funds so that money is available to distribute in low-income years. In addition, just as senior managers in a company are able to deflect requests for contributions by referring them to a corporate foundation, individual members of wealthy families can refer solicitations to their private foundation for review and consideration through a formalized grant-making process to alleviate pressure on them to accede to ad hoc requests.

Private foundations rely on funds from a single individual or family who retains control of their distribution; therefore, there is no broad base of public support. For this reason, they are not recognized legally as a public charity. The major advantage of a private foundation over other types is that the donor, together with the donor's family and friends, can control and carry out the foundation's goals in perpetuity. However, this control authority means that donors to private foundations receive substantially fewer tax benefits than they would if they contribute to other types of foundations. For example, private foundations must pay a 2% tax on net investment, must comply with regulations on self-dealing, and must meet minimal income distribution requirements. Together with the administrative and professional expenses and the bank or investment fees associated with operating a private foundation, these consequences have persuaded many donors to opt for the alternative of establishing an advised fund with a community foundation. This fund enables them to qualify for the full amount of tax benefits because technically they are only advisers to the fund that the board of directors of the broad-based community foundation ultimately control.

These financial costs have led to a substantial decline in the role of private foundations. The decline has been reinforced by the recognition that the children of many of the families who have established private foundations have shown little interest in assuming responsibility for the foundation's management. By the third generation, their descendants may not even live in the area.

Despite their reduced significance, there are many thousands of private foundations, and they remain a potential source of funds for park and recreation agencies. Examples include the following:

- The Charles Stewart Mott Foundation in Flint, Michigan, granted $200,000 to the Alaska Rainforest Campaign to support the protection of Alaska's temperate rainforest ecosystem.

- The Timken Foundation of Canton, Ohio, is a private family foundation that awarded approximately $6 million in grants each year in cities where the Timken Company had facilities. For example, it contributed $200,000 to the Timken Wing of the Carter-Witherell Center, which provides recreation and fitness services to the community of Lebanon, New Hampshire. Other projects included walking tracks, clubhouses, lodging for campers, swimming pools, and ballpark lights.

- The Packard Foundation is a family foundation established by the co-founder of the Hewlett-Packard Company. In the mid-1990s, its endowment was $2.5 billion, and it disbursed $116 million in grants. Conservation is one of its focus areas, and in a typical year in the mid-1990s, its grants included $300,000 to the Center for Marine Conservation, $234,000 to the Trust for Public Land, $200,000 to the National Audubon Society, $200,000 to the Rails-to-Trails Conservancy, and $125,000 to the Environmental Defense Fund.

- The Henry Luce Foundation gave $1.1 million to the Central Park Conservancy for an educational program in Central Park in New York. It was conditional on the Conservancy raising a matching amount from other sources. Henry Luce III, who was an avid bird watcher and member of the Audubon Society, led the first class, teaching children about turtles and pond life. The program was intended to reach 30,000 primary and secondary school children and to teach them about the park's ecology.[32]

Summary

Operating foundations are foundations that spend all of their income directly on actively conducting the services for which they were organized. Many of the recreational activity clubs, especially youth athletic organizations, that use public facilities are organized as operating foundations, but operating foundations also have emerged in response to four other types of stimuli. First, some were expressions of corporate philanthropy. Second, some were formed by groups or organizations that wanted to cooperate on a venture and needed an umbrella vehicle to do this efficiently. Third, many natural resource agencies have established cooperative associations or friends groups to provide auxiliary services, which government regulations make it inefficient or impossible for the agencies to deliver directly. Fourth, in a growing number of situations, operating foundations have assumed responsibility for the management of selected public facilities, which often is stimulated by the withdrawal of public funds from those facilities.

Support foundations are foundations whose mandate is to secure additional resources exclusively for enhancing park and recreation services. The types of foundations within this general category can be differentiated by the geographic scope of their operation and by their institutional affiliation. The two most prominent national non-affiliated support foundations are the Nature Conservancy and the Trust for Public Land. They pioneered many of the acquisition and financial mechanisms that foundations now have adopted widely, and they remain at the cutting edge of these techniques. The National Park Foundation is the only organization that qualifies as a national agency-specific support foundation.

A surge in interest at the local level in adopting a more pro-active stance to acquiring resources has resulted in rapid growth of local support foundations working at the regional, state, county, or community level. Many of these are known widely by the generic name "land trust." Facility-specific foundations may be established by friends-of-the-park groups to enhance a park's amenities, as interim vehicles specifically to enable land to be held for a period of time before passing it to a public agency, or by a bequest from benefactors. The mission of a local agency-specific foundation is to support the park and recreation services that its affiliated agency delivers. Often, agency personnel instigate them. Local non-affiliated foundations pursue their mission without having exclusive allegiance to a single agency. Rather, they cooperate with any institution that can assist in fulfilling their park and recreation goals.

When submitting a proposal to grant-aiding foundations, three guiding principles are especially germane. First, grants are likely to be awarded to innovative programs rather than to traditional offerings, and they are unlikely to be forthcoming if the funding request is for a service that government tax dollars have supported in the past. Second, most grant-aiding foundations confine their philanthropy to specific geographical areas. Third, they give to clearly defined fields of interest, even those whose articles of association have broad statements of purpose.

Four types of grant-aiding foundations are recognized. Corporate foundations are less independent than the others because the grants that they award must not only be in the public interest but also in the company's interest. Companies funnel their donations through their own foundations so that proposals can be evaluated by experienced grant managers who direct funds to projects that will serve the company's interests. Therefore, senior managers are able to deflect solicitation requests. Most grant-aiding foundations are general or special-purpose foundations with a mission to support philanthropy in fields of interest that either are specified by the board of directors or mandated in the foundation's articles of association.

Community foundations are the fastest growing category of grant-aiding foundations. Their mission is to serve the needs of a local, regional, or statewide area. They provide a vehicle for donors who prefer to contribute to a field of service or to the general welfare of their community rather than to a specific organization. Community foundations also offer an alternative to establishing an independent foundation by encouraging donors to establish specific funds with them that achieve the same end.

Private foundations are established by individual donors, and they enable donors to exercise maximal control over disbursement of the funds. However, they offer fewer tax benefits to donors than community foundations do, so many donors now elect the latter option.

References

1. Drucker, Peter F. 1991. It profits us to strengthen nonprofits. *The Wall Street Journal*, December 19, A14.

2. Drucker, Peter F. 1969. *The age of discontinuity*. New York: Harper & Row.

3. Havitz, Mark E. 1996. *Models of change*. State College, PA: Venture Publishing.

4. Callaghan, Charles. 1994. Selling First Coast golf: The tourism boost that a property tax hike wrought. *Business Journal—Jacksonville* 9(39): 14.

5. The Conservation Foundation. 1985. *National parks for a new generation: Visions, realities, prospects*. Washington, DC: The Conservation Foundation.

6. Hartman, Skip. 1995. Neglected park facility turned into tennis center. *Friends of Parks & Recreation* 5(1): 3-4.

7. International City Management Association. 1989. *Service delivery in the 90s: Alternative approaches for local governments*. Washington, DC: International City Management Association.

8. Simon, Donald E. 1979. The urban park plazas project: A proposal for Madison Square Park. Unpublished manuscript. New York: Urban Park Plazas.

9. Richardson, Jan. 1996. Built on trust. *The Leisure Manager—Open Air Supplement* March: 8-10.

10. Gilbert, Bill. 1986. The Nature Conservancy game. *Sports Illustrated* 65(17): 86-100.

11. Endicott, Eve. 1993. Preserving natural areas: The Nature Conservancy and its partners. In *Land conservation through public-private partnerships*, edited by Eve Endicott. Washington, DC: Island Press, 17-42.

12. Badger, Curtis J. 1995. A revolution in the business of conservation. *Urban Land* 54(6): 40-45.

13. Salvesen, David. 1993. Brokers for the environment. *Urban Land* 52(9): 23-25.

14. *Nature Conservancy* 46(3). 1996. Where the steer and the antelope play. 30.

15. *Building the American commons: 25 years at the Trust for Public Land*. 1997. San Francisco: Trust for Public Land.

16. Poole, William. 1993. Preserving urban and suburban gardens and parks: The Trust for Public Land and its partners. In *Land conservation through public-private partnerships*, edited by Eve Endicott. Washington, DC: Island Press, 61-82.

17. Pottharst, Kris. 1995. Urban dwellers and vacant lots. *Parks and Recreation* 30(9): 94-101.

18. Trust for Public Land. 1988. Hudson River Valley, New York. *Update* 21: 9.

19. National Park Foundation. 1996. *Annual report*. Washington, DC: National Park Foundation.

20. Wright, John B. 1992. Land trusts in the U.S.A. *Land Use Policy* April: 83-86.

21. Endicott, Eve and contributors. 1993. Local partnerships with government. In *Land conservation through public-private partnerships*, edited by Eve Endicott. Washington, DC: Island Press, 195-218.

22. LaPage, Wilbur F. 1994. *Partnerships for parks*. Tallahassee, FL: National Association of State Parks.

23. Morris, Richard I. and Daniel A. Biederman. 1985. How to give away money intelligently. *Harvard Business Review* 63(6): 151-159.

24. General Motors. 1995. *General Motors philanthropy report*. Detroit, MI: General Motors Foundation.

25. Environmental Grantmakers Association. 1997. *Environmental grantmakers association directory*. New York: Environmental Grantmakers Association.

26. National Association for Olmsted Parks. 1996. *Field Notes* 14(3): 7.

27. Kukolla, Steve. 1995. GTE cuts hit arts groups. *Indianapolis Business Journal* 16(2): 1.

28. Alperson, Myra. 1995. *Corporate giving strategies that add business value*. New York: The Conference Board.

29. Brown, Warren. 1993. Public-private land conservation partnership in and around national parks. In *Land conservation through public-private partnerships*, edited by Eve Endicott. Washington, DC: Island Press, 104-128.

30. National Fish and Wildlife Foundation. 1996. *Annual report*. Washington, DC: National Fish and Wildlife Foundation.

31. Harrison, Barbara M. 1994. Your community foundation: Partners in philanthropy. *Parks and Recreation* 29(11): 50-53.

32. Teltsch, Kathleen. 1993. Park is classroom but turtle is truant. *New York Times*, July 21, LB3.

INDEX

Note: The letter *f* after page numbers refers to figures; the letter *t* denotes tabular information.

ABOUT THE AUTHOR

John L. Crompton, PhD, is a professor of Recreation, Park and Tourism Sciences at Texas A&M University and a former president of both the Academy of Park and Recreation Administration and the Society of Park and Recreation Educators (SPRE).

Considered the leading authority in his field, Professor Crompton has authored more than 300 publications. He also has traveled extensively, keynoting the Annual National Park and Recreation Conferences in Great Britain, Canada, Japan, Australia, South Africa, and New Zealand. He's a recipient of the Outstanding Literary Award and the Outstanding Research Award from the National Recreation and Park Association (NRPA), and he received the Distinguished Colleague Award and the Outstanding Teaching Award from the SPRE.

In 1979, Crompton and Dennis Howard co-authored *Financing, Managing and Marketing Recreation and Park Resources*, which became the definitive text used in the curricula of more than 100 colleges. Since its publication, Professor Crompton has continued his research, conducting workshops around the world and gathering practical information from across North America for this book.

Professor Crompton earned his doctorate in Recreation Resources Development at Texas A&M University in 1977. He also is a member of the Board of Trustees of NRPA.

Related Books From Human Kinetics

Effective Leadership in Adventure Programming

Simon Priest, PhD, and Michael A. Gass, PhD

1997 • Hardbound • 336 pp • Item BPRI0637
ISBN 0-87322-637-2 • $38.00 ($56.95 Canadian)

This is the first book to provide in-depth information on the key elements of effective outdoor leadership. Authors Simon Priest and Michael Gass go beyond the technical skills of outdoor leadership to address the equally important facilitation skills and metaskills essential to highly effective leaders.

Outdoor Recreation in America
Fifth Edition

Clayne R. Jensen, EdD

1995 • Hardbound • 288 pp • Item BJEN0496
ISBN 0-87322-496-5 • $35.00 ($48.95 Canadian)

This fifth edition of the classic text Outdoor Recreation in America *has been revised and updated to provide comprehensive coverage of the development, regulation, and management of outdoor recreation in America. This book is also an excellent reference for recreation, outdoor education, and natural resource management professionals; park and recreation administrators; and employees of government and private resource management agencies.*

Outdoor Recreation Safety
A publication for the School and Community Safety Society of America

Neil J. Dougherty, IV, Editor

1998 • Hardbound • 304 pp • Item BDOU0944
ISBN 0-87322-944-4 • $35.00 ($52.50 Canadian)

Outdoor Recreation Safety *is the first single source to provide practical safety guidelines for a broad range of outdoor recreation activities. The 19 contributors—each an expert in his or her chosen field—offer indispensable information that can lead to better experiences for participants and reduce the likelihood of injuries and expensive litigation.*

More Fantastic Fundraisers for Sport and Recreation

William F. Stier, Jr., EdD

1997 • Paperback • 232 pp • Item BSTI0525
ISBN 0-88011-525-4 • $16.00 ($23.95 Canadian)

Breathe new life into your fundraising efforts! Author William Stier once again comes to the rescue with More Fantastic Fundraisers for Sport and Recreation. *Loaded with creative ways to generate much-needed cash for your program, this unique fundraising and "fun raising" guide will provide you with fresh ideas for years to come.*

The Story of Leisure
Context, Concepts, and Current Controversy

Jay S. Shivers and Lee J. deLisle

1997 • Hardbound • 224 pp • Item BSHI0996
ISBN 0-87322-996-7 • $36.00 ($53.95 Canadian)

The Story of Leisure *takes a detailed, and sometimes controversial, look at the meaning of leisure—what it is, how it developed, what it has become, and where it is going. Not only is* The Story of Leisure *an outstanding textbook; it's also an enjoyable read for recreational specialists, sport historians, and sport sociologists.*

Recreational Sport Management
Third Edition

Richard F. Mull, MS, Kathryn G. Bayless, MS, Craig M. Ross, ReD, and Lynn M. Jamieson, ReD

1997 • Hardbound • 344 pp • Item BMUL0808
ISBN 0-87322-808-1• $38.00 ($56.95 Canadian)

Now in its third edition, this comprehensive text and reference has been updated and expanded to reflect current trends in sport management and recreational sport. This edition contains new chapters on fitness, risk management, and marketing. The book also features special elements that provide computer applications for programming and administrative functions, descriptions of model programs, and suggestions for mainstreaming individuals with disabilities.

To request more information or to order, U.S. customers call 1-800-747-4457, e-mail us at humank@hkusa.com, or visit our Web site at http://www.humankinetics.com/. Persons outside the U.S. can contact us via our Web site or use the appropriate telephone number, postal address, or e-mail address shown in the front of this book.

 HUMAN KINETICS
The Information Leader in Physical Activity
P.O. Box 5076, Champaign, IL 61825-5076
2335